COMPANIES AND MEN

Business Enterprise in America

This is a volume in the Arno Press collection

COMPANIES AND MEN
Business Enterprise in America

Advisory Editors

STUART BRUCHEY
VINCENT P. CAROSSO

*See last pages of this volume
for a complete list of titles*

FORD

Expansion and Challenge

1915-1933

ALLAN NEVINS

AND FRANK ERNEST HILL

Volume II

ARNO PRESS

A New York Times Company

1976

Editorial Supervision: ANDREA HICKS

———◆———

Reprint Edition 1976 by Arno Press Inc.

COMPANIES AND MEN: Business Enterprise in America
ISBN for complete set: 0-405-08062-X
See last pages of this volume for titles.

Manufactured in the United States of America

———◆———

Library of Congress Cataloging in Publication Data

Nevins, Allan, 1890-1971.
    Ford.

    (Companies and men)
    Bibliography: v. 1, p.
    CONTENTS: v. 1. The times, the man, the compa-
ny.--v. 2. Expansion and challenge, 1915-1933.--
v. 3. Decline and rebirth, 1933-1962.
    1. Ford, Henry, 1863-1947. 2. Ford Motor Com-
pany. I. Hill, Frank Ernest, 1888-1969, joint
author. II. Series.
[HD9710.U54F654 1976] 629.2'092'4 [B] 75-41775
ISBN 0-405-08089-1

FORD:
EXPANSION AND
CHALLENGE: 1915-1933

BY ALLAN NEVINS
with the collaboration of FRANK ERNEST HILL

FORD: THE TIMES, THE MAN, THE COMPANY
*A History of Henry Ford, The Ford Motor Company, and
The Automotive Industry 1863–1915*

BY ALLAN NEVINS

STUDY IN POWER: JOHN D. ROCKEFELLER, INDUSTRIALIST AND PHILANTHROPIST

THE DIARY OF JOHN QUINCY ADAMS *(edited by Allan Nevins)*

THE ORDEAL OF THE UNION, 2 *vols.*

THE EMERGENCE OF LINCOLN, 2 *vols.*

A CENTURY OF CARTOONS *(in collaboration with Frank Weitenkampf)*

THIS IS ENGLAND TODAY

JOHN D. ROCKEFELLER, 2 *vols.*

Published elsewhere: THE AMERICAN STATES DURING AND AFTER THE REVOLUTION; THE EMERGENCE OF MODERN AMERICA; *biographies of Grover Cleveland, Hamilton Fish, Abram S. Hewitt, Henry White, and John C. Fremont;* THE DIARY OF JAMES K. POLK; THE DIARY OF GEORGE TEMPLETON STRONG (*4 vols.*); AMERICA, THE STORY OF A FREE PEOPLE; *and* AMERICA THROUGH BRITISH EYES.

FORD

Expansion and Challenge

1915-1933

BY ALLAN NEVINS

AND FRANK ERNEST HILL

RESEARCH ASSOCIATES: WILLIAM GREENLEAF
AND GEORGE B. HELIKER

NEW YORK

CHARLES SCRIBNER'S SONS

PREFACE

THE PERIOD extending from Woodrow Wilson's reelection through the First World War and the post-war boom into the Great Depression saw the release of powerful new forces in American life. Progress along the social and economic frontiers of the nation more than offset the political inertia which followed the advent of Harding and Coolidge. One of the effective spear-points in this progress was the Ford Motor Company. By the year of the Panama-Pacific Exposition in 1915, when this story begins, the company ranked high among the major industrial organizations of the world. It was then doing more than all other companies combined to make Americans an automobile-using, automotive-minded people. It was ready for an expansion matching the country's eager appreciation of the possibilities of the new motor age. This expansion came. The development of mass production into the instrument of a new industrial revolution first took place in Ford's Highland Park factory. The rise of the Model T as the most widely used vehicle in human history, the building of the great Rouge plant, the progress of vertical integration until the company held its own mines, forests, foundries, steel mills, glass factories, railroad, and shipping fleets, the promotion of bold new ventures in making airplanes and tractors, the challenge to Model T in a dynamic automotive era, its passing and the coming of new Ford cars—all were part of this expansion. So was the planting of factories or assembly plants, and sales offices, in every important nation abroad.

Alongside this history of material growth ran the erratic yet nevertheless valuable experimentation of the company in socio-economic fields. At times Henry Ford and his associates advanced far into unknown territory in their wage and sales policies; at times they fell back further than they should. Startling new changes, largely unseen, were taking place in the nature of American capitalism. The Ford Motor Company, even while its founder was making himself an industrial autocrat, assisted in these changes; for with all his short-comings he never ceased to believe in a future of high wages and abundant inexpensive goods, to repudiate mere money-getting ("private fortunes are reservoirs of public wealth"), and to insist on constructive pioneering ("We'll build this as well as we know how, and if we don't use it somebody will"). In an age of confusion the new technology was a conspicuous element of planning and order, and among technological products the automobile had the most immediate and pervasive impact. The Ford operations united the old American method of rapid improvisation and ad hoc invention with the new method of careful technological planning in a fashion which illuminates the fast-changing nature of the economy and the society.

The first volume of this history of the Ford Motor Company (*Ford: The Times, the Man, the Company*) covered the period from the beginnings of the automobile to the Five Dollar Day and the dawn of mass production in 1913–14. This second volume covers the crowded years of war, boom, and incipient depression. Like the first, it is the product of an agreement between Columbia University and the Ford Motor Company Fund in the interests of business history. It has been written under the auspices of Columbia University, in its offices, and with the counsel of a special University committee; the work has been done by University employees, under ordinary academic conditions and with normal University salaries; all royalties are paid to the University. Thus the independence of the authors is completely guaranteed. For the contents of the volume, however, Columbia University has no responsibility, and all omissions, errors of fact, and faults of interpretation must be laid at the authors' door alone.

These shortcomings would have been more numerous but for the unwearied assistance of the Ford Archives, a model institution of its kind, which will eventually, it is to be hoped, find many imitators in the industrial field. We owe a special debt to Dr. Henry Edmunds, its highly skilled and patient head; to Mr. Owen Bombard, whose long series of interviews with men high and low in the Ford organization and the automotive world generally, and careful exploration of the archival material, have given him an unrivalled knowledge of company history; and to Madeleine Felix, Richard Ruddell, Stanley Graham, and Winthrop Sears of the Archives staff. Many executives and former executives of the company have been helpful. Of these we may especially name Charles E. Sorensen, whose published volume of memoirs, supplemented by personal interviews, has been helpful; Ernest C. Kanzler; William A. Ryan; and Lord Perry, prominent in foreign operations. Conferences and correspondence with men only briefly in the Ford organization, or never—Wilfred C. Leland, R. C. Getsinger, Harold H. Emmons, and J. Bell Moran—have also been of high value. We are grateful to Mr. Irwin P. Halpern for his help with the appendix on Ford activities in Russia.

The authors owe a special debt to two men whose names have been included on the title page: Dr. William Greenleaf, now Associate Professor of History, Colorado State University, whose careful research, constructive vision, and able written reports on diverse sections of this history have been invaluable, and Dr. George Heliker, Assistant Professor of Economics, Montana State University, whose expertness on labor and economic questions, expressed in interviews, reports, and critical comment, has been highly important. We gratefully acknowledge the support and aid of the University committee appointed to give general guidance to our work. To many others, whom considerations of space forbid us to name, we tender our thanks.

A.N.
F.E.H.

Columbia University
New York
January 15, 1957

CONTENTS

fleet; his Brazilian rubber adventure; Ford aircraft (1926–1934) as a
pioneering force in modern commercial aviation. Ford's contribution as a
social and industrial experimenter.

under Edsel, Sorensen: plants in France, Denmark, Germany, Spain, Italy. The prosperous Canadian Ford Company—its work in Australasia, South Africa. Notable Ford expansion in Latin America.

England, Italy, the United States. The Ford legend: Ford's skill in fostering it; his capacity for pithy utterance. Books about him: Merz, Marquis, Crowther. The actual Ford: his social vision as to effects of industrialism, genius in the mechanical realm, faith in future and experimentation. His many-faceted personality; influence of his rural youth important; his unhappy attitude toward his son Edsel. Ford's total accomplishments, including those of his many associates, in balance against his defects.

ILLUSTRATIONS

Maps and diagrams by Frank Wilimczyk. All other illustrations are reproduced through the courtesy of the Ford Motor Company.

FORD:
EXPANSION AND
CHALLENGE: 1915-1933

Henry and Edsel Ford examining a model of the River Rouge plant. The slip and turning basin can be seen, with the steel-making units to the left, and the storage bins, coke ovens, power house (tall stacks), blast furnaces, and foundry to the right.

I

SCENE AND ACTORS: 1915

EARLY on the afternoon of February 20, 1915, a dense crowd filled the Palace of Transportation at the Panama-Pacific Exposition in San Francisco. It was opening day, and the throng had gathered to inspect the chief exhibit of the Ford Motor Company, a replica of the assembly line for Model T cars at Highland Park near Detroit, then in its completed form only a few months old. Everyone in the building knew of this symbol of industrial magic, but few if any had seen it in operation: frame after frame moving along an endless conveyor, to acquire axles, springs, gasoline tanks, engines, transmission shafts, steering columns, windshields, and bodies, and to roll off the line as complete cars to be started and driven away.

The scene was fully set. Months earlier conveyors had been shipped westward, installed and tested by Ford employees in San Francisco. Materials for the first day of assembly had been brought in the night before; workmen now stood beside them. A nickel-plated railing set on moveable posts held the crowd at a distance.

At length the signal was given, and the first frames began their march. The crowd, packed tight on a level floor that made observation difficult for those not in the front rows, stirred restlessly; finally, as drivers gunned the engines of the first completed cars, men and women surged forward. The railing went down and the spectators swept up to the conveyors.

"You'll have to shut this thing down until we get the crowd in hand!" shouted a Fair representative to Frank Vivian of the local Ford office, who had charge of the exhibit. The line stopped, and against the vociferous protests of spectators the uniformed guards began to push the throng toward the exits.[1]

1

2.

Mass production had been unveiled. That night the posts supporting the rails were sunk through the floor and anchored firmly to contain the crowd, while a three-tier platform soon permitted four rows of spectators to view the exhibit in comfort. Operating three hours each afternoon, the assembly line turned out twenty cars a day for the next nine months. It was the most striking industrial demonstration at the Fair, and one of the most popular.

The exposition had taken its name from the fact that six months earlier, on August 15, 1914, the steamer *Ancon* had left the port of Christobal on the Atlantic and moved through the just-completed Panama Canal, to arrive less than ten hours later at Balboa on the Pacific. As Secretary of War Lindley M. Garrison had cabled to George W. Goethals, directing the completion of the canal, this realized "the dream of centuries." A triumph for engineering, it cut the distance from Hong Kong to Hamburg by 5166 miles, and that from San Francisco to Liverpool by 5666—saving some weeks of sailing time for any steamer of that day.[2]

As the exposition opened its gates, half the world was already at war. Never before had so many millions sailed or marched to battle, and mounting technological skill made the scale and pace of the great conflict possible. Mechanized transport bore armies to the combat zones; modern communications, including the telephone and the wireless, quickened the delivery of orders; steel plants spewed out metal for armor and ordnance; factories disgorged their torrents of uniforms, weapons, and ammunition. With the submarine, the Zeppelin, and the airplane men enlarged the areas of combat, maneuvering not only on land and water, but also beneath the oceans and in the air. Grimly, the war proclaimed the power of man and his machines.

Where the world was still at peace men were making new technological advances. In January, 1915, telephone circuits were joined across the American continent, and men in San Francisco and New York for the first time spoke with each other. Later in the year operators of the wireless station at Arlington, Virginia, conversed with technicians in Honolulu and Paris. A few weeks before the exposition opened, New York aldermen were discussing limitations upon the height a skyscraper might rise above street level without a stepback—a restriction suggested by the fact that engineers were already pushing the steel frame of their structure almost a thousand feet above the earth.[3]

We can see today that the power of the United States in 1915 was strategic in a way not understood at the time. If Europe had produced the machine, America from an early time had fostered it, and the American contribution, growing with the years, by 1915 had become of major importance. Led by inventors and pioneering manufacturers like Whitney, Colt, Morse, Bell, Edison, and the Wright brothers, America had created new implements and processes, among them the telegraph, electric light, rotary press, and the airplane.

More important, Americans had taken leadership in large-scale production. They had made machine tools their special concern, and by the late eighteen-nineties had built up an industry superior in volume and dynamic quality to that of Europe. By 1900 the United States led all nations in volume of manufactured products, and by 1915 produced as much as Britain and Germany combined.[4] Americans either shared or had taken undisputed leadership in railroad construction; in structural engineering; in factory, business, and modern home architecture; in the quantity manufacture of motor vehicles; in the development of sanitary water systems; and in the new art of highway construction adapted to automobiles.

If it was just to say that the world in 1915 was the world of the Curies, Rutherford, and Einstein; of Croce and Bergson; of Matisse, Klee, and Picasso; of Hauptmann, Shaw, and Gorki; of Ravel, Stravinsky, Sibelius, and Puccini, it was a world whose culture was dominated by Europe. But if it is also just to say that this world was the world of wireless, the airplane, the motor car, the suspension bridge, the electric light, and the skyscraper, then it was one increasingly influenced by America.

To be sure, culturally America was still immature. Despite its hundred million inhabitants, its new overseas possessions, and its proud tradition of representative government, its character as a nation was in process of formation. Its political leaders were still struggling with the problems attendant on furious growth—widespread business abuses, the exploitation of the rural population, and the complaints of un-unionized office and industrial workers. Material accomplishments on a dazzling scale—pure milk and water for millions, the world's greatest railroad system, the spread of electric lighting, modern plumbing, automobiles—were part of a social pattern of startling contrasts. The Manhattan skyscrapers shadowed the pushcarts of the lower East Side; the few rich and well-staffed universities of the land towered above struggling and often mediocre colleges; the rich estates of the prosperous areas shouldered cheap bungalows. Here too were the first chain newspapers with comics and screaming headlines, the roaring baseball and prizefight crowds, jazz music, the emerging motion picture; and along with these crass novelties a lingering puritanism that forbade smoking to women, opposed the simplification of the bathing suit, and shuddered at innocuous art like the nationally notorious "September morn." * The melange confused intelligent foreign visitors like Arnold Bennett and André Siegfried, who found America crude and bewildering, and "organized to produce things rather than people, with output set up as a god." [5]

Actually there was high capacity in various fields, with notable figures like Theodore Roosevelt, Woodrow Wilson, Jane Addams of Hull House, the philosopher John Dewey, the novelists Willa Cather and Theodore Dreiser, the painters Albert P. Ryder, Thomas Eakins, and John Sloan, the jurists Holmes and Brandeis, the editors William Allen White and Adolph Ochs, the scientists Irving Langmuir and Robert Millikan, and the architects Cass Gilbert and Frank Lloyd Wright. The promise of accomplishment in numerous areas was rich, the reality of industrial power plain. It too was infused with promise. Commanding unmeasured reserves of raw materials, the greatest machine plant in the world, bold and gifted captains, and masses of adaptable and ingenious workers, America was the happiest of all environments for the growth of mechanistic enterprises.

3.

Of the many American activities that expressed industrial power, automotive manufacturing was becoming preeminent both in size and influence. Nonexistent twenty years earlier, a mere collection of sheds and shops in 1900, it had grown with the rage of Iowa corn in July and the solidity of an oak. Producing only 89,110 vehicles in 1910, it had multiplied that product tenfold (880,489 in 1915)—an output

* This painting, by the French artist Paul Chabas, showed a nude female figure, decorously turned toward a sunrise sea.

valued at $691,778,000. Another year, and the value would exceed a billion.

But the social and technological impacts of the industry had been even more remarkable than its rapid development. It had created a wholly new type of transportation. Some two and a half million Americans now possessed automobiles, and the life of the nation was changing because of this fact; for the motor vehicle was the first free-ranging form of inland transportation, not tied like locomotives to rails, or steamboats to piers. Remotely situated farmers, miners, or shop owners were no longer isolated economically because they were far from railroad stations or ports. Social isolation was disappearing. The complex of highways that served the nation was being replanned and expanded, with 2340 miles of new concrete-surfaced roads already built, and a vision growing of a future system of 4,000,000 miles.[6]

The manufacture of motor cars had also made its contribution to the improvement of industrial tools and processes. "The real revolution in American consumption, involving not only radical changes in ways of living but also profound industrial consequences," wrote Ralph C. Epstein some years later, "is in large measure a function of the automobile." From the late eighteen-nineties, starting from the point reached by the successive advances of the arms, sewing machine, and bicycle industries, the automobile makers had taken over the development of machine tools. They had diminished the margin of tolerance for precision elements from a few hundredths of an inch to ten thousandths; they had experimented with alloy and heat-treated steels, immensely extended the possibilities of forgings and stampings, and developed the use of electricity to provide magnetos and batteries, self-starters and lighting systems. Their work in the provision of raw materials and spare parts, of factory layouts, and of mass production methods had been revolutionary.[7]

We shall do well to note at this point the meaning of that term, "mass production." Had an ordinary American been asked in 1915 what was the greatest achievement of the Ford Company, he would erroneously have replied, "The universal cheap car, the Model T." Its most remarkable exploit was actually the creation of the womb in which modern industry was to be reshaped, mass production. If asked to define mass production, the ordinary citizen would again have replied erroneously, "It means large-scale production by the use of uniform interchangeable parts." Indeed, most people still confound mass production with quantity production, which is only one of its elements. Actually, as Henry Ford himself wrote, mass production is the focussing upon a manufacturing operation of seven different principles: power, accuracy, economy, continuity, system, speed, and repetition. When all seven are used to make a car, tractor, refrigerator, airplane, or other complicated commodity, then mass production throws open the door to plenty, low prices, and an improved standard of living. Arming a people in peace against want, in war against enemies, it becomes an instrument to alter radically the shape of civilization.

By the end of 1915 the alteration had begun. Mass production had made its first appearance in the world at Highland Park in 1913–14. It was there that the seven principles named were combined in three great creative components. The first was the planned, orderly, and continuous progression of the commodity—the car—through the shop. The second was the systematic delivery of the work to the mechanic, instead of bringing the mechanic to his work. The third was the analysis of all the operations into their constituent parts, with a suitable division of labor and materials.

Each one of the components of mass production was in itself more complicated than any amateur student would suppose. We may instance the orderly and continuous progression of the growing commodity through the factory. The assembly line had to move at just the right speed, on just the right level, through just the right sequence of activities. Or, still more complex, we may instance the delivery of the work to the mechanic. This meant that a multitude of subsidiary assembly lines had to feed into the main assembly line at precisely the proper points and pace. A car-spring, for example, did not suddenly appear out of thin air beside the workman charged with fastening it to the chassis. No, the spring (which consisted of seven leaves) had itself passed through a variety of subordinate operations: punch press, bending machine, nitrate bath, bolt insertion, fastening of nuts on bolts, application of two clips, painting and inspection, every operation controlled by automatic gauges. This subsidiary line for providing springs (before long 50,000 a day) had to move without halt. It had to flow into the main assembly line as a small stream flows into a river. But a half-hundred other streams had to flow in, bearing each its vital part, at the same time; and the flow of every one had to be accurately controlled. The whole plant was in motion. Meantime, geared to this motion, every mechanic had his scientifically-ascertained fraction of the labor to perform; for the efficiency expert had found just how much he could best do, and what was the optimum time-allowance for doing it.

A kinetic plant!—moving, moving, moving; every segment—presses, furnaces, welders, stamps, drills, paint-baths, lathes—in use every minute; not an ounce of metal or a degree of heat avoidably wasted; and the economy in time and labor matching the economy in materials. Fascinating in its intricate intermeshing of activities, it meant a new era.

It meant a new era not only because mass production turned out far more goods at much lower prices than ever before, but for still larger reasons. It required the constant adoption of new methods and new machines, with the ruthless scrapping of all that was obsolete—even if it had cost a large sum but a few months earlier. It thus stimulated constant advances in the making of better machine-tools, and the installation of an ever-widening variety of single-purpose specialized machines. By lifting more of the load of work off men, and placing more of it on these complex mechanical tools, it reduced the really *hard* labor of the world. Samuel Butler had predicted a civilization in which machines would control men; but mass production implied that men constantly changed, improved, and more fully mastered machines as their servants. Under mass production, if it were properly administered, more skilled artisans and more creative designers would be needed than before; for every large factory would require busy departments devoted to invention, engineering, and art. In a world moulded economically by mass production, the control of industry would be more and more largely withdrawn from the mere financier, and more fully placed in the hands of the engineer, technician, and practical planner.

These were at any rate among the larger results which Henry Ford hoped would flow from this tremendous new force in human affairs. Another result he had already helped give reality. A rich abundance of inexpensive mass-produced goods would require a fast-expanding body of consumers. People must be given the means to buy; and Ford had possessed the insight and the courage to make high wages the concomitant of mass production. The five-dollar day had rung in a new economic era as the moving assembly line had ushered in a new industrial age. All this, could men but have seen it, was bound up in the Ford exhibit at the San Francisco Exposition, and, from that time forward, in most of the assembly lines of other automotive manufacturers.

By 1915 these manufacturers had passed the first experimental period, and their vehicle was emerging from the ugly duckling stage. At its best it was no longer an uncertain, rattling contraption, but an enclosed, well-shaped, reliable unit, protecting its occupants from weather, noise, shock, and breakdowns. Declared one trade journal: "Nineteen fifteen marks a turning point in American automobile design. The automobile, considered as an object viewed by itself, has ceased to present . . . a conglomeration of inharmonious and badly assorted shapes and has begun to move toward a distinctive and appropriate form." Six and eight cylinder engines were popular, and "streamlining" was becoming a common term in the discussion of design. The cheaper cars, including the Model T Ford, although not uninfluenced by this trend, were still angular and functional in appearance, like maiden aunts in a throng of soigné and beautifully costumed women. The open car and collapsible top were still widely prevalent, but a norm combining grace and improved performance had been accepted. The industry of 1915 was also maturing in sales and distribution, for it boasted of its branch factories, display rooms, newspaper and magazine advertisements, its 26,000 disciplined dealers, its abundant supplies of low-priced parts, and its extensive servicing facilities.[8]

Like most other great American industries, automotive manufacturing was in a process of concentration. Writing in *Motor Age* Darwin S. Hatch asserted that the 270 manufacturers and 400 models of 1911 had been reduced to 119 companies and 200 models. Most outstanding firms had been leaders for half a dozen years or more. The Ford company in the field of the cheap car; the Willys-Overland, Studebaker, Maxwell, and Buick in the $600–1000 range; the Chalmers, Paige, Hudson, Cadillac, Oldsmobile, and Oakland in the $1000–2000 group; and the Packard, Pierce-Arrow, Peerless, White, and Franklin in the luxury class—these were all notable. Among the newcomers W. C. Durant's Chevrolet, a crude forerunner of the car which William Knudsen was later to make famous, was the most remarkable, with its $625 Baby Grand and its $750 Royal Mail; while the Dodge was rapidly winning place with its $785, 4-cylinder, 24 horse power car. The Reo, Hupmobile, and Kissel all maintained a standing. General Motors was the largest combination in the field, manufacturing the Buick,

Oldsmobile, Oakland, and Cadillac; but John N. Willys (Willys-Overland) claimed a business second in volume only to Ford.

With fewer manufacturers and an increasing total product; with lighter, speedier, more reliable and comfortable cars; with factories adapted to the new moving assembly line; with the new system of installment buying affecting sixty per cent of its total output and creating hundreds of thousands of new customers, the industry was ready for expansion on a larger scale. Retiring as president of the Society of Automotive Engineers, Henry M. Leland, manufacturer of the Cadillac, prophesied in the spring of 1915 that automobiles would increase "in number and utility until they cover the face of the earth." [9] Indeed, with each year the potential market seemed to enlarge, like a landscape expanding with every step toward the horizon.

4.

In this growing industry the Ford Motor Company towered above its associates like a massive skyscraper soaring upward from a village, to contain almost as many people and as much activity as the rest of the community combined. Of the 880,000 motor vehicles produced in 1915, Ford made 308,000, or 35 per cent.* The company marketed four times as many cars as its strongest rival, the Willys-Overland, and as many as any six other automotive firms. On October 1, 1915, it celebrated its millionth car, and a few months later the millionth Model T. The fifty-six acre home plant at Highland Park made an imposing center for its activities. With dozens of buildings, 5500 humming machines, fifty miles of belting, one and one half of conveyor track, and 18,000 workers, the area, announced the *Ford Times* of April, 1915, was "the most productive acreage of equal extent in the world." Yet it was only the nucleus of an industrial empire comprising twenty-five branch plants in the United States (with other branches that did no assembling), factories in Canada and England, and seventeen foreign headquarters "in the principal cities of the world." Ford cars were driven everywhere "from sunny California to Thibet and Siberia, from Alaska to Siam, and from Greenland to India—and in the isles of the sea." In the United States alone more than 7000 dealers were busy marketing Ford products.[10]

---

* This figure was for the fiscal year ending June 30, 1915, while the total for the industry was for the calendar year. Ford production for that period was about 390,000, or 44.6 per cent of the national total.

When founded in 1903, the Ford Motor Company had issued shares of $100,000 total par value, but began operations with only $28,000 in cash. Except for a dribble during the first year, all other financing had been effected from company earnings.* The growth of the young organization had been fabulously rapid. The Ford Motor Company had soon moved to a larger factory, progressed from its first car, Model A, through improved types to the popular Model N, which brought it a net income as early as 1906–1907 of $1,163,184; and in 1908 presented its Model T. Early in 1910 it had occupied its new plant at Highland Park. Its improved production methods had brought an increasing yearly output of cars, and with the establishment of the moving assembly line in 1913, the company had been able to price its car at $500 —long a cherished goal of Henry Ford. Further reductions in price and a mounting output followed. In 1914–1915 more than 250,000 Model T's were produced, and the 1915 runabout was procurable for $390! By that year stock dividends had increased the original capitalization twenty-fold, to $2,000,000. The directors would soon vote a fifty-fold increase, for earnings and plant justified the total of $100,000,000.† All the stock was held by eight persons, with 58.5 per cent in the hands of Henry Ford. Up to 1914, dividends in cash and stock had amounted to $26,113,000. That year $12,200,000 more had been voted, and in 1915 $16,200,000 would be distributed. Over the years tens of millions had been spent on construction and improvements.[11]

As the one who had provided the original car and lent his name to the company, Ford had always exerted a strong influence on policy. This had increased after 1906, when he acquired a majority of the stock. However, thus far he had worked with his fellow directors, notably James Couzens and John and Horace Dodge. On numerous matters he had accepted their judgment, the more readily because they had always supported both his idea of a cheap, durable car, and a related program of steady plant expansion.‡ But although Couzens in particular had been a co-builder with Ford of the company, supervising

---

* Later in 1903 several small stock payments were made by stockholders, $2000 in all. For further details, see *Ford: the Times, the Man, the Company*, Chap. XI.

† They so voted on June 4, 1915, but discovered that the increase was impossible, as Michigan law limited capitalization to $25,000,000.

‡ Alex Y. Malcomson, chiefly responsible for financing the young company, had favored a high-priced, high-quality product. The Ford-Couzens group opposed him, and in 1906 he sold out to Ford for $175,000. This ended opposition to the small car, and gave Ford 51 per cent of company stock, which he increased by purchases from some of Malcomson's supporters.

closely its organization, finances, sales, and advertising, Ford was beginning to show a desire for a larger executive role.[12]

He and Couzens were alike in important respects, sharply different in others. Both gave a relentless energy to their work. Both had a strong sense of obligation to their workers and the public. Otherwise they showed contrasting characteristics.

Immensely able, independent, truculent, and exacting, Couzens drove or smashed his way to a goal. The business efficiency of the company had been attributable chiefly to him, and was his continuing concern. Ford, in contrast, believed that the heart of his or any other enterprise was its product, and regarded the business office as an evil to be tolerated—and less necessary than most people imagined. Long appreciative of Couzens's ability, he had begun to be irked by his economies and his domineering manner. President of the company, Ford had a spacious office at Highland Park, but used it little. Instead, he cruised about his immense plant, watchful, appraising, contemptuous of routines; and while capable of great incisiveness and firmness, was usually pleasant in manner, and likely to issue orders in the form of suggestions.

Moreover, while Ford's passion for improving both the design of his car and the processes of production was increasing, Couzens, in contrast, was now inclined to give less time and interest to his work: already he had the idea of turning from business to public life. Ford was aware of this changing attitude. "I have had a check kept on Jim," he said later, "and he has been at the plant only eighty-four days during the past year." [13] Thus the two, long in close harmony, had become less congenial. Big as the Ford Motor Company had become, it was not big enough for two leaders at once so dynamic yet so opposed in instincts, habits, and general disposition.

So successfully had Ford emphasized the importance of the factory as compared with the office that when the two spheres of activity clashed, the factory was likely to win. Partly this was because the engineers and production executives, close to Ford, many already widely known in the automotive world, made a larger and abler group than the business officials controlled by Couzens.

C. Harold Wills, Ford's associate in the development of the company's first car, exercised more influence on design and production than anyone except Ford himself. (He had no title, for Ford frowned on specific designations of authority, preferring to indicate certain duties for each of his lieutenants, and to let them develop their own spheres of activity in competition with each other.) Highly-gifted, original-minded, and energetic, Wills had been important enough to receive a part of Ford's own dividends—an arrangement made in 1902 which had lapsed, but was to be revived in 1917. Wills's work touched car design but extended beyond it to studies in metallurgy and to the planning of factory layout and routines. He had been Ford's strong right arm in the past, and to all appearances still was. At the same time, Ford harbored an uneasy feeling that his associate might some day cut loose and design a car of his own.[14]

Already fully capable of sharing authority at the planning level was William B. Mayo, a self-taught engineer of broad knowledge, with many personal friendships in the larger industrial field. In erecting the Highland Park factory in 1908–1915, Ford and Wills had commissioned the Hoover-Owens-Rentschler Company to build the engines for its powerhouse. Mayo had acted as their agent. Edward Gray, then Ford plant engineer, had opposed Ford's plan for immense steam-gas genera-tors, asserting that they could never be successfully constructed. Mayo assured Ford that they could be, and won the confidence of the manu-facturer, who liked a man to dare and accomplish the supposedly im-possible. He wanted Mayo with him, and an arrangement was made for the engineer to give part of his time to Ford affairs. By 1915 he was busy with ambitious plans for company expansion, and would soon lend his full effort to this and other Ford work.

Associated with Wills and Ford as head of the research laboratory was William H. Smith, an official acquired when the company bought the Keim Mills in Buffalo in 1911. His was the directing hand behind many experiments. Hungarian-born Joseph Galamb presided over the engineering department, and under him served his able compatriot Eugene Farkas. Both men had European technical school training. The equally gifted German-born Carl Emde was in charge of tool design. One of Smith's assistants, John Wandersee, had been developed from a promising subordinate into an able metallurgist.

Strategically situated because of his personal relationship to Ford, a young man of German descent, Ernest G. Liebold, was rapidly making an important place for himself in the company. Trained in financial routines, Liebold had been employed by Couzens in 1912 to organize a bank in Highland Park for the use of the Ford company and the community. He successfully discharged this task, joined the organization, soon took over Ford's personal finances and his correspondence, and began to act as his agent in important matters like the new Henry Ford Hospital and the tractor experiments. From the beginning he gave complete and expert devotion to his employer—a difficult feat, particularly outside the factory, as the precise wishes of Henry Ford were seldom easy to ascertain. Liebold showed a rigid mind and the disposition of a Prussian martinet, but Ford did not object to these qualities: the test was successful accomplishment, and Liebold met it.

In fact, his cold, ruthless intensity often served him well. Once he set a course he was pertinacious and if need be truculent in following it through. He did not cultivate his associates. One of them quoted him as saying: "I make it a rule not to have any friends in the company. You are then in a position where you don't give a God-damn what happens to anybody." Another told of wishing him a "Merry Christmas!" as he left the office on Christmas Eve. Liebold looked up from his work, hesitated, and finally responded, "Well, all right." [15] In 1915 he did not seem to stand as high among the group about Ford as he actually did, but with his ability, industry, and grim temper he was already making much of his favorable position.

John R. Lee, who like Smith had come to the Ford Motor Company from the Keim Mills, occupied an important post as the head of the Sociological Department, organized in 1913 to promote the welfare of company employees. After the establishment of the five-dollar minimum wage in 1914, this unit had increased immensely in importance, for it investigated every Ford worker and his family in relation to the wage, and organized a growing number of services for them. To high executive ability, Lee joined a winning personality, and exerted a happy influence throughout the organization and on the public. Dean Samuel S. Marquis, who late in 1915 took over the sociological work, called Lee "the soul of the organization," a man of "ideas and ideals," without whom the entire relationship of the company to its employees "would have taken its course along lower and conventional lines." In the spring of 1915 Marquis, a clergyman then unconnected with the company, was working with Lee as a volunteer to improve the quality of Ford welfare work. [16]

Potentially as important as any of the men high in engineering and executive work stood Edsel, Henry Ford's only son. Since completing high school three years earlier, he had been working in various departments of the factory. While Edsel Ford had a sense of humor and a youthful love of fun and adventure, as he was about to show in driving across the continent to the exposition in a Ford car, he also had unquestionable talent as an executive, and a grave sense of responsibility. "There are no frills, either in dress or manner, about E. B. Ford," wrote a St. Louis reporter who talked with him on his transcontinental journey. The newsman noted that Edsel serviced his own engine, displaying "a pair of well-developed forearms." The young man spoke of his role as Ford's son with factual directness. "I am twenty-one years old and am working in the factory to learn the business." Later in the year he was to assume his first executive position as secretary of the company.[17]

In the Highland Park factory, the heart of the Ford Motor Company, two men controlled the tens of thousands of workers and the routines of production. P. E. (Pete) Martin was nominally in charge, but his assistant, Charles E. Sorensen, wielded an authority almost if not quite as great.

Martin, a stocky French-Canadian, gave long hours to his work. The plant dominated his life: seldom was he able to be present at the birth of any of his thirteen sons and daughters because some situation in the factory demanded his attention. He knew every important fact about his domain, or could find it quickly in a little book he carried about with him. Somewhat cautious if faced with a new problem, when given time he made a sound decision or a creative suggestion. Always he kept production, with its exacting and interrelated demands, rolling smooth and full. He was a strict disciplinarian—in the minds of many workers a petty tyrant, ready on occasion to punish men for trifles. Some employees felt "cramped" in dealing with him. Others, while conceding that he was watchful, firm, and sometimes harsh, gave him respect and even affection. "I don't believe I ever heard anyone say anything against him, from the top down," said the engineer Frank Hadas years later. Another worker felt that Martin's attitude toward the thousands under him was that of a father. He exacted obedience, but he "seemed to take a paternal responsibility for every person in the shop."

In appearance the Danish-born Sorensen made a vivid contrast to the dark, stocky, severe, but quiet Martin. Tall, blond, powerful, he was so handsome that Percival Perry, head of Ford activities in England, called him an Adonis. The fire-darting Apollo would have been a truer image, for Sorensen was masculine energy incarnate. Beginning his Ford career as a worker in the foundry pattern shop, he had soon become its head, and won the confidence of Henry Ford by his quick ability to discern what the industrialist wanted, and his promptness in embodying it in a model that could be seen and touched. He was shifted to the larger arena of the factory, and as Martin's associate played a role in developing mass production. Combining a complete belief in and devotion to Ford with a burning passion for advancement, he drove both himself and others. Legends of his fury when challenged, and of his harsh whip-cracking on the factory floor, were already forming.

In his later years the tall Dane scornfully denied these tales, and reports of his violence were certainly exaggerated—it seems clear, for instance, that he never struck an associate or a worker. But there is no question of his ability to lash out verbally, to act with disconcerting abruptness, or to sweep men along with his purpose. He never questioned Ford's wishes, and carried out many unpleasant assignments for his employer, whether definite or inferred. For these actions he always took full responsibility. "I suspect many times," recalled J. L. McCloud, one of his associates, "Sorensen insisted in a very dictatorial fashion on the maintenance of a sacred cow which in reality was Mr. Henry Ford's cow, but you could never get Sorensen to say it." If he, like Martin, was resented and hated, he had his supporters, and if feared, was fully respected. His wide knowledge of factory processes, his resourcefulness, his bold judgments, and his general soundness on large policies as well as on details, marked him for advancement. In October, 1915, he would leave the Highland Park factory to direct tractor experiments in Dearborn, and for almost four years would have no official connection with the Ford Motor Company. But he remained close to Henry Ford.[18] *

Next to Martin and Sorensen in power stood three men: William S. Knudsen, Clarence W. Avery, and Charles Hartner.

Knudsen, also Danish-born, was another official who came to the company by way of the Keim Mills. Like Sorensen, he was tall and physically powerful; while a greater admirer of Henry Ford, he tended

---

* For Sorensen's own version of his early years with the Ford Motor Co., see the first third of the recently issued book, Charles E. Sorensen with Samuel T. Williamson, *My Forty Years with Ford*, New York, 1956, hereafter cited as Sorensen, *My Forty Years with Ford*.

to use more independence of judgment in serving him than did his fellow Dane. Knudsen confessed freely that he had a violent temper, but he had taught himself to control it completely. He was quieter, pleasanter, and less aggressive than Sorensen, winning rather than forcing the cooperation of his subordinates.* He knew factory layouts, machines, and processes, but had managed to avoid the tensions of Highland Park, attending instead to the construction and operation of the branch assembly plants. But he would soon return to Detroit and Dearborn, there to show brilliantly the abilities which were later to carry him, as a rival and not as a lieutenant of Ford, to a high place in the automotive world.[19]

Avery was responsible for assembly and the development of the new technology of mass production. He had once taught Edsel Ford manual training at the University School, but when he left the classroom for the factory he quickly proved his high practical capacity. His had been a dominant role in the planning of the moving assembly line. Quiet and pleasant in manner, he could deal firmly with a shop emergency, but was particularly gifted in devising new processes of manufacture, with their new machine tools and routines, or in ironing out the complex difficulties of production.

Hartner presided over all machine operations and other aspects of heavy manufacture. His was an energy little short of Sorensen's, and a knowledge and judgment in his narrower field that were comparable.

All three men had gifted lieutenants: Knudsen the able Frank Hadas, Avery the energetic William C. Klann, and Hartner the resourceful John Findlater (another Keim man). Associated with the factory but operating outside it was Fred Diehl, in charge of purchasing, a vital activity affecting company supplies and costs. He had developed this work since 1908, and was assisted by A. M. Wibel, a well-trained and able executive, who eventually succeeded him.

Under Couzens, Frank L. Klingensmith was already well acquainted with the business routines of the company; Norval A. Hawkins had charge of advertising and sales, and Charles A. ("Daddy") Brownell of advertising routines under his guidance. Hawkins had come to the company in 1907 to lift the growing sales problems from Couzen's shoulders. As if born to the task, he had built up a magnificent or-

---

* Said one Ford worker who knew both men: "Sorensen was a wild man, and Knudsen was a mild man." (C. J. Smith, *Reminiscences*.)

ganization of branch managers and dealers, had launched the lively *Ford Times,* had brought order into shipment routine, and infused the entire public relations work of the company with his optimism and originality.[20]

5.

When the San Francisco exposition opened, Henry Ford was fifty-one. His light brown hair was graying, but his body and mind were both at the peak of vigor. As lean and sinewy as in his thirties, his color clear, his light blue eyes alive and searching, he seemed wholly unaware of the success he had achieved. Encountering this quiet man of little more than medium height, friendly and unoppressed by worries, a stranger might have passed him by as a fellow-citizen of no particular importance.*

Any extended acquaintance would have altered this impression sharply. Ford possessed one of the most original personalities in all the history of a land that had produced its share of "originals." Relaxed in manner, he was nonetheless a dynamo of energy. He could walk for hours, whether through his beloved Dearborn countryside or the aisles of his plant, with springy step and alert glance that never showed fatigue. He might vault a fence, climb a tree, or strip off his coat to tinker with a machine, as the whim seized him. He believed that every moment, every experience, could be creative. "Everything is in flux, and was meant to be," he declared a few years later. "Life flows. We may live at the same number on the street, but it is never the same man who lives there." Recognizing more clearly than any of his contemporaries what he had accomplished, he regarded his success merely as a stepping stone to more important achievements. "It could almost be written down as a formula," he said, "that when a man begins to think that he has at last found his method he had better begin a most searching examination of himself to see whether some part of his brain has not gone to sleep."

Ford acted out this philosophy. Proud of the Model T, he believed its future could be more remarkable than its past, and in 1915 was mak-

---

* An incident illustrates Ford's casualness. At the San Francisco Fair exhibit Frank Vivian had gone down beneath the floor of the moving assembly line with a worker to inspect some machinery located there. Only a few loose boards provided footing above the waters of the bay. Suddenly he looked up, and in the light of an electric torch held by the worker saw Ford standing beside him. Vivian exclaimed: "Gosh, you better look out. This is a dangerous place for you." Ford replied calmly: "It is not any more dangerous for me than for you."

ing plans to validate that conviction. He had plans also for his 18,000 workers. Now that they and their families represented a sizeable city, his interest in them could not be so personal as in earlier years, when he knew each man by name, and often had a smile, a jest, or a slap on the back for him. But he talked with the men busy with experimental work, and every Saturday noon put his office at the disposal of the young women of the administrative staff. He would bring oranges and bananas. "It was sort of open house on Saturday noons when the plant would close," recalled Liebold.

His interest in his workers ran strong at this time; he remembered his own years as a mechanic and operational engineer, wanted his employees to share in what they helped to create, and prided himself on an active relationship with them. Edsel joined in this feeling. It was a halcyon period in the company's labor policy, with special services for workers, the employment of handicapped persons, and liberal profit-sharing. The *Ford Times* announced in June, 1915, that approximately $10,000,000 had been divided that year among employees, while the company proposed to share $15,000,000 more with the buyers of its cars through reduced prices.[21] Of course, Ford's attitude and acts were paternalistic, and like most employers in the industry, he was firmly opposed to labor unions. However, since he gave much more than unions of the day demanded, his disapproval of them was little noted.

Ford asserted that his generosity was not charity, but justice and an opportunity for the worker to help himself. Of the men who designed and built his cars he demanded both diligence and initiative. Every engineer and executive knew this, and was prepared to attempt the impossible. "If Mr. Ford brought in a new idea," said C. J. Smith, who worked on experimental projects, "none of the workmen dared to tell him it wouldn't work." This attitude permeated the organization. Logan Miller, who about this time played a responsible role in production, tells how Hartner asked him when he could be ready to produce a unit for the first Model T self-starter. It was a complicated task, and Miller, calculating quickly, named a date several weeks distant. "Hell, no!" retorted Hartner. "I'll give you a week. Can you do it?" Miller agreed. "You never said No," he remarked years later. He went back to tell his men, and they leaped to perform prodigies so that he could keep his promise.

With hawk-like sharpness Ford watched each new experiment, feel-

ing out the mood of his men, pushing them toward the goal. He liked
to see individuals grow, and, says Farkas, often purposely set a man a
problem that would "stretch" him. He also liked to see every worker
from the top down compete. "It was a combination of competition and
cooperation that he required. It was very hard for an outsider to understand that, but the condition existed right along. He would have them
compete with ideas and then coöperate in carrying out the one that was
selected as the best." But if too much friction developed, Ford would
perceive it, and if necessary break the tension by sending one of the
men involved "to England or South America for a while." [22]

Ford had a "mean streak," which might be expressed indirectly, or
occasionally reveal itself in sharp words or action, but in this period it
was little in evidence, while his positive qualities were frequently
shown. A few years later John Burroughs wrote an impression of him
on a vacation camping trip which shows the effect he made upon admiring friends. Doubtless in the factory he was different, but the description applies partly to work as well as to leisure hours. The camping
party had set up its tents by a stream:

Mr. Ford is . . . adaptive, . . . indifferent to places. . . . His interests in
the stream is in its potential water power. He races up and down its banks
to see its fall, and where power could be developed. He is never tired of
talking how much power is going to waste everywhere, and says that if the
streams were all harnessed . . . farm labor everywhere could be greatly
lessened.

. . . Mr. Ford always thinks in terms of the greatest good to the greatest
number. He aims to place all his inventions within the reach of the great
mass of people. . . . In building his tractor engine he has had the same end
in view. He does not forget the housewife either, and plans for bringing
power into every household that would greatly lighten the burden of the
women folk. . . . Mr. Ford is a runner and high kicker, and frequently
challenges some member of the party to race with him. He is also a persistent walker, and from every camp, both morning and evening, he sallies
forth for a brisk half-hour walk. His cheerfulness and adaptability on all
occasions, and his optimism in regard to all great questions, are remarkable.
. . . Notwithstanding his practical turn of mind, and his mastery of the
mechanic arts, he is through and through an idealist. This combination of
powers and qualities makes him a very interesting, and, I may say, loveable
personality. He is as tender as a woman, and much more tolerant. He looks
like a poet, and conducts his life like a philosopher. No poet ever expressed

himself through his work more completely than Mr. Ford has expressed himself through his car and his tractor engine—they typify him—not imposing, not complex, less expressive of power and mass than simplicity, adaptability, and universal service.

This was the Ford many knew in 1915. His reputation was established; from Dearborn to Russia admirers sang his praises. Declared an Irish writer: "When you study the Ford Company you have before you a great state, perfect in every particular—the nearest that anything on the face of this earth has got to Utopia"! Edgar Guest, with the five-dollar day in mind, grew sentimental over the Ford achievement:

'Tis a happier world for his living here, there is joy where but grief was
    known,
Contentment reigns where misery once builded his hateful throne.
The children laugh where they used to wail, and the eyes of parents glow
With the happiness they used to think only the rich could know.
And this is the work of Henry Ford—all this shall the future scan,
And find in him a friend who lived and thought of his fellow man.[23]

These were voices in a chorus, usually less extreme, which approved Ford's attitudes and accomplishments. Only a man of remarkable modesty would not have been affected; Ford was. Tacitly he accepted the implication that his was a wisdom extending beyond machines and industry. Several years earlier his love of birds had prompted him to work for the passage of the Weeks-McLean bill for their protection; he had summoned his dealers to help, and Congress had passed the measure by a triumphant majority. With the onset of the European war he had become concerned over possible American participation, and as early as January had shown his conviction that the war was as unnecessary as it was tragic: "If there had been work enough there would have been no war," he told a group of New York newsmen.[24]

As his reputation increased, Ford had made distinguished friends who helped to broaden his experience and increase his interest in the world beyond the factory. Thomas A. Edison, John Burroughs, Harvey Firestone of the Firestone Tire and Rubber Company, William Livingston of the Detroit Dime Savings Bank, and John Wanamaker were among them.[25]

The Fords were building a new residence appropriate to their increasing wealth and reputation. Fair Lane, named for the area in Ireland where the Ford family had its home, stood on the banks of the Rouge River, in a wooded tract remote from the highway. A four-story power plant had been erected on the river a hundred yards to the south, to supply garage space, electricity, heat, and water. Both this structure and Fair Lane itself were built of Kelly Island limestone, with thick walls. The residence, a blend of architectural styles, and undistinguished in design, was redeemed by its simplicity and its happy situation.* Its western rooms and piazza afforded views up and down the river, with a northward vista of tall trees reflected in quiet water, and southward glimpses of the stream as it dropped eight feet over the power house dam. For years the Fords had spent weekends on the Dearborn estate, occupying a six-room bungalow near the river, north of their later residence. Early in 1915 they moved into the Ten Eyck house, a two-story structure near Michigan Avenue, not far from the site of the present gate house of the estate. Here they lived while supervising the completion of the new house, which was not finished until December.[26]

6.

But while he gave time to Fair Lane, to his new friends, and to public affairs, Ford in 1915 was centering his principal energies upon automotive production. He was following with particular interest the development of his tractor. "The planning of the tractor," he said later, "really antedated that of the motor car." From boyhood he had nursed an ambition "to lift farm drudgery off flesh and blood and lay it on steel and motors." As a young man he had used portable steam engines for simple tractor work, and once the Ford Motor Company was established he had begun experiments with motor-propelled machines. Joseph Galamb declared that "in 1906 or 1907" Ford came to him and said: "Joe, we have to build a tractor in three days." This, shown by a surviving sketch dated 1907, was the first of several models constructed under Ford's supervision. All worked well enough to please him temporarily, but all developed serious defects. However, in 1915 Eugene Farkas, whom Ford sent to Dearborn to direct work on a fresh design, began to evolve a more promising model. Kroll, Galamb, and Sorensen (who supervised the overall project) took a hand in the work, which Ford watched closely.[27]

* There are faint traces of early Frank Lloyd Wright, and of English Gothic in the building; but in general it is simply a rather plain, oblong structure, broken by a few abortive irregularities.

The tractor was a project with immense business and social implications. Ford was already planning to manufacture it in a temporary Dearborn factory, which would later be superseded by a plant of mammoth proportions. The site of this latter plant would also provide space for the manufacture of the Model T on a new and greater scale than anyone but Ford had then imagined; for the current annual production of some 300,000 cars, while the wonder of the contemporaneous world, seemed to him pitifully inadequate.

A new site had been considered because the 56-acre tract at Highland Park would not be adaptable to much expansion. Additional land might be acquired at a high cost, but water supply was much more the problem, and limited future production to about 500,000 cars a year. Both Ford and Wills felt that a million cars should be the minimum goal, for this would permit immense savings and dispel any immediate threat of competition. Ford had long eyed the area southeast of Dearborn where the Rouge River wound its way toward the Detroit. In the spring of 1915 he began buying land there. For a time he did not plan to abandon Highland Park. Rather he envisaged the Rouge area as a site for the smelting of iron and the making of coke, and for his tractor plant. It would also permit him to shift some units from Highland Park, such as the foundry and the power house.*

Ford had spoken to his associates about the expansion he contemplated, but none of them except Wills, and later Mayo, seems to have grasped its magnitude. However, they approved the Rouge as a site for supplementary activities, and on June 16, 1915 Couzens joined with Ford in a statement about the new development. "Nothing will be done there for three or four years, probably," he told reporters. Ford gave a different impression, and several days later pictured a great industrial center as a certainty for the future. If he was vague as to details, it was doubtless because he did not wish to alarm his associates, but actually he was already planning to cut dividends and plow back profits into expansion.[28]

Such a policy, he knew, would particularly disturb the two Dodge brothers, who had a special reason for desiring dividends to continue on their recent princely scale. For some years they had manufactured parts for Ford cars—in 1912 their factory had turned out 180,000 sets valued at $10,000,000. The Ford Motor Company was their only cus-

* For details as to the genesis of the Rouge, see Chap. VIII.

tomer. Perceiving that their situation was vulnerable, they had decided to manufacture a car of their own, had served notice, as was their right, that they would terminate their contract to supply parts, and already in 1915 had a model on the market. The $1,100,000 in dividends they had received in 1914 was extremely helpful to them in their present position, for in May they were planning overseas establishments. Naturally they looked forward to receiving further large sums as Ford stockholders.[29]

They were not worried about the Rouge development. Couzens was treasurer of the company, and the Dodges felt he could be depended upon to control disbursements for expansion. He had always done so.

But as the year advanced, Couzens's position in the organization ceased to be as unshakeable as they had supposed. While Ford was restive under the growing differences in attitude between him and his chief associate, Couzens was annoyed by the growing frequency of Ford's pronouncements against war. Canadian-born and of English parentage, he was vigorously pro-Ally. He must have heard bitterly the remark attributed to Ford about the men and women lost when the *Lusitania* was torpedoed in May: "Well, they were fools to go on that boat, because they were warned." Couzens doubtless wished the company to manufacture for the Allies, but Ford had declared that he would rather burn down his factory than supply materials for war.[30] On August 22nd Ford gave out a statement denouncing "murderous, wasteful war in America and in the whole world." He declared: "I have prospered much and I am ready to give much to end this constant, wasteful 'preparation.'" (He referred to the movement to prepare the Army and Navy against possible conflict.) And again: "I hate war, because war is murder, desolation, and destruction."

Such utterances expressed Ford's feelings, and probably incorporated phrases he had used. But he had no gift for public speaking or for extended written statements, and his published opinions were being prepared by Theodore Delavigne, a Detroit journalist.[31] Couzens was indignant when Ford's tirade was reprinted in the *Ford Times* for September, with a note: "To no better purpose can the pages of the 'Ford Times' be given than to voice the mission of peace." As the company's organ for advertising, the *Times* was closely related to Couzens, for Hawkins and Brownell were technically under his supervision. When he saw further pacifist copy (apparently that for the October issue, which comprised an editorial and another article quoting Ford), he ordered it killed, and told his partner he had "stopped it."

"You can't stop anything," retorted Ford. "It's going to stay in."

"All right. Then I quit."

"Better think it over, Jim," advised Ford.

"I have. I'm through."

Ford hesitated a moment, then said, "All right." [32]

A few days later he explained to Edwin G. Pipp, then on the Detroit *News,* that he had really let Couzens go because he had neglected his work as an officer of the company. "If Jim is on the job, I'd rather have his judgment than anybody's, but Jim's judgment off the job isn't as good as somebody else's on the job." He added that Couzens had political ambitions that "didn't mix with holding a job in the Ford Motor Company." He had come to the office that day to discuss the matter, Couzens had raised the issue of the material in the *Ford Times,* and Ford had said to himself: "Fine. That's a dandy way out of it," and had "stood pat."

Couzens gave a statement to the press in which he termed Ford's views on "peace, and the Allies' war loan and national preparedness" the cause of his resignation. "The friendly relations that have existed between us for years have been changed of late, our disagreements daily becoming more violent."

> I finally decided that I would not be carried along on that kind of a kite. . . . I have never in my life worked for any man. Even when I was a car checker, a few years ago, I had no boss; but I was, and am today, willing to work with any man. I will be willing to work with Henry Ford, but I refuse to work for him.

He sent in his resignation as vice-president and treasurer that very day, October 12; it was accepted by the directors on the 13th. He retained his post as a director.[33]

Ironically, a dividend of $5,000,000 was declared on the 13th, and Horace E. Dodge wrote Frank Klingensmith to thank him for "the lovely dividend just received." (The Dodges' share was $500,000.)

The situation thus altered to increase the likelihood of a clash between Ford, with his plans for expansion, and the Dodges, with their assumption that the flow of dividends would not diminish. Couzens, the logical restraining hand, was no longer a company official.

For the time, however, no conflict developed. Early in October Ford announced that he would set up a corporation wholly owned by his family to manufacture his tractor. This announcement seemed to the Dodges to assure the maintenance of the *status quo,* for John Dodge later testified that he thought the entire Rouge development related to the tractor project.[34] Although this was not the fact, Ford's keen interest in his new machine absorbed much of his energy for a time, while his concern with peace propaganda was increasing. This would soon pass from the stage of statements and private conference into action.

II

PEACE CRUSADE

Ford's intensive peace activities really began in November, 1915, when a company car drew up at the Ten Eyck house, his temporary home on the Fair Lane estate, bringing two guests. One was Rosika Schwimmer, Hungarian author and lecturer, a dark, stout, vibrant woman in her late thirties who had served such causes as woman suffrage, birth control, and trade unionism. Her companion, Louis P. Lochner, a slender, blond young American, had recently acted as secretary of the International Federation of Students. Both were now workers for world peace.[1]

From the beginning of the war an advocate of mediation by neutrals, Rosika Schwimmer in April, 1915, had helped persuade the International Congress of Women at The Hague to support such a policy. She assisted Jane Addams and others to gather evidence that both neutrals and belligerents were receptive to mediation. When she came to the United States as a lecturer later in the year, she brought documents that allegedly proved the existence of such an attitude. Madame Schwimmer noted Henry Ford's declaration in August, 1915, that he was prepared to dedicate his fortune and his life to achieving peace, wrote to him, and through Edwin G. Pipp of the Detroit *News* eventually procured an interview. She aroused Ford's interest. He brushed aside the objections of counsellors like Dean Marquis and William Livingston, and after he had seen her documents remarked: "Well, let's start. What do you want me to do?"

Lochner arrived in Detroit at this time, also seeking an interview with Ford. He came fresh from a conference which he and David Starr Jordan, President of Stanford University and chairman of the Fifth International Peace Congress, had held in Washington with Woodrow Wilson. Lochner felt that if a greater popular demand for peace could be demonstrated, Wilson might call a peace conference at Washington, where representatives of neutral nations would appoint a commission to work unremittingly ("continuous mediation") for a peace acceptable to all belligerents. This plan had been publicized by Julia Grace Wales of the University of Wisconsin.[2]

After the two had arrived at the Ten Eyck house, Ford left Madame Schwimmer with Clara "to talk things over," and hustled Lochner off to his experimental tractor shop. There he took him aside and demanded: "What do you think of Madame Schwimmer's proposal? Is it practical? How much will it cost to maintain a neutral commission in Europe?"

Lochner warmly supported the idea of continuous mediation, and also suggested that Ford seek an interview with President Wilson at which he could offer to maintain an official commission abroad until Congress made an appropriation; this failing, he could support an unofficial body which would perform comparable work. Ford listened closely, and seemed to approve. When they returned to the Ten Eyck house, they found that Clara Ford had been won over to the cause of "continuous mediation." Appealing to her as a mother, Madame Schwimmer had proposed that she finance a barrage of telegrams to the White House supporting that policy. These would fortify a personal plea which Schwimmer and Mrs. Philip Snowden of England were to make to Wilson on November 26. Ford approved the estimated expenditure of $10,000. Then Madame Schwimmer left for New York, Ford and Lochner agreeing to follow her the next afternoon.

As the two men were borne eastward the following day, Ford was as happy as if he had hatched an idea for a revolutionary new motor car. He bubbled with talk. Lochner noted his keen instinct for publicity. "Whatever we decide to do," declared the manufacturer, "New York is the place for starting it." He revealed a gift for epigram, striking off such crisp pronouncements as: "Men sitting around a table, not men dying in a trench, will finally settle the differences." He watched Lochner closely, and if he detected a favorable response would say: "Make a note of that; we'll give that to the boys when we get to New York."

He established himself at the Biltmore Hotel, and on the following day, November 21, lunched with a group at the McAlpin. It included Jane Addams of Hull House, Chicago, Dean George W. Kirchwey of

Columbia University, Paul Kellogg of the *Survey,* and of course Lochner and Madame Schwimmer. All approved the plan of sending if possible an official mediating commission to Europe; failing that, a representative private group. Ford and Lochner would go to Washington to seek Wilson's cooperation, which would invest the project with an official status.

In the talk at table, Lochner half jestingly suggested: "Why not a special ship to take the delegates over?" Ford's approval flashed like a light to the click of a switch. In vain Jane Addams objected to the plan as flamboyant; Ford liked it for that very reason. Men could see it; it would lift talk into action and arouse a sharper interest. He sent at once for representatives of steamship companies, and posing as "Mr. Henry" inquired what it would cost to charter a vessel. The agents stared at him, but when told his identity quickly made their calculations. Having started negotiations, Ford waved them over to Rosika Schwimmer, and by evening she had chartered the Scandinavian-American liner *Oscar II.*

Through Colonel Edward M. House, then in New York, Ford procured an appointment with President Wilson for the following day. Promising a group of reporters that he would see them Wednesday, he and Lochner left for Washington.

The conference with the President began pleasantly. Lochner contrasted it with the one Dr. Jordan had conducted. "Dr. Jordan came attired in a somber Prince Albert coat; Mr. Ford wore a plain business suit. Dr. Jordan used collegiate English; Mr. Ford talked 'plain American.' Dr. Jordan remained standing respectfully until urged by the President to take a seat; Mr. Ford slipped unceremoniously into an armchair, and during most of the interview had his left leg hanging over the arm of the chair and swinging back and forth."

Ford complimented the President on his appearance; how did he keep so trim? Wilson replied that he tried to forget business after business hours, and to enjoy a good joke. "Some of them Ford jokes, I hope?" suggested Lochner. Ford then told one such story he had invented himself.* Wilson chuckled and capped it with a limerick.

---

* The story: one day, driving by a cemetery, Ford noticed a huge hole being dug by a grave-digger, and asked him if he were going to bury a whole family in one grave. The man replied No, that the grave was for one person. Then why was it so enormous? The grave-digger explained that the deceased was a queer fellow, and had stipulated in his will that he must be buried in his Ford, because the Ford had pulled him out of every hole thus far, and he was sure it would pull him out of this one.

Then Ford explained his mission. He urged Wilson to appoint a neutral commission, offering to finance it.

The President replied that he did not feel able to take such a step. He approved the idea of continuing mediation, but a better plan might be offered. He could not be tied to any one project; he must be free.

This was too equivocal for Ford. He said that he had chartered a steamship, and had promised the press an announcement on the following morning. He offered the ship to the president. "If you feel you can't act, I will." Wilson was startled, but stood by his first statement, and Ford and Lochner soon found themselves on the White House grounds. Ford shook his head, but if his companion feared for the fate of the expedition, he was quickly reassured. Ford was only regretful that the President had missed a great opportunity. "He's a small man," he said.[3]

2.

Even before the appointed hour of ten on Wednesday the 24th, reporters began to arrive at the Biltmore. With Lochner and Oswald Garrison Villard, whom he had expressly asked to be present (the *New York Times* reported Jane Addams and Ida M. Tarbell also there), Ford chatted with the newsmen until forty had gathered, a number which somewhat abashed him. He began rather haltingly: "A man should always try to do the greatest good to the greatest number, shouldn't he?" He went on:

"We're going to try to get the boys out of the trenches before Christmas. I've chartered a ship, and some of us are going to Europe."

Lochner and Villard supplied details. Asked about the ship and its voyage, Ford stated that he would assemble a group "of the biggest and most influential peace advocates in the country, who can get away, on this ship." He would also have "the longest gun in the world—the Marconi." Jane Addams, John Wanamaker, and Thomas A. Edison would sail with him.[4] *

The interview was page one news for New York papers, and, in consequence, for most others. But from the beginning a vein of satire was apparent:

* Villard, in his *Fighting Years* (New York, 1939), 304–305, gives an account differing in particulars from the text above. He says that Ford began with, "Well, boys, we've got the ship." However, in fundamentals Villard agrees with Lochner and the news accounts. He states that he never received $20,000 which Ford promised in this interview for a campaign against preparedness.

GREAT WAR ENDS
CHRISTMAS DAY
FORD TO STOP IT

announced the *Tribune.* The *World, Times,* and *Evening Post* were more factual. Only a flicker of humor lit the news accounts. For two days there were no editorials.

When they came, satire was more pronounced, often veering toward invective. American opinion, molded by the *Lusitania* and other submarine sinkings, and by skilled Allied propaganda, was increasingly anti-German. Also, men tended to believe that only a clear Allied victory could insure a satisfactory peace. However, the *New York Times* of November 27th pictured Ford as "thoroughly well-intentioned" and likely to do "as little harm as good;" and perhaps capable of learning in Europe that "immediate peace, enormously desirable as it is . . . might be attained at costs in comparison to which those of continuing the struggle would be negligible." The *Evening Post* (controlled less by its owner, Villard, than by its editor Rollo Ogden) defended the expedition. The plan would of course be ridiculed. "But we must venture the prediction that his [Ford's] generous act of knight-errantry will be acclaimed by thoughtful hundreds of thousands the world over as a bit of American idealism in an hour when the rest of the world has gone mad over war and war-preparedness." The Jewish press, and some Jewish rabbis from the pulpit, praised Ford's courage and idealism, and the socialists approved it.

But the general chorus was condemnatory. The *World,* usually friendly to Ford, called the peace ship an "impossible effort to establish an inopportune peace." The New York *Herald* termed it "one of the cruellest jokes of the century." The Hartford *Courant* remarked that "Henry Ford's latest performance is getting abundant criticism and seems entitled to all it gets." The Baltimore *Sun* suggested that Bryan take command of the ark: "If a brutal German submarine should sink her nothing would be lost."

Along with such cutting comment by editors ran a *leit-motiv* of raillery in news reports, letters, and verse. John O'Keefe dashed off "The Flivvership," which the *World* printed on the same day and page as its editorial:

I saw a little fordship
Go chugging out to sea,
　And for a flag
　It bore a tag
　Marked 70 h.p.
And all the folk aboardship
Cried "Hail to Hennery!"

The author described the purpose and lack of plans of the crusaders, and finished:

And so, without a quiver
The dreadful task they dare
　Of teaching peace
　To France and Greece
And Teuton, Celt, and Bear.
Ho for the good ship Flivver,
Propelled by heated air! [5]

3.

It is only just to note certain factors bearing on the peace ship which were ignored by most commentators at the time, and have never been given the attention they deserve. Particularly should Ford's pacifism and his project be considered in relation to the peace movement of his day.

While his aversion to war flared out intensely in 1915, we have no direct evidence as to how it had developed. A year later one writer asserted that it had been implanted from childhood by his mother, Mary Litogot Ford. Her personal experiences in the Civil War, including her son's birth during it, were represented as so affecting her that "she gave to Henry Ford an inherited aversion to war." [6]

This statement is more than plausible.* It is also possible that both Mary Ford and her son were influenced by Mary's adopted father, Patrick O'Hern, who deserted from the British army in Canada, and presumably had no love for things military. Furthermore, an aversion

---

* Of Mary Ford's three brothers, two became soldiers, and John was killed at Fredericksburg, Va., on Dec. 12, 1862. Barney was wounded at Gettysburg, not a month before Henry Ford's birth, and although he was discharged, to marry and have two sons, one of these later testified that the war was the indirect cause of his father's death in the early 'seventies. (*Ford: the Times, the Man, the Company,* 22, 39.)

to war may have marked the Ford side of the family. Of a dozen Fords of military age in the Dearborn area in 1861, including Henry's father William, not one volunteered to serve the Union.

School may have influenced Ford. The McGuffey readers, which he used and later esteemed sufficiently to reprint in quantity, contain lessons depicting soldiers as murderers (*Fourth Reader,* "Things by Their Right Name"), questioning the usefulness of military victories (*Sixth Reader,* Southey's "Battle of Blenheim"), and challenging the roles of noted heroes. So in "How Big was Alexander, Pa?" a son protests:

> But, Pa, did Alexander wish
> That some strong man would come,
> And burn his house, and kill him, too,
> And do as he had done?
> And everybody calls him great
> For killing people so;
> Well, now, what *right* had he to kill,
> I should be glad to know.

Other selections were designed to promote an aversion to war. Evidently McGuffey felt with Washington, Franklin, and Jefferson that war was a scourge mankind should strive to abolish. Still, the editor was no pacifist, and included selections that extolled patriotism and the warlike deeds of patriots.[7]

Actually, Ford grew up in an era marked by an increasing devotion to peace. When he was beginning his experiments with the automobile in the eighteen-nineties the few faltering peace societies of the early nineteenth century had become many, strong, and influential. The cause of international arbitration, receiving its first great impetus from the successful work of the Geneva Tribunal in settling Anglo-American differences in 1871, and supported by Quakers, Manchester Liberals, and international business interests, had enlisted many authors and editors. When in 1899 Czar Nicholas II called a conference at The Hague to codify the laws of war and establish a Court of International Arbitration, the event seemed to confirm the value of their work, as did a second conference in 1904.

In seeking to avert war, Nicholas had been influenced by the powerful novel *Lay Down Your Arms,* by the Austrian baroness Bertha von

Suttner, and also by *War* (1898), an attack by Jean de Bloch, one of the czar's own subjects, on the character and cost of armed conflict. Even before the first Hague conference Alfred Nobel of Sweden had established a Peace Prize of 150,000 kroner for "the man or woman who, during the year, has contributed most . . . to the cause of peace." [8] Ideas of the humanization and prevention of war continued to grow. A brilliant Englishman, Norman Angell, attacked motivations for war in *The Great Illusion* (1908), arguing that the victor as well as the vanquished lost by it. In the United States the American School Peace League (1907) fostered peace sentiment in the public schools, peace societies multiplied, and peace magazines flourished. Theodore Roosevelt had won the Nobel peace prize in 1904 for helping to end the Russo-Japanese war, and two institutions had been founded in 1910 to combat war: Edwin Ginn's World Peace Foundation and Andrew Carnegie's Endowment for International Peace. From 1903 onward American secretaries of state and presidents had pushed arbitration treaties with other nations, John Hay negotiating thirteen in 1904–1905, Elihu Root twenty-seven in 1908, and Taft and Bryan (under Wilson) continuing the effort. Unfortunately most of these pacts had been emasculated by the Senate.

Pacifism in the United States on the eve of World War I was thus not only respectable but little short of triumphant. An atmosphere of faith in the goodness of mankind hung over the country like a spell of golden weather. The Hague conferences, the adjudication of fourteen disputes by the International Court of Arbitration, the signing of arbitration treaties—such events seemed milestones leading to a glorious goal. Young intellectuals earnestly discussed the probable span of time—10, 25, or 50 years—before war would become extinct.[9]

These talks did not live by the ideal of peace alone. New winds of thought and aspiration from other sources were then blowing across the United States and the world. The ideas of Theodore Roosevelt on social justice, and Woodrow Wilson's New Freedom, fortified all believers in a nobler world. Henry Ford had not read Upton Sinclair's *The Jungle,* Jack London's *People of the Abysses,* or John Spargo's *The Bitter Cry of the Children,* but he knew that the protest against human exploitation was gaining volume. He knew something of what Tom L. Johnson of Cleveland, Ben Lindsey of Denver, and Jane Addams stood for, and if he had never heard Vachel Lindsay's "Eagle That is Forgotten," with its praise of Altgeld's championship of the poor, or known of Romain Rolland in France, Karl Liebknecht in Germany, or H. G. Wells and Keir Hardie in England, he moved among men and women who had, and who carried the dream of a more just, serene, and joyful world through their hours of work and leisure. Great hopes were in the air; a new age was being born when the war of 1914 lurched across it like an artillery caisson over a bed of flowers.

If the war shattered the mood of the time, it also aroused fierce resentment, and intensified bruised hopes. Pacifists proclaimed the conflict to be merely a frightful demonstration of the rightness of all they had said. Peace societies were more aggressive than ever. In verse and prose American writers lifted voices of protest. An immense section of the public was receptive toward any step likely to hasten the end of the slaughter. Ford himself, who had hitherto been silent, but like others had now stepped forth to testify, spoke in the spirit of the time. His was no wild, perverse crusade; he was marching along the same road that Hay, Root, Taft, Bryan, and others had travelled, and millions in spirit marched with him.

He had already won an important objective: he had aroused the widest possible attention. Could the venture, even if born in ridicule, be so managed as to impress the watching world? One element was time: time for effective organization, time for eminent individuals to adjust their affairs to the voyage. It would have been wiser to postpone a public announcement until a number of distinguished guests had been pledged. But the announcement having been made when it was, Ford could still have associated the project with the new year rather than with Christmas, gaining a month or more. He and his associates could then have planned the cruise more carefully, enhanced the chances of success, and safeguarded the dignity of the enterprise. Instead, announcing December 4 as the date of sailing, he left only nine days for assembling guests and planning the expedition. This was stacking the cards against his project from the start.*

---

* It is interesting to note Jane Addams's attitude. As previously noted, she opposed the idea of a ship. Later, she objected to the slogan, "Get the boys out of the trenches by Christmas," and as she perceived its effect she telephoned from Chicago to Lochner, "and begged him to keep the enterprise in hand." She believed later that the ridicule heaped on the cruise resulted in "three leading internationalists who had seriously considered going, and . . . two others who had but recently accepted" withdrawing from the expedition. Nevertheless, she recognized some force in the argument that anti-war movements had been "too grey and negative, that the heroic aspect of life had been too completely handed over to war." She noted later that the Dutch Minimum Program movement, very circumspectly conducted, had not (cont'd on p. 35)

Why did Ford set himself this all but insuperable challenge? The answer lay in his own character. He had never followed conventional paths, and delighted in the seemingly impossible. Doubtless he felt that he and his associates could rise to the emergency, and that the sensation would be the greater. Again, he craved action. For half a year he had been writing and talking against preparedness and war, and had built up a reservoir of explosive energy. Moreover, something could be said for speed. It might accomplish more than a deliberate procedure, with its delayed impact. As to the dignity of the expedition, had anyone mentioned it, Ford would have responded with a snort.

4.

At Ford's suite in the Biltmore, headquarters for the enterprise, Gaston Plantiff, manager of the New York branch of the Ford company, began to plan the administration of the cruise, and soon staffed it with dozens of workers. Ford and Rosika Schwimmer began to send out invitations.

Characteristically, Ford himself did not help organize the crusade. Schwimmer and Lochner were at hand. Schwimmer regarded the crusade as a project of her own to which Ford had attached himself, and she was eager to manage it. Tacitly he let her do this (apart from matters in Plantiff's hands), shunting Lochner into the post of her general assistant. In this the manufacturer was following his factory policy, by which he let men find their own places. To take charge of cruise publicity Katherine Leckie, a journalist who was also a peace worker, was engaged. Ford's personal publicity was still handled by Theodore Delavigne, who soon arrived from Detroit. In leaving chief authority to Madame Schwimmer, Ford made a serious error. She was an enemy alien, a fact which many Americans and other neutrals never forgot. Intelligent enough to perceive the delicacy of her status, she made a pretence of keeping in the background. This proved impracticable because of her striking appearance and aggressive manner.

Work began at once with the invitations to prospective guests. Within a day of Ford's first announcement both Edison and John Wanamaker denied that they would go. Jane Addams, however, still planned to sail. Ford appealed to John Burroughs, Luther Burbank, William Howard

---

been successful (*Bread and Peace*, 36–37). She continued to support the expedition because it led to the continuous mediation in which she had faith.

Taft, Bryan, David Starr Jordan, and other distinguished Americans. The full list numbered 115. Invitations were sent by telegram, and generally were signed by Ford himself, but in some instances a briefer form was signed by one of the staff.[10]

The work was scarcely begun when Schwimmer, Ford, and Lochner went to Washington for the interview which Mrs. Philip Snowden and Schwimmer had obtained with Wilson on November 26. At a preliminary mass meeting in the Belasco Theatre, Ford sat on the platform while the two women addressed the audience. Finally there were calls: "We want Ford!" He was terrified, and whispered to Lochner, "You say it for me." Lochner urged: "Just say a few words!" At length Ford rose, cried, "Out of the trenches by Christmas, never to return!" and darted off the stage as if the applause were a pursuing monster.[11]

Ford left that evening for Detroit. Despite his absence, despite haste and confusion, the expedition gained recruits. Within three days thirteen guests had accepted, among them the Rev. Jenkin Lloyd Jones, widely known throughout the Middle West, and the Rev. Charles F. Aked of San Francisco, formerly pastor of John D. Rockefeller's Fifth Avenue Baptist Church in New York. In May Wright Sewall, President of the Women's Peace Congress in Chicago, and Mrs. Joseph Fels of Philadelphia, widow of the millionaire soap manufacturer and a single tax leader, the expedition acquired two able women. Progress had been made in recruiting a contingent of college students, and various eminent individuals and minority groups approved the venture. But many American leaders attacked it. Alton B. Parker, Democratic candidate for President in 1904, called Ford "a clown strutting on the stage for a little time," and Theodore Roosevelt, remarking that he rarely found himself agreeing with Parker, declared that "Mr. Ford's visit abroad will not be mischievous only because it is ridiculous." President John Grier Hibben of Princeton University refused to send a student; Dr. Charles W. Eliot of Harvard said that the mission must fail because it was wrong. The *Detroit Saturday Night* proclaimed Ford's voyage "a humiliation to his city and his country." [12]

Refusals from distinguished men and women poured in: William Dean Howells, Col. E. M. House, Cardinal Gibbons, William Howard Taft, Louis Brandeis, Morris Hillquit, and others. However, many in declining sent heartening messages. "I cannot too highly commend you," telegraphed Governor Hiram Johnson from California; Ida M. Tarbell disagreed only with the means of seeking peace, not the end. The poet Vachel Lindsay wired: "I am in full sympathy with your expedition . . . Am particularly in favor of anything that has the endorsement of Miss Jane Addams, our best woman and queen." Luther Burbank declared: "My heart is with you," and Helen Keller, declining because of speaking engagements, announced that she was with Ford "heart and soul." Acceptances grew: S. S. McClure, noted magazine publisher, now editor of the New York *Evening Mail;* Governor Louis B. Hanna of North Dakota; Inez Milholland Boissevain, Junoesque beauty and feminist. Others of some reputation included Andrew J. Bethea, Lieutenant-Governor of South Carolina; Judson King, lecturer; Mrs. William Bross Lloyd; B. W. Huebsch, publisher; Mary Alden Hopkins, magazine writer; Herman Bernstein, editor of the Yiddish newspaper *The Day;* and Berton Braley, writer of popular verse. Elmer Davis, then little known, was among the reporters.

On December 1 came word that Jane Addams, suddenly taken ill, could not make the voyage. She might have to undergo an operation. "It is even doubtful if she can follow later," reported her associate Dr. Alice Hamilton. The loss to the expedition was a bitter one. As an experienced counsellor and a person deeply respected both in America and Europe, Miss Addams might have contributed a stability which the leadership of the crusade sadly lacked.

For a time it seemed that William Jennings Bryan would become a delegate. He arrived in New York on December 2, just after Ford returned from Detroit with Marquis, Clara Ford, and Edsel. The two were already acquainted; earlier in the year Bryan, then Secretary of State, had sent Ford a paper weight made from the steel of plowshares. (He had presented such souvenirs to foreign diplomats on the signing of arbitration treaties.) Bryan waited patiently for five hours to see Ford, the two men all but embraced, and Bryan gave out a statement approving the expedition and proposing to join it at The Hague.[13]

Despite the loss of Bryan and Miss Addams, by the eve of sailing the group of delegates was as large and distinguished as Ford and his associates had a right to expect on nine days' notice. No first-rank American leaders like Taft, Edison, or Bryan had joined the party, but McClure, Aked, Judge Ben Lindsey of Denver, and others were nationally known. That so large a group, many of intelligence and reputation, would leave their work for a long trip on scant notice, often making financial sacrifices, was a tribute both to Ford and to the appeal of the undertaking.

Meanwhile, in Detroit a determined effort had been made by Dean Marquis and Clara Ford to dissuade the manufacturer from boarding the *Oscar II*. Marquis from the start had distrusted Schwimmer and Lochner; as refusals multiplied he was convinced that the peace ship delegates would not properly represent America. Mrs. Ford opposed the voyage on more personal grounds. She made Marquis promise that if, despite their efforts, Ford insisted on going, he would accompany and protect him. Failing in Detroit, they came to New York still hopeful, and "sat up all night" with Ford on the eve of the voyage, expostulating, arguing, cajoling. With Marquis's resourceful eloquence and Clara's tears, it was a powerful attack. The very fate of the voyage hung in the balance, for without Ford the ship would have lacked its most powerful symbol and moral force. But he withstood the assault.[14]

The day of sailing was as busy as any preceding it. John Burroughs came to wish his friend well, although he thought the cruise a mistake, and the two spent an hour together. Ford then saw Baron Shibusawa, "the J. P. Morgan of Japan," who termed the voyage "a great undertaking." At the Biltmore, Ford faced a group of reporters. Had he a last word for the public?

"Yes. Tell the people to cry peace and fight preparedness."

"What if the expedition fails?"

"I'll start another."

As he left the hotel in a Model T touring car for Hoboken, where the *Oscar II* rode, with Clara, Edsel, and the sculptor C. S. Pietro, he announced: "We've got peace-talk going now, and I'll pound it to the end."

At the Hoboken dock, despite a raw, cold day, a crowd estimated at 15,000 had gathered for the sailing. People filled the pier, with more constantly arriving. The Fords appeared, greeted by resounding cheers. Soon afterward, Bryan approached the ship. The band struck up "I Didn't Raise My Boy to Be a Soldier," the crowd roared, and the commoner made "many sweeping bows" as he went smiling up the gangplank. On board, he acted as a witness at the marriage of the poet Berton Braley and Miss Marian Rubicam. The reporters revelled in the episode as fully in the spirit of the cruise, and were almost as enthusiastic about two caged squirrels, dispatched to Ford on the ship by some prankster to live happily among the "nuts." (One was later christened "William Jennings Bryan" and the other "Henry Ford" by the reporters.)

The Fords chatted with the Edisons and other friends. According to William C. Bullitt of the Philadelphia *Ledger,* Ford urged Edison: "You must stay on board, you must stay on board." Then with a quizzical smile but (thought Bullitt) "intense seriousness," he said: "I'll give you a million dollars if you'll come." Because of his deafness Edison couldn't hear; Ford repeated the offer but the inventor smiled and shook his head. However, he assured his friend that he was heart and soul with him. Later Edison and his wife left with Edsel and Clara Ford, down whose cheeks tears were streaming. Dean Marquis, as he had promised Mrs. Ford, had taken passage with her husband. The Fords and Edisons stood on the pier until the ship left.[15]

It was delayed, in part by the crowd, in part by the late arrival of delegates and students, who had to be provided with tickets. Scheduled to sail at two o'clock, it did not swing out into the river until well after three. As it did so, in a final touch of the mad circus atmosphere of the occasion, a figure leaped from the pier and swam stoutly after it. Rescued, he announced himself as "Mr. Zero," and explained that he was "swimming to reach public opinion." Meanwhile the crowd, oblivious to most of these decorative incidents, warmed to the departure. It stood waving and roaring: it "cheered and yelled until it had no voice left." According to Lochner, Ford was exalted. "Again and again he bowed, his face wreathed in smiles that gave it a beatific expression. The magnitude of the demonstration—many a strong man there was who struggled in vain against tears born of deep emotion— quite astonished and overwhelmed him. I felt then that he considered himself amply repaid for all the ridicule heaped upon him."[16]

5.

As the *Oscar II* slipped out of New York harbor in the fading light and pointed her nose northeast, she was perhaps the first physical missile ever launched against a war. Nobody was sure what effect she would have. Dozens of reporters described the vessel's progress in day-to-day stories; later it provoked magazine articles, chapters in books, and at least one complete volume. Significantly, its ideological character dominated all these accounts. It was not a ship, but *the* peace-ship. Actual details about vessel and mission are hard to come by, for it was the pilgrims and their quest that fascinated every observer.*

The group was a strange one—not, as Mary Alden Hopkins tried to persuade herself, "representative: a cross-section of America." Almost half the delegates were writers (many suffragists, socialists, single-taxers, or pacifists); the next largest segment comprised lecturers and workers for causes; there were a few government officials, ministers, teachers. No business men, farmers, industrialists (except Ford), scientists, engineers, or labor officials were included. While a few delegates like S. S. McClure and Governor Hanna were "practical," the great majority were social evangelists of some kind. The reporters, who never gave the finer personalities the respect they deserved, probably pronounced the careless American's appraisal in terming the shipload "a bunch of nuts." [17]

Naturally, the center of interest for both delegates and journalists was Henry Ford, for all hoped that on shipboard he could be studied at leisure. Ford was cooperative. When a wave drenched him one morning as he was briskly walking the deck and he caught cold, he was of course no longer available. But the reporters, skeptical at first, by that time had been converted. Ford's complete sincerity, his friendliness, his pithy, quotable comments, won them all. Bullitt says they were convinced that the manufacturer was "an absolutely unselfish egoist." "Ford is really Christlike," Bullitt recorded. He liked the realism with which Ford appraised the voyage.

Don't you feel that this is a holy cause?" a minister asked him.

"No," Ford replied. "I don't know what you mean by holy. Instead of a holy cause I consider this expedition a people's affair."

"Are you not sailing with faith?" persisted the other.

"Yes," agreed Ford, "but it is faith in the people. I have absolute confidence in the better side of human nature . . . People never disappoint you if you trust them. Only three out of six hundred convicts in my factory have failed to make good."

Mary Alden Hopkins gives a brief, vivid picture of Ford:

* Take the number of persons comprising the expedition. Lochner lists 83 delegates, 54 reporters, 3 photographers, 50 technical staff and 18 students (*Henry Ford*, 48)—158 without technical staff. The *World* noted 77 delegates, 25 students, 46 newsmen. The list published on shipboard gives 67 delegates, 36 students, 3 foreign participants, 28 journalists, 23 business staff, 2 photographers, and 7 miscellaneous.

This silent man with the scholar's brow, the dreamer's wide-set eyes, the executive's mouth, the flickering humor, and the absolute simplicity of thought and action which comes from following high ideals to their logical conclusions—this personality grips the imagination.

Ford stated frankly what he expected from the expedition. It was not to bring peace immediately, but to hasten it. "The chief effect I look for is psychological." The peace ship was an advertisement for peace. "I consider that the peaceship will have been worth while if it does nothing more than it has done already in driving preparedness off the front page of the newspapers and putting peace on the front page."

On the third night out Ford sent an exhortation to members of Congress by wireless, urging them "to give the peace mission your support and encouragement so that it may succeed at the earliest possible moment." The following day he radioed messages to a number of rulers, pleading for peace. "Enough blood has been shed, enough agony endured, enough destruction wrought." He begged them to declare a truce, and by "mediation and discussion" to settle what was not being settled by the guns.[18] These bulletins made good copy for the reporters. Ford had unlimbered his "longest gun in the world," and the peace ship seemed not altogether futile.

On December 9 occurred the most sensational event of the voyage. Two nights before, McClure had read President Wilson's message to Congress. It was a plea for preparedness, advocating an increase in the standing army. A committee of delegates had been appointed to draft resolutions on the message, to be signed and sent to Congress. On the 9th, after Lochner had made a plea for immediate disarmament,* Dr. Aked rose and read the Declaration of Principles of the Ford Peace Party, the work of the committee. Deprecating military preparedness, it pledged all delegates to work for international disarmament. The Declaration was to be left four or five days for "examination and signing," the assumption being that all delegates would sign. But a number, although eager to see the war ended, did not favor critical comment upon their president or congress. Said McClure:

* Reported Bullitt: "Mr. Lochner never intends to offend any one. He is a gentle soul. He looks like the rabbit in 'Alice in Wonderland,' recuperating from a dreadful fright which has scared off all his hair and popped his eyes. But he has the ability of the 'unco guid' to get on people's nerves."

For years I have been working for international disarmament. I have visited the capitals of Europe time and time again in its behalf. But I cannot impugn the course laid out by the President of the United States and supported by my newspaper. I should like to be able to go on working with the party, but I am unable to sign that part of its declaration of principles which would place me in opposition to my Government.

Judge Lindsey took essentially the same stand, with Governor Hanna, the journalist John D. Barry, Herman Bernstein, and others. Madame Schwimmer and Jenkin Lloyd Jones, according to Bullitt, accused McClure of corrupting the students of the party by talking preparedness to them, while Lochner exclaimed: "Any one who accepted the invitation of Mr. Ford, and now refuses to sign this resolution, came for a free ride!" This comment was resented. Barry protested bitterly: "If you push through this resolution and cause a sharp split in the party, we shall be the laughing stock of the whole of Europe."

The conflict should have been foreseen before the voyage began. Ford, it is true, was as fervidly against preparedness as war. But the success of the expedition was his objective. To win it he was seeking the coöperation of all neutral nations and was heartened by Madame Schwimmer's documents indicating that even the belligerents were receptive to peace talks. He was pledged to seek *their* aid. How then could he logically object to peace-lovers who believed in a measure of preparedness? But the policy of the expedition had never been thought through, and such extremists as Jones, Schwimmer, Lochner, and Aked stood ready to demand that everyone approve the Declaration or leave the party at the first possible port. "Pacifist," remarked Bullitt, "means a person hard to pacify."

In the end, a statement signed by Ford, while stressing the point that to work for peace and even tacitly condone preparedness was impossible (a wholly illogical assertion, of course), emphasized that all delegates were welcome in the crusade. But the reporters joyfully advertised the rift in the party. "The dove of peace has taken flight," cried the Chicago *Tribune,* "chased off by the screaming eagle." The press throughout the world carried accounts of the quarrel. "Thank heaven," newsmen were quoted as saying, "at last a story has broken!" Later the journalists were accused of having magnified the dispute. "The amount of wrangling has been picturesquely exaggerated," wrote Mary Alden Hopkins on her return to New York. "A man does not become a saint by stepping on a peace boat." Lochner, recalling how before reaching Norway the entire delegation re-pledged itself to its purpose (peace by continuing mediation), termed the whole episode "trivial."

With more justification, the delegates resented the persistent levity and ridicule which marked many reporters' dispatches, and the downright falsehoods occasionally perpetrated. "The expedition has been hampered at every step by the direct and indirect influence of the American press, by the Atlantic seaboard press," declared one of the party who returned to write about it while its work was still going forward. Lochner in his book fully agreed. He tells how Captain J. W. Hempel of the *Oscar II,* who read everything sent out by wireless from his ship, brought some of the more obnoxious dispatches to Ford, asking if they should be sent. Ford replied, "Let them send anything they please. They are my guests. I wouldn't for the world censor them." Later he insisted: "Our work will speak for itself." Some reporters repaid this courtesy by forcing their way into Ford's stateroom during his illness to see if he were actually alive![19]

The ship approached the British Isles by the northern route above Scotland on its way to Norway. As Ford, exhausted and suffering from his cold, kept to his cabin, the position of Madame Schwimmer became somewhat clearer to the correspondents, but also a matter for suspicion. Was she tampering with their dispatches? What was in her little black bag? Schwimmer finally agreed to show them, then became angry at some disparaging comment, and called the exhibit off. Again, she accepted an invitation to tea, only to become incensed at some new report, and to send word that she refused to meet with persons who had insulted her. The journalists remonstrated: they had done nothing of the sort, wanted to be friends, and she should come. She did, to be greeted by hearty applause as she entered the room. "Don't be hypocritical!" she snapped, effectively quashing any good will. She completed the job by accusing the reporters of telling Ford that she listened at keyholes!

The delegates looked forward to their landing in Norway, where Schwimmer promised them a rousing reception. Doubtless many, like Mary Alden Hopkins, were stirred by soaring hopes:

One hundred and fifty everyday people have been brought face to face with a great idea—the thought of world disarmament. There's no escaping it, short of jumping into the sea. The idea pervades the ship. Groups talk of it. . . . Reporters are nervous lest there's no news value in it. . . . At times the vision comes to all of us—mystic, veiled, and wonderful. Then common sense revolts. Yet we dare not treat the vision with contempt. A ship of fools crossed the Atlantic in 1492. A ship of fools reached Plymouth in 1620. Can it be that in this ship of common fools, we bear the Holy Grail to the helping of a wounded world?

Norway appeared, rocky, snowbound, forested. As they ran along the coast the delegates stood on the deck, and "for a while there was sublime peace, even on the peaceship." Now the time had passed for aspirations alone; henceforth salvation must be won by works as well as by faith.[20]

6.

It was 4 A.M. on December 18, with the temperature 12 degrees below zero, when the ship docked at Oslo. Later that morning a few Norwegians appeared to welcome the expedition, but there was no reception such as Schwimmer had promised. After breakfast, the delegates took an electric train to a city park, where they enjoyed several hours of sun, fresh air, and crisp snow—their first touch of earth for two weeks. That afternoon they attended a reception by the Women's International Peace League, and in the evening a meeting at the University of Christiania.

The crowd had gathered partly to see Henry Ford, and was disappointed; for he, after insisting on walking from the boat to his hotel, had collapsed and gone to bed. He was never to appear in public while in Norway. According to Bullitt, the meeting was unsuccessful in other respects. Jenkin Lloyd Jones, after beginning with a pretentious "Hail, Nor-rrway! Hail, Nor-rrway!" bored the intelligent audience with platitudes, and ensuing speakers showed a similar tendency. Fortunately Lochner, clearly outlining the proposed activities of the pilgrims, pleased the Norwegians.

On December 20, the day following the arrival at Christiania, the five newspapers of the city indicated the attitude of the public. Two favored the expedition, and three frowned upon it (one was later to become friendly). The *Tidens Tegn,* the most influential, ridiculed the party but praised Ford. "He is a Tolstoi in a modern edition. He has a personality which we shall remember long after the expedition is forgotten." Unquestionably one unhappy influence upon the Norwegians was the leadership of Rosika Schwimmer. The Norse thought it wholly unfitting for a citizen of a belligerent power to direct the peace mission of a neutral country. Again, because of a misunderstanding, the local representatives of the International Committee of Women remained aloof. Finally, the Norwegians were in general pro-Ally, and felt that a just peace could be concluded only after the German military position had worsened.

The popularity of both Ford and the expedition was increased by his gift of approximately $10,000 for a student club house at the University of Christiania. On the other hand, people were disappointed that he did not appear in public. On December 22 he called in the press of the city, but to their surprise discussed not mediation but his new tractor! The machine and not man, he told them, would now be the drudge. He pointed out that his invention was unpatented; he would try to convince the armament makers that they could realize a greater profit by manufacturing tractors than by making guns. The newsmen were mystified. "He must be a very great man who permits himself to utter such foolishness," pondered one of them.[21]

Ford had made no progress in overcoming his illness. The weather had been cold and the rooms he occupied faced north. According to Lochner, they could be entered only through those of Dean Marquis or Ray Dahlinger. "Mr. Ford was practically incommunicado." Lochner believed that Marquis, originally opposed to the cruise, had worked steadily on Ford to abandon it, and was supported by other Ford employees, both on shipboard and in Detroit.* In his weakened state, the manufacturer was of course susceptible to suggestion. Lochner saw the drift of his feeling when he remarked: "Guess I had better go home to mother . . . You've got this thing started now and can get along without me." Lochner protested that Ford's presence was imperative. Besides, should he leave at the first stop in Europe, his act would be interpreted as an admission of failure. Why not go to Finse, a Norwegian health resort, recover there, and rejoin the party later?

Ford agreed to consider this possibility, but his decision had probably been made. If we can trust his statements then and later, he never

---

* Lochner was mistaken in thinking that Marquis continued to oppose the expedition. "Just let me say that this is a great thing," he wrote to his wife on December 16, from the ship. "I believe in it." (Acc. 63, Box 1.) However, he later urged Ford's departure because of his health. In general, Ford's company associates did oppose the peace ship. Plantiff worked loyally to make it a success, but thought it a mistake. "I'm with the old man," he told Miss Hopkins, "but why did he do it?"

regretted having launched the expedition. But he probably recognized that it had been badly managed, and that riding herd on the fantastic individualists who composed the party was a difficult task. He was as lost among them as Schwimmer would have been on the assembly line at Highland Park. However, his physical condition seems to have been the determining factor. He was simply not in a state of mind or body to take an active part in the enterprise, and realized that he must break away to effect a recovery. That he should do so was also the advice of the Norwegian doctors who attended him.

At any rate, under Marquis's urging, Ford decided to leave on the morning of December 23 for Bergen, where he could catch the *Bergensfjord,* just sailing for America. As it happened, the delegates were departing a little later that morning for Sweden. Marquis wanted no trouble about Ford's departure. He "spirited" his charge out of the hotel, with a "flying wedge" to make sure that there would be no interference. Lochner and others became aware that something was happening, and rushed down to find Ford getting into a taxi. They attempted to question him, but Marquis and his group interposed; there were "a lot of fists flying." Ford and Marquis slipped away in the cab, drove around the delegates' train to their own, and got away as few realized what had happened. Most of the delegates assumed that Ford had boarded *their* train, and were astounded when they learned that they had lost him.[22]

When Ford's flight became generally known, the effect was much what Lochner had feared. The party felt depressed—even betrayed. For some hours no one knew if Ford were on land or sea. However, the situation improved when Gaston Plantiff on Christmas day issued an explanation that Ford had been in poor physical condition to undertake the voyage, that it had precipitated a breakdown, and that he had left for home on the "absolute instruction" of Dr. Kuren of the Red Cross Hospital, Christiania, to "immediately leave the party and seek rest and quiet." Plantiff indicated that Ford would return. "Before leaving, he expressed to me his absolute faith in the party and . . . the earnest hope that all would continue to cooperate to the closest degree in bringing about the desired results which had been so close to his heart—the accomplishment of universal peace."

While this statement reassured the delegates and checked malicious comment, it did not soften the staggering blow of the departure. Of

all the party, Ford alone had been of sufficient stature to impress and
hearten neutrals. The Christiania *Aftenposten* of December 20 had
praised him but lifted its eyebrows at his companions. Bullitt said
bluntly that "so far as making an impression on Europe was concerned,
the personality of Henry Ford was the party's chief asset." Lochner felt
that his going left "a void." Ford's absence also affected the day-to-day
conduct of the expedition. While he was with it, there was never any
trouble about financing. Furthermore, while not preeminently an
executive, his judgment in emergencies was usually sound. But with
the ocean between him and the party, financing became precarious,
disagreements began to divide those in charge, and uncertainty developed as to Ford's own wishes. In short, his withdrawal impaired both
the prestige and the management of the project.

On returning to New York, apparently with restored health, he
denied emphatically that he had "deserted." Illness had hastened his
return, but he had never intended to remain long abroad—in fact, had
promised his wife to be back "in about five weeks." (He had been gone
a month.) He asserted: "I don't regret a single thing I have done. . . .
I believe the sentiment we have aroused by making the people think
will shorten the war." And when a *Tribune* reporter asked him if he
thought the peace ship worth what he had put into it, Ford replied,
"I do." Was the kind of publicity he had received satisfactory? "It suited
me all right," replied Ford with greater shrewdness than the reporter
suspected. "I was bothered only because my wife didn't like some of
the criticism. My son, Edsel, didn't mind, and I am really strong for
it." He hoped the criticism would continue. Why? "Well," drawled the
industrialist, "the best fertilizer in the world is weeds." [23]

In Europe, the expedition had done well. Following Ford's instructions, a committee had been set up "for the management of the trip
and policies." It consisted of Jones, Aked, Huebsch, Frederick Holt
(Ford's representative), Judge Lindsey, Mrs. Lloyd, Mrs. Fels, and
Plantiff, with Lochner as secretary. For a time it worked effectively.
What was better, the reception in Sweden was as cordial as that in
Norway had been cool. Despite the fact that Christmas holidays were
under way, with shops closed and other activities suspended, the resi-
dents of Stockholm saw that the pilgrims were well-quartered, organized meetings on their behalf, and showed a warm sympathy with
their purpose. Mayor Carl Lindhagen was especially active in welcom-

ing the party. He and others who aided him were for the most part
Socialists; the Conservatives were less cordial. But Sweden's fear of
Russia made her favorable to a strong Germany, and to a peace that
would penalize none of the chief combatants.

Told by Lindhagen, "You have brought us a wonderful Christmas
gift; you have brought us nearer the hope of peace," the delegates were
happy also to receive a buoyant message from Ford. Mass meetings,
dinners, and other gatherings embodied enthusiasm and good will. The
Swedes showed as much eagerness to end the war as their American
guests, and when the expedition left for Denmark on December 30,
some fifteen hundred people were on hand to provide an impressive
demonstration.

Denmark was cordial, but unofficially. A recent law forbade addresses
by foreigners on the war, and only at "private" meetings of clubs or
societies could the delegates present their case. Meanwhile, the problem
of getting to Holland loomed up as formidable. A journey by water
meant the hazard of mines, while land access was possible only through
German territory. Finally, by the unofficial action of the American
minister to Denmark, the Germans permitted the entire party to cross
their country in a sealed train, and the greater part of the group thus
arrived at the Hague. (Aked and Hanna were ill, Canadian-born Julia
Wales and the Finnish Mrs. Malmberg were left behind as citizens of
belligerent countries; McClure had quitted the expedition.) The Dutch
were not wholly enthusiastic about the party, for they had a peace society of their own which had worked along less sensational lines, and
plainly felt that Ford and his associates were muddying the waters.[24]

After the first golden days in Stockholm, the party had manifested
its old disunity. When the personnel of the administrative committee
had been announced, Inez Milholland Boissevain had wrathfully protested against undemocratic procedures, and withdrew. Plantiff felt
that she was piqued at not having been put on the committee. He had
his difficulties running the business end of the enterprise, and was
worried about the bickering. He concluded that Schwimmer, who
ignored the committee and assumed full authority when it pleased her,
was "a woman of a strange and suspicious personality." Some delegates
supported her, but she was antagonizing a growing number—particularly Aked, Mrs. Fels, and Barry. "Her presence prejudices every city,
her spirit and methods stir up bad blood," Aked was soon to write. The

Dutch took the trouble to protest directly to Henry Ford against her.[25]

From Stockholm Fru Elizabeth Bugge of that city took B. W. Huebsch to the country home of Ellen Key, the Swedish feminist and social reformer. She received them graciously, greatly impressing the American: "She is the great mother heart—mother of all the world." Writing in English to the delegates, she declared that she could not join the peace party in her "present state of despondency," but praised its purpose and spirit: "Your own strength to hope against all mountains of difficulty . . . makes your pilgrimage beautiful." [26]

Having brought the pilgrims through the three Scandinavian countries to Holland, the full circuit of accessible neutral territory, those in charge had now only to choose five delegates to represent the United States on the Neutral Conference for Continuous Mediation, and select the site for conference meetings. Jane Addams and William Jennings Bryan were supposedly willing to act as delegates, and there was no question of their being chosen, along with Henry Ford. Plantiff had already arranged with Aked to serve. Mrs. Fels made the fifth representative. As alternates Judge Lindsey, Jenkin Lloyd Jones, Dr. George W. Kirchwey, Emily Greene Balch, and John D. Barry were designated. Of these Americans only Aked from the regular group and Miss Balch from the alternates served for any extended period. Stockholm was selected as the seat of the conference.

The peace party had now completed its task. Plantiff arranged that the students should return to the United States on the *Noordam* (January 11, 1916), the delegates on the *Rotterdam* (January 15). Both groups came back with a variety of attitudes, all praising the purpose of the expedition, but many deploring mistakes in management. The gist of their comment was expressed by (state) Senator Helen Ring Robinson of Denver: "The leaders did not measure up to the bigness of the idea." The reporters took a more satirical view. "The comedy of errors is over," proclaimed T. N. Pockman of the *Tribune*. "During its two months' run the show has aroused more lively interest, cynical amusement and sheer pity than possibly any other in history."

Oddly enough, the return of the pilgrims seemed to be accepted generally as the collapse of Ford's project, although actually it marked the beginning of the real work. This was the task of continuous mediation. One delegate, Florence L. Lattimore, pointed out this fact, adding that "if you have any regard for facts you cannot say that it [the expedition] failed any more than you can as yet say that it was a success." Actually, the conference which developed from the cruise was to labor for a solid year, seeking to halt the war.

The organization of this body was a minor triumph. Hardly had the *Oscar II* docked at Christiania when it was prophesied that Norway would never furnish delegates, while later it was said with equal assurance that no eminent Dutch or Swiss would be available for service. Yet largely through Lochner's efforts, representatives from six countries, including the United States, were chosen, and by late February, 1916, the Neutral Conference for Continuous Mediation was ready to begin its work.[27]

Meanwhile the feeling against Rosika Schwimmer had continued to grow, the Ford representatives acted to curtail her power, and she finally cabled her resignation. Lochner later discussed her place in the enterprise. She had prodigious capacity for work, "eloquence, wit, *savoir-faire*, forcefulness . . . a genuine personal charm," with an ability to speak English, French, and German fluently. She had enjoyed Ford's confidence. Why did she fail? Lochner concluded that she did so because she was an autocrat, and could not adapt herself to the open, frank personalities of the Americans. They (with the Dutch and Scandinavians) despised intrigue; her instinct was to guard her secret documents and work indirectly for what she wanted. She even stationed an agent outside meetings to be sure that nobody eavesdropped!

She felt that she had been badly treated. Years later she asserted that all the opposition she encountered arose from "petty jealousies and misunderstandings." The idea grew upon her that she had rendered immense services to Henry Ford, and she went so far as to charge Liebold with poisoning his employer's mind against her—otherwise "Mr. Ford would have provided some means of subsistence for her during the rest of her life." She seems to have tried to start another conference, then to have retired to a sanitarium to rest.[28]

The conference quickly developed a character and a program. It was a hand-picked group. In no instance were the delegates chosen by a government, or by popular vote. A group of societies, advised by the Ford personnel, selected the Norwegian representatives; the peace ship pilgrims chose the American contingent, and other countries acted with a similar informality, peace societies assuming the chief responsibility. Nevertheless, the men and women who assembled included mayors, members of parliament, professors, and officers of peace organizations. Their first notable act was an appeal in March, 1916, to the neutral powers, urging them to take the initiative in offering mediation. As a result, bills to implement it were introduced in the parliaments of Sweden, Norway, Switzerland, and Holland; but no action was taken by any neutral government.

A month and a half later the conference issued an Appeal to the Governments, Parliaments and Peoples of Belligerent Nations. This document not only again stated the case against continuing the war, but also offered a set of principles which might form the basis for peace. These included the right of self-determination by peoples, guarantees of economic freedom (to make wars for commercial advantage pointless), freedom of the seas, parliamentary control of foreign policy, an international organization to promote cooperation between nations and peaceful settlement for all disputes, and a program of world disarmament. A world congress was to deal with these questions.

After this appeal, on instructions from Dearborn, the five delegates per nation were reduced to two, and the site of sessions was transferred to The Hague. The conference stimulated pro-mediation gatherings, encouraged appeals for peace by eminent writers like Georg Brandes, and indirectly stimulated others like Ellen Key, Selma Lagerlöf, and Arne Carbourg to serve the same end. Representatives of the group communicated with prominent citizens of belligerent countries, suggested that the German Government endorse the idea of a league of nations (which it soon did), and planned an international magazine devoted to peace.[29]

Ford meanwhile had vigorously pursued his opposition to war and preparedness through large advertisements in various American newspapers. Apparently he was pleased with the work of the conference in Europe. In October, when Lochner visited the United States, Ford was cordial, but wanted a shift to direct mediatory efforts—contacts with belligerent nationals, attempts to find a common ground for action, and so forth. Lochner was heartened. He felt that all the belligerents were showing a desire to negotiate, and that overtures toward action would soon be made, either through the conference or through President Wilson.

An overture soon came, but not in a form that Lochner welcomed. Emperor Wilhelm of Germany announced his willingness to negotiate, but in so arrogant a fashion as to antagonize the Allied governments and peoples. Wilson, who had been about to act, was embarrassed by the imperial gesture. However, apparently eager to be heard before a reply could be made to the Kaiser by others, the President on December 18, 1916, sent to all belligerents notes identical in text suggesting that each declare the terms on which it would consider peace. The Germans promptly expressed a willingness to confer; the Allies rejected the suggestion. Thus two peace tenders (the German and the American) had been made, and their failure had the logical effect of stimulating German activity, including the more intensive use of submarines. This really wrote finis to the activities of the commission (as the conference had become), although as yet no one perceived the fact.

Lochner, still hopeful of peace, was recalled to the United States on January 3, 1917; he saw President Wilson twice and Henry Ford oftener. Wilson made his famous "peace without victory" speech. Ford felt that with this utterance the Government had taken over his crusade. As submarine activity assumed a more ruthless character, he also saw the possibility of our being drawn into the war; but apparently his dominant feeling was that Wilson was doing all for peace that he could, and more than anyone else could do. On February 7 Liebold told Lochner that the work in Europe would stop.[30]

7.

Thus the peace crusade ended. Having made his decision, Ford could not detach himself from the project too quickly. With his approval, Liebold took over the termination of the work at The Hague, brushing aside Lochner's protest that an abrupt suspension of activities would work hardship upon some of the commission's foreign members, and ignoring other suggestions.[31] The drive for peace had lasted fourteen months; what had Ford accomplished in that period?

Opinion on that question varies almost absurdly. Mark Sullivan in *Our Times* declared bitingly of the project: "After its failure, dying down to an echo of gigantic and exhausted laughter, it deprived every other peace movement in the country of force and conviction." Although Sullivan in a footnote reported Jane Addams's vigorous dissent and admitted that the peace movement retained force despite the peace ship, his judgment has been endorsed by some responsible journalists, including Elmer Davis, who reported the cruise, and even historians.

But others have differed sharply. Walter Millis, in his *Road to War,* deplored the fact that "the Peace Ship was launched, to the undying shame of American journalism, upon one vast wave of ridicule." Merle Curti, in his *Peace or War, 1636–1936,* felt that the expedition, particularly through the work of the conference, "coordinated the scattered efforts of publicists and idealists in neutral countries engaged in an effort to formulate and popularize terms for a just and lasting peace." Upton Sinclair praised the crusade, while there was scarcely a pilgrim, from Schwimmer to B. W. Huebsch, who did not believe that it justified itself. Those who ridiculed the project had indeed little to support their ridicule, while those who defended it could point to the worldwide dramatization of the peace hope through the cruise, and to a definite effect on public opinion in Europe through the activities of the conference. Aside from the promotion of the idea that peace was desirable, by fomenting discussion and offering specific plans this body anticipated and probably somewhat influenced two important later developments. One was Wilson's theme of "peace without victory," and the other was the settlement at Versailles. The conference made more familiar various ideas which came to be factors in that settlement, such as the self-determination of peoples, the league of nations, and plans for disarmament. Of course other individuals and organizations also promoted such conceptions.

As to Ford himself, he pointed out later that in a time when no bold effort to end the war was being made, he had acted. "I wanted to see peace. I at least tried to bring it about. Most men did not even try." [32]

In the popular mind this was the merit of the cruise and of the ensuing conference. True, they attempted the all-but-impossible, but impossibles are sometimes accomplished. And although the crusade failed, it had held aloft before the world the ever-desirable alternative to war. A large body of Americans respected Ford's idealism, and in less than two years after the conference closed, the industrialist showed amazing strength as a senatorial candidate, and was persistently talked of for president.

Ford perceived other practical gains. Although he did not charter the peace ship to make himself or his car better known, the cruise publicized both. When Liebold told him that the total costs were $465,000, he remarked: "Well, we got a million dollars worth of advertising out of it, and a hell of a lot of experience." Later he confided to Edwin G. Pipp that on the voyage he had discovered potential markets for his tractor. He also asserted that he had learned the cause of the war—an illusion he was later to act upon most unhappily.[33]

Was Ford humbled in spirit by the ridicule he encountered—under which he undoubtedly smarted despite his smiling denials? No evidence supports such a possibility. He never conceded error. The experience did not deter him from attempting other "impossible" projects. He never once remarked: "Well, I went a bit too far on the peace ship venture." The effect of the experience on his thinking and character was rather in the direction of convincing him that his own instincts were sounder guides than outside judgments. Certainly from this time forward he was to show a stubborn and at times even a bitter reliance upon his own ideas and feelings. The peace ship episode was the first to mold him in this direction, and it did so sharply. He knew that war was wrong and that working for peace was right; how then could he respect those who ridiculed his efforts? Other experiences were soon to nourish in Ford a certain cynicism, and to accentuate a firm and even arrogant reliance upon his own untrammeled judgment.

III

PRODUCING FOR WAR

THE transformation of Henry Ford from peace angel to Vulcan took less than a week. Late in December, 1916, he telegraphed his "most hearty greetings and support" to Emily Greene Balch, who was arranging a peace demonstration in New York for New Year's Eve, and had invited him to attend. On January 6, 1917, he dispatched a blistering denunciation of preparedness activities to Edward F. Cragin at the Republican Club in New York. He still hoped for peace when Lochner saw him on January 30. But on February 3, when President Wilson severed diplomatic ties with Germany, Ford indicated a change in attitude. "At first he laughed at the idea of any danger of war," Lochner recalled, "but when everybody pointed out to him the significance of a breach in diplomatic relations, he said, 'Well, we must stand behind the President.'" Two days later, while declaring that "I cannot believe that war will come," he stated that "in the event of a declaration of war [I] will place our factory at the disposal of the United States government and will operate without one cent of profit." [1]

The shift amazed Lochner, yet it was quite understandable. Ford had never preached pacifism to the point of non-resistance, and during the previous year a number of forces had played upon him. The country had become more anti-German as a result of increased submarine sinkings and the exposure of Teutonic plotting in Mexico. Many of Ford's friends were pro-Ally, notably John Burroughs and Thomas A. Edison. Furthermore, Ford had completely revised his earlier opinion that Woodrow Wilson was "a small man," and had come to applaud and trust him. In refusing to fight a war with Mexico, Wilson had shown a firm anti-imperialist attitude; he had later made two bold attempts to mediate in the European war—his note to the belligerents on December 18 and his "peace without victory" speech of January 22. Both had

55

failed, and Ford was deeply impressed. If Wilson could not succeed, who could? "I am a pacifist," he said some months later in a statement that may indicate his earlier thinking, "but perhaps militarism can be crushed only with militarism. In that case I am in on it to the finish." [2]

However, the great factor in altering Ford's mind seems to have been the prospect of American participation in the war. "We had, up to the time of the declaration of war, absolutely refused to take war orders from the foreign belligerents," he wrote later in *My Life and Work*. ". . . it is at variance with our human principles to aid either side in a war in which our country was [sic] not involved. These principles had no application, once the United States entered the war." He also saw in the conflict the possibility of winning permanent peace. "I had hoped . . . that it might be a war to end wars." This hope was doubtless important, yet it seems to have been secondary to Ford's resolve to support his president and country.

To be sure, he had been unusually quick to change. He did so two months before any of his pacifist friends. Lochner continued to work for peace even after the United States came into the conflict, and both Miss Balch and Dr. Jordan strove until the end to pull the nation back from belligerency. But Ford acted in character, for once he had appraised a situation, he moved quickly. Ultimately many lovers of peace came to the same position. Dean Kirchwey did so on April 3, and on the 7th William Jennings Bryan asserted: "A declaration of war closes discussion. . . . There is no country in the world whose citizens would be so willing to die for their liberty as this one." [3]

After Wilson's presentation of the case against Germany on April 2 and the declaration by Congress on the 6th, Ford maintained the attitude he had already taken. To a Detroit reporter he said simply: "Everything I've got is for the government and not a cent of profit." Later in Nova Scotia he repeated this declaration. Actually, at that time he was already aiding the Allies.

In the first month of the war scant attention was paid to Henry Ford the patriot. Americans of all types, including former pacifists and pro-Germans, were pledging full allegiance to the nation. Already in February Ford had put forward again an idea first suggested in 1915 —a one-man submarine. "Carrying a man apiece, they will run out below the biggest battleship afloat, touch off a bomb beneath it, and blow the ship out of existence." A rear-admiral had declared the idea "worth less than a snap of the fingers," and now the renewal of the suggestion was ignored.* At this moment Ford was less interesting than persons like Hugo Munsterberg and George Sylvester Viereck. He got an occasional word of approbation, but also an occasional reminder of his former pacifism. "Today he stands ready to turn his plant over to the government for military purposes without profit," gibed the *Detroit Saturday Night*. "Henceforth it is to be forgotten that he ever spent his time and his money to prevent his country from arming itself for proper defense against aggression." [4] Throughout April there was little interest in what war materials Ford might manufacture. Attention was centered upon food conservation under Herbert Hoover, the proposed draft, the ship-building program, the general plans of the Army and Navy, and Theodore Roosevelt's dramatic proposal to lead a division of volunteers.

Actually, Ford and his company had more to contribute to the war effort than any other automotive firm, while few organizations of any kind were potentially so important. Besides the many branch plants and the home center at Highland Park, there were two important sites for manufacturing, one for tractors in Dearborn (Ford's personal development), and the other on the Rouge. Even more important than factory potential were Ford's resources in manpower. He commanded a group of engineering and business executives with as much brains, resourcefulness, and audacity as any other working force in the country. Wills, Knudsen, Sorensen, Galamb, Liebold, Avery, Lee, Martin, Mayo—to name the leaders—not only represented a reservoir of high and varied skill, but all were trained to do the impossible. With them, no idea was too extraordinary to test, no problem too difficult for solution. The American role in the war required such men. The nation had joined the conflict with little preparation in any field, and would need all the originality, daring, and productive drive that it could command.

2.

Meanwhile Ford was already working for Britain. That nation for some time had faced an increasingly desperate problem: scarcity of food. The British Isles lacked the land area to raise sufficient produce for their more than forty million inhabitants; as a rich manufacturing

---

* Jonathan Daniels, in *The End of Innocence* (New York, 1954), 176, quotes Franklin D. Roosevelt, then Assistant Secretary of the Navy, to the effect that Ford, "until he saw a chance for publicity free of charge, thought a submarine was something to eat."

nation they had felt no need to raise it. But with war there were fewer vessels to import food, and U-boats were sinking many and cutting down deliveries. Clearly all idle land should be put to work; however, a shortage of both man-power and horse-power seemed to make any quick expansion of cultivated acreage impossible. A miracle was needed. Suddenly the tractor loomed large as the machine that might perform one.

Percival L. D. Perry, in charge of Ford affairs in Britain, was consequently interested in the new tractor model Ford was preparing to produce. Perry had already purchased the site for a tractor factory at Cork, Ireland. He was influential in getting the Food Production Department, where he served, to conduct experiments through the Royal Agricultural Society with a number of tractors, among them two Fords. The judges, who included authorities on engineering, were impressed with the American machines, and as a result Perry on April 7 cabled Edsel Ford in part as follows:

Would you be willing to send Sorensen and others with drawings of everything necessary, loaning them to British government so that parts can be manufactured over here and assembled in government factory under Sorensen's guidance? Can assure you positively this suggestion is made in national interest and if carried out will be done by the government for the people with no manufacturing or capitalist interest involved and no profit being made by any interest whatever. The matter is very urgent . . . National necessity entirely dependent Mr. Ford's decision.

Ford himself replied the following day:

Have received your telegram #208 Government to Edsel Ford dated April 7 . . . Will comply with every request immediately. In full accord with principle, we will work night and day. . . . Get all information possible on gear cutting, cast iron, malleable foundrys and drop forge plants. We are sending full organization depending on your assistance at earliest possible moment.

Other cablegrams followed. With characteristic energy the Ford men took hold of their difficult job, and in different circumstances England might have become the first site of quantity production for the Ford tractor.[5]

We have seen that the tractor was an early dream of Ford's, according to him earlier than the automobile, and that he had experimented with working models since 1907. Others too had experimented. Various types had been evolved: the International Harvester Company had several models and the Emerson, Case, Moline, Little Giant, and Rock Island were well-known. In the summer of 1917 a total of 46 types were shown at Fremont, Nebraska. But although 1911–1912 had seen a big boom for tractors with internal combustion engines as opposed to steam (which had been utilized in England since the mid-nineteenth century), the machine the farmer wanted had not yet appeared. Arnold P. Yerkes, an official in the Bureau of Plant Industry, wrote Ford in January, 1915: "I find among farmers a heavy demand for a *cheap* tractor." Having studied the situation for three years, he felt that "a small, cheap tractor, with merit, will find a tremendous sale." (Cheap tractors had been made, and sold well, but did not stand up.) Yerkes wanted to submit his ideas about design to Ford.

Form 178A 2M 12-17   Cable Address "FORDSON"

TELEGRAM

Henry Ford & Son. Inc.
Dearborn, Mich.

Duplicate

32740

Sent: FEBRUARY 15   **Via**

PERRY

WE WILL GIVE FURTHER DECISION ON YOUR REQUEST FOR FIVE THOUSAND ADDITIONAL TRACTORS MARCH FIFTEENTH.   HAVE ACCEPTED ORDER FOR ONE THOUSAND WITH OPTION OF ANOTHER THOUSAND FROM CANADIAN GOVERNMENT, TO BE DELIVERED IMMEDIATELY AFTER YOUR SIX THOUSAND.

SORENSEN

COPY

Ford was quite as well aware as Yerkes that all existing durable models were big, heavy, and therefore expensive, and that they were unmaneuverable as well. From the start his objective in tractor engineering had been similar to that which he had realized in automobile manufacture with the Model T—a light, sturdy, cheap machine that the masses of farmers could afford. He had experimented with one model after another, and at times seemed close to what he wanted. By

1915, as we have seen, he seemed to have it. The *Ford Times* for November hailed the new model as "an accomplished success," and Ford exhibited it the following summer, preaching his gospel of light weight and effective traction. "A cat runs up the side of a tree, and it isn't its weight, but its traction, that makes it possible," he was quoted. The improved machine of 1917, which Farkas designed, shocked the conservatives by its lightness, its relatively small wheels, the enclosure of all working parts, and other novel features. But most experts hailed it. "A lightning flash from the clear sky of tractor engineering," said one authority.[6]

The machine was of the wheel, not the recently developed caterpillar tread type, which was highly regarded by some authorities. It weighed 2500 lbs.; used its 42 inch rear wheels for driving power and the 28 inch front wheels for steering; was powered by a 4-cylinder, 20 h.p. motor; had three speeds and a reverse operated by a multiple disc clutch; started on gasoline but ran on kerosene; and was designed to eliminate unnecessary weight.*

The tractor was a Henry Ford and not a Ford Motor Company enterprise.† As we have seen, Ford at his own expense had established an experimental shop in Dearborn. On July 27, 1917, a company was organized as a Michigan corporation under the title of Henry Ford & Son, to manufacture tractors, agricultural implements and appliances, and "self-propelling vehicles and mechanisms of every description." An issue of 10,000 shares with a par value of $1,000,000 was divided among Henry, Clara, and Edsel B. Ford, and on July 30 (his birthday) Henry Ford was elected president.[7]

However, before the incorporation Ford had taken steps to fulfill his promise to Perry. Early in May Sorensen set sail for England to organize the production of tractors there. Perry had resigned from the Food Production Department "in order to be able to devote my whole time to the necessary superintending of the Government manufacture of tractors." The arrival of Sorensen in mid-May dramatized the Ford contribution. "He is young, tall, handsome, athletic," pronounced the

---

* One striking feature of the 1917 model, says Farkas in his *Reminiscences*, was the lack of a frame, which most previous models had used. Farkas convinced Sorensen that he could "design the castings so that they will be strong enough to support the entire tractor." Ford was dubious. He still believed that he ought to have a steel frame "to bolt on the parts and hold them together." Eventually he gave way.

† C. Harold Wills emphasized this fact to Sorensen in 1915, protesting against the removal of some machine units from Highland Park. "This must be stopped. . . . These are separate concerns. . . . We intend to render your company a bill for these items." (Acc. 38, Box 139.)

Westminster Gazette. "Given a wig and gown he would pass well for a barrister; put him in a frock coat and he would look like a surgeon." Of the financial value of the young Siegfried the writer said: "I have heard on good authority that this gentleman's remuneration is equal to that of close on half a dozen minor cabinet ministers, and that he is worth every penny of it to the Ford organization."

Thus Ford was ready to coöperate with the British government. However, events dictated otherwise. German air raids in June resulted in the shift of much British heavy industry to aircraft engine manufacture. Facilities marked for tractor production were withdrawn: Perry was informed that no tractors could be made in England, and was asked if Ford would produce them for Britain in Dearborn. Ford agreed, making a proposal for 6000 units which the Director of Munitions, P. Hanson, accepted on June 28. Amid apologies from him and other British officials, Sorensen was ordered home and readied a Dearborn factory (at Brady Street and Michigan Avenue) for producing an improved model. No plans were made for installing a moving assembly line, but the building was equipped for a limited amount of production, and for assembly.[8]

According to Ernest C. Kanzler, with whom Edsel had become acquainted—the two were engaged to sisters, Edsel to Eleanor and Kanzler to Josephine Clay—and whom Henry Ford had persuaded to abandon his law practice and become Sorensen's assistant at Henry Ford & Son, Ford was reluctant to go into production with the tractor. Kroll and Voorhess confirm this fact. Ford felt that the model he had could be improved, and wanted to work on it until it was "right." However, in the fall of the year Lord Northcliffe, head of a permanent British mission in the United States, appeared at Dearborn and urged that production begin. Kanzler recalls that when Ford explained the reason for delay Northcliffe replied: "We understand your objection. We ourselves have many new military devices in blueprint, but we have to use the weapons and machines we have, and try to beat the Germans with what we've got. We need a tractor. Yours is the best we can get. We can't wait for the perfect tractor, we need what's available and we want you to produce it." Ford agreed.* Meanwhile he demonstrated

---

* Kanzler had prepared for a legal career at the University of Michigan and Harvard, and had joined the firm of Stevenson, Carpenter, Butzel and Backus, where he was assigned by Stevenson, attorney for the Dodge brothers in a suit against Ford and soon also for the Chicago *Tribune* in Ford's suit against that paper, to do research on both cases. (See Chaps. IV, V.) Meanwhile Kanzler was frequently a guest at Fair Lane, where Ford often discussed his (cont'd on p. 62)

the machine for Northcliffe, who at once became a zealous partisan, and as one of the world's most successful journalists, made his championship dramatically effective. "What a tremendous time you gave me with the tractor," he wrote Ford on October 19. "Not till the end of my days shall I forget the spectacle of your mechanical miracle romping across Mother Earth with the speed of a trotting mule." Northcliffe reported in the London *Weekly Times* of October 26 under the title, "Ford's Mechanical Miracle: the Wonderful Tractor:"

The tractor itself is a small piece of machinery about the length of a Ford motor-car. It can be used either as a stationary engine, or to propel ploughs, mowing machines, reapers and binders. . . . It is literally true that a boy or girl with neither mechanical nor agricultural knowledge can drive it. I mounted the tractor and ploughed a half-mile furrow with ease and accuracy at a speed between three and four miles an hour,* and with no time lost in turning. . . . It is low, steered by a wheel, and when pulling a set of disc harrows seems fairly to romp across country. . . . It has a strong electric head light, so that it may just as easily plough by night as by day.

Northcliffe was impressed by Ford as well as by the tractor. "He is the master mind of a great factory where 41,000 lately drew up to salute President Wilson, and whose chief owner pays a super-tax on a private income of £7,000,000 per annum." As Northcliffe was leaving after having inspected the factory Ford remarked: "I hope you observe one thing about the establishment."

Northcliffe said that the workers seemed of healthier physique than most.

"Not that only," replied Ford, "but I hope you noticed that there is no hustling. I don't allow it." [9]

(cont'd from p. 61) business freely. Kanzler would protest, explaining that he was working on the suits, and could not ignore what he heard. "Please, Mr. Ford, don't talk about your affairs when I am here." Ford would laugh and say: "You ought to be on my side. Why do you want to be a lawyer, anyway? They're parasites. Come to Highland Park and I'll give you a job." Kanzler replied that he had spent six years preparing for legal work, and liked it. Finally, when Ford was ready to launch Henry Ford & Son, he proposed that Kanzler join him and grow with this new and important activity. Kanzler agreed, and Ford took him to Dearborn, gave him a seat on the opposite side of Sorensen's desk, and said: "Charlie, show this young fellow the business." Kanzler had always had an aptitude for mechanics, and an interest in it. From technical training in high school, he had the ability to read blueprints. Now, under Sorensen's guidance, he worked at a variety of factory jobs to get a first-hand knowledge of all aspects of the business: factory routines, shipments, and the office. His work on production and shipment soon became outstanding, with important consequences to be noted later. (Interview, Ernest C. Kanzler with the authors, New York, June 11, 1956.)

* Actually, as noted by J. Edward Schipper, "Ford Tractor Ready to Help the Farmer," *Motor Age*, XXXII, Aug. 23, 1917, 28, top speed at this time was 2.83 m.p.h. Later it was somewhat increased.

Production at the Dearborn tractor plant was slow at first: the end of the year saw only 254 machines completed; but the rate rose rapidly with January, 1918, and by April the entire British order, raised to 7000, had been delivered. Ford turned to the American market, where he took orders from distributors for individual states, some buying 1000 machines each, others combining to share that number. By June, 1918, he had 13,463 American orders, with 5067 already delivered.

The British were grateful to Ford for his prompt and successful service. H. C. B. Underdown of the Munitions Department, in thanking the Ford Motor Company in England for its role in assembling the machines, stated that without them "the food crisis would in all probability not have been surmounted." While the Fordson was demonstrated in France in the spring of 1917, no tractors were supplied directly to that country. Production in Dearborn mounted: by April, 1918, an output of 64 units per day had been reached, which rose to 131 per day by July.[10]

But by that time the tractor was only one of a number of military products which were challenging the ingenuity and energy of the Ford organization.

3.

The American government first turned to the Ford Motor Company when it inquired on May 10, 1917, about procuring 2000 Ford chassis for ambulances. Because of Ford's pacifism, Highland Park had previously filled no orders for belligerents. However, Perry in England shared none of Ford's scruples, and assembled vehicles for military use by the thousand. The Paris branch of the Ford Motor Company prepared ambulance bodies on Ford chassis for French units. Even in the United States Harvard and Yale students raised money for seventeen ambulances, all Fords, which went to France. There was no question of the excellent performance of such cars; Lord Leigh, who had seen them in action on the Western front, extolled the work of 4000 Ford models in France, as did Sir Crawford McCullagh, Lord Mayor of Belfast.[11] The American government's order, officially given on May 30, required few changes on the part of the Highland Park factory, which from that time forward made cars, trucks and ambulances for the American forces.

Early in the war various Ford executives adjusted their work to the changing situation. Norval Hawkins entered government employ. John R. Lee moved to Washington, D.C., to act as a liaison man for the company. Mayo, widely acquainted with industrialists and engineers, discussed projects with Army or Navy men, while Liebold, as Ford's personal representative, was soon participating in many similar conferences. Upon Edsel Ford and Frank Klingensmith fell an increasing share of the purely business responsibilities of the company. Production activities were handled by Wills, Martin, Avery, Hartner, and their assistants. Sorensen at Dearborn was making tractors; Knudsen would soon head one of the most spectacular of war performances.[12]

After its May 30 order for ambulances, the Highland Park plant did little war work for a time, its next order being for 820,000 steel helmets in October. Ford was restive. He had immense facilities, a superb body of workers, yet was practically idle. Apparently by late August he perceived a solution: he would make his great contribution through the quantity production of airplanes, turning them out on a moving assembly line like Model T's. On the 30th he announced his intention by cable to Perry in England. Twenty-five years later Franklin D. Roosevelt was ridiculed for proposing to build 50,000 airplanes; already in 1917 Ford outdid him three to one: he proposed to manufacture 150,-000! He asked Perry to get the British government to send him a captured German fighter of the best type (obviously to help him set a design, although he later said this would not follow the German craft very closely). "Let no jealousy or excuse stand in the way!" he admonished. Perry was bewildered. The number Ford mentioned, he reported, was "deemed incredulous [sic] and unattainable." No, Ford replied, the number was correct. Aircraft could be manufactured as easily as motor cars. Perry then reported that a plane was available, but could be sent only on the request of some American governmental agency. "I presume you are working in conjunction with Government," he added.

Meanwhile Ford was publicizing his idea in the United States. In an interview with Joe Toye of the Boston *Herald,* he proposed to overwhelm Germany with airplanes, "thousands and thousands."

"Where are we going to get the airplanes?"

"Build them."

"Can we build them as fast as you build automobiles?"

"Easily . . . I could turn them out by the thousand."

Ford thought he could do it for twenty-five cents a pound. Replying to a question by Toye, he ended the interview on a personal note. No, he had no daily program. "Suppose a man gets an idea. How is he going to develop it if the programme calls for his seeing somebody at 5 minutes to 3 or 16 minutes past 4?" Ford polished his point off with a simile. "A man with a program," he concluded, "is like a dead fish floating down a stream." [13]

Ford had no governmental sanction for his aircraft proposal, and soon dropped it. Another reason for doing so lay in a more pressing undertaking which had the fullest government backing: the manufacture of Liberty motors.

The Liberty motor, a new aircraft engine supposedly conjured into existence in a few days by a group of American engineers, was actually in large part the creation of J. G. Vincent (later Colonel), vice-president in charge of engineering for the Packard Motor Car Company. He had been experimenting with it for two years, and his third model seemed so promising that in May, 1917, he and Alvan Macauley, president of Packard, decided to submit it to the War Department, volunteering to manufacture engines in quantity, and to permit their manufacture by other companies.

The War Department called in representatives of the British and French, and E. J. Hall, an engineer who had worked on aircraft engines for the Russian government. In a five day conference at the Willard Hotel in Washington, modifications of Vincent's design were agreed upon, and the Liberty Motor was officially born, June 4, 1917.

The Liberty was balm upon wounded national pride. Europe, long at war, had gained such proficiency in the design and manufacture of armament that the United States seemed unlikely to originate anything that the belligerents could use. But the new aircraft engine was an exception. Foreign as well as domestic experts prophesied its success, most of the 22,000 planes that the Aircraft Production Board proposed to build were to be powered with it, and both the British and French wanted it in quantity.

The production of the engine was the ultimate responsibility of Colonel Edward A. Deeds, Chief of Aircraft Procurement for the Army Signal Corps, and as his deputy immediately in charge of the Engine Production Section he chose Harold H. Emmons, a young Detroit lawyer and Naval Reserve officer, with some automotive experience, who was assigned to him on request. Emmons was eager for active duty, wanted no "desk job," and protested vehemently when he reported to Deeds. The latter said: "There is a desk in the next room with your name on it and a bushel of mail to be answered." Then with a smile, "Will you do it, or shall I be obliged to report you to the Secretary of the Navy for insubordination?" Emmons thereupon began to discharge his new duties with unusual foresight and energy.[14]

It seems clear that the Ford Motor Company first appeared in Liberty production in connection with the manufacture of the engine's cylinders. Despite Vincent's years of work, numerous technical problems required solution before quantity production could be successfully pushed, and cylinder fabrication was one of them. In the summer of 1917 all cylinders were bored out of solid steel forgings, or billets, a process that Deeds and his associate Sidney D. Waldron found "tedious and laborious," as well as highly expensive. They asked themselves: "Why not put the problem up to Henry Ford?"

They went to Detroit, apparently in late July, won Ford's cooperation, and three weeks later in Deeds's Washington office were presented by Mayo with a sample cylinder which embodied the Ford answer. Apparently the new method was evolved by Wills, Findlater and Emde; Wibel insisted that Findlater's was the dominant role, other Ford officials gave this to Emde. The solution was reached by substituting steel tubing for the billet. This tubing, of required thickness, was shaped to cylinder size, cut off on a bias, and the upper portion folded down at the top to form the head and provide space for the valve ports. The side and top were welded. The operation required a machine tool of special design, and the government inspectors regarded the entire process with complete contempt. But it worked magnificently, saving material and time, and cutting the cost per cylinder from $24 to $8.25.* The Ford Motor Company was asked to make all cylinders for Liberties, wherever manufactured. Eventually it contracted for 700,000, of which 415,377 were actually delivered.[15]

The solution of the cylinder problem led to a contract for the Ford Motor Company to produce 5000 complete engines. This was under negotiation in October, and signed November 22. The other companies then manufacturing Liberties were Packard (6000), the Lincoln Motor

---

* Isaac F. Marcosson, *Colonel Deeds, Industrial Builder*, 247, sets the new cost at $7.00. This may have applied to the early 8-cylinder motor, or to a cylinder which was later enlarged to increase the "twelve's" horse power from 330 to 440.

Company (6000), and Nordyke & Marmon (3000). Later General Motors (Buick-Cadillac) also produced the engine.

Emmons later recalled how he was directed to enlist Ford's aid in the Liberty program, and through Mayo, whom he knew, procured an interview. Ford asked him: "Are you sure of exactly what you want?" Emmons, although he already knew that the work had its unpredictable aspects, had to say that he was, and proposed that Ford manufacture 8-cylinder Liberties developing 225 h.p. "All right," replied Ford. "We'll do the job."

Wills took charge of the project, alloting space in the Highland Park plant, finding suppliers, and selecting machine tools for the complicated operation. However, hardly had he got well under way when the Aircraft Procurement Division received a cable from General John J. Pershing in France stating that if American participation in the air was to be effective, all aircraft motors supplied to overseas forces must be of at least 400 h.p. This meant that the 8-cylinder Liberty could not be used abroad, and that the 12-cylinder must be redesigned for greater power. Ford would have to build twelves, and Emmons was told so to inform him.

Considering Ford's insistence earlier on knowing exactly what he was to do, Emmons was doubtful if the manufacturer would accept the change, and so was Mayo. However, the latter took Emmons to the lunch room in the Highland Park Administration Building, and placed him in a chair next to Ford's customary corner seat. Entering presently, Henry asked the visitor how all his work was progressing. "Oh, fine, Mr. Ford," replied Emmons, and then explained the altered situation and the request that Ford cooperate by making twelves instead of eights. There was a momentous hush while Ford considered the matter. Then he remarked quietly: "Well, Harold, that's just darned good common sense, isn't it?"

As the two came out of the lunch room, Wills pounced upon them and began to remonstrate with Ford. "We don't want to do those twelves," he protested. "Those engines are brutes. Look at the tolerances on the crankshafts—down to ten thousandths of an inch." Ford merely looked at him and said: "Wills, show 'em some speed." [16]

The enlarged Liberty proved to be quite as formidable an undertaking as Wills had feared. The amount of floor space required at the Highland Park plant eventually comprised 521,000 square feet. Of the

14,000 machine tools used on the Ford car only 420 were adaptable to engine manufacture, and eventually 980 new ones had to be purchased. Numerous jigs, fixtures, gauges, and other devices were also designed for the engine by Ford mechanicians. Changes in specifications, fuel shortages, poor priority ratings for materials, and inexperienced inspectors compounded the difficulties of production.

In addition to solving the cylinder problem, the Ford experts developed bearings which stood up so well in tests that after June, 1918, these were supplied by Government request to other manufacturers.

The Liberty contract was one of the most important war assignments undertaken by the Ford Motor Company. At the peak of production, it absorbed more than 11,000 men, and the total cost mounted to $35,-399,900. The officials in charge of production attempted to make the engines an assembly line job, and partly succeeded. They established a moving piston assembly, a conveyor system for cleaning and washing crankcases, and a partial moving assembly for the remainder of the work. The first contract for 5000 motors was eventually increased to 12,000, but in the end only 3940 were completed. The Ford plant did not begin to produce until May 7, 1918, but then steadily increased its output, reaching 1242 for the month of October, with a daily output of seventy-five just before the armistice. By that time the goal was 100 motors every sixteen hours. In September, October, and November Ford production was the highest among the five contracting companies.[17] *

4.

Meanwhile, little had been done toward developing the great production site on the Rouge. During the remainder of 1915 Ford was busy

* Liberty engine production is covered in two reputable sources, "Judge Hughes's Report and Recommendations on the Aircraft Production Investigation, Transmitted to Attorney General Gregory," Congressional Record, LVII, Appendix A, 65th Congress, 3rd Session, 883 ff., hereafter cited as Hughes Report, and "Aviation Engine History," a MS. in the National Archives, Washington, which the Archivist terms "a history of the Production Division of the Air Service, or possibly a history of the Service itself." (Elbert L. Huber to the authors, April 7, 1955.) The Hughes Report covers production only up to October 11, 1918. Both sources credit the Ford Motor Co. with the highest production for the three months preceding the armistice. "Aviation Engine History" records motors shipped by the two leading companies as follows: September, Ford, 811, Lincoln, 687; October, Ford, 1059, Lincoln, 1050; November, Ford, 1201, Lincoln 818. Figures for motors *produced* differ (see the figure in the text, which is for production, not shipments), but also show Ford leading. In December the Lincoln Motor Company shipped 1109 units and Ford only 125 (he had stopped work as quickly as possible after the armistice). Both the Lincoln and Packard companies exceeded the Ford company in total production, each completing 6500 engines. Figures on Ford production in a memo from Leister to Liebold, Aug. 3, 1923, are 807 for September, 1060 for October, and 1214 for November (Acc. 572, Box 26).

with the new tractor and peace activities; Mayo and Wills apparently continued to plan the development. Early in 1916 the clash between Ford's ideas of expansion and the Dodge Brothers' desire for dividends became open. While a beginning was made at the Rouge site, and work on blast furnaces even commenced, such activity languished with a suit brought by the Dodges and the early activities of the war.[18]

In the summer of 1917, Ford was summoned to Washington for a conference with President Wilson, who hoped to get Ford to serve on the United States Shipping Board. Liebold, who went along, advised him not to accept the proposed appointment. He had information about poor work done by the Emergency Fleet Corporation (an arm of the Board) on the West Coast. "He [Wilson] only wants you on the Board to put it back into the good graces of the public. I don't see how you can do it."

However, Ford and Liebold discussed the situation with Edward N. Hurley, chairman of the Board, who felt that the Detroiter with his knowledge of mass production could immensely speed the building of ships in quantity. As a matter of fact, Ford had recently given an opinion on such activity. "What we want is one type of ship built in large numbers," he had declared. Wilson and Hurley doubtless noticed this statement. Finally, on November 7, Ford accepted membership on the Shipping Board and an active advisory role.

Before this Hurley, in discussing the shipbuilding situation with Ford and Liebold, showed them some charts on production and U-boat sinkings, and remarked, "Well, if the submarines keep sinking ships as they are now, it will just be a matter of months until they can be sinking more than we can build."

Liebold objected: "What's the idea of building more ships to feed the submarines? Why don't you think about building something that will cope with the submarines instead?"

"We've got destroyers," Hurley pointed out.

"They're designed for a different type of warfare," replied Liebold.

This, he says, was the beginning of work on a boat to hunt down submarines. Hurley became interested. Ford, although not proposing to build such units himself, thought he might show how to produce them in quantity. Soon Hurley, Ford, and Liebold discussed the matter with a commander in the British Navy, Sidney Houghton. He told them of the P-boats—small, open vessels employed by the British to hunt submarines. Because of their size they were limited as to armament, lacked cabin and adequate galley facilities, and had to return to port every four or five days. Houghton felt that a larger boat was needed, with better armament and adequate eating and sleeping quarters. The idea grew, and soon the Navy, which at first held aloof, took over the project. Commander Robert Stocker, a naval designer, worked out a hull for the proposed vessel in association with Admiral D. W. Taylor, while other naval experts (Admirals Griffin and Dyson, and Commander S. M. Robinson) worked on the power plant. By mid-December they were making rapid progress toward a satisfactory design.

Ford, as an adviser, urged that all hull plates be flat so that they could be produced in quantity, and persuaded the Navy men to accept steam turbines instead of reciprocating steam engines. Secretary of the Navy Josephus Daniels, who had been drawn into the project, now discovered that he had no facilities for building new craft at the Navy yards; similarly, the Shipping Board could find none. Ford was asked if he would undertake a contract, and agreed. He told Liebold: "We can't go back without doing something. We've got to be of some service." *

Ford's plan for building the boats was revolutionary. Establishing his plant on the Rouge River, he would turn them out as factory products, using mass production techniques, and employing factory workers. He would then send the boats by the Great Lakes and the St. Lawrence to the Atlantic coast.

Had other facilities been available, he would never have been permitted to proceed with the project, which, when finally announced, amazed the public and shocked the shipbuilding world. But the exceptional conditions gave Ford his opportunity, and he was supremely confident that he could meet the challenge.† Of course at this time the boats were relatively small.

---

* Norman Beasley, *Knudsen: A Biography*, 84–85, says that Daniels was making inquiries about building submarine-chasers, called for bidders, but found none available. Knudsen heard about the situation and told Ford: "We can make those boats on the Rouge." While there is no doubt of Knudsen's ability, and while he eventually directed the project, this version of its inception is unique.

† So confident was Ford that Knudsen, in charge of the job, was worried, once it was underway, about getting some Navy experts to assist him. He appealed to Lieutenant Julius A. Furer (later Admiral), who had come down to see if the program could be speeded up, to get Ford to agree to the idea. "You get him just to nod his head, or just to say yes," urged Knudsen, "then you start talking about something else right away." Furer agreed. Ford, when the two conversed, was quite contemptuous of Navy men. "After the war you can throw that uniform away," he told the young officer. "We won't be having armies and navies then." As to production, he declared that Navy personnel just didn't understand mass methods. "You go on in the same old ruts." Furer seemed to agree, but suggested that a few Navy experts would be useful to give information on special points. Ford nodded dubiously, and said, "Yes, yes." Furer felt Knudsen's large hand squeeze his shoulder, and hurried on to another subject. Knudsen had his authorization! (Interview of Allan Nevins with Admiral Furer, March 25, 1955.)

They grew. Anti-aircraft guns seemed desirable, then four-inch guns to sink submarines. The result was a larger and stouter hull, and a larger crew. A listening device developed by Edison which would locate enemy underseas craft was incorporated. Radio apparatus was installed to maintain contact with other ships. "Before we finally got through," recalled Liebold, "we had a young battleship." [19] It should be remembered that Ford had little part in the design of the boat. Except for insisting on plans that could be adapted to quantity manufacture, and persuading the Navy to accept steam turbines, he seems to have contributed nothing fundamental. It was a Navy job.

Opposition developed in Congress to an appropriation for the improvement of the Rouge and the building of a plant there at Government expense. According to Liebold, in December the boats acquired the name "Eagle." * However, it was not until January 14, 1918 that the Ford Motor Company wrote Secretary Daniels that it was willing to accept a contract for the construction of from 100 to 500 Eagle boats. The first vessel was to be delivered in five months or less, ten in the ensuing month, twenty in the next, and twenty-five or more each month thereafter. A tentative price of $275,000 per vessel had been set; Daniels apparently thought it high, and the company agreed that perhaps it was, but could be revised later. It warned the secretary: "We are not boat builders and will not assume responsibility for the performance of the boats." It estimated the cost of plant facilities and other improvements to be met by the Government at $3,500,000, and noted that at the end of the war the plant would be sold to the Ford Motor Company or another purchaser. The letter ended: "An order from you to proceed at government risk will set our whole organization in motion on this job without awaiting the rather slow process leading up to a formal contract."

Daniels telegraphed on January 17: "Proceed with one hundred submarine patrol vessels. Details of contract to be arranged as soon as practicable." [20]

Ford had already decided to put Knudsen in charge, had briefed him

* Liebold had followed all the conferences, and was worried about the appropriation. With the idea of bringing influence to bear on Congress, he sat down and wrote an editorial, telephoned Ira E. Bennett of the Washington *Post,* and asked him to consider publishing something like it. Bennett printed the editorial practically unchanged on Sunday, Dec. 23, under the title, "A Challenge to America." It described the destructive work of the U-boats and declared: "the crying need of this hour is an eagle that will scour the seas and pounce upon and destroy every submarine that dares to leave German or Belgian shores." This was apparently the origin of the term "Eagle Boats," by which the submarine chasers were known. (Liebold, *Reminiscences.*)

accordingly, and had seen the Dane begin building operations before the contract was drawn. The site chosen for the plant lay on the east bank of the Rouge. The stream was widened and dredged to permit access from below, a creek was diverted, and gullies and swampy places were filled. Concrete was poured for the foundations of the buildings. The work site, covering eighteen acres and stretching along the river for a mile, would soon include storage yards, shops, an assembly building, fitting-out sheds, docks, and—in a slip which ran from the river northward into the factory area—an enormous launching platform.

Dominating the development was the immense assembly building designed by Albert Kahn: 1700 feet long, 350 feet in depth, and 100 in height. Knudsen's biographer, Norman Beasley, writes of the interior: "Inside, he [Knudsen] fashioned three production lines, each capable of carrying seven boats, or a total of twenty-one boats in the stocks at a time. Figures he had worked out showed that sixty-three shifts could build a boat of 200 tons, 200 feet long, with a twenty-one foot beam."

Construction was ingeniously rapid. The *Ford Man* for May 18, 1918 described the process: "As soon as the foundations are ready the superstructure of steel and concrete and glass shoots up; floors are laid while the roof is going on and the glass going in the windows; as the floor progresses machinery is installed; so that when the last arching rafter is in place the roofer is at hand and when the last shingle is laid all floors, runways, assembly conveyors, machinery, lights, every essential is in place and the big plant is at once at work." [21]

At first Ford and Knudsen believed that boats could be sent down an assembly line like motor cars. Why not? Designate the parts, number them, assemble them—it was purely an exercise in planning. However, both men soon perceived that the task was not so simple. They compromised on a "step-by-step" movement. The hulls moved forward down the 1700-foot line with an impressive regularity. Knudsen had the advantage of some general experience in shipbuilding as a young man in Denmark, and of experimenting with a mockup hull at Highland Park. On May 7 Liebold telegraphed Daniels: "Keel for the first boat has been laid on blocks and side frames are now ready to go up," and announced on July 10: "First Eagle successfully launched seven P.M. today."

The launching of a hull, 204 feet long and 25 wide, was a formidable operation. These boats were not built on ways, from which they could slide into the water. From the assembly building they had somehow to be conveyed to the water's edge, then transferred from land to river. Two devices made the shift possible. The first was an enormous flat car—"probably the longest car in the world"—on which the hull moved down the assembly building. The second was a launching platform—a 225-foot steel trestle which could be sunk 20 feet by hydraulic action—designed by Mayo. This adjoined the launching dock in the slip, its top surface at the same level. The hull was drawn on tracks laid for this purpose from the assembly building to the dock on its flat car by a tractor, and then on to the trestle. We have an eye-witness account of what happened next:

Out upon this trestle the 'Eagle' moves majestically until the proper point is reached. Then the tracks are disconnected, the great hydraulic pumps are set to work and almost imperceptibly the 'Eagle' drops into the water as softly as a summer breeze. . . . As the trestle sinks deeper and deeper into the water the boat presently finds her level and floats away from the wooden cradle and braces which have supported her since the keel was laid. As the 'Eagle' drifts off the trestle—a boat ready for the emplacement of boilers, engines and other equipment—the launching trestle rises with the empty trucks, which return to the assembly building by the way they came out, and are immediately ready for the keel of the next 'Eagle.' [22]

With the launching of the first Eagle the enterprise seemed to be off to a triumphant start. Such was not the fact. Despite the tremendous effort made and the great ingenuity shown, troubles steadily beset the project. Not only were the workers unfamiliar with naval construction (a more important fact than Ford or Knudsen would concede), but few had experience in riveting or welding. Charles C. West, superintending engineer for the Navy, noted poor bulkhead work, and defects in erecting, bolting, riveting, and welding. Another inspector cited the lack of experienced supervisory personnel, patching, poor paper work, and poor inspection by the company.

Frank Riecks, assistant to Jack Bergner, superintendent of outfitting, who put the machinery into the boats, later gave an account of Eagle activity which bears out the Navy officials' criticism. However, Riecks felt that much difficulty stemmed from design: the steel hulls were in his opinion too light. Riecks thought the finished boats "not seaworthy;" they were built, he felt, for speed only. He says that the Navy crews shared his opinion. However, Liebold had perfect confidence in the toughness of the boats, and later took a group of prominent De-troiters for an extended ride on the Lakes St. Clair and Erie.[23]

Production continued to be besieged by difficulties: the need of hous-ing for employees; scarcity of manufacturing materials; the impossi-bility of getting enough workers. A great supplementary plant at Newark Meadows (Kearny), New Jersey, which was to receive Eagle hulls towed by lake, Erie Canal, Hudson, and Passaic Rivers, on which several million dollars were spent, was not completed in time to speed the project. By July, 1918, the labor force on the Rouge had risen to 4380; it was increasing at that time, and the peak almost touched 8000. Apparently the first boat was finished on schedule, but the others did not follow so rapidly. Daniels in May had hoped for one boat by Au-gust 1, ten by September 1, twenty by October 1, and twenty-five or more per month after November 1. After producing the first Eagle, the Ford organization never came within sight of these goals. It appears to have dispatched seven boats for the Atlantic coast by Armistice Day, although only two had arrived. This result reflected the difficulties the company had encountered. In time these lessened, and by November, 1918, the job was evidently getting in hand. No. 13 was launched through the ice on January 9; on February 17, reported the *Ford Man,* fifteen boats were lined up at the outfitting dock, and "Since New Year's no week has passed in which two boats were not launched." The contract had been raised from 100 to 112, then cut to 60. Tempo in-creased as the end came in sight, and the *Ford Man* boasted that No. 59 was complete less than ten days after the keel was laid:

Efficiency was raised to the nth power. The inspectors followed closely on the heels of the riveters, inspecting the work as soon as it was completed. Immediately their approval was put on the job, the painters were busy, painting the work almost before the rivets were cold. So eager were the men to complete their part of the work that they would often start back on the job before lunch was over with a sandwich in one hand and some neces-sary material in the other.[24]

Henry Ford had struck his pace just a year after the work had started, and half a year later than he had hoped.

The entire Eagle Boat operation came briefly under challenge when Senator Henry Cabot Lodge late in December, 1918, introduced a reso-lution to investigate it. He acted after the *Daily Iron Trade and Metal*

Market Report had made "charges and disclosures." The *Detroit Satur-day Night* took up the matter with enthusiasm. However, at the hearings naval officials defended the boats as a necessary experiment, and as well made, while Ford profits were proved to have been modest.

The chief fault lay in Ford's initial optimism: if to hope for miracles and not to produce them were a crime, he was guilty of it. As Admiral Robert S. Griffin of the Naval Bureau of Steam Engineering remarked: "Mr. Ford found the job a little more difficult than he anticipated." Still, when it is recalled that the first building went up in February, 1918, that the first real construction on boats dated from April, that the type of boat and the design were both wholly new, that labor and supervisory personnel were inexperienced, and that changes in design slowed the construction for a considerable time, to turn out the first seven vessels in as many months, and fifty-two in a year and a half, was a rather remarkable performance for that day. Edsel Ford testified that the changes by Navy personnel were numerous and constant, and "made a big difference in the time it took it complete the work." [25]

The final product undoubtedly had its faults. *The Daily Iron Trade and Metal Market Report* called them glaring ones, and that charge has been echoed ever since. Ford officials denied it. The *Ford Man* called the project "one of the most successful jobs ever accomplished as a result of the war," and even Charles C. West, the Navy superintendent whose severe remarks are quoted above, reported of the first Eagles on their voyage east: "Eagles 1, 2 and 4 encountered considerable heavy weather and their behavior in a seaway has been pronounced excellent." Finally, a letter from the commanding officer of Eagle 1, written from Brest, France, on August 17, 1919, stated that during the first six months of service "there were no defects in the hull, hull fitting, and equipment of this vessel." The boat had been "almost constantly under way" since April 11, 1919, serving mostly off Russia in ice-covered waters. "It speaks very well for the construction of this vessel that in bucking heavy ice, no damage was experienced to hull, frames, or bulkheads." Eagles 2 and 3 encountered the same conditions and behaved creditably.

The task essayed was audacious, the cost of $46,104,042 was the highest for any Ford war contract, and had the chasers been turned out in quantity somewhat earlier, they might have launched one of the great

American activities of the war. Although the glowing promises made by Ford were not realized, his performance was creditable to all who were involved.[26]

5.

Throughout the war the legend of the Ford company as the symbol of mass production continued to work on both military and civilian minds. The Ford plants were homes of industrial magic. In these buildings, in the men who operated them, lay a kind of modern philosopher's stone which could convert any bold idea based on mechanical efficiency into an effective measure for war.

Ford never denied that he possessed the magic; rather he continued to propose new ways of using it. And again and again he was urged to do so. The British Navy constantly sought his assistance; he manufactured for them a submarine detector, and carried out other minor activities. Farkas designed for the American air force a robot airplane bomb which anticipated the V-1. The War Department begged Ford to produce new armor plate for tanks, and he did, devising a type half the weight of that in use, but of equal strength. The Ordnance Department begged the assistance of the company in developing a two-man, two and a half ton tank, and later a larger type of six tons in weight. Ford fully lived up to his promise to turn his plants over to the Government; assembly units at Cambridge, Louisville, Philadelphia, St. Louis, and Washington were entirely in federal hands, and part of the Detroit plant was government-controlled.[27]

The tanks were the final war adventure of the company. Ford showed an enthusiasm for the small tank which matched that for the midget submarine. However, with the tank he was on relatively familiar ground, for both the Ford car and the Fordson tractor had qualities in common with small tanks, while the Ford organization seemed well equipped to evolve a successful design and produce machines in quantity. Ford on March 25, 1918, practically elected himself tankmaker by calling for 90,000 two-man machines, assuring the public that such units could "resist the hail of machine gun bullets and shrapnel splinters," and that the two men inside "would have the offensive power of fifty soldiers with rifles."

The Ordnance Department encouraged the Ford company to design and test such a machine. Galamb worked on it, while Eugene Farkas soon began to evolve a three-man, six-ton model. The smaller tank used Model T engines, the larger ones tractor engines. In both types the tank was turned by racing one power unit while the other was idling. Apparently the Army was satisfied with the smaller model, which maneuvered successfully about the muddy Rouge area, for on October 1, 1918, it gave the Ford Motor Company a contract for 15,000 machines. Under a separate contract, fifteen similar tanks were completed for experimental purposes, some being dispatched to France. Work on the larger order was about to begin when the armistice halted production.

The company signed early in November a contract for 1000 six-ton tanks, to cost $6000 each. Company records show that 203 subcontractors had been lined up for this work, and the liquidation of the contract just after the armistice was an intricate and harassing piece of business.[28]

Tank production, involving $87,000,000 had these contracts been completed, would have taken its place with Liberty engines and Eagle boats as one of the major Ford war activities. These three enterprises, with the making of cars, trucks, ambulances, and other products already mentioned, completely engaged the factory space, machines and workers which the company could command. By November 26, 1917, the main Highland Park factory had sharply reduced its automotive work, assembling only 527 cars a day, and on December 14 Liebold wrote Josephus Daniels that he expected the demand for motor cars to "automatically subside," and that "as this gradually takes place we will take men off motor car production and put them on government work." By July 31, 1918, the parent factory was producing no motor cars whatever, and the assembly plants only 2967 per day. According to Edsel Ford's later testimony, by October the monthly total was only 9326, and in November sank to 5954, or about 300 a day. These cars were practically all for governmental use.[29]

During the more than nineteen months of war, certain company employees had come under serious attack.

The first criticism had focused upon Edsel Ford. In his twenty-fourth year when his country entered the conflict, he was subject to military service. He appealed to his draft board for exemption because he was needed by the company; on October 7, 1917, his plea was denied. An appeal was taken from the board's decision to President Wilson. However, new draft regulations put Edsel in Class 2-A, as having dependents, and 3-L, as being indispensable to a war industry, and he was never called. Henry Ford in July, 1919, frankly stated on the witness stand that he had needed Edsel in the factory. As early as September, 1918, he had publicly taken responsibility for keeping him there. "He has wanted to go from the day we declared war," stated the older Ford, "and he wants to now. When the duly authorized authority says his services are more needed in the army than here in these industries, he will be found at the front fighting, and will not be found sticking his spurs into a mahogany desk at Washington."

Certainly Edsel rejected the advice of one acquaintance that he escape service by purchasing a submarine patrol boat, donating it to the government, and receiving a commission in the Naval Reserve. Conceding that the plan was "to my mind a good way of actually evading active service in either the Army or the Navy," he stated that he had claimed exemption because "I believe I will be of far greater service to my country right here in the plant," and that "if the Officials see fit to deny my exemption I am perfectly willing to be drafted with the rest of the young men of this community." Later Edwin G. Pipp, who was then criticizing Henry Ford, spoke of Edsel's war service with admiration. "It took more courage for Edsel Ford not to put on a uniform than it would have taken to put on one." Pipp pointed out that Edsel could easily have been commissioned and assigned "right back to the duties he was performing." [30]

Other Ford employees were challenged because of their birth or even their descent. All these men were completely loyal to Ford and to the United States, but the mere fact of their having German or Hungarian names, and sometimes accents to match, was enough to make Detroit patriots suspicious. The local branch of the American Protective League was watching for sabotage in Detroit. Liebold, although born in the United States, came under question because in taking a young woman who lived near him home in his car, he remarked, "Well, I think the Germans will quit before they are licked." His passenger thought the remark showed inside knowledge of German intentions, and reported it, adding that an unusually large number of people had been calling at the Liebold home, and that mysterious packages had been delivered there. Naturally, the callers were people interested in seeing Henry Ford or his personal representative, and the packages were the normal number delivered to any American home.

In the case of Carl Emde, however, the company was employing a German-born worker in the development and production of the Liberty motor. The Hughes Committee appointed to investigate aircraft production discovered this fact. It reported that while "nothing conclusive could be established against Emde in relation to this work, the advisability of removing him from his position of strategic importance was clear to some of the most important men in the management." A conference was held, says the report, and some Ford officials urged Emde's removal, but Henry Ford overruled them. The investigators concluded: "There has been a laxity at the Ford plant with respect to those of German sympathies, which is not at all compatible with the interests of the government."

Ford officials termed these remarks political, for Ford was a supporter of Wilson, and was even then a candidate for senator from Michigan. In any event, the Republican State Central Committee promptly published a full-page advertisement in the Detroit *Free Press* saying in part: "Carl Emde, a German alien and sympathizer [Emde was not an alien but a citizen, and emphatically protested his loyalty], is boss of the drafting work on the Liberty motor at the Ford plant. . . . If Carl Emde wishes to make plans and photographs of the Ford plant or the Liberty motor for use by the enemies of the United States, Henry Ford is willing to give him the chance to do it."

The attack, carried widely in papers throughout the state, was printed Sunday morning, November 3, two days before the election. It called for an immediate reply. Ford first telephoned Emde. "Don't worry, Emde," he told him. "I know . . . you are honest and faithful. If they try to hang you they'll have to hang me first." He then worked out a statement in which he announced, "Our policy is to make men, not to break them." He pointed out that great injury might be done individuals "in times of panic," and that Emde was an able employee of twelve years' service who had helped improve the Liberty motor "with a saving of $345,000 a month to the Government." The statement ended: "From the beginning of the war we have taken the greatest precaution. We have had no interference with our work that could be in any way traced to enemy aliens."

Ford's action was characteristic. He had complete confidence in his men. He told Eugene Farkas: "I don't care what they are: Hungarians, Austrians, Germans. As long as they work for me and do a good job, they're all right with me." Judged by the complete record, he was wholly justified in his attitude, and the Hughes report was mistaken.[31]

The war record of the company, in totality, was impressive. As was to have been expected, the Ford factories had supplied a large number of cars, ambulances, and trucks to the American and Allied forces— about 39,000 all told. It had dispatched 7000 tractors to Britain, and 27,000 to American farms. It had produced caissons, helmets, submarine detectors, tubes for use by Allied submarines, shells, armor plate, and helped to develop gas masks. It had produced 3940 Liberty motors and 415,377 cylinders for such motors. It had built 60 Eagle Boats and developed two types of tanks which it was ready on Armistice Day to produce in quantity. It had furnished half a dozen plants to the Government.[32]

Many of the products on which the company toiled never figured importantly in the war. The Eagle boats ran down no submarines, the Liberty motors were used only in the final months of the struggle, and peace halted tank production. On the other hand, Ford tractors helped to meet the food needs of both Britain and America, while Ford cars, trucks, and ambulances won wide applause for their behavior in battle zones.

Altogether, Ford factories in the United States furnished 6000 ambulances, and more were supplied by the company's Paris branch, and by the Ford companies of Canada and Great Britain. Most American-made vehicles implemented the work of the American Field Service, which had charge of all activities at the front related to the wounded. Ford vehicles were used both in the United States and in Europe (25,000 cars and 8000 trucks), for liaison, carrier and miscellaneous service. They were of course intensively used by the British. In March, 1919, Gaston Plantiff urged Liebold not to miss Lowell Thomas's lecture on the Palestine campaign, the success of which General Allenby attributed to "Egyptian laborers, camels, and Ford cars." According to Thomas, Allenby rode in a Rolls-Royce, but always had a Ford on hand as a kind of insurance.[33]

On May 31, 1918, Perry sent Edsel Ford a rhyme composed by an ambulance driver and published in the American Field Service Bulletin. A parody on Kipling's "Gunga Din," it remarked that

It's mighty good to feel
When you're sitting at the wheel
She'll be running when the bigger cars are broke,

and concluded with a rattling stanza onomatopoetically fully worthy of
its subject:

Yes, Tin, Tin, Tin,
You exasperating puzzle Hunka Tin,
I've abused you and I've flayed you,
But by Henry Ford who made you
You are better than a big car
HUNKA TIN!

Perhaps the most widely publicized Ford was a car attached to a
Marine unit, whose activities were described in a letter written from
Corps headquarters in Washington to Clyde Herring, a Des Moines
Ford dealer. In this letter Major Frank E. Evans described how this
Ford truck had carried "everything from sick men to hard-tack," in-
cluding rations, ammunition, flares, and water. It was constantly under
enemy fire, constantly hit, but as constantly repaired by the devoted
Marines. Said Evans: "She is our own Joan of Arc and if it takes six
old cars to make her run again we'll get those six and rob them." Wallace Irwin celebrated the car in verse, telling how

Recruited into the Corps she was—
She came of her own accord.
We flew at her spanker the globe and the anchor
And named her Elizabeth Ford.

After retailing Elizabeth's adventures in various situations, the poet
continues:

But 'twas on the day of those murder-woods
Which the Yankees pronounce Beloo;
We were sent to knock silly the hopes of Prince Willie
And turn 'em around p.d.q.
We prayed for munitions and cleared our throats
With a waterless click—Good Lord!—
When out of a crater with bent radiator
Climbed faithful Elizabeth Ford.

Such lines reflect the immense affection which the motor car often aroused in men battling for their cause and their lives.[34]

6.

From the war work of the Ford Motor Company developed a controversy concerning war profits. We have already seen that even before the war Ford had emphasized that if it came he would "operate without one cent of profit." He had consistently denounced munitions makers as "exploiters of humanity," men who often "gamble, speculate, and manipulate with the wealth provided by honest industry."

When the Government was negotiating its first contracts with the Ford Motor Company, he accordingly proposed to produce at cost. But Lucking, his attorney, explained that such a course would not be satisfactory to the Government, or to other company stockholders, who expected all work to show a profit. Ford agreed to follow the usual procedures, but stipulated: "Well, I will return fifty-eight and a half per cent to the Government." (That is, the same percentage of profits as Ford's stock bore to the full total of shares.) [35]

Now and then allegations were made as to the profits of the company as contrasted with the professions of its chief owner. For example, on January 17, 1919, the Los Angeles *Times* argued that in the case of the Eagle boats, the Detroiter had been the beneficiary of a $3,500,000 expenditure for plant and river improvement, advanced by the Government, and was making $20,000 a boat, which in the end would mean a total profit of $1,200,000. Further gains would accrue by the purchase after the war of the buildings on the Rouge site at a reduced price— about $2,000,000 in all.* Similar assertions were made by other critics about Ford Motor Company profits on different contracts.

Ford continued to protest that he would return all war profits. During the senatorial campaign of 1918 Pipp, formerly of the Detroit *News,* was preparing publicity for Ford, and raised the question of his gains from war work. Ford was emphatic. "I don't want any of it," he insisted. "It's like taking blood money. You can tell anybody and everybody that I am going to return it all." Pipp was satisfied, and prepared publicity which reiterated Ford's promises.[36]

---

* The Los Angeles *Times* estimate was not greatly exaggerated as to profits on the boats: the company made $907,605.86, an entirely proper return on the vast undertaking. However, the improvement of the Rouge was a Detroit harbor improvement, approved before the war, and if Ford gained by acquiring the Rouge plants after the war, these were charged to him by the Government as profit.

The manufacturer finally set out to discover what his war profits were. There was difficulty in getting at the facts. The non-war activities of the company had to be separated from its war activities, and the profits on both figured—for the minority stockholders and for Ford himself. Then war taxes on profits had to be deducted, with the personal income tax that Ford himself had paid. So complicated was the task that on June 23, 1919 Ford telegraphed Carter Glass, Secretary of the Treasury, asking him "to appoint a reliable accountant . . . to go over the figures and accounts of our people and to aid in reaching correct figures so that I may immediately turn over the amount." (That is, the profits he had made.) The Treasurer appointed Albert M. Colegrove, one of the Department's agents, and apparently Colegrove assisted the Ford business office in its continuing researches.

Meanwhile the legend of the returned profits became public property, and Ford was credited with already having done what he had frequently promised to do. When Sarah T. Bushnell in *The Truth About Henry Ford* stated that Ford had given all his war profits—$29,000,000—to the government, Andrew W. Mellon, now Secretary of the Treasury, had his records searched. He wrote to Ford on March 16, quoting her, and remarking that "the records of the Treasury do not show any such sum received, and in fact there appears to be no record whatever of such a donation." What did Ford know about the matter? Liebold replied on the 22nd, saying that Ford had never seen Mrs. Bushnell's book, or authorized its publication. "Consequently, he feels no responsibility in connection with its circulation." [37]

Two important facts were clear: 1) that Ford had often said he was going to return his war profits and 2) that he had not done so. Pipp, now editor and publisher of *Pipp's Weekly,* went into the matter diligently, dredging up Ford's old promises, and demonstrating that he had never redeemed them. Under such prodding, the work of estimating the exact profits, which had been suspended, was resumed, and Ford indicated that he would make a payment. The *New York Times* of October 14, 1923, stated that the refund would be about $1,750,000.

Actually, the sum involved was less. Ford's profits before taxes had never approached the $29,000,000 grandly set by Mrs. Bushnell; the company's gains totalled $8,151,119.31, and when taxes had been deducted, stood at $4,357,484.97, Ford's own share amounting to $2,483,766.43. However, the deduction of personal income taxes left only $926,780.46. [38]

But Ford never paid this or any other sum. After his many promises, why did he fail to do so?

During the next few years Ford was to show a tendency to revoke his outright or implied promises. He would charge into a situation, gain favorable publicity by pledges of what he would do, find his role unexpectedly complex and difficult, and suddenly abandon it in stubborn disgust. The case of war profits is often cited as the perfect example of this tendency. Actually, it is not.

In the first place, in closing out his many war contracts at the time of the armistice, Ford made generous settlements with the Government. By his order, the company never disputed a Federal estimate or charge unless it was palpably in error. For example, in its letter to the Navy Compensation Board on July 21, 1920, about Eagle boats, it notes several instances in which it has not claimed reimbursement for expenditures, or has accepted Navy estimates open to question. Of one ruling the company remarks: "We believe that a great portion of this could be legally recovered from the Navy under the contract, but in order to facilitate final settlement . . . we are absorbing the entire loss of nearly three quarters of a million dollars." Ford was well aware of such concessions, and there is every reason to believe that if, after disposing of his contracts, he could have estimated his war profits with the assurance that the figures would have been final, he would have re-paid them at once. His request for a government expert in June, 1919, indicates that he meant to do so.[39]

But soon afterward it became apparent that he could have no final figures for some time to come. For early in 1919 the Dent Act for terminating war contracts had been passed by Congress, and this prescribed routines which delayed the settlement of the Eagle contract until August, 1920. Moreover, it was then clear that by the act any contract, even after settlement, could be reopened by War, Navy, Treasury, or the Attorney General's personnel, up to March 1, 1924. As a matter of fact, with the change of administration came a resolute policy of re-examining all war settlements, the Treasury showing exceptional zeal in questioning the adjustments made by the Navy and War Departments. (For a striking example of such practice, see the case of the Lincoln Motor Company as described in Chapter VII.) Treasury officials came to the Ford Motor Company to re-check its settlements, and did not finish their work until well into 1923. While their recommendations added little to the company's governmental obligations, until March, 1924, there was the possibility of further investigation and revision. Any return of profits made before that date might later be proved to be inaccurate.

The fact that an accounting was thus postponed until more than five years after the war was naturally annoying to Ford, as office correspondence indicates, and the visits of probing government officials were more so. Ford detested this particular type of interference. Mellon's first letter came at the very time that his own agents were examining company books, and must have infuriated the Detroiter. He believed that Mellon was opposing his offer to develop Muscle Shoals, since its acceptance might involve a threat to his control of aluminum production.[40]

By the time he was able to calculate his war profits accurately, Ford was not in his earlier state of mind. He was resentful of the delay and annoyances that had been imposed upon him. He had had ample time and many occasions to recall the generous concessions he had made to the Government. The single item cited above in connection with the Eagle Boat contract almost covered the amount of his outstanding net profits. Furthermore, company profits in 1915–1916 had run to more than $57,000,000, while for the almost two years of war they did not average $20,000,000, and only reached that figure because of the manufacture of motor vehicles for civilians. Thus Ford could perceive that he had lost heavily because of the war. How far did patriotism extend? Doubtless he was sick of the war profits controversy, but he also had a basis for satisfying himself that he had sacrificed from twenty to forty times the sum he had promised to return.

His error, of course, was in failing to make a frank public statement of his case, or, better and simpler, paying the $926,780 involved. For him the sum was relatively negligible, and would have been worth many times its face value in advertising. Not to pay, in fact, imposed a penalty, and probably indicates Ford's conviction that he had more than discharged the moral debt that he had so positively assumed.

IV

DRIVE FOR POWER

EVEN before eight o'clock the lights of the Hudson mansion on Boston Boulevard East, Detroit, were ablaze, and guests had begun to arrive for one of the important weddings of the year, that of Edsel Ford and Eleanor Lowthian Clay. At eight-thirty that evening, November 1, 1916, the ceremony would be performed, and at nine a reception would be held for the friends of the two families.

The event had been announced in the Detroit press as a union of wealth with "society," a characterization unduly simplified. The wealth of the Fords was incontestable; but Mrs. William Clay, the bride's mother, as sister of the late J. L. Hudson, founder of the city's largest department store and prominent in automobile companies, was no stranger to it either; and while her family was socially one of distinction, Eleanor Clay had made no debut, and had told reporters: "We'll live simply." The wedding, indeed, was marked by an absence "of the ostentation, show, glitter and display of wealth usually associated with the union of scions of great and wealthy families." [1]

For Edsel the evening marked the culmination of years in which increasing responsibility in the company, adventure, and courtship had been happily blended. As secretary of the Ford Motor Company for a full year, he had been learning the administrative routines of the expanding Ford empire. But in leisure hours he had been interested in finely built automobiles, golf, popular music, and dancing.[2] He had met Eleanor Clay a number of years before. As young people the two had lived within a mile of each other; during the winter of 1915–1916 they had attended dancing classes together, and Edsel had been her "devoted admirer." An understanding had been reached by March, but the engagement was announced June 15.[3] *

---

* Up to 1915 the Fords had lived on Edison Avenue, not far from the Clays. Edsel's fiancee did not remember just when she had met him—"I guess it was at some minor social affair

86

Edsel's mood in the spring of 1916 glows pleasantly in a letter he wrote his parents from Hot Springs, Virginia, early in April. He had just done eighteen holes on the golf course in 101, a score he considered good for his first try of the season, but he was happier over some days recently spent in New York with Eleanor, her sister Josephine, and Ernest Kanzler. "We had a slick time . . . with Eleanor and Josephine. We went shopping with them two afternoons. Were in Lucille's —saw some beautiful gowns. Eleanor is buying a trousseau, fancy that." They had gone to the theater every night and danced afterwards. "The funny part of it was that with all the late hours and strenuousness I feel great. Haven't had a pain or ache since I left Detroit."

In September he wrote his closest friend, Thomas C. Whitehead, then at college, urging him to be his best man. "You really must, you know. I would rather have you than anyone else and I am sure you can arrange your classes so that you can make it." Whitehead had crossed the United States with Edsel in June, 1915, in a Ford, when the three visited the Panama-Pacific Exposition by the Golden Gate.[4]

The older Fords must have had the mixed feelings many parents know at a wedding, particularly those parting with only sons. Some regret would have been natural, for Edsel had been unfailingly considerate—a diligent, sunny, reliable boy and adult. Yet on the whole it was a happy occasion. Edsel would reside at 439 Iroquois Avenue, in a fashionable neighborhood eastward from central Detroit in the direction of Grosse Pointe, and near the Detroit River. More important to Henry Ford, marriage meant not only further maturity for Edsel, with perhaps a deeper interest in the Company, but also the prospect of control by a third generation of Fords. Edsel was the Ford future.

A sense of such possibilities must have stirred Henry Ford during the ceremony. He stood beside his wife, his hands behind his back "and the wraith of a smile hovering about his lean face." Later he chatted with old friends—the Edisons from New Jersey, the Dutee Flints from Providence, the Gaston Plantiffs from New York. These and a few associates from the plant were subtly pushed into the background by the friends of the bride and groom, who gave the affair an air of spontaneous youthfulness.

Among those with whom Ford talked pleasantly were John and

long, long ago. I just remember I had my hair down my back, so . . . it was five years ago at least." (Detroit *News*, Oct. 31, 1916.)

Horace Dodge. His disagreement with them about factory expansion apparently had engendered no lasting ill will. For the lord of Highland Park this particular night was one of promise and happiness.[5]

The next afternoon brought a shock. After Edsel and his bride had departed for California and Hawaii, Ford learned that suit had been filed in the State Circuit Court by John F. and Horace Dodge against the Ford Motor Company, Henry Ford, and others. Protesting against what they termed Ford's one-man control of the company, the Dodges denounced alleged plans to acquire iron mines and a lake fleet, asked the Court for an injunction to halt the Rouge project as hazardous and wasteful, and sought an order to compel the defendants to distribute 75 per cent of the company's cash surplus, or about $39,000,000, as dividends. On the same day, at their request, the Court had issued a restraining order which forbade the use of company funds for plant expansion.[6]

2.

Henry Ford professed surprise at the suit, but this could only have been because it had been brought sooner than he had expected. Actually, he had heard on October 31 that it would be filed, and for ten months he had been aware of attitudes and events likely to precipitate a clash between him and the Dodges.

As we have seen, the plan for the Rouge development had been outlined by both Ford and Couzens in June, 1915. Later the same year Ford, in announcing his new tractor company, had implied a dislike for stockholders who gave nothing but money to an enterprise. He had been quoted by the *Dearborn Independent:*

In the new tractor plant there will be no stockholders, no directors, no absentee owners, no parasites, declared Henry Ford the other day, in a discussion of modern industrialism.

"That is, there will be no incorporation. Every man employed during the period of his employment which the aim will be to make permanent will share in the profits of the industry, but there will be no dividend to 'stock,' either at face or market value."

Implicit in such words were opinions that Ford was to express with increasing frequency and conviction, and while this particular statement did not refer to individuals, it did apply in theory to all his fellow stockholders in the Ford Motor Company. None was now active in the organization: all merely held their stock and drew dividends—a practice Ford felt to be anti-social. "I do not want stockholders in the ordinary sense of the term," he said several years later. "They do not help forward the ability to serve." [7]

The announced dream of the Rouge, the declaration that non-working owners were drones and *personae non grata,* might have alerted the Dodges to possible trouble. It did not, and the tractor project at first actually lulled them, for, as already noted, John Dodge associated the entire Rouge development with it. However, disturbing rumors soon drifted in upon the Dodges. Ford, it was whispered, was going to use the Model T motor in the tractor; he was even going to employ various company facilities in tractor work "and still own the tractor plant himself." (Actually, there was a basis for this rumor in that Ford had freely used men and materials from Highland Park for experiments with tractor models, although he had kept account of costs.) John Dodge bristled at these rumors. He was half persuaded that the entire tractor project was a violation of what he called Ford's promise not to organize a separate company unless the other stockholders were included. Early in 1916, according to him, he telephoned Ford and suggested that he come to the Dodges' office. "The object of the interview," said John Dodge, ". . . was to discuss his tractor plant." C. Harold Wills and Ford later gave somewhat different versions of how the meeting came about, but agreed with Dodge as to its general character.[8]

Wills came with Ford, and the four men spent the entire afternoon together. The tractor was easily disposed of. Ford explained that he would not use the Model T motor, or Ford Motor Company materials or facilities. The tractor firm would be wholly independent of the older corporation, and entirely owned by Ford and his family. John Dodge then gave the enterprise his blessing. "I told him . . . I had not the slightest objection of his going ahead with it."

But like a patient who has come to consult a doctor for indigestion and is told that he has appendicitis, the Dodges saw the menace of the tractor fade only to face a much greater danger. John Dodge happened to say that Couzens's leaving was "to the Company's disadvantage." Ford, he asserted, at once disagreed, and stated emphatically "that it was a very good thing for the company that he [Couzens] had left, and that now they would be able to do things that before Mr. Couzens had prevented; that his restraining influence was gone and that they were now going to expand . . . he said that they were going to double the size of the Highland Park plant and double the output of cars and sell them at half price."

The Dodges alleged that Ford, setting forth such sentiments "with the aid of Mr. Wills," went on to say that he wanted no stockholders in his tractor project, and as for the Ford Motor Company, "he said he did not propose to pay any dividends except the nominal dividend [that is, 5 per cent per month on the book capitalization of $2,000,000]; that the stockholders had already received a great deal more than they had put into the company, and that he did not propose to pay any more; he was going to put the earnings of the company back into the business so as to expand it." [9]

This statement astounded the Dodges. They had established their own plant for manufacturing the Dodge car only two and a half years earlier. Edwin G. Pipp had estimated that as early as 1913 their properties were worth from $30,000,000 to $40,000,000, and that the brothers had $12,000,000 in cash. John F. Dodge later admitted that they had expanded their plant. All this had originated from profits made in the manufacture of Ford parts and from Ford dividends. The total of these by 1915 was $5,450,000—all from an original investment of $3000 in cash and $7000 in work and materials. Of course the Dodges had been able to prosper partly because of their own ability; still, the continuation of impressive Ford dividends was important in their plans for the future.[10] *

Ford's proposal shouted catastrophe: $120,000 a year instead of $1,200,-000 might embarrass the new Dodge enterprise. John Dodge's reply to Ford showed how seriously he viewed the situation. "I told him," Dodge testified later, "that if he proposed to carry things to such an extreme as that he should buy out the other stockholders, then he could run the business as he saw fit."

Dodge had seized the one alternative that would bring money. To keep his stock and receive large dividends would be preferable, but an outright sale would bring a large sum for immediate use. According to Ford and Wills, Dodge set a price—his stock was worth $35,000,000.

---

* John F. Dodge stated this in August, 1913. Asked if the brothers would sell their Ford stock, he said No. "They are highly valuable interests. We received $1,100,000 dividends this year, and over a million the year before." (Detroit Free Press, Aug. 17, 1913.)

"I don't believe there was any figure mentioned," Dodge testified. Whether or not he named a figure, Dodge did suggest selling, and according to him Ford sharply replied that he wanted no more stock since "he had control and that was all he needed." Ford later denied mentioning control.[11]

Two points of view had been set forth, each extreme, each motivated by a selfish interest. Each had a certain validity.

The Dodge attitude was sound in so far as it protested against using the nominal capital of $2,000,000 as a basis for dividends. The real capital of the company, as already noted, was much higher—in the hundred millions. Indeed, the annual report of July 31, 1916 showed that the net profits of the company for the preceding year had been almost $60,000,000, and that its accumulated cash surplus stood at more than $52,000,000.[12] In normal circumstances, a dividend of at least $25,000,000 would have been declared.

However, on other matters the Dodge attitude was both arbitrary and illogical. By implication at least, they assumed that factory expansion should be limited and the price of the car should not be lowered. They assailed the entire Rouge project as preposterous. Yet in the past the company had prospered by vigorously expanding its plant facilities and steadily lowering the price of its car. As we shall see, there was more reason than ever to follow that policy now. But there was a further question—assuming that expansion was justified, was this a time when $25,000,000 or $30,000,000 available for dividends should be put into expansion and price reduction instead?

When Ford's position is examined, it becomes clear that powerful arguments could be advanced for expansion. It is equally evident that, once the necessity for expansion was conceded, the development of the Rouge was a logical corollary. In fact, it can be said without exaggeration that in 1915 the Ford Motor Company must either increase its output greatly, or risk rapid withering of its prosperity.

We have already seen that the industry, nourished by a variety of forces, was growing rapidly. Steady technological progress in which the skills of a thousand inventors and engineers were involved had made automobiles both cheaper and more reliable. Better roads were being built for these cars, although not yet sufficient in mileage to exert the influence they would command ten years later. Finally, Ford himself had immensely stimulated the growth of other firms while speeding that of his own.

He had been teacher to the industry. The doors of Highland Park had been open to observers, all free to study and adapt. They caught also the possibilities for continuing change which the moving assembly line symbolized. "It was so simple and logical, so easy to comprehend in its ideal operation," wrote one commentator, "that it quickly became a subject for discussion by everybody who was given a glimpse of it. . . . Once the idea had kindled the minds of men who [were] making the industry it spread like wildfire." By 1916, the year which saw the production of automobiles first pass the million mark, many firms were manufacturing moderate-priced cars, and most of these were planning to increase their output. Among them were Willys-Overland, Chevrolet, Briscoe, Buick, Maxwell, and Studebaker.

Willys promised in the summer of 1915 that by the following spring he would be turning out 1000 cars a day, little short of Ford's 1915 production of 308,213. Chevrolet, low-priced champion of General Motors, and deliberately a competitor of the Ford, manufactured only 230 cars a day, but might soon double or even quadruple its production. A list of trade names and prices for 1916 shows that at least eight well-known cars were sold for less than $1000, and as many for $1000 or a little more.* The situation was defined by Harold Wills when he testified early in 1917: "I class as a competitor of the Ford Motor Company anybody selling a car under $1000. I mean to say that people hesitate between buying a car at $360 and $1000." According to this interpretation any of more than a dozen cars might dart from the pack to challenge the Model T's supremacy.[13]

True, none had as yet done so. Giant of the low-priced field, the Ford could still offer the consumer so much that he would seldom turn to other cars, which were either higher in price or poorer in quality, or both. Yet the menace of one or more rivals was there. The mere number of cars now being turned out enabled competitors to make some headway. In 1914, with 248,307 units, the Ford Motor Company produced 42 per cent of all the automobiles made in the United States; but in 1916, its 523,929 cars were only 32 per cent of the total.

Ford professed indifference to competition: "The minutes we spend on other people's business we lose on our own." Yet he conceded when pressed that "if we can't [undersell competitors] we don't belong in

---

* Sold for less than $1000 were Chevrolet, Dort, Dodge, Overland, Saxon, Buick, Maxwell, and Studebaker; for $1000 or a little more, Velie, Jeffery, Briscoe, Oldsmobile, Reo, Hupmobile, and Paige.

the business." It may be assumed that if he was indifferent it was because he saw keenly the way to keep well ahead. He himself gave the recipe neatly: "Expand the operations, and improve the article, and make more parts ourselves, and reduce the price." [14] Thus Ford had an urgent reason for wanting to expand plant facilities instead of paying dividends. If the company's prosperity depended upon expansion, then the money should go to that essential growth rather than to the stockholders. But how rapid must expansion be?

Thus each party to the quarrel had some support for his position. With reason on both sides, the two might have reconciled their differences. But neither wanted reconciliation. Needing money by the million, the Dodges clamored for the highest possible dividends. Seeing expansion as the company's need and a cheaper car as a public service, Ford proposed, except for token payments, to ignore dividends altogether.

3.

For the time, nothing happened. In February, 1916, Ford carried out his promise to settle the debt he owed the Ford Motor Company for services and materials used in tractor development. During the spring he did nothing to alarm the Dodges. He was busy with the tractor; as to the Rouge, it was in the planning stage. But in August, 1916, Ford took two steps that thoroughly aroused John and Horace Dodge.

The first was to slash the prices of the Ford car, although these were already low. The most popular model, the touring car, was reduced from $440 to $360; the runabout, hitherto available at $390, could now be purchased for $345; the chassis dipped from $360 to $325; and the sedan from $640 to $545.

These cuts were bitter fare for the Dodges. To date the Ford Motor Company had been able to sell all the cars it could make. Simple arithmetic showed that at one sweep Ford had skimmed about $40,-000,000 of profits from company income. Why? The Dodges felt that he might as well have tossed it out the window.[15]

But hardly had they absorbed this jolt when they received a severer one. When Ford talked in January, 1916, of ending all special dividends, his remarks had after all been only talk. In the ensuing months he had neither said nor done anything further. Perhaps, the Dodges may have hoped, he had heeded John's protest. But in late August all questions of intention were answered. In an interview in the Detroit *News* he announced that no more special dividends would be declared, and that $58,000,000 of accumulated profits would be plowed back into the business. The results? A tremendous increase in factory space, a larger working force, more and cheaper cars. Work on the blast furnaces at the Rouge would soon begin. "This is Mr. Ford's policy," ran the story, "and it is understood that other stockholders cheerfully accede to the plan."

The Dodges at once sought an interview with Ford, to urge prompt distribution by the directors of "a large part of the accumulated cash surplus as dividends to the stockholders, to whom it belongs." Unable to make an appointment, they finally resorted to a letter. In this they termed Ford's attitude "entirely unwarranted." They asked permission to present their views to the directors. They made sure that their fellow-stockholders knew their position, sending copies of the letter to them.

Taking almost three weeks to reply, Ford answered that while "it would not be wise to increase the dividends at the present time," he would set the Dodges' views before the board. This promise did not satisfy them; they wrote at once, citing reports that the Ford Motor Company had "ambitious plans" for expansion, and asking for full information. "Of course," they pointed out, "it would be idle to have the Board of Directors consider the question of disbursing the cash assets of the company in dividends if, before the Board had considered our request, the same have been appropriated in the direction referred to." This sentence guessed shrewdly at what was actually happening, and the brothers prepared to take the question to the courts.

On the 4th of November they finally received a letter from Ford enclosing as the "desired information" the company minutes for October 31 and November 2. These confirmed the Dodges' worst fears. The directors had approved an expenditure of $5,150,000 for enlarging the Highland Park plant, and noted a further $4,500,000 for possible future allocation; they had purchased 27 acres directly north of the factory for $270,000, had acquired a Rouge site from Ford for $700,000, and had approved such projects as blast furnaces, a foundry, and other buildings with an estimated cost of $11,325,000. Altogether, about $23,000,000 had either been allotted or tabbed for spending.

By the time this information reached the Dodges, they had already filed suit. Some of the directors' expenditures of November 2 may have been sanctioned after this fact was known, to tie up a part of the money the Dodges were demanding as dividends. On November 8 Ford made a conciliatory gesture when he and his associates declared a special dividend of $2,000,000. This did not propitiate the Dodges, nor did later dividends up to April, 1918, totalling $5,000,000.[16]

4.

It should be clear by this time that the suit involved the management of corporations. What were the powers of the representatives of a majority of stockholders, and what rights had a dissenting minority? There was no doubt that the majority could vote to take certain actions; there was also no doubt that the minority could protest to the courts. What then?

But if the issue of power was almost savagely argued by counsel, Ford and the Dodges were courteous in their references to each other on the witness stand, and the suit did not rupture the social relationships of the three families. After the Dodge brothers died in 1920, their wives came to Henry Ford for business advice. The other minority stockholders took little part in the dispute, although in voting appropriations for expansion they had accepted Ford's immediate program. Ford went so far as to upbraid Couzens for his noncommittal attitude. "You can't be on both sides, Jim." "I'm not trying to be. I'm neutral," retorted Couzens. "You *can't* be neutral," insisted Ford. Rackham's testimony actually made it pretty clear where the entire group stood. When asked on the stand why the directors should stop paying special dividends, he replied:

We didn't intend to stop. I don't think we know now the extent of what it will cost to make these extensions [at the Rouge and Highland Park]. I was in favor of not paying any large dividends, but paying small dividends along each month or at intervals as we could safely do it, and if any mistake was going to be made, I should prefer to have a large surplus rather than a small one.[17]

The opposing lawyers kept the clash of attitudes sharp and even rancorous. For the Dodges, Elliott G. Stevenson, adroit and dynamic, led the attack; Ford's counsel was Alfred Lucking, a former congressman who had practised thirty-five years in the Detroit courts. These men had both been born in Canada, in the same year, both came early to Michigan, and both then moved from up-state communities to Detroit. Stevenson became a partner of Don M. Dickinson, postmaster-general in Grover Cleveland's second cabinet. He entered politics briefly in the eighteen nineties, but turned to banking and business operations. Lucking, like Stevenson a Democrat, served in Congress 1903–1905, and in 1912 was the party choice for senator, ardently supporting Woodrow Wilson. William C. Maybury, mayor of Detroit and a friend of the Ford family, was a member of Lucking's law firm, a fact which may have led to his becoming Ford's counsel in 1914.

Stevenson, by 1916 a giant in the profession, carried himself with the dignity of an Episcopal vestryman, but could assume a startling variety of roles. He surpassed even Lucking in mastery of the telling word, and his versatility of manner was astounding. Wearing a cherubic if inscrutable smile, he could flay a witness with cutting sarcasm, or confuse him with blunt accusations. Again, he could purr softly through a series of courteous questions, only to spring on his victim at the psychic moment with the fury of a wildcat. Few could keep their composure under the gibes, deft thrusts, and downright blows that made the pattern of his more extended cross-examinations.[18]

The suit was one in equity, and the bill of complaint as filed on November 2, 1916 and modified on April 26, 1917, listed some extreme charges in addition to those already noted. One—the allegation that the total capitalization of the Ford Motor Company exceeded the limit fixed by Michigan law—seemed unlikely to carry force. The distinction between the company's authorized capitalization ($2,000,000) and its capital assets (which as we have seen far exceeded $100,000,000) was generally accepted. Another charge, that if the company were permitted to enlarge its plant capacity and reduce the prices of its cars, it would illegally establish a "complete monopoly" in the low-priced field, was unlikely to move the court to more than a smile. Again, the contention that the Ford Motor Company had exceeded its charter powers in pro posing to smelt iron seemed questionable, although it was true that companies conducting such activities *for commercial purposes* had to be chartered under a special statute.

However, the Dodges soundly argued that while a 5 per cent monthly rate on the book capitalization of $2,000,000 might seem generous, it was in reality pitifully small, since $2,000,000 was little more than one per cent of the company's actual investment. Again, they were at least

plausible when they asserted that their stock had a minimum value of
$50,000,000 but that so long as Ford refused to pay special dividends,
it could not be sold except at a decided loss. Still, their request for a
compulsory dividend amounting to seventy-five per cent of profits was
startling, and more so since it was joined to a demand that all future
earnings "except such as may be reasonably required for emergency"
should "be similarly distributed to the stockholders." Such a limitation
would permit Ford little independence, and might even prevent him
from producing much profit for distribution.[19]

Characteristically, Ford at once took his case to the public. In an interview published in the Detroit *News* of November 4, he defended his
plans in a manner likely to brighten his image as an American folk
hero. He wanted a small profit on more cars rather than a large profit
on fewer:

I hold this because it enables a large number of people to buy and enjoy
the use of a car and because it gives a larger number of men employment at
good wages. Those are the two aims I have in life. But I would not be
counted a success . . . if I could not accomplish that and at the same time
make a fair amount of profit for myself and the men associated with me in the
business.

Every time the price of a car was reduced, the number of purchasers
was increased—"less profits on each car, but more cars, more employment of labor, and in the end we get all the total profit we ought to
make."

And let me say right here [Ford continued], that I do not believe that
we should make such an awful profit on our cars. A reasonable profit is
right, but not too much. So it has been my policy to force the price of the
car down as fast as production would permit, and give the benefits to
users and laborers, with resulting surprisingly enormous benefits to ourselves.

Ford ridiculed the charge of potential monopoly, defended the smelting of iron, and derided the Dodges for challenging a policy that had
multiplied their original $10,000 worth of stock to a value they now
claimed was $50,000,000. Moreover, he pointed out, "I can't injure them
$10 without at the same time injuring myself $58." He added: "My
present course is precisely in line with what we have been doing in the
past, and nowhere near as venturesome."[20] In another interview on

March 14 Ford was still more explicit on his struggle to hold income down: "We could easily have maintained our price for this year and cleaned up from sixty to seventy-five millions; but I don't think it would have been right to do so; so we cut our prices and are now clearing from $1,500,000 to $2,500,000 a month, which is all any firm ought to make, maybe more—unless, as I said, the money is to be used in expansion."

The first testimony was taken November 14, in closed session, on the application for a preliminary injunction. On December 18 the circuit court upheld an injunction forbidding the company to use its surplus funds for the erection of a smelting plant at the Rouge, although the writ was modified by the Supreme Court on the 22nd so that by posting a $10,000,000 bond, the company could continue work already started. Of course, its eventual usefulness depended on the final court decision. For instance, if the company built a smelter, but the decision forbade smelting, the unit could never be operated. Additional testimony was heard in open court beginning May 21, 1917.

A distinguished file of witnesses appeared: Ford, the Dodges, C. Harold Wills, William B. Mayo, Edwin G. Pipp, and others. The clashes between Ford and Stevenson, which fill more than a third of the record, supplied the highest moments of excitement. Facing the wiles, sarcasm, insults and accusations of the resourceful lawyer, Ford so handled himself as to rate at least a draw. He was on the home ground of the mechanical world which was his daily life. He defended his ideas confidently, with a shrewd sense of humor that often frustrated Stevenson. For example, the attorney questioned the feasibility of making castings direct from iron ore—Ford's plan at the Rouge:

STEVENSON: Who is doing that sort of thing now?
FORD: Nobody.
STEVENSON: You are going to experiment with the Ford Motor Company's money, to do it, are you?
FORD: We are not going to experiment at all; we are going to do it.
STEVENSON: Nobody has ever done it?
FORD: That is all the more reason why it should be done.
STEVENSON: Therefore, you are going to undertake to do something that nobody else has done, that nobody else has even tried to do?
FORD: Oh, certainly. There wouldn't be any fun in it if we didn't.

To Stevenson's charge that Ford was "it" in the company, pulling the strings that jerked "a lot of dummies," the industrialist made a simple denial. On the defensive, he was both temperate and firm; it is doubtful if Stevenson's pyrotechnic attack, assailing this quiet and rather simple Ford as a tyrant, made much headway.

Ford denied that he had ever been inconsiderate of the other stockholders; he had paid them "a lot of dividends."

STEVENSON: You have called them parasites, on occasions, haven't you?
FORD: Not Mr. Dodge, no, sir; not the Dodge brothers; I learned that word from Mr. Dodge.*

Sometimes he took the offensive in a way surprising to Stevenson. On one occasion he burst out suddenly:

"If you sit there until you are petrified, I wouldn't buy the Dodge Brothers' stock!"

"I didn't ask you to buy the Dodge Brothers' stock?" half declared, half queried the startled Stevenson.

"Nor any other stockholders' stock," continued Ford. "I don't want any more stock."

"Did I ask you anything about that?"

"No, but that is what you are talking for, and nothing else."

Ford also parried skilfully the attempt to show that his policy was Quixotic.

STEVENSON: Now, I will ask you again, do you still think that those profits were "awful profits?"
FORD: Well, I guess I do, yes.
STEVENSON: And for that reason you were not satisfied to continue to make such awful profits?
FORD: We don't seem to be able to keep the profits down.
STEVENSON: . . . Are you trying to keep them down? What is the Ford Motor Company organized for except profits, will you tell me, Mr. Ford?
FORD: Organized to do as much good as we can, everywhere, for everybody concerned.

Such answers tended to frustrate Stevenson and to please the public. On another occasion when Stevenson asked whether the Ford Motor

* Marcus T. Woodruff, publisher of the Dearborn *Independent,* in which the word was printed, testified that Ford had used it, but had not applied it to any individuals. (Dodge Suit Record, I, 519.)

Company was still making money, Ford replied that it was: "Just because we didn't have money in mind, I suppose."

What, demanded Stevenson, was the purpose of the company?

"To do as much as possible for everybody concerned," replied Ford. ". . . To make money and use it, give employment, and send out the car where the people can use it." He added: "And incidentally to make money."

STEVENSON: Incidentally make money?
FORD: Yes, sir.
STEVENSON: But your controlling feature . . . is to employ a great army of men at high wages, to reduce the selling price of your car, so that a lot of people can buy it at a cheap price, and give everybody a car that wants one.
FORD: If you give all that, the money will fall into your hands; you can't get out of it.

These clashes were germane in that they showed Ford's attitude and his justification for his policy. Stevenson made his most effective point when he got Ford to admit that special dividends were suspended *for an indefinite period.* Had Ford put a term to the suspension, his case would have been ten-fold stronger; but he would not. Presumably he wanted the right to use all profits for expansion for some time to come.[21]

Ford's testimony comprised only a part of the defendant's case. Wills, Mayo, and others demonstrated ably the need for expansion. Wills's testimony was impressive. He showed the basic character of the Ford Motor Company, which was tied to quantity manufacture. "[In] production up to a certain point there is no profit; it is beyond this point—after you reach a certain quantity per day." With its existing facilities the company had not been able to produce the number of cars it aimed at, while its truck program had been halted, since the same engine was used for both vehicles, "and it would be robbing the car production to supply the truck production." He suggested 4000 cars a day—1,000,000 a year. This would permit great economies where the company manufactured parts itself. It could save $9 or $10 on each transmission it made (about $3,000,000 for the year 1915); $153,258 on push rods, and $582,635 on a special bolt. Wills cited fires or other disturbances in parts factories which had held up the deliveries of Ford cars.

But for a million cars a year, much expansion was necessary. Highland Park could be enlarged, but not sufficiently; it could meet the requirements for acreage, but lacked adequate water and sewage facilities. The smelting of iron on the Rouge, Wills testified, was wholly practicable, and would save "a number of millions of dollars." No other automotive company could take the entire output of a furnace—another advantage of size for the Ford organization. As for shortening the manufacturing process by making cast parts for a car direct from the iron ore, this was "entirely feasible and practical and in no sense experimental." [22]

5.

The decision, rendered October 31, and filed December 5, 1917, came at a time when the nation was settling into its role in World War I as an associated power. Ford, having recently accepted a contract to produce Liberty engines, and being already enmeshed in the daring project to produce Eagle boats for the Navy, was busy with plans for installing new machines and building new factories. Edsel was sparring with the draft board. Meanwhile, on September 4, 1917, with the birth of Henry Ford II, he had become a father and Henry a grandfather.

The pronouncement of Judge George S. Hosmer of the state circuit court went far toward accepting entire the complaints of the Dodges. To be sure, it waved aside the charge that the Ford Motor Company was achieving an unlawful monopoly in the cheap car field, and it did not grant as high a percentage of dividends as the complainants asked, but otherwise it accepted their entire case. It declared the smelter project illegal on the narrow ground that it exceeded the powers expressly granted the company in its charter. Even more astonishing, the court concluded that there was no distinction between capitalization and capital assets; the company, with hundreds of millions of the latter, was therefore exceeding the new capitalization ceiling of $50,000,000 only recently set by the legislature!

Finally, as if to emphasize the seriousness of these pronouncements, it ordered the Ford Motor Company to declare within ninety days of the decree (entered December 5, 1917) a special dividend of $19,275,-

385.96. This was fifty, not seventy-five per cent, of the accumulated profits. The previous withholding of this money from the stockholders, declared the Court, was an "abuse of discretion." [23]

The Detroit papers headlined the decision with little excitement; they noted that it would be appealed, as it was on December 6. Lucking and his associates bent to the task of strengthening their case. Busily they dug up citations favorable to Ford; and both on capitalization and on the legality of a smelter they were able to offer impressive support for their contentions. They also produced an opinion by "former Judge William H. Taft" which fully sustained their position on these points.

Lucking argued strongly that expansion had always been the company's policy, and cited Wills and Mayo to prove that it was a wise policy now. The law, he pointed out, put decisions on policy in the hands of a majority of the directors, so long as there was no abuse of their power. In the present case, what was the abuse? The degree of expansion proposed? The erection of a smelter? The reserving of adequate cash for emergencies? All such measures had long been in contemplation, and had been unanimously voted "upon the full advice of the manufacturing department," and the complainants had not offered "a single word of counter evidence" to show their impracticability. He suggested that had the Dodges opened their books, as he had earlier requested, their own practices both as to expansion and cash surplus would be seen to be parallel to those of the Ford Motor Company. As for Ford's humanitarian motives, these held not the slightest significance if his acts were for the long-run benefit of the company. Dividends? Already it had been demonstrated that the company had not adopted a policy of declaring no special dividends.

In opposing Lucking's arguments, Stevenson for the most part reiterated the basic contentions that had brought him victory in the lower court. He emphasized especially the extremity of Ford's actions. Ford, he conceded, should as majority stockholder exercise a determining influence on policy, *if the policy remained reasonable*. But, argued Stevenson, it had become anything but that. Ford was tyrannically proposing to pay an absurd minimum of dividends, *for an indefinite period*, for purposes "worthy in themselves but not helpful to the Ford Motor Company." The remedy for this manifest injustice? "Reasonable" dividends, using the greater part of the surplus, before an orgy of expansion dissipated the money.[24]

The decision of the state Superior Court was prepared by Justice Russell C. Ostrander, and filed on February 7, 1919. In general, it was far broader in outlook than the opinion of the circuit court. Completely reversing the ruling made by that body on capitalization, Ostrander held that capital stock on the one hand, and capital assets or working capital on the other, were not the same.

The justice also quickly dismissed the contention, accepted by the lower court, that the smelting of iron by the Ford Motor Company was illegal. "To make castings from iron ore rather than to make them from pig iron, as defendant is now doing, eliminating one process, is not beyond the power of the corporation." He had already noted with approval that the operation would probably save nine or ten dollars per car.

As to the alleged danger of monopoly, proof of that must rest upon the case against expansion and for the distribution of dividends. On the question of court interference to compel dividend payments, there was fairly clear judicial precedent, all against it "unless fraud or a breach of trust" were involved. A breach of trust might include a manifestly wrong withholding of dividends.

Judge Ostrander reviewed the main points of the case. He observed that Ford's testimony "creates the impression . . . that he thinks the Ford Motor Company has made too much money, has had too large profits, and that although large profits might still be earned, a sharing of them with the public, by reducing the price of the output of the company, ought to be undertaken. We have no doubt that certain sentiments, philanthropic and altruistic, creditable to Mr. Ford, had large influence in determining the policy to be pursued by the Ford Motor Company." But, the jurist went on, "A business corporation is organized and carried on primarily for the profit of the stockholders. The powers of the directors are employed for that end . . . and do not extend to a change in the end itself, to the reduction of profits or to the non-distribution of profits among stockholders in order to devote them to other purposes."

However, he was not persuaded that the court should interfere "with the proposed expansion of the business of the Ford Motor Company. . . . The judges are not business experts. It is recognized that plans must often be for a long future, for expected competition, for a continuing as well as an immediately profitable venture. The experience of the Ford Motor Company is evidence of capable management of its affairs. . . . We are not satisfied that the alleged motives of the directors, in so far as they are reflected in the conduct of the business, menace the interests of shareholders."

Thus all the allegations of the Dodges had been rejected, and the fundamental tenets of Ford policy approved. However, Judge Ostrander had not finished. Expansion being accepted as a sound policy, "What does it amount to," the jurist asked, "in justification of a refusal to declare a special dividend, or dividends?" Were all the appropriations for expansion withdrawn in a lump from the company's accumulated profits, he pointed out, there would still have remained on August 1, 1916 nearly $30,000,000. Nor was this required for immediate disbursement; rather, more cash would be coming in to augment it, or partially to replace it as it was paid out. He therefore concluded that, accepting the policy affirmed by the directors as a wise one, "it was still their duty to distribute on or near the first of August, 1916, a very large sum of money to the stockholders. . . . The decree of the court below fixing and determining the specific amount to be disbursed to the stockholders is affirmed." [25] *

The Dodges had lost all along the line, but had won on the final and all-important point: the Ford Motor Company was adjudged prosperous enough to expand and pay large dividends at the same time. However, Ford had been delivered from the jeopardies of the circuit court decision, and of course he himself would get the greater part of the $19,275,385, with interest, to be distributed. Momentarily he may have felt almost cheerful. "Under the circumstances," wrote Liebold to Gaston Plantiff in reply to the latter's commiserations on the result, "I believe that the Dodge decision was all we could expect. It could have been worse." [26]

It could also have been better had Ford cooperated with Lucking.

---

* Judge Ostrander's decision may be noted in the light of remarks on directors by two modern experts. Adolf A. Berle, Jr. and Gardner C. Means, in *The Modern Corporation and Private Property* (New York, 1932), pp. 189–190, state: "The primary device permitting directors to control participations in earnings arises out of an ancient and fundamental common law right. This was the right of directors to determine the *time* when dividends should be paid; and refrain from declaring dividends when, in their judgment, the corporate purposes to be subserved by retaining earning in the business. Only one limitation has been imposed by the law on this process. Earnings must not be withheld to an unreasonable degree. But 'unreasonable' is a word admitting of very wide latitude; in practice, save under exceptional circumstances, no lawyer advises a shareholder to sue to compel declaration of dividends on the ground that they had been unreasonably withheld. Almost any sensible showing by the board of directors that they intended to expand, or foresaw difficulties, or envisaged opportunities, would defeat the action." However, the Ford case is cited as one where dividends were adjudged to have been "unreasonably withheld." (p. 261.)

Suppose he had said, for example: "Our entire policy is for the ultimate good of the stockholders. Expansion is purely a business necessity. In the long run it will be immensely profitable to the company [as, indeed, history proved it to be]. The facts that it provides new jobs and makes possible a lower-priced car for the nation is incidental. As to dividends, we have already resumed payment of special ones, and as the company's position permits, these will be larger." Such a statement would have left Ostrander, considering his attitude on other points, small ground for interference. But Ford wanted credit for serving the public, wanted to be a hero to the millions. He also had a firm instinct against paying further large sums to the stockholders. He won the plaudits he craved, but was penalized for refusing to pay "the parasites."

Before the decision was rendered, Ford had left for the West, accompanied by Clara, Edsel, Eleanor, and the infant Henry II. In the southern California town of Altadena, he brooded upon his situation. The more than $20,000,000 assessed against him rankled, but as a gate of entry for further levies. He could attempt nothing radical without risk of interference. The experimenter was under watch, the innovator suspect.

6.

While John and Horace Dodge smacked their lips over the $2,081,-213.58 which would soon be dispatched to them, Ford studied intently all possibilities for freeing himself from future threats to his independence. While his factories climbed back to a respectable peacetime output, reminding him that there would be new profits to deal with, he finally found a solution.

Perhaps he had perceived it two months earlier. On December 30, 1918 he had submitted to the directors his resignation as president of the Ford Motor Company, pleading his desire to be relieved of routine responsibilities, and "to devote my time to building up other organizations with which I am connected." The directors on December 31, "with regrets," complied with Ford's wishes, and elected Edsel to the post he had vacated. Ford retained his seat on the board of directors.[27]

The resignation startled both automotive circles and the lay public. What did it mean? For two months there was no answer; then one came as sharply as out of a sunny noon black clouds build up to a thunderclap.

The Los Angeles *Examiner* of March 5, 1919 launched the bolt.

"Henry Ford Organizing Huge New Company to Build a Better, Cheaper Car," blazed the headlines. "His idea," reported Otheman Stevens for the *Examiner* "is to make a better car than he now turns out and to market it at a lower price, somewhere between $250.00 to $350.00, and to do it through another company than the Ford Motor Company." Edsel, said Stevens, would "surely join his father in the new undertaking."

Ford explained that the recent Dodge suit decision had been responsible for his astounding plan. He explained that the court decision was causing him to violate his principle of having plenty of cash on hand; true, he received $12,000,000 of the $19,000,000 that would be paid, but he could not put this sum back into the business because he could not force his fellow stockholders to do likewise. His only recourse was "to get out, design a new car," and win anew his freedom to operate according to his judgment. "The present Ford car was designed twelve years ago," he reminded Stevens. In the new company all stock would be owned by the Ford family. The old company? "Why, I don't know exactly what will become of that; the portion of it that does not belong to me cannot be sold to me, that I know."

"I must do business on the basis I think is right; I cannot do it on another," concluded Ford. ". . . I hope eventually that [for?] some system of common partnership wherein those who work as a result of investing their money and those who work otherwise will be partners."

His words set industrialists, financiers, and editors chattering. "Mr. Ford's recent announcement has created quite a stir in this community," blandly confided Liebold in Dearborn to Plantiff in New York. "In fact, I do not believe any of the stockholders are at all pleased over it." For the Dodges, Stevenson voiced more than displeasure. Neither Henry nor Edsel Ford, he asserted fiercely, would be *permitted* to withdraw from the Ford Motor Company for the purpose Ford had announced. "Henry Ford is under contract to the Ford Motor Company and he will not be allowed to leave the firm and start a competitive business." From the attorney for two men who had withdrawn from the same company to manufacture a competing car, this utterance must have been read with amusement by those who knew the facts.[28]

Ford fed out sensation on sensation. "The present Ford Motor Company employees number about 50,000 in the actual manufacture of its

cars. Our new company will have four or five times that number."
Again, "The new company will be owned entirely within our own
family, and thus can be directed without outside interference." And
still again, "None of the old car will be used in the new manufacture.
. . . It will have a new motor and new fixtures."

If such statements excited the public, among those connected with
the Ford Motor Company, including stockholders, they produced
alarm. This was scarcely dispelled by Edsel's remark that "We expect
to make it a competitor of the street car rather than the Ford." In
Detroit, Liebold struck a grimmer note. "The Ford Motor Company
has no mortgage upon Mr. Ford's body, soul, or brains," he told reporters who referred to Stevenson's remarks. "He is a free agent." One
newsman asked if the $250 car was merely "a club with which he
[Ford] hopes to force the Ford Motor Company stockholders to cleave
closer to his personal desires?" "Mr. Ford never threatens," replied
Liebold. But wouldn't the cheap car force the Ford out of business?
"Mr. Ford is not interested in that phase of the problem," Liebold explained. He pointed out that Ford was simply in a position where he
was not master of his own company. He was therefore forming another
company where he would be master.

As showers of letters came from potential customers, panic grew
among the Ford dealers. Edsel was forced to issue a calming letter.
Rumor, he said, had distorted the facts: the wonder-vehicle would be
manufactured, but not for some time. "We know that a new car could
not possibly be designed, tested out, manufactured, and marketed in
quantity under two or three years." [29]

Meanwhile agents of Henry Ford were preparing to take advantage
of the situation. One version of what occurred credits William B. Mayo,
Ford's chief engineer, with suggesting the purchase of all minority Ford
Motor Company stock. R. T. Walker, his assistant in 1919, states that
Mayo investigated this possibility, and one of his sons, Dana, agrees.
This is also the positive statement of Stuart W. Webb of the Old
Colony Trust at Boston. Another possibility is suggested by Ford's
own statements later. As early as July, 1919, he put the full responsi-
bility for the attempted acquisition of minority stock upon Edsel. Asked
by Stevenson in the Chicago *Tribune* suit if he himself had not begun
to negotiate "under cover" shortly after the Dodge verdict, he replied:
"Not me, Mr. Stevenson. . . . My son. My son, and Mr. Lucking." His

assertion tallies with a press release issued on July 11, 1919, by the Mt. Clemens News Bureau (a Ford unit) which ran in part:

All credit for the successful efforts to centralize the control of the company in the hands of Mr. Ford and his son is given to the young president. He it was who persuaded his father that this was a better method of carrying out their established policies than creating and organizing a new corporation.

What seems probable is that the undertaking, launched by Mayo, was quickly championed by Edsel, and won Henry Ford's approval. A glance at Mayo's earlier life is desirable at this point. Reared on Cape Cod, as a youth he had acquired training as an outdoor sign painter, and in the process gained some familiarity with mechanical drawing and blueprints. Eventually he became a salesman for the Hoover-Owens-Rentschler Company of Hamilton, Ohio, and rose rapidly in this firm, absorbing a variety of engineering knowledge. As we have seen, by 1914 he stood high in his company, and dealt with Ford in constructing the Highland Park power plant. One of Mayo's tasks at Hamilton was to train the three sons of Rentschler in business after their graduation from Princeton. One of these young men was Gordon Rentschler, who left his father's firm to become a banker, and in 1919 was an officer of the National City Bank in New York.[30]

Thus through his professional work Mayo had one powerful banking relationship. He had quite as important a connection through marriage, for his brother-in-law, Fred Holmes, was vice-president of the Everett Trust Company of Everett, Massachusetts, a bank affiliated with the Old Colony Trust of Boston, of which he was also vice president. It was with his New England connections that Mayo, according to Walker, began negotiations, confining them at first to oral and highly confidential discussions of the proposed purchase.

The situation was favorable. Actually there had been considerable interest during recent years in the stock of the Ford Motor Company. Ford himself had been approached in 1916 with a suggestion for recapitalization on a basis of $500,000,000. The Dodges, Anderson, Couzens, the Gray heirs had all conferred or corresponded in 1916 or 1917 with prospective purchasers. In April, 1919, the Dodges had granted an option to E. L. Berger, an investment broker, at $12,500 a share. Thus a show of further interest could astonish nobody.

Stuart W. Webb, a vice president of the Old Colony, took charge of the campaign for Ford. Arrangements were completed secretly in Detroit, in early April, 1919, for Webb to obtain options on the 8300 shares of stock which represented the full 41½ per cent not held by Henry Ford. Unless all the shares were obtainable, none would be purchased. The Old Colony apparently managed the entire project itself, with Webb, Fred Holmes, and Albert and Roland Boyden all engaging in the work. However, Webb apparently conducted all of the really crucial negotiations. Complete secrecy enveloped Ford's part in it. There were rumors that Durant or General Motors were back of the activity.[31]

Webb began by offering as little as $7500, but finally raised his bid to $11,000—a good price considering the uncertainty that had now been created as to the company's future. But he made no headway whatever. The shareholders were not unreceptive, but none would sell without knowing the value that the Government would put upon the stock as of March 1, 1913, the date of incidence for the Federal income tax. This value would be used by the Commissioner of Internal Revenue in determining the profit made on sales of stock in 1919.*

Undaunted, Webb engaged Arthur A. Ballantine, a Boston attorney who had served as advisory council to the Treasury Department (1917) and as solicitor of internal revenue (1918), to discuss the valuation of shares with Treasury officials, including Daniel C. Roper, Commissioner of Internal Revenue, and persuade them to make a ruling. The Bureau of Internal Revenue checked the Ford Motor Company's books, and its expert, P. S. Talbert, set a figure. Roper wrote Ballantine that although the Bureau did not usually give such information, in the circumstances it would. "It [the Bureau] is disposed to regard $9489.34 [Talbert's estimate] as a fair valuation of the stock on March 1, 1913." [32]

One by one options were now obtained. It was necessary to buy Berger's option on the Dodge stock for $675,000. The $12,500 figure set by this option became the eventual price paid all the stockholders except Couzens, who received $13,000. All the options, except those of Couzens and his sister, were made out to Stuart W. Webb of the Old Colony Trust Company, but most of the stockholders now knew that Webb

---

* When Webb made an offer to Rackham, the latter said: "I won't even make a note of the price, I must know definitely the amount I am to receive net to me." (Additional Tax Case, *Transcript of Hearings*, 762–763. Horace H. Rackham, Jan. 17, 1927.) Despite the care taken by the minority stockholders to get an official valuation, the government eventually sued them, claiming a higher figure. Couzens, e.g., was alleged to owe $9,000,000 in taxes. The additional tax case, as it was called, was won by the former stockholders, and Couzens was shown to have overpaid $989,883. (*National Cyclopaedia of American Biography*, XXX, p. 32, Couzens article.)

was acting for Ford. Couzens for himself and his sister (Mrs. Rosetta Hauss) signed a personal option to Edsel. When all the options were lined up, Holmes and his associates waited on Henry Ford, William B. Mayo breaking the news. Ford was exuberantly happy, and "danced a jig all around the room." [33]

The total cost of the transaction to Ford can be clearly shown:

Holder	No. of Shares	Purchase Price
Dodge Brothers	2000	$ 25,000,000
John W. Anderson	1000	12,500,000
Gray Heirs	2100	26,250,000
H. H. Rackham	1000	12,500,000
James Couzens	2180	29,308,857.90
Rosetta Hauss	20	262,036.67
Total	8300	$105,820,894.57 [34]

This transaction would make the total value of all shares, with Ford's, about $255,000,000, which most stockholders regarded as considerably less than their actual worth. Why then did they sell?

It may be asked in reply, "What was the alternative?" David Gray made the fundamental answer when he remarked that the company was "practically a one man management" and he "did not know what the man would plan." The Dodges had always been willing to sell, and could not complain when they received the full value of the option they had given. Rackham and Anderson both agreed because of regard for Henry Ford, Anderson considering also the interests of the other stockholders. He later told of sitting alone at night, asking himself, "John Anderson, are you going to be an ingrate or are you going to be a man?" Couzens struck a similar note in making over his option to Edsel: "In executing this option I recognize that it is desired by said Ford for special reasons particularly for the purpose of obtaining for himself and his father through personal ownership and stock controlled as nearly complete ownership of said company as may be possible." Nevertheless, the realization that Ford might if defied really go through with his plans to make a new car, or execute some other incalculable maneuver, probably influenced all sellers. They must have sighed with relief when the news of the complete transaction was proclaimed in the newspapers on July 11, 1919.

Meanwhile, on July 10 the directors declared the dividend of $19,275,-385.96 ordered by the court, together with $1,536,749.89 interest.[35]

7.

Thousands of men in America had been the sole owners of businesses; hundreds like Ford himself had owned majority blocks of stock in titanic enterprises. But never had one man controlled completely an organization of the size of the Ford Motor Company. John D. Rockefeller never held more than two-sevenths of the Standard Oil Company certificates, and J. P. Morgan, who presided over the birth of the United States Steel Corporation, owned a much smaller percentage of its shares. Ford wielded industrial power such as no man had ever possessed before.

And what a consummation it represented! What a rise had been his from the status of half-despised tinkerer who in the fall of 1902 could count only two victories on the automobile race track, and the hope of a car still to be designed! Eight months later he had put nothing into the toddling Ford Motor Company but that completed yet still imperfect vehicle, and his intense conviction of what it could become. Now he owned a complex of factories worth approximately half a billion dollars.*

The financing of the purchase was a complex transaction. In order to buy, Ford procured a credit of $75,000,000. (He never used the full amount. See Chapter VI.) The loan was made by a financial syndicate composed of the Chase Securities Corporation (New York), the Old

---

* In Great Britain, a manufacturing business which in some respects paralleled Ford's had been more slowly and modestly built up by William R. Morris (the future Lord Nuffield), who announced his first car, the Morris-Oxford, in 1912. "The success of Ford in this country [Britain]," write Lord Nuffield's biographers, "was a challenge to British manufacturers." Within a few years after the First World War the Morris Motors Ltd., with a plant at Cowley near Oxford, was an important corporation with a worldwide business, while Morris also controlled a credit company (Morris Commercial), a carburetor company, and Wolseley Motors. But he never wished to wield the absolute power which Henry Ford had achieved. Preferred stock of Morris Motors Ltd. was widely held. "Morris's management had never been a one-man affair," state his biographers. What he called "the organization," included department heads, met frequently with him to discuss policy questions. Its leading members also met regularly to debate day-to-day problems of management, such as the coördination of supplies and the output for the next period. Above the "organization" was a board of directors, which also met regularly and which had a real influence in all the affairs of Morris Motors Ltd. (P. W. S. Andrews and Elizabeth Brunner, *The Life of Lord Nuffield*, Oxford, 1955, 181–184). William Morris learned much from Ford, with whom he had cordial relations; in company management Ford might have learned much from him—as from numerous American corporations.

Colony Trust Company (Boston), and Bond and Goodwin (Boston).[36] * At the same time that the loan was arranged, a corporate reorganization of the Ford interests was undertaken, with two main objectives: an escape from the Michigan limit on capitalization, and a merger of all Ford activities into one immense but compact unit.

The first step was the incorporation on July 9, 1919, of the Eastern Holding Company. This unit began its life with 1000 shares of $100 stock, a total capital of $100,000. However, on July 14, changing its name to the Ford Motor Company, it expanded its shares to 1,000,000 and its capitalization to $100,000,000. On February 16, 1920 the name was changed to the Ford Motor Company of Delaware and on June 5 back again to the Ford Motor Company.

On April 19, 1920, Klingensmith notified the Chase corporation and its associates that on May 1 the Ford Motor Company of Michigan would transfer all its assets, valued at $300,000,000, to the Ford Motor Company of Delaware. This corporation would then assume responsibility for the completion of loan payments. The process was completed in June, 1920, when notices of the dissolution as Michigan corporations of the Ford Motor Company and Henry Ford & Son were filed with the Secretary of State of Michigan.[37]

Meanwhile all Ford enterprises had been integrated with the Ford Motor Company of Delaware, and stock in this corporation had been issued to replace all stock in former concerns. These were Henry Ford

---

* An account by Merrill F. Cross, attached to the Accounting Department of the Ford Motor Company at that time, gives a glimpse of the physical activities connected with a large transaction like the making of the loan to the company. Cross assisted Klingensmith, starting after hours and working then and Saturday afternoon, to check and sign the notes that were being issued against the loan. Klingensmith used a multiple check-writing machine, which signed five or six checks simultaneously. Then on Saturday they summoned Edsel from a golf game (for his signature was required) and he came in on Sunday and completed his part of the work. Cross was then given the notes in a small grip—$60,000,000 worth—and instructed to buy $2000 worth of Federal revenue stamps in New York when the train brought him there. By noon the notes were ready to deliver, and Cross and Al Todd started down town in a car. "Going down, they had about four cars following us and two cars ahead of us. . . . We were going down through the toughest neighborhood in New York."

Arriving at his destination, says Cross, "I got out, grabbed my bag and went into the bank. I knew the man's name, I've forgotten now, the vice president I was supposed to see. I walked in there and I told him I was from the Ford Motor Company in Detroit with some securities.

"He said, 'Where are they?'

"I said: 'Right between my feet.'

"I put the bag right down there. He pressed a buzzer and I looked around and there were about fifteen guys running for me. They rushed me right down into the directors' room. There were about a dozen other men came down and checked the notes, found them okay, and I got a receipt for them and bid them good-bye and went back to the hotel and went to bed." (Merrill F. Cross, *Reminiscences.*)

& Son, the Dearborn Publishing Company, the Hamilton and Rossville Hydraulic Company, and the Dearborn Realty and Construction Company. Total stock issued against them comprised 5413 shares, with an overall value of $541,300. By a series of transfers shares were distributed to Henry, Edsel, and Clara Ford, giving them respectively 95,321 shares, 71,911 shares, and 5413 shares. The percentages were, Henry 55.212; Edsel, 41.652, and Clara, 3.136.[38]

Thus Ford activities became one massive unit, entirely owned by the Ford family. There could now be no challenge to company policy. The payment for the minority stock seemed to be merely a matter of routine, for in July, 1919, the demand for motor cars of all types was raging, and even in June, 1920, the outlook was good. Ford held in firm hands the tools to implement his many ideas of industrial and social change. He was no longer merely a dreamer; he could act with massive power. He meant to do so. In the new Ford Motor Company he would be complete master.

But men like James Couzens and John Dodge must have wondered about the Ford future. With no restraint upon him whatever, would Ford with his unorthodox plans for expansion, manufacturing, and marketing be able to steer a successful course through the still uncharted shoals, reefs, and narrows of the automotive world? And what would be the effect of his augmented power on Ford the man? Certainly the Dodges, with their suit for dividends, had started a chain of cause and effect that had worked to a startlingly different ending from what they had envisaged, transforming beyond expectation ownership, corporate structure, and the roles of individuals.

V

FORAYS IN POLITICS

ON Monday, July 10, 1916, with the battles of Verdun and the Somme rising to their height in Europe, and the presidential campaign opening at home, Woodrow Wilson paid a visit to Detroit. Dense crowds cheered him as he drove through the streets to address a salesmanship congress, before which he defined his Mexican policy, defended the Federal Reserve Act, and discussed the democracy of business. But he met his most enthusiastic welcome when he paid a brief visit to the Ford plant in Highland Park. Tens of thousands of workmen, dismissed from their machines, jammed Woodward Avenue and John R. Street, raising a shout at sight of their President. A huge banner strung along the side of the main Highland Park building proclaimed, "He Kept Us Out of War," and before Wilson left the city Ford gave him a personal message of confidence in his main policies.[1]

All spring Ford had commanded the public's attention as a pacifist leader. "It is better to spend money for peace than for preparedness" —this was the thesis he kept hammering home in printed statements. After Wilson had demanded that Congress strengthen his hand by measures to arm the country, many pacifists had turned toward Ford as a symbol of their hopes. Popular petitions put him on the presidential-preference ballot of the Republican Party in Michigan. He dismissed the movement as a joke, but early in April, in a light vote, he actually defeated another preposterous nominee, Senator William Alden Smith, 83,000 to 78,000. Two weeks later, despite his emphatic public statements that he was not a presidential candidate, he came close to winning over Senator Albert B. Cummins in the Nebraska preferential primary. Many German-Americans fearful of war had voted for him. When the St. Louis *Times* in May conducted a poll on candidates for the presidency, Ford topped it; and in the Ohio preferential primaries, some 5000 voters wrote his name on their ballots.[2]

Nearly every day Ford's name was in the news. Now he was announcing that he planned New York headquarters for his peace work; now he was publishing anti-preparedness advertisements; now he was ostentatiously *not* meeting Theodore Roosevelt in Detroit. In May the Navy League brought suit against him for alleged libel. Hudson Maxim bitterly rebutted his charge that Maxim's book, *Defenseless America,* and a film he helped sponsor, *Battle Cry of Peace,* were intended to produce munitions contracts. Meanwhile, Jenkin Lloyd Jones compared him to Socrates and Christ, and Eugene Chapin, twice candidate for president on the Prohibition Party ticket, announced that he would work to put Ford in the White House. His championship of peace pleased a considerable number of newspapers, farm journals, and church organs, and even the intellectual New York *Nation.*[3]

Henry Ford's reputation and that of the Ford Motor Company were almost as indissoluble as Chang and Eng, the Siamese twins. Every Model T, every article on the engineering achievements at Highland Park, every discussion of Ford labor policy, helped lay a foundation for the industrialist's fame. Three elaborate company exhibits at the San Francisco Exposition—the automobile assembly in the Transportation Building, the sociological exhibit in the Main Building, and the lectures, motion pictures, and pamphlets in the Education Building—contributed to the founder's renown. That year more than a hundred thousand visitors went through the Highland Park plant.[4] Circulars, press advertisements, and agency displays helped make the Ford name familiar, and fortified the democratic impression conveyed by Ford jokes. The company distributed a cinema film called the Ford Educational Weekly which was seen regularly by millions. So much did Henry Ford personify the company that no history of it can neglect the public adventures into which his restless energy drew him.

These adventures, 1916–1926, seem a hodge-podge. However, a certain unity was given them by two basic principles: Ford's stubborn devotion to peace, and his attachment to agrarian ideals in politics and society. Not one of them could be called the central focus of his attention: that was always in the automotive industry. Like his hobbies and recreations, his farms, schools, mines, and steamships, they were subordinate to or divergent from his chief activity. Hence, in part, the casual, unplanned, erratic nature of some of these adventures; hence, also, the indulgent attitude of the public.

2.

Both as a pacifist and an admirer of the President, Ford naturally supported Wilson in 1916. Though his father had been a Republican and he had cast his first vote for Blaine, he approved Wilson's desire to keep America neutral in a war-harried world. When the campaign opened he made an explicit statement for the President which delighted Democrats. Late in the summer Wilson invited Ford to Shadow Lawn, where the two had a long talk.[5]

All this encouraged Democratic leaders to apply to Ford for a large campaign gift. Early in October Secretary Josephus Daniels and Vance McCormick, head of the Democratic National Committee, met Ford and Thomas A. Edison for lunch in a private room of a New York hotel. The first course ended, Daniels watched in fascination as Edison challenged Ford to a kicking match, and the inventor shattered one chandelier as the manufacturer grazed another.

Then McCormick and Daniels eloquently sketched the financial straits of the party in the Eastern States. They almost fainted, writes Daniels, when Ford responded: "All this campaign spending is bunk. I wouldn't give a dollar to any campaign committee."

He showed himself more amenable to persuasion, however, when Daniels described the urgent need for newspaper publicity. Over the coffee, Ford yielded sufficiently to remark: "I sincerely hope that Wilson will be elected, and in my own way I will see that the reasons why he ought to be elected are presented in the papers of large circulation in the pivotal States." On October 7 the press announced that Ford and Vance McCormick were working together on Democratic publicity. Ford insisted that the actual placing of the advertisements be kept in his hands, and Liebold applied characteristic system to the undertaking. Tabulating the state election returns for the past twenty years, he analyzed the party trends and selected the doubtful areas where votes might be won. "I immediately came to the conclusion that the decision was going to be in California," he states. "I felt therefore that we ought to concentrate on California." [6]

Before the end of October a series of signed Ford advertisements for Wilson, published in five hundred newspapers, began to appear, some filling a full page. They were largely concentrated in New York, New Jersey, Illinois, Indiana, California, and other closely-fought states; Michigan got due attention, though it was regarded as strongly Republican. Altogether, Ford spent $58,800 for the cause, receiving an effusive letter of thanks from Wilson's secretary, Tumulty. Perhaps as helpful to Wilson as the advertisements was an enthusiastic interview which he gave the New York *World,* aimed at workers and farmers and widely reprinted.

"About politics as a business I know nothing at all," said Ford, "but about Woodrow Wilson I know a lot. I spent four hours with him the other day and found him the most human man, the most sensible man, the most businesslike man withal, I ever encountered." As an advocate of shorter work days and higher pay, Ford endorsed Wilson's acceptance of the Adamson eight-hour law for the railroads and his declaration that labor is not a commodity but a form of cooperation. "The keeping of Americans alive, out of war, and alive properly, with comfortable working hours and decent wages, is Woodrow Wilson's passion." Ford proposed for the workmen of the country a slogan, "Out of the shops in eight hours." On November 11, when Wilson, carrying California by less than 4000 votes, was safely reëlected, Ford telegraphed congratulations.[7] It is barely possible that his advertisements had shaped the decision of 2000 Californians, and had thus kept the President in the White House.

Political feeling, high even during the war, became bitter as the end approached. The Republicans in 1918 were determined to wrest control of Congress from the Democrats. Party leaders on both sides looked about for the strongest candidates. To Wilson, bent on achieving American leadership in a league of nations, the Senate was of paramount importance in peace-making. Every seat would count. Although Michigan was traditionally Republican, one Wilson man could very possibly be elected there—Henry Ford. Naturally the President and his friends turned to Ford.

A number of Michigan men eagerly coveted the senatorship. The Republican aspirants included two former governors, Chase Osborn and Fred M. Warner, a former Secretary of the Navy, Truman H. Newberry, and James M. Couzens; the principal Democratic aspirant was James W. Helme, the state Food and Dairy commissioner. By March, Newberry was taking the lead among the Republicans. Meanwhile,

talk of Ford as a bi-partisan nominee increased. He was still nominally a Republican, but Wilson was concerned only to get men who
would sustain his principles in peace-making; he had endorsed Knute
Nelson of Minnesota, a liberal Republican, for reëlection. It soon became clear that Administration leaders were anxious to use Ford to
defeat such anti-Wilson men as Osborn and Newberry. Word went out
to a Democratic conference at Lansing, which on June 12 endorsed
him "although he is not in our fold." Next day, by urgent invitation,
Ford arrived in Washington for a talk with Wilson.

Josephus Daniels had been trying to overcome Ford's reluctance to
run. "Bring him over to the White House," Wilson told Daniels, "and
I'll see what I can do." When Ford came, the President gave him a
hearty handshake.

"Mr. Ford," he said, "we are living in very difficult times—times
when men must sacrifice themselves for their country. I would give anything on earth if I could lay down this job that I am trying to do, but I
must carry on. . . . You are the only man in Michigan who can be
elected and help to bring about the peace you so much desire. I wish
you therefore to overcome your personal feelings and interests and make
the race." [8]

Ford had gone to Washington reluctant but open to suasion, for the
office tempted him. Next day the newspapers announced his consent,
with a statement that he wished to do everything possible to assist the
President. Although these words identified him as an Administration
candidate, he was still nominally a non-partisan independent, and was
entered in both primaries. Most Democratic newspapers were enthusiastic. Bryan and Barney Baruch congratulated both him and Michigan
on his decision. The Republican and independent press, however, was
tartly critical. The *New York Times* remarked that for all his ami-
ability, he lacked the type of mind to grasp national or international
problems; his election "would create a vacancy both in the Senate and
in the automobile business, and from the latter Mr. Ford cannot be
spared." The Senate, grumbled the Grand Rapids *Herald,* made laws,
not lizzies; and the *Detroit Saturday Night,* while conceding that he
would carry an immediate election, declared that he had not known
what the war was about until it began.[9]

Could Ford win both party primaries? He would certainly sweep
the Democratic field; but the Republican entrenchments were harder

to storm. Party regulars closed their ranks behind Newberry, though some resolute Bull Moose veterans clung to Chase Osborn.

And Newberry would be hard to defeat, for all the forces of conservatism, all the groups made resentful by war pressures, all the haters of Wilson, gathered under his banner. He was essentially an estimable, canny, parochial-minded businessman. The son of a successful attorney, a Yale graduate, a protégé of Russell A. Alger of match trust and Spanish War fame, he had been associated with Henry B. Joy and others in buying the Packard Motor Company (1902) and bringing it to Detroit. Theodore Roosevelt had made him Assistant Secretary and then, briefly, Secretary of the Navy. In the war with Germany he had become a lieutenant-commander with a desk job as aide to a shore admiral. Once the primary contest began he returned to Michigan, and spared no effort to win. He made speeches, mobilized the party press, and saw to it that money was spent lavishly. In fact, his campaign committee spent $176,568, chiefly on advertising and publicity.[10] Ford meanwhile made no speeches, gave out no statements beyond a declaration for woman suffrage, and spent not one copper.

The war had set people's tempers on edge, and the primary campaign soon became bitter. If the gentlemanly Newberry wished to keep it on a high plane, his lieutenants grabbed every weapon within reach. They sent an emissary to New York to gather ammunition against Ford, ferreted out disaffected employees, and featured attacks by conservative businessmen on the five-dollar day. They charged that the three Detroit newspapers which supported Ford did so because they were afraid Ford would help Hearst establish a rival journal if they opposed him. The *Detroit Saturday Night* gave currency to this wild idea. Above all, the opposition press harped on Edsel Ford's draft deferment.[11]

Henry was more successful, sneered one newspaper, in keeping his boy out of the trenches than in getting other boys out by Christmas. Why not send the indispensable Edsel to the Senate? asked another. One editor acidly recalled that on the day Quentin Roosevelt was slain in an air battle, Edsel and his wife were entertaining friends at a fashionable club. Political advertisements for Newberry emphasized his long support of preparedness measures, and his son's ready enlistment. Answering these gibes, Ford gave out the statement already quoted, taking full responsibility for retaining Edsel at Highland Park. His remark that if Edsel went he would be found "fighting, and not sticking his spurs into a mahogany desk in Washington," was a sharp thrust at Newberry.[12]

With the regular Republican organization fully mobilized for New-berry, Ford could not have won in that party even had he made a spirited battle. At the close of August, Newberry carried the primaries by a vote of 114,963 against Ford's 71,800 and Chase Osborn's 47,100. On the Democratic side, however, Ford defeated Helme 30,791 to 8414.[13] Michigan being strongly Republican, Ford was left at a great disad-vantage in the final race. His handicap was presently increased by the President's appeal for a Democratic Congress, which hardened party lines. Nevertheless, his popularity among workers and farmers gave him a good fighting chance.

To aid Wilson in writing a constructive peace (for one more vote in the Senate would have been invaluable) Ford should have exerted every ounce of strength. Instead, he remained inert. The National Security League, Theodore Roosevelt, Elihu Root, and even ex-President Taft appealed for his defeat. The Newberry forces continued to use money extravagantly. But Ford again announced that he would not conduct an active campaign. A non-partisan Ford-for-Senator Club in Detroit told the voters just before election that, holding public office too sacred to be scrambled after with money, and feeling too much respect for the law to violate its spirit, he "refuses to spend a cent." This club reported receipts of $1866, of which only $140 came from Ford employees. When the Democratic committee, with the approval of E. G. Liebold, ap-pealed to the 268 Ford agencies in the state to lend their aid, only 63 of them (probably all Democratic anyway) responded favorably. Ford himself offered not the slightest hint that his workers or dealers should stand behind him. To have done so, of course, would have been very bad politics.

As the party battle rose to a climax, Ford's friend Harvey Firestone sent a competent attorney, Bernard M. Robinson, into Michigan to help knit the Democratic forces together and put some fight into them. With Alfred Lucking, attorney for the Ford Company, Robinson toured a good part of the State. At least one of his crisp reports on the situation was forwarded by Firestone to Ford. Democratic speakers and editors, meanwhile, denounced Newberry for his excessive pri-mary expenditures, and in mid-September Senator Atlee Pomerene of Ohio gained national attention by a resolution for a Senate investigation. With a dark scandal gathering around Newberry's name, Democratic advertisements pressed strongly the charge of corruption. But the Republican campaign was better organized, more energetic and alert, and more unscrupulous. The progressive and standpat wings of the party had partially healed their recent breach, and fought in close harmony. Wealthy business interests which feared a return to the advanced program of Wilson's first administration supplied ample means. Now that the end of the war was coming into sight, Theodore Roosevelt, Henry Cabot Lodge, William E. Borah, and others violently indicted the President and called for the election of a Congress able to defeat his program. Republican leaders appealed to all the deep irritations over wartime burdens, all the resentments of the German, Irish, and other stocks, and all the desires for change after six Democratic years.[14]

On election day, Newberry won by a narrow margin. On the face of the returns, Michigan gave him 220,054 votes against 212,487 for Ford. The heavy Detroit vote for Ford, who carried Wayne County by more than 35,000, had been expected, but his strong showing in the upper peninsula was surprising. Considering the traditional Republican sympathies of Michigan, and the general reaction against Wilsonian policies, he had done well. His secretary intimated that if any special evidence of irregularities appeared he would ask for a recount. "We feel confident that if the people of the State had known Mr. Ford personally as do the people of Wayne County, he would have been elected by a tremendous majority."

Whatever might be done about a recount, an investigation into primary expenditures was inevitable. Many in the disappointed Republican faction led by Chase Osborn called for it; while Henry Ford, convinced that Wall Street and war profiteers had played a large role in his defeat, and bitterly hurt by the attacks on Edsel, was determined to force action. Obviously the Newberry forces had violated both the Federal law limiting expenditures in a primary campaign to $10,000, and the Michigan law fixing a limit of $3750 exclusive of advertising. Officers of the Ford-for-Senator Club at once asked Senator Pomerene to renew his drive for an inquiry, and submitted open letters by Osborn, ex-Governor Dickinson, and other disgruntled Republicans, with additional evidence. As soon as Newberry's election was certified on December 4, 1918, an acrid Senate debate began. Ashurst of Arizona, denouncing the large Republican disbursements in both Colorado and Michigan, and asking just who had contributed Newberry's $176,000, defied the Chamber to seat men who knocked at its door with such stained and dishonorable credentials. Ford not only petitioned the Senate to look into the primary expenditures, but asked it to recount the November ballots, and took steps to contest the election.[15]

When the Sixty-ninth Congress assembled in special session the following May for its consideration of the League, the Republicans held 49 seats in the Senate, the Democrats 47. Had Ford been elected, the division would have been 48 to 48, and with Vice-President Marshall's deciding vote, the Democrats could have organized the Senate and its committees. In the Republican-dominated chamber, Henry Cabot Lodge became head of the Foreign Relations Committee, and Wilson's Gethsemane began. Action on Ford's petition and Pomerene's resolution was slow, so that the Senate did not vote the investigation until December, 1919. Meanwhile the Federal Department of Justice had empanelled a special grand jury in Michigan, which after hearing some very plain evidence, indicted Newberry and 134 other men connected with his primary exertions. The main counts against the Senator were that he had conspired to violate the Federal Corrupt Practises law, and broken the Federal statute against bribery; while his co-defendants were charged also with converting part of the campaign funds to their own uses.[16]

Behind this action by the Federal grand jury lay much inspired labor on the part of Robinson, the Firestone attorney. Convinced that Newberry's victories had been bought, he eagerly responded to Alfred Lucking's appeal for aid. Ford, his fighting spirit aroused, authorized the two men to spend up to $40,000. He felt certain that Wall Street "interests" were responsible for his defeat. "If they would spend $176,000 to win a single Senate seat," he blazed, "we may be certain they would spend $176,000,000 to get control of the country." When Robinson began work, the Administration was apathetic, the public indifferent, and Newberry loud in deriding his assailants.

"I took rumors," later wrote the attorney, "and within eight weeks, personally directing, twenty-four hours of every day, a Statewide investigation in the camp of the enemy, with forty men in the field, ran these rumors into a case." It was Robinson who drafted a report explaining in just what ways and at what places Newberry and his associates had been guilty of felonious conspiracy against sections of the Federal code. It was he who insisted on the appointment of a special assistant to the Attorney-General, the employment of Federal investigators, and the calling of a grand jury. He induced the Department of Justice to accept his view that Newberry could and should be driven from his seat. Finally, he suggested a personal friend, Frank C. Dailey, to undertake the prosecution.[17]

The trial of Newberry early in 1920 naturally aroused nation-wide attention. Henry Ford and his supporters rejoiced when on March 20 the Senator was found guilty of the main charge, conspiracy to violate the Federal Corrupt Practises Act, and sentenced to two years' imprisonment, with a fine of $10,000. (All the minor charges had been dropped.) Sixteen co-defendants were convicted on the same count, and sentenced to varying penalties. At this time no substantial action had yet been taken by the Senate. The constitutionality of the Federal law, as Newberry pointed out to the country, had never been reviewed by an appellate court, and he immediately took his case to the Supreme Court. Arguments were heard early in 1921. On May 2 the court ruled five to four that Congress had exceeded its powers in trying to regulate primary contests, for its authority to control elections did not extend to nominations. Newberry's conviction was therefore reversed. He had contended all along that he was not even morally guilty—that the Federal and State limits on spending applied to him individually, but not to his campaign organization.

By the time of the Supreme Court's decision, Ford's effort to upset the Newberry victory by a recount of the ballots had also broken down—as most recounts do. A considerable staff had gone to work in 1920 combing the county returns and sending their findings to Ford's agents in Washington. Certain Republican county clerks were obstructive, demanding outrageous sums for their extra labor. In precinct after precinct gross carelessness was exposed, and in some places gross fraud as well. Ford ballots in one ward of Benton, for example, had been altered to Newberry ballots. As his gains mounted, Ford had hopes that he might win after all—hopes and fears, for his friends say that he wished to win, but did not really wish to leave Detroit and occupy a senate seat. The final count, however, stood Newberry 217,-

088 against Ford 212,751. Ford had to get what consolation he could from the fact that a change of fewer than 2200 votes would have elected him.[18]

3.

The senatorial campaign, like other events which made Ford a controversial public figure, stimulated his desire to own a personal journal. The mixed reception given the five-dollar day, the ridicule showered upon the peace ship, and the denunciation of his pacifism by the Chicago *Tribune* and other militant sheets, had caused him even before the United States entered the war to think of creating his own editorial organ. In 1916 he made a confidant of Edwin G. Pipp, editor of Detroit's best paper, the *News*. Pipp, an able journalist of progressive political and social views, became an informal press counsellor, and was often favored with an exclusive story dealing with Ford or the company. The two confidentially discussed two projects, the purchase of a weaker paper, the *Journal,* or the founding of a new daily. Neither came to anything, and when the country went to war, Ford announced that he would have to devote his whole energies to war work. Pipp, himself, after a disagreement with the publisher of the *News,* resigned and entered a Washington office for the duration of the conflict.

But immediately after the armistice, smarting under his defeat at the polls, Ford decided to revive the project. He believed that a great part of the press was bent on misinterpreting his opinions and activities, and that it was owned body and soul by bankers. "When they tell it to bark, it barks. The capitalistic newspapers began a campaign against me. They misquoted me, distorted what I said, made up lies about me." He thought he had something important to say. "I have definite ideas and ideals that I believe are practical for the good of all, and intend giving them to the public without having them garbled, distorted, or misquoted." A keen young salesman whom he and Pipp had used to collect information on publishing costs, Fred L. Black, was again called in, and asked to find an available secondhand printing press or newspaper plant. He discovered a large press which had been used to print *The American Boy,* and took an option on it.

Before the end of November, 1918, Ford had bought not only this equipment, but the *Dearborn Independent,* a little country weekly which, leading a precarious existence since the beginning of the century, had achieved a subscription list of about 1200. Ford liked the name; he meant to be independent, and he felt that the fame of Dearborn was intertwined with that of his industrial enterprises. One Saturday afternoon he, Pipp, and young Black looked over quarters in the new tractor building. Ford delighted Pipp by saying he meant to make the weekly the greatest organ for national and international liberalism in the world, and both startled and delighted Black by exclaiming:

"Say, we've got to have somebody run the business end of this thing. How would you like to come out and work on it?"

Black, assenting, became chief assistant to E. G. Liebold, who was appointed General Manager.

Pipp, Black, Liebold, and Ford in his spare hours labored strenuously getting ready to start early in the new year. They incorporated the Dearborn Publishing Company, with Henry Ford as president, Clara vice-president, and Edsel secretary-treasurer. They obtained a stock of paper, in those postwar days a difficult matter. They collected an editorial, business, and operating staff. Initially, all costs were paid by Henry Ford's personal checks. Pipp had an understanding that he would enjoy complete editorial control, with one exception: Liebold was to have the responsibility for "Mr. Ford's Own Page," a weekly feature on which Ford would collaborate with a forty-year-old journalist of Canadian birth whom Pipp had brought from the *News*, William J. Cameron.

Cameron was to play a notable role in publicizing both Ford and the Company. Largely self-educated but extremely well-read, with a brilliant mind, this Scot possessed an evangelical temperament which enabled him to infuse editorials, sermons, radio talks, and brief essays with an inspirational quality. On the *News* he had written an editorial, "Don't Die on Third"—an exhortation to get to home base on any undertaking—which was frequently quoted and reprinted. Pipp, who correctly thought him one of the best newspaper writers in America, said that he would "be lost without Billy Cameron." With something of the directness of Arthur Brisbane and the studied grace of Alexander Woollcott, Cameron commanded a religious eloquence quite his own. He then belonged to one of the most curious sects on earth, the British Israelites, who believed themselves descendants of the Lost Tribes, and based an esoteric interpretation of history and eternity on data derived from the Great Pyramid. In mundane matters, however, he had a practical idealism. During his service on the *News,* he had for years done social work among derelicts—all the more effective because he himself knew the power of drink—and had delivered weekly homilies at a religious center on Randolph Street, then Detroit's "skid row" or section for outcasts.

Highly characteristic of Ford was his treatment of the mechanical aspects of his project. The press he had bought was in poor condition, its base cracked and other parts missing. But he thought its purchase a good risk, telling Black: "If we can't make it run, we can put it in the cupola [of the blast furnace at the Rouge] and make tractors of it." He selected the position for it in the tractor plant. When the work of erecting it was nearly finished, mechanics suddenly began disassembling it! Ford had come in, looked it over, and ordered that the wheels and other parts be polished. The explanation he gave Pipp revealed his deeply ingrained love of machinery. "It's an old press, but a good one," he said. "If you polish up the edges of those cog-wheels you can tell whether any of them are cracked or not. Besides, you can't expect men to keep a piece of machinery neat and clean unless you start it that way." Repolished, refurbished, and reassembled under Ford's eye, it ran as if charmed. Never in its old days, vowed its former operator, had it done such good work; and it was used for years without ever breaking down.[19]

On January 11, 1919, the first issue of the *Independent,* sixteen large pages on calendared paper, appeared; five cents a copy, a dollar a year. Ford and Pipp had agreed that it would champion the gospel of social harmony, and the Wilsonian ideals of post-war reconstruction at home and abroad. Its subtitle, "The Ford International Weekly," indicated that its range would be wide. Cameron wrote a large part of the first issue. Besides two signed articles, the editorial page bore unmistakable marks of his rhetoric. Throughout, the trumpet of "social justice" pealed resonantly, but as used by Cameron the term had a wooly vagueness. "Into the new time with all its prophetic forces," declared the leading editorial, "the Dearborn *Independent* comes to put its shoulder to the car of social justice and human progress." It was not a medium for publicizing the Ford enterprises. "The paper owes its establishment to Henry Ford's desire to serve the new freedom of the future." The new freedom, of course, was Woodrow Wilson's phrase.

Some articles in the first issue, fortunately, made a more solid contribution to internationalism and reform. Postmaster-General A. S. Burleson advocated government ownership of telegraphs and telephones, while Josephus Daniels, in a full-page interview, called for an adequate navy but an end to competitive naval programs. An unsigned article, "Obeying the Dictates of Humanity," threw down Ford's gage in the League battle, declaring that however Congress might stand the people of America were behind Wilson. A cartoon showed Wilson bidding a ruffian-like "International Reactionary" enter his School of Democracy. The first "Page" signed by Ford held a potpourri of notions: the omnipresence of opportunity, the superiority of production to pelf ("I would rather hear that a man made a million plows than that he made a million dollars"), the evils of absentee ownership, and the wisdom of Wilson's world plans. "I can talk with plain Americans in a way that we can understand each other," Ford hopefully remarked. Subsequent articles enlarged upon progressive and pacifist themes. Various essays argued for better housing, conservation, progressive education, and the rehabilitation of disabled soldiers. Of course Ford trenchantly advocated prohibition and women's rights.

If all this was on the general side of sweetness and light, it was also a bit dull. The *Dearborn Independent,* with its anti-profiteer, anti-monopoly, anti-reactionary articles, had the flavor of a muckraking periodical ten years after muckraking went out of fashion—without the basic research which had given the first muckracking point and bite. Pipp, for all his capacity, failed to impart to the hodgepodge any central purpose. In price, the *Independent* was a bargain. But its format was as unsuccessful as its editorial policy. In aspect it was a weak, hybrid adaptation of the *Saturday Evening Post, Collier's,* and *Harper's Weekly.* Its numerous illustrations tended to be muddy; its layout was crowded; in the table of contents gleamed no shining literary names—no Kipling or Wells, no Edith Wharton or Dreiser. One weakness was an excessive stress on foreign topics, ranging from the development of Singapore to the lot of German farm women.

"Mr. Ford's Own Page," staring from every issue, reflected the ferment of several minds, but chiefly those of Ford and Cameron. Ford would stroll into Cameron's office, and, while the editor took notes, fire off in his "telegraphic style" a broadside of opinions. This material, hammered into shape by Cameron, with assistance sometimes from Black and Liebold, reached the printed page as Ford's own. As yet, Ford and Cameron had not developed complete intellectual sympathy, but the seeds of this rapport were being planted. The encounters gave Cameron a deep insight into Ford's unpredictable mind, so that he could deduce from a few laconic words a whole range of anterior thinking. For the most part, the "Page" verged toward the Ralph Waldo Trine-Dr. Frank Crane pabulum of the time. Frequently it was studded with cliches and third-hand anecdotes; sometimes, however, Ford struck off sparks of shrewd wisdom or an idea of striking originality, for he did think, and often along unconventional lines.[20] His idealism, if erratic, was very real.

Ford was prepared to lose money on the weekly, and did. From the first he denied the paper the most important of all sources of revenue, paid advertising. This, he felt, might compromise its position as "an organ of unbiassed opinion." While a year's subscription was sold at a dollar, the cost of filling it ran well above five. Promotional charges were also high; when the *Independent* conducted a circulation campaign early in 1919, the cost of each subscription averaged about forty-eight cents. Newsstand sales were weak, dealers understandably showing scant enthusiasm for a colorless publication which sold for a nickel and thus yielded little profit. An astute member of the early staff, John W. Smith, later the mayor of Detroit, began at one point to perform miracles for the weekly. By obtaining 3000 subscribers at only twenty cents' cost each, he demonstrated that a more astute type of promotion could pay. But he became disgusted by backbiting within the organization, and left. At the end of 1919 the *Independent* had a net circulation of just under 72,000, and during its first year it lost $284,000.[21]

Unlike Bryan with his *Commoner* and La Follette with his weekly, Ford commanded no marching army of political followers to snatch eagerly at his publication. Neither did he have an effective gospel with which to attract readers. Like countless other magazines, his began to fail because it did not have anything much to say. Although the Ford purse was too deep to feel the drain, Liebold and Black were worried and sent out representatives to make a survey of newsstands. They discovered that the *Independent* was so lacking in popular appeal that it was practically unknown in many areas. Sales on stands in New York City amounted to fewer than one-tenth of the copies sent to dealers.

Agents who visited 175 cities and towns in 11 states to talk with wholesale and retail sellers sent back uniformly discouraging reports. It was evident that both the editorial and business management would have to be overhauled.

The best thing that could be said for the *Independent* in its first two two years, 1919–20, was that it fought a sturdy battle for the Wilson Administration and the League. Ford in his page even compared the League covenant with the Decalogue. Editorial after editorial praised Wilson's high purposes and denounced both his European and American antagonists. On both continents, declared one editorial, "he has had the masses with him, always believing, always trusting." Ford had to admit some months later, when the President was being reviled by some noisy sections of the European population, that this was not strictly true. By December, 1919, the weekly was lamenting that the Republican plan to make the League the political football of the coming presidential campaign had succeeded, and that much of the German, Italian, and Irish vote would be anti-League. But the initial defeat of the peace treaty was accepted as only temporary, and Ford by editorial, cartoon and article continued to rebuke and reproach its opponents.[22]

4.

It was during the *Dearborn Independent's* first year that the Chicago *Tribune* suit inflicted upon Ford perhaps the cruellest mortification of his career. It grew out of an editorial that even in the history of the *Tribune* stands forth as peculiarly silly and obnoxious.

In June, 1916, Wilson had called the National Guard for duty along the inflamed Mexican border. Soon after they were mustered, the *Tribune,* in a burst of hyper-patriotic fervor, began questioning some large employers to learn whether they would continue paying workers thus mobilized. When the paper instructed a correspondent in Detroit to interview Ford or his spokesman, the reporter telephoned Klingensmith, who, apparently without consulting Ford or any other officer, replied that Ford employees answering the President's call would forfeit their positions, and receive no company aid. Actually, this was inaccurate. The company gave each of the eighty-nine Ford employees who went to the border a numbered badge stamped "M.N.G.," entitling him to his job upon completing military duty. Some returning workers, as events proved, were given better places than they had held before. The Sociological Department took care of needy families of absent soldiers.

Without pretending to make any real inquiry, the *Tribune* on June 22 published the correspondent's story under a headline, "Flivver Patriotism," and next day ran an editorial, "Ford is an Anarchist," which made the kind suggestion that Ford should expiate his "ignominy" by moving his factories to Mexico. One of its many offensive sentences declared: "If Ford allows this rule of his shop to stand, he will reveal himself not merely as an ignorant idealist, but as an anarchistic enemy of the nation which protects him in his wealth." Ford might well have ignored this characteristic pasquinade of Colonel McCormick, but Alfred Lucking thought it intolerable, and urged the manufacturer to protest against the indignity.

"Well," replied Ford, all too casually, "you'd better start suit against them for libel." When a demand was sent to McCormick for a retraction, he replied with a patronizing insult. "You are reported as saying that militarism may have to be fought by militarism," he wrote. "Possibly no difference exists between our views. If so, I shall be glad to congratulate the nation on the repentance of one whose former opposition to preparedness may cost it heavily in lives unnecessarily sacrificed." This naturally added fuel to Ford's slow anger.[23]

Ford filed suit for a million dollars against the *Tribune* (September 7, 1916) in the Federal district court of northeastern Illinois, and in the spring of 1917 presented the case before Judge Kenesaw Mountain Landis in Chicago. Then, deciding that an impartial trial was impossible in the area served by the *Tribune,* his attorneys took steps to transfer the suit to the Michigan circuit court in Wayne County, doing this by making three newspaper distributors of Detroit codefendants. The *Tribune* lawyers, protesting that this was grossly unfair, asked for a change of venue on the ground that articles in the Detroit press had been generally hostile to them; and eventually the case was transferred to the circuit court in Macomb County.[24] Two and a half years had been spent in preliminary wrangling, and the attention of the whole country had been excited.

Early in May, 1919, the county seat, Mt. Clemens, a little town twenty-two miles by rail northeast of Detroit, previously known only for medicinal springs beneficial to rheumatic patients, throbbed with a new importance. Carpenters swarmed into the red brick courthouse on the public square and began remodelling the cramped, bare little white-walled courtroom to accommodate more lawyers and stenographers than it had ever seen. Space was reserved outside the rail for nearly fifty newspaper correspondents, representing leading journals and all the larger news agencies. The Western Union and Postal Telegraph installed batteries of telegraph instruments to maintain touch with leading cities of the Union by direct wire. The hotels were crammed not with invalids, but with correspondents, photographers, expert advisers to the principals, and thrill-hunters. Yet even as Mt. Clemens became a cynosure of national curiosity, it retained its small town ways. A sign outside the courtroom admonished visitors: "If you spit on the floor in your own house, do it here. We want you to feel at home."

Like armed bands establishing rival fortresses, the *Tribune* and Ford forces entrenched themselves in hotels and business buildings. The newspaper's crew of well-dressed lawyers and raffish journalists, captained by the tall, martial figure of Colonel McCormick, took possession of a suite of twenty rooms at the Park Hotel, with two tons of munitions in the shape of books and papers. The largest room in this stronghold, noted a reporter for the Detroit *Free Press,* resembled "the library of someone who had gotten hysterical over war writings." Ford's legal and personal staff took over the Colonial and Medea Hotels, meanwhile moving decks, books, and records into a neighboring office building. During most of the trial the Medea, with direct telegraph connection to the Ford plant, was the business center of the Ford Motor Company. Here Liebold and other executives bustled about officiously.[25]

The panoply of weapons and ammunition in both camps was a necessity under the broad terms of reference which the case presented. Lucking and other Ford counsel had made at the outset a cardinal error. If they had sued merely on the ground that the terms "anarchist" and "anarchistic" were libelous, under the common law they would have had an ironclad case, for the courts had already decided that these words could be penalized. They could probably have held the judge to a strict limitation of evidence. The trial might have been ended in two or three days. But they had cited the whole editorial, thus throwing the gates wide open for the admission of evidence to prove that Ford was an "ignorant idealist" and an unpatriotic man.

It was with good reason that Ford established his own news bureau in Mt. Clemens, officered by a *Dearborn Independent* group headed by Pipp, and a few journalists recruited from metropolitan newspapers, notably Joseph J. O'Neill of the New York *World*. This bureau looked like a staff headquarters behind a battlefront. On its wall hung a map of the United States, bristling with colored pins; the blue pins representing towns and cities whose newspapers were favorable to Ford, the red pins centers of unfriendly papers. Typewriters quickly began to clatter over news handouts and the material for boilerplate releases to small newspapers which lacked a news agency service. The same reasoning that underlay the purchase of the *Dearborn Independent* had created the news bureau: Ford feared that the press would misrepresent his cause. He was going to need all the assistance the bureau could give him.[26]

As special trains ran into the station, automobiles clogged the streets, and crowds seethed about the courthouse, the trial began on the afternoon of Monday, May 12, 1919. Judge James G. Tucker, a shaggy-browed, middle-aged jurist of mild temper and oldfashioned rural mien, presided. A dozen attorneys, more distinguished than any gathered into a Michigan courtroom since Theodore Roosevelt had marched into the Upper Peninsula to vindicate himself against a charge of habitual drunkenness, sat elbow to elbow at two great tables crowding the space in front of the bench.

On Ford's panel of six, former Congressman Lucking shared the leadership with ex-Judge Alfred Murphy, fresh from a distinguished career on the Detroit bench. A man of eloquent tongue, Murphy possessed a voice which he could make throbbingly tragic even in requesting a glass of water, and a courtroom presence like that of a sensitive gentleman pleading in harrowed distress for a condemned friend. Having come into the case on Ford's insistence, he was to miss few opportunities of tossing garlands of purple rhetoric about Ford's neck. Underneath his oratory lay real ability. Among the nine Chicago *Tribune* lawyers were a brilliant young Chicagoan, Weymouth Kirkland, and Elliott G. Stevenson of Detroit, who had shown his mettle as a foe of Lucking in the Dodge suit. His caustic courtroom encounters with Henry Ford three years earlier had caught the attention of the *Tribune* and been recalled when the paper was seeking for counsel. The two sets of attorneys glowered at each other, and at times barely avoided personal collision.

To expedite the trial, both sides agreed to a struck jury (names being struck out of the jury list until twelve remained), which was completed on the third day: ten working farmers of the county, one retired farmer, and one roadbuilder. Questioned at length about military preparedness and anarchism, they made it evident that they would bring shrewd, homely common sense to the issues. One of them, admitting to the ownership of a Ford car, added: "That would not prejudice me against Mr. Ford." Judge Tucker announced that in deference to the home duties of the farmers, he would hold court only four and a half hours daily and omit Saturday sessions. He also made it plain at an early stage that, wide as was the door which the unwary Ford attorneys had opened to the introduction of general evidence, he would hold it still wider. He had the unhappy idea that all issues appurtenant to the case, rather than just those directly pertinent to it, ought to be threshed out.[27]

In extenuation of Tucker's failure to keep the trial concentrated within a narrow area, it should be said that the very nature of a libel suit gave the *Tribune* wide room for diversions. Anglo-American libel cases traditionally admit a free range of testimony bearing upon personal views and character, and often put the plaintiff no less than the defendant upon trial. That is a fact which many public figures, from Fenimore Cooper and Oscar Wilde to Harold J. Laski and Alger Hiss, have learned too late.

The judge's attitude precisely suited the predetermined strategy of the *Tribune* attorneys. Pleading justification, absence of malicious intent, and legitimate comment, Kirkland in his opening argument dragged in appeals to patriotism, Americanism, and national vigilance. Lucking at once took exception and asked the court for a ruling on the limits of the case. If the testimony could be held close to the offensive language in the editorial, and particularly to the word "anarchist," the newspaper would be stripped of its major defenses. Argument on this subject dragged through five days of legal wrangling while the jurors, temporarily excused, worked happily on their farms. The torrent of words overwhelmed Tucker. "I have been talked almost to death," he complained.[28] Then, as the long procession of witnesses,

120 in all, began their march through the courtroom, he took the problem under advisement. At last, on June 26, he handed down his formal
decision: anything which indicated that Ford's views or actions had
justified the *Tribune's* criticism was material to the case.

Lucking indignantly protested. Could such testimony be admitted
even though it bore no relation to the direct charges made in the editorial? he demanded. Tucker cooly replied: "I don't think that makes
any difference. I think anything [that] indicates Mr. Ford's anarchistic
tendencies is material. I don't care where it comes from . . . and on
the proposition I feel that anything that was said, or anything that was
done, or any overt act or opinion expressed, that was done for the purpose of hindering or delaying or preventing the Government from
making such preparation as it saw fit to make, whether much or little
or adequate or inadequate, is material." [29] These words meant that
Ford, not Colonel McCormick, was arraigned. They meant that the
Tribune lawyers could seek to establish their contention that Ford's
pacifism, his anti-preparedness utterances, were the heart of the case,
and could haul in anything even remotely related to that thesis.

The *Tribune* attorneys at once took the offensive. Even on the
narrow issue of anarchism, Stevenson intended to put Ford into the
culprit's box. It was ideas like Ford's which had actuated Vallandig-
ham and the Civil War copperheads, he proclaimed, which had inspired the Haymarket bombing, and which had tended to every sub-
version of law and order. Ford, "by his insidious, vicious propaganda,"
had nerved the arm which hurled a bomb into the preparedness day
parade in San Francisco in 1916. Henry Ford was no mere philosophical
anarchist; he was the most descructive type, "as dangerous as the kind
who throw bombs." The *Tribune* lawyers even struck at Edsel's exemption from military duty. In the initial exchange of blows Kirkland
launched into a eulogy of McCormick's valor, recounting how the
over-age publisher went to France and saw a full half-year of fighting.
As he spoke, Kirkland glared significantly at the chair Edsel had just
quitted, and grimaced at Lucking. This cheap gesture showed that no
blows would be spared Ford. Simultaneously, the *Tribune* was asserting editorially that the Mt. Clemens battle was no mere private dispute;
it was a contest of principle, which involved issues of the greatest moment to the country. Should pacifism and internationalism triumph
over patriotism?

Whether the *Tribune* libelled Mr. Ford or not is a legal issue in which the American public would show little interest. But whether Mr. Ford expresses the philosophy of the American people in this generation, whether his views or those of the *Tribune,* his public conduct or the *Tribune's* throughout the critical events of the last few years, are to indicate the policy of the American people, is and must be momentous.[30]

Powerless in the face of Judge Tucker's ruling to hold the case to the original issues, the Ford attorneys tried to deal counterblows along peripheral lines. They charged, for example, that the *Tribune* had favored intervention in Mexico because a near relative of McCormick had held stock in the Standard Oil, which obtained crude oil from Mexico. "Greed for money," cried Murphy, actuated the editor. This was preposterous. The attorneys showed more astuteness when they brought Edsel to the stand to give a lucid account of the creditable work the Ford Motor Company had done on government contracts during the war. They were also wise enough to put Dean Marquis of the Sociological Department before the jury to prove that the Company had held open the jobs of national guardsmen called to the Rio Grande.

When Henry A. Wise Wood took the stand as a *Tribune* witness, reporters sharpened their pencils, for as one of the noisiest big-army and big-navy nationalists of the time, he seemed certain to furnish a sensation. Ford, he said, was "a rotten American." He related how, in a two-hour interview in 1916, Ford had told him that if a hostile army landed on Cape Ann (as Wood said it might), the farmers would immobilize it; how Ford had spoken of national flags as tribal emblems— "Wood, when this war is over, these flags are coming down"—for, like H. G. Wells and others, Ford dreamed of a world flag; and how Ford had declared that wars were made by great financial interests. As a crowning insult to loyal Americans, testified the witness, Ford had said: "Patriotism is the last refuge of a scoundrel." Wood had not recognized the familiar quotation from Dr. Johnson! The promised sensation hardly materialized.[31]

But the central focus of interest in the trial was Ford's appearance as a witness. Called to the stand for cross-examination on July 14, he was subjected to eight days of merciless inquisition by Elliott G. Stevenson. Setting verbal traps, and playing upon the manufacturer's ignorance in general fields of knowledge, Stevenson essayed to prove that he was totally unqualified to serve as a guide in politico-social fields. Ford, so self-confident, alert, and expert in his own plant, soon became a reluctant, discomfited, and shamefaced witness. His very honesty played into Stevenson's hands, for where anybody with a little more of the serpent's guile would have been shrewdly evasive, he was naively frank. Nervous and flustered, he realized that he was caught in a trap. As Stevenson probed deeper, Ford made an unhappy spectacle. He sat slightly slumped forward, cupping his chin in hand, his body turning from side to side, his feet twisting nervously. In the Dodge suit he had talked fluently and interestingly about familiar technical and corporate subjects. But at Mt. Clemens, led into a bog of cultural knowledge and dictionary definitions, he floundered helplessly.

Not that his showing was wholly discreditable. Here was a man of slender common school education, too busy to have read much, too engrossed in engineering and business to explore other fields, inarticulate and timid in public appearances, who did not quail before a highly trained attorney. He wore an air of amiable patience suggesting the country-store philosopher; he never lost his temper; if an ignoramus outside his chosen field, he was an ignoramus of sense and integrity. His courage made him rash. Sometimes, after his counsel made an objection, he plunged into an answer before the judge could rule. Occasionally he motioned Lucking to silence as he proceeded. Once when Lucking protested against Stevenson's return to a damaging admission, Ford interjected: "If I said it, it's in the record." Such a man was easy to "expose," but the exposure revealed lack of learning, not lack of character.[32]

As the *Tribune* editorial had charged that Ford was "an ignorant idealist," and as in his ghosted statements and articles he had assumed a knowledge of history and politics, Stevenson demanded an opportunity to prove ignorance. Ford had spoken as an educator of America; now, said Stevenson bluntly, I shall inquire "whether you were a well-informed man, competent to educate the people." At this point Ford's attorneys should have interposed to say that they did not deem the phrase "ignorant idealist" libelous, and that Ford, as he himself presently admitted, was "ignorant about most things." They should have made more of the argument they shortly advanced, the relativity of knowledge; no man, fortunately, knows a thousandth part of the facts in the *Britannica*. But the wide terms of their original charge estopped them from pressing this point. Moreover, Judge Tucker, himself floundering, supported Stevenson's line of attack, saying crudely that the defense had a right "to get all of the man's trend of thought, his educational condition and the whole business." When a man, said Tucker, "is charged with being an ignorant idealist, musn't he submit to an inquiry as to all things that would go to make an ignorant idealist?" This ruling, as we have said, made the trial one on the "charges" against Ford, not the *Tribune*.

Ford scored telling points for himself in asserting that he had opposed not preparedness but over-preparedness, and that he was for adequate armaments if the League failed. He refused to retreat from his conviction that war is murder. While he might have justified that term as applied to the general institution, however, he got into trouble when Stevenson made him deal with Grant, Sheridan, and Pershing. Led into definitions, he was soon answering like a truant schoolboy. A mobile army was "a large army, mobilized;" the Monroe Doctrine was "a big-brother act;" treason was "anything against the government;" an idealist was "a person that can help to make other people prosperous." His idea of anarchy was that of most untutored Americans in those anti-Bolshevist days: "Overthrowing the government and throwing bombs." [33]

Sorriest of all, however, was Ford's exhibition when confronted with what to him was the virgin expanse of American history. Too late, his attorneys attempted a frenzied coaching. At the end of the day's trial, Lucking would conduct an hour of patient instruction. Ford, his arms folded, his face resigned, submitted like a victim led to the rack:

Lucking [wrote E. G. Pipp later] would begin with, "Now don't forget this; remember the evacuation of Florida . . ."
But Ford would be out of his seat, looking out of the window.
"Say, that airplane is flying pretty low, isn't it?" he would ask.
Again Lucking would steer him to the chair, but Ford would hop to the window with: "Look at that bird there; pretty little fellow, isn't it? Somebody around here must be feeding it, or it wouldn't come back so often." [34]

On cross examination, Ford could not say when the United States was created. Asked what the United States was originally, he gave an answer as sensible as the question: "Land, I guess." But in reply to a query on the Revolution, he ventured the date 1812 before hitting on 1776. Apparently, he confused the word revolution with wars against Great Britain; he thought the War of 1812 was "about aggression," and when Stevenson told him that no revolution took place in that year, he said, "I didn't know that." Stevenson asked him about a statement reported by Charles N. Wheeler of the Chicago *Tribune* in an interview of May 25, 1916: "History is more or less bunk. It's tradition." Ford replied: "I did not say it was bunk. It was bunk to me . . . but I did not need it very bad." This was sensible enough. He of course had his own values in history, and in fact within the year would plan to serve them by a technological and industrial museum. He might have quoted Napoleon's famous remark that history is a lie agreed upon, or Carlyle's dictum that history is a distillation of rumor. But then followed one of the memorable exchanges of the trial, blazoned far and wide by the press:

STEVENSON: Did you ever hear of Benedict Arnold?
FORD: I have heard the name.
STEVENSON: Who was he?
FORD: I have forgotten just who he is. He is a writer, I think.

Smirks and chuckles among the *Tribune* lawyers greeted this response. Lucking, his fists clenched, hissed: "Outrageous, cruel, a shame to subject that man to such an examination." The explanations later made for Ford—that he was tired after hours of grilling, that he was fussing with his shoelace and inattentive, that the associative name of Arnold Bennett or Matthew Arnold popped into his head—do not excuse him. He had failed a question which a grade-school pupil would blush to flunk. The most plausible of these explanations states that he was thinking of Horace L. Arnold, long a familiar figure at Highland Park while helping write *Ford Methods and the Ford Shops,* the standard text on the Company's engineering practice. After court adjourned Ford remarked, "I thought Stevenson wanted to know about the Arnold who used to write for us;" and his use of the present tense in his testimony, "He *is* a writer," lends color to this theory.[35]

With Ford's departure from the stand, the trial settled back into its humdrum routine. More witnesses droned away the summer hours. Tired reporters coined a phrase: "Out of Mt. Clemens by Christmas." Not until nearly mid-August, the fourteenth week, did the attorneys sum up. Alfred Murphy's address, liberally plummed with biblical quotations for the benefit of churchgoing jurors, portrayed Ford as a champion of social justice whose pacifist teachings followed the message of Christ; and his rhetorical peroration brought a gust of applause from supporters of Ford in the audience. Stevenson pounded away at his major motif: "Does anybody have to argue to you about the ignorance of Henry Ford in this case? . . . . They forced us to open the mind of Henry Ford and expose it to you." Charging the jury, Judge Tucker declared that preparedness had not been an issue in the case, a statement that excited wonderment why he had let so huge a segment of the testimony be devoted to it.[36]

The case went to the jury August 14, and was decided that night. The twelve hard-headed farmers, after ten hours of deliberation, found the *Tribune* guilty of libel and fined it six cents. Lawyers for each side hastened to toss hats in air and proclaim victory and vindication.

Actually, Ford, the *Tribune,* and American jurisprudence had all lost the case, for all emerged heavily injured in public esteem. Although the *Tribune* trumpeted its confidence that it had been exonerated "in the forum of public opinion," it had really been convicted of reckless and spiteful utterance, and the huge sums it had to pay in fighting the suit offered a needed lesson in decorum and reasonableness. "The *Tribune* was silly," said the Nebraska *State Journal.* Estimates of the cost to the newspaper ran well over half a million dollars. Judge Tucker, after being given the opportunity of his lifetime, bowed a diminished head. Newspapers and lawyers agreed that the suit had been made needlessly protracted and extravagant by his rulings. Had he held the issue somewhere close to the question whether the epithet "anarchist" was libelous, the trial might have been ended in a quarter the time.

As for Henry Ford, editorial comment upon him was withering. "The State of Michigan was spared a great humiliation when it failed to elect Ford to the United States Senate," said the Portland *Oregonian.* The *New York Times* observed that the manufacturer, subjected to a severe examination of his intellectual qualities, "has not received a pass degree." Typical of Mid-Western press comment was the statement of the Sioux City (Ia.) *Journal* that the revelation of Ford's deficiencies was startling. "He is disclosed as a man with a vision distorted and limited by his lack of information. The public has been disillusioned, and if Mr. Ford has not been, he has failed to learn one of the most valuable lessons of the trial." Perhaps the feeling of judicious men was best summed up by the *Nation,* which sadly reported that the veil of glamour which had gathered about the miracle-working industrialist had in great part been torn away:

Now the mystery is finally dispelled. Henry Ford is a Yankee mechanic, pure and simple; quite uneducated, with a mind unable to 'bite' into any proposition outside of his automobile and tractor business, but with naturally good instincts and some sagacity. . . . He has achieved wealth but not greatness; he cannot rise above the defects of education, at least as to public matters.

So the unveiling of Mr. Ford has much of the pitiful about it, if not of the tragic. We would rather have had the curtain drawn, the popular ideal unshattered.[37]

Yet many plain folk retained their old illusions. As the *Tribune* suit progressed, Ford received hundreds of letters, mostly from people in humble walks, which attested the hold he possessed on the popular imagination. That image of Ford the benefactor, creator of cheap transport and author of the five-dollar day, persisted undimmed in the minds of working people harried by wartime inflation. A New Jersey housewife praised him as the only rich man she knew of willing to give the poor a decent chance. A correspondent in Havre de Grace, Maryland, happily believed that the world could be made over if they only had more "real constructors" like Henry Ford. A Brooklyn woman praised him for helping thousands of men and women enjoy the ordinary comforts of life. While many of the encouraging letters were penned by cranks who pictured the industrialist as a St. George lifting his spear against such dragons as "Wall Street," "the money power," and "the subsidized press," others came from true idealists, humanitarians, and pacifists. Plain Americans of the kind who had not been disturbed by Andrew Jackson's bad grammar, Lincoln's backwoods stories, and McKinley's tobacco chewing were not worried by Ford's haziness about the War of 1812. Hosts of them, studying the *Ford Manual* before they climbed into the loose-jointed Model T, were still ready to make him a folk hero.

Ford, now nearing sixty, was little inclined to ask himself the question he often put to others who had undergone a scathing experience: "What did it teach you?" Unquestionably the rough buffets he took in

THE CHICAGO TRIBUNE

July 30 1941

Dear Mr. Ford

    It occurs to me on this, our
birthday, to write you and say I regret
the editorial we published about you
so many years ago. I only wonder why
the idea never occured to me before.

    It was the product of the war
psychology which is bringing out so many
similar expressions today.

    I am not planning to publish
this myself, but you are perfectly welcome
to use it in any way you wish.

                    Yours sincerely,

                    Robert R. McCormick

Mr. Henry Ford
Dearborn
Michigan

m

these years—the Dodge suit verdict, the ridicule of the Peace Ship, the misrepresentation of the five-dollar day, the cheating and name-calling in the Newberry campaign, the slaying of the League, the *Tribune* trial—blunted the edge of the fine idealism so marked in him just before the World War. Other men were changing too. The nation, as Wilson's towering vision crashed into dust and Harding, Coolidge, and Mellon opened an era of selfish materialism, grew cynical; and Ford had some excuse for sharing its mood. His experience on the witness stand left him with something more than a conviction that Lucking had badly failed him, that lawyers were to be distrusted, and that courtroom appearances must be avoided; it gave him a sense that the world was a more brutal, malign place than he had supposed and that self-protection was its first law. Thus the trial, which did not break the closed system of his thought or persuade him to seek a broader cultivation, tinged his mind with wariness, bitterness, and cynicism. This change took place just as his intellectual isolation was accentuated by his industrial eminence and great wealth. It strengthened the arbitrary and arrogant elements in his nature which would have been nourished in any event by his dictatorial power in the Company.

The scars which the *Tribune* suit left upon Henry Ford were thus a public misfortune. It was a greater public misfortune that his quest in these years for an occupation outside his company which would satisfy his altruistic impulses did not open some modestly suitable field and give him some really helpful associates. He was thrown back upon himself.

His opponents had their own wounds to lick, but in time resentment died away. In 1941, when the two men saw more nearly eye to eye on the international situation, Colonel McCormick sent Ford a letter. "It occurs to me, on this our birthday," he wrote (both were born July 30), "to write you and say I regret the editorial we published about you so many years ago. I only wonder why the idea never occurred to me before." [38]

VI

POSTWAR CRISIS

WHEN Edwin G. Pipp, editor-in-prospect of the *Dearborn Independent,* conferred with Ford at the Dearborn tractor plant on armistice day, 1918, about the forthcoming periodical, he noticed tanks on the floor of the factory. By noon, after news of the armistice had been received, "they were out of sight and large machines were being hauled into place to enable the men to begin work on tractors." At the Highland Park luncheon table half an hour later, Ford calmly advised his associates that he had telephoned Washington and stopped all war work at Dearborn. He urged them: "You call Washington and get permission to stop."

"You will lose a million dollars on the work you are doing," he was told.

"Peace will be worth it," retorted Ford.

The following day he strolled into the Liberty Engine section, where work was still going on as usual. He asked William Klann why. "I guess they want to fill the contract," Klann replied. "You go and tell Mr. P. E. Martin," commanded Ford "that the war is over, and that we should stop this job." [1]

Many observers have found in these abrupt actions only the convinced pacifist's satisfaction in the cessation of a devastating conflict. While Ford undoubtedly knew such an emotion, in starting peacetime production he was much more Ford the industrialist, impatient to resume activities that had been suspended for almost two years. Despite the fact that the Dodge suit was still unsettled, that his factories were geared to war, and that economic prospects were unpredictable, Ford was already concentrating on motor car production, confident of the future.

No leader in the industry had acted more promptly, and some had been doubtful of what was now in store for them. The collapse of Germany had come as a surprise, to many as a blow. Like an intricate machine, the entire thinking and producing of the nation had to be put in reverse. New jobs must be provided for hosts of war workers and four million returning service men, materials must be channeled to new uses, financing devised for new industries. Charles Evans Hughes, with an anticipation of New Deal practice, urged a vast program of public works to take up the "labor slack," and *Automobile Topics* in November foresaw "the most absolute and abysmal uncertainty of which the mind can conceive." Fortunately a number of automobile manufacturers did not share such forebodings. Some had facilities to start limited production, and five days after the armistice shipments of finished cars were made. Alvan Macauley of Packard announced that only access to raw materials was needed—with these, "the automobile industry will reassert and reestablish its former splendid proportions." [2] He was soon justified. Difficulties and anxieties began to vanish as the Government lifted restrictions on raw materials, canceled war contracts, and through the Federal Reserve System established a low discount rate. A sustained European demand for American goods (paid for by American loans), a general shortage of civilian goods and housing, and a flood of ready money provided by savings from wartime wages, bonuses for service men, and cashing of Liberty bonds all united to establish an active market in most commodities.

Because of the curtailment of automotive production during the war, the motor car was especially in demand. Within a month its manufacturers jubilantly anticipated a prosperity never before attained. The Government rapidly freed them to exploit their market by reducing its war contracts with automotive firms from $673,000,000 on armistice day to $62,000,000 on February 1, 1919, and by so disposing of its surplus vehicles that they did not become a factor affecting motor car sales. [3]

The Ford Motor Company moved rapidly to reëstablish production at Highland Park. Since at the time of the armistice it was still manufacturing trucks, ambulances, and Model T's for government use, its assembly line was intact. According to Pioch, retooling required only three weeks; E. A. Walters, also engaged in it, thought it covered a longer period. For the first time since 1908 important changes were to be made in the Model T, most of them necessitated by the installation of a self-starter and generator. However, by December 7 the plant was already producing 1000 vehicles a day, and pushing rapidly toward a higher quota. Meanwhile the total output for the industry was also rising, from 43,244 cars in November to 93,779 in January. Ford and his competitors were on the way to new production records.[4]

2.

As peacetime activity was resumed, Henry Ford had yet to acquire full control of company stock. However, he was already planning to achieve complete ownership, and that some anticipation of his later autocracy should now be manifest can scarcely be a matter for surprise.

Ford, as we have seen, looked back with distaste on the period of Couzens's activity in company affairs, when he had been unable to move freely. The Dodge suit had of course intensified his desire for absolute authority. He was therefore irritated by the presence of anyone in the company who might not work with him in complete harmony. The departure in the spring of 1919 of three of his ablest lieutenants seems to have been related to this state of mind. The men who left were C. Harold Wills, on March 15, John R. Lee, a few days later, and Norval Hawkins, some time in April. None of the three was discharged, yet we have reason to believe that Ford viewed the resignations with satisfaction.[5]

To be sure, he said nothing publicly to indicate such a feeling, and Edwin G. Pipp later pictured him as regretful with respect to Wills and Lee. "It is my fault," Ford told the editor. "They are very able men, and you have got to keep something in sight ahead for men of that type. I wasn't able to do it, and they can't be blamed for going into it [the automotive business] for themselves." This referred to Wills's brief statement on the day his resignation was announced: "I am anxious to do something worthwhile and this seems the opportune time to start." With Lee, he was soon developing a new car, the Wills-Sainte Claire. But we may question whether Ford had spoken his full mind to Pipp. Ford disliked taking responsibility for unpleasant acts, while there were elements in the situation which he was unlikely to discuss, even privately. Wills in particular aroused instinctive feelings which Ford would have found difficult to explain.

Wills had taken an important role in developing the Ford car of

1903, and its successors, including the Model T. *Automobile Topics* called him the "mechanical genius of Highland Park," and intimated that he deserved as much or more credit than Ford, and that the two had at times been in conflict. "There were occasions . . . when Wills was made to feel that an individual course would not only be more agreeable but more resultful." A certain tension between Ford and Wills had been observed since 1908 or earlier. "They used to watch each other, those two," said Max Wollering. Sorsensen later noted that Wills was always working at a tangent from Ford's wishes, trying again and again to evolve something different from and better than what the industrialist wanted. Another element in the relationship had been the already-noted arrangement by which Wills was to receive a part of Ford's dividends. Just as he was irked by minority stockholders who drew large returns on an original investment absurdly small, Ford was perhaps annoyed at the idea of paying Wills special sums in addition to a very high salary. Was he now more valuable than Mayo, Knudsen, or Sorensen? Yet after leaving, in a final settlement the engineer collected $1,592,128.39.[6]

As to Hawkins, the evidence of friction is clearer. Brilliantly as he presided over sales and advertising, some Ford officials, Wills among them, felt that his methods at times were too sharp. Ford himself had other objections: he did not like Hawkins's systemization of company forms, disapproved of his leaving the company during the war to serve the Government, was annoyed by a feud between him and Gaston Plantiff, and in general felt that Hawkins took authority too readily, and even acted at times in opposition to Ford's expressed wishes. Two years later, when Hawkins suggested through Liebold that he might return and help stimulate sales in a dead period, Ford remarked: "Well, you tell Hawkins that if he ever gets to the point where he'll do what we tell him to do, why, we might talk with him." Hawkins was maneuvered out rather gently. During the war his work naturally shrank to nothing, and on December 31, 1918, the directors appointed his assistant, William A. Ryan, sales manager, designating Hawkins a special sales representative for Europe and South America (and thus out of Ford's hair!). His salary was not reduced, but he was offended, and left the company.[7]

Lee's motive was different. He stated later that he had left voluntarily, "with a rather indefinite idea," and that he was urged by Alfred

Lucking to remain, a fact that suggests Ford's desire to keep him. Lee was in all probability aware of Ford's hardening temper, and Wills's departure undoubtedly influenced him. But it is significant that the popular executive who, with Dean Marquis, had been the symbol of liberal Ford welfare policies, should leave the organization at this time.

If the public and the automotive experts expected the departures to affect the company adversely, there was no sign that it had done so. Ford of course still had a staff rich with talent, with Mayo, Knudsen, Martin, Galamb, Sorensen, Avery and others ready to carry on. Early in the year Highland Park was turning out 2000 cars a day, and by May was producing 3100. Meanwhile, work at the Rouge was proceeding vigorously, although this enormous plant would not begin to affect Ford output until 1921.[8]

In his plans for a bigger future, Ford was only one amid a throng of ambitious rivals. By March, 1919, *Automobile Topics* announced that all companies "are increasing production as rapidly as possible and expect more business than they can possibly deliver this year." Willys-Overland announced a yearly quota of 180,000 cars, Dodge and Studebaker 150,000. Franklin, Marmon, Maxwell-Chalmers, Nash, and others were enlarging their factories. In General Motors, the brilliant William C. Durant was scheduling extensions for the Buick, Chevrolet, and Olds, a completely new Cadillac plant, and a fifteen story office building and research laboratory, both in Detroit. With an expenditure of $37,398,000 the engineers promised to double the General Motors output.

The hopes which inspired such activity appear in prophecies made at the time by various automotive leaders. Charles Clifton, President of the National Automobile Chamber of Commerce, predicted in January a demand for three million cars. G. C. Hubbs of Dodge Brothers declared that "the immediate future could scarcely be more encouraging." As to the further horizon, Ralph Kaye, advertising manager of Kissel, predicted in *Automobile Topics* an era of special motor highways, mass garages, and automobile classes, since "to be unable to drive an automobile would be as bad as an inability to write a legible hand."[9]

Buying, which now rose sharply, was stimulated by a sales device of increasing prevalence: the installment plan of paying for automobiles. First emerging as important in 1910, when the Morris Plan banks began to finance car purchases, by 1913 it had come into general use. Since the usual down payment ranged from 25 to 40 per cent of total value, a cheap or medium-priced car could be "bought" for from $125 to $300.

The sale of Ford cars on credit had never received the company's official blessing. Henry Ford firmly opposed the practice. Edsel, in contrast, recognized its effectiveness, and quietly encouraged its use. Ford dealers often employed it.[10] *

Supported by strong demand, the drive of the industry for high production surged on triumphantly, until the Ford Motor Company in May was aiming at 4000 units a day (well over 1,200,000 a year). A flood of unfilled orders (143,751 in July) was an incentive in pushing the output upward.

But the Ford goal was never reached that year, and few of the other companies met the quotas they had set. The consumer was not to blame, for appetite raged. "There were never enough cars to meet the demand," says one expert, pointing out that used cars could easily be sold for the price of new ones, and sometimes brought more! The trouble lay in an epidemic of strikes which affected the supply of raw materials and automobile parts.

That labor disputes should affect the automotive industry was ironical, for its wages were relatively high, and early in 1919 most of the companies had announced bonus, profit-sharing, or stock-distribution plans. Furthermore, except for one strike that took 14,000 men out of three Willys-Overland plants, disagreements within the industry were few, and like that of the Studebaker Corporation and its workers, were settled quickly.[11]

However, American industry in general was not so fortunate. With

---

* Edsel's position was clearly defined late in 1919. Clarence H. Booth, president of the Motor Bankers Corporation, a company holding commercial paper for motor vehicles, wrote on November 10 to Richard P. Joy, president of the National Bank of Commerce, Detroit, protesting the bank's coolness to MBC paper. He sent a copy of his letter to Edsel, saying: "I do not know whether you are aware of the fact that the Motor Bankers Corporation . . . are handling a large amount of this paper from many of your dealers in the city . . . If this method does not meet with your approval, and if the security we take and offer to the banks with our indorsement is not proper security for them to handle, the automotive business is working on a rather unstable basis." Edsel replied on the 18th, "I believe, as you do, that a corporation such as yours is a very necessary adjunct in the financing of motor car sales, and . . . it may be interesting to you to note that at least sixty-five per cent of our cars and trucks are handled by the dealers on a time payment basis. I also feel that the time payment plan will become more important as time goes on." (Acc. 6, Box 34.)

the cost of living moving upward, organized labor made a desperate effort to lift wages to a level with prices. Beginning with a walkout of harbor workers in New York on January 9, a succession of disputes plagued employers and public alike. A number affected basic production or transportation, and as early as April the Wadsworth Manufacturing Company, which made sedan bodies for Ford cars, was at odds with its workers. This strike quickly impaired production by the Ford Motor Company, which strove to keep the Wadsworth factory going, using its own employees as strike-breakers. Concurrently a strike at the Wilson Body Company, which supplied Ford bodies for open cars, further crippled company operations.

Not less disruptive were three national strikes outside the motor car field: those of the railroad shopmen in August, of the bituminous coal miners on October 31, and of the steel workers, beginning September 22, 1919, and lasting until the surrender of the men on January 8, 1920. All caused scarcities which slowed the assembly lines of automotive factories, and delayed the construction of additions and new plants.

These disturbances profoundly affected Henry Ford. We have seen that early in 1919 he stood at a crucial point in the development of his new Rouge project. Now after a long battle he seemed likely to win complete control of the company. But suppose he did? If parts-makers, railroads, coal-miners, steel mills and glass plants could wreck his schedules, what security could he have in pushing his larger program? He had long planned to acquire a control of raw materials, and now began to do so: timber tracts to supply wood for car bodies; iron mines to produce ore for axles, wheels, transmissions; coal properties to feed Ford furnaces and factories. And he moved at once to manufacture his own car bodies in B Building at the Rouge, where production began July 18.[12]

In view of their difficulties, the automobile manufacturers did well. For the calendar year they achieved a production of 1,876,336, a new record by a few thousand cars (the best previous mark was 1,873,949 for 1917). Ford's share of the total was 750,000, slightly above his record of 730,041 in 1917, and 40 per cent of the national output.* How-

* The figure for 1917 was for the year ending June 30. However, on any basis of comparison the Ford Motor Company production set a record. As to other manufacturers, Studebaker, aiming at 150,000, produced only 29,356; Willys-Overland, its quota 180,000, reached only 94,800, and the Dodge Brothers, also hoping for 150,000, turned out 124,000.

ever, he had aimed at 1,000,000. In falling short of his proclaimed objective, he stood with other firms like Studebaker, Willys-Overland, and Dodge.[13]

Nevertheless one shining fact relieved this failure. The heap of unfilled orders had now become a towering mountain: in September it was set at 2,500,000 cars, while the Secretary of the National Automobile Chamber of Commerce in December 1919, dared to predict that, including trucks, the production for the coming year would reach a total of 3,450,000 vehicles. The first months of 1920 confirmed such estimates. In March, all previous records were smashed with an output of 220,000 cars. On the 27th of the month the Ford Motor Company assembled 4256 Model T's. (Yet so great was the demand that Ford dealers were refusing to guarantee deliveries before fall.) A shortage of freight cars that threatened to prevent the delivery of finished automobiles was met by a great "driveaway" operation. "During the month of March," reported the *New York Times*, "more than 46,000 cars were driven from Western factories to points as far distant as 1000 miles. It is the largest number of automobiles ever driven over the roads to dealer agencies. On one side, it is an object lesson of the inability of railroads to handle the shipments, while on the other side, it demonstrates the increasing demand in all parts of the country for motor vehicles." [14]

Unfortunately, various economic forces were already in operation to check the tide of production. The post-war prosperity of the nation was largely the result of artificial elements already noted: government spending, war savings, a low discount rate, and a temporary European market. These now were fading or disappearing. The result was inevitable: no matter what the demand for cars, it was bound to shrink as jobs and incomes decreased, and other commodities fell in comparison with the prices of automobiles.

The first blow had been struck in November, 1919, when the Federal Reserve Board raised its discount rate. For this act the rash installment selling of cars had been partly responsible. The Board expressly condemned its volume and character. "A well-managed bank does not want to become a dealer in second-hand automobiles," sharply remarked W. P. G. Harding, its governor. The higher rate meant that a customer would soon be asked for something like half of the price as a down payment, instead of a fourth or a third. However, the effect of the new rate was not felt immediately. General commodity prices were still rising, and reached their peak only in May, 1920 (at 121.7 per cent of the November, 1918 level). The index for cars, reflecting the unusual consumer demand, actually continued to rise until August, reaching 124.9. But already in June a weakening was apparent, reflecting the economic situation of the country. Used cars were much less in demand, and fewer orders were being received for new ones. The credit situation had so deteriorated that bankers in the Middle West were reported in July to be forbidding the purchase of automobiles altogether.[15]

Dealers now began to urge price reductions. Manufacturers united in opposing the idea. A number, the Ford Motor Company among them, had just been forced by high materials costs to increase their quotations, and *Automobile Topics* declared that lower prices were impossible not only for the present but for the foreseeable future. In August Willys-Overland and Reo made further increases of from $50 to $100 a car! Rather than produce cheaper vehicles, the manufacturers proposed to persuade the bankers to adopt a more liberal attitude, and as late as August the Ford sales organization suggested "a campaign to educate the country banker and sell him on the tractor, and more fully sell him on the automobile as an essential to the industry and the welfare of our country." [16]

The time had indeed come for a lesson, but it was the automotive industry and not the banker that would receive it.

3.

Other warnings of trouble had accompanied the slackening of sales in June and the slight fall of commodity prices beginning in May. The Federal Reserve Board had consistently urged all banks to reduce still further their financing of the installment buying of cars. At about the same time, in April, stock exchange quotations of automobile company shares began to fall, and on April 21 the market broke. General Motors dropped 42½ points that afternoon. A continuous decline ensued.[17]

Although the greatest single precipitant of the decline had been the attitude of the Federal Reserve Board, that body, and through it the banks, had only responded to influences that affected the entire country. The car makers, keeping their eyes on the strong demand for automobiles, simply forgot that however great the demand, it could not operate in a sagging economy. Men had to have jobs or dependable incomes in order to buy automobiles.

Henry Ford had watched the situation. Describing it later, he pictured himself as fully aware of its significance even in early 1920. "Our own sales kept right along," he stated, "but we knew that sooner or later they would drop off. I thought seriously of cutting prices, but the costs of manufacturing everywhere were out of control." This was of course hindsight. Ford and his associates may have discussed reducing prices, for low prices and high volume of production had long been standard Ford policy. But by no action during this period did the Ford Motor Company indicate that it had appraised the complex situation more shrewdly than its rivals. Like the others, it had raised prices and pushed sales.

However, Ford had special reasons for wanting to maintain production and income. His financial situation was delicate; for not only had he been forced to pay more than $20,000,000 in dividends and interest, and to undertake the repayment of what he had borrowed to buy out the minority stockholders, but he was also involved in a program of expansion requiring large expenditures. On the Rouge in the preceding three years he had spent $60,453,000, while he had paid out from $15,000,000 to $20,000,000 for mines and timber tracts, and for the necessary repairs, construction, and personnel to make these properties usable. The total expenditures would more than have paid off the loan, which was being reduced, but Ford was bent on building a greater company, and ample income had seemed in prospect to take care of both debts and expansion.[18]

But by midsummer the situation had become menacing. Sales were falling off, yet the costs of raw materials continued high. To maintain production and income, some kind of wizardry was required. Ford now perceived that inflation must be met boldly. He would reduce prices. He recognized that since he was still paying high rates for materials, any drastic reduction in car-prices—and he knew that a drastic step was necessary—would mean that for some time he would sell every model at a loss. But he could neutralize much of the loss through the sale of parts; his act would compel his rivals to reduce prices; costs of materials, sure to fall in any case, would be deflated more rapidly; and over the long period the operation would be profitable.

He called a conference of high Ford Motor Company officials (Edsel, Kanzler, Sorensen, Knudsen, Ryan, William H. Smith among them), informed them of his intention, and bade them plan reductions. They worked out a set of figures. Ford glanced at these, and announced abruptly that the cuts were too small.

They tried to argue with him, and he got mad. He pulled out a piece of paper with pencilled prices on it and said: "There, gentlemen, are your prices."

The men were astonished. They told him the Company would go broke on those prices. He asked for the paper back and reduced two cars five dollars more.

The first leader in the industry to act, Ford startled the nation and his competitors on September 21 by the size of the cuts, some of which were:

Unit	Old Price	New Price	Amount of Cut
Chassis	$525	$360	$165
Runabout	550	395	155
Touring Car	575	440	135
Coupe	850	745	105
Sedan	975	795	180

Ford said in a statement accompanying these figures:

"The war is over and it is time war prices were over. . . .

"Inflated prices always retard progress. We had to stand it during the war, although it wasn't right, so the Ford Motor Company will make the prices of its products the same as they were before the war.

"We must of course take a temporary loss because of the stock of materials on hand, bought at inflated prices, . . . but we take it willingly in order to bring about a going state of business throughout the country." [19]

The reductions, the largest in the history of the trade, seemed the more bewildering because Ford declared that he had a bank of 146,065 orders for cars and tractors. The immediate response of a number of rivals was hostile. One group, including Dodge, Maxwell-Chalmers, Hupp, Hudson, Essex, Paige, and General Motors, conferred in Detroit and announced that prices should not be lowered, because buyers would then expect further reductions, and all buying would cease! "You can expect anything from him!" remarked one competitor. "We're disposed to look at it just as we looked at his peace ship," shrugged another, "an eccentric matter, which he is perfectly able to pay for, and therefore is entitled to enjoy as much as he can." But in two days the Franklin Automobile Company followed the Ford lead, and soon too did Studebaker and Willys-Overland. "It was said that we were disturbing conditions," Ford remarked later. "That is exactly what we were trying to do."

Other manufacturers got into line, including five of the group that had agreed to preserve the old price level. By October 9, twenty-three companies had lowered prices, and twenty-eight had not. *Automobile Topics* explained Ford's plan of operations: he lost $20 a car on every vehicle he sold, but with each he sold $40 worth of parts at no reduction, the profit on which went far toward canceling his loss.[20]

For a time it seemed as if his strategy might succeed. The Ford purchasing department immediately put pressure on parts makers and suppliers of raw materials, and obtained reductions, although they were not proportionate to the lowered prices of cars. Another favorable influence was the diminishing output of automobiles. A number of manufacturers had begun to lay off men—Willys-Overland in August—and their plants were operating with reduced crews; by October Detroit had 54,000 unemployed automotive workers. Ford was running with a full force, and following his price cuts the company was receiving new orders. "We are going along in very good shape," wrote Plantiff from New York to Liebold on October 10; "in fact, most all the Eastern Branches are close up to their estimates and consumers are taking the cars off their dealers' hands in good order."

But the flurry of buying soon fell off, and the sales letters from the company to the branches show that the Detroit officials were worried. The record for October was excellent, 106,669 cars and tractors, but November showed a decided drop to 93,956, and it may be assumed that an increasing number of cars had begun to pile up with the dealers. In December the sales sank to 42,492. The tractor plant at Dearborn, now a Ford Motor Company unit, was closed about October 1—a reflection in part of the weak purchasing power of the farmers, but also an act consonant with Ford's long-standing plan to move it. "In spite of the concentrated efforts of our entire organization," wrote Ryan early in December to his branch heads, "unfilled orders have steadily diminished each ten day period while dealers' stocks have increased making it evident that to successfully go through with our original plan of maximum production we must obtain increased selling strength." [21]

Thus the long-term strategy of maintaining production at a loss, and sustaining consumer demand by low prices until the costs of raw materials fell and profit was again possible, was rapidly running toward failure. Temporarily, buying power had all but disappeared. Looking back on the period later, Ford liked to think that if all manufacturers had promptly followed his lead, cutting to the bone, the situation could have been saved. "Hanging on in the hope of high prices simply delayed adjustment. Nobody got the higher prices they hoped for . . . and . . . [all] lost the profits they might have made working on a more sensible basis." But whatever the validity of this view, the situation continued to deteriorate as the year advanced. For General Motors, the sensational Ford price reductions resulted in a sharp depreciation of its shares. Durant strove to maintain its position by buying huge blocks of stock, but he was soon faced with complete disaster. The DuPonts bought 2,500,000 shares from him late in November. It was a $27,000,000 operation, and the DuPonts borrowed from J. P. Morgan & Co., thus partially delivering General Motors into the hands of the bankers. Durant was forced out, the company reorganized, and its previous expansive policy sharply modified.[22]

Meanwhile, the Ford executives were attempting to strengthen the company by a program of severe economy. Ernest C. Kanzler, who had left Henry Ford & Co. at Henry Ford's request to supervise production and shipments at Highland Park, had been carrying on this work, and with Edsel was directing company activities there.* Only a few days after the price cuts Edsel announced a campaign of "waste elimination." "We are confident," he wrote branch heads, "of the many economies, now overlooked, that can be instituted," and bade them act

---

* As Sorensen's assistant at the tractor plant, in charge when the Dane was absent, Kanzler became fascinated with the relationship between production and shipment. He perceived that failure to synchronize the two built up "inventory," or money tied up in goods not promptly used (also, it tied up valuable space). Millions of dollars might be lost in this fashion. He worked out routines which eliminated confusion and adjusted the influx of parts from suppliers to the making and shipping of Fordsons. So exact were his schedules that supplies arrived practically as needed, and freight cars bringing in wheels, radiators, castings, etc. were utilized a few hours after their arrival to dispatch completed tractors. Ford was immensely impressed, and after acquiring full control of the company, brought Kanzler to Highland Park to apply his methods there. For further details of his work, see Chap. X. (Interview with authors, June 11, 1956.) Edsel and Kanzler had been at work since the spring of 1919 on company organization, and had employed the efficiency firm of Thompson & Black to study activities and make recommendations.

promptly. *Automotive Industries* pointed out that while the company was not laying off employees, "wherever one does leave he is not replaced. Employees in the Ford offices and administration buildings are given opportunity to go to the factory, on account of the slack work in the offices." By November, Edsel and Kanzler were working out a definite plan in conjunction with outside experts. Henry Ford approved. "We planned a thorough house-cleaning," he recalled later. ". . . The office force had expanded and much wastefulness and scattered production had set in." Ford was determined to throw out "everything that did not contribute to the production of cars." If Edsel and Kanzler planned a systematic procedure, they were soon to be startled at the sweeping character of what was done.

The drive for economy went forward through October and November, while *Automobile Topics* reported that "production is once more at a low ebb," and that employees in most companies were being reduced. For a time the Ford organization seemed to be little affected, but with December its plight became clear, for although the 78,000 cars produced represented a quota twenty per cent below normal, the total was some 35,000 more than the dealers could take.[23]

In one final effort to "obtain increased selling strength," Edsel and Ryan announced to all Ford dealers that "effective immediately, all territory lines will be eliminated." The plan was described as an opportunity: "Present large dealers will be benefited by being permitted to reach out into unlimited territory," while small dealers could "expand and grow . . . by intensively covering territory just over the line which they have constantly claimed could be handled best by them."[24] This open territory system brought few complaints at the time, but later, in more intensive form, was to cause much resentment.*

It did little to increase the revenue of the company, which was now as much in the grip of the increasing depression as most of its rivals. They began to accept the necessity of a complete shutdown. On November 22 the Nash Motor Company closed its plant at Kenosha, Wisconsin, "to allow an inventory and completion of plans for readjustment of labor conditions." As December advanced, other companies followed suit: Willys-Overland, Packard, Dodge, Studebaker, Reo, Maxwell-

---

* The company felt that the fixed territory plan represented both an abuse and a nuisance: a nuisance, because when an energetic dealer made a sale in another's territory, the company had to fix percentages of profit, often in dispute; an abuse, because lazy dealers were inclined not to push sales, but to demand their "take" on a more industrious agent's work. Today, all companies operate on an open territory basis.

Chalmers, and Buick. Finally on the 24th the Ford Motor Company stopped work "for inventory," promising to reopen on January 5, 1921. Such plants as remained open carried a negligible working force and produced little. Automotive employees in Detroit, 176,000 in September, now shrank to 24,000.[25]

4.

Commodity prices struck bottom in January, and even in that grim month a number of firms completed "inventory" and reopened, manufacturing on a small scale. The Ford Motor Company did not join this rather tentative procession. In a series of announcements on December 28, 30 and 31 its officials postponed the reopening, and finally stated that the plant would be closed indefinitely. A "lack of orders" and "general financial and business conditions" were given as reasons for the delay. One official, irritated by questions, snapped: "The Ford Motor Company has been operating while other concerns have been laying off men or working them part time."

This was of course true. All during the late summer and fall, while its competitors had been discharging "inefficient workers" and slowing their assembly lines, the Ford factories had been pushed to the limit. December production was short only because it represented a three-week month. Cars were now piled up by the tens of thousands in the form of parts at the branches, or finished models in the hands of the dealers. Henry Ford later asserted that both the full production and the accumulation of surplus stocks were deliberate. "We wanted to have as much as possible of our raw material transformed into finished product before we shut down. Then the new cars could be built out of material bought at lower prices." [26]

Doubtless this was part of a plan, although the probability is that the company did not develop it until mid-October at least. Another feature of the situation that suggests planning was the position the company held after the shutdown. It had stopped buying raw materials, thereby cutting expenses sharply. As the backlog of cars was sold, money would come in, but very little was going out. The big reservoir of unsold cars would later be used, however, in a way Ford was not likely to have foreseen in the fall and early winter.

Meanwhile the shutdown took on aspects that few in the company and no outsiders had foreseen.

First of all, the working force was stripped to a skeleton crew of managers and superintendents. Klann tells how Edsel Ford, Avery, Hartner, Findlater, Ernie Davis and he laid a machine shop floor. The regular salaries of these men amounted to hundreds of thousands a year, and the product of their work was called "the million dollar floor." When it was finished, some of the former executives asked if they would now be laid off. "No," they were told, "you can act as watchmen."

For several months they sped around the empty factory buildings on roller skates or bicycles. Klann, Degener, and Wandersee were thus employed. They also swept the floors, and as orders were received for parts, packaged them for shipment. Who would remain and in what capacity —indeed, what would be the entire structure of the new company soon to emerge—were matters apparently undecided.

The fate of the office force was even less certain than that of the research and factory crews: soon the survivors in the empty factory perceived that little would be left of it. The lot of the travelling auditors illustrates this point. In October they were recalled from their field work and employed in making surveys of all company departments, listing personnel, and preparing charts. The task was directed by Herbert L. Leister, assistant to Louis H. Turrell, the chief auditor. Then on December 30 the men were called into Turrell's office, where he explained that the company had no further work for them. The following day Turrell himself was discharged! Leister with the aid of the charts then worked out a startling simplification of the entire accounting system, both at home and at the branches.

Ford, who had always regarded the office force with an executioner's eye, as mostly parasitic, thus joyfully cut the total from 1074 to 528, or by more than half. Departments were merged and sections eliminated. The cost-keeping department on which factory officials had depended was drastically simplified—"If you want to keep costs," men like Klann and Hartner were told, "keep them on your desk." The telegraph office vanished and the telephone operator in the information room took over its functions. The Tax and Controller's departments were merged into the Auditing Department. The Stock Department became a shadow of its former self.[27]

Simultaneously, Ford made a relentless drive to collect and sell all useless or surplus material. Every tool or fixture that could be spared was disposed of: lamps, tables, files, typewriters, hand and machine tools. "We literally took out a trainload of desks and furniture and sold them!" he exclaimed gleefully half a year later. Much of this material was sold at a store established on Miller Road. Among the items removed were six hundred extension telephones, and every pencil-sharpener in the place. "If you wanted to sharpen a pencil," said Klann, "you had to sharpen it with your knife. You buy your own knife." The entire Rouge plant cafeteria equipment, a survival from the war, was sold. Theodore Mallon, still employed during this period, had the impression that the sale netted $7,000,000.

Meanwhile attention was given to improving factory equipment and methods, so that fewer men would be needed. Richard Kroll states that many new tools were brought in as the old ones were sold. "Half the men were let go, and still they made more cars and parts." [28]

5.

While Henry Ford was brooding over problems of production and sales in the summer of 1920, he never forgot the financial reckoning he would be called upon to face. The remainder of the $60,000,000 he had borrowed was due in the spring of 1921.* The company had repaid $35,000,000, leaving $25,000,000 to be paid in April, 1921. Ford was determined to distribute a $7,000,000 bonus to his employees in January. He owed from $18,000,000 to $30,000,000 in taxes. Ford himself put the total required at $58,000,000; it may have been no more than $50,000,-000.

To meet these obligations the Ford Motor Company in the fall of 1920 had $20,000,000 in cash. Its situation was generally known, and with the closing of the Highland Park plant on December 24 the opinion grew in financial circles that Ford would need a large loan to meet his obligations. [29]

In retrospect, Ford always spoke as if he had never seriously considered such a possibility; actually, ample evidence exists that his associates had thought much about borrowing, and that Ford was aware of various exploratory efforts made by them on his behalf.

As early as October 29 Edward A. Rumely, an independent financial expert who stood high in the regard of the Ford executives, proposed,

* Ford had established a credit of $75,000,000, but had used only $60,000,000, plus $7,000,000 of his own money. (See Acc. 352, Box 1, which contains a full record of the transactions).

apparently on his own initiative, several plans by which Ford could raise money: a farmers' credit company to finance tractors and cars, and a $200,000,000 issue of company stock. Neither plan seems to have appealed to Ford, and the latter would have been anathema to him. He had just got rid of his minority stockholders, was in jeopardy because of the transaction, and would only create new stockholders—a vicious circle in policy. Of course the plan would have had wide public support. From this time on Ford was receiving contributions and offers of assistance from a wide variety of persons, from the Detroit woman who wanted to lend him $100 to a fellow industrialist who tendered several millions.*

He returned all unsolicited contributions and declined offers of aid. On January 21 the *New York Times* ran a headline: "FORD CO. SAID TO SEEK LOAN OF $50,000,000 OR MORE." This speculative article named several New York banks which would float a bond issue to meet Ford's needs, estimated at $30,000,000 owed the banks, and $40,000,000 due the Government for taxes. As we shall see, there was some basis for the article, although it greatly exaggerated Ford's requirements.

On January 25 Arthur Brisbane, the Hearst editor, always a warm friend of the Fords, reported to Liebold an earlier declaration by a Detroiter: "In a day or two they will get Durand [sic] of the General Motors, and a little later they will get Henry Ford." Brisbane commented: "Of course I know they are NOT going to get Henry Ford. But I thought it might interest you and Mr. Ford to know that some of his 'friends' have the thing in mind." [30]

The period had been so critical that some Ford executives felt sure that Ford would be obliged to borrow. Liebold says that Klingensmith took such a view, and Klingensmith may have influenced Edsel. Early in January Edsel was in touch with the Detroit banks, and was encouraged by one correspondent to borrow, putting in a treasurer "who has the confidence of the financial world." Edsel probably never gave this message to his father, for he knew Ford's aversion to bankers.

---

* The *N.Y. Times* of Feb. 9, 1921 cited the case of Mrs. M. D. Brown of Detroit, who could not afford a Ford car, but wanted to lend its maker $100, and hoped that other Detroiters would follow her example. As to the industrialist, on Jan. 27 Benjamin Briscoe wrote Ford: "I could get together a few million dollars in a short time and would be glad to turn it over to you." Briscoe was an old automotive man who with W. C. Durant had tried to buy the Ford company in 1908, and later organized the United States Motors Company. He strongly advised Ford not to "put yourself in the hands of any 'banking group.'" Various other suggestions, some accompanied by cash, were made to Ford. (See Acc. 62-2, Boxes 1 and 9).

Even Liebold had been dallying with two groups, one in Detroit, one in New York. The latter even drew up an elaborate plan by which money could be advanced against the production of Ford cars. But Liebold, who saw Ford daily, knew his sharp hostility to financiers, and kept the negotiations tentative.[31]

Meanwhile, Ford had been groping toward a solution. He indicated later that the situation had begun to affect the company soon after the price cuts had been made, that it developed as a crisis "not of money but of men," with Klingensmith heading one faction in the organization, and Liebold and Sorensen another. Klingensmith, according to Karl Bickel, news manager of the United Press, who talked with Ford, had disapproved of the price cuts and felt that borrowing would be mandatory. Ford, of course, firmly believed in the soundness of the price reductions, and was averse to seeking a loan. Liebold and Sorensen automatically lined up with him. Edsel was represented as holding the two factions in balance. But on January 3 a stormy conference was held, and it seems certain that Ford, if not yet seeing his way clearly, categorically refused to consider a loan (although he may have toyed with such possibilities as Liebold explored), and that as a result Klingensmith resigned.[32]

Already the situation was clarifying. As it stood early in 1921, it had certain potentially favorable aspects. In the first place, company expenses for salaries and wages were low, for only a few executives and men were employed, who could be carried on the proceeds from the sale of surplus goods. Again, production having ceased, the branches and dealers were working off surplus stock. A third advantage existed in relation to the suppliers, who had now lost their chief customer, were eager to quote lower prices, and with commodities at rock bottom, could do so. They were also willing to take trade acceptances of from sixty to ninety days on the delivery of goods, thus permitting Ford to be paid for completed cars by the dealers before he made payment to the suppliers. A fourth favorable circumstance lay in the fact that Ford was receiving cash from outstanding bills collected by the branches, and for spare parts. Finally, he had 30,000 cars for which he would receive cash when they were sold. (Cars in the hands of dealers, being already paid for, would of course bring him nothing.)

As to the future, it would clearly be favorable to Ford as soon as a normal demand for cars again existed. This condition in turn rested on the economic condition of the country. Had the depression run its course? Would cars again be saleable in a few weeks? And if these questions could be answered affirmatively, how rapidly would the dealers work off the cars they had and be able to accept shipments of new ones?

Early in January these questions could not be answered. However, even by the end of December there were some encouraging signs, and Ford was aware of them. From New York on the 31st came a letter written by Gaston Plantiff:

... I see by the papers that you are going to shut down indefinitely in Detroit, and am wondering if it is true, as we have just received word here to start assembling what stock we have, on January third, which I believe we will be able to consume without much trouble, as the territory is getting in better shape all the time, and think we can run along fairly normal. . . . One thing is that it will certainly create a shortage of cars, which will be good and will give us a chance to reduce our old stock and turn it into cash, which we need.

The letter indicates that conditions in New York were already on the mend. Within a week other automotive plants showed returning confidence. Packard reopened on January 3, Reo on the 5th, Studebaker on the 6th, Willys-Overland on the 15th. These events must have been reassuring to Ford. He was of course receiving reports from all his branches, which doubtless showed some improvement in the situation. Alvan Macauley stated not long afterward that the upturn had begun in January. Soon after the conference of January 3 Ford seems to have begun to feel out the situation by shipping parts and cars to dealers in limited quantity. He must move in this direction if he was not to accept a loan. He later noted that January was marked by a heartening revival, with a sale of from 50,000 to 60,000 cars.

However, as the month advanced the Ford home plant remained closed, and Ford gave no public intimation of what he would do. Representatives of various banks were now coming to Detroit. Ford told Liebold to talk to some of them. "You'll get a lot of experience out of it," he said, adding significantly, "We are not going to borrow any money."

Ford seems to have felt satisfaction in seeing the bankers' representatives waiting in Company offices. He eyed them as he would so many respectable vultures. He said nothing to check the rumors as to his borrowing. "We are having lots of fun," he wrote Benjamin Briscoe when declining the latter's offer of "a few millions" to improve the situation.[33]

The culminating event of this fortnight of uncertainty was an interview with Ford by a banker who managed to get an appointment at Fair Lane. Liebold, Harold Hicks, Ford himself, and the *News* reporter James Sweinhart have all described the conference. The visitor seems to have been Joseph Bower, vice-president of the Liberty National Bank of New York (a Morgan-controlled institution). The story in each instance is essentially the same. The banker began by mentioning the loan that Ford would need.

"But I don't need to borrow money," objected Ford quietly. "I can finance all my Company's operations myself."

"I think not," countered the visitor courteously. "We know your obligations, we know your cash reserves, and we know you need money."

He explained that he had worked out a plan, a copy of which he had brought with him. He began to read it, then suddenly broke off. "Who is going to be the new treasurer of your company?" he demanded. (Klingensmith had not yet been replaced.)

"That makes no difference to you, does it?" inquired Ford, puzzled.

"Oh, yes, it does. We'll have to have some say as to who the new treasurer shall be."

Ford got his visitor's hat and showed him to the door.* Next day he told Edsel to take the office of treasurer as well as that of president. The occurence shocked him. It bore out his belief in the predatory character of bankers. "They did not suggest putting in an engineer," he pointed out two years later; "they wanted to put in a treasurer." [34]

Meanwhile Ford had continued the shipment of parts and cars to dealers, from reserve stocks. Now he resolved upon more drastic action. Liebold says that one day late in January Ford, Edsel, Martin, and he were discussing the loan question.

"Well," said Ford, "I don't think we need to borrow any money. Ed," and he turned to Martin, "you know the best way to do is to start the plant going right away Monday, getting those cars out to the dealers. People want cars, and they need them. That's where we'll get our money."

---

* Sorensen, in *My Forty Years with Ford*, 167–168, states that he was present, and at a nod from Ford gave Bower his briefcase and told him to go.

The decision was made about January 26th. On January 28 the *New York Times* announced that Highland Park would reopen, and on February 1 a force of 15,000 men reported for work. Ford now gave an interview to Wilbur Forrest of the New York *Tribune*, doubtless to quiet persistent rumors. "I have never sought a loan for any amount in Wall Street," he declared, "nor has anyone done so with my authority." (As we have seen, this statement was technically but not substantially true.) Ford explained that the shutdown had been primarily for the purpose of disposing of "stocks on hand." "We will steadily work back to near normal production. In the meantime, Ford employees will not have been hard hit by their layoff, because it came at a time when their bonuses were being paid." [35]

A high hurdle had yet to be cleared. Ford was assuming that dealers had now sold most of their surplus cars, and could accept the new production which was steadily increasing in volume. But while probably no one then knew the exact number of cars the dealers had on hand, and while certainly no one knows today, the total was still considerable. This was confessed by the Sales Department's general letter of February 5, 1921, to the branches. It mentions "large stocks of both cars and tractors still in dealers' hands unsold," and continues:

We have been remarkably successful the past few months in wholesaling cars and tractors to our dealers, as is evidenced by their present stocks, but it is one thing to wholesale our products and another thing to retail them, and so we are confronted with the biggest job we have ever tackled in our lives, THE QUICK RETAILING OF OUR DEALERS' stocks. . . . Follow up your dealers as you never have followed them before.

Thus the move was recognized to be something of a gamble. "Wipe out the cloud of pessimism hovering over the dealer who has not sold a car or tractor lately by staying with him and closing a few sales," exhorted Ryan. The cloud was undoubtedly darkened and enlarged by the arrival of new consignments of cars, to be paid for at once in a period not yet marked by strong economic recovery. Ford did not wholly ignore the difficulties of the situation. While in the last resort the dealer had to pay or forfeit his franchise, the company, as indicated by Ryan's letter, stood ready to work with him closely. It assisted him to reassure his banker, assisted him to sell. Success was vital, for if he met the crisis the company would collect both on its dwindling store of reserve models, but also on the growing production for February, March, and April.

As Ford calculated, the plan was a success. Many dealers raised cries of protest, but although the company maintained steady pressure, in extreme cases it was forbearing. In most instances the dealers went to their bankers, got the money needed, and gradually saw demand overtake supply. As one commentator put it: "Instead of borrowing money himself, Ford compelled his dealers to borrow." [36]

The method was normal in the industry: all firms shipped cars collect. Ford simply shipped at a difficult time. Some dealers later said that they had no particular difficulty in disposing of their consignments; more admitted that they had. Kanzler, then responsible for both production and shipments, stated emphatically in 1956 that all consignments to dealers were carefully made, with their stocks and sales prospects in mind, and that he never heard of a Ford agent who found himself in jeopardy because he could not finance the cars he received. Kanzler termed all allegations that dealers were unjustly treated at this time "sheer nonsense." *

If any actually went to the wall for such a reason, there is no record of such a case. Some dealers were undoubtedly replaced in this period; they were every year. The figures indicate a very low percentage. In December, 1920, the company had 6345 dealers; in January, 6340; in February, 6486. To be sure, those figures are not conclusive. We know that the company was dissatisfied with some dealers, and also that it began about this time to add new ones.† What is clear is that the company and the dealers cooperated, that all those who have testified came through safely, and that many did so with company aid. For example,

---

* It should be noted that while Ford production for January and February was 3000 and 35,000 respectively, sales were 57,000 and 63,000. Although dealers were undoubtedly working off previously unsold cars, the increasing demand is clearly indicated.

† General Sales Letter, Mar. 16, 1921 (Acc. 78) points out that the preceding months provided a test for dealers, with "fair weather" and "order taking" types showing up poorly. "Our organization would be considerably strengthened through their elimination and replacement." It asks the branch heads to report poor dealers and recommend cancellation of their contracts. "In some cases, conditions will no doubt warrant the appointment of two or more dealers to replace one eliminated."

General Letter 1174, Oct. 19, 1921, speaks of "our campaign for new dealers," apparently under way for some months. It was primarily designed to extend Ford representation into new territories, but of course increased the total of dealers.

It is interesting to note that 1920–1921 was not a period of numerous dealer failures as compared with other years. One expert states that 13 per cent failed in 1920, 21 per cent in 1921, and 26 per cent in 1923—the latter a prosperous year. (James L. Collins, "Management Problems in the Automotive Industry," *Bulletin of the Taylor Society*, X, Aug. 1925, 192–195.) Collins of course referred to the dealers of all companies.

a dealer near Kansas City was thunderstruck when the local station agent telephoned him one morning, "We have some cars for you down here—about eighteen on the track." He went to a small neighborhood banker for advice. The banker said, "You'd better take them. We'll make up a note for those eighteen cars and we'll send it down to the Kansas City bank and let them handle it." They did so. "That is the way we got by," the dealer recalled. Again, in Ohio, Willis Hakes found one morning that he had seven carloads of automobiles on the railroad siding. "I called up and raised cain and . . . they sent a traveler out and the traveler went with me to the bank. Before we left we had raised the money and I unloaded them [the cars] *with the promise that they wouldn't send any more."* (Italics ours.) [37]

Thus with a combination of shutdown, ruthless economy, opportunistic delay, and pressure on his dealers and suppliers, Ford won through. Even on February 23 he could announce: "We are calling our men back to Highland Park as fast as we can possibly take care of them." On April 12 he asserted that "we were never in a better position than now," and that he was producing at a rate of 1,000,000 cars a year.[38] The very fact of his reopening, as Liebold asserted later, probably gave a lift to public confidence. So did the fact that he did not borrow. In general, the public saw only that Ford had outwitted the bankers, and applauded him.

Sales rose steadily: 42,492 in December, 57,208 (plus 1138 tractors) in January, 63,603 (and 1932 tractors) in February, 87,221 (and 4708 tractors) in March. These represented an important source of funds. Ford himself said that he realized $24,700,000 from car and parts sales, saved $28,000,000 by cutting down inventory and speeding deliveries,* cashed $7,900,000 worth of Liberty bonds, and procured $6,700,000 from the sale of by-products and collections from foreign countries. With a cash reserve of $20,000,000 this amounted to $87,300,000, and Ford needed $58,000,000 or less. In April he paid his debts in full and had cash on hand.[39]

---

* The schedules Kanzler had set up, synchronizing the arrival of materials used in production with the productive process, and that process in turn to shipments, were the basis of savings on inventory. The acquisition of the D.T. & I. at this time helped to insure the promptness of shipments. H. L. Maher in his *Reminiscences* describes the general process. Utilizing the D.T. & I., Ford shortened the period during which goods were in transit, cutting the amount tied up in inventory from $60,000,000 to $20,000,000. As already stated, by paying suppliers with 60-90 day trade acceptances, Ford was able to collect on completed cars by the time bills for the materials used in their construction were due.

6.

The "panic" was over. It had sharply slapped down a brash young industry, but with more of a shock to its egotism than to its fundamental well-being. In the period 1920–1921, only six firms went out of business for good, while seventeen new ones started up. These were fairly normal statistics for deaths and births. Most companies went through a healthful period of pruning and reorganization. Some cancelled welfare and profit-sharing activities, and some, like the Willys companies, faced difficulties that had been intensified by the depression. Many had expanded plant facilities and laid out high-priced inventories on the assumption that prosperity would endure. They took severe losses, which temporarily crippled some, but nearly all survived.[40]

Ford had emerged triumphant, improving his stature as a folk hero. Technologically he profited also, clearing his factories during the six-week shutdown of junk and obsolescent machines, and improving the methods and layout. His handling of the office problem was in contrast both cruel and inept. An orderly reorganization such as Kanzler and Edsel could have conducted would have benefited the company immensely. Ford may have lopped $2,000,000 of the company payroll, but it was by smashing and hacking, and not in accordance with a constructive plan. Here he completely missed the opportunity which General Motors seized and developed under Alfred P. Sloan, Jr.

It has been said of the 1920–1921 depression that labor in the main paid for it; and in the case of the Ford Motor Company, labor and the dealers helped Ford through his difficulties. The great force of more than 55,000 men at Highland Park and the Rouge was for the most part sent home, and lost its wages for that period. While there were no cuts in pay, individuals were often assigned to lower paying jobs. Those affected were superintendents, foremen, and office workers; in no instance the run of factory employees.[41]

During this period of crisis, or immediately after it, Ford parted with other executives than Klingensmith, as well as with workers. Among them were some of his most widely known lieutenants; others were relatively obscure. The departures of Klingensmith and Turrell have already been noted; even before they left, Charles A. Brownell, in charge of advertising, had been dropped. Warren C. Anderson, Ford European representative, was recalled and discharged late in January.

Dean Marquis went at about the same time, and with him the vital role of the Sociological Department. Finally, Hubert E. Hartman, Assistant Secretary and General Attorney, resigned about the middle of February and William S. Knudsen followed him on the 28th of that month.

Some of these men, like Wills, Hawkins, and Lee in 1919, had shown an independence displeasing to Ford. Now in full control of his great enterprises—motor cars, tractors, extended parts manufacture at the Rouge, and the outlying railroads, mines, timber tracts, mills, glass plants, and village industries which he was integrating into one vast operation—Ford was impatient with individualists and humanitarians.

Klingensmith had shown an independence that Ford disliked, and Lord Perry believed that the industrialist was also jealous of the treasurer's influence over Edsel, whom he had taught the business routines of the company. Ford wanted no one closer to Edsel than he. Again, Klingensmith had frankly expressed the opinion that the Company should accept a loan, and according to Liebold, Ford regarded him as too much a banker's man. He also suspected him of being particularly friendly with New York Jewish bankers—"He was half Jewish, you know," Liebold added in making this point.[42]

The exit of the redoubtable William S. Knudsen, seems to have reflected dissatisfaction on both sides. Ford objected to some of Knudsen's personal habits; Knudsen found that Ford was countermanding his orders or telling Ford employees and officials to ignore them. He had no objection to Ford's controlling his own company, but resented the method, and felt that he must protest or quit. He didn't want to quarrel with Ford, but "I can't avoid it if I stay, and I can't stay and keep my self-respect." According to Liebold, the precipitating incident involved Sorensen. Edsel directed Knudsen to go to Europe, apparently to oversee Ford activities there. Sorensen felt that European affairs should be under his direction, appealed to Ford, who spoke to Knudsen, and the latter left.*

Others who were discharged, like Brownell, Anderson, and Turrell, were apparently regarded as lacking the vigor and originality that Ford

* Kanzler gives a version of the actual discharge which shows Ford deputing the task to others. Kanzler relates that he was summoned to Fair Lane, where he found Ford ill, with a fever of 102°. The manufacturer told him to discharge Knudsen. Kanzler protested, pointing out the Dane's high abilities. Ford said at length: "I see that you don't want this job—I'll give it to Sorensen—he'd love to fire Knudsen." In the end, Sorensen and Kanzler sought out Knudsen together and told him he was discharged. Kanzler, however, later returned, told Knudsen that he objected to the manner of the discharge, wanted him to know that he had challenged its wisdom, and was sorry that Knudsen was leaving.

demanded. For while he wanted men who would carry out his orders, he also demanded alertness, resourcefulness, and energy. The men he kept had such qualities, and the best of them, if told to do so, could develop and administer large and complicated projects with high skill. But they were deferential to Ford's wishes, and made every effort to carry them out promptly and triumphantly.

The discharge of the executives was unnecessarily arbitrary and even cruel. W. C. Anderson wrote Edsel a letter which shows his deep hurt at the manner in which he was treated, and indicates the general atmosphere in which others left. Anderson had been an employee for sixteen years, then was summoned from his European post abruptly.

When I received the cable to report, at once [he wrote to Edsel], at the factory in Detroit I was very much surprised to note Mr. Liebold's name at the foot of the message, as this is the first time, in my many years of service, that I had ever received an order from anyone but an executive of the organization. Then, upon my arrival in Detroit, to have been shifted around from one to another, finally to receive my instructions from Mr. Ryan was more than I could understand. Not one time during my stay did I see Mr. Ford (appreciating your position, I felt it was impossible to see you), and I want to go on record as saying that I feel I have been treated anything but fairly in my leave-taking.

It was no easy task for me to give up my friends and go to a strange country, but I did, and I gave the Company the very best that was in me while in Europe and left no stone unturned to further its interests while there . . . and in leaving it seems to me that it would have been fitting and proper to have been accorded the same courteous consideration that I have always been shown in the past. I feel that I should have been at least granted an interview with Mr. Ford personally.

Anderson, Klingensmith, and probably Knudsen received no bonuses. A cold letter from Liebold to Klingensmith explained that they were a matter for the company officers to decide, and that as he had left before the time of their distribution to executives, "we cannot recognize that you are entitled to a bonus." [43]

Ford was to have occasion to regret the departure of some of his executives; Hawkins and Knudsen, in particular, were to play vital roles in the rise of General Motors. In the struggle between the Ford and the Chevrolet which developed in the middle 'twenties Ford may well have thought bitterly of his break with Knudsen. But in 1921, he was following his deepest instincts and his own interpretation of his past experience. He was working toward the concentration of power, to be exercised by his own intuitive judgment. He wanted a responsive organization, a smooth-running company unimpeded by brilliant individualists. While he did not consciously shut out contributions from others, in practice he himself was tending to supply the ideas and the chief decisions.

VII

THE LINCOLN STORY

In the autumn of 1921, when Highland Park was breaking production records and the Model T was once more in high demand, Henry Ford became aware of a crisis in the affairs of another firm, the Lincoln Motor Company. Headed by two Detroiters of reputation, Henry M. Leland and his son Wilfred, the organization had launched its new car, the Lincoln, and maintained production for more than a year, only to be caught in financial entanglements that threatened to throw the company into a receivership.

The tale of the Fords and the Lelands is difficult to recount. Throughout a conflict of testimony, with overtones of confusion, impedes the effort to tell an objective story. Even on the question of how Ford became interested there is disagreement, the Ford account varying sharply from the Leland.

Let us begin with the Ford version. According to this, William B. Mayo, the Ford chief engineer, was approached late in October, 1921, by Harold H. Emmons, attorney for the Lincoln Company. (Emmons will be remembered as the chief of procurement for aircraft engines, including the Liberty, during World War I.) He outlined to Mayo the desperate condition of his company, pointed out that the Lincoln car was superior in design, workmanship, and performance, and that the Lincoln plant was admirably laid out and equipped. He stressed the personal tragedy which now threatened the Lelands: the loss of their factory, impairment of reputation, and personal bankruptcy, for both had signed notes for large sums. A disaster for Henry Leland, now seventy-eight, might be final, and would be a disaster for Detroit and the automotive world. Emmons appealed for Ford's aid, and Mayo promised to lay the facts before his employer.

He soon reported that there was little prospect for assistance; but

171

shortly afterward Emmons, who relates the following incident, encountered Henry Ford on the street near the Grand Central Station in New York. "Harold," said the industrialist, "I'm glad you're here. I've been thinking about this Lincoln business. Frankly, I can't see why I should have anything to do with it." Emmons remonstrated vigorously, and Ford, impressed, finally remarked: "Well, I'll think it over."

Edsel Ford later said that his father discussed the matter with him "three or four times," but "never seriously." On reflection, Ford must have perceived attractive possibilities: to intervene would be a dramatic act, and he loved the dramatic; and were he to acquire the Lincoln company, he could offer the public both a cheap, reliable car for the masses and a luxury car for the few. Also, he could not have forgotten that nine months earlier he himself had faced a financial crisis. However, he took no action until after the Lincoln Company had gone into a receivership.

According to the Fords, the Lelands then came to Fair Lane to discuss their problems. Ford was still inclined to take no action. However, his wife had overheard much of the conference. Edsel Ford says that she had just received a letter from Mrs. Wilfred C. Leland asking for aid. After the visitors had left she took up their cause. "Can't you do something to help them?" she demanded. "It's a shame that all Detroit should stand by and see that company wrecked."

Clara also spoke to Edsel, knowing his interest in quality cars and his readiness to support any cause, especially in the industry, that he considered in the public interest.* By the time the Ford executives met for lunch the following day, Edsel had talked with a number of them. He brought up the matter of the Lelands. His father asked if Edsel and the others thought the Ford Motor Company should take over the Lincoln. Edsel replied that they "would like to."

"Like to, nothing!" retorted Ford. "The question is, will we or won't we?"

"Tell the Lelands to come out and talk it over," suggested Edsel.[1]

The Leland version, as given by Wilfred C. Leland in 1955, is that he and his father knew nothing of Emmons's talks with Mayo and Ford. They themselves had confessedly approached Ford in July, hop-

---

* According to J. Bell Moran (letter to authors, Dec. 6, 1956), it was Edsel, with the support of his mother, who was responsible for the Ford interest in the Lincoln Company. Moran quotes Edsel (who played golf with him) as saying: "Father made the most popular car in the world; I would like to make the best car in the world."

ing that he would make a loan to the Lincoln company, or purchase one of its properties. He had refused to do either.* However, they became aware that Ford's interest had been aroused when in September he paid two visits to their country home at Lake Angelus, one on the 10th, the other the following week. He was told of the situation of the Lincoln Company, which the Lelands regarded as sound, but threatened by a group of their directors. Ford merely remarked: "Well, when you get through with those fellows, come and see me." Mrs. Wilfred Leland, her husband believed, wrote no letter.† After the receivership had been declared, the Lelands were working on a plan for a loan, and approached Ford among others. Then came a telephone call from him, asking them to come to Highland Park.²

No matter which version is accepted, Ford had taken a step which was to alter profoundly the lives of the Lelands, and to have important effects upon the now expanding Ford empire.

2.

In Detroit, or wherever in the United States men worked with automobiles, the figure of Henry M. Leland loomed as a symbol of the industry's growth, for he had been both a distinguished business leader and an apostle of high mechanical standards. For twenty years he had set these in the manufacture of engines, and for sixteen in that of cars.

Actually, Leland at seventy-eight linked three generations of technological progress in America. As the youngest child of a Vermont teamster who reared a family of seven under rugged conditions, he had become a tool-maker in the old Springfield, Massachusetts, armory, in the Colt factory at Hartford, and in the Brown and Sharpe plant in Providence, where he rose to high executive responsibility. Moving to Detroit, he became head of his own factory, and in the eighteen-nineties evolved the precision methods which made possible the Columbia chainless bicycle. Finally, he manufactured engines for Oldsmobile, and in 1904 captained the newly formed Cadillac Company, successor to the Henry Ford Company which Ford left in 1902. Under his leadership the Cadillac in England twice won the Dewar Trophy for auto-

---

* This was in accord with Ford's usual practice of refusing to interfere in similar situations, even when they involved close friends or relatives.
† Although the Fords preserved most significant letters received by them, including one from Mrs. Wilfred Leland written on May 23, 1922, no letter written by her in late 1921 has been found.

motive excellence. His feat in 1908, when from three disassembled
Cadillacs, their parts mixed with other surplus parts, he reassembled
three complete cars which ran successfully for five hundred miles,
astonished the mechanical world.[3]

After the purchase of Cadillac by Durant in 1909, Leland and his son
Wilfred continued to operate the company as a division of General
Motors. As its president, the older Leland introduced the first fully
successful self-starter and all-electric system in 1912, and in 1914 the
first 90° V-8 engine to appear in an American automobile. When in
1917 Durant refused to permit the division to manufacture the new
Liberty engine, the Lelands left General Motors and founded the Lincoln Motor Company (August 29, 1917) to produce them. The appearance of the Lincoln car in 1920 demonstrated the persistence of Leland's
capacity as a manufacturer. It is significant that two outstanding quality cars of America today were both originally brought out by him.[4]

Wilfred C. Leland, associated with his father for twenty-five years,
had served as Vice President and General Manager of Cadillac for eight
years, and of the Lincoln Company for four.[5]

In addition to his professional eminence, recognized in 1916 by his
election as president of the Society of Automotive Engineers, Henry
M. Leland had won distinction as a civic leader. As president of the
Detroit Citizens' League, he helped to effect a number of electoral, edu-
cational, and court reforms. He shared two convictions with Henry
Ford: that both tobacco and intoxicating liquor were evils.[6]

Unlike other firms producing Liberty engines during the war, the
Lincoln Motor Company took its first contract (for 6000 units, August
31, 1917, two days after incorporation) with no other assets than a
factory site and the technical and administrative skill of its officers.
However, many Cadillac employees joined the Lelands, and their
new venture had the confidence both of bankers, who with the stockholders provided $2,000,000, and of the Government, which advanced
$10,000,000. One reason for the large outlay was Henry M. Leland's
conviction that intensive machine tooling would insure highest quality
and eventually the greatest possible volume of production.[7]

Undoubtedly he was right, and had the war lasted six months longer
the Lelands would have gone far toward paying for their plant, although it was erected in a period of high prices, high wages, and

scarcity of materials.* But the contract was terminated in January, 1919, with 6500 engines completed.[8]

The company was thus left with a considerable indebtedness, its plant, and 6000 employees. Unlike Ford or Packard, it could not convert overnight to the manufacture of motor cars. However, the Lelands decided when peace came that they would produce an automobile, and began work on the Lincoln car. They now pushed this with all possible vigor. On January 26, 1920, they formed a new corporation, the Lincoln Motor Company of Delaware, to produce the model, and elected officers. It accepted the "property, business, and other assets" (with the debt, scaled down by the Government) of the Lincoln Motor Company of Michigan, the assets being set at $5,237,033; and issued new stock. This, subscribed practically on issue, brought in about $6,500,000. The company at once turned to the difficult task of re-tooling for the manufacture of a car. Some $4,249,000 for machinery and $1,750,000 for special machine tools had been expended before the first car was delivered on September 16, 1920.† These were large sums, swelled by Henry M. Leland's insistence on thoroughness of equipment, and the high prices prevalent in the boom period of 1919–1920. Had prosperity continued, such outlays might not have been crucial; but although the outlook in the industry had been bright in January, it had darkened by September. Further financing was necessary, and on September 22 the officers were authorized to borrow $3,700,000. In April and July, before production began, quarterly dividends of $1.25 a share had been declared. These added about $400,000 to the company's obligations. The October dividend was wisely deferred.[9]

Public enthusiasm for the unborn Lincoln had been marked; early in September the company held 1000 orders. The finished car, exhibited in August and shipped the following month, as a mechanism justified

* The original "bogey cost" per engine was fixed by the Government at $6087. Fifteen per cent of this was paid the manufacturer as profit ($913.05). He also received 25 per cent of the difference between bogey and actual cost—e.g., if he manufactured engines for $4000, he would receive $522 in addition to 15 per cent. However, in Dec., 1917, the bogey cost was reduced to $5000, and on July 31, 1918, to $4000, while profit was fixed at 12½ instead of 15 per cent. The Lelands produced no engines under the $6087 schedule, and only 1064 under the $5000 one. However, had they maintained an output of 1500 motors a month and had the war continued to July, 1919, they would have completed 15,000 units, for a total profit of $10,000,000, with additional profits on spares. (See Hughes Report, 906,907.)

† While its machine tool equipment was impressive, the company by no means made the complete automobile. Like other producers, it depended on suppliers, who furnished axles, gears, brakes, frames, bodies, lighting and ignition, and other parts.

the high popular expectations, but the body, lacking style, was a bitter disappointment to the sales manager and the dealers. The unattractive appearance of the car, the slowness of production, and the deepening depression, caused cancellations; in the remaining three and a half months of the year only 752 cars were sold. Nevertheless, with factories closing their doors and the demand for automobiles falling sharply, the sale was creditable. The early months of 1921 continued to show a poor market, but in April, after a Lincoln had won the Los Angeles-Phoenix contest, the factory was producing 400 cars—still too low a number.

What happened in the ensuing months is in question. The Lelands picture a strong upsurge in manufacturing and sales. They point out that in September they had 151 dealers, and in that month Henry M. Leland told his dealers in convention: "We've turned the corner. From now on, it's forward!" The majority of his fellow directors did not agree. Led by Dr. Fred T. Murphy, a nephew of William H. Murphy, they saw the situation worsening rather than bettering: * the company was selling too few cars, continuing to need financing, and showing no prospect of a happy future. Ralph C. Getsinger, the Lincoln sales manager, indicated in 1956 that the situation was not so favorable as the Lelands asserted, but was susceptible of improvement as attractive custom-made bodies were supplied.[10] †

The Lelands, supported by William T. Nash, the company treasurer, and to an extent by G. Hermann Kinnicutt, whose firm, Kissell-Kinnicutt, had marketed the company stock in 1920, argued that with modest additional funds, sales in volume could be assured, with a profit. The debt could then gradually be paid off. In contrast, Dr. Murphy asserted that the company required a comprehensive program of refinancing. At a directors' meeting on October 10, 1921, Wilfred Leland proposed to sell certain company properties and outstanding bonds. His pro-

---

* William H. Murphy, chief investor in the original Cadillac company, was a director of Lincoln along with John Trix and Joseph Boyer (long president of the Burroughs Adding Machine Co.). Dr. Murphy became a Lincoln stockholder and director, says J. Bell Moran, son-in-law of W. H. Murphy, about July, 1921, at his uncle's request, relinquishing a directorship in another automobile company (letter to the authors, March 19, 1956). W. H. Murphy supported his nephew.

† Getsinger (*Reminiscences*) says that the dealers were unanimous in condemning the first Lincoln bodies—"They were pre-World War I Cadillac designs." He remonstrated with H. M. Leland, who admitted he was unqualified to pass on body design, and told Getsinger to remedy the situation. The latter ordered bodies from Judkins, Fleetwood, Brunn, and others, and finally arranged for Brunn to design an entire Lincoln line. But deliveries were sporadic up to the receivership, and were not made in volume until some months after Ford bought the company.

posals were blocked, and a committee appointed to investigate the possibilities of refinancing. It reported on the 20th, to no good effect. Kinnicutt, however, asked for further time to work out a plan he had devised. The Lelands were also active, leaving Detroit on November 5 for New York with Henry R. Platt, attorney for an interested Chicago bank, to seek a large loan. At a meeting of the Lincoln directors on November 8 a government claim, dated November 4, chiefly for taxes, was noted. Platt reported that he and the Lelands had failed to procure a loan. Wilfred Leland vainly renewed his proposals to sell company properties. Murphy pointed out that there was apparently now no hope of re-financing, for Kinnicutt, while urging by telegram that a receivership be avoided, said nothing about a loan. Over the protests of the Lelands and Nash a resolution was passed stating that the operations of the company "have been and are now conducted at a substantial loss," and asking for a receivership.[11] *

3.

The Lelands did not accept this action as final defeat. They announced that they had opposed the receivership, would attempt to buy and revitalize the company, and would reimburse both creditors and stockholders ($50 a share). The last step was a *sine qua non* with the Lelands. "I didn't want to die with people saying that they had lost money through me," declared Henry M. Leland later.

There were two possibilities before them. One was to obtain a loan with which they could buy the company at a receiver's sale, and finance it until operations, now all but suspended, could be resumed and made profitable. The second, less desirable in their view, was to find another person or company able and willing to buy the Lincoln properties, who would permit the Lelands to operate them, as they had under General Motors, and from profits reimburse both creditors and stockholders. Obviously, the second possibility assumed a remarkable disinterestedness on the part of the hypothetical buyer.[12]

* For a more detailed account of the Leland-Murphy clash, see Note 11. There is no doubt that cars were being produced at a loss, and that the insufficient volume of sales was responsible. Walter T. Jacobowski, who was a Lincoln purchasing agent in 1920–1921, in his *Reminiscences* states: "They were losing money on every car they sold," and "It wasn't production that was holding us back; it was sales." Getsinger's testimony agrees with these statements. Both he and Harold J. Robinson (*Reminiscences*), who was also at that time with Lincoln, note that about Nov. 1, 1921, H. M. Leland reduced the regular hours of workers from 50 to 30, showing that production was slowed down to match a low sales volume. The time of year was of course also a factor, as the active selling season had passed.

When Ford appeared, he seemed to have the resources and the generosity required. Was not the Model T selling as never before? Was not Ford the father of the five dollar day, an evangelist with a gospel of business service, a professed friend of the Lelands? Did not his altruistic ideas on village industries, Muscle Shoals, and war profits make stimulating discussion throughout the nation?

According to a statement drawn up by Wilfred Leland on March 8, 1923 (for possible distribution to Lincoln stockholders), he and his father at once began to consult "men and groups of men of large financial responsibility" who might work with them. He states that their proposals "created undisguised interest" in several quarters (unnamed). Ford was included among those whom the Lelands proposed to consult, and, apparently on their initiative, a meeting with him was arranged at some time between November 8 and 14.* This was undoubtedly the conference overheard by Clara Ford. Wilfred says that Ford was "manifestly impressed," but merely promised that within a few days he would send someone to confer with them.

However, on the following afternoon, says Leland, Ford telephoned and asked him and his father to come to Dearborn. There the two found a group of Ford executives assembled, among them Mayo, Sorensen, Kanzler, and P. E. Martin. Ford asked Wilfred Leland to recount the events leading to the receivership, and the latter did so. He felt that his listeners were "manifestly impressed" with the unusual opportunity the Lincoln situation offered. Ford himself took a positive stand. "Your troubles are over," he said in effect. "We are going to work out a wholly satisfactory situation." Edsel Ford refers to this meeting in a statement, saying that "we agreed to go into the matter in detail at once," and that a series of conferences followed. These, he says, first concerned the Treasury claim of November 4. But by his account the Fords soon held out hopes for the payment in full of legitimate creditors and for a plan "to give all parties a dividend on their investment." [18]

Concerning other details of what followed there is sharp disagreement. Wilfred Leland states that he and his father continued to meet with financial groups in Chicago, Pittsburgh, New York, and else-

* In a letter to Ford, May 23, 1922 (Acc. 6, Box 276), Wilfred stated that the meeting took place the day the receivership was voted; in his 1923 statement he indicates it was later, and in a Chronology he prepared in Aug., 1924 (copy given to authors) he fixes the date as Nov. 14. It does not greatly matter which date is taken.

where. He asserts that a tentative understanding had been reached with Ford, who would pay all creditors and all stockholders, "good and bad" —that is, the original purchasers of stock at $50 a share and any who had later bought shares on speculation for as little as $2 each. In 1931 Henry M. Leland told a somewhat more detailed story, which his son then adopted. He stated that he had continued to negotiate with others while Wilfred dealt with Ford, and finally received assurance of a loan (for $10,000,000, Wilfred said, and from Kissell-Kinnicutt), with which he personally could buy the company at a receiver's sale, and finance the resumption of manufacturing. He told Wilfred, who assured him that Ford wanted the plant. Henry M. Leland, he himself says, was at first not favorable to cooperation with Ford:

Then Mr. Ford came to see me. He sat down in a chair in front of me, his knees touching my knees. I told him I was going to buy the plant, but I had arranged a loan and was going to pay back these old stockholders. He moved both hands up and down in rapid fashion and pleaded with me to cooperate with him, stating, "Yes, I know you can get all the money you need to buy the plant, but if you borrow the money and do that it will take you years to earn enough profits to pay off the loan before you can even start to take care of the creditors and stockholders. I can do it right away; it would take you years."

"You run it for me," urged Ford. On consideration, both Lelands felt that this proposal represented a surer way than the loan of achieving what they wanted. There was also the possibility that if they did not cooperate with Ford he might bid against them. They decided to try to work out an arrangement with him. According to Wilfred Leland, they insisted on an explicit understanding of what should be done. He himself drew up an agreement which covered all the points on which he and his father insisted, including the payment of creditors and stockholders. This agreement he read aloud to Henry, Edsel, and Clara Ford, and Henry approved it in its entirety. Wilfred then remarked that the only remaining formality was to sign the statement. Ford protested at once: "Mr. Leland, that isn't necessary." His sole desire, he said, was to rehabilitate the company and put the Lelands in charge of it. He would bid strongly; if someone outbid him, and the Lelands could not work happily with the new owner, he would establish them in a separate firm. So emphatically did he speak that it seemed ungra-

cious to insist on a signed contract; besides, had the Lelands not worked
for years in General Motors on a purely oral understanding? Accordingly, they expressed their satisfaction with Ford's assurances.[14]

Edsel Ford has commented upon this stage of the negotiations, and
while his remarks are brief, they leave no doubt of his complete disagreement with important items in Wilfred's account. He states that
the Lelands had made several "visits down east before even approach-
ing us and were entirely discouraged with their efforts. As far as I can
remember no negotiations of any kind were discussed or considered
after we once stated we were interested. It was really a great relief to
the Lelands to feel that we would consider buying the plant, and *it
never was a question of considering our offer against any other offer.*"
(Italics ours.) Edsel admitted that the Fords stated "we would like to
take care of the merchandizing creditors" and hoped that "all parties
interested" would receive "a dividend on their investment," but denies
that any further pledge was made.[15]

For the Lelands, and for all who would like to have a clear record of
what happened, their reliance on verbal assurances was unfortunate.
Their sole evidence of the alleged promises lies in their own statements;
and the fact that Wilfred in 1923 failed to note any offer of a loan, and
that it was first cited by his father in 1931, is a singular fact which
indirectly supports Edsel's version of what occurred. No letter or other
written statement incorporates the pledges which the Lelands attribute
to Henry Ford, and in announcements before and immediately after
the sale, no outline of these pledges was offered.* Edsel firmly and on
numerous occasions denied any pledge to pay the stockholders.[16]

It must be pointed out that the agreement the Lelands ascribed to
Ford was almost incredibly generous, and did not tally with his past
actions. Although he constantly voiced a progressive attitude toward
labor, he had thus far exacted much from his workers for what he gave.
He had put severe pressure upon his dealers, had been quick to part
with able executives who questioned his methods or objectives. He had
bought out the minority stockholders to achieve absolute control. The
arrangement the Lelands describe was one which no other wealthy man

---

* Getsinger states that when Ford became a probable purchaser of the plant, Wilfred Leland
assured him that he had promised to repay both creditors and stockholders. This confirms the
Lelands' understanding of what had been promised, but of course does not indicate that this
was the Fords' understanding.

would have been likely to accept, and Ford as he had revealed himself was not the man to carry it out.

One observer took account of the situation as it existed in January, 1922, and made a prediction. Edwin G. Pipp in *Pipp's Weekly,* in an article confidently titled "The Passing of the Lelands," asserted that should Ford obtain the Lincoln plant, "it will become a Ford plant and not a Leland plant."

> There is no disposition to question Ford's intentions as to the Lelands now, but good intentions now will not be permitted to interfere with business success later.
>
> Ford's men can be depended upon to . . . put to use whatever there is good in the Lincoln designs and organization, but it will all be made over to conform to Ford methods, the method of having many stop watches held on men and push bosses speeding them up.
>
> The Lelands if they stick will find their desires overridden by young men placed there by the Fords for the purpose of getting production and not to pay too fine a regard for the feelings of others.
>
> It will be the passing of the Lelands.[17]

Pipp was of course both a knowledgable and a skeptical witness. His prophecy would soon be tested by events.

4.

The period from late December, 1921, when the role of the Fords as deliverers was definitely assumed, until the receiver's sale about six weeks later, was a honeymoon in this marriage of volume and precision manufacturing. All parties soon agreed that the first step should be to request Judge Arthur J. Tuttle of the United States District Court to fix a date for the sale. Tuttle had appointed the receiver, the Detroit Trust Company, and had authority to act.

At a meeting in Henry M. Leland's Detroit home, Emmons, acting for both the Lelands and the Fords, told Tuttle that Ford would make a minimum bid of $5,000,000, and pay all Lincoln creditors. Tuttle remarked that if all the creditors were to be paid, the minimum bid should be $8,000,000, and he later fixed it at that sum, saying that "when it comes to protecting the creditors I feel the duty rests with the judge to do it by form of decree rather than relying on statements made to him privately." He set the date of the sale as February 4, 1922.[18] The

New York Times of January 12 predicted that if necessary Ford would pay $11,000,000. Either figure was well above what others would have bid: Ralph Stone of the Detroit Trust later stated that a normal price would have been $5,000,000, although the Trust appraised the property at $9,490,811, and the Lelands claimed a much higher value.[19]

News stories during the month of January romanticized the sale. Ford was pictured as the rescuer of the Lelands. He was quoted: "It would be a stain against the motor car industry and against Detroit to permit outsiders to secure control of the Lincoln plant merely because the Lelands have been caught in a pinch." Ford called Henry M. Leland "one of the greatest motorcar men in America." He intimated that the Class A stockholders would be "protected." "These original purchasers bought Lincoln's stock because they believed in Henry Leland," he said. "I believe in him too."

By the day of the sale, a Saturday, friends of the two families, Lincoln and Ford employees, and the public all regarded the event as a happy one. Proceedings at the plant took on "the air of a festival." Henry M. Leland appeared with Mrs. Henry Ford, Ford and Mrs. Wilfred C. Leland made a pair, Edsel and Wilfred a third. The crowd which had assembled jubilantly cheered them and others. And when Emmons, who was known to be acting for Ford, bid $8,000,000, when no other bid was made and the sale was consummated, the spectators rushed up to the third floor of the building, formed a line and shook hands with Henry M. Leland, who was "visibly affected."

An announcement promptly issued stated that while the Lincoln Motor Company would be affiliated with the Ford company, "the executive personnel of the two concerns will be held separate and distinct, the management of the Lincoln company continuing with Henry M. and Wilfred C. Leland," as "insisted upon by Mr. Ford at the outset of negotiations."

At the first meeting of the new Lincoln Motor Company of Michigan, organized to take over the properties of the older firm, the independent status of the corporation was confirmed, although its shares were held by the Ford Motor Company. Officers were elected: Henry M. Leland, president; Wilfred C. Leland vice-president and general manager; and William T. Nash secretary and treasurer. Edsel as second vice-president and B. J. Craig as assistant secretary and treasurer represented the Ford interest. But by that time, in May, 1922, the

Lelands were already beginning to feel uneasy as to their position in the Ford organization.[20]

5.

When production was resumed on February 6 after almost three months, 241 cars were on hand in the plant. A work force had to be created and various changes made to bring the new company into alignment with other Ford activities.

According to Wilfred Leland, while he and his father were seeking aid in November, 1921, they had proposed to reduced the price of Lincoln cars. Such reductions were now made: specifically, the $5400 passenger car was priced at $4200, the $6000 model at $4900. A bank of sales orders totalling $2,000,000 accumulated in a few days. Again according to the younger Leland, with the use of only $250,000, production was lifted to thirty-five cars a day in the ensuing four months, with fifty a day and a profit of $10,000,000 a year in prospect.

Edsel Ford later gave a different version of conditions during this period. He felt that the company was a "very stagnant organization." The price for cars on hand had to be cut "in order that they might be moved," because their bodies were "obsolescent and old-fashioned." Getsinger confirms this version in the main—most of the cars on hand had the older, unattractive bodies. These were difficult to sell—during the receivership he had sold a few cars daily with custom-made bodies, but such bodies were coming in slowly.* Again, Edsel questioned the alleged production of thirty-five cars a day, pointing out that after plant enlargement and improvement the maximum production later, under Ford management, was only 40 cars a day, while profits at that volume ran from $5,000,000 to $6,000,000. Actually, what was done in the spring of 1922 was to realize the potential production of 30 cars a day which the factory had when reopened.[21] The maximum production for 1922 was reached in June, when shipments totalled 734.†

With the reopening of the plant, we again reach a chapter in Lin-

---

* Getsinger in the spring of 1956 stated that he had sold perhaps five cars a day during the receivership, paying running expenses, and keeping a small factory force. He thought that sales in the earlier fall had perhaps averaged 15 cars a day, and that at 20 operations might have become profitable.

† The minutes of the company, Feb. 21, 1921, show production then to have been put at 30 cars a day for 9 hours. It would have been potentially that after the reopening in Feb., 1922. An article, "Lelands Quit the Ford Lincoln Organization," *Automotive Industries*, XLVI, June 15, 1922, 1345, states that production was then "about 30" per day. For Ford June, 1922 shipments, see *Ford News*, II, June 15, 1923, 1.

coln history in which there is a disagreement as to exactly what happened. Ford officials immediately appeared in the factory; according to the Lelands they "overran" it. But these visits, according to Ford officials, had a double purpose. One, says Klann, was to observe Lincoln methods of operation, and to adapt some to Model T manufacture. Again, Sorensen, Martin, and Kanzler came on Ford's instructions to observe the plant and improve processes of manufacture.* In principle, the Lelands had agreed to changes if these were justified, and Ford executives quickly suggested a number. Liebold states that the axles of the 1922 Lincoln showed an undue tendency to break, and that Ford told Sorensen to employ AAA Ford steel in their manufacture. Henry M. Leland was outraged at the suggestion, says Liebold, but after a visit to the Ford laboratory, agreed to the change. The Lelands accepted Ford methods of accounting and purchasing, and Ford wage and employment practices. They resisted Ford plans for sales. Wilfred Leland and Getsinger both say that the two Fords promised to make existing Lincoln dealers the nucleous of sales activity, but that this arrangement was ignored by Ryan.† The latter felt that the Lincoln force was inadequate in size, should be merged with the larger Ford organization, and that Wilfred Leland in opposing the amalgamation was obstructive. In manufacturing, again, the Lelands, proud of their past accomplishments, resented suggestions for change, while Ford officials felt that changes were both helpful and inevitable.[22]

The reality of the situation should be emphasized. The Lelands had developed the Lincoln car, and firmly believed that its production and marketing should follow the patterns they had established. Ford, while respecting the Leland name and accomplishments, felt that with the car brought to its present stage of development, the Ford organization

---

* Getsinger says that the Ford officials assumed authority at once: on their first visit Martin ordered a call system taken out, and it was. Kanzler agrees that they "overran" the place: Ford had ordered a survey looking toward greater efficiency: "We are not going to throw away any more money on this company." Kanzler felt that the plant was outdated. "I remember the first thing I saw was a group of workers sawing off a piece of bar steel from which to machine a part. But they needed a number of parts, and why saw off one piece at a time? They could have done five at once." As to the adoption of Lincoln methods, Klann says that Ford adopted the Lincoln process of balancing the flywheel, and those of checking pistons and cylinders by weight.

† Getsinger argued that separate Lincoln salesrooms should be maintained in forty centers, because buying a Lincoln at a Ford agency was like buying expensive jewelry at a Five-and-Ten store. Henry and Edsel agreed, but Ryan told him the next day that it should be all Ford, and put that system into effect. However, Lincoln dealers were retained, and got adequate allotments of cars. Later, says Getsinger, Ryan changed to the system Getsinger had advocated, but by that time thought he had evolved it himself!

could improve both manufacture and sale. Actually, Ford resources and experience for any type of automotive work were much greater than those the Lelands commanded. The larger company's knowledge of raw materials and its ability to procure and use them effectively were greater. Its machine tool equipment was more varied and in general more modern, its technicians in this field more numerous than Lincoln's, and as ingenious if not more so. Its knowledge of factory layout and assembly methods was unequalled. Its metallurgical experts were more active and experienced than those the Lelands commanded. Its purchasing division was more effective, for to produce the Model T the Ford buyers had been forced to cut costs to the bone while preserving quality. Ford had a larger and more seasoned sales organization than the Lelands. Henry Ford was aware of these facts, and from his point of view he would have been a fool not to seek to improve the Lincoln plant. The Lelands never acknowledged the facts, tending to belittle or ignore them.*

We have evidence showing the two attitudes in clash. Wilfred Leland refers to the merging of departments and to orders by Martin and Sorensen; the latter are not specified: the point is that orders were alleged to have been given without consultation with the Lelands. Bourne, the Lelands' secretary, asserts that Ford officials ordered defective cylinders used, and that Henry M. Leland promptly commanded these parts to be destroyed. We have noted Getsinger's testimony as to the sales organizations. On the other hand, E. A. Walters of the Ford pressed steel department relates two incidents indicating Ford helpfulness and Leland resistance. He states that on one occasion Henry M. Leland informed P. E. Martin that the company supplying Lincoln hub caps had broken its master punch, a precision tool of special steel, and that production would be slowed for a week until the punch could be replaced. Martin told Walters to see what he could do; the latter checked the dimensions and the type of steel required, and in a day delivered a new punch to the amazed supplier, Ireland & Mathews. On another occasion Martin, at Ford's request, noted what steel stamped parts Lincoln was buying outside, then told Walters to plan a punch-press unit at Lincoln to make these. Walters drew up

* Such factors, and the incidents soon to be noted, have never been considered by authors like Keith Sward (*The Legend of Henry Ford*, New York, 1948), who simply follows the Leland version of what happened. Obviously, any attempt to get at the truth must consider all factors and attitudes.

his plans, procured an appointment with H. M. Leland, was kept waiting an hour, then explained the project to Leland, who "didn't like it." Martin took up the matter with him, and Leland said "No." [23]

The Leland attitude was that they were operating the plant, and would accept only such changes as they felt to be constructive. Manufacturing was Henry M. Leland's special province, he was doubtful if the Ford organization could contribute anything helpful, and had not Henry Ford stated that the Lelands were to be in control?

In contrast, Henry and Edsel Ford doubtless regarded "control" as something more elastic, with the stretch in their favor. The Lelands were now on salary. The Lincoln plant was a Ford, not a Leland property. "You run it for me." There are two parts to that sentence, and "for me" is not necessarily less important than "You run it." Knowing Ford, which way should we assume his mind was slanted? Pipp, familiar with his talk and acts, felt sure that the Lincoln factory would become a Ford and not a Leland plant. Ford would doubtless have agreed from the start to the extent that the plant should be improved in any way that Ford methods could improve it. He expected, as Liebold said later, that the Lelands would "line up" with the Ford organization. So did Martin, Kanzler, and Sorensen.[24]

We must bear both attitudes in mind. Wilfred Leland complained in 1924 that "the plant was over-run with men from your various departments." We have seen that these officials came at Ford's command, with what he considered a constructive purpose. Wilfred Leland pictures them as abrupt, indifferent to him and his father, and eventually rude and insolent.* It is clear that they assumed a certain authority and were persistent. Sorensen, says Liebold, went over to "kind of look things over and supervise their [the Lelands'] activities." Yet we have seen from Klann's account that Henry M. Leland was consulted on axle steel, that Martin acted on the hub-cap press only after Leland had told him about it, and that Ford's suggestion of setting up a unit for stamped parts was carried to the head of Lincoln and vetoed by him. Conferences on sales covered a long period, with Wilfred Leland taking a very active part. Thus there is ground for believing that the Leland insistence on their authority and methods may have helped to promote

* From Wilfred Leland's 1924 Chronology, while he clearly felt that there were too many Ford officials around, one gathers that for several months there were friendly conferences, especially with Edsel and Kanzler, and that the situation did not seem unpromising.

the insolence of which Wilfred finally complained. Certainly Sorensen would resent what he considered stupid obstruction, and was not to be awed by the Lelands. "The general impression is that you think yourselves exclusive," Wilfred himself quotes the Dane as saying. "You are no different from me or anyone else—no different from any other Ford plant." It would have been Sorensen's attitude. He did not see why Henry Ford should buy the Lincoln Motor Company only to have the Lelands put up a sign, "Keep out." His behavior was not tactful, but as he and other Ford officials saw the situation, the Lelands were drawing into the shell of their reputation and refusing sensible cooperation.[25]

The Lelands finally appealed directly to Henry Ford. As we have already seen, he was adept at subtly promoting conflicts, but disliked to be directly involved in them, and was doubtless evasive. Wilfred Leland says that Ford told him and his father that they were in full control of the plant, and that he would support them. He did not like to "remove" his men because it would "destroy their initiative," but he urged the Lelands to assert their authority. Bourne later testified that he told Henry M. Leland: "Mr. Leland, you mustn't let them do it. You are in charge here. Don't let them do it." What did not take place was an honest discussion of the situation, bringing out and reconciling the conflicting attitudes. The Lelands were concerned about their authority. Ford on the other hand did not encourage definitions of authority, and doubtless thought it healthy that Martin and Sorensen should crowd the Lelands. Things would work out. When Henry Leland complained to him that his force was a good one, but had never had a chance, Wilfred quotes Ford as saying, "The way to show that is to get production coming right." Edsel apparently tried to harmonize the situation, but to judge from his later comments, he found the Lelands difficult.[26]

About the middle of May several inconclusive conferences seem to have been held; then, on May 23, 1922, Wilfred Leland wrote a five-page letter to Henry Ford reviewing the situation. He reminded Ford of his public statements that the Lelands would control the plant, that his purpose in buying it was to aid them. "These assurances constitute a contract with the people," he insisted. "There are many fundamental reasons why they should be fulfilled one hundred per cent." He claimed credit for rebuilding the work force, for orders that exceeded production, for keeping costs down. (Ford officials would not have regarded these as mainly Leland accomplishments; they would have said that Ford reputation and Ford assistance had been vital.)

Leland now made a startling proposal. If Ford and Leland methods could not be harmonized, the Lelands would buy back the company "at the price paid for the same, plus a reasonable interest rate." * He closed with an emotional appeal: "The Lincoln car, as the finest in the world, and the Lincoln Company with its reputation for high quality, are the culmination of the life work of Henry M. Leland, myself and several of the men associated with us. While with all your vast interests the Lincoln may not be of great importance and may easily be swallowed up within the Ford organization, we assure you . . . that with us it is the most important thing in the world."

No reply was received to this letter, and conditions at the factory apparently continued difficult. On May 26 and 27, Leland wrote two more letters, in the second again urging the Fords to sell the plant.

Having had no reply to any of these communications, or any opportunity to see Ford, Wilfred Leland now drove to Fair Lane. Halted by the guard, he says that he merely smiled, saluted, and pushed on. He found Ford and talked with him for two hours, again urging him to sell the company back to the Lelands.

According to Wilfred, Ford replied: "Mr. Leland, I wouldn't sell the Lincoln plant for five hundred million dollars. I had a purpose in acquiring that plant." But, he continued, Leland had made good on production, and he, Ford, could perceive that the actions of Ford employees were "unjust." "I'll come over to the Lincoln plant with Edsel tomorrow morning," he promised. "We'll make the Lincoln an independent organization and you and your father will be in full control." Leland replied: "Very well, Mr. Ford. That is all we ask. If you do that, great things will be possible."

Ford came, but without Edsel, and, says Wilfred, reiterated his promises, assuring Henry M. Leland that he would spend two hours daily with him. This promise was never kept. Meanwhile the activity of Ford employees, with Sorensen in command, became more aggressive. "He gave orders," wrote Wilfred later to Ford, "with absolute disregard of our authority. . . . His actions seemed to confirm the statement of

---

* Wilfred Leland told the authors in 1955 that he hoped to get the money from Kissel-Kinnicutt. Getsinger says that he and the Lelands investigated the possibility of a loan, and that Budlong, the New York Lincoln dealer, thought he could arrange it.

one . . . high in authority in the Ford organization, that your chief of staff is retained by you largely for the purpose of applying drastic methods of making life unbearable for those whom it suits your purpose to eliminate."

The Lelands resisted, countermanding Sorensen's orders. At length he "sullenly withdrew," but on Saturday, June 10, Liebold and Mayo appeared,* informing Wilfred that they had been delegated by Ford to tell him and his father to leave the plant that afternoon. (Liebold says that only Wilfred was told to leave, but that his father at once resigned.) Mayo made an appointment for the Lelands in Ford's office on the following Monday, when, he promised, a full settlement would be made. Ford, says Wilfred Leland, did not keep the appointment, and after the vain promise of another interview, the Lelands heard nothing further from the Ford Motor Company except a routine request for the transfer of two shares of stock held by them.[27]

Most of the foregoing account is Wilfred's. There is no evidence but his as to his conversations with Ford, and Ford officials give a different version of what occurred, which we shall soon consider. But first we must note certain happenings during this period which relate to the creditors and stockholders of the former Lincoln Motor Company (of Delaware).

Soon after the sale of February 4, 1922, the Ford Motor Company began to receive inquiries from such stockholders. Some came to Henry Ford's office, more to Edsel's. Replies to these letters were discouraging. Even before the sale, on January 21, 1922, Edsel's office advised a young Canadian veteran that "Mr. Ford . . . does not think there will be anything left for the Lincoln stockholders when all the Company's debts are cleaned up, except that something may be done for the people who invested their money in stock when the company was organized, and also at the time of the sale of Class A stock." Most answers were less encouraging. Liebold, replying for Henry Ford from March 6 to May 2, 1922, simply stated with variations that "up to the present time no plan has been worked out for the purpose of taking care of the stockholders of the Lincoln Motor Company."[28]

Letters to the Lelands met with similar responses. Later Bourne, their secretary, deposed that he had answered these, signing the Le-

* Wilfred says Sorensen came with them; Liebold, and Getsinger, who saw them arrive but was not at the conference, say that he did not.

lands' names, and at Emmons's direction had offered no encouragement to anyone. One such letter quoted Wilfred Leland: "The stock lost its actual value when the company went out of existence at the Receiver's sale. . . . Anything that might be done to relieve the situation would be entirely gratuitous." Wilfred Leland later declared that neither he nor his father had ever signed such letters, and that they were entirely unaware of Bourne's replies. Emmons later stated emphatically that he had never told Bourne to sign the Lelands' names to letters, and never had advised him to keep any type of correspondence from them. He stated that he probably gave general instructions as to how letters from stockholders should be answered, and told Bourne to trouble the Lelands as little as possible, since they were busy with production problems, and to avoid phrasing which might be used by any stockholder as a basis for a claim for reimbursement against the Lelands personally.[29]

In Wilfred Leland's reproachful letters to Henry Ford in May, 1922, one might expect to find references to Ford's alleged promises to pay creditors and stockholders, but none exists. However, the omission should be considered in relation to Ford's actions with respect to the Lelands, Nash, and others in February and March, 1922.

On February 16 Henry M. Leland was seventy-nine years of age. A birthday dinner party was held for him at the Lincoln plant, and there Ford presented him with a check for $363,000. Bourne describes the event:

> There was quite a jubilation. Mr. Ford was very happy, and Mr. Henry Leland was very happy. They stood in front of the restaurant while the employees were all eating. Everybody was happy, because the rumor of that check had gone through the factory like a flash, quite naturally, and its implications were understood by everybody.
> When I got to Mr. Leland, I overheard Mr. Ford say to him, referring to the men standing by, "Show it to them, Mr. Leland, show it to them. Tell them that they are all going to get them just the same." Leland then produced the check which I had seen in his room before as the one Mr. Ford had given him.

Bourne's references to Lincoln employees—the excitement among them, the assurance that they would "get them just the same"—take meaning from the fact that many had bought stock in the old company. The $363,000 represented the par value of Leland's B shares—if he was being paid, they might be. Ford would undoubtedly have been sympathetic to the idea that workers holding stock should be reimbursed. Wilfred Leland later asserted that the check marked the beginning of repayment: he wrote Ford that "this was only the first installment of your agreement to repay all qualifying Lincoln stockholders." Edsel would have been quick to deny that. The Ford Motor Company later termed the payment to Leland a special one for services in starting Lincoln production under Ford control.[30]

A further presumption with respect to Ford's intentions was established in the Lelands' minds when payments of $206,349.19 were made on March 25, 1922, to Henry M. Leland, Wilfred C. Leland, and William T. Nash, representing a coverage by Ford of their obligations as guarantors of notes comprising part of the debt of the old company. The money of course went to creditors, and Wilfred Leland later held that this was a partial discharge of Ford's promise to pay all of them.

Thus it is understandable that the Lelands were hopeful in May, 1922, about both creditors and stockholders, whom they regarded as in process of being recompensed.* The process could not be rapid, government claims still remaining unsettled. Full payment of creditors was not made until March, 1923. However, there is no evidence that Ford officials shared the Leland view. None of them had encouraged the hopes of stockholders, and Liebold and Edsel were apparently of the opinion that the $8,000,000 paid for the Lincoln Motor Company at the receiver's sale discharged Ford's full legal obligation. Anything further he might do would be pure generosity.[31] †

Liebold has given the only description by a Ford representative of the departure of the Lelands. He simply states that Ford was irked by Wilfred Leland's efforts to see him (and, we may be sure, by his letters, if Ford read them). "He didn't want to be involved in their disputes

---

* In connection with stockholders, Getsinger relates that he was lunching with the Fords and Lelands in the spring of 1922, and Henry Ford said to the older Leland that Mrs. Ford had asked him what he was going to do about the stockholders. "You know what I told her? I told her if they would come out to Dearborn we'd give them a badge and put them to work." Apparently the Lelands took this as a joke.

† This attitude took account of the fact that Judge Tuttle had raised the upset price *in order to protect the creditors.* If the higher price was supposed to take care of them, why did Ford have an obligation? Thus his finally paying them was "an act of generosity."

John Trix, one of the important stockholders of Lincoln, reflects this opinion in a letter to W. H. Fisher, March 14, 1923 (unclassified material, Ford Archives): "Yes, you are correct about Henry Ford paying all the obligations of the endorsers and the material creditors of the Lincoln Motor Co. My share of the endorsement was $360,000.00, and I still have at stake the common stock and the A stock. If he would come once more, I would just about be even with the game, *but of course he is not obliged to pay this, any more than he was obliged to pay the endorsers and creditors, whom he did pay.* (Italics ours)

over there. He thought our organization could handle that, and if Mr. Leland didn't want to line up with them, that was going to be his problem, not ours." Edsel evidently came to the same conclusion as his father. In December, 1923, he replied courteously to an appeal that the Lelands be taken back, or aided to start anew for themselves, with an assurance of his "profound admiration" for Henry M. Leland. "However, the suggestion that these men be taken back into the Lincoln Motor organization, or financed in a new venture, is something we cannot consider. We have in the past endeavored to cooperate with Mr. Leland, and after several months of close association found that it was impossible to agree on business methods and procedure, and this association cannot be renewed."

Liebold, Kanzler, and Edsel thus agreed on the fundamental difficulty as the Fords saw it. Wilfred's letters and his efforts to force Ford may well have been a determining factor. "Ford had a lot of respect for Henry Leland but not too much for his son," says Walter Wagner, head of the tool section for Lincoln. The industrialist was now willing to listen to Sorensen and others who felt that Wilfred was a "fussbudget." Finally he told Mayo and Liebold, says the latter: "Well, you'd better go over and tell Wilfred that we don't want him any more." Here he was of course within his rights, and acting as did other employers when they felt that they were being shut out of the management of their own property.[32]

Was there more in the situation than a failure to harmonize? Had Ford never intended to keep the Lelands? * It is possible, but improbable. The evidence indicates that Ford expected Martin, Kanzler, and Sorensen, working with the Lelands, to bring about a satisfactory relationship. In the case of William B. Stout, important in the story of Ford aviation (see Chapter IX), such an adjustment was made, and Stout remained with Ford for many years. He adapted himself to the merger; when the Lelands failed to adapt, Ford wanted no more of them.

---

* There were rumors that Ford "got even" with Henry M. Leland because he felt that when he was chief engineer of the Henry Ford Company, Leland had prejudiced Murphy against him, and interfered with his work. Wilfred Leland noted such reports in his letter to Ford on March 19, 1924, and denied that his father was responsible "for your dismissal in 1902" (Ford of course was not dismissed), although there is evidence that indirectly H. M. Leland was a cause for the break. (See interview with C. T. Bush, June 9, 1955, Ford Archives). Liebold says that Ford felt Leland to have been responsible, but if he nursed a grudge he had apparently dropped it, for his many professions of interest in the Lelands, and his acts, indicate sincerity.

So Pipp was proved a good prophet. The only flaw in his prediction was that it came true much sooner than he expected.

6.

Once the Lelands left the Lincoln Motor Company, Edsel and Kanzler took their places, Edsel showing a keen interest in the Lincoln car. There were no discharges of key Lincoln officials: with few exceptions these remained at their posts. For a time production fell off, but with the early months of 1923 it began to climb, rising from 5503 for 1922 to 8541 for 1926.

The chief reasons for the drop after the departure of the Lelands were a further integration of the Lincoln plant with Ford methods, and new construction. Both Sorensen and Edsel had ideas for improvements, the former in the factory, the latter in styling. As early as July, 1922, Lincoln cylinder blocks were being produced at the Rouge, while all aluminum parts were soon turned out there. In September, 1922, a large plant addition was begun, and was operating by the fall of 1923. Conveyor systems for some operations were installed. In November, 1922, Edsel was studying the car, and suggested various changes to improve its comfort and appearance.

Hardly had the Lelands left when Lincoln was "discontinued as an operating company, and all matters pertaining to the manufacture and sale of Lincoln cars, parts, etc." were handled by Ford executives. Ford dealers took over from the Lincoln sales force, and Ryan in September was directing his branches to select men able to handle the new de luxe product, and to provide prompt and efficient service to owners.[33] *

There was never a question of lowering standards; rather, with Edsel watching operations, the effort was to raise them. *American Machinist* in December, 1923, published the first of three articles on "What Ford Has Done at the Lincoln Plant," and the conclusion was that "not only has quality been maintained but . . . many refinements and improvements have been added." The articles reported a progressive assembly, with conveyors, a decrease in employees because of better planning and delivery of parts, and the finishing of bodies "under ideal conditions and strict supervision." While the account reflected to no small extent the attitude of the new owners, Jacobowski, then in purchasing, states that quality was "maintained plus," adding: "They

* Many of the former Lincoln dealers became Ford dealers.

were getting better specifications. I was writing these for purchasing."

For custom-made bodies Edsel enlisted special manufacturers: Judkins, Brunn, Le Baron, Willoughby, Dietrich, Locke. While prices for ordinary Lincolns (which were styled, as Getsinger had arranged, by Brunn) ranged from $3300 to $4900, those for the special types ran from $4600 to $7200. The effort was to adapt these to "quantity" production—that is, to manufacture up to several hundred of a model; and the body-makers were paid a high price, say $9000, for a product that could be turned out successfully in numbers. Such cars were described to branch offices in company sales letters, and orders invited in advance.

Ford-made Lincolns, built to exacting specifications and so finely machined as to working parts that Litle, chief engineer of the plant, boasted that they required no period of breaking in at low speeds, won increasing prestige in the United States and abroad. The New York and Detroit police departments used them for speed cars; English experts commented favorably on their speed, smoothness of operation, and novel gadgets (the cigarette lighter among them), and prizes for high quality were awarded them in centers such as Madrid and Milan.[34]

7.

After leaving in June, 1922, the Lelands began to feel concern for the payment of the creditors and stockholders of the former Lincoln company. According to Wilfred Leland, he eventually discussed these matters with the Ford legal staff and found a disposition to deny any obligation with respect to either group. He protested, insisting that Ford's pledge to pay all creditors had been made to Judge Tuttle before the receiver's sale. In any case, Ford paid the creditors in March, 1923, but asserted that the act was voluntary. Altogether, he paid $4,018,699.21, including the $363,000 presented to Henry M. Leland—a total of $12,018,699.21 with the purchase price of the company added. These payments won golden opinions in the industrial world. One payee wrote:

We want to take the occasion to express our sincerest thanks for your action in settling the balance of the obligations of the Lincoln Motor Company of Delaware. As far as we know, this is the first time any such action has been taken; at least on any . . . such magnitude. By this action of yours we feel that you have done more for the morale of business in general at one stroke, than could be accomplished by all the preaching in the world.

Automotive Industries reported that Ford's deed "has gained for him the esteem of the whole industry." On the other hand, *Pipp's Weekly* remarked: "This is in keeping with the pledge given by Henry Ford when he was permitted to buy the Lincoln plant for $8,000,000, and given by his representative to Judge Tuttle."

Ford's admirers, obviously encouraged by the industrialist himself, extolled his act in newspaper, magazine, and book publications, often with startling exaggerations of what had been done.[35]

The Lelands now began to press for the payment of stockholders. The first gun in what may be called their active campaign was a long public letter from Wilfred Leland to Ford, dated March 19, 1924. In this he reviewed the entire history of the Ford-Leland relationship, and stated that in 1923 he had told Ford officials: "No man ever made a more emphatic agreement than Henry Ford made to pay the qualifying stockholders. I shall leave no stone unturned to compel him to fulfill that agreement."

Leland's letter was published in the *Detroit Saturday Night* of April 5, 1924, and he may have hoped that by acquainting the public with the Leland claims, and bringing to bear the force of public opinion, he would constrain Ford to act. There are indications that Ford had considered the matter; Pipp on March 3, 1923 reported that he was doing so. Winnowing out the original stockholders from the speculators, conceded Pipp, was no easy task. He concluded: "Much as we disagree with Mr. Ford on many things we are going to give him credit for acting in good faith in this for we know he has men at work on it, and that they have a difficult task to perform."

But in this matter Pipp was not a good prophet. Time passed, and Ford took no action. The very effort to constrain him may have been self-defeating, for he had already proved stubborn under pressure, as with war profits. Moreover, as we have seen, he had now passed the problem to others, and they were asking: "What is Mr. Ford *compelled* to do?" They would of course do the minimum, and Ford would support them.

The Lelands formally acquainted the stockholders with their position and intentions. They engaged two attorneys, William Henry Gallagher and Kenneth Stevens, who were willing to work in part on a contingent fee basis. Some 1,800 stockholders were found to participate in a suit. "Each stockholder," the Lelands wrote, "will thus bear his just share of the expense if a recovery is had and will not be liable for any expense whatever unless a recovery is had in his behalf." [36] The suit was filed November 16, 1927, in the state circuit court at Pontiac. It asked for the repayment in full of all Class A and Class B stockholders. Gallagher, who led the attack for the Lelands, had already tilted successfully with Ford in the Sapiro case. He admitted that no written evidence existed of an agreement to pay the stockholders. "However," he noted, "we have witnesses to the fact that a verbal promise was made before Mr. Leland would consent to the sale of the Lincoln company to the Fords.* . . . This case will be largely based upon the word of Henry Ford against that of Henry M. Leland. Mr. Ford will be called to the stand to tell his story."

Gallagher was never able to produce Ford as a witness; indeed, the suit never reached the point where witnesses took the stand. Liebold in his *Reminiscences* explains why. He confirms Pipp's statement that Ford personnel were studying the reimbursement of Class A stockholders, and recalls that "we couldn't find any way whereby we could make an equitable distribution to the stockholders without speculators getting some material profit on it." This investigation seems to have suggested the principal defense developed by the Ford attorneys during the suit.†

It was this: they did not concede that Ford had made a verbal contract, but argued that if he had, it was illegal! The Lelands, in a statement just after the receivership, promised "to secure a reorganization which would protect the creditors from loss." But their suit was based upon an alleged promise by Ford to pay *bona fide* stockholders, *and not "speculators."* After making an agreement with Ford on this basis (their own contention), they had become officers and directors of the Lincoln Motor Company, and had thus, argued the Ford attorneys, entered into a relationship whereby they would serve themselves and a special group, the original stockholders. Since they had previously promised publicly to protect *all* stockholders, such action was manifestly illegal. Ford was therefore justified, his counsel submitted, in

---

* Leland's consent was of course quite unnecessary. As Wilfred Leland noted, even had the Lelands been able to bid, Ford had he wished could have outbid them and acquired the company. Of course, their support strengthened him morally, and might have resulted in his paying less. As to types of stock, B shares were of no par value; but the Leland bill of complaint demanded that their owners be reimbursed, the total value of all B shares to be $1,500,000. Class A stockholders were to receive $50 per share, the original par value of their stock.

† Emmons was not a Ford attorney. He stated later that he had no first-hand knowledge of the Ford-Leland personal conferences, and decided that having served both groups in the past, he would act for neither in the 1927 case, although both sought his services.

refusing to carry out such an agreement, if indeed he had ever made it.

This defense evaded the question of Ford's alleged promise. At first the Lelands seemed likely to crash through it to what they held was the fundamental issue. In March, 1928, Judge Frank L. Covert of the state circuit court denied a motion by Ford counsel to dismiss the suit on the ground they had taken, and because, they alleged, no consideration had been involved. Covert ruled that there was a definite consideration. The Ford attorneys appealed to the state supreme court, which on February 1, 1929, through an opinion by J. Fellows, ruled in their favor. Of the Lelands he said: "After they publicly announced that they were going to look after the interests of the stockholders, if they acted at all, their duty required them to act for all." Men who acquired stock at three dollars a share "acquired the same interest in the company as the man who paid $50 for his share of stock." No proper action could be brought to enforce an illegal contract. However, while denying a rehearing, the court permitted the Lelands to file an amended bill which might cure the defects of the first one.[37]

Such a bill was filed, but the Lelands did not claim that a contract had been made to pay all stockholders and first Covert, and then the supreme court, ruled that the second complaint failed to cure the faults of the first. After more than three years of litigation (it was now 1931), Henry M. Leland notified the stockholders that he had exhausted all possible efforts in their behalf. He died the following year.[38]

8.

The story of Ford's acquisition of the Lincoln company is one which no dispassionate reader can follow without regret and pain. The ability and distinction of the Lelands stand beyond question. Their union with the Fords was justly hailed as an event bringing together high and diverse talents—"Ford as the master manufacturer in quantity production, and Henry M. Leland as the master of fine things mechanical." [39]

What ensues has been set forth by some writers like a tragedy in the classic mold, with industry in the background, Ford as the villain, and the Lelands as the heroes. But the story does not fit into this pattern. It is rather one of two groups with differing conceptions of business, who in the factory found it difficult to work together, and as to financial commitments did not agree as to what had been pledged. That the Lelands were ready to do all they could for the Lincoln Company and the Fords on their own terms may be conceded, and so may their belief that Henry and Edsel Ford understood those terms. But it is equally clear that the Fords did not understand them, and that they could reasonably have expected the Lelands to be more flexible and realistic in fitting into the larger organization they had joined. Again, that the Lelands believed Ford had pledged himself to pay the former Lincoln stockholders may be accepted, but it is questionable if Ford believed he had made an irrevocable commitment. That he hoped to do something he stated, and that he investigated the possibility of doing so is clear; but when it became certain that he must pay "speculators" as well as investors, he rejected further action.

Ford did much both for the Lincoln Motor Company and for the Lelands. He purchased the company, put the Lelands in charge of it, paid all creditors, and paid the Lelands themselves $775,698. True, $412,698 of the total went to redeem their pledges as guarantors, but the payment, protecting their reputations and possibly saving them from suits, must have been welcome. Ford did so much for the company and the Lelands that many men in the automobile industry felt he had been exceptionally generous, and that it was of no consequence that he did not pay the original stockholders, since it would be difficult to cite a comparable instance in which such stockholders had been paid. Here the question is what Ford said he would do. Either the Lelands are correct, and Edsel Ford misstated what occurred, or the Lelands read into Ford's talk more than he said, or with time imagined a firmness of commitment that was never a fact. In any case, they were in error in not insisting on a written agreement.

There remains the question of Ford's public pledge to keep the Lelands in the industry, insuring the continuance of Henry M. Leland's contribution to automotive progress. Ford began well; then came the clash of differing practices, and the departure of the Lelands after four troubled months. We have seen that there were two points of view with respect to this period. We have seen that neither group seems to have shown a commendable eagerness to avoid friction. But granting that the attitude of the Lelands was superior and "exclusive," Ford and his officials seem to have acted with unusual speed and pertinacity in pushing changes which were galling to an industrial leader of Henry M. Leland's reputation. True, we can say that Ford officials saw these as essential. We can say that the Lelands were given as much consideration as or more than Ford officials gave each other. We can say that, considering the character and methods of the two groups, eventual disagreement was probable if not inevitable. All this being noted, had Ford made the effort that might have been expected of him in view of his public statements?

The answer must be that he had not, and to understand why, we must go back to Pipp's remark that good intentions would not be permitted to stand in the way of business success. This remark leads us to Ford's changing personality. He was building an empire. Undoubtedly from the start he thought of the Lincoln Company not only in terms of the Lelands, whom he esteemed and wished to aid, but also in terms of how the property he was buying would fit into the complex of his expanding organization. As the work of the company was resumed, Ford inevitably made his plans for improving his new property. The Lelands blocked them in numerous ways. He had the legal right to eject them, and did (a process which the Lelands themselves, and Wilfred in particular, undoubtedly hastened). He found a safe method of dropping any plans to reimburse the stockholders. By this time it may be doubted if Ford recognized the inconsistency between discharging the Lelands and his earlier promises to keep them in the industry. He was simply on his way to an objective: a more efficient company to produce a quality car under Ford auspices.

The Lelands had collided with the dynamic, increasingly ruthless Henry Ford who was in the full current of industrial accomplishment. Unhappily, for them this meant the ending of a career, and for the public the elimination of a fine and constructive influence in the industry, although much of what they had accomplished up to this time was to survive in the Ford-produced Lincoln car.

VIII

THE ROUGE:

CONCEPT AND GROWTH

ONE day in the fall of 1914 Fred Gregory, Henry Ford's realty agent, drove down into the district southeast of Dearborn and to the east of the Rouge River. He was looking over the area on Ford's order; his 'teen-age daughter Mary Louise was with him. The country unfolded in small truck farms and pastures, dotted with trees and clumps of cattails, for the land was low and easily flooded. When they got out of the car Mary Louise, who wore a new frock and white shoes, wrinkled her nose and exclaimed at the muddy terrain. Her father already knew why Ford was interested in the territory. "You'll live to see when it won't be all mud like this," he told her. "There will be a big factory almost as far as you can see."

Mary Louise didn't believe him. She saw only the sweep of empty land, isolated, inert. "I thought there would be a factory," she confessed years later, "but that it would never be big." [1]

At the time her thought would have been shared by most people in Detroit or Dearborn. The whole Rouge area was remote, and this part of it, lying more than three miles north of the Detroit River, seemed the least promising. It was not near the navigable Detroit; it was not even near Dearborn; it was nowhere. But Ford, who had been associated with an early attempt to develop the region as a residential district, had gradually fixed upon it as the center of a great industrial project.* By 1915 he was ready to act, and at a word from him Fred Gregory and four assistants soon purchased some 2000 acres of land, most of it east of the river.[2] As we have seen, blast furnaces and a tractor plant were Ford's immediate objectives, but beyond these he

* Ford was a member of a "Citizens' Committee of Fifty" which in August, 1891, issued a pamphlet for Oakwood, a community just south of where the Rouge plant's turning basin was later located. An electric railroad was to provide rapid transit to Detroit. Oakwood developed, but slowly and obscurely.

envisaged a super-plant—an industrial complex rising from the flat land to serve a new Ford empire and alter the work habits of the world.

Among the varied influences which motivated him two have been noted: the inadequacy of Highland Park and the scarcity of raw materials during the war. The latter, of course, came after the Rouge was conceived, but it was a goad to action. From 1915 on, Ford had seen steel frames, malleable iron, steel for springs and motors, leather and glass all more than double in price. Control of raw materials seemed to him "buying insurance against non-supply." Wibel, Liebold, Walker and many others heard him express fears of shortages, high prices, inspired strikes. The Rouge, symbolizing self-sufficiency, became a prime objective with him.[3]

But the most vital pressure for the project came from the depths of his own restless imagination. He knew that Highland Park, although it had fathered the moving assembly line, would soon be outmoded. For years his mind had played with the potentials that might shape a more advanced type of manufacturing. With probing insight he saw the larger relationships of iron, lumber, water power, coal; rivers and railroads; power plants, foundries, assembly units. As elements of production all were in a large sense one, and he believed the company could relate and control them, forging a new and superior type of industry. The Rouge provided the setting. If from 1915 onward Ford was blocked by war and minority stockholders, if he moved gropingly toward the final form of his experiment, in his conviction that the Rouge was the ordained site of his new creation he was never to falter.

2.

Even by 1915 the project had achieved scope and detail in Ford's mind, for in June of that year he talked to reporters not only of blast furnaces and a tractor plant, but of employing more than 20,000 workers and building a great inland port. "He will make the Rouge a harbor for craft that will bring ore from the upper lake district and for craft that will carry the Rouge cargoes of motors direct to England, France, Germany, South America, Australia, and the Orient," ran one account of his plans. The imposing scale of the final operation was suggested by his assertion that "we may take ten years to bring things to the point where we want them."[4]

That he was working intently on details at this time is also revealed in letters written to him by William Livingston, one of Detroit's business statesmen,* who indicates that he and Ford had talked about the "canal" (later called the slip) which Ford was to excavate, and discusses the relationship of the Rouge to the numerous railroads near it. "I assume," Livingston remarks at one point, "that you will have a belt line tract of your own running around the plants, with proper leads or switches, to . . . make connections with the various roads in shipping." [5]

Important elements were thus being considered even at this early date. A preliminary blueprint of the Rouge, dated January 29, 1917, indicates that the plan continued to grow both in general character and in detail.† Liebold stated later that "he ultimately conceived the idea of doing it all [that is, his automobile as well as iron, steel, and tractor operations] at the Rouge." William F. Verner, who was in charge of power house construction under Mayo when this began in 1919, indicates that by then he and others had the same impression. [6]

What did Ford have in mind, and how did it differ from other developments in the United States at the time?

A superficial observer might say that there was no originality in the mere size of the project; and, to be sure, other American companies had achieved bigness long before Ford first thought of the Rouge. Rockefeller and his associates had fashioned the Standard Oil—a network of wells, pipelines, refineries, by-products plants and marketing companies that covered the United States and thrust tentacles into five continents beyond it. The United States Steel Corporation, the Du Pont industries, General Electric—all represented large industrial structures. In the automotive field General Motors was evolving its own impressive group of motor car plants and subsidiary units. But Ford was projecting bigness in a new and more intensive form than any of his contemporaries had achieved.

The basic element in his conception was flow. He and his associates had already demonstrated in the moving assembly line that flow in

---

* In 1906 Livingston had helped Ford finance the purchase of Alex Y. Malcomson's Ford stock. In 1915, at seventy, he was president of the Dime Savings Bank, an official of the Lake Carriers' Association, a newspaper publisher, and a vigorous yachtsman.

† This blueprint shows coke ovens, blast furnaces, the foundry and associated facilities, indicates a steel-making group, and bears an arrow designated: "Flow of Materials." (Ford Archives). Sorensen, *My Forty Years with Ford*, 156, is undoubtedly right in saying that for a time Ford thought of the Rouge as a feeder to Highland Park, but even by 1915, as the Livingston correspondence and the press interviews show, its greater role was already taking shape in Ford's mind.

the factory was of vital importance, but Ford recognized that without the flow of materials *to* the point of manufacture, the flow *at* that point might be impeded or stopped. This recognition led him and his associates beyond the Rouge to long distance transportation, and to the raw materials required for the manufacture of cars—iron and steel, lumber, coal, limestone, silica sand (for glass). Ford meant to control transportation, at least by water, and to possess the sources of raw materials.

These basic services and materials would not need to be supplied in full by the Ford Motor Company. To have the power to supply a considerable percentage of the chief ones would be enough. Later Ford defined his purpose: "We make nothing for the sake of making. Our operations all center about the manufacture of motors. If those who sell to us will not manufacture at prices which, upon investigation, we believe to be right, then we make the articles ourselves." [7]

He was also confident that he could devise new and better processes of production for almost *any* product. He could then persuade those who wished to manufacture for him to adopt these superior routines. As a part of the grand flow of supply, Ford even planned to develop latent water power on various streams, carrying the factory to the country. Another aspect of Ford's conception was the strategic location of his plant. We have seen that the acreage he had acquired lay close to the Detroit River and deep water navigation; with the widening and deepening of the Rouge it would surround an inland harbor. But the Rouge harbor might be thought of as the center of a circle, with transportation radials extending in all directions, while had the plant been located on the Detroit River, as Couzens was said to have proposed, it would have commanded only an arc, with its effective outlet waterwards only. Rail and road connections would have had to be brought down at great expense, and a labor supply would have been less available. In contrast, the site actually chosen lay in a network of transportation. Trunk lines and highways ran above and below. Ford had only to hook up with the Michigan Central and Pere Marquette in the manner Livingston had suggested.* As to transportation, his situation was superior to that of General Motors and other automotive plants.

---

* In the area were also the tracks of the Detroit Terminal, the Wabash, the Grand Trunk, and the Detroit, Toledo & Ironton.

Again, in a tract free of surrounding city congestion, Ford could lay out his plant with the fullest freedom. He could place there a large number of producing units, and the ample space made possible one-story buildings, without the cumbersome elevators that impeded operations in four or six story structures.* Finally he could make these units serve each other in constructive ways, as we shall see, and link them by rail or conveyor. This close inter-relation of its units was to be one of the Rouge's points of superiority. "As the result of the high degree to which fabrication [that is, the actual shaping of an article] has been mechanized," an expert was soon to point out, "the attention of management is now turning to the *transportation* of materials. . . . The biggest cost savings of today and tomorrow are likely to come from *moving* rather than from *making*." [8] (Italics ours.) No one had perceived and applied this truth so fully as had the Ford engineers at the Rouge.

Their conception of size thus included control of raw materials, control of their transportation to and from the plant, space for all the chief units they might desire, and a close interrelationship among such units. They could then command flow throughout the entire manufacturing cycle, and make bigness creative not only in its separate parts, but as a whole.

3.

The end of World War I freed Ford as to money, men, and materials to develop the Rouge; with the entire stock of the company in his hands by mid-1919, he was also free to employ these as he desired. The construction of the super-plant now went forward rapidly.

Actually, the war had contributed to the growth of the Rouge. The building of Eagles at the new site had required the completion of the slip and turning basin, and the erection of B Building. This structure was now, in early 1919, remodelled for automotive and tractor production, and worked into the overall Rouge plan. In addition, four other small buildings stood available for use. Many acres that had been muddy wallows in wet weather had been filled and paved for railroad tracks or factory streets. In September, 1918, the Government had granted priorities for materials needed in the construction of the blast furnaces,

---

* On Nov. 13, 1916, Julian Kennedy and William B. Mayo wrote letters about the Rouge site to the Ford directors, bringing out the advantages described in this section. Mayo also emphasized the level nature of the land and the possibilities of housing for workers.

and work on them, never entirely halted even during the Dodge suit, was pushed ahead. By late 1918 the blast furnace repair shop had been completed, and as men were released from the Eagle project they swelled the furnace construction crews, which soon comprised 3500 workers. Furnace A, as the first unit was called, was rising, and the foundations of B had been laid. Near by, the site of the foundry was being excavated, and one for the coke ovens had been chosen.[9]

The Rouge River flowed just south of the plant site, meandering in a general easternly direction from Dearborn, seven miles away. Just beyond the site, it turned south toward the Detroit. A turning basin had been dredged out near the bend, and the slip extended from it a little west of north for more than a third of a mile. The two made an inverted capital T of water. This was the plant's harbor, and construction was going forward along its eastern side. Here, for some distance back from the water's edge, space was reserved for concrete bins which would receive limestone, coal, and iron ore from incoming barges or from railroad cars. Back of these bins, and at the northern end of the slip, the blast furnaces were rising; just back of them, the foundry. The furnace repair shop lay near the slip's southern end, and behind it the coke ovens were being installed. Late in 1919 the foundations of the power house were laid between the ovens and the foundry.[10]

In early 1919 no ships came up the undredged river, only a few barges. Most materials were delivered by rail; cars clanged in bearing coal, iron, cement, sand, steel beams, machinery; while trucks, cranes, tractors, and thousands of workmen were active. The noise of machines, the voices of men, the walls and stacks lifting everywhere from the flat land, advertised a great industrial center in the making.

At this stage William B. Mayo, working closely with Ford, supervised the planning and construction. He had a considerable staff of his own: R. T. Walker, his executive assistant; Charles Turner, in charge of mechanical engineering; Ralph Shreve, mechanical engineering; Everett B. Arnold, architectural engineering; Stewart Bullock, in charge of construction, and G. R. Thompson, who succeeded him in 1919; William F. Verner, in immediate charge of power house and mechanical engineering details; his son, Dana Mayo; L. B. Breedlove, who would later write about the Rouge; Theron C. Taylor, Frank C. Riecks, and others—250 in all, says G. R. Thompson. Mayo's wide knowledge of basic industrial units, his foresight, his skill in overall planning—

these gave the Rouge much of its basic character. Ford, of course, approved each step, and Knudsen, Martin, Sorensen and others took their definite roles where production was involved.[11]

The method of planning was fixed in this early period, and was never altered fundamentally. It began with a study of function. What in each instance—the power house, the foundry, the coke ovens, B Building—was the objective? The unit was discussed at this point by

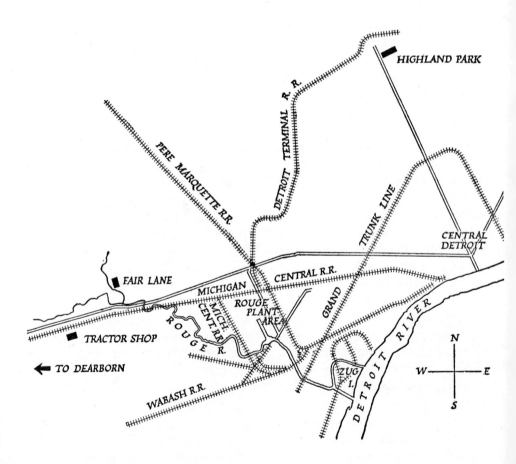

Rough map of the Detroit-Dearborn area, showing the location of the Rouge Plant area in 1917, and its relationship to other Ford holdings and to rail and water facilities.

all the executives who might later be concerned. Then came the blue-print stage. But Ford was no blueprint man,* and for him an idea had to be embodied in a model made to scale. Such a model would show windows, machines, pillars, conveyors. In conference, elements were pushed about to test possible arrangements, often revealing defects or potential improvements. Only then was the industrial architect brought in to make plans for the structure. These in turn were examined, discussed, and altered if necessary.[12]

For most buildings the architect was Albert Kahn, who had built the Highland Park factory and B Building at the Rouge. He worked in complete harmony with the Ford staff ideas on function and layout. Moritz Kahn of his organization later wrote illuminatively of the relationship between industrialist and architect. "A manufacturing building may be built to fit the job," he noted, "at no more cost than if it does not fit." He insisted that the participation of production engineers was vital. "An architect is not qualified to make process layouts. Only the works management can do this." But having the functional layout, "the architect should be able to plan a factory around the scheme of production." He could even provide solutions for technical problems which an industrialist might not find, for his experience in fitting machinery and men into buildings was much broader.

The Ford staff drew on other experts for special units. Julian Kennedy of Pittsburgh designed the Rouge blast furnaces, while the Riter-Conley Company made the steel for ovens and stoves. The coal and coke-handling plant and coke ovens were designed by the Semet-Solvay Company, and erected by the Heyl-Patterson Company.[13] However, in selecting and supervising such firms, Mayo's broad knowledge was invaluable.

But while the planning for the first phase of the plant was bold, and true to Ford's basic conception, it did not cover the entire complex he envisaged. There were "manufacturing facilities" still to be placed, and while he doubtless had ideas about them, his cut-and-try instincts prompted him to proceed slowly. "Let's feel it out," was his motto. As a result, growth seemed to be haphazard, one step leading to another. "I think the Rouge was pretty much like Topsy," remarked R. T. Walker of later developments. "I think that it pretty much just grew." Such

---

* See *Ford: the Times, the Man, the Company,* 199n. There is disagreement as to whether Ford could or could not read blueprints, but none as to his demanding models.

comment was sound in that growth was opportunistic, but opportunism was deliberate, and related to the constant changes in the industry. As W. F. Verner points out, both Ford and his associates knew that the automobile was altering its character from year to year. By relating what was already built to the next steps to be taken, they could ride with the evolutionary character of the business.[14]

As construction advanced, Ford slipped in and out of work sites, now with a casual glance at routine construction, now with a brooding appraisal of some detail that disturbed him. On one occasion he stepped into the compression room of a coke oven unit, nearing completion. Standing by Frank Riecks, who was in charge, he studied a huge wall about 35 feet high and 200 long. "That wall is off." At first the engineer didn't agree, but Ford kept looking at him, "egging me on to admit it." Riecks finally conceded that the unit was half an inch out of line. "Take it down," snapped Ford as he walked away.

Down came the wall. "It was a kind of expensive lesson," Riecks recalled, "because he paid for it himself." But Ford, while a guesser and cut-and-try man in many matters, was a perfectionist in others, and knew that the "lesson" would alert the entire organization. It did. "We watched for those things and we were very fussy about them ourselves. I'm still fussy about them." [15]

Already one of those most active in planning and checking was the tall, blond Sorensen. He was looking for a new home for his tractor plant at Dearborn, but appeared at various work sites, asking a sharp question, or assertively taking a position as to some feature of a unit. Even at this time he wore a confidence born of his close relationship to Ford, the manner of a grand vizier who knew his sultan.[16]

The work went forward at a rapid beat. The No. 2 block of coke ovens was completed and in operation on October 15, 1919, and No. 1 came in on December 6. Work on Blast Furnace A was nearing completion as the year ended, and Furnace B was well under way. By January 17, 1920 a network of 24 miles of railroad tracks had been laid.[17] The concrete bins beside the slip, extending from the tracks at its edge back for more than 250 feet, with a capacity of more than 2,000,000 tons, had been completed, and the High Line at their eastern edge had been built. Since basic materials started their journey toward the plants from these units, we may look at them for a moment.

The bins were basic storage units, representing Ford's greatest concession to stockpiling. However, the bins were chiefly used to accumulate a reserve of materials for the winter months, when transportation by lake was impossible.

They were supplied by railroad car and barge, ships largely replacing the barges as the Rouge was improved. Two Hulett ore unloaders and a Morrison coal unloader ran along the tracks at the margin of the slip. They reached down to incoming vessels, taking up their cargoes in "eight and ten ton bites," and depositing them in the bins. Two enormous Mead-Morrison transfer bridges also operated along the slip, lifting materials from one bin to another to "ballast" the contents, and also transferring coal, iron, or limestone to empty cars coming up the High Line.

The High Line, heart of Rouge transportation, was a concrete structure 40 feet high, extending the full length of the slip. On its flat top it bore five standard gauge railroad tracks. At the northern end, however, a ramp connected it with the intra-factory railroad system below. Nearest the slip the outer track, laid on open grating, overhung the bins; on the other side the line ran close to the blast furnaces, and was underlaid at points by "active storage" bins or hoppers, into which materials needed at once by the coke ovens or furnaces could be dumped. Railroad cars coming into the plant could move under remote electric control along the track nearest the slip and drop their loads into the bins (these cars were of the bottom-dumping type). Or they could move up the opposite side to feed the coke ovens or furnaces. Empty cars could come up the Line to be loaded from the bins. Thus the Line dealt smoothly and easily with the main problems of distribution. But it was also a building as well as a transportation unit. Under its tracks many small shops were located, servicing various Rouge units.[18]

The first productive activity of the Rouge was established in B Building. As the last Eagle moved out of the huge structure its foundations were reënforced to support two stories on either side of the central bay, and by August, 1919, a body-making plant was installed on part of the main floor. It began operations on the 5th, when the first touring car body was turned out. On the 16th sedan bodies began to come through, and by November 800 units a day—300 sedans and 500 touring cars—

were being manufactured, delivering the company, as we have seen in Chapter VI, from the strike-harried outside plants on which it had heretofore depended.

The coke plant began operations late in the year; early in 1920 a saw mill, designed to prepare wood for body-making, began to function. Finally, on May 17, 1920, occurred the "blowing in" of Blast Furnace A. The occasion was celebrated with a drama worthy of the launching of an ocean liner. A pile of cordwood and coke was placed in the furnace, and Henry Ford II was designated to light it. Held in his grandfather's arms, he approached the unit while his father Edsel, his mother, and Clara Ford looked on, together with Ford officials and workmen. Meanwhile, some pieces of oil-soaked excelsior had been tossed into the furnace.

"The fun of playing with matches," reported the Detroit *News,* "was almost too much for Henry II, who is only three years old, and he had some difficulty, but with his grandfather's aid the blaze was started and then he sat perched on grandfather's shoulder while everyone cheered. He entered into it by clapping his hands and shouting gleefully, too." [19]

4.

When with the fall of 1920 the entire automotive industry slid into the sharp depression of that year, and the Ford factory at Highland Park closed, construction at the Rouge was all but suspended. But as Henry Ford weathered the financial crisis of the ensuing winter, and began to manufacture again, the Rouge took on new life.

The first important event was the arrival of the tractor plant, and Sorensen. Dearborn had stopped making Fordsons even before Highland Park had shut down the assembly line for Model T's, the plan being already to transfer operations to the Rouge; the idle period was a convenient one in which to reëstablish them there. Tractor manufacture went into B Building, occupying a large part of the first floor. Here new machine tools and a new assembly improved its character. As the foundry increased production a number of parts previously supplied by outside firms were made at the Rouge. The first tractor came off the new line on February 23, and before the end of the year a total of 36,000 had been produced.[20]

Sorensen took command on arrival. With his assistant Mead L.

Bricker, Harry Bennett,* and others, he looked about and noted a structure near the power house called the Wash and Locker Building. A few draftsmen and engineers were occupying it. Says Riecks: "That was the only place where there was anything that looked like an office building in the Rouge plant, and they said, 'We don't need any Wash and Locker Building. We'll just move in.' So they took the two floors over. They then threw the draftsmen out. I remember trucks driving up outside, and they opened the windows and poured the drawings right . . . into the trucks."

It was an entrance true to the growing Sorensen legend. At once he took charge not only of the tractor plant, but of the entire Rouge, including all planning activities. "The minute Mr. Sorensen moved from Dearborn to the Rouge he was chief engineer as well as production manager." He brought Harry Hanson, a gifted layout engineer, down from Highland Park, who now became, under Sorensen, the chief of planning. Stanley Hill, acting independently, and later under Pioch in tool design, undertook specific tasks. Mayo continued his work with the power plant, in which Sorensen had scant interest, but otherwise faded from the picture.[21] As we have seen previously, Sorensen believed implicitly in Ford's genius, and developed the Rouge as his agent. He was quick to remodel a just-completed section of a building if it would promote better production, and followed Ford's policy of leaving ample space for future development. "Well, push it over plenty far," he would say to a layout man placing a new unit. "We don't know what we're going to put around it."

---

* In 1919 Henry Ford began to take an interest in a small, wiry young man with reddish hair, sharp blue eyes, and rather handsome features named Harry Bennett. An ex-sailor, an athlete, and a skilful amateur pugilist, he had come into the plant the previous year. Employed at first in the commercial art department, he began his upward climb when the head of the photographic service, lunching with Knudsen, recommended him as an assistant in handling some of the work on the Eagle boats. Knudsen liked his agile industry. Ford began to assign him various special tasks. Bennett, proud of these assignments, executed them without regard to plant routines. He had no title, no desk, and apparently no stated salary, but Ford saw that he was adequately compensated. As early as the acquisition of the D.T. & I. he was able to use squads of his service men in ways that deeply offended older and more responsible executives in the plant; for the journalist James Sweinhart tells how he defied the foreman of the blast furnaces by stopping the use of slag as track ballast. (Detroit *News*, Sept. 30, 1945.) Like Plunkett of Tammany Hall, Bennett saw his opportunities and used them. He had been active at Ford headquarters during the Chicago *Tribune* trial, and on coming to the Rouge took over the service duties for that unit—at first a modest task—and was eventually to seek the full control of personnel matters—the employment, watching, and discharge of workers. When Harry Hanson arrived in 1921 to take charge of planning under Sorensen, he thought Bennett of little consequence, but soon revised his first impression. However, Bennett did not become much of a factor as compared with Bricker and Sorensen until 1927. (H. B. Hanson, *Reminiscences*.)

Hardly had the new tractor plant been established when the Rouge foundry and the power plant came into operation. Both were the largest units of their kind in the world.

The foundry spread over a space 595 feet in width and 1188 in length. In height it was dwarfed by the chimneys of the blast furnaces and the stacks of the power house. But here the greatest working force in the Rouge assembled, already 10,000 by 1922. The first big operations began in November, 1921, with the casting of Model T cylinder blocks, and soon 24 cupolas, later to be increased to 30, were preparing molten iron for the molds, to be mixed with hot metal brought directly from the blast furnaces.[22]

The power plant supplied light and current for manifold work operations. Covering a ground area of approximately 225 by 350 feet, it rose 120 feet above the ground, and its stacks reached a height of 325. Eight in number eventually, these became one of the recognizable features of the Rouge profile. By 1922 the plant was generating 30,000 kilowatts, and had a horsepower of 40,000. It was furnishing one-third of the Highland Park current, the power house there, once the pride of Henry Ford, now being termed a "sub-station." A tunnel twelve and a half feet in diameter and almost a mile long brought water from the head of the slip for the plant, discharging the residue into the Rouge. However, from 1920 on eight turbogenerator units were being built at the Rouge, each to generate 30,000 kilowatts. The complete plant would have a potential horsepower of more than 500,-000. A number of sub-stations—seven by 1923—were erected in the Rouge area to facilitate the distribution of power. In the 1930's the capacity of the plant was to be still further increased.[23]

While the Rouge was thus expanding, the deepening and widening of the river was in process. In August, 1917, Congress had passed a bill for the improvement of the stream under Federal auspices, and on August 14 the directors of the Ford Motor Company had voted to guarantee, with Henry Ford personally, the availability of land along the banks for this work, and the construction of a turning basis "at the head of improvement." The company also undertook to insure the altering or rebuilding of bridges, although eventually three of the seven involved became the responsibility of the railroads using them. The entire project was one of harbor improvement, as the port of Detroit would benefit from the work as well as the Ford Motor Company.

Sufficient dredging had been done during the war to permit the low-draft Eagles to negotiate the river, but in 1920 the main task still remained to be accomplished. In the spring of that year Secretary of War Newton D. Baker instructed Col. Edward M. Markham, U.S. Engineer for the Michigan District, that the target date for completion of all work was October, 1921.

The river varied in width from 75 to 100 feet, and in depth from 10 to 16. It was to be dredged to a bottom width of 200 (225 at one bend), and to a depth of 21 feet. However a canal with a bottom width of 400 feet and a length of 3000 was authorized as a cutoff about two and a half miles south of the Rouge plant, where the river turned west and ran for some distance in that direction before again flowing south. The canal continued the straight southernly course to the Detroit, saving two miles. The entire improvement scheme would add six miles to the Detroit waterfront, and would cost $10,000,000.[24]

The project would have fitted neatly into the development of the Rouge plant, which, had the work been completed on time, would have enjoyed ample cheap water transportation just as its chief productive units came into operation. But the dredging and bridge-building were only well under way by the time of the target date.

There were, to be sure, several distracting developments—a Congressional resolution for investigating the entire project (a political maneuver), and difficulties with the owners of lands and buildings which were involved in river improvement. Still, none of these activities seems to have caused any appreciable delay, nor was there any question of the high ability with which Markham had conducted his operations. The task was simply greater and more complicated than had been foreseen.[25]

Meanwhile, like a city newly built that waits for the completion of trunk highways, the Rouge was struggling desperately to maintain an adequate service of supply. Rail transportation was expensive and in the confused post-war period cars were not available to bring in the vital supplies of coal, iron ore, limestone, and building materials. In July, 1922, a drive was made to increase deliveries by water. Flocks of small ships and barges able to negotiate the channel were assembled to take shipments from Lake carriers at the mouth of the Rouge, and bring these to the hungry storage bins. This stop-gap operation supplied 425,000 tons of ore and 140,000 of limestone during its first year,

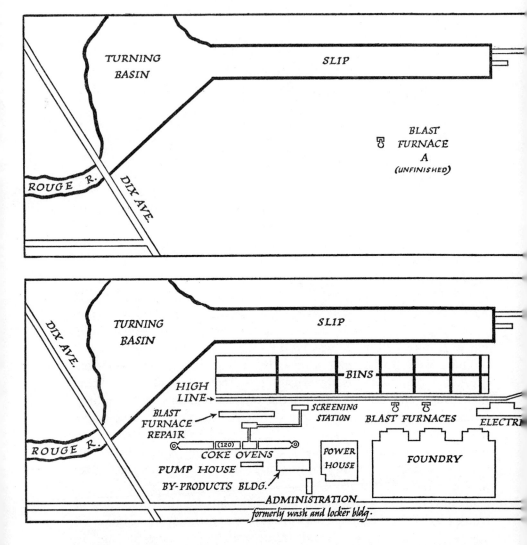

but with the blast furnaces now consuming 750,000 tons of ore alone, the deliveries, even when supplemented by rail tonnage, barely sufficed.

However, by the early summer of 1923 the engineers were in sight of their goal. The channel had been deepened and widened, the dredging having provided much fill for marshy areas. (Contractors by the terms of their agreements were required to dump mud and silt under Army direction.) The bridges had been improved or rebuilt, although

KILNS

B BUILDING

POWER
HOUSE

A BUILDINGS

SAW
MILL

POWER
HOUSE

KILNS

B BUILDING

A BUILDINGS

FURNACE BLDG.

MILLER ROAD

The Rouge in 1918, top, and
1922, bottom, showing the rapid
progress in the construction of
buildings and other facilities.

supplementary work had to be done as late as December, 1923. One
road, the Detroit, Toledo & Ironton, was unable to provide the $300,000
required for its bridge, and in the end Ford bought the entire railroad
and completed the structure himself. The D.T. & I. was to become of
considerable importance in the development of the plant. In June, 1923,
before the route was officially open, three carriers a week were able to
make their way up the Rouge with light loads. Finally, on July 2 the

steamer *Oneida* made a trial trip, bearing a cargo of happy Ford and Army officials. A week later, on July 11, the *Cletus Schneider* finally discharged the first full load (of iron ore) into the bins beside the slip.[26]

The Rouge could now operate according to the original plan. "Great Lake ore carriers can now bring cargoes to the Ford Motor Company's docks," exulted the *Ford News*. The flow of supply fed the flow of production. Almost two years later, on July 6, 1925, the Polish steamer *Anders* demonstrated that the harbor was fully a world port, steaming in from Antwerp with 1400 tons of rails for the D.T. & I. Meanwhile the volume of water-borne tonnage swelled. During 1924, 141 ships brought 800,000 tons to the slip, as compared with 565,000 transshipped in the year ending July, 1923. The total continued to rise month by month. All the lumber and ore from Ford mills and mines on the upper peninsula were now pouring in by water, while from the south Ford coal was arriving, although at first by rail.[27]

PROJECTS IN EXPANSION

ONE day in July, 1919, E. G. Kingsford, a real-estate agent in Iron Mountain on the upper peninsula of Michigan, found himself talking by long distance telephone with Henry Ford. The latter wanted Kingsford, a relative by marriage and a Ford dealer, to join him on a camping trip and discuss the reserves of iron and lumber in the northern part of the state. Kingsford protested that the summer was his busiest season and he couldn't possibly go. However, his assistant, Miss Jennie Folley, promptly told him he was making a mistake. "You are going to miss the chance of a lifetime," she said. Kingsford reconsidered, and in a few weeks joined Ford in Buffalo.[1]

This episode reveals Ford at the beginning of a group of activities which he seems to have considered as early as 1912.* Most of these projects were related to Highland Park or the Rouge; all exemplified the larger ideas about industry and society in Ford's quicksilver mind. So challenging did some of them become that this one phase of the Ford story could fill half a dozen volumes—sagas of mines, timber empires, railroading, glass furnaces, fleets, aircraft factories, and rubber plantations.

Ford by 1919 had proved his industrial originality with the mass-production of Model T. But for him this was merely an incident in a social revolution, and he was prepared to effect other startling changes. His tractor and the Rouge illustrated the range of his thinking, and with the Rouge had come the vision that moved him to telephone Kingsford: a vision of acquiring the raw materials for his factories—coal, limestone, silica sand, iron, timber—and bearing them to Ford plants on Ford ships. Almost simultaneously, perhaps earlier, Ford had

* A. G. Wolfe, *Reminiscences*, tells how his father examined ore and coal properties for Ford at that time. As will later appear, he was also considering water power sites in this early period.

considered how he could extend his main factory by scattering little plants over rural areas wherever rivers provided adequate water power.

By 1919 he was eager for action. He had the money for bold experimentation, and even in the spring was confident of acquiring full control of the Ford Motor Company. When he talked then with Upton Sinclair at Altadena, California, he radiated this sense of power. "Does the possession of great wealth make you happier than you would be without it?" Sinclair asked.

Ford replied: "Yes, of course; because I can do things with it that I could not do otherwise. . . . In those days [before his success] I was struggling to do something. Now I am in a position to do it, and do it exactly as I want to do it." [2]

That summer, with all the minority stock purchased, Ford was ready to undertake his quest for the sources of raw materials.

2.

With Kingsford, Ford joined Edison, Burroughs, the Firestones, and others for a trip through upstate New York and New England. They visited a power site he had purchased at Green Island on the Hudson. He had ample opportunity to talk with Kingsford about lumber and iron, and on his return made a quick survey of the Iron Mountain region. He was already familiar with it from earlier visits, but now regarded its dense stands of hardwood and hemlock, its busy sawmills, mineheads, and harbors through the transforming lens of a new purpose.

That fall, through Liebold, he investigated possible purchases. "You know very well," wrote the secretary to Kingsford, "that from the timber standpoint Mr. Ford would like to get a block of land large enough to create a permanent supply and that he would like to farm whatever land may be cleared to build a community and at the same time utilize the mineral rights and mine the ore and use the scrap wood in making charcoal iron. This, of course, is a very big undertaking and requires large holdings." Kingsford and Liebold looked for the immense tract Ford wanted. Kingsford found one of 140,000 acres in October, 1919, but this was rejected, and in January, 1920 a larger one (313,447.35 acres) belonging to the Michigan Iron and Lumber Company was optioned, and an agreement to purchase signed on March 30,

1920. The sale was completed in the fall at a cost of $2,540,421. Ford had meanwhile purchased additional acreage at a cost of $412,459.[3]

In the early summer of 1920 Ford took Edsel, Liebold, Mayo, Avery and others north in his steam yacht *Sialia* to examine the properties. They disembarked at Escabana on the northwestern shore of Lake Michigan and went to Iron Mountain by automobile. There an additional tract was acquired for a sawmill, which was erected in August. Early in September, 1920, Ford incorporated the Michigan Iron, Land, & Lumber Co., which took over all existing activity as a subsidiary of the Ford Motor Company. Clarence W. Avery assumed charge of the Iron Mountain development, with Kingsford as his advisor and lieutenant. By November, 1921, the Rouge was receiving "regular shipments" of lumber for the body assembly unit in B Building.

Iron Mountain, the headquarters for all lumbering and mining in the area, had been in a depressed state; however, the Ford invasion quickly lifted it to vigor. The sawmill, built under the supervision of Avery and Mayo, was equipped with the most modern machinery and laid out for activities of original types; a chemical plant was designed for the conversion of residues into useful products; and large kilns were erected to dry the green wood. At Sidnaw Camp, the first center for tree-felling, rose offices and living quarters which dazzled and for a time appalled the lumberjacks. These moveable structures were equipped with electric lights, steam heat, shower baths, and individual beds, and were connected by cement sidewalks. Dining rooms and club rooms were provided. With food comparable to the quarters, the development seemed the stuff of a backwoods fairy tale.[4]

Along with his first large purchase in 1920, Ford had acquired the Imperial mine at Michigamme, some eighty miles north of Iron Mountain. This property, reconditioned according to Ford practice, began operations on a limited scale in October, 1921. Its ore was not of the best quality, and later elicited complaints from technicians at the Rouge; however, it established Ford as a producer of iron. Late in 1922 Ford purchased dock facilities at L'Anse on the southern shore of Lake Superior, a sawmill, and timber holdings, and in September, 1923, he acquired port facilities at Pequaming, ten miles to the northeast, buying a sawmill, docks, towing outfits, tugs, scows, a town, and 400,000 acres of standing timber in four counties! Later he also bought 2200 acres of ore-bearing land about twenty-five miles east of the Imperial. However, the Blueberry mine, developed there, did not come into operation until 1929.

Ford liked to create the impression that through such purchases he was fully controlling the raw materials for his cars. Actually, his mine could furnish "only a fraction of what we need," as one of his officials stated in 1924. The Imperial did not supply enough ore to keep one blast furnace in operation. As to lumber, then used extensively in the Model T, Ford's forests and mills in an emergency could have produced more than the Rouge and Highland Park consumed, but the company was then buying 80 per cent of what it required from contractors, and conserving its own supply. (It also let contracts for the cutting of its own holdings.) By 1925 the upper peninsula mills and factories were valued at more than $23,000,000, mostly plant. Since wood was destined to give way to steel in motor vehicles, the company had concentrated on the less crucial of two materials; but its vigorous exploitation of sources was a warning to producers who might be tempted to raise prices too high.[5]

3.

In July, 1920, before buying the first large timber tract, Ford had purchased two coal mines, the Banner Fork properties, at Wallins Creek and Tisdale, Kentucky. Later the same year he bought a mine at Nuttalburg, West Virginia. These mines could have supplied sufficient fuel, if worked at full capacity, for the chief Ford factories and the D.T. & I. railroad, although apparently they did not furnish all the varieties required.

As it proved, they were only a beginning of the Ford coal adventure. Early in September, 1922, the *Ford News* announced that a fuel shortage would force a shutdown at the Ford plants. Ford was indignant. "The coal shortage has not come about naturally," he declared. "It has been brought about artificially by the Wall Street interests that own the railroads and coal mines. We have to shut down, but I can tell you one thing—it won't be long before we can get all we need at an honest price." He and others also denounced the Interstate Commerce Commission's order (No. 23,) which allotted cars for the transportation of coal to public utilities, food manufacturing plants, and "essential industries," *not including automotive companies*. After Ford closed his plants the Commission rescinded the order, and issued Order 25, which gave priority to coal cars, and removed all restrictions on allocation. The Ford factories then reopened, after a shutdown of five days.*

Between November, 1922, and April, 1923, to safeguard his coal supply, Ford bought three groups of mines in Kentucky and West Virginia, and incorporated the Fordson Coal Company, with a capitalization of $15,000,000, to manage all the shafts. The coal resources of the Ford company were now of such size that in 1928 one quarter of its product had to be sold to the public, while all along coal and coke had been offered to employees at low prices.[6]

Even before acquiring timber, iron, and coal, Ford had considered the factor of transportation. He had been impressed by the economy of waterborne cargoes, and in 1917 he gave orders that all new Ford branches and subsidiaries should be placed where they could use deep water facilities. The next step was to acquire his own ships, and apparently he was considering such action in 1919. But for a number of reasons nothing was done at this time, and another form of transportation was to make the first demand upon Ford's resources.[7]

When the government prepared immediately after the war to widen, straighten and deepen the Rouge, it served notice on all railroads in the area to reconstruct or replace their bridges over the stream. Among these was the Detroit, Toledo, & Ironton, a corporation which had bounced in and out of receiverships, was yearly losing money, and for the coming year would show a deficit of $1,896,523. Klingensmith had conferred with Frederic Osborn, son of the road's largest stockholder, about a new bridge, which would cost about $350,000. Young Osborn came to see Ford. He explained that the D.T. & I. had mortgaged all its available property, even its rolling stock, and could not possibly finance so expensive a project; but if Ford would agree to take bonds issued against construction, the road could proceed.

Ford was aware that the D.T. & I. had developed little passenger service, and that its future as a freight carrier was dubious. Started in 1874 as a local line in Ohio, it had pushed south to Ironton on the Ohio River, then north to Detroit, sending a spur east to Toledo. Its chief revenues had once come from hauling Ohio and southern Michigan coal and iron ore; the beds were now exhausted, and the condition of

---

* Edsel Ford announced on Sept. 21, 1922, that the new I.C.C. order permitted the reopening of Ford plants. (Detroit *News,* Sept. 21, 1922).

the line had not recommended it to shippers from Kentucky and West Virginia. To guarantee its bonds was much like underwriting a loan to an ailing octogenarian who could repay it only from what he earned.

However, Ford perceived that if he could acquire the tottering enterprise, he might find uses for it. To be sure, the road wandered across Ohio without touching any big cities, but this was actually an advantage, for it had no freight bottlenecks. Ford could ship his coal north by the road in record time. Again, the D.T. & I. crossed all the northern east-west trunk lines, and to the south connected with the Baltimore & Ohio, the Chesapeake & Ohio, and the Norfolk & Western, thus providing access to Kentucky and West Virginia. Quite as important, freight could be sent to Toledo, and thence north across Lake Erie to the Rouge, or up through Lakes Huron, Michigan, and Superior to upper peninsula plants. But perhaps the most valuable characteristic of the road in Ford's eyes was its usefulness in starting and speeding company shipments. As we have seen, he quickly employed it to cut "inventory float" and reduce the money tied up in the process of transportation, whether of coal or of motor vehicles.[8]

Ford knew that if he acquired the D.T. & I. he would have to remake it. As a matter of fact, while he had never meant to enter railroading, he had ideas about that activity as well as about water power, shipping, iron, and steel. Once he began seriously to consider the purchase, the itch to exhibit a showcase railroad undoubtedly became a factor in persuading him to buy.

There was little difficulty in acquiring the road. It had never paid a dividend. Its stock and bond holders, when told that an unknown buyer had appeared, were almost as eager to sell as would have been holders of Confederate currency in 1866. Ford paid less than $5,000,000 all told. He would have liked to acquire all stocks and bonds, but some holders could not be traced, and a few, including two New Yorkers, Leon Tannenbaum and Benjamin Strauss, refused to sell. They rejected bids of $20 a share, saying that they preferred to "participate in the earnings of the road." Later they acted to prevent Ford from drawing off any profits without including them, bringing suit to set aside a lease he could otherwise have taken. From time to time they took further action to protect or promote their interests as minority stockholders, much to his annoyance.[9]

The road's condition on July 9-10, the dates of purchase, was precarious. Although the estimated value of plant and equipment was set at from $16,000,000 to $20,000,000, its 456 miles of roadbed were defective, its rails light and badly worn, its locomotives and cars inadequate in number and in poor condition, its stations and shops in disrepair, and the morale of employees low.* "For years," wrote one expert in 1921, "the D.T. & I. had been a defendant before the Ohio Public Utilities Commission to answer complaints brought by shippers and passengers concerning irregularities and inadequate service." One expert estimated in 1920 that to rehabilitate the road, $8,000,000 would be needed, "with no assurance that its prospects would improve." [10]

Railroad and business circles regarded the purchase with sardonic amusement. Some called it Ford's "new tin Lizzie;" others grimly remarked that he had found a bottomless hole into which to pour his money.

Ford met such comments with silence. During the remainder of 1920 he studied the situation, with Liebold as his deputy. Up to December 24 he advanced $521,000 for interest payments on the bonds of the Toledo-Detroit Railroad Company and for "reconstructing tracks and other purposes." These expenditures were increased in January, and a program of improvement requiring from $10,000,000 to $15,000,000 was announced.

On March 4, 1921, intensive work on the road began when James A. Gordon retired as president, and Ford took his place. A number of D.T. & I. officials were released and Ford men brought in, including Stanley Ruddiman as engineer and W. C. Cowling as Director of Traffic. Worn 56-pound rails were replaced with 85-pound stock, the roadbed was put in order, with heavier ties, and ten new locomotives and 800 new freight cars were acquired. Hazardous curves were reduced, useless flag stops abolished, stations and shops repaired and painted; the legal department was expunged and its work turned over to Claims, while paper work was halved. The employees were reduced from 2760 to 1650. At the same time, the Ford minimum wage of six dollars a day was introduced, resulting in increases for most of them.

---

* This estimate of value is given in "Henry Ford's Railroad Experiment," *Railroad Magazine*, XXIV, July, 1938, 9–28. The *N.Y. Times*, Nov. 13, 1921, "Accuse Henry Ford of Rail 'Freeze-out,'" Sec. 2, gives the same figures. However, the *N.Y. Times* of June 27, 1929, states that in 1926 the I.C.C. put a tentative value of $11,826,300 on the road, but that Ford's attorneys claimed it was worth $23,061,208. Ford had then put some $8,000,000 into the road, so a $15,000,000 valuation in 1920 may have been reasonable. The road had 75 locomotives, 2800 freight cars, and 27 passenger cars.

A drive was made to enlist the men in avoiding accidents and delays, and in establishing a standard of alertness and industry. "Every man had to work every minute of his eight hours' stint [the standard working day for the road]. If a crew stopped on a siding every man except the flagman had to apply himself to the task nearest him: in the case of the enginemen, to polish the engine, in the case of the trainmen, to washing the caboose windows and walls. . . . Nobody was expected to go out on a run without a shave, clean overclothes, a white cap, goggles." Smoking and chewing were prohibited, with severe penalties.[11]

As a result, the costs of operation were drastically reduced, the amount of traffic handled was increased, and breakdowns and accidents were all but eliminated. A report submitted to the Board of Directors on July 21, 1921, boasted that the railroad had been so improved that it could "easily be made to pay a profit larger than was its annual deficit in the past." * Meanwhile Ford had announced a 20 per cent reduction in freight rates, which the I.C.C. held up amid the indignant shouts of other roads that this was for the benefit of the Ford Motor Company! Finally the rate was permitted to become effective on July 1, 1922.

It may be added that the employees were satisfied with their eight hour day and higher wages. In October, 1921, the road was the only one not affected by a nation-wide strike. T. C. Cashen, President of the Switchmen's Union of North America, stated that D.T. & I. men would not affiliate with the brotherhoods. "Because of his [Ford's] treatment of them there is no need for organizing among them," he stated. However, employees were free to join any labor organization they chose.

The new policies began to show their effect. The $1,896,523 deficit of 1920 shrank in 1921 to $530,556, rose to $1,018,741 in 1922 because of improvements, then became a profit of $1,417,036 in 1923, and $1,719,-290 in 1924. Undoubtedly, as rival railroad executives asserted, the gains were partly due to company traffic. "Henry Ford, the shipper, gives his freight to Henry Ford, the railroad man," stated one critic. Yet, as the *New York Times* stated editorially, this was only one phase of "shrewd investment and skilled management." Ford's officials worked hard to

---

* An amusing result of improvements in service was a flood of letters denouncing them! One woman wrote to Ford complaining of the strict adherence to schedule now observed in passenger service. She was only two blocks from the station, she noted, when the train began to draw out. She waved to the conductor to stop, he saw her, but would not wait! This was unprecedented on the D.T. & I., and therefore indefensible! (Hoagland, as cited in Note 14.)

get freight from other roads, and earned it by greatly improved service. If they drew on Ford shipment to work an apparent miracle, their accomplishments could be and were studied by other railroad men, who came to Dearborn to watch operations.

The company continued to operate the line with success. Ford had early organized the Detroit and Ironton Railroad to build and own new lines, and the Ford Transportation Company to purchase equipment. Both these units leased their holdings to the D.T. & I., and through them Ford avoided expending money for the old road, and cut down the profits to be divided with the few outside stockholders. The D. & I. built the Flat Rock-Rouge cutoff (double track, 15 miles), which cut shipping time by from 17 to 22 hours, and the Durban-Malenta cutoff (56 miles), which shortened the main line route. Ford introduced a radio dispatching system, and electrified portions of his railroad.

However, he found the regulations of the I.C.C. and compliance with Federal law annoying,* and in 1928 began negotiations with the Pennroad Corporation (associated with the Pennsylvania), finally selling the D.T. & I. to that company for $36,000,000, more than seven times what he had originally paid for it.† In addition, his road had returned him rich profits from 1923 through 1926, these ceasing in 1927 when the gestation of Model A cut down traffic and caused a deficit of $134,000. Ford sold just in time to escape the depression.[12]

Meanwhile the dream of a Ford fleet had not been abandoned. By 1923 the American Shipbuilding Yards at Lorain, Ohio, and the Great Lakes Engineering Works at Ecorse were building twin freighters for the Ford Motor Company, the *Henry Ford II* and *Benson Ford*. These vessels, about 612 feet in length, 62 in beam, and 32 in depth, ‡ differed somewhat, but both used powerful Diesel motors (3000–3500 hp.), with auxiliary engine equipment, and were among the largest lake boats in operation, with cargo capacities of from 12,500 to 13,500 tons, and speeds of from twelve to fourteen knots.

---

* In 1928 Ford was sued for a violation of the Elkins Act, and was fined $20,000. (*N.Y. Times*, July 20, 1928.)

† Liebold, *Reminiscences*, denies Harry Bennett's colorful account (*We Never Called Him Henry*, New York, 1951) of sending cash to New York in an armored car as an incident to the sale. Transfers, he pointed out, could be made by wire or letter from Detroit in any amount. "It only indicates Mr. Bennett's ignorance of how financial transactions are carried out."

‡ Dimensions as given in the *Ford News* and elsewhere vary slightly.

The *Henry Ford II* was launched at Lorain on March 1, 1924, with Edsel's oldest son flashing a signal from Detroit; the *Benson Ford* took the water on April 26. However, Ford had meanwhile purchased two smaller vessels, the *Oneida* and *Onandaga,* and when these left Toledo on May 27 with coal for Menominee, they were the first company ships to go into operation.

First of the larger vessels to make a voyage, the *Benson Ford* early in August, 1924, bore Ford coal from Toledo to Duluth, picking up iron ore for the return voyage at neighboring Allonez. (It will be recalled that Ford's own mine produced low grade ore in limited quantity, and that some ore of better quality was needed at the Rouge.) A dozen vessels were soon added to the fleet, among them the *East Indian* (12,500 tons); the *Twin Cities* and *Twin Ports,* two smaller vessels for lake and barge canal traffic to New York; and six barges. Later the 4000 ton *Lake Ormoc,* diesel-powered, was salvaged from ships Ford bought from the Government for scrap. Some Ford vessels were later assigned to European and South American service.

For the period 1925–1929 the *Henry Ford II* and *Benson Ford* showed a profit of $887,810. On the whole, the barges also were profitable. A memorandum of November 12, 1926, states that the Ford shipping venture had provided valuable information on water transport, had forced other boats to liberalize their carrying practices (for example, they finally agreed to handle unboxed motors and parts as well as boxed goods), and had met the rates of outside carriers. Apparently Ford costs were somewhat higher than those of rivals, but the memorandum asserted that if shipments and sailings could be "regular and consistent" the company's boats could operate "very favorably" in comparison with others. They had also brought about a reduction of rates, and were they withdrawn, a return to higher tariffs could be expected.[13]

4.

Ford's interest in water power sites was keyed to his concern for rural America. "I am a farmer," he told Frank Stockbridge in 1918 as the two stood one evening by Ford's birthplace. "I want to see every acre of the earth's surface covered with little farms, with happy, contented people living on them." His tractor would work towards such an end. But to dot streams and rivers with water-driven factories would supplement the mechanization of the farm. These centers would offer employment to farmers and their families, and make their lives more profitable and varied.

In 1919 Ford moved from theory to action, buying sites in Lenawee County, Michigan, and on the Rouge, and acquiring others at Green Island on the Hudson and Hamilton on the Miami River in Ohio. "I am going to . . . establish plants for manufacturing parts of Ford cars and Fordson tractors," he announced in September in an article under his name, "in places where they will be within easy reach of farming districts, and provide employment for farmers and their families in winter. And these plants are going to be operated by water power."

A year later his plans, further expounded in "Mr. Ford's Own Page" of the *Dearborn Independent,* were attracting keen public interest. In part this stemmed from a faith in Ford: millions were convinced that if the wizard of Detroit proposed to act, this was tantamount to success. Furthermore, Ford said what men wanted to be true. For years youths had been leaving the farm for the city factory, and Americans, steeped in a great agricultural tradition, found the movement painful if not tragic. But now came Ford with a simple but powerful magic; he would take the factory to the country! The city, Ford pointed out through the pen of Cameron, had been a mistake. It meant high land costs, high taxes, poor housing, congested transportation. The country, in contrast, was an area of hope. "Factory and farm should have been organized as adjuncts one of the other, and not as competitors." Since with modern machinery a farmer could now plant and reap in twenty-four working days, he and his children could man the rural factory. He would be given time off for his farm duties, and throughout the rest of the year earn six dollars a day! [14]

The theory of the rural production center was not new in America. It went back to nineteenth century experiments with self-sustaining communities like New Harmony in Indiana and Brook Farm in Massachusetts (inspiration for Hawthorne's *Blithedale Romance*), and the more successful center at Oneida, New York, which created a wide market for its products, Community Silver among them. In Ford's own day Elbert Hubbard was successfully administering the crafts and printing shops of the Roycrofters at East Aurora, New York, while at Garden City on Long Island Doubleday, Page & Co. had established both its editorial offices and its press (which soon would publish Ford's own works). But Ford was launching a far more challenging development, designed to alter the basic character of American life, and if anyone could work such a transformation, he had the practical knowledge, experiences, and resources to effect it.

He began modestly with an old mill at Northville, twelve miles up the Rouge from Dearborn. Leaving the frame as it stood, he installed machinery and was soon employing three hundred men. The plant utilized water power, small at this point; but eventually supplemented it with a steam turbine. At Nankin Mills, also on the Rouge, available power again was low—from 30 to 50 hp.; at Phoenix below, it was possible to generate 100 hp. Waterford could provide 50, Plymouth 26. Northville made valves, Nankin rivets and other small parts, Waterford gauges, Phoenix generator cutouts, and Plymouth small taps for threading operations.

These and other small factories were the norms of village industry activity. But Ford also utilized water power for larger plants. The Flat Rock and Ypsilanti units on the Huron River developed greater power and employed more men. Flat Rock, for example, used 500 men in two shifts and could make 500,000 headlights per month. Larger still was the Hamilton plant on the Miami, which utilized 5000 hp., had a work force of 2500, and made 14,000 steering wheels daily. Green Island, utilizing a dam built by the Government, developed 10,000 hp. and used 1000 men. At St. Paul, Minnesota, another former Federal dam provided the factory with 28,000 hp. None of these units were "village industries," but they exemplified Ford's desire to scatter his productive centers and use available water power.

The smaller plants operated in strict accord with Ford's basic ideas. Eager to prove that water power was effective, he installed the turbine at Waterford in a glass case outside the factory. He was opposed to supplementing that power by steam or gasoline. Avery, for a time in charge of the village industries, discovered that one plant lacked power for the production it was attempting, and installed a Lincoln engine. Ford was outraged. He ordered the engine and generator delivered to Avery's house, where they were left on his front porch at night. "We built these plants to run on water power," he pointed out. "When I want any other kind of power in I'll let you know how to do it." He was also insistent on reducing office personnel to a minimum. "None of them have offices or clerical staffs," he boasted. This was not the fact, as the manager had responsibility for accounts, and sometimes even used an assistant. But the white collar element was cut to the bone.[15]

Ford believed that his experiments with decentralization were successful. Time and again he quoted figures to show that the costs of manufacture were low and the quality of work performed unusually high. Since most of the parts made were small, materials could be delivered to the plants cheaply, and hauled away as finished products at a low cost. The work was so simple in character that little supervision was required. Ford argued that to manufacture partly at a main plant and partly elsewhere was desirable.

He was particularly pleased that farmers and their families gladly came to work. "We have not drawn men from the farms," he boasted, "we have added industry to farming." (However, once farm boys worked at a plant, they often wanted to forget the soil and stay there!) Workers were given leave of absence for farm work, but, Ford pointed out, "with the aid of machinery these farmers are out of the shops a surprisingly short while—they spend no time at all sitting around waiting for crops to come up."

Ford pointed out that rural factories would tend to distribute purchasing power more evenly. His village industry workers could buy tractors for their farms and cars for transportation. Thus they purchased more Ford products, and more products in general, expanding the manufacturer's market while making a better life for themselves. "We have never put a plant anywhere," he asserted, "without raising the purchasing power of the community, nor without increasing our own sales in that community." He was hopeful that his experiments would foster sweeping changes in society. "It is far from impossible that with automatic machinery and widespread power the manufacture of some articles may be carried on at home. The world has proceeded from hand work in the home to hand work in the shop, to power work in the shop, and now we may be around to power work in the home." Actually, the practical effect was negligible, since never even a thousand families were affected, but Ford loved to contemplate the possibilities involved.

He did not live to see the idea develop; his own village industries remained few and of only theoretical importance. Nor can it be said that his experiment was a financial success. He was breaking ground, and did not count what he spent. Liebold estimated that the Waterford unit, the building of which Ford directed personally, cost $450,000—a ruinous price for a tiny plant. Were the unused properties and those unfinished or abandoned figured into the basic cost, along with units that ran profitably, the village industries would have shown a loss. Nor were they a really important part of the Ford effort. Even including Green Island and the Twin Cities development, the factories operating on water power made a negligible fraction of the total Ford activity.[16]

Nevertheless, they embodied a challenging idea, and with no small success. The problems of making farm life more remunerative and factory life less grim still exist, and if they are eventually solved, not a little of Ford's philosophy about factory and farm may be found to have vitality.

5.

Even while lumber, iron, coal, a railroad, a fleet, and a flock of rural factories engaged Ford's attention, he was never too busy to undertake additional enterprises which seemed essential to his role as manufacturer. At a relatively early date his attention was attracted to glass.*

Liebold says that just after the war Ford saw a Model T sedan with wavy glass in the rear window. He was aghast. He summoned Knudsen. "We can't put that kind of stuff into our cars! Where the hell do you suppose our business will go to?"

Scarcity of glass and the high prices demanded in war and post-war years were even more important influences on Ford than poor quality. He decided to produce his own glass, and to improve existing practices of manufacture. He and his assistants questioned particularly the method of spreading the molten glass. The ingredients were heated in clay pots, which were lifted by cranes from the furnace and poured on tables to be rolled, trimmed, cleaned, and polished. Avery hit upon the idea (which Riecks says H. B. Hanson developed) of doing away with the pots and pouring the glass directly from the furnace upon a moving table, which would take it under the rollers and through the processes required for its manufacture. Apparently experimentation

---

* In addition to the activities described in this chapter, Ford operated a lead mine for a time, took steps to produce abrasives, explored the Pokegma Range for new iron deposits, prospected for oil, and purchased dolomite lands with the production of magnesium in mind. He also experimented with the development of power by the burning of coal at the mine, and with the making of charcoal iron!

began in 1919, and by November, 1921, the glass-house at Highland Park (another was later established at the Rouge) was turning out an excellent product on an assembly line plan.

It was one of Ford's most successful excursions into a strange field. Like men who saw new light, the glass-makers scrapped their cranes and pots and adopted Avery's system. Ford, to expand his glass-making facilities, acquired in 1923 the Allegheny Plate Glass Plant at Glassmere, Pennsylvania, which covered a sixty-acre plot, offered 300,000 square feet of floor area, and produced 7,000,000 square feet of glass annually —about one-third of that used in Ford and Lincoln cars. By 1926 a glass-house, the greatest of all, had been established at the Twin Cities Ford branch. The four combined produced about 26,000,000 square feet of one quarter inch glass, more than enough for increasing company needs.[17]

Meanwhile, Ford's attention had been called by Harvey Firestone to a situation in the field of rubber production which affected both their companies. On November 1, 1922, the Stevenson rubber restriction scheme, endorsed by the British Colonial Office and the governments of Ceylon and Malaya, became effective. Designed to protect planters in the Far East from ruinous rubber prices, the act restricted output to 60 per cent of the 1920 production, permitting an increase of 5 per cent if the market averaged 30 cents, and a decrease of 5 per cent if it were lower. The British in 1922 supplied 66.85 per cent of all crude rubber, and controlled overall production, although the Dutch, who refused to accept the Stevenson scheme, were increasing the output of their Indonesian plantations. Brazil, once dominant in the rubber world, now supplied only 4.6 per cent of the total—all "wild" rubber from jungle trees.

The possibilities of price increases under the Stevenson scheme were explosive, and Firestone took a militant stand. "I am going to fight this law with all the strength and vigor that is in me," he told his associates in October, 1922, before it became effective. Early in 1923 he called a conference of American rubber, automotive, and accessory manufacturers to meet in Washington and organize to oppose the plan. In his letter of invitation to Ford, he pointed out that in a little more than three months the price of rubber had risen from 15 to 37 cents a pound. "This means an increase of $150,000,000 to the crude rubber bill of the United States for 1923." Firestone was confident that "coöperation and organized effort" by American industrialists could bring about the repeal of the act, "for it is admittedly unsound economy and contrary to British government policies and traditions."

Firestone made his fight without the help of his fellow rubber manufacturers, who deplored the Stevenson scheme, but accepted the promise of the British planters that it would not push prices to unreasonable levels. (Actually, it did.) Before his conference opened, he had won the support of Secretary of Commerce Hoover, of the War and Agricultural Departments, and of a strong bloc in Congress. A bill was introduced providing $500,000 for an investigation by the Department of Commerce of rubber-growing possibilities in Latin America or the Philippines. The conference, when it met, approved this step and denounced restriction. Not waiting for Government action, Firestone enlisted both Ford and Edison in a project most likely to shake the British —the development of an American-controlled supply of crude rubber.[18]

Such a goal seemed realizable. After all, the best types of rubber-bearing trees were native to the Americas, where rubber had first been gathered and used. After Charles Goodyear's discovery of vulcanization, patented in 1844, which brought rubber into wide commercial use,* Brazil had long enjoyed a monopoly of production, gathering the sap of the *Hevea brasiliensis,* superior to the little-used *castilloa* and *ceará* trees, direct from the Amazon jungles. At the river ports of Santarem and Manaos rubber merchants waxed rich, and fine avenues, villas, government buildings, parks, docks, and theaters decorated these remote centers of trade. The Brazilians gave little attention to the possibility of developing rubber plantations, but a few British merchants and botanists perceived the opportunity, and Sir Joseph Hooker, director of the Royal Botanical Gardens at Kew, determined to experiment with the culture of the *Hevea* in Ceylon, India, and Malaya. After one unsuccessful attempt to grow trees in the Gardens from a small number of seeds, he arranged with Henry A. Wickham, then active in the rubber trade in Brazil, to procure a large number, and Wickham succeeded in getting a shipment of 70,000 out of the country.† From these more

---

* Up to that time, rubber had been a curiosity and oddity, not adaptable to steady use. It became soft in summer and brittle in winter.

† Hooker, according to Wickham (Henry A. Wickham, *On the Plantation, Cultivation, and Curing of the Para Indian Rubber, Hevea brasiliensis, with an account of its introduction from the West to the Eastern Tropics,* London, 1908) saw a drawing of the *Hevea* leaf and seeds in Wickham's book, *Rough Notes on a Journey Through the Wilderness* (London, 1871). Hooker arranged with Wickham to supply seeds for the government of India. He was to be

than 7000 young trees were successfully grown at Kew Gardens, dispatched to the Far East, and set out in Ceylon, India, and Malaya. Later the Dutch were given seedlings and established plantations in the East Indies.

The results of these experiments were felt slowly; it was not until 1910 that the Far East supplied 12,000 long tons of rubber, only 8.52 per cent of world production. But then in four years the percentage mounted to 52.17, and it continued to increase. Brazil was soon expunged as a vital factor in the crude rubber trade.[19]

Firestone, familiar with this dramatic story, persuaded Edison and Ford that what the British had done, Americans could do, and perhaps more. Soon the three were pursuing two projects. One was to experiment with trees, vines, and plants containing rubber (the goldenrod and milkweed are common examples), find one or several types that could be cheaply raised and processed, and thus create a rubber supply independent of the climatic conditions which the *Hevea brasiliensis* required; the other was to find suitable places in Latin America, Africa, or the Philippines for establishing American-controlled plantations.

Ford and Firestone financed the first undertaking, conducted by Edison at Fort Myers, Florida, where he experimented with thousands of specimens. Finally he selected a specially developed variety of goldenrod which he asserted would provide rubber, although of inferior quality and costly to manufacture.

The search for a satisfactory plantation area first led Firestone to the Philippines, where Leonard Wood, then governor, was enthusiastic; however, the Filipino leaders feared that to establish a great American industry in their islands might act as a deterrent to independence, and the bill which they introduced in the insular legislature to pave the way

---

"left quite unhampered by instructions as to ways and means. A straight offer to do it and pay to follow the result." Located near Santarem, where he had "turned to planting" on the plateaux between the Tapajos and Madeira rivers, Wickham in 1876 chartered a ship "for the government of India," collected his seeds, and sailed down the river. He now became concerned about clearing the vessel at Para, fearing that if the character of its cargo were known, "we should be detained under plea for instructions from the Central Government at Rio, if not interdicted altogether." However, the British consul at Para explained to the Brazilian customs officer that the ship was "taking a botanical cargo of delicate specimens . . . for delivery to Her Britannic Majesty's own Royal Gardens at Kew," and the vessel was promptly cleared. Wickham, who had packed the seeds carefully, and kept them in the best condition throughout the voyage, had them conveyed by a special train from Liverpool to Kew Gardens, where the young trees were grown. He gave good advice about the planting and care of the specimens. He was deservedly knighted for his work: he was indeed the father of modern rubber culture. Apparently he operated as a planter in the Far East; in 1908 he gave sound advice in his book about the spacing and tapping of trees.

I am experimenting on the giant milk weed you found in Michigan. I will send results when finished. It grows all along the road on which I came back to Orange, except I saw none in limestone soils. There I found another variety resembling the giant but it's not so high. It was ripe and had another shape of leaf - ; I also saw two other kinds of milk weed. Am making rapid progress on the Ford Starter.

I inclose a piece of rubber I extracted from the Guayule. It can be further purified.

Sincerely,

Thos A Edison

Concluding paragraphs of a letter from Edison on his rubber experiments

for Firestone was never brought out of committee. In Liberia, the Negro republic established in 1823 with American aid, Firestone found a better area, which he was eventually to develop.[20]

He seems never to have considered a Latin American site; perhaps he hoped that Ford would develop one. For some time both men moved slowly, with an eye on Edison. Late in 1924 Liebold told a correspondent that "we have not really reached a position where any decision can be made." Actually, they had already received an appeal from Brazil. Its consul-general in the United States, J. C. Alves de Lima, had heard in the spring of 1923 that Ford was interested in producing rubber. To de Lima, Ford must have appeared as a delivering—and avenging— angel, well able with his limitless wealth and industrial genius to create a Brazilian plantation industry which would restore the position and prosperity stolen by the British and the Dutch. In April, 1923, he wrote to Ford, without effect, about the special advantages his government would offer to American capital interested in cultivating rubber in the state of Para. In 1925, when the price of rubber was rising spectacularly, he came to Detroit and conferred with Ford personally. On July 8 he outlined the concessions that the state of Para, through its governor, Dionisio Bentes, was prepared to offer. These included free land, tax remission, and police protection.[21]

The price of rubber had continued to rise, and both Ford and Firestone were thrown back on their original resolve to check the British monopoly by growing rubber themselves. Since Edison had not shown an effective way to do this in the United States, it must be done abroad. Still, Ford was not inclined to plunge into Brazil on the bait of a few suave promises.

He sent one of his engineers, Hudson McCarroll, to the Far East, and dispatched an American scientist with experience in the Dutch rubber plantations, Dr. Carl La Rue, on a survey of the Amazon valley. Meanwhile he received a report of the United States Rubber Commission, headed by W. L. Schurz who had conducted one branch of government activity while La Rue had directed another. It became clear that a South American plantation industry would suffer from the remoteness of its site (long river travel added to ocean shipment), that labor was scarce and high in comparison with Malaya or Sumatra, and that a complete agricultural-industrial community would have to be established, with emphasis on sanitation and the control of diseases. However, other factors seemed favorable, and Ford soon had an expedition headed by W. L. Reeves Blakeley looking for a plantation site in the Tapajos area, which La Rue had recommended, and, toward the end of more than a year's work, seeking a concession from the state of Para. Finally, in the summer of 1927 O. Z. Ide of the Legal Department went down to review and complete the work Blakeley had begun.

Excitement over the great project was mounting in Ford Motor Company offices. Edsel Ford grasped Ide's hand and exclaimed: "I wish I were going with you!" At Para, Ide found the situation more complicated than it had appeared to be in Dearborn, but he eventually procured a tract of 2,500,000 acres on the east bank of the Tapajos River, a main tributary of the Amazon, with a frontage of twelve miles on the river, and an area (3906 square miles) four-fifths that of the state of Connecticut. It lay directly across the Tapajos from the district where Wickham had gathered his seeds for the Far East in 1876.

By the final agreement, Ford was to import machinery and other materials for his plantation duty-free, and was to pay no export duty on his rubber, but would share seven per cent of his profits with the state after twelve years. He received permission to dam the Tapajos, and to operate railroads, airports, banks, stores, schools, a hospital, and other essential activities. The Federal government also gave certain concessions to Ford, who in return engaged to plant about 1000 acres to rubber trees during the first two years, and as many more in the two succeeding ones.[22]

The site had much physical beauty. From the river, in places seven miles wide, and, in contrast with the yellow Amazon, a clear blue, the shore mounted sharply to a height of fifty feet, and the land continued to rise gradually inland. Forested with tall and lovely trees, the castanheira or Brazil nut, the Spanish cedar, the amargose, uxy, and itauba among them, it was not the swampy terrain most Americans might have pictured, but a fertile, rolling plateau. The forest not only clothed the land with green beauty, but offered a variety of timber for the building of Boa Vista, as the headquarters of the plantation was named.

When the final agreement was approved in October, 1927, the Ford Engineering Department promptly drew up a plan of operations for 1928–1929, a special company was organized in Brazil to operate the enterprise (Companhia Ford Industrial do Brazil), and the tract was named Fordlandia. In the spring of 1928 a crew of twenty-five men was dispatched to begin clearing the land. Blakeley, in charge of the work, was recalled later in the year. Meanwhile the *Lake Ormoc* was remodelled to serve as a headquarters ship (a hospital, laboratory, machine shop, and refrigerating plant were all fitted into the vessel), the *Lake Farge* was selected to carry most of the supplies, and the two boats left Detroit in the summer of 1928, reaching the mouth of the Tapajos in late September. Here it was discovered that neither could go up stream loaded except in the season of high water, and Captain Oxholm of the *Ormoc* was obliged to transship most of their cargoes, which included tractors, stump-pullers, a sawmill, and a portable powerhouse.

Oxholm, who took charge of the entire Fordlandia project after Blakeley's departure, found that the advance crew had cleared a site for buildings, erected shelters for the workers, and constructed a temporary dock. Blakeley had arranged with planters across the river to set out 1000 seedlings, which were to be used as Fordlandia acreage was cleared. Oxholm continued the work of development, but was soon in the midst of difficulties. A new governor at the capital of Para was making trouble, taxes were unpredictable and annoying, the Brazilian workers were dissatisfied to the point of revolt, and the planting and cultivation of seedlings was a perplexing and discouraging labor. Three Ford officials successively sent by Sorensen to report on the situation must have added to the confusion.[23] *

Physically, progress was rapid. Acreage was steadily cleared for plant-

---

* Bentes, the original governor, had been helpful; Valle, his successor, denounced the Ford project as a monopoly and imposed duties on all Fordlandia exports. The workers demanded higher pay, violently opposed the use of West Indian Negroes as labor, objected to American food and cafeteria service, and demanded the right to buy liquor from river steamboats. The Brazilian government would not permit a plantation police force, but furnished only a squad of soldiers. In general, Ford officials had to adapt their policies to local practices. (Kristian Orberg, *Reminiscences; N.Y. Times,* Oct. 16, 20, 1929. See also Note 23.)

ing; a hospital, powerhouse, refrigeration plant, sewage system, and residences for Ford officials were completed. Particular care was given to sanitation, for the district was subject to yellow fever, malaria, and hookworm.

Tree-culture was the problem. Although by August 28, 1929, less than a year after the *Ormoc*'s arrival, 1440 acres had been cleared and much of it planted, the seedlings were already dead or in dubious condition. Unfortunately the young trees across the river (Blakeley's contribution) could not be used. The state of Amazonas, in which they had been set out, forbade their export to Para, and Para refused to permit their entry, saying that local stock was as good or better. The case was carried to the courts, but in vain. As a result, good seedlings were in short supply. Moreover, all the stock proved vulnerable to both climate and diseases. Seedlings imported from the Far East, although of course South American by ancestry, were particularly susceptible to root and leaf blight. The chief trouble seems to have been that the *Hevea* was a jungle tree, used to shelter, and when exposed in the open to pelting rains and long hot dry spells, could not survive.[24]

Oxholm was relieved in May, 1930, and was succeeded by Victor Perini, who soon returned to Detroit, leaving John Rogge, under J. S. Kennedy of the Para office, in charge at the plantation. Late in 1931 Archibald Johnston took charge. The new manager wrote Sorensen: "Everyone agrees that a great amount of work has been done at Boa Vista, and a great deal of money spent, but . . . that very little has been done, along the lines of what we came here to do, 'namely, plant rubber.'" Johnston threw himself into that task with great energy, while his experts studied and experimented. The acreage of planted trees was greatly increased, but the seedlings still did not thrive as desired.

The depression had now fallen on America, and Ford must have been tempted to write off his rubber plantation as a loss. But he pushed ahead, trying to find a market for the timber it produced, and in 1934 trading 703,750 acres for a site at the mouth of the Tapajos, eighty miles downstream. Here Belterra was created, accessible to ocean-going ships. Fordlandia became a mere research station. The problem of seedlings was finally solved by using a native root stock, poor as to rubber production but resistant to diseases, on which fine Malayan stock was budgrafted. Effective sprays checked the leaf blights.[25]

In 1941 the Ford plantation contained 3,651,500 rubber trees, and the following year a number were tapped, yielding 750 tons of creamed latex. By 1950 a product of 7500 tons was expected, with an eventual goal of 38,000, the amount required yearly by the Ford Motor Company. Success thus seemed within the company's grasp. However, in 1945 the plantation still needed financing, although an estimated $20,000,000 had been poured into it, and on December 22 of that year the company sold its holdings to the Brazilian government. The development of artificial rubber during World War II and the condition of the company just after the war were both factors in the sale.

The Ford project had undoubtedly created a healthful, orderly work-site for the growing of rubber, and, according to one observer, "has proved that Brazil can grow rubber on plantations, successfully and economically." The costs, it was asserted, would compare favorably with those of Far Eastern plantations "and rubber will move to market only 4000 miles, over seas the United States can keep safe from attack." Incidentally, despite the many years of difficulty and experiment, Ford had achieved the beginnings of production in about 14 years, as compared with 24 required for the establishment of promising plantations in Malaya. But the real test of the project, year-in and year-out operation, was never made.[26]

6.

In the autumn of 1922 William B. Stout, an ingenious promoter and engineer with bold ideas in the field of aviation, organized the Stout Metal Airplane Company and enlisted the financial support of a number of prominent Detroiters in the building of a duralumin commercial monoplane. He collected altogether $128,000 in contributions of $1000 each, saying to each stockholder, "You will get one very definite promise, and that is that you'll never see your money again!"

Stout, who had designed one promising airplane finally rejected by the Government,* was appealing to local pride (Detroit led in auto-

---

* Stout, an engineer trained at the University of Minnesota, had served as a reporter, designed toys, motorcycles, automobiles, and airplanes. During the war he had held a key post under Col. J. G. Vincent at McCook Field, and his "Batwing" monoplane, while never accepted by the Government, had a number of sound and at that time startling features. Stout had a genius for clarifying complex ideas in talk or writing, aroused enthusiasm for his projects, was a hard worker, and became a popular speaker with a happy vein of humor. (Stout, *So Away I Went*, 60–144.)

motive production, why not in aeronautical?) and the hope of establishing flying on a practical civilian basis. Millions of Americans had dreamed of such an achievement. With dramatic progress in the design of planes and motors during the war, the swift development of aviation as a business when peace came had seemed inevitable. The first air crossing of the Atlantic in May, 1919, by the Navy NC-4, the first non-stop crossing in June by Alcock and Brown, and the maintenance of air mail service begun in May, 1918, by the United States Post Office—these and other accomplishments seemed to bring the goal nearer. Yet in 1923 no aircraft could carry a respectable load either of passengers or freight for any considerable distance, landing fields were few and wretchedly equipped, weather service for flyers was embryonic, and the guiding radio beam of a few years later was unborn. Stout was proposing to mend this situation by solving the first problem—that of an airplane of increased speed with a respectable carrying load.[27]

Edsel and Henry Ford and William B. Mayo had all eventually become supporters of Stout. Henry Ford had watched aeronautical progress closely since he had ceased manufacturing Liberties, and as early as 1920 had toyed with the idea of building dirigibles, sending Mayo to Europe to study conditions and progress there. Edsel had an even keener interest in flying. However, they had been slow in coming to Stout's support, and as stockholders continued to be cautious, although Mayo had urged them as early as 1923 to give him assistance, "either in cash, a free lease . . . of a piece of property, a free lease of some building we may not be using, or any other combination that may occur to you." One of Stout's chief desires was a good landing field in the Detroit area, where up to 1924 none existed. He had outlined to Edsel his plans for the future, the first step being the establishment of an air freight service, passenger carrying to follow. Stout strikingly anticipated in his plans the later practices of successful commercial flying companies.

His sixth airplane and the second designed for commercial use, a craft powered with a Liberty motor and punningly called the *Maiden Detroit,* proved its capacity to carry 1500 pounds of freight as well as fuel and a pilot, and won favorable comment from Paul Henderson, Second Assistant Postmaster General in charge of the air mail. As a result, Mayo in the early summer of 1924 was able to invite Stout and his business manager Glenn Hoppin to confer with the Fords about a possible landing field. Henry Ford met them at Dearborn, showed them several available tracts of land, and then asked Stout to pick a site for a field.

When Liebold objected that the place the engineer chose was a potential housing sub-division on which a large sum had been spent, Ford snapped: "Oh, Liebold, maybe it was a sub-division yesterday, but it is a landing field today." He insisted on ample dimensions: "We'll make this the finest landing field in the world." Within twenty-four hours Fordson tractors were grading the land, 260 acres adjacent to the Engineering Laboratories, between the Michigan Central Railroad on the north and Oakwood Boulevard on the south (now the Ford Proving Ground). The completed airport, with runways 300 feet in width and 3400 and 3700 feet in length, ample hangar space for visiting planes, and parts and shop service, was one of the finest in the world. It was only twenty-five minutes' drive from the main Detroit post office. The name "FORD," in letters of crushed white stone 200 feet high, could be seen from a height of 10,000 feet. Ford extended a public invitation to all flyers—Army, Navy, Marine, Air Mail, or private—to use the field.[28]

Soon afterward he also approved the construction of a factory at his expense for the Stout organization. The *Maiden Detroit* was sold to the Post Office, and Stout at once began the construction of five new aircraft, although he had no prospects for their sale. They were, actually, far superior to any existing cargo planes of American design. At about this time Ford sauntered into the shop one morning, took Stout outside, and sat with him on a pile of lumber while the engineer outlined his plans for the future. Finally Ford rose, saying, "Stout, I'm very much surprised. . . . This whole picture looks to me as if it was something that somebody has got to put a lot of money behind to make an industry out of it. I don't know why the Ford Motor Company shouldn't do just that." He told Stout to talk to Mayo about putting the operation "on a production basis."

Stout was elated. "In my opinion," he wrote later, "the greatest single thing that I accomplished for aviation was getting Mr. Ford into it." He conferred with Mayo, and discovered that because of his earlier experiences with minority stockholders, Ford wanted complete ownership or nothing. He would pay two for one to all who held stock in the Stout Metal Airplane Company, but he must have every share of stock. Stout was thus called upon to break his promise to investors that they would never see their money again; they would see it doubled—but they must sell out!

Anticipating difficulties, Stout proposed that Ford should take over the manufacture of aircraft, but permit him to form an independent company which would operate as an airline, in which he could invite his stockholders to invest. Ford agreed. Even so, the engineer met stubborn resistance—not from his directors, who supported him fully, but from a few individuals. One told him: "Bill, I'm your friend. You're out there and all the Fords are going to do is take you and everything you have and wring you dry and throw you out in the street. I'm not going to stand for it. You can't get my stock." But in the end Stout won the unanimous approval he needed.

Although the negotiations for purchase were handled discreetly, rumors of the impending sale soon flew about. Ford, already interested in aviation, was going into it actively! To many it meant that aviation would now come of age. The Detroit *Times* remarked that "if the Fords, father and son, undertake the building of all-metal airplanes in quantity production, one great problem will be solved." The *Michigan Manufacturing and Financial Record* thought that it might mean "the centralization of the industry in Michigan." Arthur Brisbane in his column of February 13th declared that "the Fords have the power, knowledge, industrial genius and money to put this nation ahead of all others in air defense. Let them do that, and their fame will outlast the memory of war." He then wrote Edsel to ask if the rumors were true. Edsel replied cautiously, acknowledging interest, but making no definite statement.[29]

But Henry Ford, although always declaring that Edsel was the prime mover in flying activity, now pushed farther into the field by announcing in March, 1925, that the Ford Motor Company would establish a pioneering commercial airline for its own guidance and that of others. "We are going to tell the public what happens from stage to stage as we go along." He promptly took an option on all of Stout's air transports, and after the first was completed in March and tested, he put Mayo in charge of organizing a Detroit-Chicago flying service for mail and goods. The planes were to leave at specified times. For the inaugural flight of April 13, 1925, Clara Ford carried the first small package of a consignment from the truck to the pilot's cabin. Edward G. Hamilton, who flew the plane, took off at 9:22 A.M. from the Dearborn airport, arrived at Maywood, Illinois, at 12:14, and was back in Dearborn at 5:36 P.M. The Ford operation was of course not designed as a substitute for Stout's projected airline, which duly came into being more than a year later. Operating with only one plane at first, and therefore every other day, Ford on April 27 was able to start daily services and inaugurated a Detroit-Cleveland airline when a third plane became available on July 1, 1925.

On that very day Mayo reported to Edsel Ford that Stout had at last completed arrangements for the sale of all Stout Metal Airplane Company stock on a two for one basis. The purchase and transfer were soon effected, Stout and his chief backer, R. A. Stranahan, receiving special and additional consideration. With this event the Fords stepped into the full stream of aviation pioneering. The Stout organization was now a part of the Ford complex, and new directors and officers were elected, Edsel assuming the post of president, Stout and Mayo acting as vice presidents, and B. J. Craig becoming secretary and treasurer. Mayo was actually the operating head, but Henry Ford, of course, held the final power. Stout was continued on the Ford payroll as a consultant, while his assistant, George Prudden, acted as chief engineer.[30]

On February 2, 1925, Congress passed the Kelley Act, which permitted private companies to bid for the carrying of United States mail over certain air routes. This legislation had stimulated the formation of a number of organizations which hoped to get contracts and develop gradually into successful commercial airlines. All were in need of modern airplanes, superior to the obsolescent DH-4's then used by the Post Office. Although the Stout Air Transport promised to meet their demands in part, Stout and Mayo both agreed with Henderson, who discussed the general situation with them in Washington early in June, that it was not adequate for the future. What was really required, all agreed, was a tri-motored plane which could carry larger loads, operate at higher speeds, and sustain flight on two engines, or prolong it on one. If the Ford organization could develop such a product, it would dominate aircraft manufacturing. Stout and Mayo promised that they would undertake its design.

Edsel's approval was promptly secured, Stout laid out a design, and Prudden and his assistants carried it forward. Unfortunately, a mistake on Prudden's part soon lost him his post, and Harold Hicks was told by Ford to take his place.* Hicks had worked brilliantly on such projects as a gasoline-motored streetcar which Ford had planned and Edsel's "999" motorboat, and had experience with aircraft engine design.

While the experimental tri-motor was being completed, additional air transports were constructed, and received recognition because of their performance in the first Air Reliability Tour, which was initiated in 1925 by the Detroit Aviation Society. Sixteen aircraft took off from the Ford field for the contest on September 28–October 3, following a course of 1900 miles through thirteen cities. Any plane that finished was a "winner," and eleven did; but a Ford air transport showed the greatest speed, a little more than 100 miles an hour, with a Fokker tri-motor second (98.5 miles). As a result, the first commercial sale of a Ford all-metal monoplane was made to the John Wanamaker Company, followed by one of four planes to the Florida Airways Corporation, a new firm headed by the World War ace, Eddie Rickenbacker. In December Mayo announced orders from Western Air Express and National Air Transport as well. The National Air Reliability Tour became a yearly event with rules that permitted only one winner. Ford aircraft were victorious a number of times.[31]

Meanwhile the tri-motor model, the Ford hope for the future, was ready to be tested. In general lines it followed the Air Transport model, but the central section and the landing gear had been widened and strengthened, the wing extended, and two of the three Wright air-cooled motors mounted in its leading edges. The enlargement of the central section and the elevation of the cockpit had given the nose a bulky and awkward appearance. Unfortunately the tests were highly disappointing, and Ford was outraged. He ordered Hicks to take charge of engineering "and keep Stout out of the design room." He said: "I've bought a lemon and I don't want the world to know it." This was unjust to Stout, whose work formed the basis of the entire Ford activity, but Hicks was better able to develop aircraft manufacturing in the Ford organization. He began work on a new tri-motor design.

Ford's desire to eliminate the unfortunate plane was dramatically realized on January 17, 1926, when a fire mysteriously broke out in the

* Prudden had been assigned to report on the disaster to the airship *Shenandoah* (Sept. 3, 1925), and permitted the Detroit *Free Press* to take a picture of him writing a report to Henry Ford. This violated common Ford procedure of never featuring employees, and also linked the Ford name with the airship accident.

airplane factory, consuming the entire building, the tri-motor, three Air Transports under construction, and a vast amount of engines, jigs, and tools. The monetary loss was high, but the strategic loss, halting all production just as Ford products were in demand, was even greater.

But Ford took the disaster with a kind of stoic buoyancy. That morning, when he saw Stout gloomily poking around amid fragments of engines and the metal dust of wings, he beckoned to the engineer. "Stout, don't look so sad," he advised. "It is the best thing that ever happened to you. Now we can start and build the type of factory and hangar that we should have built in the first place." [32]

Actually, it was the beginning of Ford aviation on a new scale, and of higher quality. While the tri-motor was pushed ahead in a temporary shop, a factory of 60,000 square feet of floor space arose, "laid out expressly," noted the *Ford News,* "to accommodate the Ford system of progressive production." At this time, in March, 1926, the Fords announced also that they would henceforth build only multi-motored airplanes—a somewhat astonishing declaration, since there were then less than half a dozen such craft in the entire country. But the decision was not lightly taken, and merely anticipated the needs of the growing industry.

By June 11, the second tri-motor (commonly called the first, since Ford liked to forget the failure that was burned) was ready for testing. Hicks and Tom Towle, his chief assistant, had taken account of the weaknesses of the first design, although keeping the general lines of the air transport type as earlier developed. In particular, the new model used a wing curve that provided greater lift, eliminated the bulky nose of its predecessor, showed more graceful lines, and had its two outer engines located in nacelles or pods under the wings, to avoid alleged interference with wing areas caused by their installation in the wing edge. The plane had a wing spread of 70 feet, carried eight passengers, and provided separate space for freight. It was the largest multi-motored type designed in the United States to date for commercial use. After a successful flight in the morning, the ship was demonstrated in the afternoon before representatives of National Air Transport, Colonial Airways, Western Air Express, and Florida Airways, all hopeful that it would provide an answer to their future needs. [33]

It did so, but the plane was ahead of passenger-carrying activity. The

Fords therefore proceeded with the construction of their new factory, and their output for the remainder of the year comprised only two planes, one of which the company kept. The other went to National Air Transport. However, once the new plant was occupied (November, 1926), a growing crew of factory employees began to deliver planes more rapidly. Tri-motors were put into Ford airlines operation, sold to the Navy, the new Stout Air Services, the Maddux Air Lines, Skyview Air Lines, the Army, and private companies such as Standard Oil and Royal Typewriter.

In 1925 the Fords had bid for two air mail routes, were awarded contracts, and on February 15, 1926, initiated service between Detroit and Chicago and Detroit and Cleveland. During the first year their planes completed 963 of 979 flights, for an average of 98.3 per cent in more than 260,000 miles of flying.[34]

The year 1927 witnessed steady expansion in various ways. A third airline to Buffalo was inaugurated on March 28; the tri-motor was improved by the installation of more powerful Pratt & Whitney engines; the use of a radio beacon was established, and both the engineering and factory forces were enlarged. The crossing of the Atlantic by Charles A. Lindbergh that summer gave an impetus to aviation in general, and for the Fords the culmination came on August 11, when Lindbergh himself visited the Ford airport and took both Henry and Edsel aloft in the *Spirit of St. Louis*. It was Henry Ford's first flight.

By 1928 production was getting further under way, with 36 tri-motors —a large number for that day—finding customers with new lines like Juan Trippe's Pan-American, Northwest, and Transcontinental Air Transport, then called "the Lindbergh line," which was experimenting with a combination of rail-plane transport that cut the distance across the country by several days. (Eventually TAT became the modern TWA.) [35]

The distinction of the Ford organization was that alone among well-established aircraft manufacturers it was studying production as a commercial problem. Through its own intra-company airlines, its mail contracts, and the operation of its airport it acquired valuable experience which it could apply profitably to design and construction. The spirit of the entire undertaking in these years, Hicks later testified, was one of freedom and initiative (under Ford's supervision, but with his approval). A number of special projects emerged. One was the "flivver plane," a small 40 hp. craft which was first tested in the summer of 1926, and later, with an engine designed by Hicks, broke the world's endurance record for small airplanes (986 miles). Ford became hostile to this model because Harry Brooks, a popular young pilot, lost his life in it. He showed an interest in the 14-AT, a huge passenger airliner which was one of Mayo's favorite projects. Hicks vehemently opposed it, but Mayo told him: "Well, Hicks, if you don't superintend the design of that, I am going to get somebody else who will;" and Hicks proceeded with the task, which occupied him for three years. The 14-AT represented immense progress in provision for passenger comfort, but Ford eventually saddled it with heavy water cooled motors, and it never left the ground.

The aircraft division, as it was now called, reached its highest activity in 1929, when it sold eighty-six planes. Relatively speaking, production had been mastered: in June alone eighteen units were completed. Soon afterward the factory capacity was doubled. The tri-motor had been steadily improved, chiefly by the introduction of the new and more powerful Pratt & Whitney motors, and improvements in structural design, including cowling for the motors. The 5-AT, as the improved model was called, cruised at 122 miles per hour, and in October, 1930, achieved a high speed of 164.43 miles per hour. Ford during 1929 was selling aircraft to practically all the commercial companies, to the Army and Navy, and to individuals and companies who wanted planes for publicity or the convenience of their chief executives.

Unfortunately the oncoming depression quickly deflated flying activity, which had only recently become profitable by a narrow margin. The demand for planes fell off rapidly; sales dropped from 86 in 1929 to 26 in 1930, 21 in 1931 and 3 in 1932. All air activities included, the Ford project had been a losing operation, but as production facilities and personnel had grown (the factory now employed 1600 men), the losses were bound to be greater. Ford also had begun to interfere with design; Hicks felt that he foresaw the end of the entire adventure, and was "sabotaging it to a certain extent." Stout had been gently dropped in 1930; in July, 1932 Ford ordered the engineering and factory forces discharged, except for men with automotive experience who could be routed to the Ford Motor Company. Mayo left in August, Hicks in November.[36]

Ford flying had covered a period of more than seven years, and had contributed notably to the progress of American aviation.* The Fords had accepted from Stout and his associates the metal monoplane, which became the unit for commercial flying. They had pushed on to establish the routines of a regular air service, and to develop the first tri-motor successfully built in the United States for commercial purposes. The work was original, for although Fokker later claimed that the Ford aircraft was an adaptation of his own, ample evidence exists that in inception, design, and methods of construction it was independent. The Stout-Ford plane appeared at a time when it was desperately needed; and the subsequent tri-motor enabled the new American air lines to function successfully during their infancy. The Ford air freight lines made a convincing demonstration for many years of the possibility of regular, dependable flying.

Ford might have gone much further. There is evidence that had he permitted a continuing initiative such as his engineers had enjoyed at first, they would have greatly improved the planes he manufactured. With these improved types, and the will to weather the depression while still developing commercial aviation, Ford might have fulfilled Brisbane's prophecies and played a role in flying parallel in part at least to that which he played in automotive progress. Edsel and Mayo, given greater freedom, might have contributed to such a result.[37]

But this is conjecture. The facts are that with time Ford tightened his control over the air division, that he interfered with design, that he lost the first enthusiasm he had shown, and that the depression posed a grave problem. Ford had lost his money on aviation from the beginning.† In 1932 he had accumulated a total operating deficit of $5,627,996, while his expenditures (plant, equipment, and losses) aggregated $10,369,825.[38] Ford was primarily concerned with the manufacture of motor cars, and no one can argue that he was foolish, in a time of stringency, to abandon an unprofitable side-activity. Of course, full success in aviation would have meant a glorious extension of the Ford legend.

* A number of Ford tri-motored planes were still employed in 1955 in forestry work in the Far West. Their moderate speed made them useful for cruising low over forest areas to look for fires, insect infestations, illegal timber cutting, and the like; while it was easy to throw equipment from them to fire-fighters below. In 1955 a project for reviving manufacture of the airplanes was being canvassed.

† Technically, he made a profit on the airplane division of $4,437.27 in 1925 and $187,748.03 in 1929. But his total expenditures (on non-profit lines maintained as experiments, factories, landing field, etc.) naturally more than cancelled out such gains.

7.

Ford at Iron Mountain, Ford on the D.T. & I., Ford at Boa Vista or the Dearborn airport, was Ford in a succession\ of creative phases. No one can follow these extra-automotive activities without recognizing the daring and flexibility of a mind that could also, at times, be limited and sterile. Here Ford is fully the industrial and social pioneer.

The public recognized him as such. Not without intention, he was immensely successful in fostering through these projects a wide conviction of his originality and technical skill, and of his will to serve mankind. In half a dozen different areas, Ford was an industrial angel, bringing light and order to dark places. It did not matter that he fell short of the goals he set himself. He achieved enough to command respect and a chuckling popular enthusiasm. "Henry Ford showed them," his admirers could say with considerable justification, whether of lumbering, railroads, village industries, glass, or airplanes.

Financially, a number of these forays into strange fields—notably the rubber and airplane adventures—brought heavy losses. Others were profitable. Ford didn't care. To his credit, he was concerned with what could be accomplished. He thus appears, in his reach toward newer patterns of industrial and social life, in his happiest role—that of the experimenter who was glad to risk greatly, and if necessary to accept partial or even total failure, because of the high value of the attempt.

X

THE GREATER COMPANY

"It is difficult to comprehend the vastness of this industrial enterprise," a veteran of the automobile world wrote of the Ford empire, "for it reaches from the depths of the earth in the iron mines of northern Michigan to the heart of the jungles of Brazil, and its plants and buildings are found in thirty-three countries of the globe." [1] This magnitude, however well-known in the industry, was scarcely grasped in the mid-nineteen-twenties by most Americans, who identified the Ford Motor Company with Model T and the Fordson. Yet scope and intricate variety were vital aspects of the organization, and neither its products nor its personalities can be understood except in relation to the complex that produced them.

Ford activities in the period 1922–1928 can be divided into six main areas: raw materials, transportation, research, and engineering, plants and production, marketing, and administration. We can relate here certain elements previously treated to the whole body of company facilities and work, and round out the picture with an examination of other areas not yet fully explored. These comprise chiefly research and engineering, some vital but neglected aspects of production, the Ford marketing organization, and administration.

2.

If the processes of manufacture began for the Ford Company with raw materials and their transportation to the centers of production, the articles to be manufactured were determined by engineers in the experimental rooms which Ford habitually haunted. In its early days the company had probably spent more time and money than any of its rivals in improving the basic character of its cars, the materials used, and the machine tools, fixtures, and factory layouts for their produc-

249

tion. Ford himself, Wills, Galamb, Farkas, Emde, Wandersee, Pioch and others had labored on automotive design, metallurgy, heat treatment, and productive devices. Fred Allison, Ed Huff, and later Pat Maher had worked in the electrical field, George Holley on carburetors. Little of this was research in the modern sense. Ford was confessedly a tinkerer, a cut-and-try man, and Wills too believed in testing by practice.* A few Ford employees had formal training as engineers—Galamb, for example, and his fellow-Hungarian Farkas. But both worked easily in the Ford shops, never emphasizing their special schooling. In contrast, Galamb's assistant, Walter Fishleigh, who had taught at the University of Michigan, never shook off the academic manner. McCloud, a college-trained engineer himself, felt that Fishleigh was always a square peg in a round hole. Eventually he left.[2]

A great deal of practical experimentation and testing was carried on in the factory. Here Findlater, Avery, Klann, and others evolved numerous processes and devices, sometimes with the help of Emde or other engineers, but often on their own. They had the tools, equipment, workers, and above all the initiative, to carry on such activities.[3]

During the war and just after a number of younger men appeared —Philip Haglund, J. L. McCloud, Laurence Sheldrick, Harold Hicks, Allan Horton, Howard Simpson, and Hudson ("Hud") McCarroll. In the early nineteen-twenties they worked along with the older men.

As company enterprises multiplied, and production of both the Model T and the tractor mounted, Ford strengthened his research and experimental facilities. The first step was the erection of an Engineering Laboratories Building in Dearborn near the site of the old tractor plant. On March 16, 1923, construction began on the unit, worthy in size of the new Rouge and the almost two million vehicles that Ford plants were now producing annually. The building, one storied, 200 by 800 feet, provided ample space for experimental work of all types.

A second important step was the installation here in 1924 of a special department for the Johansson gauges. These metal blocks still represent the finest units of industrial measurement, accurate to a millionth of an inch.† Their manufacture was now a Ford enterprise, like glass-

---

* But they encouraged systematic efforts by the men to acquire information and training. Dozens of Ford engineers and officials, Sorensen, Haglund, Wandersee, Klann, and Lumsden among them, made special studies and took International Correspondence School courses to improve their knowledge in various fields.

† For the general reader who may wonder how blocks can be used for gauges, it should be

making, lumbering, and mining, for in the fall of 1923 the company had acquired the C. E. Johansson Company, their makers, along with the services of Johansson himself, the inventor and producer.* For a time Ford maintained the Johansson plant at Poughkeepsie, New York, but established the research and eventually the manufacturing, at Dearborn. The rough steel blocks were made at the Rouge, but finished in the Laboratories Building under Johansson's supervision. Air-conditioned quarters kept the temperature, to which the gauges were sensitive, at a constant 68 degrees Fahrenheit.[4]

The Laboratories Building also provided quarters for the *Ford News,* the *Dearborn Independent,* and the Ford radio stations—both the broadcasting studios of WWI and the central unit for the wireless network which Ford had developed for communication with remote plants like those at Iron Mountain and L'Anse, and with the ships of the Ford fleet. The early Ford experiments with wireless had been of a pioneering character, and there was a parallel opportunity to develop a contribution in broadcasting, but Ford eventually lost interest in the work.[5] †

After the completion of the Laboratories Building late in 1924, Ford could boast of research facilities that potentially were second to none in the automotive field. Unfortunately the shell was much bigger than the meat. While General Motors had appointed Charles F. Kettering to direct its research, with the result that the work was ably organized and staffed, provided with modern facilities, and prosecuted with originality, Ford in important respects still clung to the habits of horse-and-buggy days. He was skeptical of if not hostile to formal professional

---

explained that the blocks, oblongs of many sizes, and each exact in dimensions, were so finely made that when placed one on another, they adhered. To test the dimensions of a mechanical unit, several blocks could thus be put together, the total representing the precise measure, to the millionth of an inch, to which the object being tested should conform.

* Born in Sweden in 1864, Carl Edward Johansson had come to the United States as a young man, working in factories here, and attending Gustavus Adolphus College at St. Peter, Minn. When twenty-one he returned to Sweden, and worked at the government arsenal at Eskilstuna. As toolmaker and foreman there, he became increasingly dissatisfied with the existing gauges, and began to develop his blocks, producing a set in 1897. He improved them, and resigned from government service in 1911 to manufacture them commercially. Returning to the United States in 1917, he established his Poughkeepsie plant, winning wide recognition for the merits of the blocks, but apparently not thriving commercially. (See "Johansson, Apostle of Mechanical Accuracy, in America," *Automotive Industries,* XLI, Sept. 25, 1919, 608–610; Liebold, *Reminiscences.*)

† One event affecting his attitude toward radio was the establishment of government control with the Federal Radio Commission (which eventually became Federal Communications Commission) in 1927. Ford did not like regulation from Washington.

training, and never appointed a research director, but clung to the reins of authority himself without providing adequate direction. Aside from the Johansson quarters, the radio stations, and the offices of the *Dearborn Independent* and the *Ford News,* the allocation of space to specific groups or activities was confusingly haphazard. As Howard Simpson recalled the same situation: "There wasn't any reason for each spot; you just happened to be there." [6]

By the organization chart of November 1, 1919, W. H. Smith was designated Director of Research and Joseph Galamb Director of "Experimental." In practice, neither had more than routine authority. Ford decided what important experimental work should be undertaken, and who should develop a particular project. Often he dealt directly with an engineer or a workman, assigning tasks and checking on progress. At times he had men working in a private laboratory built over the garage at Fair Lane; he also had a special room in the new building—"the Green Room" (from the color of the partitions). But he kept track of the groups scattered throughout the building, although many were busy with the mere testing of metals, paints, individual car parts, and devices. The engineers had desks but no chairs. "Mr. Ford . . . detested anybody just sitting around on a chair, and according to him doing nothing." They were not encouraged to keep records. The chief experimental work in the early nineteen-twenties included that on the "X" engine and car, on tractors (to improve the Fordson, and later to investigate wholly different types), on a gas turbine, on transmissions, and other car improvements.[7]

So far as routines of testing were concerned, the Ford shops set varying standards. There was a startling lack of dynamometers—a shortage which slowed basic research. In contrast, the quality of many important elements—their strength, and their behavior in operation—were all checked by devices of the latest available type. Ford was exacting in his search for superior materials. He was also insistent on maintaining close tolerances, and the Johansson blocks were only one of a number of gauges used in the laboratories and factories. But Ford's personal direction of research left small leeway for initiative in the larger sense, and none for organized progress. He launched a number of projects which wasted time and manpower—the Alco fuel press, the tomato juice extractor, the gas-engined street car, a variety of motor boat designs, and even the possibility of deriving fuel from water. (Ford personnel never admitted that *anything* was impossible!) His captiousness also interfered with effective design or development. He would start a man or group on a new project, but limit possibilities by insisting that the final product must be adapted to one of his fetishes, such as the planetary transmission, or avoid elements that he made taboo, such as the chain drive. For a time the mere mention of hydraulic brakes in his presence was highly dangerous. Again, he would appear just as a designer was making progress with an idea, and suggest several incompatible features, or an entirely new approach, which of course had to be undertaken. "I could have gone ahead and designed a job if he had left me alone long enough," said Simpson of tractor possibilities. Ford was also impatient of explanations, and in the midst of a complicated and important statement would say, "I'll be back pretty soon," and vanish for three weeks! [8]

Thus the two great weaknesses in experimental work and design were deficiency in trained men, and the failure to use wisely the strength actually available. "There was a lack of depth in engineering ability in plant engineering, production engineering, and advanced design engineering," states McCloud. And again: "There was no advanced planning as far as I can understand. When we'd compare it with the engineering departments of other automobile plants, we didn't have an engineering department." Ford had thus confused and frustrated the activity he had been at great pains to promote.

In one particular respect he was far behind his chief competitor, General Motors. In that organization Alfred P. Sloan, Jr., had established an adequate proving ground by the mid-nineteen-twenties. Ford would not hear of one, continuing to use the plant yards and public roads to test new vehicles. It was another ten years before the growing congestion of highways, the laws governing motor traffic, and the possibility of needless accidents forced him into modern practice.[9]

3.

By 1921 most elements in the Ford production network had been established, but many were incomplete and operating only in fragmentary fashion. The Upper Peninsula iron mines and saw mills were just starting, the D.T. & I. was in process of renovation, and the Rouge, except for its body plant and coke ovens, was producing only a few castings. The depression of course crippled all activity for the first few months of the year, and the branch assembly plants, although open for most of the time that Highland Park was closed, were operating on a reduced schedule. The production of 1,050,740 cars, trucks, and tractors for Ford factories throughout the world in 1921 (928,750 for the United States) set a record, but did not express the potential strength of the company. Neither did the 1,425,830 units produced in 1922; but 1923 exhibited the power of the giant for the first time. In that year, with the Rouge blast furnaces and foundry active, the Upper Peninsula and the D.T. & I. efficiently operating, and the branch plants coming into new productivity, Ford factories soared to a mark of 2,201,188 (2,120,-898 domestic). In four years the output had been doubled.[10]

The Model T was of course the backbone of the accomplishment, but the output of trucks and tractors had been anything but negligible. The Ford truck as a unit of manufacture had not existed until the fall of 1917. Actually, merchants and dealers throughout the country bore it to Highland Park as a gift. They had constructed delivery wagons and truck bodies of various types on Model T chassis, thus demonstrating the feasibility of a commercial vehicle. The company accordingly began to build truck chassis, especially of the one-ton type. In 1921 67,796 were manufactured, and in 1922 production rose to 127,322, advanced to 268,411 in 1925, and 355,453 in 1929. One-ton trucks became available in 1923 in several body types, and with open and enclosed cabs; and a half-ton pickup appeared in the spring of 1925. The truck chassis was also used for school buses. Ford trucks were victorious in endurance contests, a one-ton model winning a six-day contest in North Africa.[11]

Tractor production, which had stood at 70,000 in 1920, dropped to 36,783 in the depression of 1920–1921,* but rose to 68,985 in 1922, despite the fall in farm prices and the consequent lower buying power of the rural areas. It then climbed to 101,898 in 1923.

Success was achieved in part by adaptation to non-farm uses. The tractor hauled baled cotton on Virginia wharves, served as a snow plow in northern states, dragged logs, and was used for everything from coal-mining to a government campaign against the corn borer.

Farmers employed it not only for plowing, harrowing, seeding, and spraying, but also for sawing wood, pumping water, and operating small machine shops. The *Ford News* boasted that the Fordson had

---

* This period was also that of the move to the Rouge, when tractor production was suspended for six months.

1700 potential uses, and had taken over work that would have required 1,500,000 horses. The tractor won numerous plowing contests in the United States and Great Britain. One evidence of its success was its wide use in Russia. The Soviets ordered Fordsons in large lots, the total for the period 1920–1926 amounting to 24,600. The tendency of the machine to tip over backwards had been countered by several devices, although the company always asserted that such accidents were "operational" in character. In February, 1928, tractor manufacture in the United States was abandoned, the greater part of the production machinery at the Rouge was shipped to Ireland, and the Cork plant became the chief Fordson unit for the company. The reduced duties on parts importations, the lower labor costs in Ireland, the opportunities of the European market, the need for more space at the Rouge for Model A manufacture, and increasing competition in the United States were all factors in this shift.[12]

Meanwhile, a sweeping modernization of assembly centers was affecting Ford production as old plants were rebuilt and a vigorous program for constructing new ones was launched.

In March, 1916, the company had operated twenty-eight branch factories in the United States, most of them developed by Knudsen and his assistant Frank Hadas. In addition, it had fifty-one non-producing branches. However, even before American entrance into the war the assembly units were unsatisfactory because of improvements in factory layout and assembly methods. The Ford executives decided that a formidable program of remodelling and new construction would have to be undertaken. Branch plants were essential: they provided convenient shipping points for outlying territories, and would be vital also in raising Ford production toward the two million mark. On the other hand, to use most of the older units would be impossible. They had been prepared for stationary assembly, and were not expected to produce more than a hundred cars a day. Many were buildings of several stories, too small for conveyors or moving assembly lines. Others, though roomier, contained central elevator shafts which blocked effective layouts. "They were right in the middle of the floor," recalled Frank Hadas, "where you couldn't put any conveyors or progressive machinery or equipment."[13]

The program of new branch construction was approved by Henry Ford and carried out by Edsel and Kanzler. The first indication of the immense project came to the public in late 1921, with an announcement that the Ford Motor Company would build a $6,000,000 assembly plant in Chicago. Henry Ford, stated the news release, regarded each branch factory as "the hub in a great wheel of industry that he eventually hopes will cover many cities in the country." The company soon added that it would increase the domestic assembly units to thirty, thus raising its productive capacity by 600,000 cars and trucks.[14]

The character of the new branch factories was determined by experience at both Highland Park and the Rouge. "We had decided," says Kanzler, "that the multiple story buildings were not effective. We wanted lots of ground for parking, railroad sidings; and Mr. Henry Ford insisted that every plant be on navigable waters." Ford, says Kanzler, not only appreciated the cheapness of water transportation, but also had found that the railroads were at times undependable: even the D.T. & I. on occasion "was just not allowed to favor his shipments." Edsel and Kanzler made numerous trips to survey possible sites, and chose their locations. The new plants were designed by Albert Kahn, took account of the improved moving assembly, employed the latest machine-tool equipment, and provided paint spray booths and drying ovens. In some instances it was possible to remodel existing structures: for example, in Cleveland, Atlanta, Denver, Los Angeles, and Portland. The two largest of the new plants rose at Chicago and Minneapolis. The first, with a floor space 500 by 1360 feet, could assemble 600 cars a day, while the Twin Cities unit, 600 by 1400 feet, eventually had a capacity of 750 cars, or 225,000 annually. All the new buildings were low, trim, and functional in appearance, with ample light, efficient floor arrangement, and the most modern equipment. They had been located and designed with freight shipment, to and from them, in mind. Attractive sales quarters and offices, waiting rooms for dealers, and other features proclaimed that all the branches were sales and administrative as well as assembly and shipment centers.[15]

By 1923–1924, construction on the new factories was under way in seven cities. The cost of the program has been estimated at between $110,000,000 and $150,000,000. By 1925, the company had thirty-six branch factories, which undoubtedly contributed notably to the increase in total Ford production. The program had been hastily planned, apparently without any central board of strategy, and certainly without market research. On the other hand, past sales in various areas and the opinions of branch managers were good practical guides, each new plant was studied for possible improvements in the next, and the results in general were good. The branches were of course in constant communication with Edsel's and Kanzler's offices, as well as with Ryan's, and they had a consistency and efficiency of operation which, as we shall see, was lacking in company units in the Detroit area.[16]

By 1926 the entire productive activity of the company had been impressively developed. Raw materials were now flowing from the iron mines and lumber mills of the Upper Peninsula, from Ford coal mines in Kentucky and West Virginia, and from Ford glass plants in Pennsylvania and Minnesota, much of the product travelling on Ford ships or over Ford-owned rails. Ford manufacture of parts had been expanded—starters and generators, batteries, tires, artificial leather, cloth, and wire had been manufactured by the company in increasing quantities.* The Rouge was producing coke, iron, steel, bodies, castings, engines, and other elements for Highland Park and the assembly plants, and also manufacturing the full quota of Fordsons. The entire operation was synchronized on a grand scale, greater than any automotive firm had ever attempted. Indeed, Ford production in 1925 was more than one fifth larger than that for the entire industry in 1920.

4.

In the end, the transformation of the company, 1919–1925, at a cost of at least $360,000,000, had to be justified by sales.† The branches and the thousands of Ford dealers received the never-ending spate of trucks, tractors and Model T's (and the smaller consignments of Lincolns), and disposed of them. How had the marketing organization of the company adjusted itself to the productive network?

In form, this organization consisted of branch offices, headed by managers, who controlled their dealers through roadmen, or travelling inspectors. Each branch had an assistant manager, a wholesale manager (in charge of the roadmen) and a superintendent (who operated

---

* In all these activities Ford personnel contributed improvements in manufacture paralleling those in their glass, iron, steel and railroad operations.

† The Rouge represented an expenditure of about $116,500,000, the branch plants may be estimated to have cost $125,000,000, and the outlying activities (Upper Peninsula, Glassmere, the D.T. & I., the Ford fleet, Ford aviation, the Brazilian plantation, Fordson Coal Co., etc.) make a total estimated investment of $360,000,000 from July 1, 1919 to Dec. 31, 1925, and about $376,000,000 if Jan. 1, 1919 is taken as a starting point. (Figures prepared by O. H. Husen for the Ford Archives, May–June, 1956.)

the assembly plant). It was served by from 150 to 500 dealers, who in turn were watched by from 10 to 25 roadmen. In addition, the Detroit office maintained six supervisors, each of whom watched a number of branches, and reported on them regularly to Detroit. The six were themselves branch heads, who while absent from their regular posts left their assistant managers in charge.

They were men of exceptional experience and energy, able to advise branches constructively, and to report with ruthless candor to Edsel Ford on every phase of the areas they visited. Among the were A. L. Gilpin of Houston, P. F. Minnock of Kansas City, Gaston Plantiff of New York, and S. A. Stellwagen of Minneapolis. Evidently they exerted great influence on promotions or discharges. Their reports contain comments such as "With more experience, Jones [as assistant manager or wholesale manager] will make a good branch head," or, pointing out that the manager was not delegating enough responsibility, "I asked him to put Mr. Burroughs on his own to ascertain if he is the right material for the position," or even, "He's a nice guy, but he isn't doing his job. Get someone else." The supervisors also watched the roadmen, recommending some for assistant managers, or wholesale managers. They even reported on individual dealers. Ryan found that a number of branch managers, busy with administrative and assembly problems, took too little time for field work among their dealers, or even for conferences with their roadmen.[17] The 6484 Ford dealers active in February, 1921, rose to 9800 four years later.[18]

The control of the Ford branches, both as to manufacturing and selling, was centered in Detroit. The supervisors reported to Edsel, and he and Ernest Kanzler watched closely the branch heads, particularly in administration and manufacturing. Henry Ford gave little attention to them except in times of crisis. Edsel and Kanzler also watched sales, and Edsel as president of the company not only signed some general letters, but also made himself familiar, as we shall see, with the chief problems of selling. Ryan, of course, was directly responsible for sales policies and routines. A tall, enterprising, ruddy man, he lacked the breadth of knowledge and inspired ingenuity which had characterized Hawkins, but brought an aggressive, confident energy to his task. It was to be a difficult and complicated one, for during this period the Model T was to encounter its first (and final) challenge. He followed the work of the branches and dealers with unremitting vigor, and issued most of the frequent letters which went from Detroit to the branches.

Control was authoritarian, and designed to preserve the line of relationship from dealer to roadman to branch head and to Detroit. Even the branch managers were not encouraged to assume a broad initiative. For example, they were categorically forbidden to exchange information with each other, or to discuss common problems—unless specifically told to do so. Consultations between branch heads, declared the company, represented "neither the proper way nor a healthy condition." Similarly, dealers were enjoined from discussing their problems with each other. Ryan in 1921 pointed out to branch heads that clubs and associations of dealers had been formed. "While these meetings might have originally been productive of good results, in most cases they have developed into more or less time-takers, and have brought about discussions and agreements between dealers along the line of hiring each other's salesmen, divisions of commissions between dealers working on the same prospects, and such like." He wanted competition between Ford agents, not adjustments. "If your city dealers have been holding such meetings, have them discontinued at once." [19]

Indeed, the discipline was military, each individual reporting to his superior. Dealers were firmly discouraged from complaining to the company about alleged injustices perpetrated by roadmen or branch managers, although in desperation a number of them did. The branch, severely controlled from Detroit, often controlled its dealers even more severely. Although the roadmen could tell their regional office what difficulties were encountered in selling, that office often showed no disposition to know, for fear of displeasure at the top. Detroit never admitted that any feature of the Model T or Fordson, or any defect in either, could impair sales. "It is not the car," said Edsel characteristically on one occasion, "so it must be our Organization." Thus the dealer had little opportunity to be heard. He was taught, often by bitter experience, to keep quiet about his difficulties, even when they were also the difficulties of the Ford Motor Company. [20]

During the early nineteen twenties Ryan was dissatisfied not only with the inactivity of branch managers in the field, but with the work of the roadmen. He pointed out that the company spent $2,000,000 a year on their salaries and expenses, and was "not getting results at all commensurate with this outlay." He ordered the branches to classify dealers as good, fair, and poor, reduced the roadmen by half, and bade them confine their efforts to agencies in the "fair" and "poor" categories. The roadmen who continued such activity were called "zone" men; a number of the others were kept, and they concentrated on new activities which the company was developing: trucks, tractors, Lincolns, and the handling of spare parts.[21]

Ford dealers had definite responsibilities. One was to keep a clean, neat place of business, with a pleasing show window, and attractive cars for demonstration. They must study their territories, build up files of prospects, and work on them systematically and diligently. Many dealers kept maps showing with colored pins the owners of Ford cars, non-owners who gave promise of becoming customers, and recent sales. The company stressed the importance of rendering service promptly and at reasonable prices, to create good will for both dealer and company. It instructed its roadmen to inquire into the alleged difficulties of a dealer, and to report him if he did not show resourcefulness and energy in meeting them.

Some roadmen carried cameras and photographed untidy premises. "It might be well to use this at all branches," wrote one of the supervisors to Detroit. Enterprising dealers were lauded, such as those who exhibited new Model T's at factory entrances, or demonstrated them by offering free rides to or from work. Supervisors sometimes complained of roadmen who scamped their tasks, or of branches that shipped cars in poor condition. However, the chief effort was to stimulate an aggressive, intensive effort on the part of dealers, with the building up of large files of prospects, and frequent house to house calls. The dealer who did not respond to pressure would in the end find a more enterprising agent planted near him, or, in extreme cases, would lose his franchise.[22]

Aside from its tendency to regiment the sales organization, the company in this period followed a liberal policy toward its dealers. While the supervisors and roadmen were alert and even exacting, they showed an understanding of local conditions and did much constructive work, demonstrating sales methods for dealers, helping to build up prospect files, and so forth. No cars were shipped to dealers without due notification—one branch manager was actually disciplined for having made an unscheduled shipment. The commissions were satisfactory; that for the Model T was raised in 1922 from 17½ to 20 per cent, while 25 per cent was allowed for tractors. Dealers basked also in the generally prosperous state of the country. "After 1922 sales were very good up to the end of the Model T," one recalled. "I don't think we ever discounted a Model T car." Often they had orders which they could not fill; in 1923 the company was said to have lost 350,000 sales because it could not deliver cars for which the agencies had customers.[23]

One growing problem was that of used cars. On May 28, 1921, the Ford Motor Company had produced its five millionth automobile, and the total for the rest of the industry at that time was higher. Millions of these vehicles were still in use, and millions of Americans were ready to buy new cars if they could get a reasonable allowance on their old ones.

Up to 1920 the problem had scarcely existed, in that there had been little difficulty in disposing of both new and used cars. Now suddenly, with the great yearly increases in production, the situation changed, and used cars piled up on every automotive company's (and on every dealer's) doorstep. The difficulty for the dealer was that while a sufficient allowance for a used car might close a sale, he must later dispose of it, and if the allowance had been too high, he would do so at a loss. But he was under strong pressure to make it high, for another dealer (Ford or non-Ford) might offer more and get the customer.

The chief objection to the trade-in practice, however, was that it militated against the sale of cars to new owners. The company admonished the dealers not to spend their time "in hunting up second-hand cars to *buy* from present owners instead of hunting up and *selling* Ford cars and trucks to prospects who have never owned an automobile." It pursued the matter to the point of asking the branches to investigate their dealers. If some lost on re-sales, they had probably outbid other dealers, jeopardizing their own businesses and those of their competitors, often Ford agents. "We do not propose to have the morale of our dealers' organizations lowered through any such unbusinesslike methods." This was a threat of cancellation which, by 1925, was sometimes justified. One district supervisor reported that fifty-five Ford dealers in Chicago were "all bidding against one another," and a survey of twelve agencies in that city showed that only one had profited on used car sales, while two sustained annual losses of $18,000 and $29,000 respectively.[24]

The dealers also suffered from the "driveaway" system of delivery. The "driveaway" had been used as early as 1916, and will be remembered as a popular device during the railroad strikes of 1920. After the building of the new Ford assembly plants, it was made a standard Ford practice. The dealer, if not too great a distance from branch headquarters, took many of his cars as they were assembled and drove them to his establishment, thus presumably eliminating short hauls by rail. Unfortunately various abuses developed in connection with the driveaway. The dealer rarely appeared just as his cars were completed; they were therefore stored for him, usually in a yard. In New Orleans a district supervisor found a hundred cars in the open waiting to be driven off; they had suffered marked deterioration. Again, cars that were driven away showed definite effects of their journey. Nor, aside from damage to the vehicles, was the operation economical for the dealer. The Milwaukee branch office estimated that driveaway cost from $12 to $13 a car more than rail shipment; a serious cut in agency profit, since this was as low as $60 per car.[25]

In addition, Ford agents resented the necessity of getting subscriptions for the *Dearborn Independent,* selling fertilizer produced as residue at the Rouge, and marketing tractors in areas where the farms were few, or not of the type to use the Fordson.[26]

During the early nineteen twenties the Ford Motor Company laid an additional burden upon the dealer in advertising. From 1903 to 1911, its first eight years and the period of the Selden patent case, the company had advertised aggressively. Such slogans as "Watch the Fords Go By" had achieved a national currency. The five-dollar day had probably raised the question in Ford's mind whether advertising was necessary. According to Charles A. Brownell, then Ford advertising head, this step gave the company "more than 2,000,000 lines of favorable advertising on the front pages of newspapers and thousands and thousands of editorial endorsements." And in the next few years Ford was publicized without expense in connection with his Rouge plant, his war-born tractor, the mythical $250 car of 1919, Muscle Shoals, his political possibilities, and his escape from the bankers in 1920–1921. A dozen other Ford activities of the nineteen twenties received comparable attention.[27]

As a result, the Ford advertising department, inactive in 1917–1918 because of the war, ceased work for five years. But while the company could ignore the need, the dealers could not, and they advertised at an expense of about $3,000,000 a year. Naturally they furnished their own copy and decided where and when to place it. Small dealers employed local newspapers; those in larger cities usually combined in "cooperative" advertisements. Ford became firmly opposed to advertising by the company, which he felt was unwarranted. By eliminating "useless advertising," he argued, the manufacturer reduced his overhead and passed the saving on to the consumer.

But while Ford took this complacent attitude, Ryan, and doubtless Edsel and Kanzler too, soon showed a keen interest in advertising. This early took the form of guiding and controlling the dealers, who after all were using the Ford trademark. As early as 1920 the home office prepared and distributed copy to assist dealers in the selling and servicing of tractors. It also paradoxically raised the question whether the dealers were advertising sufficiently, and asked the branches to report on that point! Later it prepared plates for advertisements, which the dealers paid for if used.

Finally, in the summer of 1923, after a conference of branch managers on the question, the company reestablished its advertising department, and on September 15 set up a coöperative arrangement for financing a program directed by the home office. An assessment of $3.00 for each vehicle delivered was levied on dealers, and the company matched this dollar for dollar. Newspapers, magazines, and billboards were to be used, and of a $7,000,000 total to be expended, the company contributed $3,500,000 for the first year. Two-thirds of this was to be spent locally, but the dealers had no voice in the type of copy or the time of its appearance. Concentration of effort, they were told, would mean economy, uniformity, and evenness of distribution, and would relieve them of a time-taking responsibility. However, some local initiative was permitted if the copy was supplied by the national office or approved by it.[28]

The dealers soon voiced dissatisfaction. The chief cause was the elimination of all individual agents' names, and their special copy. The company explained that these details offered supplementary information which "does not bring increasing sales," and also tended to reestablish the territorial limitations which had been abolished in 1920. Thus the advertisements merely stressed the Ford product and urged: "See the Nearest Authorized Ford Dealer." The dealers asserted that in operation the plan was inequitable, often ill-timed, and badly adjusted to local conditions. The district supervisor who covered North

Carolina wrote early in 1924 that the dealers wanted advertising at that particular time, had asked for it in vain, and "are very much dissatisfied." He suggested: "Someone should go to Charlotte and discuss the matter with them." However, the company did not modify its position.

One further step was taken by Detroit: in 1924 it adopted a supplementary policy of national advertising, apparently suggested by Edsel Ford. In June it began double-page color advertisements in the *Saturday Evening Post* and *Country Gentleman,* "to familiarize the public with the Ford industry, its vast facilities for the manufacture of quality products on a production basis and to point out that by owning and controlling its own sources of raw material greater value can be passed on to the consumer." For a time this appeal was also used in newspapers, but was discontinued because the results were not encouraging. But the effort was impressive: in 1925, stated the *Wall Street Journal,* the Ford budget of $2,000,000 was the highest in the country.[29]

It should be remembered that in 1921 the Ford Motor Company had occupied an enviable position. The cars of its chief competitors were then all much higher-priced than the Model T, and the low-income public was still primarily interested in price and reliability. The Ford offered both. In 1921, of all the cars sold in the United States, the Ford Motor Company manufactured almost 56 per cent. As we have seen, its production increased in 1922 by about 27 per cent, in 1923 by almost 55 per cent. Its proportion of the total national production of cars rose to 57 per cent. But by 1925 it had fallen—to 45 per cent. Despite the increases in Ford production, those of other firms had been even greater. Chevrolet, producing 240,000 units in 1922, had shown a 220 per cent gain as opposed to 27 per cent for Ford. Already comfort and appearance in somewhat more expensive cars were attracting a growing body of Americans.

The company responded to this challenge by the procedure always followed in the past: the reduction of prices without a lowering of quality. Indeed, during this period quality was definitely raised in various ways, to be described in a later chapter. The combination of an improved commodity and lower prices (six price cuts were made from 1921 to 1925) kept the Ford car in demand up to the end of 1925. The final cut of December 2, 1924, found the runabout selling for $260, the touring car for $290, and the four-door sedan (an enclosed model) for $660. No competitor could approach these prices and values.[30]

The popular impression was that successive cuts merely represented improvements in engineering and production routines by which Ford had effected savings, passed on to the public. Actually, the order was reversed: price cuts were made *before* any reductions in costs were effected! The reductions were indeed a series of nightmares for purchasing and production officials. "There have been times when Mr. Ford cut prices," stated one company executive, "when everybody shivered around there, when they figured they could not make ends meet. . . . Mr. Ford himself does not pay a whole lot of attention to costs. . . . Probably 97 per cent of the time we did not give much attention to costs when it came to cutting prices."

However, reductions having been made, someone had to see that a margin of profit was insured. One means was to "go out and hammer down the suppliers," with the threat of withdrawing orders. This measure brought limited results. Production economies were also enforced. In addition, the greatest reductions were made where competition was strongest (for example, on the touring car and the sedan), and it was not expected that a profit would be made on every type of car. Some models might show a slight loss; others, a profit of 5 per cent, and still others of 15. The highest rate was 40 per cent—on the Ford truck. Prophetic of things to come was the fact that although from 1920 to 1924 the price cuts preserved the Ford position, the Chevrolet, by style and engineering changes, could *raise* its price by $15 and still increase its sales by a percentage greater than the Ford's.

Actually, Ford was able to maintain his favorable position largely from two sources of gain outside the income from the sale of cars: savings on freight, and the sale of spare parts.

The management of freight involved a number of factors. The basic element in the situation was the synchronization of supply, production, and shipment which Kanzler had effected at Highland Park. One aspect of this was the making of ten day reports on dealer stocks and sales, inaugurated by Kanzler soon after he took up his work. It was a vital service from the dealers to the company. Kanzler was of necessity in close touch with supply and production, and could regulate these as they affected each other. But production also involved the marketing of cars. How many would be sold? When? The ten day reports indicated the answers to these questions, and were important in maintaining a rapid flow *from* the factory as well as to and through it. If the entire cycle from suppliers to dealers could be maintained steadily and expeditiously, it would cut inventory to the minimum, and save millions.

Again, the thirty-six branch assembly plants were in a very real sense a part of the manufacturing process. They received freight cars containing Model T parts, and assembled finished cars. It was therefore essential that they receive parts promptly and in relation to their needs. When Kanzler arrived they were operating amid considerable confusion, receiving their shipments irregularly and in jumbled form; but his reorganization of the supply, production, and shipping problem immensely improved the service to them, permitted them to increase their production, and cut inventory float some $40,000,000.* This great saving was of crucial importance in cutting the total costs of manufacture and enabling the company to lower prices.

But the company also profited directly on freight shipments. Automobiles were *billed* as complete units f.o.b. Detroit, at the rate of six models per freight car. But by shipping parts instead of completed Model T's the company could get the equivalent of ten automobiles into the same space that six assembled cars would occupy. It pocketed the freight charges for the four extra units. By using double-decked box cars and routing assignments over the D.T. & I. it made further gains. Its profits on shipments were estimated at from $24,000,000 to $30,000,000 a year.

The sale of spare parts was about equally profitable to it. As the total of Ford cars manufactured rose from 5,000,000 to 10,000,000 (a goal reached on June 4, 1924), the number in use in the United States was estimated at 7,000,000, and profits on replacements became a great source of income. Every year's production added to the potential. From the early nineteen-twenties, parts and accessories for the Ford car could be found in dime stores or procured from mail order houses. As Leister observed, you could buy a Ford part on practically any street corner.[31]

---

* The shipment program as devised by Kanzler divided the Model T parts into thirteen groups—engines, transmissions, wheels, radiators, etc. with in some cases related units. Complete automobiles had not been shipped for some time. However, previously there had been no regular classification of parts. A branch assembly plant would receive a freight car containing certain parts it had urgently requested, and filled in with other miscellaneous items, often those which the shipping force found it easiest to procure. Branches might receive 50 freight cars before they got the materials for assembling even one Model T. Under Kanzler's system, they needed but 13 cars to assemble 400 Model T's. The result was order instead of chaos, and a doubling of the branch plant's capacity to assemble. Kanzler summarized the result: "The saving was such that we were assembling 10,000 cars a day, domestic, with as I recall an inventory float of $33,000,000 compared to a former 5000 cars and a $75,000,000 inventory float." (Interview with authors, June 11, 1956, and letter to authors, June 26, 1956.)

By 1924 there were 41,800 outlets for the sale of authorized parts—
9800 dealers and 32,000 approved service stations. However, parts for
Ford cars were manufactured by independent concerns, which had
appeared as early as 1915, and which turned out dashlights, windshield
wipers, tire repair kits, batteries, spark plugs, and many other items.
The company fought this competition, suing manufacturers who put
"Ford" on their products, and disciplining those Ford dealers who
stocked imitation parts, often of inferior quality, because they could
make a higher profit on them than on authorized parts. The home office
urged branch managers to police their agencies. "This business properly
belongs to us and can readily be obtained by a little sales effort," it
admonished. Monthly parts quotas were assigned to the branches, who
in turn assigned quotas to dealers.

In its drive against the "pirate or spurious parts evil," as Edsel termed
it, the company employed two chief weapons—low list prices and
generous commissions. In January, 1922, the commission was raised
from 25 to 33⅓ per cent on quantity lots. Later in the year it was increased to 40 per cent. Apparently such measures checked "pirate" sales
to Ford dealers, and in general reduced the sales of outside manufacturers.

The company profited handsomely from its spare parts sales. For
the year ending February 29, 1924, its net gain on all activities was
$82,260,000, and $78,150,000 of this came from by-products, freight
charges, bank balances, securities, and spare parts. At $4,110,000, the
profit on car sales was less than two dollars per unit. As for spare parts,
"it is estimated," ran an analysis of the Ford financial statement in the
Boston *News Bureau*, "that the average amount of parts purchases per
Ford owners is in the neighborhood of $40, of which the Ford Motor
Company sells $28. This would make the gross on Ford parts at retail,
on the basis of 7,000,000 Ford cars in operation, total $196,000,000." The
net revenue on all this was estimated at $29,000,000, or about 35.3 per
cent of all Ford profit.[32]

In its effort to keep car sales abreast of production, the company
finally resorted to an unusual arrangement for the purchase of Ford
cars. We have seen that Henry Ford opposed all time-payment plans,
although Edsel had always favored them. By 1923 from 75 to 80 per
cent of all automobiles were sold in this fashion, including a large share
of Fords. However, in contrast with its rival General Motors, the Ford

company had never established a special corporation to finance its customers. Liebold in 1921 gave the official explanation of its policy:

> The fact that Ford products sell so readily and our dealers make a reasonable profit, enables the greater number of them to carry our products without any financing in addition to what they readily can obtain from their banking connections.

The statement was both true and untrue. Dealers could and did obtain financing for sales, and at times the demand for Ford cars made time-payment arrangements of relatively small importance, but many could not handle the problem as easily as Liebold indicated, and would have welcomed a Ford financing company.

The pressure for some kind of action, and perhaps the desire to keep demand well ahead of production, resulted on April 7, 1923 in the launching of the Ford Weekly Purchasing Plan. Actually, this was no time-payment scheme. It merely permitted an individual to register with a Ford dealer as a possible customer, make a first payment of at least $5 to a bank, and continue successive weekly payments until he had accumulated the price of a Ford car. He might almost as well have put the money into a savings account, for he received the same interest on his deposits, and could withdraw a part or all of them at will.*

A great flourish of publicity marked the beginning of operations. Posters in bank windows and dealers' show rooms proclaimed: "$5.00 Will Enroll You in the Ford Purchase Plan. Start Today and Before You Realize It You Will Have a Car of Your Own." Ryan hailed it as a device for aiding people of $1000 and $2000 incomes, heretofore not buyers of cars, to become owners.[33]

But the results were disappointing. The plan was not pushed by dealers, for they were interested in quick turnovers, or by their salesmen, to whom it offered no commissions. During the first eighteen months of operation, 400,000 persons enrolled, and 131,000 of these completed payments and acquired cars. This total was less than a month's regular sales. More significant, the number of persons registering steadily declined. "It was bad," said a Ford dealer of the plan, "because $5.00 a week doesn't accumulate enough money to buy an automobile very fast. We often had to refund it. After people would

---

* The idea had been promoted by Edsel and Kanzler. Henry Ford of course gave his sanction, but later specifically disclaimed authorship. "The boys at Highland Park worked it out," he stated. (*New York Times,* May 30, 1923.)

get $50 or $75 they would want a vacation or something and they would withdraw it." [34]

Of course, the scheme had the grave defect of not giving what the installment plan gave: possession of the car. With that, the purchaser had a prime incentive to pay: he also acquired the habit of using an automobile. Had Ford liberalized the plan so as to deliver the car when a considerable part of the total had been paid, he might have tapped the lower stratum of the population where price was still more important than style or comfort. But this would have amounted to a form of time-payment, which he was not yet ready to accept.

Despite its difficulties, despite its rigidity, its abuses, its errors in long-time strategy, the Ford Motor Company in the early nineteen-twenties had done well. It had achieved a volume of production never before approached, and had successfully marketed its outpouring millions of tractors, trucks, and Model T's. Improving quality and cutting prices, it had been able to continue the manufacture of what was essentially the same car. But each year the fight would become fiercer, and the victory more uncertain.

5.

The immense Ford organization, its factories and offices in the United States alone covering more territory than the combined trunk railroads of the nation, its subsidiary enterprises embracing mills, farms, ships, rails, and factories, cried for a unifying administrative control. This would require dozens of gifted executives and a sound plan for relating the many separate activities to a central directing office.

Even after the departure of Ford executives in 1919 and 1921, there was ample talent in the company from which to assemble a brilliant administrative corps, and for a time it seemed as if a coherent administrative plan might be evolved. The "housecleaning" of early 1921, if savage and haphazard, had at least provided an opportunity for building. Edsel and Kanzler perceived it. "Mr. Kanzler was trying to set up a corporation structure which would have a central administrative system similar to any corporation," said Herman L. Moekle, then in the Treasurer's office. "Particularly he wanted control to be in the office of the president."

At this time no apparent difference in purpose and method existed between Edsel, holding that office, and his father. Even some years later

Edsel recognized none. "I have not worked out a separate business philosophy for myself," he stated. "It has not been necessary, for on all material points I agree absolutely with my father's philosophy. I do not merely accept his beliefs; I feel as strongly about them as he does." Undoubtedly he had in mind such conceptions as durability, high volume of production, low price for products, high wages, short hours, bonuses for labor and willingness to explore new materials, methods, and mechanical devices in manufacture. In 1921 Henry Ford was the living symbol of all these concepts, and Edsel, who had grown up with the Ford plants and models, had no impulse but to applaud.[35]

But in the field of administration a great although unrecognized contrast actually existed between the father and the son. Edsel worked in a constructive, judicious manner on any question, examining all available facts, consulting with those who had assembled them, discussing important aspects of the matter, and then making a judgment. His instinct was to draw out and utilize the abilities of others, and always to be fair, although never soft, in his treatment of them. As a business man he could intelligently build an organization, encourage the originality of others, and work successfully as a part of the whole.[36]

In contrast, his father was a believer in the inspired leadership of one man. "My idea," he told Upton Sinclair as early as 1919, "is that a man ought not to have to give an order more than once in six months, but that when that order is needed he ought to know it will be carried out. . . . I don't see any other way to get things produced, except that some person who knows shall have the power to give orders." This philosophy contemplated a plant in which officials subordinated themselves to a single will, carrying on in accordance with the leader's known ideas, and in emergencies turning to him for solutions. When Edwin G. Pipp suggested to Ford that Woodrow Wilson's administration would have profited from more team work and less "one man rule," the industrialist promptly corrected him. "That's the only way to get anywhere—one man rule," he snapped. Ford had his way. "From 1915 on I have heard it said that no one ever contradicted him," said Alex Lumsden.* By 1921, when he had freed himself from all restraint by acquiring the minority stock, and had parted with such independent-minded men as Wills, Hawkins, and Knudsen, he was particularly

---

* This was not strictly true, for men remonstrated about closing war contracts and the September, 1920, cuts in prices. But no one persisted once Ford made the final decision.

unlikely to be receptive toward an elaborate organization. He felt that danger lurked in it, while there was a creative fluidity in loose procedures which he could alter at will.

"Mr. Ford," remarked one employee, "didn't believe in administration." This statement should be qualified and interpreted. Ford's attitude went back to his long experience as an automotive creator, which satisfied him that the car and its efficient manufacture were the keys to success. In the factory, as we have seen, he respected organization, and had improved it by brilliant comprehensive measures and many a detailed stroke. But organization in the company offices, he felt, must be kept in hand, lest the tail wag the dog. And even in the factory he wanted men who worked out not their ideas, but his. He had no patience with committees or with extended discussion. While Edsel was orderly, analytical, and democratic, Henry Ford was intuitive, inspirational, impatient, autocratic. (Of course an immense experience and capacity lay back of his "intuition.") His was the greater talent, but it lay chiefly in the field of production, and what he should have perceived was that the company, with its increasing complexity, was now at a stage where Edsel's mind and methods were more likely to serve it well.[37]

Ford's procedure had one important feature: since he rarely exerted his power, he left large areas in which power was bound to be exerted most of the time by somebody else. In the early nineteen-twenties he was busy developing the Rouge, the Upper Peninsula, the village industries, the D.T. & I., his inns and Greenfield Village, and the Ford fleet. Accordingly he left the factory at Highland Park, the business offices, and marketing to Edsel and Kanzler. From 1921 to 1926 Kanzler supervised production, helped develop the branch assembly plants, and consulted with Edsel and Ryan about sales. A dark, tall, dynamic young man who could lay out a complicated production schedule, appraise sales possibilities, or write a letter of clarity and literary distinction with equal facility, he seemed early destined for leadership. He rapidly took on broad powers. "Kanzler was the general manager of the whole plant," recalled Galamb, and Klann testified to the same effect. Martin took his orders from Kanzler. In 1924 he was elected second vice-president of the company. Edsel meanwhile presided over the business, branch, and marketing relationships of the company, over all foreign developments, and over the Lincoln Motor Company. The result was that, despite some rigidities and minor faults of operation, what Edsel and Kanzler covered was well integrated and worked smoothly.[38]

During these years the young president assumed an impressive burden of work. While Henry Ford was issuing spectacular statements that kept him in the public eye, Edsel was shouldering the day-in-and-out responsibilities, making decisions on administration, manufacturing, taxation, and sales. His was the eye that perceived weakness in the company, and his the hand that quietly but effectively (except when blocked by his father) remedied them. "He had a hundred thumbs stuck in as many leaks in the boat," said Kanzler of such work. All who knew him agree as to his talents and personality. Pipp, observing him during the first years of his presidency, described him as "a very human, very sensible, very capable, very modest, very energetic, and well-balanced young man who . . . had responsibilities that would stagger many a man twice his age." Liebold, Walker, McCloud, Black, Voorhess, Gehle, and Hicks all have noted similar qualities. Kanzler in retrospect stated: "There are no words to describe adequately the great modesty, honesty, and gentlemanly fineness of Edsel, coupled with extraordinary intelligence, judgment, broad knowledge, ability and plenty of nerve to face his crises."

Edsel's testimony at the Chicago *Tribune* trial shows that even in 1919 he had the fullest grasp of company affairs, and expressed himself with a confidence and clarity painfully lacking in his father. Again, he had a keen eye for good lines in a car, quickly perceived important trends in automotive construction and production, and frequently urged Henry Ford to consider promising devices and alterations. According to Harold Hicks, he gave many Ford employees the courage to stick with the company when conditions were difficult. "You always figured there was one person who was a perfect gentleman and that some day he was going to run the place, and that it would be a fine place to work when he was running it. You stuck around because of him." Hicks felt that the confidence in Edsel Ford had "a lot to do with the success of the Ford Motor Company." His was a "moral influence." [39]

But while Edsel bore the title of president, and worked with industry and distinction, he never assumed the full power of that office. Neither he nor any of his associates doubted that Henry Ford was the ultimate source of authority. And because he was, and because he exercised that authority only sporadically, opportunity was afforded others besides

Edsel and Kanzler to assume considerable powers. Two men in particular stepped into the vacuums he left, one in the executive sphere, the other in production. They were Liebold and Sorensen.

Neither could have assumed authority had he not possessed Ford's confidence, and neither would have enjoyed that confidence had he not shown an ability to discharge important and difficult tasks, with or without specific orders, to Ford's satisfaction. So devoted were they to his interest and wishes that they might almost be called extensions of his personality.

As Liebold grew, power was literally thrust upon him. Ford refused to read correspondence and was impatient of office routines; Liebold of necessity dealt with both. In fact, he strove constantly to win his chief's attention to important matters. Ford was a poor collaborator. "If he saw any amount of correspondence . . . that he thought I was going to tell him about, . . . he'd get up before I had hardly got started, and walk away. I tried at all times to conceal what the matters were that I wanted to bring to his attention." In the end, Liebold had to assume many responsibilities without guidance from Ford, and also to work out plans and details for large undertakings which Ford tossed to him with a casual word. He negotiated for most of the Upper Peninsula properties, bought and managed D.T. & I., supervised the planning and construction of the Ford Hospital, handled all Ford's personal finances, directed the *Dearborn Independent,* and watched over the manufacture of the Johansson blocks. In particular, he acted as a buffer between Ford and the numerous individuals who wanted to see him. Until the mid-nineteen-twenties, when Cameron took an increasing role in that field, Liebold was completely in charge of the manufacturer's public relations, including his political activities and his contacts with the press. Occasionally he spoke for Ford to reporters, he scrutinized all interviews, had the final responsibility (although Cameron wrote most of the copy) for "Mr. Ford's Own Page," and guided the collaboration between Ford and Samuel Crowther.[40]

Liebold had a genius for cooling off the importunate. In handling correspondence, the phrase, "Mr. Ford is out of town" marks thousands of letters Ford never saw (and never wanted to see), while Liebold's frequent definitions of Ford's attitude on a variety of questions disposed of numerous other suggestions and queries. With the press, the secretary was not popular. "Mr. Liebold was very heavy-handed and the typical Prussian type," remarked one competent observer. However, this was of small importance, since it did not diminish the desire of the press to reach Ford, and since when they did reach him he had charm, friendliness, and usually something of high news value.

No one questioned Liebold's ability; the charges against him were that he shut off access to Ford, and that he manipulated his power for personal ends. "No king was ever so hedged about, none but the Grand Lama of Tibet was ever so inaccessible," exclaimed Dean Marquis, while John Brisben Walker wrote Ford that "you are the only man I have ever known, who so surrounded himself with secretaries that he was unreachable." A Michigan publisher who held a grievance against Liebold wrote Edsel that the secretary "has become a real menace to your father, yourself, and your business. His great greed for power and more power have driven him to action akin to Kaiserism." As we have seen, Liebold was credited with fostering Ford's anti-semitism (a charge he denied) and encouraging his political ambitions. Liebold does not seem to have affected greatly the larger industrial policy of the company. In general, he carried out orders, many of them unpleasant, and while he did so coldly and abruptly, the decisions he enforced were usually his master's and not his own.[41]

Sorensen did not have power thrust upon him; he acquired it. He had earned the headship of the Fordson factory; if he stepped into the command of the Rouge with Ford's approval, it was also by right of his superb industrial knowledge and his force of personality. There is no doubt that as he climbed rapidly up, he aspired to be first among Ford's lieutenants, Kanzler and Edsel included. (According to McCloud, Edsel at first had a high opinion of Sorensen's abilities, and favored his advancement.) Like Liebold, the Dane found a vacuum left by Ford's sporadic leadership, perceived there was ample room for manipulation, and utilized his opportunities. As we have seen, he early took considerable responsibility for overseas operations, and as the Rouge grew and began to use the products of the Upper Peninsula, he gradually took over the supervision of activities there.

Thus from 1921 onward, Liebold and Sorensen were building up, with the tacit blessing of Henry Ford, centers of authority which covered increasing areas of company activity. For some time these did not touch the large area in which Edsel and Kanzler worked. Nor does Liebold seem to have clashed with the younger men in dealing for Henry Ford with business or financial matters. With Sorensen, the clash was almost inevitable. Up to 1926 he did not invade activities at Highland Park, or exert much influence on branch activities. But as unit after productive unit moved from Highland Park to his domain at the Rouge, he was obviously a threat. Kanzler's area of authority was being diminished, and as production would eventually all pass under Sorensen, this would affect the branch assemblies. Actually, Kanzler left in 1926, and Bricker, as Sorensen's agent, took over Highland Park. From that time forward Sorensen moved into branch and sales affairs, and by the late nineteen-twenties his orders were obeyed from the Sault-Sainte-Marie to New York and San Francisco, and overseas to Buenos Aires and Yokohama.[42]

The strain of competition permeated the Ford organization. "I have seen the intrigue, men literally pushing each other in a scramble to get close to the throne," reported Pipp, "and to get away from it at times I have gone for relief to the wholesome atmosphere of the foundry, the blast furnace, the heat treatment, the machine rooms, the assembly room." Pipp won his sense of peace, and doubtless in some departments it was real, but in most, had he known it, a contest, latent or overt, was in progress, the top man always menaced by an assistant of comparable abilities, who sometimes displaced him. The device of competition was never really successful; energy that might have been merged into constructive accomplishment was siphoned off in useless friction. Like two mechanics trying to repair the same engine at the same time, each keeping his own counsel, each interfering with the other, the rivals often slowed down tasks that might have been smoothly cooperative.

Ford spread uneasiness throughout his vast organization in other ways. He would take a keen interest in one man or project, then would drop it completely. He was a creature of moods ("If he saw three black-birds in the morning, all birds were black that day"); he cut off explanations with a sudden decision; walked out of a discussion remarking: "I'll be back when you get through talking about this." His officials, all without title, were never sure of their standing; favored one day, they might be ignored the next. Indeed, one of Ford's habitual treatments was "the silent cure." He might work closely and continuously with an employee, then for weeks give him not a glance. Was it deliberate hostility or disapproval? Sudden indifference? A test of the victim's toughness? Or had the master merely become lost in a new problem? Nobody knew. But the effect of these unpredictable actions was to produce a tautness in the entire work force, so that a word, a gesture, an act would set it vibrating, as a sound or a touch might affect some delicately adjusted mechanism of bands and wires.

Ford's methods sometimes approached the sadistic. Men whom he wished to discard were informed of their removal in humiliating ways, and never by a frank talk with the leader they served. Some were sent on vacations, to receive telegrams or telephone calls of dismissal from Liebold or Sorensen. One was notified of his discharge by the local sheriff! In another instance a tarpaulin was flung over the victim's desk, and workmen removed the roof of his office. When he returned he hastily submitted his resignation, remarking: "Well, I didn't really think they wanted me to leave, but when they pulled the roof down over my desk, I decided they didn't want me any more." [43]

Edsel did not escape the tension his father created; in fact, he was signally a victim of it. With him as with others Henry Ford took the indirect way. He emphasized Edsel's position and authority. "Do whatever he says," he would tell an executive. "He's got to run this company." But when Edsel had made a ruling, Ford might take postscript action: "The old man was back in the harness, reversing Edsel's decision about things." Or again, after discussion, Ford would agree that a certain project should be undertaken, and his son would start it. Then Ford would direct Sorensen or another official to stop the work, even if a considerable amount of money had been expended. When Edsel would learn of such an action, the muscles of his jaw would tighten, his face would cloud over, and he would say: "Well, I thought father understood this. Apparently somebody's talked to him about it who doesn't believe in this, or believe in this way of doing it. Well, I guess there isn't anything we can do about it at the present time."

Edsel might have improved his position by making an issue of such occurrences. He did not lack courage; in fact, he showed more than his father. He never evaded unpleasant duties. "I'll do my own dirty work," he remarked once when he undertook to make an explanation to a Detroit business man who was bound to resent it. His correspondence shows that time and time again he dealt directly with difficult situations that he might have evaded. He took up voluntarily with Henry Ford questions that no one else dared to discuss. However, once he had a decision from his father, he bowed to it. (He might, to be sure, reopen the matter at a later and more propitious time.) To Fred Black he explained why. "Well, after all, my father built this business," he pointed out. "It's his business." So the result, as Frank Hadas phrased it, was that "Henry Ford was a very dominant father over an obedient son." [44] Consequently, executives lost confidence in Edsel's authority, recognizing that his was not the final word; and when in doubt talked with Henry Ford, Liebold, or Sorensen.

There is ample evidence that Sorensen consulted Edsel on policy, and Logan Miller stated that he had seen Sorensen take orders from him. "I think, personally, that Sorensen liked Edsel very much. . . . He was between the devil and the deep blue sea, I'd say. He had to try to satisfy both Edsel and Mr. Ford." On the other hand, some executives felt that Sorensen's behavior toward Edsel was hostile and overbearing. He would snap out biting remarks "in order to humiliate him and show him who was boss around here." Once, after a policy meeting in which Edsel had opposed his father, Sorensen, runs the account, turned and gave Edsel a derisive smile as he went out. "Edsel was now president of the Company with no authority. Sorensen just as much as said, 'To hell with you. What do you amount to?' " [45]

Ray Dahlinger, according to Hicks, explained the relationship as one deliberately created by Henry Ford to hammer his son into the type of executive his father thought he should be. "Sorensen's job in the Ford Motor Company is to train Edsel Ford for the big job when he can take it over. Edsel just isn't tough enough. Sorensen is being employed here to toughen up Edsel, and that's why Mr. Ford let Edsel go ahead [on a construction project] and then had Sorensen stop him." Black and Hicks also felt that Ford was trying to mold his son into a harder, more aggressive executive. Needless to say, the treatment was unsuccessful.

On at least one occasion Henry Ford took peremptory action. Once after luncheon, Edsel brought up a project to which he knew his father was opposed. "Now, father," he remarked, "I think the time has come to take up the matter of hydraulic brakes." There was a silence, and Ford flushed, rose, blurted: "Edsel, you shut up!" and walked away.[46]

The atmosphere was not always so uncertain and strained, the dark moments so frequent, as the foregoing account might indicate. Henry Ford was proud of his officials and workers and their accomplishments, and proud of his son. He had many pleasant periods, many days of elation. Often he appeared with Edsel, chatting cheerfully and observing progress in the research rooms or the factory. Those with whom he spoke and worked found him wholly unpretentious in manner, if often exacting as to the activities he touched. It was simply that as the nineteen-twenties advanced, as the Ford work scene expanded, as Ford became at once more powerful and more remote, there was an increasing atmosphere of tension, with the factory chiefs driving their workers to meet difficult objectives which price cuts and high volume production imposed.

Undoubtedly the opportunity to achieve administrative unity was lost. Undoubtedly Henry Ford failed to use fully Edsel's notable talents, and Kanzler's. The sidetracking of Edsel and the elevation of Liebold and Sorensen made for a less happy and less integrated company. But the practical effect of opportunities lost should not be exaggerated. The Ford Motor Company in these years was an effective organization, as its accomplishments clearly show. One cause for its success lay in the fact that each separate enterprise was capably organized and operated. Liebold and Sorensen, if disliked by many of their associates and subordinates, were highly talented and resourceful, and were prodigious workers. Under them the outlying Ford activities and the increasing power of the Rouge were developed with notable ability. Edsel and Kanzler in their spheres worked well. Ford was undoubtedly satisfied with this tripartite control, the fluidity of which suited his mind and habits. In so far as he was aware of drive and tension, he regarded them as necessary and up to a point desirable. Could he have been brought to foresee their ultimate effects in the factory and particularly upon Edsel, he might well have recoiled. But Ford shut his eyes to much; he was now the prisoner of his own great power, both that which he wielded himself and that which he let others wield by default. Moreover, the effects of his mode of operation were not to reveal their destructive character for some years. Even after the purges of 1927–1928, which cast out many able executives and workers, the Ford organization was still a chief force in the industry.

One factor in making it so was Ford's own personality, for along with its sinister aspects it showed an originality of general outlook, a confidence, and a vitality which were unique. With a word or gesture Ford could still lift his great work force to superb activity. If many officials and men recalled days when their participation was more spontaneous, they could still exult in rising to his challenges.

XI

THE ROUGE:

INDUSTRIAL COLOSSUS

BY the beginning of 1924 the Rouge had taken its place as one of the two principal Ford plants. It was the chief reception depot for coal, iron ore, and lumber used in the company's manufacturing. It processed all the coke for its own furnaces and foundry, and supplied coke to Highland Park. Its blast furaces produced from 35 to 50 per cent of all the iron used in Model T's and tractors. It provided lumber for Model T bodies, and cardboard for these bodies and for shipments. Its power house supplied current to both main Ford plants. It made most of the parts and housed the final assembly of the Fordson. Its foundry fashioned practically all the iron, brass, steel, and bronze castings used by Ford factories anywhere.

The Rouge workers made a large army. Altogether, they comprised 42,000 persons, 12,000 in the foundry alone; and although the Highland Park force was larger, 68,285, it would not long remain so. To the west, just south of Michigan Avenue in Dearborn, the company was laying out an extensive residential district to provide homes for its increasing workers. Seven thousand five hundred now came to work in their own cars, which they parked at the edges of the plant. The majority used street cars, private buses, and jitneys. The company encouraged the establishment of street car and bus lines, and late in the 1920's would provide special parking facilities. More workers would soon surge in as additional activities were shunted to the Rouge. Highland Park was bound to decrease and the Rouge to increase; like some inflexible, calmly feeding steel monster it was already detaching and absorbing, unit by unit, the proud home of the first moving assembly line. The end was inevitable, for in site, planning, construction and mechanization the Rouge symbolized a new industrial era, while that of Highland Park was passing.[1]

No acute observer could fail to read what was happening. Many officials at Highland Park were doing so, and already a definite rivalry was growing between the two plants. This had crystallized slowly, for at first Edsel, Martin, and Kanzler had assumed that with time they would move to the Rouge and take it over. After all, in 1919 Sorensen, then heading Henry Ford & Co., had not seemed a dominant figure. In most companies he would have operated the Rouge under some chief executive, and actually for several years Martin, himself acting under Kanzler, was conceded to be Sorensen's superior, and gave him orders. But as we have seen, the lines of authority in the Ford Motor Company were never formally fixed; and once established at the Rouge, the Dane more and more assumed the role of complete master. In practice he exerted large authority from the start, as his correspondence while on a European trip in 1921 abundantly indicates. He received reports on all Rouge activities—planning, engineering, production—and issued orders in reply. Soon, doubtless because he knew that to assume authority meant to defend it (was not Ford's policy "Let's you and him have a fight and see who comes out best"?) he began to scrutinize the officials who came down from Highland Park as a new unit was shifted, and replace them with men of his own. "When they brought Mr. Martin's men down to the Rouge plant there was a collision," said Philip E. Haglund, who himself came down in 1921 to install and operate the electric furnace at the new plant. Haglund had no difficulty, for he was a specialist, and not particularly a "Martin man." "Mr. Sorensen and Mr. Bricker replaced the Highland Park men with Rouge men. The Rouge plant was a Sorensen outfit."

Gehle thought that this policy developed because "P. E. Martin tried to lord it over Sorensen; he wanted the Rouge organization under him." Frank Hadas in contrast felt that "Charlie was rather aggressive and he just butted in anywhere that he could and took whatever he could." Opinion varied on other points of character: Haglund felt that you knew where you were with Sorensen; Fred Black in contrast felt that he "would lie like hell if it suited his purpose." In general, the men who worked directly under him respected and admired him. "He was hard," they would admit, "but if I had to choose again he'd be the man I'd work for." [2]

Certainly Sorensen was aggressive, arbitrary, abrupt. If he thought a desk unnecessary, he threw it out. If drawers were locked, he broke them open. If he saw a group of men standing idle, even if with reason, it infuriated him. "Go and fire those guys," he told Haglund on such an occasion when the two were going through the foundry.* If an official had a chair, he might find it suddenly gone, or even jerked out from under him. Sorensen writes in his memoirs that superintendents should be walking about the plant.

Sorensen abominated collections of odd materials that a number of workmen tended to accumulate. One day he and Haglund came upon a man who had one. Sorensen stopped and asked for a screw of a certain size. The man began searching his box while the two officials watched, but had no luck. Finally Sorensen exclaimed: "Look, this fellow has been looking here fifteen minutes and he can't find the screw. There is a crib over there. He can go over and get it in two minutes. Take that box and throw it in the cupola—tools and all."

Haglund did; and he and Sorensen went around breaking open tool boxes and dumping their contents—except for the tools—on the floor.[3]

However, Sorensen should not be thought of as merely captious and impulsive, merely an arrogant driver. His was a complex personality, with two chief facets. One showed him as an impatient, explosive man, with a consuming and ruthless energy. In small matters, his activity was directed against slovenly habits, laziness, disobedience (although he sometimes punished the innocent with the guilty, and struck harder than the offense merited). In larger affairs, such as his elimination of gifted personnel, he acted in part to protect and extend his own authority, in part to execute Henry Ford's directives or suggestions. In either role he was abrupt, implacable, devastatingly thorough. But there was another Sorensen, more temperate and judicious. With his own chosen assistants, men like Bricker, Gehle, and Hanson, he was reasonable. In matters of plant and company policy, except when he acted to augment his own power, or as Ford's divisive or destroying agent, his judgment was usually sound. His knowledge of production was broad and detailed; he saw beyond the factory to the marketing of the product, both at home and abroad. And it should be said that if his aggressiveness and harsh decisions were disruptive and costly, he got spectacular results. His demonaic energy matched the furious growth

---

* Theodore Mallon explained this type of outburst. Sorensen told him: "I figure it this way: I probably don't get out into the yard more than once a month, or once every two months, and when I do come there, I don't want to find a bunch of men standing around doing nothing." (Mallon, *Reminiscences*.)

of the new plant. Another might have been awed by its complexity and size. Not Sorensen: he was not afraid of the Rouge. He grappled with the monster and tamed it, machines and men.

Sorensen also satisfied Henry Ford, who demanded an excess of vigor rather than too little. "Take it easy and do not throw too many things around," he cabled Sorensen jocularly in November, 1921. On a later occasion he remarked to Galamb, "Joe, we have to have a man like Sorensen in a big organization like this, to raise the dickens once in a while." [4]

2.

Sorensen ruled over a domain that was without parallel both in size and in sheer mechanical efficiency. In 1924 it covered an area more than a mile and a half long and three quarters of a mile broad, and was still in process of growth. It contained forty-four buildings. The total effect on the observer was both unique and impressive. Here was the fulfillment of the Belgian poet Verhaeren's earlier cry:

"The hungering city spreads out and devours the plain!"

for if ever a tract of soil had been tamed, paved, and molded in steel and concrete into the geometrical forms of an industrial design, here such a conversion of land into machines had been effected. The forms of the plant had an authority of their own, severely functional. The concrete-lined oblong of the slip, the storage bins with their dark hills of coal or iron ore or white hills of limestone, the sheer bulk of the foundry, the stacks of the blast furnaces and power house, the authentic sweep of the High Line, the covered conveyors twisting like angular snakes from building to building—all gave a picture of designed power, at once strange and convincing to the lay observer. Coming to them from England, J. A. Spender, a distinguished editor and historian, felt that "if absolute completeness and perfect adaptation of means to end justify the word, they are in their own way works of art." And, he added with a wry glint of humor, "they have the artistic quality of stirring the imagination till it falls back exhausted." Even to the trained engineer John H. Van Deventer, who wrote thirteen articles on the Rouge, the first impression was "one of vastness and complexity." * He found this

---

* For the Highland Park plant, *Ford Methods and the Ford Shops*, by Arnold and Faurote, gave a clear yet humanized picture of that unit as it functioned in 1915. There is no com-

effect intensified by his second impression—one of "motionless quiet."
He saw few workmen about the vast exterior scene: all action went
forward within the factory units. Even the conveyors were covered,
and only the electrically controlled cars on the High Line, a few trucks,
and the passive vessels in the slip from which the mammoth arms of
the unloaders dipped up ore or coal, suggested the complex activities
inside the cubistic furnaces, plants, and towers.[5]

We have said that Ford's objective at the Rouge was a flow of transportation, associated with the integration of key producing units. Along
with this central purpose went the determination to improve machines
and processes to the utmost. For example, take the conversion of coal
to coke as a case in point, where "approximately 2000 tons of coal . . .
and 1500 tons of coke are handled daily . . . by machinery every foot
of the way." The processes were elaborate, and dominated by conveyors
of various types; they also illustrated the ingenious use of waste material, for gas from the coke ovens supplied tar, benzol, illuminating
gas, and ammonia sulphate, most of which was utilized in Ford plants.
The finished coke, of course, went directly to the blast furnaces—a ride
of only a few minutes by conveyor.[6]

We have seen that Ford had promised to improve the manufacturing
of iron at the Rouge, skipping the production of pig, and shunting the
molten metal direct from blast furnace to foundry. He did not fully
redeem this promise, for where quality was essential, as in automotive
castings, the blast furnace product was unpredictable—the "analysis,"
or dependable character of product, could not be maintained. However,
by mixing it with foundry cupola metal (made of scrap and pig) and
treating the lot in electric furnaces, Ford technicians were able to use
from 30 to 50 per cent of it in any batch of metal (that is, the blast
furnace iron comprised that percentage of the whole), with considerable
savings in equipment and labor.[7] Moreover, his furnaces were unique
both for their cleanliness and for their utilization of waste. 'As an example of the latter practice, some thirty tons of ore dust were collected

---

parable report on the Rouge. However, Van Deventer's articles, written 1922–1923, give an
admirable technical description of the newer plant, although unfortunately one gets from
them not even a fleeting glimpse of the men who operated the complex. Abundant charts and
illustrations recreate the look of the Rouge and picture its work. In 1927 Faurote came to
the scene, and wrote ten articles on what he saw there. These are good reporting, with some
personal quality (Arnold and not Faurote was evidently the better informed of the two
collaborators, and the better writer), and help fill out a complex picture for us. Both series of
articles, with other less comprehensive descriptions, are freely used in the ensuing pages.

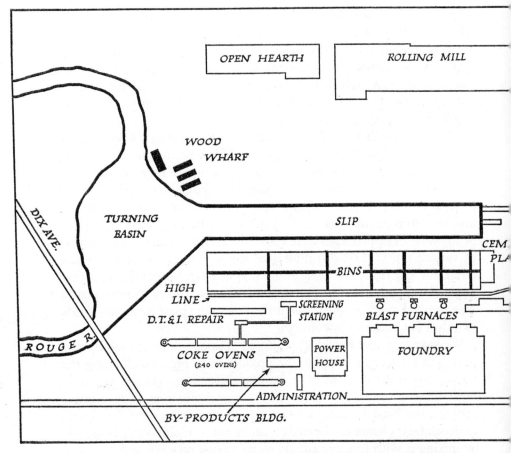

daily from the stacks, mixed with iron and steel machine borings from Rouge and Highland Park shops, and wetted and agglomerated into chunks of metal at a nearby sintering plant. Normally, such stuff could not have been used—it flew up the chimneys and was lost. Ford also employed furnace slag to make cement to be used in Ford construction projects.[8]

The foundry (including its machine department) was the most impressive single unit of the Rouge. It not only produced almost all Ford castings, but also machined them. In both castings and machining processes a high degree of mechanization was employed. For example, at the entrance of the machining department, the various castings were routed mechanically to 32 different groups of machine tools, each unit

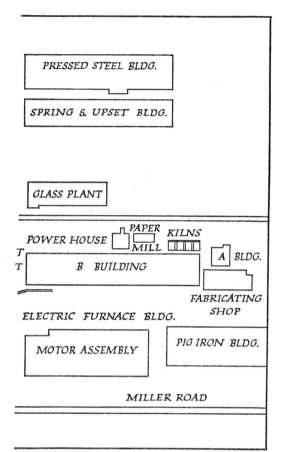

The Rouge in September, 1926, showing the steel units, the Motor Assembly Building, and the Glass plant.

then passing through a series of machine-tool operations—43 in the case of the Ford cylinder block—before the finished shining element emerged, ready to be routed to assembly.[9]

Foundry equipment and foundry crews had been moved from Highland Park to the Rouge as the plant there became ready to receive them. Piling up an excess of production, the officials would transfer a unit at night or on a Sunday, picking up activity at the new site with scarcely a hitch. Equipment went with the men, some of it being utilized with the new machinery already installed. With the entire transfer made, production steadily mounted. In the summer of 1922 the foundry was casting 7700 motor blocks a day for Model T's and Fordsons; a year later it produced 9000, and by 1924, 10,055. Here was one of the basic volume operations which made possible the high production totals in Ford cars and tractors during the middle nineteen twenties.

Fundamentally, the practices described above were repeated in such operations as body-building and the fabrication and assembly of tractors —that is, precise layout, ingenious tooling, and the coordination of diverse operations achieved flow in production. Spender has given a description of tractor operations as he saw them several years later:

The 'conveyors' cross the building at right angles to the assembly line, and in a corresponding endless procession bring to each station just that part— motor, wheels, steering gear, etc.— which has to be fitted in at that station, and at the exact moment when the embryo arrives. At each station there is precise teamwork, different rivets being assigned to different individuals or two men working together to lift a part into position. Often I held my breath for fear that a team should not complete its work before the embryo moved on, but I never saw any fail, and the time was apparently sufficient to enable the work to be done without hustling. . . . At a certain point the tractor was so far completed as to be ready for painting, and then it entered a covered space in which men in masks sprayed on the paint, completing the work in about two minutes. . . . In the last stage a little gasoline was fed to the infant now coming to life, and someone mounted its seat and drove it gaily out of the building to the railway siding, where a freight car was waiting to take it West. The whole process, from the raw ore to the finished tractor, takes 28 hours and 20 minutes.[10]

In departments of the Rouge the processes of production were never frozen. The plant was dynamic. "It does not matter in this plant," stated one expert observer, "what the equipment cost to install or how long it has been in operation; for if a more efficient method presents itself, it is immediately tried, and, if found successful, the old method is disposed of and the new installed." Ford dramatically affirmed the practice: "We tear out whole departments, perhaps, to make one or two changes that would not be noticed by the customer, but which are of vital importance to us because they produce a better machine, give it greater durability on the road, make it last longer in the hands of the consumer." [11]

Ford himself was responsible for the greatest error in Rouge planning: the use of direct instead of alternating current. His preference for DC dated back to his days as operating engineer in the Detroit Edison Illuminating Company, and to the influence of Edison himself.

While the development of alternating current (it came later into use than direct) was marked by some disadvantages, by 1920 these had been wholly overcome. Ford however argued that the higher voltage required for AC transmission was a plant hazard, and insisted upon the conversion of all Rouge generators, which were geared to AC. This resulted in a loss of fifteen per cent of power, but Ford's engineers dared not oppose their employer. In time however not even Ford could ignore the waste and its attendant evils. The armatures of the partially open DC motors became clogged with dust and grit causing the units to burn out. As more and more motors were installed in the foundry and foundry machine shop, the problem became alarming. "Nobody could keep them going," recalled Frank Riecks, then an assistant plant engineer. Finally Ford gave in, and ordered a complete changeover, which was supposed to have cost $30,000,000.

But Ford, or his engineers, extracted a compensatory satisfaction from the change. "Well, all right," they said to General Electric and Westinghouse. "We're going to use AC. But we want a superlative, totally enclosed, fan-cooled motor." It did not exist at the time, but the manufacturers produced it.[12]

3.

The variety and completeness of mechanical equipment at the Rouge impressed even the technical experts. In conveyors alone it was a wonderland of devices. Gravity, belt, bucket, spiral, pendulum, gravity roller, overhead monorail, "scenic railway" and "merry-go-round," elevating flight—the list was long both in range and adaptation to special purposes. The machine tools were as notable. These, numbering 43,000 in 1926 (with the coming of Model A they increased to 53,000), comprised standard types adapted to Ford routines or redesigned, and a large number of special Ford design. New uses of tools abounded at the Rouge, and the pace of the machines was increased "far beyond the point believed desirable by conservative tool manufacturers." Special crews oiled, sharpened, and otherwise serviced such equipment. The roll of Ford employees contained 8000 tool-and-die men. Dozens of inspection devices were adopted or developed to supplement the basic Johansson blocks and the tests of the laboratories of the basic materials used. These, incidentally, comprised 49 types of steel, 4 of iron, 22 of brass and bronze, and 5 of aluminum.[13]

The layouts of the Ford factories won the astonishment (and later the approval) of visiting technicians. Astonishment, because as Van Deventer pointed out in 1923, "a man who is accustomed to the space usually allotted between machine tools in average shop practice would say that the River Rouge departments were crowded and congested." Faurote a few years later wrote that to cross the floor of a Ford factory was all but impossible. However, both experts agreed that the apparent congestion was actually efficiency in a plant where "the work moves and the men stand still." As to crossing the factory floor, Faurote noted, "One is not supposed to traverse the shop in this manner. There are overhead metal platforms and tubular-railed metal runways provided for visitors and for general shop inspection. Each workman in the machine shop has ample room to perform his operation or series of operations, but there is no waste space. If a machine which has too long a table or base is purchased, it is cut off. The saving of one step to the right or to the left; the reaching up instead of down; the deliverance of material at a waist-high altitude—these are some of the little things which, individually, do not amount to so much, but which, in the aggregate, bulk big."

Thus the Ford staff had produced the flow in manufacture which was one of their great objectives. Van Deventer described the total effect: "He [a visitor] sees these units not only in their impressive individual and astounding collective magnitude, *but he also sees each unit as the part of a huge machine*—he sees each unit as a carefully designed gear which meshes with other gears and operates in synchronism with them, the whole forming one huge, perfectly-timed, smoothly operating industrial machine of almost unbelievable efficiency."

There was another way of describing the process which the Ford Motor Company emphasized in its publicity. At eight o'clock on Monday morning, it pointed out, ore arriving in the slip was transferred by way of the High Line to the Blast Furnace. At noon on Tuesday it was molten iron being poured into a foundry mold, and later that afternoon a finished motor travelling by trunk-line conveyor toward final assembly. "Here is a conversion of raw material to cash in approximately 33 hours." In several years the total time was to be lessened by almost five hours. The Rouge had brilliantly realized Ford's dream of continuous, integrated manufacture.[14]

4.

By 1924 the Rouge had fully established its character, but was still in process of growth. Units continued to be brought down: the Motor Assembly Building (January, 1925), the Pressed Steel Parts and Spring and Upset Buildings (June and July, 1925), the three requiring almost 20,000 workers, most of whom came with the equipment from Highland Park. Greater capacity and more modern tooling and processes marked all the new units.[15]

Meanwhile a great new manufacturing complex was being developed west of the slip: open hearths and mills for the making and processing of steel.

Ford had flirted with this project since 1915. According to one account, he startled a group of his engineers at the Rouge in that year by demanding: "Boys, what is your idea of the best spot in the world to build a steel industry?" and by declaring, after discussion. "It's right here where we stand. Up in Northern Michigan and Minnesota are great iron ore deposits. Down in Kentucky and West Virginia are huge deposits of soft coal. Here we stand, half way between, with water transportation to our door. You will look the whole country over but you won't find a place that compares with this."

His analysis was sound, and indeed, the first commercial steel produced in the United States by the Bessemer process had been made in 1864 by a Detroit firm, while the first American steel rails were rolled at Wyandotte in 1865. But Detroit failed to expand such activities, and other cities farther east or south like Bethlehem, Gary, and Pittsburgh had taken over the lead. It was not until after World War I that the Great Lakes Steel Corporation at Ecorse began to develop local steel-making capacity, although pig iron had been made since 1902 on Zug Island, several miles south of the Rouge site.[16]

Ford never abandoned his interest in the Rouge as 'a steel center. Both A. M. Wibel and Philip Haglund recalled his discussing it in 1918, and Haglund on request made a plan for a small steel plant about that time. In 1919 or 1920, says Wibel, Sorensen asked him what were the chief companies in the United States that designed and constructed steel plants. Wibel named the Morgan Construction Company of Worcester, Massachusetts, and the United Engineering Company of

Pittsburgh. "You get those fellows in here," commanded Ford. "We want to talk about it. . . . Our use of steel is a million tons a year. We want to make 500,000 tons of it." "Where do you want to start?" asked Wibel. "We want the whole doggone story finally, probably, but let's feel it out."

Wibel brought the experts to Dearborn. With them Ford, he, Harry Hanson, Haglund, and others discussed such factors as coal and coke, and Wibel thinks that the acquisition of coal mines and the first coke ovens were linked to these conferences.[17]

By February, 1923, Ford officials were meeting with Morgan experts at Worcester, while in July *Automotive Industries* reported that there would be "a substantial increase in steel producing capacity at the Rouge plant" (some steel was already being made by the electric furnaces near the foundry). For a time, says Haglund, the plan had been to increase electric furnace capacity for steel making, and to establish mills for the processing. However, the ten-ton furnaces which Haglund supervised were "too confined," a fifty-ton unit proved unsuccessful, and "then they started thinking about open hearths." By 1924 these were scheduled; and Sorensen delegated Hanson, Haglund and Lumsden to go down to the Central Steel Company of Massilon, Ohio, and to other steel centers, and familiarize themselves with the processes of the industry. But he warned them that he did not want merely to be told how the established steel-makers operated. "I want you to have that in the back of your head right now, that we are not following these other steel plants at all. They are going to follow us."

These instructions undoubtedly came from Henry Ford. Just as he had modified the methods of manufacturing iron, he meant to improve the making of steel. He was convinced that a flow of production could be established. For example, he envisaged open hearth operations as continuous, raw materials being added from time to time, and the molten metal drawn off as needed and made directly into castings.[18]

The entire steel development, once in operation, was to be in charge of John Findlater. After Lumsden and Haglund returned from their several months of observation, Findlater and they, with Ford, Sorensen, and Hanson, aided by experts from the steel-plant fabricating companies, planned the Ford steel complex—open hearth furnaces, blooming mill, and rolling mills (merchant, billet and sheet, and rod units). Hanson took final authority in planning, including the foundations, which required extensive and costly piling. "The Rouge River site couldn't have been worse," he noted. Hardpan was down a hundred feet. The power plant site, where rock was "practically at ground level," would have saved "millions and millions of dollars." The open hearths in the new plant were tilting hearths. "The idea was to keep a certain amount of molten metal in the furnace and just keep adding scrap to it and pouring it in small amounts." Characteristically, Ford also insisted that his open hearths and mills should be clean. In order to supply iron for steel operations, additional coke ovens were constructed.[19]

The Open Hearth Building, designed by Albert Kahn, was started early in 1925, about a quarter of a mile back from the southern end of the slip. It had a capacity of ten furnaces, although only four were constructed immediately. The rolling mills, much larger, were erected just to the north. The Pressed Steel and Spring and Upset buildings continued the line of steel units, lying end to end with the mills, and west of B Building.

The pouring of the first heat took place on June 21, 1926. For this event officials and distinguished visitors made a small group of spectators. Lumsden recalled that there was difficulty in opening the tap hole of the furnace, so that the heat dribbled into the ladle, and when ready to be poured into the ingot molds, was "considerably on the cold side." Hanson says that the fault was in the ladles. Anyhow, it proved impossible to lift the stopper of the ladle, and a hole had to be burned with oxygen lances. Then the steel gushed out, and spilled fiercely on the open hearth floor. The visitors, seeing only a fine display of fireworks, applauded. But Sorensen knew that the job had been bungled, and stormed about, his language matching the molten metal. "Who in hell invented this thing?" he finally shouted.[20]

The plant in operation, Findlater, Lumsden and Haglund strove to meet Ford's expectations as to the flow of manufacture. They tried in various ways to use the open hearth as a reservoir of metal to which scrap could be added as heats were poured, but, says Haglund, "we failed in all those ways." They also encountered trouble when they tried to pour the furnace metal into a "continuous pigging machine," then take the thirty to forty pound pigs and clap them into forging presses. "We spent thousands of dollars on that. . . . We were going to eliminate the making of ingots and the re-heating of ingots and the soaking pits and the rolling mills. . . . We were going to take the metal right out of the open hearth ladles and pour it into a pig and slap that pig into a forge press and make a forging." It didn't work. "I remember one time we cut one of those slugs and put it in a forging press and when the press came down on that pig of steel, which wasn't solidified except on the outside, it shot molten metal right through the roof of that open hearth, about sixty feet above. It was just like the shot of a gun. That scared Mr. Ford when he heard of it." They tried other experiments, and did cast gears and gear blanks successfully, but it was cheaper to machine them!

Ford was more successful in challenging the tradition of dirty hearths and mills. "An open hearth was the most God-forsaken thing any human being could work in," states Haglund. Dirt, smoke, and heat were everywhere. The Ford plant was spotless, pit and floor "slick as a whistle." Floors were scrubbed, ladles whitewashed, furnaces painted. Steel men came, saw, jeered—then went back to their plants and did the same thing! "It cleaned up every steel plant in the country, not only open hearths but rolling mills as well."

In a similar fashion, the Ford engineers revolutionized the methods of handling iron ore, limestone, and dolomite, and provided other improvements. They ran these materials on an endless belt, dropping them into hoppers at the top of the building, and drawing supplies as needed into the charging boxes. The practice was soon universally adopted.[21]

The quality of Ford steel was excellent, the amount produced creditable. In 1926 the company produced 321,476 steel ingot tons, and in 1929 was prepared to double that output. Considering their limited background for steel work, and the relatively few expert employees they imported from outside, the performance of the Ford officials was impressive. Hanson states also that on the whole the company saved money by making its own steel.

By 1926 the company had established the first link in its most elaborate conveyor system, completing a unit that connected the foundry with the motor assembly building, 3600 feet in length. Another was under construction between the foundry and B Building, a mile and a quarter apart. As a safety measure the company also constructed walkovers from Miller Road to B Building, and from there to the Spring and Upset building.[22]

The mature Rouge—it was still to change and grow—now occupied

1115.12 acres, the land having been sold by Ford to the company from time to time, at cost. In the buildings there were 159.62 acres of floor space (Highland Park occupied 229.09 acres, with 52.18 of floor space). A total of 93 separate structures stood on the site, 23 of which were classified as "main buildings." Railroad trackage covered 93 miles, conveyors 27. About 75,000 men worked in the great plant. A force of 5000 did nothing but keep it clean, wearing out 5000 mops and 3000 brooms a month, and using 86 tons of soap on the floors, walls, and 330 acres of windows. The Rouge was an industrial city, immense, concentrated, packed with power. It was ready for the culminating act in its growth —the transfer of the final assembly line from Highland Park.[23]

5.

In one sense the event was anti-climactic. Everything else of productive consequence had been moved; this last occurrence was a kind of signature to a carefully drawn and fully approved document. It took place in September, 1927, and the new unit was established in B Building. Here an improved conveyer enabled all types of cars to be assembled on the same line, the length of which was reduced from 680 to 340 feet. As the *Ford News* pointed out, the shift to the Rouge would at a stroke abolish the shipping of motor, chassis, and body parts to Highland Park. All would now go by conveyer "from the place of their manufacture to the proper point on the new line. This means that the loading, unloading, switching, and hauling of 2500 cars of freight yearly will be saved." Also, it noted, because of a thorough redesigning of operations "not a single body-truck will be employed either in building a body or in transporting it to the assembly line. From first to last the body will be handled by conveyors, hoists, elevators, and transfer tables." [24]

The time for the move was auspicious: there was no problem of continuing production to be met, for work had ceased on the Model T, and the Model A was not yet ready for quantity manufacture. In fact, the entire plant was being overhauled and re-tooled for the new car, and the transfer of the assembly line fitted into this activity.

Martin had come to the Rouge about two years earlier, and was working with Sorensen, nominally sharing the responsibilities of production, but tacitly deferring to the man who had once been his assistant. Sorensen could not discharge him, but he indicates in his memoirs that he encouraged Martin to stick to production details; and meanwhile he weeded out any of Martin's associates who might form a rival nucleus of power.

The process went forward both at Highland Park and the Rouge. When Martin came down to the Rouge, Bricker was sent up to Highland Park as acting superintendent. After surveying the situation there, he began to remove men, or have them removed, as their activities were transferred to the Rouge. "They didn't want the supervision to come [from Highland Park] to the Rouge plant," Klann later pointed out. At the same time, some men who went to the Rouge found that they had no jobs there, or inferior ones, and quit. Bricker used Klann as his deputy in discharging many men. "You know those fellows better than I do." Klann was to tell them that the company was cutting down its force. Top officials, including Klann (who did much of the firing and then was fired himself) were kept on until the final assembly was moved, or longer. Among those who were discharged, or appraised the situation and left, were Findlater, Avery, E. Burns, Hartner, Benedict, Degener, Scofield, Diehl, Hobart, and Leister. Kanzler had resigned in 1926 (see Chapter XV); Ryan, the sales manager, departed late in 1927, but his going was associated with the demise of Model T, and was not a part of the Rouge-Highland Park feud, although Sorensen had a hand in it. Diehl was let out at this time, but apparently for special reasons. Quite as important as the exodus of higher officials was the weeding out of their abler subordinates. Hundreds of these were dropped, and their disappearance left the company dangerously thin in experienced supervisors and expert workers at a time when the new car was about to demand a miracle in the speedup of production.

Sorensen and the hard-jawed Harry Bennett supervised the slaughter. Bennett, his power growing, was janissary for Sorensen. Some called him "Sorensen's little puppy-dog." He was already asserting an influence over personnel. Sorensen surveyed the working out of his program, and lent act or voice when either seemed to be needed. He told Klann: "We want to fire every Model T son-of-a-bitch!" (He was now identifying the Rouge with the new car, and Highland Park with the old one.) Klann retorted: "Charlie, what are you? You worked on the job yourself, too, didn't you?" Sorensen ignored the thrust. He was building up a scorn for the old car—"That's a Model T idea," or "That's Model T

thinking,"—which even Henry Ford himself came to share. Klann's
reply may have made his own discharge a certainty.[25]

6.

Now that the Rouge was complete as an industrial unit of power, it
quickly took on a character as a place of work. One would gladly write
that its bold planning and fine mechanization, its large, well-lighted,
clean and efficiently ventilated structures were matched by a happy
spirit among its officials and workers. Unfortunately, the reverse became true.

The fact was grimly ironic. Here Ford's hope to "lift . . . drudgery
off flesh and blood and lay it on steel and motors" had been superbly
realized. Men pressed buttons or levers instead of handling heavy loads;
the parts on which they worked came to them, the height just right for
their hands, and passed on under mechanical power as the work was
completed. Every precaution for safety was taken and enforced. Heat
and noxious fumes were artificially drawn away. The machinery was
cared for by experts, and factory and equipment freshly painted. The
Rouge was cleaner then than now, recalled Logan Miller in the 1950's.
"It was not uncommon to see a whole building shut down and everybody cleaning the machines, the floors, and starting to paint the building. Maybe it would be [shut] down all day or for part of a day, and
the night shift would come on and do the same thing until the place
was shining." This was for Henry Ford, who might appear at any moment, but it gave the Rouge a brightness strangely in contrast with the
mood of its workers.[26]

This mood was to some extent created by the size of the plant. By
its very massiveness and complexity it denied men at the top contact
with and understanding of those beneath, and gave those beneath a
sense of being lost in inexorable immensity and power. "The place was
growing so fast and getting so immense and so heavily involved," recalled Haglund, who watched it develop, "that one man couldn't possibly take care of it. When a job gets too big for a man he isn't responsible for the methods he pursues." This of course was not true, for the
Rouge later was not a sinister worksite; but sheer bigness was a factor.
In the mounting nineteen-twenties it invited a severe and even harsh
control, for it was new and complex as well as immense. And in Soren-

sen it found a master who was naturally a driver, of himself as well as of others.[27]

He instituted from the first a control that was aggressive and unrelenting, and he found stanch supporters in Bricker and Bennett. We have already noted some of his methods. Their sudden, sweeping, and often captious character created the atmosphere of the Rouge. Men coming from Highland Park, says Haglund (and many confirm his words) had to be made over. "It was a hard-boiled policy at Highland Park but it didn't compare with the intensity that was at the Rouge. Everybody was on edge. They ran around in circles and didn't know what they were doing. Physically everybody was going like a steam engine but not so much mentally. As long as their feet were on the go they were working hard. The more a man ran around the better he was." In contrast, at Highland Park, "People worked willingly there. They'd tackle jobs and try to get results without any particular pressure. There was an internal desire in the man to do a good job. . . . When he came to the Rouge plant, he had to do a good job or get his head chopped off. . . . You didn't know when somebody was going to come along and clip you one and knock your feet from under you." Officials had no offices—only desks in the open factory at which they stood. They couldn't keep records, and lower officials could not discuss their problems together. Sorensen might occasionally confer with a few top men, but otherwise an official didn't even stop to talk to another. Logan Miller called the plant "a place of fear." Fear even extended beyond working hours. Miller didn't dare cultivate Bricker socially, and one day at an airplane meet, although he was off duty, at a glimpse of Sorensen he began dodging about so that the boss wouldn't see him. He and others suffered from what came to be called "Forditis." Its symptoms were "a nervous stomach and all parts of your body breaking down. Maybe a week or two week rest would build you up, and you'd come in fighting again." [28]

What infected the officials also infected the masses of employees. Here the intensive mechanization of the plant had its effect. As early as 1923 Van Deventer noted that the flow of manufacture promoted "the elimination of any possibility of loafing or soldiering on the job when each operator is faced with the necessity of keeping up with the procession or else seeing his stock piled up to the point where it becomes distinctly noticeable by the immediate management." Faurote

commented with similar approval on the same close timing and processing of work as he saw it five years later. Both noted the packing of
machines into minimum space and applauded it. "Each workman in
the machine shop has ample room to perform his operation or series of
operations," said Faurote, "but there is no waste space."

However, what neither Van Deventer nor Faurote saw was that
limited space and measured time for work imposed a kind of physical
isolation which, combined with an atmosphere of uncertainty, unremitting pace, and harsh penalties for innocent action or inaction,
created a tension for the common worker comparable with that felt
by his boss. The worker also had his specific grievances, to be noted in
a later chapter. But the tension was the important factor. As Ford reduced prices on cars, there was inevitable pressure from Sorensen down
to weed out men, to keep the vast plant moving at its maximum pace.
The entire 70,000 felt the strain. The pace was never too fast for accomplishment, but it was fast enough to make the job relentless,
harassing, and to many hateful.[29]

Yet despite its sinister aspect, which organized labor and more enlightened management would in time cure, the Rouge stood out as
a pioneering accomplishment in industry which affected both automotive and other manufacturing processes. The Ford organization as embodied in the Rouge unquestionably took a great stride forward as
compared with any of its rivals. None so completely controlled and
related the basic elements of production. None effected a concentration of manufacturing which permitted so great an integration of related activities, along with notable economies in manufacturing. None
achieved the same degree of mechanization, or quite matched the
modernity of the tooling. In its own different fashion, more complex
and not always obvious, the Rouge influenced the motor car factories
of the late nineteen twenties and the nineteen thirties much as the moving assembly line had influenced those of the preceding period. In its
extension and refinement of mechanization it even helped to lay one
part of the foundation on which the phenomenon of today, automation, rests, although it did nothing to develop that control of machines
by technology which has been the determining factor in the revolution
American industry is experiencing in the nineteen-fifties.* To be sure,

---

* The essence of automation lies more in the electronic controls than in the mechanization
which responds to them. But obviously the controls could not be applied without the machines,
and the Rouge was the exemplar of machine equipment.

the Rouge did not prevent the Chevrolet or Chrysler organizations from challenging Ford supremacy. They too progressed in factory engineering, learning and adapting to an extent from Ford, but also developing their own layouts, processes and equipment. Knudsen was a master in production when he left Ford in 1921, and did not stop growing; Fred M. Zeder and K. T. Keller gave Chrysler distinction both in design and in the detail of manufacturing. But Ford's rivals excelled him in design and company organization and could not match him in plant; there, it may be said, the Rouge was a great counterbalance to his unquestionable weaknesses.

The factory had its limitations, which even Ford came to accept. In theory, it might have expanded geographically and mechanically, taking on an ever larger proportion of Ford production. Actually, it was apparent from the first that only a part (although it was a large part) of Ford cars could be completed at the Rouge; Ford in effect said so, and while it was under construction, so were branch assembly plants; in 1928 there were thirty-five of these active in the United States, and others abroad. The Rouge toiled for these, fabricating parts and motors. The village industries, although negligible in effect, marked a further recognition by Ford of the idea of decentralization. And eventually even castings and motors were to be fashioned elsewhere, while an increasing volume of cars were to be assembled in branch factories. This trend toward confining the limits of the Rouge and establishing other production sites was part of the change of policy which marked the reorganized company in 1946, and in the opinion of some Ford personnel represented a reaction from the practices of Bennett, Sorensen, and Henry Ford. But it could also be argued that a further expansion of the Rouge would have been unsound economically. The coming and going of a still larger army of workers and the shipping of a greater volume of raw materials and finished products to and from a single site both threatened to create problems of congestion. The Rouge probably reached its maximum effective size about 1929–1936.

But the solidity of the original achievement seems to be attested by the survival of the plant in its essentials today. A number of minor activities have been expunged, and the change in the character of the Ford products, now in total both greater and more varied and complex than the Model A, have made for new layouts and functions in many of the main buildings. Yet an astonishing amount of the original Rouge persists. Its slip, its open hearth and steel mills, its blast furnaces, foundry, glass plant, final assembly building, its coke ovens and by-products activities still throb with vital if changed activity after thirty years. Ford and his associates registered an achievement which was memorable. The world has justly given its attention to Ford's foibles, sins, and failures, but may quite as justly remember him in this aspect of industrial creation, one of the crowning accomplishments of his maturity.

XII

FROM MUSCLE SHOALS
TO ANTI-SEMITISM

THE nation in these years was in the hands of political and social reactionaries. Warren G. Harding's flabby rhetoric, "not nostrums but normalcy, not revolution but restoration, not surgery but serenity," expressed its easygoing, self-centered, gain-seeking temper. Baiting the reds, lifting every control from business, exalting isolationism as a fundamental national tradition, raising tariffs and collecting foreign debts, the Government rode carelessly on the boom of the "roaring twenties." Even though the increasing rural depression made it difficult for many farmers to buy the cheapest car, the Ford company shared in the general business prosperity. Its officers, great and small, saw no further into the future than the heads of other great American corporations; with the optimism characteristic of the nation, they expected the prosperity to continue unbroken. It was in many respects a crazy era: bizarre in such episodes as the Scopes trial, horrifying in the rampant efflorescence of gangsterism, and illogical in the avoidance of world responsibilities when American solvency required world trade and American safety rested on world peace. Although Henry Ford was increasingly engrossed in his fast-expanding company affairs, he made his own contribution to the pattern of this eccentric period.

It was to his credit that, still an ardent pacifist, he supported Wilson's policies to the end. In the presidential campaign of 1920 he was outspokenly for James M. Cox against Harding. After the Republican victory he continued to argue for the League. When the isolationists slew it he pleaded for a broadened and invigorated world court until that hope also faded.

Meanwhile, he had the satisfaction of watching in 1921–1922 a violent Senate debate on the Newberry case. Most of the Republican senators defended Truman H. Newberry against the charge of illegal campaign expenditures, but a number of the strongest members—Borah of

Idaho, LaFollette of Wisconsin, Capper of Kansas, Kenyon of Iowa, Norris of Nebraska—joined such leading Democrats as Walsh of Montana and Pomerene of Ohio in demanding his expulsion from the chamber. They pronounced his use of money intolerable. Early in 1922, by the close vote of 46 to 41, the Senate seated Newberry for that session. Nevertheless it was plain that the case would be opened again when Congress reconvened. On November 18, 1922, Newberry sent his resignation to the governor of Michigan with a letter both defensive and apologetic. Ford could feel a transient throb of exultation. He had not won—but neither, in the end, had his rival.[1]

2.

The curious mania called Ford's presidential boom, in which he took but an oblique interest, showed a rapid revival in 1922–1923. In part it was a natural outgrowth of the myth about Ford's personality which L. R. Collier summed up by saying that people liked Ford because he was one of themselves and a good deal more: "You are to them the greatest of manufacturers, the fairest and most liberal of employers, a practical philanthropist who has brought hope and sunshine into millions of homes." To millions Ford had a Lincolnian quality. Another basis for the boom was the persistent belief that he was a magician who could solve any problem whatever. The Nebraska Senate invited Ford to visit the State to develop its waterpower; a body of Michigan fruitgrowers petitioned the President to buy all the American railroads and hand them over to Ford for really efficient operation; the New York State Waterways Association called on him to persuade Congress to improve the Hudson River; the price of stock in important corporations rose or fell with reports that he would or would not become a director or investor. At the time of the Disarmament Conference in 1921, the New York *World* printed a report that he would buy the whole French fleet to help the peacemakers; later, when the Dawes Plan was launched, the *New York Times* noted a Wall Street rumor that he would buy the entire $100,000,000 bond issue.

The myth, of course, was not what it had been before the *Tribune* suit, when even so astute a man as John R. Commons had urged Ford not to run for the Senate because he was needed for the greater post of President. But it was still sufficiently imposing to enable the *Wall Street Journal,* of all newspapers, to print a serious editorial in the fall of

1922: "Why Not Ford for President?" Indeed, if a Harding could be President, why not anybody? In Michigan the neighbors were caustic about the boom. The *Detroit Saturday Night* remarked that Ford could easily qualify under the constitution, for h̀e was native born and past thirty-five. Arthur Vandenberg, conceding that Ford had to his credit perhaps the greatest single industrial unit in history, debited him with more erratic interviews, more dubious quotations, more bland ignorance of American experience, more political nonsense, and more dangerous propaganda than any other dependable citizen he had ever known. Vandenberg was then a conservative isolationist. But even in Michigan Ford had staunch adherents.[2]

At a meeting in Dearborn in the spring of 1922 about 140 men assembled wearing cardboard hatbands reading, "We Want Henry," chose committees, and organized a "Ford for President Club." The leaders of this amateurish gathering were Dearborn business and professional men, wholly without political connections. They took a tiny upstairs office in a Dearborn business block, began writing letters to friends around the country urging them to form "Ford Clubs," and sold hatbands at a dollar each. Almost or quite spontaneously, clubs began springing up across the map. Just how many finally existed we shall never know. F. S. Hammond of Elizabeth, N.J., who soon laid claim to national leadership, wrote in June, 1923: "I have now fourteen clubs in this State, and we have over one thousand throughout the United States." Most of them doubtless possessed a tailors-of-Tooley Street membership; nevertheless, the movement became formidable. By the spring of 1923 the *New York Times* was declaring that "Ford looms today a powerful and enigmatic figure on the political horizon"; that fall the Washington correspondent of the New York *Herald* asserted that "the astonishing growth of popular sentiment for Ford for President is causing deep concern to Democrats and anxiety to Republicans." Senator King of Utah predicted that in an immediate election Ford would sweep the nation, and first returns from a poll taken by *Collier's Weekly* bore him out.[3]

Most of Ford's intimates believed that his saving modesty would drive the bee from his bonnet, and this at first seems to have been true. He kept saying: "The idea is a joke." William Stidger, a minister who after a series of interviews for the Hearst syndicate wrote an obsequious volume on Ford, concluded that the manufacturer had no interest in the boom. Another man who saw much more of Ford, Fred L. Black of the *Dearborn Independent,* decided that while E. G. Liebold had a self-interested faith in the movement, for he cherished dreams of glory as a sort of assistant-president, the boss was never beguiled. What did interest Ford initially was the question of the extent to which people supported the Ford clubs so rapidly springing up—the extent, that is, of his personal popularity. Liebold sent Black to Western Michigan to make inquiries, and Black travelled from town to town interviewing leaders in the clubs. They had really spontaneous local origins, he learned, and enlisted reputable citizens who honestly believed that Ford would make a better president than Harding.[4]

Liebold records that when he first told Ford of the heavy volume of letters urging him to run for President, Ford replied that he would take no political office. "You do all you can to keep me out of this thing," he warned. "I don't want anything to do with it." Later, however, his attitude shifted. When supporters were getting ready to file petitions in the Iowa primaries, he advised against interference. "Let them go ahead with it and see what happens. We might have some fun with these politicians." Thereafter, states Liebold, the Ford offices let the movement take its course. This was for some months both unpredictable and fascinating. Headlines blazed, polls showed great strength (the *Collier's Weekly* poll, reaching a quarter of a million men, gave Ford an eight to five lead over Harding), and inevitably politicians climbed aboard the rolling wagon. In the West and South particularly members of Congress declared that if the people's voice was heard, Ford would soon enter the White House. A New York insurance firm announced that somebody had taken out a $400,000 policy against Ford's election. Clara Ford telephoned Liebold in high indignation.

"Since you got him into it," she scolded, "you can just get him out of it. I hate this idea of the name of Ford being dragged down into the gutters of political filth! My name is Ford, and I'm proud of it! If Mr. Ford wants to go to Washington, he can go, but I'll go to England!"

For a time, as William Randolph Hearst showed some inclination to back him, Ford seems to have toyed carelessly with the idea he at first derided. When *Collier's* asked him to contribute an article entitled, "If I were President," he called in Cameron and others to write it. Company associates found his conception of the presidency frightening. According to Liebold, he believed that as in Dearborn he devoted long hours to inspecting units of the plants, in Washington he could spend his time going from department to department to learn on the spot what cabinet and bureau chiefs were doing, and in talking with plain citizens. "I'd get to the bottom of things and find out," he said darkly. "No, no," expostulated Liebold. "The way the presidency is set up, you don't have much time to get out of the office." Ford was unimpressed. "You fellows could handle all that," he explained. "That's just correspondence to be answered and things of that kind." To Stidger he made an equally alarming remark. "I'd just like to be down there about six weeks and throw some monkey-wrenches into the machinery," he ruminated. He told Sorensen that he would make him Secretary of War!

It was inevitable that this little dust-cyclone should soon whirl away into oblivion. While it lasted, with more and more clubs, a New York headquarters at 1270 Broadway, men parading with "We Want Henry" placards, Liebold telling the *New York Times* that he received two hundred letters daily urging Ford to run, and Edison expressing the hope Ford would resist political ambition, the movement attracted a number of men anxious to use Ford's fame to further their politico-

FORM 717

CLASS OF SERVICE	SYMBOL
Day Message	
Day Letter	Blue
Night Message	Nite
Night Letter	N L

If none of these three symbols appears after the check (number of words) the telegram is a day message. Otherwise its character is indicated by the symbol appearing after the check.

Ford Motor Company
Automobile Manufacturers
TELEGRAM

RECEIVED AT MAIN OFFICE   VIA POSTAL TELEGRAPH CO.

WU-25-JBS   DAY LETTER   WHITE HOUSE WASHINGTON D C
12:40P M 29th

HENRY FORD

I WANT YOU TO KNOW HOW MUCH I APPRECIATE YOUR STATEMENT
THAT YOU WILL VOTE FOR ME YOUR CONFIDENCE HAS BEEN A
GREAT SATISFACTION

CALVIN COOLIDGE

1:55P M 10/29/24

economic ambitions. Collier, quoted above, a nephew of the publisher, wrote: "I should like to sound the keynote of your campaign. And I have a program in mind for it that will interest you." The same idea was entertained by George L. Record of New Jersey, a former Bull Moose leader, who urged Ford to press forward to a great success by campaigning for destruction of the Beef Trust and Anthracite Trust. Echoes of Bryanism arose. But when, on August 2, 1923, Harding died and Coolidge succeeded him, the political scene completely changed. Republicans rallied behind the new president with revived unity, new figures and issues appeared, and the Ford movement instantly lost momentum.

Ford himself finally crushed the little boom. On December 19, 1923, Liebold wrote a Memphis agent of the company: "We have recently requested the Third Party movement to call off its meeting which was to have been held in Detroit. In this connection I might give you some advance information, and that is, Mr. Ford intends to support President Coolidge as a candidate." Formal announcement of this support came next day.[5] During the 1924 campaign Ford repeated his endorsement.

3.

But prior to Ford's emergence in favor of Coolidge, and as some thought bearing upon it, lay an interesting chapter in the history of Muscle Shoals. W. J. Cameron had said early in 1923 that Ford was thinking not of the presidency but of a thousand other matters. A company employee who saw much of Ford in 1923 believed him wholly indifferent to politics. "In those days he was more interested in getting something like Muscle Shoals going." [6]

In considering the Muscle Shoals problem of 1921, we must dismiss all thought of the imposing TVA, which lay in the womb of a later and different period. We must fix our attention on certain limited, incomplete, and temporarily derelict installations on the Tennessee River, begun in wartime for the manufacture of nitrates. Ambitious plans for dams and plants had been made and dropped. They included the Wilson Dam at Muscle Shoals, commenced in 1918, which after government expenditures of about $16,250,000 was less than one-third completed at the beginning of 1922; another and smaller dam which had been planned but not even started; a nitrate plant at Muscle Shoals built under contract by the Air Nitrates Corporation at a cost, including a quarry, of about $67,500,000; and a lesser plant at Sheffield, Alabama, constructed for the government by the General Chemical Company at a cost of almost $13,000,000. Both plants were in an inert condition, with maintenance charges running about $270,000 a year. At Warrior, Alabama, the government also had a $5,000,000 steam plant which it had rented to the Alabama Power Company.[7]

It was irritating to taxpayers to see an incomplete dam deteriorating and two costly nitrate plants standing unused; irritating to critics of the Alabama Power Company to see it getting the low-rental use of a government steam plant; irritating to farmers to think that the idle nitrate plants might be selling them cheap fertilizer; and irritating to believers in government development of hydroelectric power to think of all the Tennessee River water running to waste. But what could be done about it? Unquestionably a number of greedy interests had their eyes on these facilities. Unquestionably, also, no administration of the Harding-Coolidge era was going to support a huge governmental enterprise on the Tennessee. Harding's Secretary of War, John W. Weeks, declared soon after taking office that private enterprise must do the work, and asked for bids.

Ford, at the instigation of a number of farm leaders, began inquiring into Muscle Shoals in the spring of 1921. Gray Silver, Washington representative of the Farm Bureau Federation, ex-Governor E. A. O'Neal, president of the Alabama branch of the Federation, and several editors of agricultural journals were among his chief prompters. The Tennessee Valley Improvement Association, headed by J. W. Worthington, was also desperately anxious to enlist Ford's capital in completing the facilities. On July 8, 1921, Ford submitted an offer to the Secretary of War. This fell into two parts, one for the leasing and maintenance of the dams, and the other for the outright purchase and operation of the nitrate plants and accessories. His main objects in the offer, according to his own statement, were wholly public-spirited; he wished to make a good fertilizer at lower costs to the farmers than they were paying, and to maintain the larger nitrate plant in constant readiness for war work. The offer was made, as he later pointed out, at a time when the government was selling many wartime facilities for low salvage prices. It thus disposed of the Old Hickory Powder Plant, which had cost about $80,000,000, for less than five per cent of its cost, and numerous wooden ships for less than half of one per cent of cost.

His initial bid Ford almost immediately amended. Secretary of War Weeks made objections to it, and called him to Washington. Ford then visited Muscle Shoals in company with Thomas A. Edison, and after consultation with various experts at Dearborn, on January 25, 1922, altered his terms for the better. He proposed to form a new corporation. This company would complete the two dams and their appurtenant power-houses for the government at cost, on a scale to furnish 850,000 horsepower. It would then lease the dams and power facilities for a hundred years, paying after the start an annual rental of four per cent of construction costs. The two nitrate plants and the quarry the company would buy outright for $5,000,000. It would agree to manufacture approximately 110,000 tons of ammonium nitrate a year for the farmers of the country, limiting its profits to not more than eight per cent of production costs. Moreover, it would keep the larger Wilson Dam plant always in readiness to make explosives or other warlike material, and would transfer it to the United States on five days' notice. Ford would also agree to make various smaller payments in money and services, such as $35,000 a year for upkeep of the Wilson Dam. Finally, he would pay the government a semi-annual sum for a sinking fund, sufficient to produce about $49,000,000 at the end of the lease if the government invested it at four per cent, and about $70,000,000 if at five per cent.[8]

A hot debate instantly broke out over Ford's offer. On one side it was described as the most brazen plan of robbery since the Credit Mobilier; on the other, as a constructive act of rare statesmanship and generosity.

In behalf of the plan a clamorous body of men representing agricultural groups, Southern realty and industrial interests, and mere believers in Ford as a miracle-worker pressed forward. The National Grange hastened to place itself alongside the Farm Bureau Federation; the Mississippi River Association was as enthusiastic as the Tennessee River Association. The Nashville (Tenn.) *Banner,* the Albany-Decatur (Ga.) *Daily,* and the Birmingham (Ala.) *Age-Herald* led forth a column of applauding Southern newspapers. Much of the farm press in all sections was for acceptance. A majority of members of Congress from the area, headed by Senators Joseph T. Robinson of Arkansas, William J. Harris of Georgia, and Oscar Underwood and Thomas Heflin of Alabama, were ready to sign a contract. The American Federation of Labor at its 1922 convention voted general approval. A demonstration staged in Montgomery, Alabama, on March 1, 1922, drew vociferous delegations from all over the state, Mobile alone sending a special train crammed with people and a fifty-piece band. Indeed, it seemed for a time that acceptance might be swept through Congress on a flood of favorable farmer-labor sentiment and Southern enthusiasm.

But the opposition was equally vocal and determined, and it included two powerful fighters, Gifford Pinchot and Senator George W. Norris. "The Ford plan," declared Pinchot, "is seven parts waterpower, one part fertilizer." He meant that the nitrate plants when running full-tilt would consume only about one eighth of the 850,000 horsepower furnished by the hydroelectric installations. Ford himself seemed to acknowledge this when he spoke exuberantly of building a city seventy-five miles long in the Muscle Shoals area, for such a city clearly implied a variety of industries. Pinchot was particularly indignant because Ford asked for a hundred-year lease, with preferential status in seeking a renewal, for this ran squarely counter to Theodore Roosevelt's insistence, written into law in 1920, that all Federal waterpower leases be limited to fifty years. Senator Norris already had national repute as an exponent of Federal as opposed to private development of electric power on navigable streams. Speaking as chairman of the Senate Agricultural Committee, he said on May 10, 1922, that the farmers were being deceived. "No corporation ever got a more unconscionable contract." It would be impossible to regulate the new Ford corporation, he argued, and members of Congress who voted these huge property values into Ford's hands would be condemned as severely as the men who had voted land-grants to railroads a generation or two earlier.[9]

More telling than the arguments of these men, or the broadsides delivered by the National Fertilizer Association (which Ford's adherents dubbed the Fertilizer Trust) and various public utilities journals, were the memoranda submitted to the War Department by the Chief of Ordnance and Chief of Engineers. In effect, they threw grave doubts on the proposal. They showed that to complete the dams and power plants the government must make new appropriations of from forty to fifty millions, of which Ford's company would have the benefit for a hundred years at four per cent. They also showed that although the two nitrate plants, quarry, and steam plant had cost the United States about $85,000,000, and as scrap were worth more than $8,000,000, Ford would get them for $5,000,000. To be sure, acceptance of Ford's plan would stop the rapid deterioration of the partly-finished Wilson Dam and assure the nation a wartime supply of nitrates; but the price for these benefits was high.

It was soon clear that Congressional approval would be difficult though not impossible to obtain. On May 31, 1922, Ford wrote certain amendments into his proposal, suggested by the House Military Affairs Committee. Next month that body made a majority report strongly urging immediate acceptance, on the ground that Ford would assure the farmers cheap fertilizers and the nation abundant explosives, while government ownership and operation of these complex facilities would be "unspeakable folly." But a minority of seven stood for rejection, denouncing "one of the most insidious propagandas that the nation has witnessed for many a day." [10] Bills for acceptance were introduced by Senator E. F. Ladd of North Dakota, a noted agricultural expert, and Representative W. C. Wright of Georgia. But in the Senate, Chairman Norris locked up the plan in his agricultural committee.

As the matter dragged into 1923, Ford gave out several interviews attacking unnamed corporate influences for obstructing his plan, and reproaching Secretary Weeks for a prejudiced attitude. What he meant by corporate influences was partly defined by the irrepressible Worthington: "Wall Street and its ninety million dollar chemical combine, with the fertilizer manufacturing trusts like the Virginia-Carolina, financed by Morgan & Co., along with the Barrett Company representing the byproduct coking interests, and the air nitrogen fixation interests represented and owned by J. B. Duke." It is true that various organizations brought forward competitive bids. The Alabama Power and certain associated Southern utilities companies made an offer. So did the United States Muscle Shoals Power & Nitrates Corporation, whose spokesmen included Vice-President W. Wallace Atterbury of the Pennsylvania Railroad, J. G. White of a noted engineering firm, and the politically influential Elon H. Hooker of New York. But Ford was less disturbed by them than by Secretary Weeks, whom he accused of personal hostility:

Long ago Mr. Weeks matured in his mind the plan to break up Muscle Shoals and dispose of it piecemeal. When he sold the steam plant at Gorgas he pulled the first stitch in unravelling the greatest single prospect ever held out to the American farmer and manufacturer.

The next steps are so plain that a child can see them. It only remains to sell the gigantic nitrate plant No. 1, and then nitrate plant No 2, and finally the Wilson Dam itself, and that is the end of the Muscle Shoals as a possible demonstration of the cheapness with which power and fertilizer can be produced.[11]

While unquestionably Ford's motives were mainly public-spirited, it is clear that he hoped for a certain amount of personal glory from the enterprise. He expected to create at Muscle Shoals a development that would be a memorable object-lesson to the nation. His seventy-five mile city would really (as he soon made clear) be a chain of industrial towns illustrating his idea that workers and their families should live in small communities enjoying the benefits of a semi-rural life. He intended to show how efficiently waterpower could be harnessed to run factories, lighten household work, and operate farm machinery. Within fifty years, he declared, he wished his company to turn the running project over to the people of the community or the government in such a way that no private interest would derive a profit from it. The country had depended too long on coal power.

"If Muscle Shoals is developed along unselfish lines," he said, "it will work so splendidly and so simply that in no time hundreds of other waterpower developments will spring up all over the country and the days of American industry paying tribute for its power would be gone forever. I am consecrated to the principle of freeing American industry. All I want is a chance at Muscle Shoals, and if it's the last thing I do on this earth, I'll fight for that chance." He honestly believed that as an international money power had fostered militarism before the war, so Wall Street financiers were now trying to prevent his creation of this shining object-lesson. "In a sense the destiny of the American people for years to come lies here on the Tennessee River."

For a time in 1923–1924 Ford hoped he was on the verge of success. In September, 1923, he talked with President Coolidge and Secretary Weeks. On December 3 he had another conference with each. Just what passed between him and Coolidge is unknown, but according to the *New York Times* Ford appeared well pleased with his audience. The Army Chief of Engineers, General L. H. Beach, was on the whole favorable to his proposals. On March 10, 1924, the House, by the decisive vote of 227 to 142, passed a bill authorizing acceptance of the bid.

In midsummer *Collier's Weekly* opened its pages to a confident article by Ford on his Muscle Shoals dreams.[12]

The issue had now narrowed to a choice between Ford's plan and government operation, and Senator Norris was the principal lion in the path. Of Ford personally Norris spoke kindly, but declared that his name was being misused. When the Nebraska legislature passed resolutions asking Norris to change his stand, he simply became more adamant. He fought the measure to a standstill in the Senate, which adjourned without action. And seeing that Senate approval could probably never be obtained, Ford on October 15, 1924, withdrew his bid. He would consider a counter-proposal from the government, he said —but this he knew would never come. Public sentiment for his plan, in large part artificially whipped up by regional organizations, was declining as economists subjected its implications to a merciless dissection. Sentiment for public operation was meanwhile gaining.*

The withdrawal created in Dearborn a sense of relief rather than disappointment. "I think the fact that we never got into it was a blessing, a godsend," said Liebold later. And Henry Ford told Samuel Crowther with an air of release: "We are not in politics and we are in business." [13]

4.

It would have been better had Ford never entered journalism either. The *Dearborn Independent* of May 22, 1920, featuring on its front cover an unsigned article, "The International Jew: The World's Problem," began an anti-Semitic campaign which was to place on Henry Ford's career its darkest blot. The total losses of the Dearborn Publishing Company from its origin in late 1918 until its dissolution in 1930 aggregated $4,795,000, no small sum even for Ford. But these financial losses were trifling compared with those of an intangible character which he sustained.[14]

How Ford came to stumble into this battle against the "Jewish menace" is a question to which many answers have been offered. One theory is that, brooding over the failure of his peace crusade, he concluded that an "international Jewish banking power" (the Roths-

* Senator Norris during the next seven years carried two bills for Federal operation, the germ of the TVA, through Congress, only to see them vetoed by Coolidge and Hoover.

childs, the Warburgs, and others) had started the war and kept it going. Various men quoted Ford as saying that on the peace ship the Socialist editor Herman Bernstein had told him of this sinister power (as we shall see, Bernstein emphatically denied this). E. G. Liebold declares that he never knew of any anti-Semitic feeling on the part of Ford until after he came back from Stockholm. Another theory, certainly erroneous, is that he once tried to borrow money from Jewish bankers in New York and resented their rebuffs; the fact being that he never attempted to borrow from any Jewish individual or house. It is true that in acquiring the minority stock of the Ford Motor Company, Ford's agents had been forced to pay E. T. Berger the price his Dodge option stipulated—$12,500 a share, which may have helped to raise the cost of other stock; and in addition, $675,000. Again, the refusal of Tannenbaum and Strauss to sell their D.T. & I. shares prevented Ford from acquiring full control of that line. Both experiences may have confirmed him in his view that in finance the Jews were manipulators.

One little-mentioned but powerful influence on Ford may also have been that of his close friend Thomas A. Edison. As early as October, 1914, Edison was reported by the Detroit *Journal* as stating that the commercial rise of Germany had been a cause of the world war, that the Jews had been largely responsible for German business success, and that "the militarists which govern the country do their bidding." Vociferous protests greeted these remarks, and Edison denied that he had meant to accuse the Jews of starting the war—he was merely praising their ability. However, a number of Edison's letters to Ford and Liebold show a distinct anti-Semitic bias, and he approved of the *Dearborn Independent* articles.[15]

Still another hypothesis, vigorously maintained by E. G. Pipp, is that anti-Semitic feeling was subtly implanted in Ford's mind by Liebold. "I am sure that if Mr. Ford were put on the witness stand," wrote Pipp in 1921, "he could not tell to save his life just when and how he got started against the Jews. I am sure that Liebold could tell." * Still others felt that Cameron, who as a British Israelite might have bent a jaundiced eye on other Israelites, strengthened Ford's latent prejudice.

---

* Liebold in his *Reminiscences*, while defending the *Dearborn Independent's* anti-Jewish articles, insisted that they were aimed at a special type of Jew, and denied that he had influenced Ford's basic attitude.

This, however, was denied with emphasis by Pipp, and is made improbable by Cameron's kindly disposition and outlook, and his role of interpreter rather than instigator of Ford ideas.

One fact seems certain: that Ford's spasm of violent anti-Semitism grew out of ignorance and misinformation, not out of any deep-seated bigotry or vein of malice. Very likely J. L. McCloud is right in suggesting that it stemmed in part from boyhood influences; for in rural communities where the only Jew ever seen was a roving peddler, where Christian and Jew were antithetical terms, and where such images as Shylock and Fagin were traditional, parochialism bred strange distortions of view. An anti-Semitic thread had been observable in the garment of Populism. More than one observer noted that when Ford spoke harshly of the Jew he referred less to race or religion than to certain traits for which that term seemed convenient. He would conceivably have called J. P. Morgan an "international Jew." He did call some of Morgan's gentile associates "Jews." This translation of ignorance into rancor, though highly discreditable, was less odious than some of the parallel utterances of (for example) Henry Adams. It had more of loutishness than of bigotry and malice. We must remember that talk about Jewish machinations, common in all countries, was regarded much less seriously in pre-Hitler days than it can be now. Colonel C. à Court Repington's diary for the war years repeatedly mentions the British and French gossip concerning Jewish influence around Lloyd George and Clemenceau.[16]

Perhaps one minor element in the *Dearborn Independent*'s insanity was furnished by a report of J. J. O'Neill on the reasons for the failure of the weekly to catch the public interest during its first year. He correctly pointed out that the magazine lacked plan, coherence, and force: it stood for little. "If we get and print the right sort of stuff," he wrote, "ONE SINGLE SERIES may make us known to millions. A succession of series of FEARLESS, TRUTHFUL, INTERESTING, PLAIN-SPOKEN articles, if properly handled. . . . will make a lasting reputation. . . . LET'S HAVE SOME SENSATIONALISM."[17] Another element may be sought in the social atmosphere of the time. This was the United States of the Palmer deportations and the Federal spy system under the Espionage Act; of the Lusk Committee and the expulsion of Socialists from the New York legislature; of general hysteria about

Bolsheviks; of the sentencing of Victor Berger and Eugene Debs to jail; of the Chicago race riot; and of the Ku Klux Klan, with four or five million anti-Catholic, anti-Jewish, anti-Red members.

Discussion of that mythical creature the international Jew could under no circumstances be "fair, temperate, and judicial," as certain Ford officials declared the *Independent*'s articles to be. Pipp indignantly resigned in April, 1920. Cameron then partially bent to the demands of his employer. New writers were employed who prostituted themselves to the task in hand. The weekly actually revived that hoary forgery, the "Protocols of the Wise Men of Zion," which had often been discredited, and which was shortly riddled afresh by three able articles in the London *Times*, August 16–18, 1921.* A group of Jewish leaders in New York were stirred to what in calmer times would have been a needless protest: "The Jewish people have never dreamed of a Jewish dictatorship or an overthrow of civilization." According to Pipp, Liebold employed several private detectives to try to find material discrediting the Jewish race, with no material results; and both Ford and Liebold sent Cameron to the Detroit Public Library to amass a body of information. Cameron undertook his assignment disgustedly, and shortly made an honest report to Pipp: "He told me what a wonderful race they were, and how little he had known of their history, and what a magnificent history it was." [18]

While the first series of twenty articles lasted, it covered a wide field. Its general thesis was that the international Jew, a secret leadership of the race, was bent on disrupting all Gentile life by war, revolt, and disorder, and thus finally gaining world control of politics, commerce, and finance. Many of the charges carried a flavor of outraged rural puritanism. Public and private morals had declined since the war because Jewish financial interests were striving "to render them loose in the first place and keep them loose." Intemperance was growing, for "the profits of spirituous liquors flow in large amounts to Jewish pockets." Rents were becoming extortionate: this was "the Jewish landlord" at work. Short skirts, rolled stockings, and other decadent fashions "came out of Jewish clothing concerns." It was maleficent Jewish influences which made the cheap movies of Hollywood and the vulgar

---

* Nesta H. Webster in her volume on *Secret Societies and the French Revolution* (London, 1934) describes the many 19th century adoptions of the myth of a Jewish conspiracy for world domination, especially in France and the German states. Liebold states that he invented the term "international Jew" to avoid slurring the whole race; it had the opposite effect.

shows of Broadway. Gambling, jazz, scarlet fiction, flashy jewelry, night clubs—"every such activity has been under the mastery of the Jews."

As finally the anti-Semitic articles ran on through some ninety issues of the *Dearborn Independent,* resentment rose. The weekly was making a well-organized effort to increase its circulation by street sales, concentrating on fifteen of the larger cities. In some instances its salesmen were threatened or assaulted by members of the local Jewish community or their friends. The Boston police in the summer of 1921 tried to stop sales, but being unsure of their legal ground soon desisted. In Cincinnati vigorous protests by citizens caused the city council to establish a press censorship. Petty riots took place in Pittsburgh and Toledo. Street sales in New York were so impeded by interference that Ford found it necessary to obtain an injunction. A number of public libraries removed the *Independent* from their tables. Mass meetings in various cities denounced Ford, and a resolution of protest was introduced in Congress. In 1921 the theatrical producer Morris Gest filed a five-million-dollar libel suit against Ford, soon dropped. A little later more than a hundred prominent Americans, including Woodrow Wilson, called on Ford to halt his campaign. Both in an article in the *Independent* and in a subsequent press interview he repeated that his first information about the activities of the "international Jew" had come from the journalist Herman Bernstein on the peace ship; Bernstein at once denied this, and brought a damage suit for $200,000.[19]

The leading Rabbi of Detroit, the able Leo M. Franklin of Temple Beth-El, long a neighbor of Ford, had become a warm friend, and was often seen at Fair Lane. Ford regularly gave him a new custom-built car. When, soon after the commencement of the articles, he repeated the gift, Franklin ordered the car sent back. According to Pipp, Ford was astonished. He innocently telephoned to inquire: "What's wrong, Dr. Franklin? Has something come between us?" More in sadness than in anger, Franklin pointed out in a Detroit newspaper the real character of the harm Ford did:

Few thinking men have given any credence to the charges offered against the Jews. But his publications have besmirched the name of the Jews in the eyes of the great majority, and especially in the small towns of the country, where Ford's word was taken as gospel. He has also fed the flames of anti-Semitism throughout the world.[20]

It was true that offprints of the articles, issued in four small brochures 1920–1922, gained a considerable circulation in the United States, and that a compilation entitled *The International Jew* was distributed widely and translated into a number of European languages. The German anti-Semitic leader Theodor Fritsch, editor of *Der Hammer,* was active in superintending these translations and circulating the books, which were eagerly seized upon by the nationalist and reactionary groups that from France to Russia had long attacked the Jewish people. The articles probably had little effect in stimulating the circulation of the *Dearborn Independent.* That circulation grew during 1922 to almost 270,000 paid copies, and in the middle of 1923 stood at 472,500, but the growth was based on semi-compulsory buying by branches, agencies, and dealers. Some agents, like Thomas May of Newark, protested angrily at the pressure put upon them. If Ford would put the money spent on the weekly into making better cars, said May, everybody would be happier, adding that the anti-Jewish articles had injured his business. Doubtless the campaign did somewhat reduce the market for Ford cars, but no data exist for estimating the extent of the loss.[21]

As impulsively as he had begun the series, Ford at the beginning of 1922 ordered it discontinued. Striding early one morning into the office of W. J. Cameron, who had succeeded Pipp as editor, he awaited his arrival. "You're late, aren't you?" was his greeting to Cameron, and before the editor could reply he went on: "I want you to cut out the Jewish articles." Cameron was momentarily breathless. Ford continued: "Put all your thought and time to studying and writing about this money question. The Jews are responsible for the present money standard, and we want them on our side to get rid of it." * Liebold, arriving soon afterward, remonstrated with Ford. "We can deal with both subjects," he said in effect. "No, we can't," Ford returned. "The Jewish articles must stop, and Cameron must go to work on the money question."

What lay behind this step we can never know. Edsel, always fine-spirited, had been deeply pained by the series. Too loyal to say anything publicly, he doubtless expostulated privately with his father. It

---

* Ford had been influenced by the ideas of Thomas A. Edison on the "energy dollar," and had conceived the notion that he could use Muscle Shoals to make this type of dollar popular. An interview of his on the subject had appeared in leading newspapers December 3–4, 1921.

was reported later that President Harding had privately asked Ford to halt his attacks, and had enlisted two men who possessed special influence with the industrialist, Edison and Arthur Brisbane. Ford gave an interview to the press announcing that the *Independent* would cease its articles January 14, and that the world needed a new financial system which the Jews could greatly help to create! But as yet he retracted nothing, and indeed boasted that his campaign had opened the minds of Americans to possible evils.[22]

Thereafter criticism of the Jewish people in the weekly was only sporadic, like the criticism of arms-makers, bankers, bootleggers, Wall Street, and Hollywood. One or two of Ford's Jewish friends, notably the architect Albert Kahn, had refused to break with him. They were hurt and indignant, but felt that his error was rooted in ignorance. After 1922 little was published to lacerate their feelings. The *Dearborn Independent* definitely improved in content, presenting contributions by such authors as Robert Frost, Hugh Walpole, and Booth Tarkington.

Nevertheless, in 1924–1925 it committed one of the worst of its offences. It published a series of anti-Semitic articles dealing in large part with the activities of Aaron Sapiro, a distinguished Chicago attorney who, as a counselor in farm economics, had written a standard contract binding growers in a coöperative marketing arrangement, and had done much to promote such arrangements. Sapiro correctly believed that a marketing coöperative should represent just one staple crop. The fruitgrowers of California, the wheat farmers of Western Canada, and the cotton planters of the South had learned to respect his views. Nobody in the farm-coöperative movement, indeed, was better known. Frank O. Lowden of Illinois and Robert W. Bingham of Kentucky were among the men who thought him a valuable ally of the farmers—which he was. It is true that he had a genius for controversy, for he was hot-tempered, impetuous, conceited, and sometimes dictatorial, while he was accused of a grasping temper in the matter of fees. He made many enemies and latent anti-Semitism undoubtedly accentuated these enmities. But the *Dearborn Independent* had had no just reason for the attacks it launched.

For some time Sapiro had been laboring to draw Middle Western farmers, now deeply discontented and demanding relief from Congress, into a great new wheat-marketing organization. He met sharp opposition. The Farm Bureau, now powerful, was divided in its attitude toward coöperatives. Supporters of the McNary-Haugen Bill were fearful lest coöperative action lessen the strength behind that measure. In Kentucky, certain politicians accused Bingham and Sapiro of using the farmers for political ends, and in Illinois similar arrows were aimed at Lowden and Sapiro. When an advisory committee appealed for funds, Bernard Baruch and Julius Rosenwald were among the few who contributed generously. Looking at these two men, at Eugene Meyer, another supporter, and at Sapiro, the *Dearborn Independent* leaped to the conclusion that a Jewish group was trying to gain control of American wheat farming! In April, 1924, a series of articles began in the magazine.[23]

These attacks were as offensive as they were ill-founded. Scattered through them were references to "Jewish combinations," "international banking rings," and "Jewish international bankers." The names of Albert D. Lasker and Otto Kahn were dragged in, although these public-spirited men had done nothing worse than show a sympathetic interest in efforts to help the farmers. Various men sprang to Sapiro's defence, among them non-Jewish spokesmen for the North Carolina Cotton Growers' Coöperative Association and the National Council of Farmers' Coöperative Marketing Associations. But the *Independent* persisted, accusing Sapiro of cheating his clients.

The upshot was a million-dollar suit by Sapiro for defamation of character.[24] It came to trial in Detroit in March, 1927, in the Federal District Court under Judge F. S. Raymond. Ford was represented by Senator James A. Reed of Missouri, C. B. Longley, the company's lawyer, and five Detroit attorneys; Sapiro by William Henry Gallagher and Judge R. S. Marx of Detroit. While Reed insisted that the trial must be limited to the alleged libel of Sapiro alone, Gallagher maintained that Ford's attack on the Hebrew race in general should be made part of the record. "There is no use in trying to pull the wool over our eyes and tell ourselves this is only an attack on Aaron Sapiro and that he personally and individually is being libelled." Reed maintained that the Jewish people were not bringing the suit, and that Sapiro had no right to demand damages in the name of his injured people, and then put the money awarded, if any, into his private pocket. When the court decided in favor of Reed, the main question became that of the responsibility of Henry Ford (the suit being directed against him, not the *Independent*) for the libelous matter. W. J. Cameron took the stand as Ford's chief witness. Testifying for five days, and maintaining perfect aplomb under severe cross-examination, he declared that he had the sole responsibility for whatever the *Dearborn Independent* had published; that he had never discussed with Ford any article on any Jew, had never sent Ford an advance copy of the weekly, and had never even seen Ford read a copy.

The defense, in short, took the position that Ford had given Cameron and his staff a free hand in shaping policy, and had been simply an innocent bystander when the staff allegedly used it to malign a race or an individual. The question of Liebold's relations with the staff and with Ford (he was both Ford's secretary, and general manager of the Dearborn Publishing Company) was not explored. It was unquestionably true that Ford had paid diminishing attention to the *Independent*. But a man who could believe that the ultimate and direct responsibility for the articles on Jews and on Sapiro was not his could believe anything. When the company attorney, C. B. Longley, contended that Ford had not even heard of Sapiro before the trial began, opposing counsel put on the stand a former employee of the Dearborn Publishing Company, James M. Miller, to swear that Ford had told him he intended to have Sapiro exposed.

Two dramatic events ended the trial. Gallagher was eager to bring Henry Ford into the courtroom to give testimony and submit to cross-examination; the defense, haunted by memories of Mt. Clemens, was as reluctant as Ford himself to invite the spectacle. Process servers long found it impossible to reach Ford with a subpoena, but finally one plumped a writ in his lap as he was watching planes at the Ford Airport. The trial had been a fortnight under way when Ford's turn to testify arrived. Then on the Sunday evening before the Monday on which he was to appear, he was involved in an accident. He was driving alone, or with one fellow-passenger—accounts vary—on Michigan Avenue in Dearborn. A car side-swiped his coupe and forced it down a fifteen-foot bank near the River Rouge, where it struck a tree. The only witnesses were two youngsters walking near by who gave no dependable account of the mishap, and the full circumstances were never clarified. Ford, badly shaken, bleeding, and half dazed, staggered to the gatehouse of Fair Lane and went to bed, whence two days later he was moved to the Ford hospital on orders from the chief surgeon.*

Rumors that Ford had been attacked by gangsters gained some currency. Mrs. Ford was always fearful of a holdup or kidnapping. Harry Bennett, however, rejected the idea. "Our connections with the Detroit underworld," he said, meaning his own connections, "are such that within twenty-four hours after the hatching of a plot we would know of it." [25]

The second event was a grave blunder by one of the jurors. The defense presented the court with affidavits signed by fourteen persons charging that Sapiro had hired an agent to bribe jurors, and further alleged that a woman on the panel had accepted a package. In a rash statement to a reporter, she not only defended herself, but accused Ford's counsel of showing excessive anxiety to keep the case from going to the jury. When this was published, the judge had no choice but to declare a mistrial, and he adjourned the case for six months. [26]

This gave Ford an opportunity to settle the case out of court. On July 7, 1927, he published a personal apology to Sapiro, and a formal retraction of all his past attacks on the Jewish people. He appears to have acted on his own initiative. It has been said that he did not consult Edsel; certainly Reed, his other attorneys, Liebold and Cameron were taken by surprise. Details were worked out by E. J. Davis and Joseph A. Palma as Ford's agents, and by two prominent Jews, Louis Marshall and Nathan D. Perlman. According to Palma, Ford declared to him that he had been genuinely shocked when he investigated the extent and harshness of the anti-Jewish articles in the *Independent*. "I wish this wrong could be righted," he said earnestly. Urging Palma to explain his views in Jewish quarters, he pledged himself "to act honorably and to repair the damage as far as I can." Just who wrote the text of his long retraction, which was issued through his friend Arthur Brisbane, we do not know. It was complete and emphatic if at some points disingenuous:

* All that the public was allowed to learn of the accident appeared in the *N.Y. Times* and Detroit *News* and *Times* of April 1–6, 11, and 14, 1927. It was not much. Liebold in his *Reminiscences* declares that Ford had a habit of driving slowly at times, on the side that blocked overtaking traffic; and that his hearing was about 20 per cent defective, so that he might not hear horns in the rear. He adds: "The story that I got was that a couple of kids were driving along, and Mr. Ford didn't get over. They came over and just to show their indignation they headed him off. Bennett said to me later that they found the kids, and they found there was no criminal intent." That Ford's injuries were real is shown by the statements of the doctors, who were of too high a character to connive at deception.

To my great regret I have learned that Jews generally, and particularly those of this country, not only resent these [*Dearborn Independent*] publications as promoting anti-Semitism, but regard me as their enemy. Trustworthy friends with whom I have conferred recently have assured me in all sincerity that in their opinion the character of the charges and insinuations against the Jews, both individually and collectively, contained in many of the articles which have been circulated periodically in the *Dearborn Independent,* and have been reprinted in the pamphlets mentioned, justifies the righteous indignation entertained by Jews everywhere toward me because of the mental anguish occasioned by the unprevoked reflections made upon them.

This has led me to direct my personal attention to this subject in order to ascertain the exact nature of these articles. As a result of this survey I confess I am deeply mortified that this journal, which is intended to be constructive and not destructive, has been made the medium for resurrecting exploded fictions, for giving currency to the so-called protocols of the wise men of Zion which have been demonstrated, as I learn, to be gross forgeries, and for contending that the Jews have been engaged in conspiracy to control the capital and industries of the world, besides laying at their door many offences against decency, public order, and good morals.

Had I appreciated even the general nature, to say nothing of the details, of these utterances, I would have forbidden their circulation, without a moment's hesitation.[27]

Had Ford taken a completely honest and manly course, he would never have hidden behind Cameron and other staff members. The idea that he did not know the content of the anti-Semitic articles is absurd. Liebold states that "they were prompted largely by Mr. Ford;" that "he kept in touch with every phase;" and that when warned that the attacks on Sapiro might lead to a lawsuit, he said "that would be just what he wanted." However, he did more than apologize. He promised that he would publish no more offensive articles. He engaged to withdraw *The International Jew* from the book market—though he could not stop the circulation of old copies. He discharged Liebold from the general managership of the *Independent,* and Cameron from his editorial post, though both remained in Ford employ. At the end of 1927 he abruptly stopped publication of the weekly.*

* Ford sent Sapiro a check for costs which Sapiro pronounced "ample," and which report placed at $140,000 (*N.Y. Times,* July 19, 1927). The *American Hebrew* declared in its issue of mid-July that it would "forgive and forget." Herman Bernstein, with whom Ford also made a financial settlement, praised him for his new attitude, and dropped his suit.

No doubt his motives in issuing his public apology were complex. The Sapiro suit may have brought home to his well-insulated mind the volume and force of the public criticism of his obnoxious campaign as nothing else had done. Such friends as Arthur Brisbane could speak more frankly. Ford must also have been genuinely frightened over the prospect of going on the witness stand in front of 135,000,000 Americans. Moreover, his company was in the midst of the critical change-over from the Model T to the Model A, and he knew well that Gaston Plantiff and other important distributors were complaining that Jewish hostility hurt business. Not in the East alone, but in the Middle West and California, a Jewish boycott could have important consequences. By no means least, Ford was innately a decent man, and it may be hoped that he felt a real contrition.

"I sincerely regret any harm that may have been occasioned to the people of that great race," he wrote Herman Bernstein, editor of the *Jewish Tribune*, "and am anxious to make whatever amends are possible." Unhappily, much of the harm was irreparable. In America the Ku Klux Klan had profited from the articles, and in Germany, where anti-Semitism had its own origins and a special political character which it never possessed in English-speaking lands, Ford's name and influence added some strength to a specially noxious crusade.[28]

5.

These adventures of Henry Ford in public life make an uneven, sometimes preposterous, sometimes deplorable and pathetic story, amply illustrating Dean Samuel Marquis's statement that men of great wealth and limited education readily overestimate the value of their judgment on questions outside their proper sphere. By 1928 Ford had learned his lesson. Honestly wishing to better the world, he had found that politics, journalism, and reform crusades were full of pitfalls. It would have been better for him, far better for his company, had he stuck to the automotive industry.

The extraordinary fact is that his blunders did not greatly harm his standing with the American masses, whose faith in him continued strong. They saw what sad flaws were mingled with his merits, but they perceived that he was a thoroughly unconventional man, whose originality was not controlled by a sound education; they knew that opposing forces warred within him, and that he had to be accepted as extraordinary in faults as in virtues.

The American masses outside the large cities, moreover, responded to one large motivating element in his public conduct. Ford had sprung of sturdy farm lineage. He had been reared among simple, hardworking folk who lived useful lives close to the soil. A lover of the old rural traditions projected into the industrial and urban age, he felt nostalgically that the well-tested values of the countryside were being lost; he sought for a means of saving them; and he turned to the prescriptions of the Populists he had heard in youth, the prejudices of the older American stock, and the fundamentalist moral dogmas.* Prohibition was the answer to urban intemperance, old-time dances the answer to jazz, the Victorian essays of the *Dearborn Independent* the answer to H. L. Mencken's stinging ridicule of rural simplicities. Seeing how large was the Jewish element in banking, publishing, and motion pictures, he felt their influence somehow inimical to the simple, homely, virtuous American ways. In some respects the cast of his mind resembled that of Bryan: the Bryan who crusaded against Wall Street, who fought war to the last, who at the Scopes trial championed the old religious outlooks. Because Ford's errors sprang from the same ignorance and simplicity which marked many of the plain people themselves, the masses either did not recognize that he erred, or when they did, overlooked his missteps.

* It should be remembered that Ford was a rebel against aspects of farm life, and an innovator who with his tractor, his village industries, and his later soy bean experiments, worked to change them. But about farm moral values and traditions he was sentimental.

XIII

LABOR:

A BRIGHT DAWN PALES

AGAINST a background of individualistic, aggressive and ruthless corporation activities in most areas of the nation's economy, the Ford Motor Company in 1914–1918 made an intelligent effort to achieve amity, brotherhood and prosperity within the Ford gates. By no means all American workers were as badly exploited as those in Upton Sinclair's *The Jungle;* by no means all industrial communities were as dreary as that pictured in the volumes of the *Pittsburgh Survey.* Enlightened employers—Eastman, Firestone, Studebaker, Patterson of the National Cash Register Company, Doubleday, Page in publishing, Hershey—were deeply concerned with worker welfare as well as with profits. But at Highland Park paternalism was pushed to an unprecedented point by John R. Lee, Dean Marquis, and their aides, carrying out plans partly approved by Henry Ford. The five-dollar day, the practical prohibition of discharges by foremen, the attention to plant safety and comfort, the supervision of living-standards by the Sociological Department, the employment of cripples and defectives, the English school and trade school, the medical care—all this made the Ford establishment an object-lesson of international renown.[1]

Many a mechanic, drawing his plump pay-envelope, many a social worker reading Lee's speeches, must have asked: "Will it last?" A more realistic question would have been: "How much of it will last, and how and why will the rest collapse?" The second question geared into others: "What kind of superintendents will hereafter run the factory? Can production and capital accumulation, as competition mounts, be kept adequate to high social standards? When the working force reaches scores of thousands, can it be treated as a community instead of as an army?"

When Ford announced the five-dollar day in January, 1914, in a social atmosphere warmed by Lloyd George's reforms in Britain and the progressive measures of Roosevelt and Wilson, the times seemed propitious. Nobody could foresee what cataclysms were about to shake the world, unchain new brutalities and fears, and deepen social antagonisms. The next five years were to lead millions of young men to death, disrupt all peaceful activities, loose first a wild price-inflation and then a sickening depression, and cover the fires of wartime idealism with the ashes of postwar cynicism and materialism. Social Utopianism at Highland Park even in a peaceful era would have gone through evolutionary changes. Amid the chaotic uncertainties of the World War and postwar period it could not escape violent distortion.[2]

2.

The five-dollar day had been the keystone of the arch leading to Ford's ideal factory. From Zanzibar to Peru, men heard of it who knew nothing else of what the Ford Company was doing. They learned that Ford had nearly doubled wages while reducing hours from nine to eight. But when the world convulsion began, what would happen to wages and hours?

Inflation, mild at first, became almost uncontrollable after the United States entered the war. By the end of 1918 the cost of living index in Detroit stood 78 per cent above the level of early 1914. In other words, the real value of the $5 wage had shrunk to $2.80, little better than the $2.35 average paid in 1913. Although nearly all elements of society suffered from inflation, middle class salaried workers being specially hard hit, and although the government had tried to put a brake on wartime wage increases, the Ford company saw that it must act. Some groups of employees were worse off than before the celebrated increase. A skilled mechanic in the category which in 1913 was paid $3.42 a day, for example, by the end of 1918 received $5, with a 1914 purchasing power of only $2.80. Indeed, highly trained workers, such as tool-makers, became difficult to hire and keep during the war, for they could get better wages elsewhere than in Ford employ.[3]

The Ford establishments would have lost men badly during and after the war but for two factors: their ability to turn unskilled workers into skilled, and the faith of many employees that Henry Ford would soon come to their rescue.

The traditional Ford expedient of meeting labor shortages by throwing raw men into the breach, meanwhile using ingenious techniques to simplify the job, was applied with large-scale vigor. At the Ford shipbuilding plant, for example, riveters were swiftly trained. When some began getting as much as $20 a day in busy yards, Frank Hadas, superintending the Eagle boat project, found his trained men, paid only $6 a day, vanishing by the dozen. He described how porters and floorsweepers became semi-skilled workers:

"What are you doing, Joe?"

"Sweep."

"You go home and tell your wife and mother and mother-in-law that you sweep for a living?"

"Well, that's my job. They give me that."

"Your grandmother can go out and do that job here. Sweeping, what kind of a job is that for a man?"

"What can I do?"

"Riveter. From $5 a day you will get $6."

"I don't know."

"Sure you do. Here, put him on."

For a time Hadas turned out successive batches of forty riveters in two-day training periods. Once taught, a large proportion of these men left the Ford plant for the higher pay of neighboring establishments. But Ford and Hadas knew that as the labor market grew easier, many would come back with increased skill. "Months went by before that happened," testifies Hadas, "but we made hundreds of riveters. We taught them big riveting, small riveting, angle riveting, upside-down riveting, and all the different things they had to do on the ship."

The confidence of hard-pressed employees that Ford would get around to relieving their plight did not prevent them from grumbling. An employee who described himself as "one of the many Ford workers who is obliged to wear his old clothes a long time and spread his butter awful thin" wrote the *Ford Man* in the fall of 1918 that he was tired of holding on by his fingernails. "Why can't we have more overtime and Sunday work?" The editor's answer was: "Be patient, the subject is under consideration." This did not help. Neither did a subsequent editorial in the *Ford Man,* by the well-meaning C. A. Brownell, urging Ford hands to avoid "the real riot of extravagance" sweeping the country, and copy "the frugal, modest and simple methods of living" practised by Henry Ford. But belatedly, the company did partly adjust to higher living costs.

Two concessions, in fact, were made in 1919–1920. The first increased the minimum wage, in January, 1919, to $6 a day. This gave the lowest paid workers $3.36 daily in 1914 dollars, or $1.64 less than when the five-dollar day was initiated. The inflationary spiral continued to mount throughout 1919. The company therefore announced a year-end bonus plan, graduated according to skill and length of service. In January, 1920, each $6-a-day worker of more than three months' service received $50, the minimum, while the bonus rose to a maximum of $270 for those workers on the $10.80 level who had served continuously since the summer of 1914.[4]

The bonus payment was accompanied by intimations that Henry Ford was pondering a larger scheme of profit-sharing. This would have been made effective at once, he hinted, but for the financial obligations he had incurred in buying out the minority shareholders. According to the Detroit *Journal*, he talked of putting the company on a cooperative basis, and dividing with the workers such melons as had once been cut for the cormorant Dodge brothers. But of course these dreamy exhalations vanished into thin air.* Another year-end bonus was paid in January, 1921, when it was specially welcome. The seven million dollars distributed was a generous sum in view of the current depression and Ford's special embarrassments, and it cushioned the blow of the 1921 layoff. Finally, in May, 1921, Ford employees were paid in a lump sum the accrued bonus credits for the first third of the year (again a welcome relief in hard times), and the bonus for the future was incorporated into a new wage readjustment.[5]

The amount of this wage increase was small, ranging from two cents an hour for employees just hired to eleven and a half cents for some veteran workers. The sum given depended on existing rate of pay and length of service. Most of these differential gains were probably wiped out over the ensuing years by individual wage rate changes, which were weighted against the favored workers. That is, the integration of the bonus into individual wage rates was probably merely a substitute for raises which in the normal course of events would have come to most of those affected anyway. To be sure, they got the benefit of the change earlier; perhaps the overall advance was greater; and the company was

---

* Except for the Investment Certificate plan to be described later.

raising pay at a dark period when many firms were cutting it. Comparable adjustments in salary rates were made simultaneously.

These various increases made in Ford wages in 1919–1920 were inadequate, if measured by the old five-dollar wage, for the new six-dollar minimum, with the bonuses added, did not close the gap opened by inflation. We may bluntly say that "profit-sharing" as Ford used the term in 1914 died during the war and the years just following, the *coup de grace* being administered by the depression of 1921. The Ford company could no longer boast of exceptional wages; in various categories of labor, other firms equalled or excelled it. It should be added, however, that any protracted maintenance of the five-dollar level in real wages during this period of economic storm and uncertainty would have been too much to expect. The Dodge suit, the difficulties of postwar readjustment, the slump in the automobile market, Ford's financial stringencies, and the widespread expectation that living costs would fall, all operated against any effort by the company to regain the old wage-plateau. And when the depression of 1921 came, the substantial fall in prices—especially those prices which counted most for industrial workers—did benefit the Ford employees materially. Rents dropped, the prices of bread, meat, and milk came down, clothing was reduced; but Ford men continued to get the pre-depression wage, or even more.[6] *

In other industries and a multitude of factories, the price-cuts of 1920–1921 came hand-in-hand with drastic wage-slashing. These reductions brought wages in American manufacturing as a whole to a point approximately thirty per cent below the postwar peak. Average hourly earnings in the Ford factories, on the other hand, were slightly greater in 1922 than in 1921. To some extent, of course, this was attributable to the company's retention, when it lowered its average employment by

---

* It is difficult to furnish comparative statistics of value. But readers should bear in mind that of 27,474,000 families at the time of the 1930 census, nearly 20,000,000 had possessed incomes in 1929 of less than $2500, and 12,000,000 had incomes under $1500. The National Industrial Conference Board has published the most complete series of hourly earnings in manufacturing since 1920. Its tables for some 23 representative industries show an average hourly wage in 1920 of 61 cents; in 1921 of 52 cents; in 1922 of 49 cents; and in 1923 of 54 cents. The minimum Ford wage from January, 1919, to December, 1929, was $6 a day, or 75 cents an hour. The National Industrial Conference Board found the average hourly wage of its 23 industries in 1929 to be 56 cents an hour; that year the average in Ford plants in the Detroit area was carefully computed to be 82 cents an hour. See Maurice Leven, H. G. Moulton, and Clark Warburton, *America's Capacity to Consume* (New York, 1934), 54, 55; President Herbert Hoover's Committee, *Recent Economic Changes in the United States* (New York, 1929), II, 430 ff.; Ford Motor Company, Records of the Treasurer's Office.

about twenty per cent, of the long-service employees with comparatively high wages. But to some extent it undoubtedly sprang from the upward readjustments of 1921, and in any event the company's refusal to participate in the general wage reductions of the time was commendable. Steel, coal, textiles, and general merchandising pursued a different course.[7] Mr. Keith Sward's statement that the Ford company pushed its wage scale downward by a fifth or a quarter in 1921 is simply not so.[*]

3.

It is true that a sharp speed-up of the pace of production followed the re-opening in 1921. It is also true that a good deal of wage-chiselling was perceptible in the plant in 1921, when the pressure for reducing unit costs was strongest. It was confined to the fringes of the wage structure, however, or, if it actually touched basic wage rates, was accidental and sporadic. When a ten per cent bonus for night shift work was given Ford workers in the Detroit area, and later in branch plants, it greatly pleased those who endured that disagreeable stint. Its abrupt discontinuance a little later caused a proportionate sense of grievance. The policy of paying as much as $7.20 a day to branch employees who met certain targets was also discontinued in the spring of 1921. Happily, the wages of those who had benefited by the plan were not reduced; the home office declared that $6 was a fair wage for newly employed men, but that the man receiving $7.20 daily should be continued on that basis as a reward for length of service, and for fidelity to the company when high wages prevailed in other shops.

It is evident that the company crisis of 1921 brought two partially inconsistent policies into conflict. On the one hand, it was the publicly announced intention of the company to maintain wage rates; on the other, economic necessity demanded a reduction. From this sprang the thrust for sharply increased production per capita, which was achieved

---

[*] Mr. Sward says (*The Legend of Henry Ford*, 79) that Ford "put into effect the most drastic wage reductions," and that according to the *Commercial and Financial Chronicle*, "the company 'adjusted' its wage-scale 'downward' by 20 to 25 per cent." This illustrates the pitfalls lying in wait for the unwary historian who depends on press sources—and who is handicapped by a pronounced bias. The *Commercial and Financial Chronicle* merely summarized parts of a *N.Y. Times* story a few days earlier, leaving out the *Times'* statement that it was quoting some unnamed "bankers in Wall Street." That the information of Wall Street bankers concerning the Ford Motor Company was mostly what Al Smith later called venom and apple sauce had become very clear earlier that year. The company records offer a complete refutation of the charge of any material wage cutting in 1921.

in the main by mechanical and managerial improvements, but in part by driving the men. From it sprang also some minor invasions of the forbidden area of wage economy. Individuals on the Ford payroll before 1921 did not suffer. Workers hired later, however, had a probationary period below the $6 minimum, and found some difficulty in gaining the higher rates above that figure; promotion was slower. Beginning with 1922, a tremendous expansion of the Ford working force took place. The two factors named, along with this expansion, explain why the average hourly earnings from 1922 to 1926 fell. Such earnings, of course, would have dropped along with increasing employment anyhow, for it augmented the lower echelons in the plant.[8]

In August, 1922, a more permanent character was given to the company rules respecting the hiring-in wage and the probationary period. It was decreed that all new employees were to get $5 during a probationary spell, and that those retained were automatically to go to $6. This rule seems to have prevailed until the introduction of the $7 minimum near the end of the decade; at any rate, it was still in effect during 1926. For some years the company operated on the general theory that most unskilled labor should stay at $6 a day, while semi-skilled men should be promoted shortly to $6.40, and skilled to $6.80, with higher rates for special talent.

One benefit to the workers in which Henry Ford took pride was the introduction at the beginning of 1920 of a generous employees' savings plan. Investment certificates, comparable to non-voting preferred stock in the company, were prepared in denominations of $100. Any employee could buy them as long as he stayed on the payroll. They yielded six per cent guaranteed interest, with such additional dividends as company directors might think were warranted. In spite of a provision that they were non-negotiable and non-assignable, they were clearly a desirable investment. Current purchases were limited to one third of an employee's pay, to which he might add all his bonus, and his interest and dividends. Nobody could withdraw money from bank accounts or other investments to buy certificates. This plan in general form was maintained until September, 1941, and existing accounts were then permitted to draw interest until 1947, when they were all liquidated. It was an unequivocal success.[9]

Annual returns paid on the certificates ranged in the nineteen-twenties from twelve to sixteen per cent. The company apparently did not

wish its certificate fund to exceed $25,000,000, for it halted the accept-
ance of deposits for ten months in 1925–1926 when the total threatened
to exceed that figure. If the fund was kept at or near the maximum, the
company sometimes made an annual distribution of about $4,000,000,
of which $2,500,000 represented a return over and above a satisfactory
interest on an almost riskless investment. This amount, therefore, may
be considered a form of profit-sharing or bonus. The plan was naturally popular among Ford workers, and in both domestic and foreign
plants it sometimes enlisted from four fifths of the employees to almost
the whole number. By 1923, 27,000 employees owned certificates, with
fresh accounts coming in rapidly.

Savings were important, for a great part of the working force lived
always near the danger line, defenceless in the event of a layoff or
discharge. The stoppage of operations in 1921 left a searing mark on
many men. "I was scared," succinctly states one. Most of the widespread
suffering from unemployment at that time attracted little public notice.
A workless man retired to his home, or tramped the streets, his plight
ignored. Only if he and his family were evicted, or his children appeared in school barefoot, or his wife fell ill of malnutrition, was some
public attention aroused. Indeed, most unemployment in the various
slumps from 1915 to 1930 was faced with quiet stoicism. But that it resulted in poignant distress is evident from many a newspaper item like
this one published during the 1921 shutdown:

> I rode from Dearborn to Detroit yesterday in the same street car with a
> Polish workman who had been out to the tractor plant looking for a job.
> He told me a crowd of his countrymen had chipped in thirty-four cents for
> the round trip carfare, and sent him to inquire into the truth of a statement
> in a Polish newspaper that the plant had resumed operations.
>
> When he alighted at a corner in the Polish quarter in West Detroit the
> car was held up a couple of minutes. He approached a crowd of men stand-
> ing at the curb, and I heard him call out:
> "Henry ain't vorkin' yet."
> It means a lot to Detroit when "Henry ain't vorkin'." [10]

From 1914 until near the end of 1920, employment had been steady
in the Ford factories. During the next decade it was subject, as in other
automotive plants, to checks and oscillations. Just what living standards
had the ordinary Ford worker achieved, what provision for the future
had he made, and how anxious was he to improve his position? Light

is thrown on these questions by the history of the famous Sociological Department, first under John R. Lee and then Dean Marquis.*

4.

"Mr. Ford told me," Lee had said three months after the five-dollar day was announced in 1914, "he wanted it known his plan is for every family working for him a comfortable home; a bath tub in it, and a yard with a little garden, and ultimately, he wanted to see every employee of his owning an automobile. I asked him, 'A Ford automobile?' and he said that would be going too far." Ford, Lee, and the other planners of the Sociological Department emphasized the importance of a wholesome family life; the requisites of physical and mental health; and Americanization through mastery of the English language and New World ways. They encouraged a Ben Franklin type of thrift, savings being valued not in themselves but for what they could purchase. "We wish chiefly to have our workers *use* their funds advantageously," said Lee. "Lots of fellows are helping relatives and the like, and that is more beneficial than putting money in a bank for a rainy day." The underlying assumptions were that the five-dollar wage gave employees a wide margin above subsistence, that immigrants, Negroes, and others often needed guidance in managing their surplus, and that the company had a right to fix some rules for the conduct of its workers. These assumptions, if sound in 1914, possessed no permanent validity.

---

* No adequate biographical account of the Rev. Samuel S. Marquis has yet been written, while only the scantiest crumbs of information are available on the career of John R. Lee. Marquis was born in Sharon, Ohio, in 1866, and after graduation from Allegheny College and theological study in Cambridge, Massachusetts, served for a time as an Episcopal minister in Massachusetts. He became rector of St. Paul's Church in Detroit May 15, 1906, where he distinguished himself by applying the principles of Social Christianity as expounded by Canon Barnett in England and Dr. Rauschenbusch in America, and by leading the movement for the construction of the Episcopal Cathedral in Detroit, of which he became Dean. He was a man of cheery temper, vigorous personality, and abounding energy, keenly interested in economic conditions and the lot of the workingman. His labors for St. Paul's Cathedral having exhausted him, his doctor early in 1916 ordered a year's leave of absence. He said, "A change of work would be more beneficial to me than being idle," and accepted Henry Ford's offer of the directorship of the Sociological Department in succession to Lee. Marquis had been an adviser in the early activities of the department, and as the pastor of Henry and Clara Ford knew them both intimately—Henry calling him "Mark." The Marquis Papers and the reminiscences of his two daughters and son in the Ford Archives present engaging sidelights upon him.

Photographs of Lee soon after he joined the Ford Company from the Keim Mills show a rather tall, heavily built, earnest-looking man, clean-shaven, with a good jaw and forehead and abundant black hair; wearing a gentle, persuasive look. Marquis was shorter, with a stocky figure and large head topped by curling dark gray hair; his Roman nose, close-set lips, and keen eyes gave an air of decision to his face, and altogether he looked more of a businessman than Lee. Both men were fluent of speech, and Marquis talked and wrote with a nice choice of phrase.

They would soon come into question if applied in a Prussian spirit. The initial administration of the sociological work, happily, was excellent. A capable staff was recruited, its membership varying over the seven years in which the department played an important part in labor relations, and reaching a possible maximum of 160 men. In 1917, immediately preceding a reorganization and reduction, 52 were performing regular investigative work, and 22 special tasks. Of course the size of the staff had to be related to that of the labor force, for its work was carefully systematized. In 1917 the Detroit area was divided into 77 districts with an average of 527 employees each. Each investigator, who was assigned an average of 727 employees, was expected to make about 15 calls a day, and hold about 5 daily interviews in the plant before or after shift changes. All investigators necessarily made careful written reports, and their work was closely scrutinized. To reduce the load, and lessen its inquisitorial character, the department placed nearly 6000 men on an honor list to be investigated only on specific complaint; and some 7600 on two preferred lists to be visited but once or twice a year. The roll and lists in 1921 were growing rapidly.*

Under Lee and Marquis the investigators, who were given detailed instructions and forms, were held to a high standard of accuracy. Study of the instructions reveals some interesting details concerning the company's requirements for "profit sharing." [11]

First, it was company policy to employ those in greatest need. For this reason any single employee under twenty-two (later twenty-one) was required to be the *sole* support of a close relative. Second, profits were denied a confirmed drunkard, gambler, drug-addict, or the like, though if he had a large family who would be the chief sufferers, some arrangement was made to insure them the benefits. Third, every employee was required to account for his share of the profits, above the expenditures for rent, board, and clothing. When domestic cleavages were discovered, the department sometimes withheld profits from the husband and placed them temporarily in the wife's hands.

Among the minor instructions were that documentary proof be demanded of an employee's age below twenty-six; that any prison record of an employee should never be mentioned in his investigation or held against him; and that whenever a wife was found pregnant, no note

* In 1917, Highland Park employed just under 36,500; more than a third were on these lists.

should be made of the fact unless absolutely necessary to complete the picture of the family. No employee was to be allowed to conduct any outside business whatsoever. To protect the children in families, lessen immorality, and improve home standards, wives of workers were discouraged from keeping boarders.

The Sociological Department under Lee and Marquis investigated absentees. It had also general charge of transfers. These were made from one shift to another, from the Detroit factories to some branch, or from job to job, whenever an investigation showed good reason for the action. Finally, it had wide authority over pay increases and discharges. Wage rises were given only for added responsibility, not for a mere increase in efficiency. "No man," ran the rule, "was to be discharged from the services of the Ford Motor Company until every possible effort has been made, and every means exhausted, towards lifting him up to the requirements of the Company, and to the equal of his fellow men."

The before-mentioned reorganization in the summer of 1917, after Dr. Marquis had taken charge, introduced one fundamental and healthful change in the nature of the plan. Coincidentally with a sharp staff reduction, emphasis was placed upon inquiries requested by the workers themselves. Thereafter a new employee was to be investigated only twice: when he was hired, and after five months. The second investigation was to be the only home call made. If the worker passed both tests, he was to be exempt from further investigation *unless he himself requested assistance,* or the shop management reported an intolerably bad work record. The personnel was cut down to fifty-two in all, including investigators, interpreters, and clerks. Absenteeism became the responsibility of another department. These changes were made, according to Marquis, on his own initiative, so that his staff could give more time to those who most needed help and advice.[12]

By 1920 the profit-sharing plan in its original form had disappeared, the five-dollar day having become the six-dollar day with no "profits" included. The Sociological Department continued to operate much as before, except that a home investigation was conducted immediately instead of at the end of five months. No longer, however, did it determine whether the employee would be "approved for profits." Indeed, the investigator had now been transformed into an adviser, that being his official title—though the company still discharged workers if the inquiries revealed some violation of its code, as in the instance of a

woman employee accused of interfering with the marriage of an associate. "The object of these calls and interviews," said Marquis in 1920,
"is to find if we can be of any service of any character whatever to that
man, because we feel that we have never gotten the man fully convinced that we mean exactly what we say until we do render him some
kind of service." [13]

Whether as investigator or adviser, the Sociological Department agent
lived no life of ease. He had to summon to his aid all the tact and ingenuity he possessed. Inevitably he met the suspicion of many employees and the hatred of their petty exploiters. In dealing with immigrants who, remembering police-spies in Russia or Hungary, thought
him a minion of tyranny, he had to be courteous and persuasive; in
facing viragoes who bristled at any scrutiny of their housekeeping, he
had to be firm but gentlemanlike; in his relations with *padrones* and
grasping landlords, he needed courage physical and moral. At times
he had to play Sherlock Holmes, and at other times Bulldog Drum-
mond, but always he had to give the impression of being one of the
Brothers Cheeryble.

One of his most difficult tasks was to convince irascible Slavs, Italians,
or Greeks that the company standards would be pleasanter and healthier
than those they had brought from their native lands, or had formed in
one of Detroit's tightly packed foreign settlements. Many a factory hand
liked the crowded tenement, the noisy sociability of a slum, the familiar
grime of his alleyway; he was fearful of grass, trees, and privacy. The
investigator had to persuade him of the merits of better housing, help
him summon the courage to leave old friends and associations, and ease
for his family the final plunge into a new residential quarter or even
a new town. An equally difficult task was to get employees, once they
were accepted for the five-dollar day, to maintain their efforts to learn
English, keep the home clean, buy proper food, and educate the children. As Lee put it, many lapsed into the attitude of the slang phrase,
"I should worry." [14]

Another cardinal difficulty was scattering the wolves and jackals who
preyed upon exposed workers. Petty bosses, labor agents, and brokers
of various services made the most of the opportunities given them by
ignorance, illiteracy, gullibility, and fear in the numerous foreign-
language colonies. Some were tuppenny Mussolinis and Pilsudskis—
"petty emperors," as Lee called them, who had built small political

domains based on threats and favors, and who saw that the Ford guidance work threatened their power. They had the assistance of traders of all sorts who found the five-dollar wage an irresistible lure.

Tony Giovanetti no sooner had his new money to spend than real estate agents, second-hand car dealers, insurance men, and peddlers of ice-boxes and over-stuffed chairs raced to his front porch. The company had to help Tony separate the sheep from the goats. Honest real-estate agents and furniture salesmen could cooperate in raising living standards. The company was specially anxious to encourage employees to own their homes. It therefore not only prepared a pamphlet, written by the Sociological and Legal Departments with the advice of Ford and Couzens, to warn its men against malpractices—with some telling instances and much emphatic language. It also offered to send an expert to appraise property in which any employee was interested, and to furnish free inspection of deeds, mortgages, and other legal papers. During the first eighteen months of the five-dollar wage, Lee found many instances in which Ford men had paid ridiculously high prices for real estate. The department's efforts to stop such plundering naturally aroused the ill-will of the sharpers, who did their best to foment prejudice and dislike.[15]

And as we might expect, old-stock Americans took a superior attitude toward the Sociological Department. Why teach Yankee standards to a man of colonial ancestry? One such worker recalls that he and his friends found it easy to avoid interference with their tastes, which fairly approximated the Ford ideal anyway. "I was interviewed, of course, and so was my wife. But my attitude was to keep my mouth shut and do as I pleased. This was the attitude of a great many Ford employees. They didn't stir up any resistance to the interviewing system, but they didn't pay much attention to it either." [16] This naturally led some foreign-born workers, who were under greater pressure, to feel a sense of discrimination.

5.

All in all, the work of the Sociological Department was unquestionably beneficial. It had its faults and its merits, but a fair balance-sheet shows that the good predominated.

An objection immediately offered by the critics was that its inquisitorial visitations, however benevolent at first, would soon become arrogant and autocratic. Boyd Fisher, who wrote an early report on the system for private distribution by the Detroit Board of Commerce, raised this demur emphatically. He conceded that for the initial six months the Ford plan had worked well. Few workers had protested; in fact, the amount of criticism "is very small, and only so great as might be expected in connection with an absolutely ideal scheme." This he thought explicable by the high character of the investigators chosen, and the remarkably close attention they gave to each individual case. So intent were the staff on making every case, not merely the majority of them, justify the system, that their guidance was bound to be beneficial. But no such high level of intensive work could long be maintained. The time must come when power would be delegated to paid agents who would feel an increasing sense of authority and infallibility. When that day came, "it will take only a slight change of tone and manner to make their inquisitions highly irksome and disagreeable, if not intolerable." He concluded that the Ford scheme was essentially a despotism, enforced by the high wage; and he argued for a gradual transfer of its administration to some democratic organization of workmen.[17]

The company's answer was that its plan was *not* a despotism, for its sole requirement of each company employee was that his share of "profits" should be used for constructive good. And it must be said that, as we have seen, the scheme tended to become looser and milder, not more severe.

More forcible was the objection that the investigators asked the wage-earner to stand and account for himself in altogether too officious a way. Not so, again replied the company. The Sociological Department did not demand any accounting for the regular wage, which was as high as or higher than that obtainable elsewhere, nor did its requirements as to the use of the "profits" go beyond a line which responsible, decent citizens would reach anyhow. The company proposed only to assure itself that the larger wage payments (a gratuity, measured by the yardstick of a free labor market) were not wasted by bad management or expenditures for injurious purposes.* To gain such a reasonable assurance, the inquiries were indispensable—and they were confined to

* One employee, asked how he had invested his profits, said "in houses and lots." When pressed for documentary evidence, he admitted that he had meant "whorehouses and lots of whiskey." (Report of Operative 15, October 22, 1919, Espionage Papers, Ford Archives.)

the gathering of strictly necessary information. The company insisted on no rigid formula; it allowed men a wide latitude in saving and spending. If they wished to marry, to buy a car, to acquire a wardrobe, to save up to return to the "old country," it was all one. Nor did workers find it troublesome to talk matters over with a kindly, experienced, far-sighted adviser.

The Americanization work of the department, including its English classes, did indeed put the employees to some trouble. In the long run, however, far greater trouble would have flowed from neglect of it. The education of recent immigrants was aimed at saving them from the penalties of a continued foreign status, and inducing them to accept simple household standards embracing cleanliness, convenience, and a sensible balance between a stock of durable consumer goods and savings. Officious and troublesome! The critics who parroted these words, argued the department, simply did not comprehend the terrible squalor of the immigrant proletariat of Detroit in 1914. Many Ford workers were unable to understand a higher standard of living until they had experienced it. Some resented investigation at first; but those who were shrillest in protests often became the loudest in praise once they grew accustomed to their new mode of life. Said a company representative:

. . . . the Ford Motor Company gives its employees five dollars a day so they can get away from slums and tenements. . . . The foremost duty of the Adviser is not to question employees so as to be able to disapprove of them. . . . It is his mission to teach them to live and spend according to the codes of good living.[18]

Impartial observers in the Detroit area 1914–1920 were impressed by the amelioration of living conditions among the Ford hands. The chief housing inspector of the Detroit Board of Health observed that they had been "greatly improved," particularly in congested districts. A Hamtramck official bore witness that homes once filthy had been brought up to a high standard. A Hungarian pastor in Detroit spoke particularly of the adoption of neat, cleanly ways. "I am heartily in favor of the investigation work," he declared, and other ministers echoed him. A Detroit probation worker volunteered his approval. "The good which has been done is inestimable," he said on the basis of visits to the homes of many Ford wage-earners.[19]

Especially in the first two years of the plan, the company met great success in persuading employees to better their housing. The way in which the men responded to Lee's and Marquis's encouragement was heartening. Typical of a mass of evidence on this head is the report of an investigator upon a new housing area opened in Hamtramck after the five-dollar day went into effect. Sixty-three dwellings had been built:

Thirty of these are being bought by Ford employees, which is almost fifty per cent. These houses are not a lot of poorly constructed shacks, but are A-No. 1 four and five room frame cottages. Most of them have bath, nice yard, and a garden spot. . . . we find them nicely furnished, neat and clean, and arranged with good taste. They do not only contract for these homes, but make good headway toward paying for them. Many of these same families prior to obtaining a share of the profits were living in the worst kind of old buildings, poorly furnished and crowded in some cheap tenement district. If one would care to ask these employees' wives if they had been benefited by the profit-sharing plan he would not have to wait for an answer, for it could be plainly read in their faces.[20]

A manifest elevation in moral standards accompanied the physical amelioration. Judges, police officers, and clergymen all hailed the decline in intoxication, gambling, and crime. "Perhaps the most noticeable feature is the decrease in heavy drinking," said the rector of a church in the heart of the Polish district. "Sobriety is now the rule rather than the exception." In Hamtramck the police chief called the change wrought by the Ford plan wonderful, while in Highland Park the chief termed it almost indescribable. "Previous to the inauguration of the Plan there were from thirty to forty Ford employees in the cell block each morning. . . . but now Ford employees are rarely seen in the Police Station." Judges of city courts spoke of the lightening of their loads, which one magistrate found halved.

The one really valid criticism of the Sociological Department centered in its paternalistic character. Paternal care of the weak and erring may in itself be an excellent thing, but it has a tendency, if long continued, to sap moral fiber. Professor Samuel M. Levin placed his finger on this vulnerable spot when he wrote that any industrial welfare plan rendered the worker "too conscious of his dependence and inferiority." An effort was made by Lee and Marquis to call their work "fraternal" instead of paternal; but the fact remained that it was planned and executed from the top down, and the wage-earner well understood that he had no voice in defining the standards which were to be enforced. The company declared that every individual case was considered as such, "peculiar only to its own needs and not subject to any rule of precedence or system." This simply meant that the paternalism had a personal touch—but it continued to be paternalism. For a time the good which any such welfare plan did might be immensely greater than its deleterious accompaniments; but the evil would gradually become evident. The Ford plan did not last long enough to prove this rule.[21]

The most successful of all the activities of this idealistic era were those in the educational field. Both the English School for immigrant workers, and the Henry Ford Trade School for poor boys who wanted a technical education, received wide attention from the press, and both deserved it. The English School withered after meeting an acute temporary need, but the Trade School flourished throughout Henry Ford's lifetime, winning golden opinions from educators and social workers in the Detroit area.

All national leaders in World War I, Theodore Roosevelt in the van, insisted on Americanization of the foreign-born, and some mastery of the common language as the first step in the process. The English School opened its doors in May, 1914. At the outset classes were held in the afternoon for a relatively small body of day-shift workers who lived at hand. In clear summer weather groups met in the open air near the Highland Park plant; later the program expanded into the public schoolrooms of Detroit and into such philanthropic institutions as the Franklin Street Settlement. During its first three and a half years, leading into the turmoil of war, more than 14,000 men enrolled, and 1500 received diplomas certifying that they had completed a full course of 72 lessons. These diplomas, accepted by courts as evidence of a sufficient knowledge of English for naturalization, were awarded with proper ceremonial.

Since it was a rule that immigrant employees must learn to speak English, enrolment for some time remained high. At its peak it reached 2700, with 163 volunteer instructors. As late as 1919, 38 workers were discharged because they refused to study the language. During the war, however, the shortage of space and the rapid growth of the Trade School led to a curtailment of tuition. Near the close of 1917 the allotment of rooms for English classes was cut from 22 to 3; and after this the school was continued only on a limited scale, with about 500 students and 30 instructors. Inasmuch as the war and the ensuing immigration legislation almost totally blocked the flow of aliens, the need for such special work rapidly diminished, and in 1922 the school was finally closed.[22]

The Trade School was strongly stamped with a social welfare character. Henry Ford opened it in the fall of 1916 with six pupils from his Valley Farm—"wayward" boys whom he had taken in hand to turn into farmers and useful citizens. When they rebelled against agriculture, Ford said: "Let's take them into the factory and make mechanics of them." The student body and teaching staff rapidly grew. Edsel Ford and his onetime teacher, Clarence Avery, took a sustained interest in the school, Avery helping guide its early steps. A year after the school opened, another of Edsel's teachers in the Detroit University School, Frederick E. Searle, was brought in and presently became superintendent—a title he held until his retirement in 1946. The boys gave one-third of their time to academic subjects and two-thirds to shop work,* each pupil receiving a stipend sufficient for his maintenance. From the beginning admission was conditional upon need, and in 1926 four-fifths of the boys were orphans or sons of widows.

The Trade School grew rapidly, but no matter how fast its expansion it always had boys clamoring to enter. About 1920 the enrolment stood at 400, with a waiting list of 6000. Henry Ford told Searle: "Reverse those figures. Let 400 wait!" Searle then began admitting new students at the rate of 400 a month; but when he reached 1800, he had to call a halt because the waiting list had grown to 15,000. Registration expanded with special rapidity after 1925, reaching a peak of 2900 in 1930, and then declining in the depression. During the school's career of thirty-six years it graduated 8000 boys, and when the new company management shut the doors, educational and engineering circles widely lamented the step.[23]

That the school filled an urgent need was demonstrated by the pertinacity with which underprivileged boys tried to crawl in through windows and transoms. Often Searle, arriving at his office at seven o'clock in the nineteen-twenties, would find a hundred lads in line.

---

* In 1917–1918 the student body was divided into three groups, two working in the shop while one attended classes; two days a week thus being given to academic subjects, and four to shop training. Beginning in 1919, one full week in the classroom was followed by two weeks in the shop. (Superintendent's Reports.)

One June morning, the day after school closed, he received 800 applications from boys in person for entry that fall. Although the policy was to take only boys from the Detroit area, pleas came from every State and many foreign lands. One Florida youth, undaunted by several negative answers, hitch-hiked to Detroit with a pocket full of recommendations and was accepted. Another Horatio Alger lad from Manila stowed away aboard a ship to San Francisco, worked his way across the country, and gained entry. Years later, after having grown wealthy in the Philippines, he wrote Henry Ford asking permission to found a "Henry Ford Trade School of Manila."

The guiding spirit of the school was always Searle. It soon took out a charter of its own, and had its own board of trustees, made up of company leaders. But neither Henry Ford nor the trustees interfered much with Searle's administration. Like other successful Ford executives, he tried to guess what Henry's views were. But Ford was taciturn, and Searle worked out a philosophy of his own: "I think we've got to get back to the practical in education. Education has tended to make people feel that they should have a life of ease rather than of manual work. Ninety per cent of everything we know about the world comes to us by the hands through the sense of touch." We have ample testimony from Ford that he held the same opinion.[24]

The program stated by Searle sounds narrow, and narrow the school was. It trained boys in the industrial arts, with a minimum of ordinary academic tuition; and it trained most of them for tool-and-die making. Trade School graduates who went on to study engineering or science in universities often felt that their teachers had overlooked essential theoretical knowledge. Youths who in their hearts preferred some other trade resented the heavy emphasis upon tool-and-die training. In its deliberate narrowness, the institution made no attempt, in this period, to meet the State requirements for high schools, and the pupil who wanted a high school diploma had to attend night classes in the regular educational system. There simply was no time for adequate tuition in English, geography, civics, and economics.* The heads seem to have read the testimony in the *Tribune* case, for not a single history course was included! Of course night school work was seldom a hard-

* Yet nearly all the 8000 graduates enthusiastically praised the school. Of those replying to questionnaires in 1950, 93 per cent recommended Trade School training to others, and 89 per cent wrote that if they had to repeat their education, they would choose the Henry Ford Trade School again. (Nicholson, *op. cit.*)

ship, and nearly half of the graduates really did obtain the high school diploma. Only after Henry Ford's death was the curriculum revised to meet State standards, and in 1948 accreditation was granted by the University of Michigan.

But whatever the school's literary deficiencies, there is no doubt that its vocational training for tool-and-die work was without a peer. Having the resources of the Ford Motor Company for teaching the students industrial processes, and a constant supply of useful work materials from company tool rooms, it was able far to excel the public vocational schools. After the school moved to B Building in the Rouge plant in 1930, it had its own pattern and carpentry shop, its own plating department, its school foundry, and its own machine shop. Boys over sixteen with sufficient experience could go into the company departments for their shop work. These purposeful youngsters worked twice or three times as hard as public school youngsters. They got only three weeks' vacation in summer, and one week at Christmas; for a time they had only one hour of recreation a day—later reduced, apparently, to seven hours in three weeks, not including Saturday and Sunday. Some athletic contests, chiefly intra-mural, were permitted until 1927. Then Henry Ford ordered their discontinuance on the ground that "the boys get exercise while at work"! [25]

The hard application, the practical alternation of one full week in the classroom with two weeks in the shop, and the general feeling that the school represented a brilliant opportunity, all made for highly proficient graduates. Special financial incentives were provided. Every boy received a cash scholarship, and the size of his award rose one cent an hour at the end of each month if he got a grade of "good" or better, falling by one cent if his grade was "poor." In 1928 the minimum scholarship came to $450 a year, and the maximum to $1020, with tuition free. At that time the school equipment alone was appraised at $1,000,000, while it occupied about three acres of floor space in the company plant. The average annual value of material produced by each boy was about $1000, which paid for scholarships and instruction, but did not meet any interest on investment. Jerome D. Greene of Harvard thought the spirit of the place remarkable:

Henry Ford has made a pioneer experiment in uniting theoretical book learning with practical applied adventure in the factory. . . . Each subject lives in the consciousness of the boy because he has to make a practical application of it two-thirds of his time. . . . There is nothing done which the student might feel is useless. The result is that there is creative joy in the work.

After reaching the age of eighteen, a boy entered the senior course, working regular company hours in shop and attending classes in advanced drawing and mathematics. By the time he was twenty he was receiving an employee's wages; and at that age if not earlier, he was offered a position in some department of the company if one was open. In the nineteen-twenties nearly all graduates were employed immediately and even in the depression they had a superior chance of finding good positions somewhere. Detroit newspapers often carried want-ads for "expert mechanics, graduates of Henry Ford Trade School preferred." Searle relates:

One boy came in during the depths of the depression. I asked him what he was doing.
He said, "I just got a job at Fisher Body."
I said, "How did you get in there? They aren't hiring." [26]
He said, "They told me they weren't hiring, but I told them I was from Henry Ford Trade School. They beckoned me around to the side door. They hired me and asked if I knew any more Trade School boys who wanted jobs, and they hired six of my friends."
That was the story time after time during the depths of the depression. During that period, many graduates of Detroit University School came to me wanting work. Almost *no* graduates of Henry Ford Trade School came to me asking for work. They came to me telling how they had gotten jobs, which was the difference between the training offered by the two schools.

This recollection is substantiated by Trade School reports and other data. One letter from the school mailed in 1934 to all tool shops in the Detroit telephone directory brought immediate requests for about seventy-five boys. It was sometimes hard to keep students in the Senior Course when they could get higher rewards elsewhere. Once Searle called this fact to Henry Ford's attention, pointing out that the company was losing many of the best-qualified youths. Ford's reply was characteristic: "What do you care? Get some more. Somebody's getting the benefit!" [27] *

---

* The fact that the school was a good Ford advertisement must not be overlooked. In 1933 the company sent twenty-two boys and four instructors to an exposition in the Port Authority building in New York. Searle later wrote: "At the show all the boys were doing useful work. One was at work on the drafting boards, one repairing goggles, two were winding armatures

6.

A variety of minor services in the brief golden age of the company, the Lee-Marquis era of social conscience, may be briefly dismissed. A Medical Department, at first a separate and important link in the labor relations of the Ford Company, was imbued with the progressive spirit of Lee, Marquis, and Edsel Ford. A model plant hospital was opened in A Building at Highland Park in 1916. It contained, in addition to facilities for the medical examination given all new employees, an operating room, an X-ray laboratory, a general laboratory, and a medical room. The company that year had the Life Extension Institute examine a thousand sample men of its work force. As late as 1924, when the scope of medical work had been curtailed by the economy drive, more than 23,000 medical examinations were made. Dr. Mead and his staff were proud of the work they did, and when times of stress came, fought hard to save it.

It was this medical department which, with the cooperation of Dean Marquis, undertook to solve the problem of tubercular employees by special job assignments. For a time the company even considered building a parts factory in New Mexico in order that infected workers could be transferred to a region more favorable to recovery. While this idea came to nothing, the company did make a practise of transferring tubercular employees to better climates. The Medical Department also had a close relationship with the Compensation Committee, on which Chief Surgeon Mead sat. This body reviewed all accidents, and decided how much money should be paid to injured employees. The main factors taken into account were the worker's financial condition, the number of his dependents, his period of service, and the nature of the accident (which must have occurred in the course of employment through no carelessness of his own). The rule of the Ford company was to give an injured man a compensation higher than that required by

---

or performing other electrical operations, another was repairing micrometers, a boy was operating each of the following machines: drill press, shaper, lathe, mill, grinder, and the most advanced boy was working on the bench as a toolmaker. So great was the interest of visitors that there was always a crowd watching the boys and asking them questions. . . . Many a visitor remarked, 'You have to hand it to Henry!' " (Report of the Superintendent to the Trustees, February 4, 1934; Acc. 6, Box 162.) The English company had a similar but much smaller school at Dagenham, while an imitative school was opened in Jamshedpur, India, in affiliation with an iron and steel works there, by a Hindu who had worked in the Ford Motor Company for a number of years. (Searle, *Reminiscences,* 29, 30.)

Michigan law, and sufficient to prevent him from falling in debt. It appears that he usually got the equivalent of minimum pay without "profits"—this was certainly the fact in 1918.[28]

Victims of disease or of any other disability non-compensable under the law might also be helped by the company, at least as long as recovery was possible. In some instances this assistance was as little as five dollars a week, and it was cut off when the cases became clearly incurable—a practice which brought to Clara Ford some pitiful pleas. The company argued, of course, that totally and permanently disabled ex-employees were properly a charge upon society at large.

Near the end of his term with the company, Dr. Marquis recommended, in a detailed report to Edsel obviously based on careful research and thought, that some provision be made for families left destitute by the death of a Ford wage-earner. He had looked into group insurance plans. It would cost $700,000–$800,000 a year, he found, to insure the life of each employee for $1000 by this method; and funeral costs and doctors' bills would leave the dependents only about $500. He proposed that the company employ an equal amount of money to give $500 to every family, and devote the remainder to helping such destitute households as had children so small that the mother could not be employed by the company. Others cases he would relieve by hiring the mother or oldest child, as the company had done previously, or by giving the mother light work in the home.[29] When Marquis made this proposal, however, sunset was overtaking the social welfare era in the history of the Ford Company.

That the Ford commissaries survived the close of this era is no doubt attributable largely to the fact that they met their costs and provided a shining example of successful business enterprise. We do not know on whose initiative they began. Their origin can be traced to weekly sales of fresh fish, bought in carload lots and retailed directly from freight cars, in the winter of 1919–1920. The company opened a grocery at the same time which quickly expanded, while it was soon retailing meat, coke, shoes, and drugs. Sales were made at cost, which was kept low by operating on the same principles as the super-markets of a later day, with large stocks, a minimum of personal service, and a cash-and-carry requirement. On the true Ford formula, no waste space, no waste motion, and no waste speech were tolerated. The shoppers who thronged the aisles carried their own bags. Beyond question these commissaries at the Highland Park and Rouge plants—to which the company presently added ten stores at various points in upper Michigan, Kentucky, and West Virginia—assisted employees to meet rising costs of living throughout the nineteen-twenties. At prices ranging from 10 to 90 per cent below prevailing retail rates, they still realized a profit of 3½ per cent on gross sales!

By 1923 the stores did a tremendous business. That year they sold 80,000 pairs of shoes and rubbers, 4,580,000 pounds of meat and chicken, and great quantities of work clothes. The Highland Park store alone, crowded every day, had a staff reaching 110 persons. Some of the food-stuffs came from Ford farms—wheat grown on Ford land, with such rarities to gladden the heart of food faddists as soya bean flour bread, unbleached flour bread, 100 per cent whole wheat flour, and canned green soya beans. In time the company launched a "salvage store," which disposed of tires, car-parts, paint, and hardware. Coke and cement came from the Rouge plant, soft coal from the Ford mines, and charcoal briquettes from the Iron Mountain woodworking plant. No Ford source was overlooked.

So long as the commissaries confined their benefits to Ford employees, nobody complained. When in 1926 the company dropped its ill-enforced exclusionary rule, however, and welcomed outsiders, a pained outcry arose from the retailers. Well might they complain! One visitor to the Highland Park store in 1927 found that even on a week-day morning cars were lined two deep, and that the crowd within included not only fur-coated housewives of the professional class, but liveried chauffeurs buying for their mistresses—"Thus showing that even a Packard outlook is not too haughty for a Ford economy." The Retail Merchants Associations of Michigan and other States, and the National Association of Meat Dealers, were not content with expostulatory statements, but threatened a boycott of all Ford cars and trucks. Liebold was at first truculent in defense of the company's decision, but under this pressure began to ponder the issue. A vociferous gathering of Detroit retailers, called by the Michigan Association, met at a down-town hotel on April 4, 1927, and listened to denunciatory speeches. Then it was thrown into a paroxysm of joy and relief when a Ford spokesman arose with a quiet announcement that the company would reinstate its old rule against outsiders.[30]

In the field of housing the Ford Motor Company at no time did much for its workers. Though Marquis took an enlightened interest in the subject, the theory in 1914–1917 was that the five-dollar wage would enable workers to buy or rent good quarters without difficulty. Even when rising costs and congestion in the Detroit area destroyed this assumption, the rule of inaction prevailed. Marquis called attention to housing pressures in 1916, but Ford's personal ideas—which remain a mystery, though Klingensmith stated that they would in good time be explained—blocked any action. Perhaps he had heard of the censure visited on George M. Pullman for ill-advised company housing policies.

One small experiment was made just after the war with dubious results. The Dearborn Realty and Construction Company, with Clara Ford, Edsel Ford, Liebold, and C. R. McLaughlin as shareholders, was incorporated to build houses for employees on land bought early in 1919. Stanley Ruddiman took charge under Liebold's direction. During 1919–1920 they erected about 250 houses, of three and four bedrooms each, on a large tract in West Dearborn south of Michigan Avenue. It was intended to sell them all at from $8225 to $10,000 apiece, but temporarily some were rented at $50 to $60 a month. Originally, the Dearborn Realty asked a down payment of half the price, but after the onset of the 1921 depression this was cut first to a quarter, and then a tenth. Prices were also reduced to a range of $6900 to $8500.

The project was not planned in a money-making spirit, and Liebold always wrote of it in terms indicating uncertainty whether it would come out even. At first the company treated purchasers with generosity. Those who gave up their houses received a refund of principal payments. When the Ford Company fell into financial difficulties in the winter of 1920–1921, however, this policy went the way of other liberal measures. This was a breach not of contract, but of what some purchasers thought had been a clear understanding. One man protested: "I would never have taken the house otherwise, as the price was too high for me to expect to pay with my rate of earnings. Also the monthly payments. I simply had to have a place to live and figured that the interest would be as reasonable rent as I could get." At this dark season, when a relaxation of demands might have been expected from an employer previously as liberal as Ford, the company also stiffened its attitude toward tenants whose rent fell into arrears because of partial or complete unemployment.

In its first two years, the housing company lost nearly $6000. Later, according to Liebold, it did better, and despite renewed difficulties after the beginning of the 1929 depression, yielded profits over a twenty-year period of $600,000. But even if we accept this statement, the annual rate of return on the company's investment must have been less than two per cent. Company housing has always been a treacherous quagmire, full of quicksands for both workers and companies. The Detroit area desperately needed housing for low-income wage-earners, and needed efforts by large companies there to combat the deplorable situation. But the one experiment the Ford company made did not encourage it to try others.[31]

7.

On January 25, 1921, Dr. Samuel S. Marquis announced that he had tendered his resignation as head of the Sociological Department of the Ford Motor Company. He declined to discuss his reasons. The event signalized the end of one era in Ford labor relations, and the beginning of another—darker, harsher, more Prussian, more capricious and irrational. Instead of the enlightened, progressive John R. Lee and Norval Hawkins, Dr. Marquis and C. A. Brownell, those whom Marquis called the "scavengers"—presumably he meant Sorensen, Martin, Liebold, Klann—took control. Sorensen in *My Forty Years with Ford* makes plain his antagonism to Marquis, whom he accuses of interfering with production.

Dean Marquis resigned only when his continuance had been made impossible. Ever since the consolidation of the tractor company and motor company in October, 1919, which led to Sorensen's control of the Rouge, he had met increasing difficulties in his work in the Sociological Department. The cars assigned to his staff had been reduced, his recommendations for transfers of workers had been disregarded, other proposals for helping men had been rejected, and efforts to protect hands against summary discharge had been nullified. Sorensen, who bossed the Rouge from Dearborn while Marquis kept his office at Highland Park, wanted complete authority (under Henry Ford) in his plant. He despised the Sociological Department and tried to thwart it. Repeatedly Marquis went to Henry Ford to discuss his troubles. The owner would agree that orders of the department in welfare matters should not be disregarded.

"Well," Marquis would say, "as soon as you leave the factory, my order is immediately countermanded."

"Then disregard everything that Sorensen does," Ford would reply. "I say your orders should go through!"

But of course Sorensen had his way, until Marquis became convinced that Ford was deliberately undermining him and the department. For months, his family later recalled, he would come home at night saying: "I don't know how long I can take it. I think I'll get out." Finally the denouement came. Marquis appealed to Ford in Sorensen's presence. "I have ordered so-and-so transferred to another job," he said. "Mr. Sorensen orders him dismissed. What are you going to do about it?"

And Ford, thus forced into the open, snapped: "You heard what Mr. Sorensen said!" [32]

A number of elements entered into the rapid sapping of the welfare era in company annals. One was the waning of Henry Ford's social fervor. John R. Lee had told investigators of the five-dollar wage and accompanying reforms in 1914, "There is not a thing in connection with his business life, I think, that has given Mr. Ford the enjoyment and the keen interest that this whole scheme has." But as the novelty wore off, as he drifted into politics and journalism, as his business activities multiplied, and as years hardened his temper (he was sixty in 1923), his faith in his first social goals flagged. The rough buffeting he endured in the peace ship episode, the Dodge Brothers' suit, the Chicago *Tribune* case, and his campaign for the Senate, edged his temper with cynicism; he was not the only man whose faith in human nature declined during the first World War. With lengthening years, as many testify, came a distinct hardening of the moral arteries. Marquis in 1924 might well lament that he had not manifested "the same sustained interest" in employee welfare as in some more selfish aims.

Another element in the jettisoning of welfare work was the financial troubles of the company. During the January of Marquis's departure its very survival was in question; Henry Ford was selling desks, wrenches, and files to keep its head above water. Sorensen thought that only tough discipline could meet the crisis, and Ford had no choice but to support Sorensen; his drive and skill were indispensable, while Marquis's humane vision seemed a luxury. When the company had been making profits in tens of millions, welfare measures were much easier to provide and administer than when it was against the wall, counting every penny.

Indeed, the principal foundation of the spectacularly liberal Ford policies went to pieces when wartime inflation, as we have seen, closed the once-tremendous gap between the five-dollar day and the ordinary factory wage. When Marquis had taken over the Sociological Department from Lee at the beginning of 1916, the buying power of the five-dollar wage was almost what it had been at the start. But when the war ended, unskilled laborers in the Ford plants had lost most of their gains, and skilled workers had lost all of them. What grounds now existed for watching over workers' expenditures? It is erroneous to think of the new labor regime as being suddenly scuttled when Marquis left in 1921. Rather, it had gradually lost force over the preceding three years because of the company's inability to support the high level of real wages. As the economist Dr. Samuel Levin remarked, no theoretical and slight practical justification now existed for the sociological work. Ford recognized this fact, for he moved forthwith to terminate the interesting experiment—retaining, however, some useful remnants.[33]

What happened was in retrospect perfectly clear. Henry Ford, by virtue of the immense popularity of the Model T and the flowering of mass production at Highland Park, had made lordly profits. These gains had coincided with the burgeoning of Progressivism; the old Populist ideas of social justice had suddenly quickened in Ford's lively mind; Lee and Marquis, entering the scene at a happy moment, had helped him see the possibility of remodelling capitalism by high wages, high consumption, and high production of low-priced goods. His New Order had enchanted the world. Then other automotive companies caught the secret of mass production and low-priced models; competition, war taxes, and inflation stole his fairy gold; progressivism gave way to reaction. Ford's sudden wage-increase could not long keep him ahead of other ambitious manufacturers. Men spoke of the light that failed. But this was unfair: the company's labor policies for some years remained more enlightened than most. And though the relapse might seem disillusioning, the memory of a daring effort endured.

For a short period after the war the general position of American labor worsened, as did that of Ford labor. For twenty-odd representative manufacturing industries, as we have seen, the National Industrial Conference Board found that average hourly wages dropped from 61 cents in 1920 to 49 cents in 1922. Some parallel Federal figures for twelve industries show that average full-time weekly earnings fell from $32.57 in 1920 to $26.04 in 1922. Ford wages, the minimum at $6 a day or 75 cents an hour, with bonuses and perhaps a share in savings-certificate dividends, compare well with such figures. Then the situation for industry as a whole improved. Business in 1922–1923 showed a strong revival. General wages rose, and thereafter for some years kept on a slightly ascending plateau. Employment also became more stable. Though layoffs during the postwar depression had reached a peak of 50 per cent, after the industrial revival they fluctuated between 3 and 12 per cent annually.[34]

As the sun of prosperity brightened, another announcement by Ford resounded through industry. On March 24, 1922, the company introduced the five-day week for all employees, many of whom had been working only three days weekly. Of this we shall say more later. It is sufficient here to note that although some large stores had adopted the five-day week years earlier (in New York city in the summer of 1914), and it had made headway among shoe and clothing manufacturers, most industrialists opposed it. It was most successful in plants where the cost of making ready for the day's work cut sharply into the profits of a Saturday half-day. Some garment-makers combined it with a cruel Friday speed-up. Samuel Gompers praised Ford's step as good both for labor and production. Matthew Woll was still more enthusiastic, saying that it would promote a better understanding of the fact that working hours could be shortened without loss to the community. Ford himself put the decision on a broad human basis, telling newspapermen:

"Every man needs more than one day a week for rest and recreation. The Ford Company always has sought to promote ideal home life for its employes. We believe that in order to live properly every man should have more time to spend with his family.

"Right now market demand warrants the operation of the plant six days a week, but we are satisfied that the five-day week is practical, and it has been adopted as the permanent policy of the company. Adjustments, naturally, are necessary. . . . It will mean works for 3000 more men. It will mean more machinery."[35]

It was natural for unions to lose members during the depression of 1921; what was remarkable was that they failed to regain the ground during the ensuing years of prosperity. Businessmen carried on an aggressive campaign against them. No Ford representative took part in the famous meeting of twenty-two manufacturers' associations in Chicago in 1921 to organize a campaign for the open shop. The company held aloof from the trade associations, chambers of commerce, and other bodies which fought for the so-called "American Plan." But Henry Ford, like practically all other automotive leaders, sympathized with it. Both ignorance and selfishness moulded his views on labor groups, which he regarded as predatory. "Labor unions are part of the exploitation scheme," he told the *Christian Science Monitor* in 1923. "The men probably don't know it, and maybe their leaders don't even know that they are really but tools in the hands of the master exploiters of . . . . human productive energy." [36]

Labor organization made no headway in the Ford plant, or in any other major automotive plant. It made no real headway in chemicals, rubber, iron and steel, food-packing, or other industries so highly mechanized that they employed masses of unskilled workers.

The decade 1913–1923 in Ford labor thus closed with lights and shadows strangely intermixed. Workers had been led to the top of Pisgah to see a Promised Land, but their enjoyment of the milk and honey had been brief. War, hard times, Ford's changing psychology, and other factors had cost them their double pay, their paternal "sociological" care, and their protection against hectoring, speedups, and arbitrary discharges. But they had a fairly superior wage, a short working-week, and valued fringe benefits.*

On the dark side, one token of the harsher atmosphere of the Ford shops was the conversion of the employees' weekly, the *Ford Man* (under benevolent C. A. Brownell a fearless exponent of the workers' views) into a mere house-organ. E. G. Liebold took charge of it. Renamed the *Ford News,* it rapidly abandoned all pretense of speaking for the employees. Brownell, who had done much to lift factory morale, left before the opening of 1921. "His gospel of good will," wrote Marquis, "fell into the hands of the higher critics, and they proved it not only a fond delusion but a needless overhead expense on production." On the bright side, some vestiges of the era of altruism remained. The journalist W. L. Chenery, visiting the Ford plants in 1924, found that the employment and reclamation of convicts was pursued with unabated zeal; that the sociological staff still gave valuable

---

* The report of the Sociological Department for 1924 shows: investigation of absent employees, 3131; aid to sick, checks delivered, and report of progress in the case, 1801; investigation of sick employees to see if aid is necessary, 2188; calls pertaining to crippled children, 2361; investigations pertaining to real estate, 2401; miscellaneous home calls upon request, 1647; and domestic trouble cases, 678. The company that year spent $41,294 aiding the sick, $4232 for handicapped children, and other philanthropic sums, while it loaned more than $200,000 to about 13,000 employees. Typed report entitled "Ford Industries," 1925, Ford Archives.

advice, on application; and that at least some superintendents stuck by the rule that discharges should never be made ruthlessly. The company continued to treat Negroes with more liberality than any other large corporation, and in 1923 employed about five thousand. It continued to hold an honorable primacy in employing the lame, blind, ailing, and other physically handicapped persons.[37]

The sheer growth of the company had presented new disciplinary problems, and created a new psychology among workers and bosses. The little force of 1655 Ford men employed in the first year of Taft's Administration, and even the larger force of 12,880 in the year the World War began, might be regarded as a close-knit community; not so the 60,000 men working at Highland Park and the Rouge in 1920. The army of toilers swelled until the total number of Ford wage-earners in the United States in 1925 exceeded 150,000. It became faceless and impersonal. It was a cross-section of all society, equal in size to a large city, with groups responsible and irresponsible, law-abiding and criminal, cooperative and rebellious, intelligent and stupid. It had all the contradictions of a large city. We read with sharp repugnance what one boss, Klann, says about the way he and others regimented and spurred the hands just after the depression of 1921: "We were driving them, of course. We were driving them in those days. . . . Ford was one of the worst shops for driving the men." But when we read reports of some employees thieving, malingering, gambling, and idling, we realize that discipline was essential; and when we recall how near the depression brought Ford to financial disaster, we can understand how the emphasis on driving, brutal and self-defeating though it was, got accepted.

Nevertheless, the dissipation of the bright dream of 1914–1918 provokes regret. The Ford factory, which had been one of the luminous spots in world industry, became just like any other factory. The sparkle was gone; the benevolence was a tattered travesty of what it had been when Ford said he wanted to put Christ into his establishment. "What was left," as Marquis wrote in despondent retrospect, "was what had to be done, and what any hardboiled company would do anyway." [38]

XIV

FORD OVERSEAS:
THE EXPANSIVE YEARS

By the outbreak of the first World War, the distribution of Ford cars had spread throughout the globe. The first assembly plant outside North America, established at Manchester in 1911, had flourished under the direction of that talented Englishman, Percival L. D. Perry. With a central sales office in London, Perry had enlisted a corps of brisk dealers in the United Kingdom, where in 1913 he sold well over six thousand cars. Other parts of the British Empire were served by Ford of Canada, which under Gordon McGregor met a rising demand from Gibraltar to Auckland. The American company had opened dealers' offices in the chief Latin-American cities. Marketing on the European continent had been taken in charge by H. B. White, whose Paris headquarters supervised selling outlets scattered from Lisbon to Warsaw.[1]

Initially, all American cars had to conquer a good deal of foreign prejudice. James Couzens, making a hurried tour of Europe in the early days, had decided that this fertile field would have to be tilled with an eye to special foreign needs and foreign psychology. "The Europeans are not unfriendly to American goods in general," he announced, "but they are somewhat unfriendly to American automobiles." This attitude stemmed from the fact that Europe had at first led in making automobiles, and from unhappy experiences with small American cars in the days of experimental Olds and Hupp models. No other car did so much to dispel the prejudice as the tough little Model T. Before Serajevo, the demand for it justified the opening at Bordeaux of a second European assembly plant, and Ford officials were thinking of a third in Germany or Scandinavia.

Though the war practically stopped all non-governmental orders for cars and trucks in Europe, while it raged the Ford became still more widely known. The Allies found the Model T ideal for a variety of purposes. Ontario-assembled Fords did ambulance work with Canadian troops in Flanders; British-assembled Fords carried ammunition and dispatches in the Somme Valley; American-made Fords ran on all fronts, even going to Serbia with the Columbia University relief expedition. No job was too difficult.

"We got within a mile of the fort [at Verdun]," wrote Howard A. Boyle of the American ambulance service in 1917, "when we struck a big abrupt hole filled with mud and water, and dropped. I thought we would come out in China. My Frenchman thought that the car had broken the axle, but I gave it a little more gas and put her into low and she walked right out." This was in pitch darkness on a May night. "Up half a mile, we smashed into another huge hole, and went right down to the chassis that time. Personally I thought it was hopeless even to try to get out. But still I thought I would give her a try. So I again started the motor and shoved her into first, and to my extreme surprise I went up out of this hole and climbed up the side of it like a cat, and kept agoing." [2]

Almost as soon as the Treaty of Versailles was signed, the outside world more than regained its old place as a market for American cars —for European factories had lost ground. The number of American units exported in 1920 rose to 171,644, with the Ford well in the lead. By this time the Model T was the one car, indeed, known the globe over. Sometimes an almost incredible tale, drifting back from a foreign strand, illustrated its cheerful ubiquity.

A driver from Jerusalem, for example, was bouncing shortly after the war over the stony face of Palestine, then British-ruled, following goat tracks from Jenin toward Haifa. Steering his Ford across an abrupt watercourse, he broke the drive-shaft pinion in the differential gear. He was in a quandary. The nearest town, Jenin, was ten miles back. He could trudge thither, pay ten Egyptian pounds for a horse-tow, and then wait several days for a pinion from Haifa or Jaffa. Indeed, that seemed the only course. Feeling hungry, he decided first to buy some food at a peasant village visible a half mile away. This turned out to be a collection of fifteen mud huts called Romani. An Arab there had no bread, but a bag of barley, some parched beans, and a pair of rude scales made of string and two tin pans. In despair, the driver asked for beans. The peasant placed a handful in one scale, and from a box on which he was sitting produced a weight—a Ford pinion, worn but sound! He had picked it up at a motor repair shop maintained near at hand by Allenby's army during the war.[3]

During 1922, when the United States manufactured more than 2,500,-000 motor vehicles, exports were sharply reduced by the depression abroad. But in 1923 they recovered to 152,000 units, in 1924 they set a new record of 224,000, and in 1925 they went to 303,000—Ford easily leading. The Model T had swept away all foreign doubts, and despite its ungainliness, had won the hearts of plain people everywhere.

Endless news items during the early and middle 1920's bore testimony to the cosmopolitan acceptance of the Ford. Several hundred young Chinese, many of them university graduates, arriving at Highland Park for a rapid training course in manufacturing and business methods; a Methodist missionary in Korea driving his Model T four thousand miles in two months, mastering floods, mud, and rocks as he averaged three services daily; the motor corps of the Dutch army attending classes at Ford's Rotterdam headquarters in the maintenance and repair of cars; Amtorg, placing orders in 1921–1926 for nearly 25,000 Fordson tractors; a battered Model T making a heroic run of six hundred miles from "out back" in Australia with a patient who had suffered a compound fracture of the thigh; President Calles of Mexico driving his Lincoln regularly twenty miles to his farm to plow an hour or two with one of his Fordsons—such stories became commonplace.[4]

Since the foreign business done by American automobile companies in 1923 was worth well over $100,000,000, the Ford Motor Company was naturally eager to enlarge its share. In the fall of that year an export managers' conference in Detroit produced some searching of hearts. Those present were full of enthusiasm, pointing out that the total of foreign sales amounted to more than eight per cent of Ford output, with excellent opportunities for expansion. But their discussions revealed a highly inadequate organization of the foreign field, which needed more assembly plants, more dealers, and more managers. Ford executives, in summarizing the results of the conference, declared that each of the 2174 dealers abroad ought to employ, on the average, one more salesman; that each salesman ought to make at least ten calls a day; and that a more energetic demonstration of cars, trucks, and tractors was essential.[5]

To put the matter somewhat differently, the three elements most needed were efficient oversight from Detroit, imaginative planning for the future, and a skilful selection of managers. The difficulties of conducting business in fifty different countries during the confused postwar period were forbidding, but the prize was great. Other companies, notably General Motors, were furnishing a competition which the Ford executives must if possible outstrip.

2.

Supervision from Detroit was furnished in a general fashion by Henry Ford himself, in the intervals of his other crowded occupations. He was well aware of the financial importance of the foreign field. Moreover, taking warm pride in his international reputation, he often talked of the contribution the company could make to world welfare by distributing large quantities of cheap cars. He intended to prove that Ford methods could be applied abroad. "I am glad to say that European industrialists have welcomed a complete demonstration of our principles, in the various countries," Crowther smugly wrote for him in 1930. As a matter of fact, the great error of Americans in foreign business was to insist too much on their own principles, and to give too little scope for foreign methods. Active control over operations abroad was exercised by Edsel, Ryan, Roberge, Kanzler, and Sorensen.

The first steps taken were eminently sensible. Henry and Edsel Ford sent the redoubtable William Knudsen abroad in 1919–1920 to survey the situation and draft a plan. For a time he was in control of all company affairs both in Great Britain and on the continent. His sturdy figure, massive head, and booming voice became familiar in all the offices. With advice from Detroit, he worked out an ambitious program. Though necessarily tentative, it divided Europe into half a dozen divisions which may be noted in the order of their importance:

The British Division would embrace the United Kingdom, Egypt, and Malta, with headquarters in Manchester. Managing both large manufacturing works and an assembly plant, it would receive more attention from Detroit than any other.

The Northern Division would comprehend Scandinavia, Finland, the Baltic States, Poland, and at first Germany and Holland, with offices and an assembly plant at Copenhagen. Obviously, Germany and Holland would in time demand separate facilities.

The Central Division, with headquarters in Paris, would include France,

Belgium, Switzerland, and Algeria, and would set up assembly plants as these were needed.

The Southern Division would cover Italy, Spain, Portugal, Morocco, Tunis, and Tripoli, with an assembly plant in a convenient Spanish city.

The Adriatic Division would embrace Central Europe south of Germany, the Balkan lands, and Asia Minor, and would have headquarters and an assembly plant at Fiume.

Finally, the Black Sea Division would include the Ukraine, Central Russia, Turkey, Armenia, and the Caucasus, a difficult region for which planning was shadowy, but which Knudsen hoped would develop a center in Odessa.[6]

On paper Knudsen's plan looked impressive. Its development, however, was to follow a simple evolutionary course which displayed no great vision or energy. The general rule was that first a resident agent in a given country solicited dealers to handle Ford products; then a sales and service branch or branches were established; and finally, when sufficient demand was evident, an assembly plant was opened. Except in the United Kingdom, the plants at first did little but assemble American-made parts; they manufactured none of their own. Each assembly plant thus turned out a car which in name, design, and materials was wholly American, wholly Ford, and subject to whatever antagonisms might gather about a foreign product. The development also followed another rule long since established in the United States, that the expansion of facilities in each area was to be financed from the profits made there; Detroit was rarely to be called on for any expenditure. Thus British money was to be plowed into the Manchester works; Spanish money into a Spanish assembly plant.[7]

Naturally, in that period of international turmoil, Knudsen's division lines underwent certain changes. One by one, however, assembly plants were opened. In 1919 two were established, in Copenhagen and Cadiz respectively. Three years later plants also began operating in Trieste, which had been found more advantageous than Fiume, and in Antwerp. In 1924 Copenhagen got a new and better assembly plant, and one was located in Stockholm. Next year the important French operations began at Asnières on the Seine, and in 1926 the Berlin plant threw open its doors. Knudsen himself, of course, had resigned early in 1921. The only really comprehensive supervision of Europe was that supplied from Detroit; none was exercised in Europe itself, except by occasional travelling representatives.* Each country or division, under Detroit, tended to be a law unto itself.

While the program could be called dynamic—for the Model T was popular enough to make fairly steady expansion possible—it lacked the imagination, flexibility, and unity that it might have shown under a farsighted lieutenant placed in Europe. It would have been much better had Edsel been given a free hand. Henry Ford's rigidity interfered with the proper growth of foreign activities. In Europe, as in America, he clung too long and too inflexibly to the Model T. The frequent dismissals of executives by Ford or roving Detroit officials interfered with long-range planning. When Edsel and his brother-in-law Kanzler attempted in 1923 to obtain permission to design, make, and sell a special European product, Henry refused to entertain the idea; he was too proud of the company name, too wedded to his own creation.[8]

Ford's principal rival, General Motors, showed more acumen. It had begun manufacturing in England before the First World War by establishing Bedford Buicks, Ltd., of London, which made cars with a Buick chassis. After the war it displayed redoubled energy. It opened a training school in New York for employees going overseas, set afoot a lively advertising campaign, and multiplied agencies until in 1923 it boasted of selling cars in 125 countries. As the Chevrolet gained low-priced ground at home, the company pushed it abroad, establishing plants in 1924 at Hendon near London and in Copenhagen. The British horsepower tax, however, made it advisable to find a still smaller vehicle; and General Motors therefore presently purchased the Vauxhall Company, which had a factory at Luton, England. Possessing a long-established reputation, the Vauxhall sold widely. Meanwhile, in the London area the Chevrolet and Buick, built with chassis shipped from the General Motors plant at Oshawa, Ontario, and with English bodies, were made in quantities.

In their general methods of assembling and selling cars abroad Ford

---

* To this statement one partial exception must be noted. Temporarily a Foreign Department was established, with headquarters first at Copenhagen and later in Paris, which was responsible for areas not yet under a branch or affiliated company. This department sent representatives to yet unopened countries or districts, selected resident agents and dealers, and advised them in their activities. It pushed its work energetically but always on too small a scale. (Knudsen Report; Roberge, *Reminiscences*.) For a time the Foreign Department, under A. Lie and later J. J. Harrington, exercised a considerable supervision of European operations. But beginning in 1925 Detroit took full control. Ten-day cable reports and a monthly letter kept it informed. A travelling auditor had European accounts under constant scrutiny. (L. E. Briggs, *Reminiscences*.)

and General Motors were much alike; both scattered assembly plants and sales agencies widely, both used cavalcades of cars, public hill-climbing and load-carrying demonstrations, and motion pictures. But General Motors took pains not to seem so foreign as Ford. Its control of the Vauxhall factory, followed in 1929 by its purchase of an interest in the great Opel works at Russelheim, Germany, gave it a special *locus standi*. In England the Vauxhall was considered English, in Germany the Opel was German. Both cars were adapted to local laws and tastes. Inasmuch as General Motors was a stock company, the citizens of any country could purchase shares. Moreover, while the Ford company in general refused to invest any funds overseas beyond the profits made there, General Motors did not hesitate to pour home capital into foreign subsidiaries.[9]

The Ford enterprises overseas, foreign in name, ownership, and product, were a natural target for the widespread xenophobia of the postwar period. Ford could be pictured as drawing money from a country without making a real capital investment. And while the Model T was highly saleable, modifications to suit European taste would greatly have improved its appeal.

3.

It was unfortunate for Ford operations in Europe that, for reasons too complex for thorough discussion, the company temporarily lost the services of Sir Percival Perry. One of the fundamental causes of his resignation in 1919 was a sharp difference on issues of policy. Perry employed methods of selling which Detroit rejected. After the war the Ford Motor Company refused to give a dealer a fixed territory, or a guarantee of ample warning against price changes. It required all its dealers to sell Ford products alone. But in Britain, Perry had created a system of sole distributors in large protected territories. They might handle other cars while they offered the Ford; they were not required to maintain show-rooms or demonstration cars; they often had no supply of service parts. When a customer asked for a Ford car, the distributor would get one for him, taking a profit even though he had done no work at all. The customer would then take his chances on repair parts. In the United States, again, trucks were sold on the same basis as passenger cars. But in Britain Perry had organized an independent company with almost exclusive control of new Ford trucks. In the United States dealers were free to take out insurance where they pleased. In Britain, however, dealers were required to buy insurance from a company in which Perry was a shareholder.[10]

Other differences went deeper. Perry believed concessions must be made to national feeling. Nor did he regard complete American domination of the world automobile market as a healthy situation. Before the war the automobile industry had thrived in Britain, France, Germany, and Italy, which shipped cars throughout the world; during the conflict the United States had seized most of market; now the pendulum should swing part way back.

Perry when the war ended had a vision of a great British factory in Southampton, where on Ford's authority he had contracted for two potential sites, one at the spot where the *Queen Mary* and *Queen Elizabeth* later docked; a factory using modified Ford designs but British materials, making not merely bodies and radiators but every part of the cars, and shipping them throughout Britain and the colonies. "I didn't think as an Englishman I was playing the game if I went on importing American cars," he later said frankly. He had long insisted that Britain was the logical center for supplying at least part of the Empire, for when a farmer in South Africa or New Zealand wanted a Ford, he naturally wrote to England. If Perry had had his way, the Southampton factory would have built up a large business, while allied companies on the continent made cars of domestic materials for their home markets. The business would have been partly Europeanized.[11]

For three main reasons, however, Henry Ford did not act. The activities of the Ford Motor Company in America, 1918–1919, absorbed his time and money, and made heavy new commitments abroad (even on foreign-supplied capital) seem dubious. Perry was found to have made a defective survey of the site. The European scene, moreover, was chaotic and uncertain. Ford refused to proceed with the proposed factory in Southampton. Knudsen's reports from abroad were critical of Perry's methods, which Klingensmith in Detroit (whom Perry had called simply a superior bookkeeper) also attacked. As a result of these and other factors, Perry's connection with the English company was severed, effective June 30—though he remained nominal head of the Cork tractor plant until October. From Henry Ford he received a letter expressing keen regret over the differences which led to the severance.

Within a decade he was to come back, bringing his plan with him.[12]

The temporary loss of Perry's brains and experience, though probably inevitable, was regrettable for several reasons. He knew much more about European affairs, methods of doing business, and mental habits than anyone whom the Ford Company found it possible to send from America. He had considerable influence in Great Britain, where his wartime labors with the government were gratefully remembered, and where his vivid personality made many friends. He excelled in public relations. In building up the Manchester plant he had displayed ingenuity and insight. He even had his own ideas about car design, some of them good. For example, he tried to furnish his own fore-doors for the early Model T, which had none; he conceived the happy idea that the brass lamps should be built into the body instead of being screwed on, and vainly tried to convert Henry Ford to that innovation; and he invented a radiator collar which in any collision would take the shock off the radiator pipes. Perry's organizing capacity had raised the assembly plant and body works at Manchester to a high pitch of efficiency.[13]

He had a zeal and enthusiasm, too, which had early brought him into cordial relations with Sorensen. Indeed, their friendship had been one element in his success. Before the war, complaining of faulty shipments, Perry had besought James Couzens: "Give me someone who will wear the Manchester name on his forehead as a Jew wears his phylactery!" When Perry soon afterward visited Detroit, Couzens told him: "I have the man with the phylactery." They walked out in the bitter winter cold to an exposed loading platform. "I saw a man who looked like an Adonis," later recalled Perry. It was the lithe, athletic Sorensen, toiling to get the Highland Park shipments on the cars. His grasp of Manchester needs was immediate. "He did a proper job," runs Perry's tribute. "After that, we got the materials to Manchester with the cases properly marked. We would open them, find the right parts, and assemble the cars in record time."

Though Perry had certain faults, his combination of talents was difficult to replace. Both he and the Ford Company learned something from the break.[14] Nor could it be said that the Ford Company was fortunate in the Americans it chose as managers in the various European countries; too many proved inadequate.

4.

The history of the British operations was especially interesting. Perry's successor as managing director was Warren C. Anderson, who pursued (first under Knudsen, then under Edsel and Sorensen) what he called an aggressive course. In manufacturing, he determined to spend about £1,000,000 in expanding and renovating the Manchester works, to raise the annual target at once to 25,000 cars, and to use, as Perry had wished, more British materials. The pre-war capacity at Manchester, 15,000 cars, would be doubled. As for marketing, he decided to lower prices immediately, and require dealers to handle Ford wares exclusively. He meant also to see that they were kept on tighter rein. The new marketing requirements, imposed July 31, 1919, when old contracts expired, at once raised a storm. The "exclusive" policy, which meant that a man selling Fords could not sell the Lanchester, Daimler, or any other car, was repugnant to most dealers.

A great deal of reason existed for the new rules. Anderson complained that a select group of distributors had parcelled out the Ford output to small dealers, and reaped a rich reward although they "seldom canvassed for an order." To be sure, the old system had been reasonably efficient. The 1200 dealers in Perry's sales organization had contracted before July 31, 1919, for more than 20,000 cars. Of the 1200 dealers only 400 were initially ready to renew on the exclusive basis. Some of the more resentful sent representatives first to Manchester, and then to Detroit. Anderson followed them, and came back late in 1919 accompanied by Sorensen, Klingensmith, and other Ford officials, who undertook a study of manufacturing and marketing. For the time being, no dealer was denied reappointment. But nearly all were put under scrutiny, and Anderson reiterated that he would not countenance a Ford dealer using his position as a meal-ticket while handling a half-dozen other makes.[15]

In the end the new policy was of course enforced: a Ford dealer in Britain might sell Ford products only. Something was gained, and something lost—the balance is hard to strike. At any rate, Ford policy abroad was made consistent with Ford policy at home. "Unhappily," Perry said later, "Warren Anderson almost completely ruined the marketing system which had slowly and painfully to be rebuilt. The Ford dealers had been in nearly all instances the best motor-car agents in England. After their experience with Anderson and his successor, a Ford man trained in Omaha, most of them would not handle a Ford car on any terms whatever." While this statement doubtless possesses some truth, it must be discounted. So must the complaints of various dealers who, precisely like their counterparts in the United States, grumbled that they were being forced to sell ever-increasing quotas of cars, and were meanwhile at the mercy of unpredictable price reductions. As the competition of the Vauxhall increased, they complained that this "cramming" became more intensive.[16]

Unquestionably some dealers did suffer in England, as in America, from strict contracts which meant that, after they had made a large capital investment, they would get only low profits in a moderate market, and would suffer severe losses if sales dropped. But many others did well. The English manufacturer William R. Morris imposed somewhat similar requirements. This, wrote one dealer in 1923, was quite proper. Too many men had wished the Ford and Morris companies to do all the work and hand over a check; the heads of these companies, in halting slack methods, were contributing to trade efficiency.[17]

The Model T, for all its growing deficiencies, continued to sell, the Manchester plant to grow, and profits to remain fair if uneven. In the last five months of 1920, a painful readjustment period, the British company (with the Bordeaux branch) lost approximately £120,000. Then in the calendar year 1921 a small profit was achieved, £46,245. Next year the profits rose abruptly to £695,000, for the government removed all trading restrictions and demand was enormous. Sales dropped in 1923, and profits fell to less than £338,000 that year, and to only £124,000 in 1924. But in 1924 a much improved version of the Model T went into production, giving the British market a fillip, while the able Ernest C. Kanzler was now in charge of the foreign branches. Profits therefore recovered—£432,733 in 1925, £438,655 in 1926, and £355,520 in 1927.[18]

In methods of production the English company made steady improvements, particularly after a reorganization in 1923–1924 which displaced Anderson's incompetent successor. Two years later the 250,000th car, setting a British record, emerged from the Manchester plant, to be sent immediately on a tour of the kingdom. By this time it was almost an all-British car, the engine-blocks being made at Cork, and most other parts at Manchester, from British materials. The machine shop was small but efficient; the assembly line a miniature counterpart of that in Detroit. A new plant site was meanwhile (1922) purchased at Dagenham, but without immediate intention of building.

In wages and working conditions the Ford plant held an advanced position. Perry at the end of the war had instituted a forty-four hour week, with minimum pay of two shillings one-penny an hour for office and factory worker alike; and this, he wrote Clara Ford, placed the works ahead of any similar industry in England. The five-day week was introduced in 1926. Labor unions were no more recognized for collective bargaining in Manchester than at the Rouge, though some employees belonged to the Amalgamated Engineering Union. But a man with a Ford job was generally envied. A worker sometimes offered a five-pound note to anybody thought able to get him one, in spite of the fact that Ford, Ltd. frankly coupled a demand for higher production with the higher pay. Just before Christmas in 1926 an increase of two pence an hour was given to men on assembly lines that had shown "consistent improvement"—and to them alone.[19]

5.

The Cork plant, erected by Henry Ford & Son, Ltd., primarily for the manufacture of tractors, was one of the most interesting in the foreign domain. Even before the war, Henry Ford had contemplated placing a factory in this area. The wartime demand for more home-grown food brought him and the British Government to an emergency agreement. Lloyd George had reasons of his own for establishing the much-needed tractor plant in Ireland, for he thought the island deserved a share of war industry, yet could hardly be trusted with an arms factory. Perry, the moment he got word that Ford and Lloyd George had reached general agreement, acted with energy.

"I had an interview with the War Cabinet on Monday," he said later—this being a Monday in March, 1917. "I left England on Monday night and got to Cork Tuesday morning. Before the end of the week, I made an arrangement by which I had been appointed a Cork Harbor Commissioner, and had acquired about two thousand feet of river frontage with a low water depth of about twelve feet. I had acquired also the Cork race course which adjoined this river frontage." In all, 136 acres were acquired at a cost of £20,000, a sum divided

A Ford-made Liberty engine (above),
and an Eagle boat coming out of
B Building to be launched.

Henry Ford, Lord Northcliffe (second and third from right) and the Northcliffe mission with a Fordson tractor. Dearborn, October, 1917.

Fair Lane nearing completion. In the foreground, the dam is in process of construction.

Harvey Firestone, C. Harold Wills, and Henry Ford in consultation.

Rosika Schwimmer, Henry Ford, and Louis P. Lochner.

Truman F. Newberry speaking, and Drs. Charles F. Aked and Jenkin Lloyd Jones playing leapfrog on the deck of the *Oscar II*. Below, Woodrow Wilson's arrival at the Ford plant at Highland Park, July, 1916.

The Ford Engineering Laboratories Building (above), and the Fords and Lelands at the Lincoln plant, February, 1922. Left to right, Henry M. Leland, Blanche (Mrs. Wilfred C.) Leland, Wilfred C. Leland, Mrs. Edsel Ford, Edsel Ford, Clara Ford, Henry Ford.

The New Orleans Ford branch assembly factory, a good example of plant construction in the early nineteen twenties, and (below) the Rouge plant about 1928, showing the northern end of the slip at the right, the storage bins at its left, the high line bordering it, and farther left the blast furnaces, foundry, and power plant (tall chimneys).

Charles E. Sorensen and Percival, Lord Perry (1934), and below, the Dagenham plant on the Thames.

The Ford airport, with the Edison museum buildings beyond it, at upper left. Below, a Stout transport, *Maiden Dearborn,* being loaded for flight. Left to right are Henry Ford (with **bundles**), Clara, W. B. Stout, and Edsel. Two figures in the background are not **identified**.

A contrast in Ford working conditions: above, the work crew at the Fordlandia rubber plantation, 1927; and below, Logging Camp No. 4 at Sidnaw, upper Michigan.

Ford water power developments of Nankin Mills and Flat Rock.

Group with Model A engine. Left to right, Sorensen, Edsel, Henry Ford, P. E. Martin, Gus Degener, and Charles Hartner.

Three 1924 Model T's: Tudor, coupe, and touring car; and below, Henry and Edsel Ford by a Model A Fordor.

Ford workers emerging from the factory, and below, the assembly line at the Rouge plant. The well-packed but well-lighted factory floor of the Rouge is visible in the lower picture.

Working and learning. Above, Negro employees can be seen, and below, a group of workers having an outdoors English lesson.

Henry Ford
with two of his
grandchildren

The four friends on vacation. Left, Edison standing on hub of old water wheel,
Burroughs and Ford on the wheel, and Firestone to the right of it.

The Rose
Garden at
Fair Lane

The Edsel Ford family and Clara Ford, about 1927. Left to right, William Clay
Ford, Eleanor Clay Ford, Benson Ford, Clara, Edsel, Josephine, and Henry II.

The 1932 V-8 Ford Roadster, and below, Henry Ford and Harry Bennett.

equally between the city of Cork and the Harbor Commission. Inasmuch as the land was public property, an act of Parliament had to be passed to sanction the transfer. The principal consideration which Ford and Perry offered in return for the waterfront grant was an agreement to employ at least two thousand workers for the next five years.

Behind the tract ran the Cork, Blackrock & Passage Railway. As Southern Ireland had no coal, iron, or heavy industry, many thought the site a mistake. Perry would have preferred placing the factory in North Ireland, where labor (he believed) was more efficient. But Ford, apart from a sentimental attachment to the area of his forefathers, was swayed by the fact that while very little emigration took place from Ulster, it still flowed steadily out of Southern Ireland—and he thought emigration unfortunate. His basic attitude was expressed by Sorensen, who said:

Back of it all, we are pushing forward Mr. Ford's program to increase industry wherever possible, and particularly in areas where industry has fallen back. Wherever there is an indication that industry will be of help at all in building up communities, that is where we intend to go.[20]

In a broad sense the Cork plant was simply an arm of the Manchester works. Most of its products went by sea to Manchester and other English ports. Ireland itself (and especially Southern Ireland) furnished as yet little market for tractors. Typical farms were small, modern agricultural machinery was little known, and a pair of horses or donkeys supplied sufficient power for the plows and mowers. English agriculture, however, offered a favorable area for mechanization, and the Fordson, used in World War I, was popular. Part of the assembly work was to be done at Cork. Some British manufacturers, not at all happy about the opening given to so formidable an industrial leader, predicted that the Cork factory could not begin producing machines for two years. In this they were correct. Not until July 4, 1919, did the first unit come from the Irish assembly line. But before the year ended more than 300 tractors followed, and during 1920 the production totalled 3626, so that Cork-made Fordsons began to play a part in British agriculture not long after the conflict.

Along the south bank of the beautiful Lee, the plant slowly expanded—a sprawling structure with outbuildings which by the spring of 1922 covered six acres and employed about 1800 men. Freighters loaded with raw materials and parts for assembly came eleven miles up the river to discharge their cargo at the doors, while other freighters carried the finished products to England, the continent, and the Middle East. But even by 1921 it was plain that the Irish plant was not destined to succeed on the lines first planned.

Indeed, a variety of difficult problems had to be solved before Detroit could take any real satisfaction in the Cork enterprise, and its whole basis had to be broadened. Tractors were not enough; after the first postwar demand was met the farm market in Europe temporarily sagged, and other products had to be made and sold. A relatively large capital had been invested in the plant. In the first nine months of 1920 alone more than £327,000 was spent on a machine shop, foundry expansion, new wharves, and equipment. As the total investment thus rose toward two million pounds, the plant manager, Edward Grace, estimated that to pay profits on this sum, they would have to produce about 200 tractors a week, or 10,000 a year. This was preposterous. The solution of the main problem was found in making engines and axles for the Manchester factory, and spare Model T parts for all the Ford companies in Europe.[21]

But before reaching this solution the plant executives went through much agonized effort. Under Henry and Edsel Ford, operations at Cork were directed by the masterful Sorensen, who kept close watch over details. He was the marshal at headquarters; his field commanders were Grace, an American, and two capable Britons, E. L. Clarke and Port Stewart. In the second half of 1920 these men encountered a succession of calamities. The oncoming depression began to retard sales. A seamen's strike in October tied up shipping. No sooner was this over than a British coal strike crippled transportation in England and Ireland. The "troubles" in the latter country, with a bitter struggle between Sinn Feiners and British troops, distracted the labor force. When Sorensen criticized failing returns, Port Stewart graphically described the interruptions (August 13, 1920):

Conditions in Ireland seem to be getting worse instead of better. . . It is a nightly occurrence to see armoured cars running around the streets and to hear machine guns fire all night; the next morning the shop windows in the main street can be seen full of bullet holes. My wife and children and myself were held up the other evening whilst we were out for a drive;

we were placed under arrest and made to drive to the Barracks between two truckloads of soldiers, with guns pointing all around us; but we got off all right without serious mishap.

Sorensen kept urging increased effort, and the Cork officers strove earnestly to improve their showing. But in 1922 the tractor market almost collapsed under the impact of the worldwide depression, only 1443 Fordsons being shipped from the plant. Grace then concentrated his energies on Model T engines and parts, believing that from parts alone he might make a profit of almost £100,000 a year.[22]

While the plant was struggling to make enough Model T engines, axles, and parts to balance its books, the city government of Cork launched an unexpected assault. Early in 1922 a councilor complained that although Henry Ford & Son had covenanted to employ 2000 men for five years, only 1600 were actually at work. A resolution to send the firm a stiff notice passed 18 to 8. The city solicitor announced that if the company did not hire 400 men at once, he would proceed to cancel the lease and eject the holders. This action aroused a sensation in Ireland and was telegraphed all over the world.

Inevitably, Henry Ford took a defiant attitude. He was doing his best to provide more employment, but he refused to be dragooned into making artificial work. He notified Grace that he would not submit to conditions that would be a perpetual nuisance; if the city persisted, he would discharge all hands, close the factory, and establish his plant elsewhere. He ordered construction work and installation of new machinery stopped. Early in March five hundred men were dismissed, trooping to city offices for unemployment pay; and other dismissals loomed ahead. Cork at once surrendered. The councilors unanimously rescinded their rash resolution, directed the city solicitor to meet the Ford attorney to arrange an amicable settlement, and presently gave Henry Ford & Son a title in fee simple instead of a leasehold.[23]

Though the Cork plant in 1923 showed a promise of prosperity, another threat to its solvency quickly arose on the horizon. By treaty early in 1922, the Irish Free State had been created, with the same rights of dominion self-government enjoyed by Canada. It proceeded now to establish its own customs system, while the British Parliament imposed tariffs on some goods from Southern Ireland. When it became plain early in 1923 that automobile parts from Cork would be taxed, Ford executives in England saw they could never afford a continued importation from that source. Urging dealers to buy large quantities of cars before the duty went into effect, several of them hurried over to the United States to confer with officials at the Rouge. A new set of policies had to be drafted for both Cork and Manchester.

In a series of Detroit conferences, the Ford executives decided that Cork would have to stop manufacturing Model T motors and axles for the Manchester factory, and that all such manufacturing should now be concentrated in England. A suitable site would have to be acquired, approximately a hundred acres in extent. In accordance with Henry Ford's long-standing rule, this site must have not only good rail facilities but excellent water transportation. Gould of Manchester and Edward Grace of Cork were instructed to begin scouring England thoroughly for a place. The complete Model T and its successors would be made at this new English plant, which of course would include large foundries and machine shops. Cork would fall back to a secondary place. It would still make tractors for distribution throughout Europe, and it would sell Model T's in the Irish Free State; but the manufacture of automobile motors and axles would cease as soon as the new English facilities were in operation.[24]

Thus it was that Henry Ford, Edsel, and Sorensen, with the advice of their British executives, turned back toward the path that Perry had pointed out to them four years earlier. Henry Ford never regretted his investment in the Cork plant. It continued to sell tractors throughout much of the Old World. But a great self-contained motor factory under the Ford name was in time to rise in England, using British materials, employing British workmen, and selling a large block of stock to British investors; to rise not in Southampton, however, as Perry had proposed, but on a Thames site close to London.

6.

The number of foreign assembly plants steadily grew, and so did their output. It would be tiresome to cover their separate histories—some colorful, some routine—in detail. As a rule, much depended on the brains and energy of the manager; whenever a good man was hired progress was rapid. But all foreign operations were subject to one general law. They flourished with but weak competition in the early nineteen-twenties, the Model T carrying everything before it; then the rise of the Chevrolet checked expanding sales in the mid-twenties, though most of them still prospered; and finally in 1930 the Great Depression shut down like an iron clamp on their activities.

From France in the summer of 1919 came an astonishing offer. André Citroën was in financial difficulties. He had transformed his factory to manufacture small ten-horsepower cars in large quantities, had erected a new body works, had laid down a program for building 30,000 units the next year, and had booked orders (he said) for 14,000. But his competitors were trying to undercut him, and the banks had stopped his credit. He telegraphed to "Sorensen Chez Fordson" in Dearborn: "Willing to accept any financial cooperation with Ford either partnership or as sleeping partner or formation of limited company. Shall be absolutely master of the French market and can also make very big exportations. The requirements of the business are ten million dollars." To get the ten millions he was ready to come at once to Dearborn with all his papers. But Sorensen crushed his hopes in ten words: "Impossible to secure Mr. Ford's aid in financing your company." [25]

Henry Ford wished no partnership with a French manufacturer. But he did see the importance of a better assembly branch than he had at Bordeaux, and the policy adopted in France was typical of that in most important countries. Agents were sent over in 1921 to choose a new factory site. They decided that the best point would be on the Seine near Paris. Barges could bring American or British parts up the river from Havre; other materials would be bought in or near Paris, where the Michelin and Goodrich tire companies, among others, had plants; pig iron, steel, and coke were all near at hand; and finished automobiles could be readily delivered to customers, for nine-tenths of Ford sales were made in Paris and adjacent areas. Every possible saving was important, for French makers of low-priced cars furnished fierce competition, and about three-fifths of the Ford selling price in France was attributable to duties and taxes.

The new assembly plant at Asnières, a suburb of Paris, began operations in 1925 with a capacity of 150 cars daily. It had a power plant, a main assembly building 672 feet long and 325 feet wide, its own body works, and four other buildings. Cargoes of engines and frames from the Rouge were transferred from freighter to barge at Havre, and unloaded at Asnières by a huge crane. The Ford Company had its special problems in France, as in most countries. Fluctuations in exchange made price stability difficult. The horsepower tax was increased in 1926. Three French manufacturers, Citroën, Renault, and Peugeot, who turned out a heavy majority of the French cars and fiercely resented American competition, were always ready to join hands against Ford. Methods in the plant were so careless that an inspector from Detroit, touring Europe late in 1926, discharged a number of the key employees. Nevertheless, the merits of the Model T and after it the Model A enabled the company to do a modestly profitable business. Out of a total of 205,693 new cars registered in France in 1929, the last year of world prosperity, Ford had sold almost 11,000, or 5.3 per cent, as against Citroën's 62,000, or 30.1 per cent.[26]

Much more important at first than the French plant was that in Copenhagen, which enjoyed an exceptionally rapid postwar growth. Founded in 1919, it sold to a bakers' dozen of countries, reaching southward into Germany, and beyond Scandinavia and the Baltic states into Poland and the Ukraine. The original site, selected by Knudsen, was next a coal-yard, and when the wind blew coal dust into the factory, proper painting was impossible. Another trouble lay in the fondness of the Danish workmen for beer. They brought great quantities right into the factory, and when Henry Ford ordered the practice stopped, they forthwith walked out. The building of a big saloon just across the road solved that problem.

But the Danish workers were as efficient, according to the reports of travelling inspectors, as the French were slack. Output at Copenhagen for the first eight months of 1922 exceeded 7000 cars and trucks, and grew steadily. Enlarged facilities were built in 1923–1924 on the Copenhagen waterfront, with a building big enough for an American-style assembly line, and a body factory. At the formal opening on November 15, 1924, the Danish prime minister made a speech—as well he might, for the plant, with a capacity of 600 cars a day, employed fully five hundred Danes, and used much Danish material along with American and British parts. Three-fourths of all the Ford dealers in Germany, Scandinavia, and the Baltic states attended the ceremony.[27]

Germany presently had its own assembly branch. Though Sorensen, touring the defeated and occupied country late in 1921, thought that Bremen was the best spot, the factory was eventually placed on a barge canal at Plötzensee, a suburb of Berlin. Because of the political and financial difficulties of the Reich, the plant was not established until

1926. The low initial schedules called for about 8500 cars a year. Machine equipment came from America, Britain, and Belgium.

But in Germany greater obstacles were encountered than almost anywhere else. Throughout the nineteen twenties it was almost impossible to overestimate the reputation which Henry Ford enjoyed among German businessmen as the apostle of mass production; nevertheless, German workers and technicians were decidedly frigid. As labor was cheap and plentiful, efficiency in terms of the average workman's product was less at a premium than in America. Moreover, most German engineers showed an instinctive reluctance to subordinate their individualistic leadership in research to the doubtful advantage of standardization.[28] The new Ford plant near Berlin paid wages considerably higher than those offered for similar work in German factories. But the employees in 1926 claimed their constitutional right of organizing a shop council, which German law indeed made practically obligatory; and this action collided squarely with the non-union policy of the American company. When the management learned that the workers were about to elect the council, which would have a good deal to say about running the factory, it announced that if German laws were to be introduced, then only German wages would be paid. Of course German laws triumphed.[29]

In the prosperous year 1929, Ford sold 9400 cars in Germany out of 131,500 new registrations, or 7.2 per cent. This was better than the percentage sold in France, but far lower than the results in Scandinavia, in Greece, Spain and the Baltic states, where sales that year ran between 18 and 33 per cent of all new cars registered.[30]

King Alfonso had specially asked the Ford Company in 1924 to build a plant in Spain to replace the small unit already opened at Cadiz by Knudsen, arguing that the country was importing 12,000 Fords a year; and in 1925 assembly began at Barcelona. The plant in the free port of Trieste, opened in 1922 by the Ford Motor Company of Italy ("Fordita"), sold not only to Italy but to the Balkans, Turkey, Cyprus, Tripoli, Egypt, and the Middle East. A large building here received "semi-knocked-down" cars from America, completed them, and shipped them through this wide area. Unfortunately, the Italian tariff, imposed to protect Fiat and other home manufacturers, was almost prohibitive. The $295 Model T had to be listed in Italy, after freight and duty, at $862. And in operating this company yet another of the innumerable vexations abroad had to be met, petty graft. Attempts were made to eliminate it, but it persisted. As an Italian employee graphically informed Dearborn:

Agencies are sold to people by roadmen inasmuch as the Ford agency is something very lucrative in Europe. You can see our business going to the dogs on account of that reason: It is not a responsible party who will make most success of the Ford dealership who gets it, but that one who pays the most. It might happen to you when coming to a dealer and start to advocate Mr. Ford's ideas that the dealer might tell you: "What are you telling me? You belong to an organization of biggest crooks!" [31]

7.

In the Western Hemisphere, pride of place among foreign affiliates was always taken by the Canadian company at Windsor, Ontario. Its fortunes throughout these years to a great extent paralleled those of the American progenitor. To be sure, Ford of Canada went to war in August, 1914, instead of April, 1917, and did a large war business in automotive units before America entered. It had its own overseas operations in Australasia, South Africa, India, and other British colonies and dominions.

But it used designs and models from Highland Park and Dearborn; it had American experts help lay out its new buildings; throughout the long hegemony of the Model T it imported its engine blocks from the American factory. When the American company began making Eagle boats, the Canadian company made Eagle boats too. When the depression of 1921 shook Highland Park, the Canadian chieftains conferred anxiously with Henry Ford and took his suggestions on inventory reduction. The five-dollar day applied to the Canadian plant as to the American, and Windsor saw a Sociological Department at work on the same lines followed in Detroit. The long shutdown of the Detroit factory as Model T gave way to Model A was paralleled by a similar shutdown in Canada.

Under the able administration first of Gordon MacGregor, the founder, and after his death in March, 1922, of W. R. Campbell, the Canadian company grew lustily. The Model T was just as well adapted to rural Canada as to rural America. The selling organization, modelled on that created by Couzens and Norval Hawkins in the United States, was consistently efficient. As population figures rose and demand expanded, branches extended across the continent—Montreal, Toronto, Calgary, Regina, Winnipeg, and Vancouver. Perhaps the principal difference in marketing between the two countries was that the Dominion factory depended much more upon its export trade than did Highland Park or the Rouge. In some years sales to the other wide domains under the British flag more than equalled Canadian sales. It was the Canadian company which in October, 1924, established the Ford Motor Company of Australia with a capital of $15,000,000 furnished from Canada (though Detroit did lend Ford of Canada $3,000,000 of this sum on three-year notes). It was the Canadian company which erected assembly plants there, in South Africa, and finally in Wellington, N.Z. Officers of these and other imperial operations, visiting Ontario headquarters, would be taken across to Detroit, often giving Henry or Edsel Ford their views.[32]

Latin-America was a rich field, for the Model T precisely suited large areas. In Brazil, Kristian Orberg, a Dane who took charge of the assembly plant at Sao Paulo in 1921, made a resounding success. He found an exceedingly primitive branch housed in a former skating rink. Transferring it to a new three-story structure specially built by an American engineer, he installed moving assembly lines and soon doubled the output. He bade dealers sell their quotas, or give way to hustlers who could. Travelling up and down Brazil, he advertised the car, took orders, and recruited new agents. "We had to appoint blacksmiths, dentists, doctors, whoever we could find," he later recorded. "We had to *make* dealers."

The energetic Dane also threw himself behind a much-needed movement for good roads. When Washington Luiz, an advocate of better highways, was elected president of Brazil in 1926, the Sao Paulo office devised an exhibit showing his wax effigy against a background of Model Ts, Fordson tractors, and trucks busily at work driving roads through the jungle. As passable ways were opened, the Model T—its lightness, high clearance, and toughness giving it a great advantage— became an important agency in knitting the settled areas together. The capacity of the Sao Paulo branch had been raised in 1924 to 45,000 cars a year. When the Model A came in, it possessed enough of the sturdy traits of its precedessors to please Brazilians. Argentina, with an assembly branch in Buenos Aires which by 1924 also had a capacity of 45,000 cars annually, was an even better market.

The primary difficulty in Latin-America lay in the economic and political instability of many of the countries. When prices of sugar fell in Cuba, of copper in Chile, of coffee in Brazil, Ford sales dropped. Revolutions sometimes interfered with business. The turmoil in Mexico delayed the opening of an assembly plant until 1925. Inasmuch as these southern lands had no automobile companies of their own, however, and little taste for European cars, the market was always tempting. In 1929 the Ford Company sold 27,500 cars in Argentina, 18,250 in Brazil, and 9500 in Mexico and Cuba combined, a better business than in continental Europe.[33]

To supply a widening array of overseas operations, twenty-nine by the mid-twenties, the Ford Company not only chartered freighters, but used ships of its Great Lakes fleet. The *Oneida* and *Onondaga* were placed on the Atlantic in 1924 for coastwise and trans-ocean voyages.

As company executives became aware that the feeling against the Ford car as a foreign product was often injurious, they did what they could to combat it. Under a directive sent out in 1924, efforts were made to increase the proportion of home-supplied materials. The rule was to buy such parts, from tires and gas-tanks to floorboards and electric wiring, as could be obtained in the national market at a cost not exceeding that of American materials plus freight, insurance, and tariff duties. This was good public relations; Ford officials were glad to announce how much British material went into the Manchester car, how much Belgian material into the Antwerp car. In view of the high tariffs imposed in many countries, it was also good economics. Though for obvious reasons Britain led in the proportion of home-supplied components, about seventy per cent by the later nineteen-twenties, even in Spain it proved possible to buy a good deal. But still the feeling remained.[34]

8.

Despite all perplexities and embarrassments, the overseas operations were consistently an important part of the company's whole business. A schedule dated August 31, 1923, shows that thus early the assets of the foreign plants totalled almost fifty millions. Manchester of course led with almost $15,000,000, Buenos Aires came next with $8,800,000, Cork was on its heels with $7,270,000, and Copenhagen was not far behind.[35] It must be remembered that these assets were almost entirely paid for from overseas profits. In the number of employees Manchester with 2580 and Cork with 1850 were far in the lead.

Over and above the profits drawn from foreign plants, Henry Ford and his associates took satisfaction in the prestige their products enjoyed throughout the globe. To give such vigorous competition to the Austin in England, the Citroën in France, the Opel in Germany, the Steyr in Austria, the Fiat in Italy; to receive a steady flow of letters from pleased customers; to know that the Model T was the greatest single vehicle in the history of world transportation—all this invested the business with a special aura.

The two cardinal rules given foreign managers were to keep the quality of the product high, and to hold production as steady as possible. Supervision was maintained by various methods. These managers made regular reports, which Edsel Ford, Sorensen, and occasionally Henry closely scanned. Travelling auditors and production specialists descended unexpectedly on the plants, while some auditors resident abroad were available for company meetings (for separate companies were incorporated in France, Spain, Italy, England, Ireland, and other countries) or branch conferences. They made recommendations for hiring and firing, for promoting and demoting. J. J. Harrington, long resident in Europe in charge of sales, had broad powers. In 1926 he made a tour with two American associates to reorganize operations, fortify weak spots, and install the five-day week; and he took drastic action in several places. In Belgium, for example, he called a directors' meeting, and with their authorization dismissed the manager, named a successor, and severely reduced the staff. In Manchester and Cork he effected a "general cleanup" of dirty premises. Abroad as at home, Ford discipline never lacked rigor.[36]

But what remains most memorable about these foreign activities is their color. A tourist in Fiji reported just before the war that one of the picturesque sights he met in Suva was a Model T crammed with half-dressed natives. In Upper Assam, among the Himalayan foothills, another traveller found that the wonder of the countryside was a Ford car owned by a tea-planter. In a region where the rainy season brought from 300 to 500 inches of precipitation, on rough, steep tracks formerly sacred to the pony and pack-coolie, the automobile gave rough-and-tumble service without faltering. After the great Japanese earthquake of 1923, the government asked the manager of the Ford assembly plant which had been established the previous year in Yokohama to furnish transportation for demolished Tokyo. A thousand small buses were needed immediately, and the Ford men, fitting Model T chassis to improvised bus bodies, supplied them. The world, as Kipling sang, was wondrous large, seven seas from marge to marge; but literally from China to Peru the saucy, sturdy little Ford was giving it one kind of bond.[37]

XV

WINDS OF CHALLENGE

SOME demon of unrest seemed to give Americans a thirst for more and more movement, for wider diversions at faster speeds, as the nineteen-twenties wore on. They needed more amusements farther from home; they felt a passion for broad new landscapes both social and geographical. The agents of change had appeared before the war, in the low-priced cars that dashed past frightened horses, in the new asphalt or concrete roads that slowly thrust across the landscape, and in the service stations that gradually punctuated the crossways. But now these and other factors seemed to be producing a Götterdämmerung of the old America—the Victorian America, as young people scornfully called it—and ringing up the curtain on a spectacular transformation scene. After the anxieties of the war and tensions of the brief depression, the country shot into its gayest, noisiest, and most hectic decade; a decade of exuberant expansion, its slangy motto "Boost—Don't Knock."

Everywhere the automobile, made in increasing quantities, and sold at figures within the reach of mechanics and farmhands, could be seen subtly or overtly at work. It changed the physical outline of cities; their boundaries moved outward like the margins of lakes swollen by spring floods, new suburbs, "additions," and "developments" covering fields with bungalows, streets, and garages. It changed household architecture; roomy homes on wide lawns became *passé* as apartments of two and three rooms, with "dinettes" and "kitchenettes," vied with the bungalows, their occupants living half the time in their cars. It altered the amusements of the land: roadhouses multiplied along the automobile highways, and people drove hours to dine, dance, and drink bootleg gin. Summer resorts bourgeoned on distant lakes and mountain slopes, while Florida beaches became arenas of frantic exploitation. Crime and law-enforcement were transformed. The modern Jack Sheppard, after holding up the bank or store, fled in a stolen car and was pursued by the sheriff in one still faster, while the merry moonshiner, the rum-runner, and the piratical hi-jacker all depended on the automobile. Old economic interests died while new ones were born. The once-thriving electric inter-urban lines were choked in the Laocoön-grip of "jitneys" and busses, while many an old red-brick hostelry in wayside towns saw its doom written in motor-camps and the early motels.[1]

Lord Bryce, describing uniformity as one of the principal characteristics of American life, traced it not to the influence of democracy, but to the equality of material conditions, the extraordinary mobility of the population, and the fact that so much of the country was made (and remade) all at once by the same forces. The cheap motor car accentuated these factors. It gave the poor man a chariot that millionaires would recently have envied, made Americans more migratory than ever, and laid the same molding hand on the social scene from Cape Cod to Los Angeles. Before its warning honk, isolation vanished from remote farms and sleepy villages. It brought together persons and families from all parts of the land, mingling them in the overnight haunts of the endless motor procession. "If anybody deserves a government bonus for destroying sectionalism," wrote Anne O'Hare McCormick in 1922, "it is surely the inventor of the cheap touring car." Like the radio, it helped the Georgian to talk the idiom of the Indianian; like the motion picture, it assisted Yankee mill-hand and Kansas wheat-grower to share each other's problems. By the winter of 1925 Florida had 178 registered tourist camps offering hospitality to 600,000 visitors drawn from New York to Oregon, three out of five coming by car.[2]

As never before save on the great pioneering highways—the Cumberland Road, the California-Oregon Trail—different types of Americans became acquainted face to face. While inexpensive motor camps sprang up by myriads (by 1923 two thousand American towns had such camps under municipal ownership) and while leisure increased, holiday-makers took to their Reos, Fords, and Overlands, piling them high with tents, bedding, and skillets. Once a privileged few had gone to Newport for bathing, and Pasadena for winter sunshine. Now millions went wherever they pleased.

"Turn into a through road anywhere," wrote Mrs. McCormick, "and you will become a part of the longest, fastest, and most extraordinary procession that ever raised the August dust on the face of the earth.

. . . A stream of tourists bowls or bumps along all the open trails from Maine to California. Camp fires and tent villages mark its daily course. It draws Main Street across a continent and changes a sparsely-settled countryside into a vast and populous suburbia." Historic scenes from Plymouth Rock to the Alamo, legend-haunted spots from the House of Seven Gables to Tom Sawyer's Hannibal, were lustily advertised. Billboards, roadside vendors, and souvenir shops flourished.

So omnipresent became the automobile that sharp controversies sprang up over its effect on churchgoing, on courtship, and on its use by college students. In 1922 President John Grier Hibben of Princeton, with the support of the trustees, asked parents of undergraduates to deny their sons cars. "The motor car," said the *Harvard Alumni Bulletin,* "induces idleness and is a distracting and unsettling influence." [3] Oldfashioned people associated the automobile with all kinds of changes of which they disapproved, from jazz to bobbed hair. John Dos Passos, looking back over the era in *The Big Money,* made the car a symbol of the wild flux of American life; Sinclair Lewis in *Dodsworth* chose an automobile magnate for his hero; and Booth Tarkington in *The Midlander* wistfully pictured the transmogrification of his pleasant, sedate town of Indianapolis into a noisy, smoky city of automotive factories.

But voices of criticism were drowned out by the steady drone of the gasoline engine on city street and country road. For ill or good, the dynamism of American society had taken universal form. Nothing could halt the movement of the time. In 1910 the United States had 468,000 registered motor vehicles; in 1920, registration had already reached 9,239,000. Six years later, after the industry had run up record production totals, the number of registered motor vehicles stood within a few hundreds of 20,000,000. By this date the American people were spending more than $14,000,000 annually on all costs connected with the purchase, operation, and maintenance of motor vehicles. The automotive industry already took first rank among manufactures, and the automobile was the main prop of the American economy. It was also the chief stimulant to and catalyst of urbanization.

Down to the First World War the United States had been considered backward in the building of improved highways; but parallel with the increase in the number of cars ran a development of well-surfaced roads so rapid that by 1928 the country had one of the finest systems in the world. More than a billion dollars annually was then being spent for the construction and maintenance of good highways, and not far from a half billion for the improvement and upkeep of city streets.[4]

The passage of the Federal Aid Highway Act in 1916 had done much to promote this progress. It not only furnished increasing sums from the national treasury, but required all states which had not created highway departments to do so if they were to share these funds. In the first decade under the Federal aid program almost 56,000 miles of road were completed. At the outset many states had used water-bound macadam and sheet asphalt, but as these disintegrated under bad weather and the pounding of heavy vehicles they turned to concrete roads. All the artificially surfaced highway of the nation, built by local, state, and state-Federal effort, aggregated about 522,000 miles by 1926. Though this was a creditable showing, much remained to be done. The national and state authorities had worked out a systematic plan for about 186,000 miles of arterial interstate roads in the country, but in 1928 only about a third of this network had been improved.

No longer was the railroad the principal means of overland transport. When the century began, the country had more miles of railroad than of improved highway; but the ratio steadily changed, until by 1927 more than three miles of paved road could be measured for every mile of rail. The motor bus became a dangerous rival to the passenger train, and the truck to the freight train. Down to the middle of the nineteen-twenties, to be sure, both the motor bus and the cargo-carrying truck were used almost wholly in short-haul operations, for distances under a hundred miles. Both thus to some extent operated as feeders to the railway as well as competitors. As time passed, however, railroads began to feel the pressure of the gasoline age. By 1929 a number of companies were successfully running passenger busses across whole regions, one line connecting Detroit with Seattle and San Francisco. By that date also trucks, some operated by factories, some hauling for large shippers by contract, and some maintained as common carriers, were numerous in interstate business.[5]

And there seemed no limit for the future of the passenger car, the bus, or the truck! The Iowa farmer with five dozen eggs and a bushel of Damson plums got them to the county seat by his Ford or Oldsmobile just as the Michigan peach growers sent tens of thousands of boxes of fruit to Chicago by truck. For perishable produce the automotive vehicle was far more useful than the railway. The rich truck-garden district around Norfolk was soon sending a great part of its vegetables and fruit to Baltimore, Philadelphia, and New York by road. Passenger busses ran between towns which had no railroad or at hours when trains were not available, and offered cheaper fares as well. In self-defence some railroads got into the bus business themselves; by 1928 they were operating more than a thousand motor coaches over routes ten thousand miles in length. By that year more than 3,000,000 trucks were being used in the country. One farmer out of fifteen had his own truck, and others used contract or common carrier service, while every year the sale of new trucks rose. Many people who had to move their household goods from Boston to Philadelphia or Chicago to Denver were beginning to prefer trucks.

Every year new uses for the automotive vehicle were being found. It would be hard, indeed, to say what a resourceful Illinois or Montana farmer and his wife did not use his Ford for doing, from herding cattle to cutting ice. The horse was disappearing so rapidly that the transfer of acreage from hay to other crops amounted to a minor agricultural revolution. School busses doubled in number in 1925–1926, reaching a total of some 27,000, while they were being markedly improved in design and size. Sightseeing and touring busses were becoming common —two transcontinental railroads used such busses to show passengers scenic points along their lines. In short, the motor age had fully arrived. When Americans read that in 1929 the factory sales of cars and trucks had exceeded 5,620,000, they could well believe that the time was at hand when every family would have its automobile. The home might be mortgaged, but it would possess that indispensable auxiliary! [6]

Henry Ford and the Ford Motor Company, surveying the changes connected with the automobile, could well feel a special satisfaction in them. Ford more than any other person had nurtured the vision of the car as the poor man's utility rather than the rich man's luxury; the tool of democracy, not the toy of aristocracy. The company by its pioneer work in engineering and mass production had given that vision reality. Some aspects of the automobile revolution would have pleased Ford more than others. The staggering annual total of deaths and injuries, the complication of the crime problem, the traffic snarls of great cities, the social irresponsibility bred by command over speed and distance, he deplored—while regarding them as unavoidable comcomitants of progress. But the improvement of rural life by wider markets, consolidated schools, accessible hospitals; the spread of pleasant suburbs; the stimulus to recreation; the general lifting of horizons and destruction of provincialism—these he applauded. On the whole, the revolution was good.

The prime question for Ford and the company, however, was a business question. Could they ride the swell of the movement they had done so much to initiate? Leaders in their field in 1910 and again in 1920, would they be leaders still in 1930? The competitive pace was so fierce that the answer was doubtful.

2.

In 1913–1914 the emergence of the cycle car, a miniature runabout seating two people, had made a stir in Detroit. One make was called the Mercury, another the Comet. For perhaps five years they had an unsettling effect on the sale of light automobiles. Ford decided that something should be done to stop the peddling of speculative stock in cycle-car companies. "He built a smaller model of the Model T," relates one of his associates. "It was almost what you might call today streamlined, and it was very neat looking." Edsel showed much interest in its construction. When it was completed, Henry said to Edsel:

"Now you take it down and park it in front of the Pontchartrain Hotel."

Edsel did so. A curious throng gathered and saw the name "Ford" on the car. "They immediately thought that Ford was going to bring out a cycle car," recalls the employe, "and that ended its era in Detroit."

Down to 1920 Ford, as this story suggests, was alert to competitive innovations and usually ready to meet them.* If not wholly open-minded to criticism of the Model T, he was willing to remedy glaring defects. In August, 1916, thirty-odd Ford dealers, guests of the company, met at the Highland Park plant. Norval A. Hawkins, who presided while Ford sat back and listened, asked their frank opinions on the car. A Georgia dealer got up to deliver an unabashed encomium, saying what he thought Ford wanted to hear.

"Now listen, fellows," snapped Hawkins, "we didn't bring you here for bouquets. . . . We want to know what is the matter with this automobile and why it isn't selling."

* He did resist the electric starter and generator, a basic improvement, for six years; see H. L. Maher, *Reminiscences.*

At this an Ohio dealer said just what he thought about the faulty front wheel bearings, while others briskly indicted different features of the Model T. "That's what we want," declared Hawkins. The fault-finding went on. Finally Hawkins turned to Ford: "Up to this afternoon I thought we were selling an automobile, but it seems just a piece of damn junk. What are we going to do with it?"

"Notes have been taken of everything said," replied Ford. "For most of it, something will be done. We'll investigate and go right on through." [7]

This was the earlier, more flexible, more tolerant Ford. He was as good as his word. The adjustable ball bearings on the front axle, for example, a common source of complaint, were replaced by roller bearings. Indeed, during the years 1913–1918 improvements were steadily made in the still fluid design and equipment of the Model T. Some were a response to complaints by dealers and customers; some represented an effort to accelerate production, reduce costs, or lessen the demand for replacements. But at any rate, changes were frequent, sensible, and sometimes far-reaching.

In 1914 the Model T carried for the last time a bulb horn, acetylene gas headlamps, and straight fenders front and rear. Beginning the following spring, it had a hand-operated Klaxon horn, brass electric headlamps powered by the magneto, curved rear fenders, a slight center drop in the front fender, hood louvres, and an unbraced windshield. Demountable rims were offered as extra equipment. Then in August, 1916, in response to new styling trends and the acrid complaints of buyers about "the dinky little brass-bound radiator" and other features, striking changes were made in the 1917 line. "Yes, it's a Ford," the New York *World* assured readers when it published a photograph of the hardly recognizable touring car.[8] In Chicago an excited crowd broke down the window of the show-room where it was displayed. It seemed almost a new vehicle. The spinsterish "Lizzie," shedding some of its gaunt angularity, looked more like a comely maiden, while it was sturdier than ever.

The hood had been given an approach to streamlining. The radiator, necessarily recast, was larger and of more pleasing shape; and it had a separate shell of pressed steel, which gave it greater strength than the old one-piece construction, simplified its repair, and enhanced the cooling capacity. Set higher, the radiator blended its line with the rounded hood, which swept more gracefully back to the cowl. Garish brass trimming had given way to shining nickel and black enamel. The early Model T had been recognizable at a mile by its squarish packing-box hood and brass radiator cap; they were as much a part of Gothic America as baseburner stoves and kerosene lamps. Now the Ford owner need scarcely blush as he passed an Oakland or Velie. "This comparatively tremendous advance in styling," writes a genealogist of the Model T, "served to set the pattern for most of the succeeding decade." A blight struck the business of certain body-building companies which up to this time had done well in selling crown fenders, V-shaped radiators, and other embellishments to style-sensitive owners. "More Class for Your Ford," one such firm had advertised. "Make It Look Like a $1000 Car." Dealers were delighted, and the trade value of older models significantly declined.[9]

For a time other improvements followed. The muffler of the early Model T had actually been responsible for much of its clatter. It consisted of a series of tin cans wrapped in asbestos; "when the engine backfired, away went the muffler—tin cans, asbestos, and all." Now it was replaced by a more solid muffler tightly affixed to the exhaust pipe. More important still was the introduction in 1919 of an electric self-starter. The task of cranking the Model T by hand had always been specially fearsome:

Mr. Smith. . . . climbs in by the right-hand door (for there is no left-hand door by the front seat), reaches over to the wheel, and sets the spark and throttle levers in a position like that of the hands of a clock at ten minutes to three. Then, unless he has paid extra for a self-starter, he gets out to crank. Seizing the crank in his right hand (carefully, for a friend of his once broke his arm cranking) he slips his left fore-finger through a loop of wire that controls the choke. He pulls at the loop of wire, he revolves the crank mightily, and as the engine at last roars, he leaps to the trembling running-board, leans in, and moves the spark and throttle to twenty-five minutes of two. Perhaps he reaches the throttle before the engine falters into silence, but if it is a cold morning perhaps he does not. In that case, back to the crank again and the loop of wire.[10]

Happily, the company celebrated peace by a self-starter as optional equipment. On cars so equipped, the magneto was used thereafter only for ignition.

Some notable improvements were also made in the engine, always

The
Ten-Millionth

The 10,000,000th Ford car left
the Highland Park factories
of the Ford Motor Company
June 4. This is a production
achievement unapproached in
automotive history. Tremendous volume has been the outgrowth of dependable, convenient, economical service.

Detroit, Michigan

Runabout $265 Coupe $525 Tudor Sedan $590 Fordor Sedan $685
All prices   o. b. Detroit

**SEE THE NEAREST AUTHORIZED
FORD DEALER**

The Touring Car
$295
F. O. B. Detroit

Demountable Rims
and Starter $85 extra

under Ford's watchful eye. "Nobody," testifies Galamb, "could touch the engine unless he knew about it." The compression ratio, which at first had been about 4.5 to 1, had to be reduced by successive steps, mainly because of deterioration in the quality of gasoline, until it was stabilized at 3.98 to 1; the engine then yielding twenty horsepower as against an initial twenty-two. But meanwhile, 1914–1919, finer machining of the cylinder walls improved acceleration; a tapered piston ring two one-thousandths of an inch thick improved the compression; and a new design strengthened the pressed steel crankcase. Finally, in 1922, the Ford engineers produced a new cast iron piston a half-pound lighter than its predecessor; and this gave the engine smoother operation. A little later the bevelling of the bottom edge of the nethermost piston ring created a pocket for excess oil, and the residue was carried back to the crankcase with each downstroke of the piston. The connecting rods were bettered in 1922 by the use of lighter, stronger metal, while a new carburetor, wiring system, and steering wheel were installed.

But after the opening of the new decade Ford's temper stiffened. The acceptance of the Model T by the American masses, its worldwide fame, and the huge revenues from its sale confirmed his belief in the infallibility of his handiwork. As he reached sixty, his mind became less pliant, his disposition more autocratic. Success, as Dean Marquis noted, shut him off from the free relationship with a variety of men, the give-and-take of frank criticism, the necessities of change and compromise, which he had known on his way up. He began to regard the Model T as immutable. He had standardized it for cheap universal use; very well, he would keep it standardized.

Early in the nineteen-twenties, when the unprecedented sales of the Model T were bolstering Ford's confidence in its merits, a market analyst gained an interview with him. The expert sat before Ford a detailed report on the industry, and pointed to three major conclusions. First, the production of cars would be concentrated among fewer companies. Second, women, their needs and tastes, would become a powerful factor in the demand for automobiles. Third, design and convenience would gain controlling position in the sale of cars. Unimpressed, Ford remarked coldly that the Ford Motor Company was not concerned in any way, and bade his caller good-day.[11] To him it was enough that people were still saying of the Model T: "It takes you there and it brings you back."

As his factory was unable year after year to keep up with the demand for its product, he might well fancy he held a position of absolute security. His methods were regarded as the best in the world; Highland Park had evolved modern mass production, and the Rouge had lifted it to a higher level. The company engineers, production executives, and selling staff, even after the departure of Wills, Knudsen, and Hawkins, were surpassed nowhere. Ford's complex of machines and materials— mines, forests, railroads, glass works, ships, Highland Park, the Rouge, the branch plants—had few if any equals. To be sure, his Model T was more utilitarian than attractive; but then Americans were a utilitarian people. In all matters of machinery did not men fix the canons of demand?—farmers, stockmen, mechanics, store-owners, salesmen? Then, too, Ford knew that other automobile manufacturers shrank from competing with him in his own field. He had probably heard of the remark by Pierre S. du Pont about 1917 after meeting Ford: "I would not step on his foot in the production of a small car."

A significant story is told by William C. Klann of an incident early in the nineteen-twenties. The dealers, as he puts it, "began to yell for changes in the Model T." They were again invited to visit Highland Park and speak out. A majority of them urgently requested adoption of the Bosch ignition system in place of the flywheel magneto. Klann carried this request to Ford.

"You can do that over my dead body," bristled Ford. "That magneto job stays on as long as I'm alive."

Later, Klann asked Edsel: "Don't you think your dad made a mistake?" "Yes," replied Edsel, "he did; but he's the boss, Bill."

It was probably at this meeting that Ford was called in to deliver his views. Some dealers wanted body changes, some engine changes; the group agreed that alterations were imperative. A journalist tells how Ford took the demand. "He came in presently and took a seat by the door, folding his long arms and crossing his long legs in a characteristic attitude. At such times he gives the impression of waiting for the right minute, the right word, or the right idea. In this case, when discussion was about ended, the chairman asked his opinion. 'I think,' said Mr. Ford, rising, 'that the only thing we need worry about is the best way to make more cars.'" He departed. A wet blanket had fallen on the gathering.

The Model T brake bands, which sometimes screamed like banshees and even in their best mood groaned and chattered, were one target of motorists' wrath. If they required changing, the owner at first had to remove part of the transmission assembly to get at them. In 1920 Ford engineers designed a two-piece band as part of a crankcase assembly containing a small door just below the transmission; and this made the bands readily accessible. But no basic alteration in design was made, and they continued to shriek. The Model T brake shoes were also unsatisfactory, for the cotton linings sometimes burned out when the driver went downgrade. Ford dealers were compelled to stock shoes with better linings made by outside manufacturers of parts.[12]

Beyond question, the mechanical feature of the Ford which excited the most irritation was the planetary transmission. As the three-speed selective transmission came into more general use, dealers found the Model T gear-shift one of the principal impediments to sales. They raised an overwhelming chorus for change. But Ford clung to the planetary system like a mother to a favorite deformed child, so that in 1924 an expert called it the feature that had been subject to fewest changes. To be sure, Ford experimented with the transmission—but on a severely limited scale. His attitude toward the planetary component was apparently mercurial. "I'm never going to change that," he would announce one day. The next day he would modify his attitude: "I'm going to perfect that damn thing. We'll have three speeds in there. But I'm not going to change it; I'm not going to the sliding gear transmission." In 1920 the Ford engineers did make minor improvements in the Model T device, but the boss never let them replace it by a standard selective gear-shift. Apparently Ford had a deepseated prejudice against sliding transmissions. In 1910, when he had installed one in an experimental car, the driver crashed the vehicle into a telephone pole. A possibility existed that the sliding transmission was responsible. "Mr. Ford was tickled to death," recalls Galamb. "He was glad it was smashed up, and he never had anything more to do with it [the sliding transmission] until we came to the Model A."[13]

Ford was capable of holding such prejudices in the face of the strongest evidence. In 1914 he and Frank Kulick were bowling along a sandy country road in Michigan. Their Model T suddenly overturned end for end. Ford, tossed into the ditch, was dazed but unhurt. Galamb, who was following in another car, traced the accident to the radius rod, which bent under heavy strain. Galamb designed a new rod that withstood exacting tests in sandbanks. But Ford vetoed it! "He was practically killed with the old rod," says Galamb, "but he still didn't want it changed." [14]

Of course it can be said that with all its faults the Model T was the greatest single model in automobile history. It can also be said that Ford's conservatism was often well grounded. For example, his opposition to hydraulic as distinguished from mechanical brakes was long justifiable. Until after 1924 the hydraulic brake was imperfect, and Ford was correct in saying: "If you had the slightest leak anywhere, you had no brake." Chevrolet did not adopt hydraulic brakes until the mid-thirties. But was his belief in the impregnable position of the Model T and the Ford Motor Company well founded? In theory, he was one of the greatest exponents of change; he continually insisted that a man's success lay in moving, not in arriving. Did he fail to realize how fast and how radical change could be? *

3.

The Ford Motor Company never put any obstacles in the path of competition. Its practises were an open book. Automotive engineers and manufacturers were gladly given tours of Highland Park and the Rouge, Ford imparted his ideas freely to visitors, and the heavily illustrated volume by Arnold and Faurote revealed every detail of machines and methods. In Detroit, such automobile companies as Paige, Maxwell, Hudson, Packard, Dodge, and Saxon, adapting Ford practices, had by 1916 installed conveyor belts or chains, operating in conjunction with overhead monorail carriers. The Maxwell plant that year was building 250 cars daily on a moving track 800 feet long which carried 100 cars at a time. Continuous moving assembly soon appeared at the Reo, Chevrolet, Briscoe, Willys-Overland, and Studebaker works. When the depression of 1920–1921 brought a need for tighter internal economies, lagging manufacturers discovered that they could not afford the old methods. The H. H. Franklin Company, for example, makers of a medium priced car noted for its air-cooled engine, in 1921 installed a belt-and-chain conveyor system at its Syracuse establishment. The movement continued until in the mid-twenties some factories could approach the

---

* Some changes in this period Ford could not resist: a larger radiator, balloon tires, wire wheels, and steering-gear locks, for example. See *Ford News*, September 1, 1923. But the general criticism stands.

efficiency of the Ford plants. An excellent example is offered by the Hudson Company, which built the light six-cylinder Essex, a popular car. So intensive was its use of factory space and machine tools that by 1926 it even boasted of turning out more automobile engines an hour than the Ford company! Expert use of conveyors for materials and finished components reduced stock-piling of parts (that is, inventory) to a minimum. The four final assembly lines at the Hudson plant were producing a car every thirty seconds; and the elapsed time for assembling an automobile was ninety minutes.[15]

As the total production of cars swiftly rose, as models were improved, as more elaborate machine tools were required, and as mass production whittled prices and reduced the margin of profit, small factories continued to die. Unable to stand against the technological resources and economic strength of the big manufacturers, they sold out, merged with others, or sank. In 1923 the New York automobile show had 113 exhibitors; two years later the number had fallen to 51. This was but the acceleration of a tendency evident since early in the century. "The weak and inefficient are going," said a motor executive in 1925. "Larger production and fewer plants are the tendency." Two figures for 1926 are eloquent. The Hudson Company that year completed a new ten-million-dollar plant in which steel bodies for the Essex were produced at the rate of 1500 a day. General Motors announced a $40,000,000 building program, including $10,000,000 for additions to the Chevrolet plant and $5,000,000 for a factory at Flint to make closed bodies. How could the little Davids fight against these Goliaths? Slingshots would no longer do.[16]

And while other companies worked toward Ford practice in mass production, they enlisted engineers, designers, and executives equal or superior to those the Ford Company had trained or hired. The history of one discarded Ford expert, Knudsen, is full of significance. On leaving the Ford Company early in 1921, he served as general manager of a Detroit factory making automobile parts and stove trimmings. Before long he was introduced to the perceptive Alfred P. Sloan, Jr., of General Motors. Although Sloan had no specific opening, he at once offered Knudsen a place on the general staff of the corporation. "How much shall we pay you, Mr. Knudsen?" he asked.

Knudsen might have replied that Ford had paid him $50,000. But what he actually said was: "Anything you like. I am not here to set a figure. I seek an opportunity."

Just a year after leaving Ford, Knudsen joined General Motors at $30,000 annually. He immediately set to work on an inspection of General Motors factories, including the Chevrolet assembly plant at Tarrytown, N.Y., and on a set of recommendations for improvements.[17] Within the month he became vice-president in charge of operations of the Chevrolet division, his salary again $50,000. In that position the Ford Motor Company was soon to hear of his activities.

For the American masses now wanted inexpensive cars in huge volume. Throughout the nineteen-twenties the market for costly cars was fair, that for medium-priced cars was good, and that for cheap automobiles was tremendous. Inevitably, a number of companies took over not only Ford's mass production, but his idea of progressive price cutting in a widening market. From the first years of the industry numerous models had sold for less than $1000; and there was much truth in the observation made by both Wills and Hawkins: "Every car that sells under $1000 is competing with the Ford." Two years later the Oldsmobile with six cylinders was selling below $1000; so was the six-cylinder Essex. Indeed, year after year the price advantage of the Ford over other cars was reduced.

The Model T open touring car in 1920 had sold for $440; its nearest competitor in the low-priced bracket (omitting roadsters and coupes) was the Overland touring car at $895. Thus the price spread after the war between the Ford and his nearest rival was $455, a large sum to countless Americans. In 1921 only three cars seating four and five passengers were offered to buyers at less than $1000; two were Fords, the third an Overland. The Model T touring car was the only automobile of its kind selling for less than $750. By 1926, however, the picture had radically altered. In that year 10 different firms were offering 27 models among four-and five-passenger cars, open and closed, at less than $1000. Of the 27, 11 sold for less than $750, and 3 for less than $500. If we bring roadsters and coupes into consideration, in 1926 the buyer had available 41 models priced at less than $1000.[18]

A sharp trend toward lower prices had set in with the slump of 1921, and the new models for 1922 had brought the era of the cheap car into full bloom. A simple table of price changes for five companies between

1922 and the spring of 1926 eloquently indicates the development of competition for the mass-consumption market:

	1922	*1926*	*Reduction*
Ford Sedan	$645	$545	$100
Overland 4	895	595	300
Chevrolet	875	735	140
Dodge	1785	895	890
Chrysler (Maxwell)	1485	995	490

Still another element in the fast-changing situation 1916–1926 spelled danger to the Model T and the Ford Company: the factor of public taste. The nimble, sturdy little Ford, even after the concessions of 1917–1920 to grace in design, and a further restyling in 1923, stood squarely on its reputation for utility. Nobody ever called the Model T handsome, much less beautiful; nobody ever rhapsodized over its silhouette; nobody ever praised its comfort. It could plow through bogs, surmount hills, skitter along slopes, and take stumps and rocks in its stride. Summer cloudbursts and winter blizzards merely gave it stronger heart. What more could anyone ask? As it turned out, people had begun to ask a great deal more.

Partly because Henry Ford's image of the farmer, mechanic, and shopkeeper had been formed in the pinched eighteen-eighties and eighteen-nineties, partly because he himself knew and cared nothing for art, and partly because he had an ingrained dislike of "conspicuous consumption"—fine clothes, jewelery, great mansions, paintings, race-horses, opera—he was insensible to certain broad tendencies in American life. He did not realize that as farmers, mechanics, and small professional people gained purchasing power, their horizons expanded. They wanted houses, clothing, furniture—and cars—which looked like prosperity and advancement. This was especially true of the wage-earning masses, whose ambitions in the United States have been shaped by middle-class ideals. The first Ford models were distributed in the broad reaches of the middle class. But this part of the population turned to other cars when the Model T ceased to be an outward sign of higher economic status—that is, when *any* car was suggestive of it—and in their wake the wage-earning segment showed the same tendency.

Ford also failed to comprehend two other facts. One was that the automobile naturally passed through the cycle characteristic of most products of the machine age created to meet urgent popular demands and marketed in changing forms. At first the factory-made article is the property of technicians and businessmen who concentrate on efficiency and reliability. Birmingham turned out a mass of cheap, strong, useful wares for the world, and "Brummagem" became a symbol of ugliness. Presently, as utility is assured, aesthetic considerations come into play. The Seth Thomas clock, made at first as mere machinery, garbs itself in ornamented cases. Indeed, as the market grows wider and more sensitive, beauty becomes ever more important. A comparison of early and late models in Wedgwood china, Waltham watches, Grand Rapids furniture, refrigerators, and radio sets shows that in time fashion is likely to be the main arbiter of public demand. The second fact overlooked by Ford is connected with the first. Most Americans are individualists, and however much they applaud the savings effected by standardization, they want enough variety to suit individual tastes. When Ford said, "People can have the Model T in any color—so long as it's black," they laughed—but they still wanted various colors and various styles.

It was these demands of the emergent postwar generation for style, attractiveness, and variety which inspired Will Rogers's jest in 1923: "Ford could be elected President all right. He'd only have to make one speech, 'Voters, if I'm elected I'll change the front.' He has reduced the price $50, and that will change the scenery."

As they asked for more beauty, buyers called for more convenience and comfort. The closed body, which meant an all-year, all-weather car, took the leadership in sales in 1923 from the open-body automobile. If a storm came up or a norther struck, the owner of an old car spent an arduous fifteen minutes adjusting top and side-curtains. Even then, the sagging top and billowing side-flaps failed to shut out the wind and rain. The 1924 season opened with no fewer than fifteen closed models selling for less than $1000 each. And along with the closed car came a demand for better designs, incorporating improvements which before the war had been confined largely to foreign or high-priced domestic cars. Buyers asked for roomier interiors, with better upholstery; a lower slung body; and more rounded lines outside and inside. Progressive manufacturers lowered the floors and running boards, increased the head room for tall men and for women's hats, and in some models provided adjustable seats for greater leg-room. They made the springs longer and more resilient. They made demountable rims a standard feature. Meanwhile, a wide range of mechanical improvements contributed to comfort and utility alike. Improved steering gear and shorter wheelbases made steering and parking easier; improvements in engine power and flexibility reduced the hazards of stalling in traffic.

These stylistic and mechanical improvements, in combination, became as important a stimulus to buying as price reductions. As hotly competing manufacturers made repeated price cuts 1922–1925, the cost of closed models drew closer to the cost of open cars. People began to feel that they were left in the rearward of the fashion unless they had the new model. The roomy sedan was the favorite; it kept the seating capacity of the four- and five-passenger open touring car while offering the shelter, cleanliness, and adaptibility that old designs lacked. The coupe took second place. Many Americans made haste to trade in their cars.

In 1924, when closed models made up 48 per cent of total sales, two thirds of the dealers of the country reported that from a half to the whole of their new car sales were based on such exchanges. Next year, with fresh price reductions, many more motorists traded their open models for one or another of the new closed designs, paying a small sum down. An analysis showed that more than four fifths of all used cars brought in for exchange were of the open type. In cities and towns, the dealers' lots were filled with semi-obsolete open automobiles rusting in sun and shower. Thus the maker of low-priced cars who shunned style improvements would assuredly find himself competing with a flock of his own used vehicles offered at cut-rate prices.[19]

. No other mechanical innovations were so important as four-wheel brakes and balloon tires, two improvements which after 1924 swept mass-produced cars into a new era. An importation from Europe, the four-wheel brake system had first seen American use in the Duesenberg three years earlier. Emerging rapidly from the experimental zone, it was adopted by Buick, Packard, and Rickenbacker in the summer of 1923 for their 1924 models. Other manufacturers hastened to fall into line. As a result, the 1924 season found about twenty-five firms offering four-wheel brakes of either the hydraulic or mechanical type as standard or optional equipment. Ford was not among them. The adoption of the four-wheel brake showed that American motorists wanted a safer way of meeting the risks of heavy city traffic, steep grades, and increasing road speeds. Balloon tires, which though larger had thinner walls than oldstyle tires and needed only about half the air pressure, gave a smoother ride. Ford did accept them for the Model T, but tardily. These advances reflected a growing emphasis on speed and comfort which Ford seemed reluctant to acknowledge.

A popular insistence on speed and power was also responsible for the steady supplanting of four-cylinder engines (like the Ford) by six-cylinder types. Before American entry into the war, four-cylinder makes had exceeded the six-cylinder nearly two to one, and had dominated the cheap car field. But an augury of postwar changes came in 1918, when the Saxon six was advertised at the low price of $935. After the war the trend became pronounced. "The six-cylinder motor equipped cars," reported the *New York Times* at the beginning of the 1922 season, "are in the ascendency, represented by fifty-eight cars." Four-cylinder types numbered only twenty-three. Within a year makers sharply increased the number of sixes sold at a level just above the top price of cheap fours. "Practically every manufacturer of note has a low-priced car which sells from $75 to $250 more than the standard touring car," noted an automotive expert. "This tempts the buyer who wants the closed car with open-car money. He gets it either in a four or six, at about the same price." [20] The margin in cost narrowed as firms dropped their prices from the inflationary levels that carried over from the war until the end of 1921.

Because of the immense Ford output, and the volume production of Chevrolet, Overland, and Dodge, as late as 1923 the low-priced four still accounted for seven tenths of the cars sold. The six, however, was rapidly gaining acceptance. With quicker acceleration, greater power, and less vibration at all speeds, it satisfied the desire for smoother, faster travel; and although its operating cost was higher, many motorists willingly paid the difference.[21] In 1924 the Oldsmobile and Essex were available in six-cylinder models at less than $1000. The extraordinary growth of instalment-payment plans, with liberal credit terms, helped open the six-cylinder market to buyers of modest means; while many people were happy to acquire second-hand sixes from dealers at prices about those of new Fords.

4.

"I guess female emancipation is pretty nearly here—these New Women are going to get the ballot as sure as you're born," a friend observed to Booth Tarkington just after the War. "They're going to do everything the boys do, I expect, and it looks as if it's too late to stop 'em." He had just seen the new generation of women dancing the maxixe "in a way that would have got a Knights of Labor ball closed by the police not so many years ago;" he had seen them drinking cocktails and singing "When good fellows get together." "Then three or four of the girls were smoking on the terrace without caring who saw 'em doing it. Yes, sir, right young girls they were, daughters of friends of mine—smoking and not blinking an eyelash." He had seen young women take to alarmingly short skirts and had deduced one reason for the act: "because girls can't hop in and out of automobiles in long skirts." And he had glimpsed another portent of a new era—"our colored laundress comes to work every Monday morning in her son's automobile."

Another factor which Ford overlooked, in his devotion to an immutable Model T, was the crescent influence of women upon all forms of consumption. Count Hermann Keyserling, declaring that America was a two-caste country in which women formed the superior caste, added that this aristocracy directed the whole social, cultural, and moral tradition. Women had always been more alert than men to changes in fashion, and to fresh currents in commercial and industrial design. From the days of *Godey's Lady's Book*, they had controlled a great part of the expenditure of American households. They correctly prided themselves upon using this expenditure to lift the level of national taste, and to give life more elegance and color. Nor was the power of women confined to large cities and the Eastern seaboard. The Kansas farm-wife, studying fashion magazines and newspaper advertisements, copied the dress and house furnishings of Fifth Avenue and Beacon Street.

If feminine influence on style and design counted in McKinley's time, it became far more potent as the nineteenth century multiplied the numbers and increased the prosperity of the middle class; and more potent still when the New Women who so disturbed Tarkington's friend began to exercise their authority. In the old days the distaff side of the household had said little about the choice of a new carriage or buggy. Men ruled the world of horses. Now women used automobiles as much as men; in cities often more. Women living in apartments or bungalows, cultivating gregarious habits, and working in offices, stores, and factories, learned to drive as they learned to smoke. The prosperous farm woman was constantly in the car. After the war the wives and daughters did much to set marketing trends.

A Ford executive later admitted that personal experience taught him that styling was the prime consideration in many women's minds. Negotiating with a dealer for a used Lincoln car, this executive had limited his questions to mechanical subjects. But when he got home, his wife demanded: "What kind of upholstering has it?" He replied, "I did not pay much attention to that." "Well," she pursued, "what is the color of the paint?" He vaguely responded, "I think it is a sort of blue. I did not pay much attention to that either, except that I know it is not cracked." At this point his wife gave up with a glance of withering scorn. "What I was interested in," the officer said in review, "was an automobile that would run. The other party was interested in looks." [22]

Looks—along with ease and safety of operation, and general convenience. In the "get-a-horse" period motor operation had been a man's job. But during the war, with many men away, women had learned not only to steer a car but to make minor repairs. They had studied the machine and made notes. To them it seemed noisy, bumpy, hard to guide, clumsy to park, and too easily stalled without extensive gear-shifting. No woman, without risk to frock and limb, could crank a car. As they began to help select models, they asked for self-starters. By 1919, to practically all women as to many men, "A Ford without a starter is no longer worth considering." Women, standing beside most cars, found them too high; a height under six feet harmonized best with the average woman's stature. Yet they wanted adequate headroom, even with tall hats. The manufacturers who lowered the car floor and running-board with specially designed frames got women's approval; so did those who made seats adjustable to long or short legs and provided arm rests. To any woman the closed body was an invaluable boon. A million wives and daughters who had been "blown to bits" in open cars, and who rejected dusters, veils, and goggles, would tolerate nothing else. The task of changing gears with heavy hand levers that crunched and ground was particularly distasteful, and feminine requirements had much to do with gear-shift simplification.

Women wanted grace. They wanted something of the same variety that they cherished in dresses and shoes. They liked a quiet note of elegance. Above all, they were pleased by an imaginative use of color. This fact struck Edward S. Jordan, whose cars were early leaders in styling, and made a special appeal, on a medium price level, to women purchasers. In 1918 Jordan brought out his "Sports Marine" model as "essentially a woman's car." He had a prescient comprehension of the role feminine demand was to play, as he showed in a signed advertisement of 1917:

One day, about eighteen months ago, I stood on the corner of Fifth Avenue and 42d Street in New York, and watched the motor cars go by. Nearly every one of them appeared to be in mourning, finished in dark, repelling shades of black and blue—black hoods and blue bodies. Only a few of the high-priced cars appeared in striking shades of fashionable hues. . . .

Then I recalled my experience in selling cars to women. It is true that while men buy cars, women choose them. I recall hundreds of women going through the same process of motor car selection. First, the quick glance at the body—it must be straight as an arrow . . . Next, the expert eye of a woman catching the appeal of a striking color.

A variety of colors became by 1926 the dominant styling impulse in the industry; and the use of quick-drying pyroxylin paints and varnishes, which drastically reduced the time for finishing a car, encouraged the tendency. One paint company in 1926 offered a hundred different colors and shades to automobile manufacturers.[23] Even Ford bowed in 1925 to the inevitable and brought out the Model T with a choice of colors.

Ford's Model T had emphasized utility and almost nothing else. But comparing the automobile of 1928 with that of 1908, an automotive engineer said: "It is like comparing a sleek greyhound with a mid-Victorian pug dog. . . . Our cars should be made fashionable and given style appeal, because it is our most important asset. No one cares about engines; their satisfactory functioning is taken for granted. In fact, we turn in a car with a perfectly good engine and buy a new car because the new one appeals to our style sense, our desires and our developing needs. . . . The automobile is not merely a machine. . . .

Cars produce a form of emotional thrill." To this voice of the new age even Henry Ford could not long turn a sardonic ear.

5.

Up to 1926 the Ford car still held first place in sales. After it came, in order, the Chevrolet, Dodge, Buick, Hudson-Essex, Willys-Overland, Nash, Chrysler, Star (made by William C. Durant) and Studebaker. But great shifts were occurring, which would soon declare themselves. The industry was in the throes of a sales convulsion unprecedented in its history—one that threatened to crowd the Ford Company far down in second place.

Several distinct forces were at work. One was the general concentration of most manufacturers upon a single-chassis car, with a reduction in the number of models. This made for cheaper manufacture and relieved the dealer of the hardship of carrying the complete line of his firm. Naturally the process was most forcibly applied to popular cars. In other words, makers had adopted the Ford principle of a basic unit geared to mass production methods. Their sales effort could now be focussed, with effect, on a smaller number of models.

Moreover, the cheap closed car by 1926 was definitely established in control of the mass market. In the previous year the six-cylinder Essex coach had been reduced to $795, only $100 more than the Chevrolet coach, which in turn was only $200 more than the Ford two-door sedan with balloon tires, and but $150 more than the Ford four-door sedan (also with balloon tires). A wave of price-cutting which swept over the industry in the summer of 1925, with slashes by more than twenty manufacturers in all price classes, was especially felt by closed models. "While many of the price reductions have been $100 or less," noted the *New York Times,* "in some closed models the reductions have been $500 and over." These cuts were keenly felt by the Ford Company.[24]

As a third influence, the prosperity of the nineteen-twenties was crystallizing the determination of many people to keep up with the Joneses. A survey conducted among owners of low-priced cars in 1926 indicated that more than half planned to buy more expensive automobiles the following year. The four-cylinder rivals of the Model T, as well as six-cylinder models at slightly higher cost, had adopted various refinements appealing to popular taste. As a journalist wrote in 1926: "All shades of opinion in the industry agree that the public wants a car with more power, more style, especially style. The four-cylinder, foot-driven Ford is called 'obsolete' by Ford's rivals. The new light sixes, with hand gears and trim bodies, the very embodiment of style, have sold in steadily rising numbers." The rise of instalment buying made it easy to meet the increased expense.[25]

Most remarkable of all the new factors was the way in which one segment of General Motors, Knudsen's Chevrolet Division, had shot up out of the ruck of Ford's competitors.

The Chevrolet Motor Car Company had been incorporated in Michigan in 1911 by that restless empire-planner William C. Durant, had thrived modestly after 1913 with a factory in Flint, and had been the principal lever used by Durant in 1915 to regain the presidency of General Motors. With du Pont support, he rapidly expanded the factory, which in 1916 built more than 128,000 four-cylinder cars, and in the post-war boom (1919) nearly 133,000. But when with the recession he lost control, Vice-President Alfred P. Sloan, Jr., persuaded the reluctant Pierre S. du Pont to become president, and he and Sloan together tackled the job of pruning, strengthening, and centralizing the sprawling Durant companies. The new management, concentrating upon the rehabilitation of a select number of General Motors properties, gave special attention to Chevrolet. That company, after building 144,500 vehicles in 1920 (as compared with 1,074,000 produced by Ford), had dropped production the next year to 75,700, and had chalked up a loss of about $8,700,000. A group of consulting engineers wagged their heads over Chevrolet. The Model T was out-producing the Chevrolet thirteen to one. The engineers concluded that Chevrolet could not sustain competition with other cars and should be liquidated. But Sloan had sufficient vision to perceive that a low-priced Chevrolet, with better engineering and improved sales effort, might effectively invade the mass market, and he convinced du Pont. "Forget the report," du Pont agreed. "We will go ahead and see what we can do." [26]

The reconstruction of the Chevrolet division was part of the larger regeneration of General Motors under intelligent functional direction. Sloan and his associates saw that for an administrative organization so complex, a dictatorship like Durant's (or Henry Ford's) was no longer efficient. "General Motors had become too big to be a one-man show," observes Sloan. "It was already far too complicated. The future required more than an individual's genius." Each component had its own problems. "Dictatorship is the most effective way of administration, provided the dictator knows the complete answer to all questions. But he never does and never will." The Durant regime, with its court favorites, had been feudal and divisive. Now Sloan decided that General Motors would have to be guided by an organization of expert intellects, and he, du Pont, and others labored toward that end.

The immediate problem was to weld Durant's unwieldy, incoherent empire into a well coördinated federation, first determining the facts and then developing plans through the group judgment of the ablest personnel that could be assembled. By 1927, when both General Motors and Ford were among the ten corporations in the country valued at a billion dollars and more, General Motors was pronounced alone among the ten "in that it is set up along the lines of the most modern principles of industrial management." And Sloan, then its president, could be quoted as saying, "I never give orders." The results were summarized that year by Paul Clay of Moody's Investors Service. General Motors, he said, had reorganized its system of buying raw materials, harmonized its factories, reformed its sales methods, improved its advertising, organized a department to study public demand, and developed the greatest automobile research organization in the world. In so doing it had approximately doubled its rate of profit.

Under the new policy of corporate operation, each General Motors division—Buick, Pontiac, Oakland, Chevrolet, and the rest—became a largely self-contained unit, controlled by a general manager responsible for finances, engineering, purchasing, sales, production, and other functions. In effect, the senior executives of General Motors worked as semi-independent heads of entrepreneurial ventures. Thus Sloan, first as vice-president and after 1923 president, solved the problem of unifying the organization without sacrificing flexibility. What emerged was a system resembling a staff-and-line organization. But nothing like the authoritarian pattern of military command was permitted. Instead, the divisional managers retained administrative jurisdiction and responsibility, each for his own operating unit. Each consulted and coöperated with others on manufacture, purchasing, sales, and other activities, but had his own full delegated authority. Sloan's emphasis on consultation pervaded the entire organization.

"He is as different from Mr. Ford as a man could be," wrote R. L. Duffus. "He makes suggestions. He does not give commands. If he cannot persuade his subordinates that a certain policy is wise, that policy does not go through. The same principle applies to them in turn. They must persuade their own associates."

Sloan saw to it that General Motors placed an emphasis on research in engineering, distribution, and other phases of the business that were quite new in the automobile industry. "I determined," he writes, "that my first job would be to concentrate all effort possible on making General Motors cars the very top in eye appeal, in engineering soundness, and in technological progress." He increased the budget of the engineering staff, gave them the most modern equipment, and raised their status in company councils. He himself became chairman of the corporation's technical committee. Other features of the revamped corporate structure under Sloan and du Pont were a centralized budget, an efficient inventory control, and (on the basis of thorough research) a continuous coördination of retail demand and production.[27]

In its emphasis on group policy-making, General Motors was the polar opposite of the Ford Motor Company. Moreover, while Ford accumulated the largest executive scrapheap in the industry, General Motors sought everywhere for talent and kept it. In their initial reshaping of the company, for example, Sloan and du Pont had the aid of Norval A. Hawkins, who early in 1921 joined them at a reputed salary of $150,000 a year. He went about hacking away Durant's encrustations of industrial favoritism, coördinating the various divisions, and eliminating intra-company competition. To end duplicate bidding for the same consumer markets, he suggested a reclassification of General Motors products in separate price and style categories. Among other proposals, he urged returning the Chevrolet to its original status as the low-priced volume car in the General Motors line. He also suggested cost-saving methods and shipping methods, both drawn from his experience with the Ford Company. Hawkins's services to General Motors demonstrate how executives discarded by Ford intensified competition to the disadvantage of the Ford Motor Company.

Meanwhile that other former Ford executive, the stalwart and resourceful Knudsen, was revolutionizing the Chevrolet division. He scrapped all old machine tools, introducing the newest and best. He put the production work in better sequence, introducing an efficient conveyor system. He reorganized and improved inspection, with gauges and indicators, and made accuracy a part of the production routine. With the use of alloy steels, he strengthened the metal in the car. Everywhere he overhauled and modernized the Chevrolet factory, not quite matching the efficiency of Ford at the Rouge, but using *his* Ford experience to come close to that mark. The results were soon evident. The Chevrolet, with its spare stretched cowl and the blue cross on its radiator, was far more attractive in appearance than the Model T. Its 103-inch wheel base, as against the 100-inch Model T, its standard transmission, and its annual new styling made it seem a better bargain. Knudsen was destined to have an eleven-year reign at Chevrolet, and made every year of his leadership count.[28]

From 1924 to 1925 Ford retail sales dropped from 1,870,000 cars to 1,675,000. Meanwhile, in these two years Chevrolet sales advanced from 280,000 to 470,000, Overland sales from 176,000 to 215,000, and Dodge sales from 194,000 to 209,000. The Ford was still far ahead, but the Chevrolet was becoming very dangerous. To alert watchers on the battlements of the Rouge, all the storm signals were now flying.[29]

6.

Belatedly and inadequately, the Ford Motor Company began to respond to the sweeping changes in the automobile market. Edsel and his brother-in-law Ernest Kanzler had a discerning grasp of the new trends in style and convenience. Edsel in particular possessed a keen aesthetic sense. He was more than a patron of the arts; he showed an artistic temperament, and no little artistic talent. In automotive design, he had a free hand in giving excellent advice to the outside body builders who did custom work for the Lincoln car. But in dealing with the Model T, unfortunately, he was consistently thwarted by his father.

After becoming president of the company in 1919, Edsel pressed steadily for changes in design. Joseph Galamb testifies to this. So does Kroll, who writes: "Edsel took more interest in style than his father did. He wanted nice lines on everything. The boss was more interested in making the production easier in order to get out more cars cheaper."[30] More than once Edsel dutifully carried out a design that he disliked. Galamb believes that if he had been able to take more than nominal control of the company, and to implement his ideas without obstruction by Henry Ford, the company would have maintained its leadership. "We would have been on the new model before the Chevrolet could get ahead of us," he asserts.

Certainly Edsel has left various statements which prove his sensitive appreciation of changing style patterns. "Women are a greater influence in the automobile buying field than ever before," he told the *New York Times* early in 1924. "It will be expressed particularly in the closed car sales." In framing advertisements for this year, he admirably summed up the new market conditions. Economy and efficiency were to be stressed—but also other considerations:

An analysis of our sales possibilities indicates that there is a very large field of Ford prospects among the middle classes in which women are usually an important factor. These people are able to pay more for a car and pride, vanity, a desire for something more impressive, etc., enter very strongly into the sale. . . . The object will be to build into the minds of women the impression of Ford cars as a quality product; to imply its social standing and the fact that it answers all a woman's requirements in comparison with any other car; to build about the Ford car an atmosphere of 'Pride of Ownership'; to associate it with other products which are accepted as standard high grade merchandise.[31]

Edsel at last received a belated opportunity to make style changes in 1923, when it was plain that the company must stimulate public demand. For the ensuing season the Model T, in what was called "the English job," was brought out with "cosmetic changes" in better-curved surfaces and smoother lines. The radiator was enlarged and slightly raised, its apron at the bottom was joined to fender aprons, and the hood lines were raised. Dealers at once increased their orders for the new coupe models. For the 1924 season, the company called its closed cars the "Tudor" and "Fordor" sedans—for two-door and four-door models respectively.

All this encouraged Edsel to press forward a project which employees dubbed "the Australian job," a radical alteration of the styling of Model T. It lowered the distance from the top of the body to the ground four and one half inches, thus softening the top-heavy appearance of the car. (A European visitor had told Frank Hadas, a Ford production manager: "You know, we like to sit in our cars, not on them.") Other stylistic alterations made the new design a marked improvement. "It looked all right and everybody fell for it," says Hadas. Unfortunately, Henry Ford looked at it, grimaced his disapproval, and commanded: "Rub it out." Sorensen as usual supported him. Happily, only part of it was 'rubbed out'—for it was clear that Henry Ford's conservative stand was really untenable.[32]

Thus not all the alterations suggested by Edsel perished, while in the ensuing months he was able to add more. In August, 1925, the company announced "the most pronounced changes" in the Model T since it was first built; and they certainly were the greatest refinements adopted since 1919. The body style was changed for most models; all-steel bodies were introduced for both open and closed cars; the chassis was lowered one and a half inches, the radiator was raised, and a redesigned cowl merged with the longer body lines. On closed cars color options, as we have noted, were provided, with matching upholstery. The open runabout and touring cars (which remained black) were each given a door on the driver's side, permitting him to enter without disturbing other passengers. In all models except the Fordor the steering wheel was dropped three inches, the seats were lowered and moved back for greater room, and the fuel tank was placed under the cowl instead of under the front seat. The overall height of the Tudor and the touring car was reduced four and a half inches, and the body was made three and a half longer. "Comfort and Beauty Standardized," proclaimed the *Ford News*.[33]

Although the company cautioned dealers not to use the word new in describing the improved models, for the chassis had not been redesigned, to many people the cars at least seemed a little newer. Some useful mechanical changes were effected at the same time. A wider brake band and larger brake drum afforded better braking, while a lining of asbestos composition for the brake shoes reduced the likelihood of burning them out. The pistons were reduced in weight; an improved crankcase assembly was installed. Prices remained unchanged. At first it seemed that these alterations might actually produce the brisk new demand which the company needed. In October, 1925, the Ford plants broke all production records, completing 204,827 units. For a time that fall they operated at peak capacity on day and night shifts. Then the orders for the Model T began to show flagging strength.[34] A price reduction was tried in the early weeks of 1926, but brought no improvement in sales.

Heroic measures were clearly required. Henry Ford, obstinate, imperious, persisted in his belief that the Model T still had a splendid future. He knew, of course, that it could not last forever; during the early nineteen-twenties he had conducted experiments with a "Model X" engine, to be the basis of an entirely new car. But he still refused, into the beginning of 1926, to perceive the urgent necessity for action. Edsel and Ernest Kanzler felt that they must resort to a desperate expedient. On January 20, 1926, Kanzler (doubtless with Edsel's approval) handed Henry Ford a typed memorandum of six pages describing in realistic terms the predicament of the company, and suggesting certain broad remedies. "I can write certain things that I find it difficult to say to you," ran the paper. "It is one of the handicaps of the power of your personality which you perhaps least of all realize, but most people when with you hesitate to say what they think."

A demand for action had been brought into the open. What would be done with it?

XVI

THE END OF MODEL T

"A BASIC philosophic difference," in the phrase of engineer Laurence Sheldrick, was rending the Ford Motor Company; and the years just before the passing of the Model T "could be called the years of the great debate." Ernest C. Kanzler by his bold memorandum was giving sharp definition to the far-reaching issues of that debate.

Mr. Sheldrick accurately defines the positions taken in the contest by the various company leaders. On one side stood Henry Ford, at the beginning of 1926 still adamant in his refusal to drop the Model T until he had a car of radically new design ready for production. On the other side, with differing degrees of courage, were aligned practically all the important executives but Liebold and W. A. Ryan. Openly, Kanzler and Edsel Ford were against continuing the Model T. "Rockelman was against it, not openly but quite frankly. Sorensen and Martin were against it in a very veiled way." Sheldrick, Galamb, and Farkas, although unhappy with the Model T, were discreetly silent.

Unquestionably Kanzler knew that in handing Henry Ford his shrewd, clear, plain-spoken argument for a new model he was risking his career with the company. It was much to risk. Already second vice-president, from his Highland Park office he dealt authoritatively with production, and touched sales and advertising policy. He showed tokens of becoming a new Couzens, and already Henry Ford had been overheard saying acidly to Sorensen: "That young fellow is getting too big for his breeches." Henry was instinctively jealous of anyone as close to Edsel as Kanzler or Avery, or as enterprising and sure in executive work as Kanzler.[1]

The heart of Kanzler's memorandum lay in three crisp paragraphs. Acknowledging that he was afraid his frank statement might arouse Ford's anger, he wrote:

We have not gone ahead in the last few years, have barely held our own, whereas competition has made great strides. You have always said you either go forward or backwards, you can't stand still.

In the past twelve months the other manufacturers have gained tremendously. Our production and sales in 1925 were less than in 1924.

Our Ford customers, particularly the Two and Four door customers, are going to other manufacturers, and our best dealers are low in morale and not making the money they used to.

Admitting that great hopes might be pinned to Henry's projected "X" car, Kanzler argued that its highly unconventional design could not be perfected for some time to come; that a conventional six-cylinder car was needed at once to hold the market against rising competition; that the company owed an obligation to its 180,000 and more employees; that it would cost only $100,000 to design and develop an experimental motor; and that this step would give the company a safe and reliable product, which it could make more cheaply than the Chevrolet. "We have made over 100 million dollars the last two years each and will probably make 100 million next year"—but an abyss lay ahead. Every officer was restive:

The best evidence that conditions are not right is the fact that with most of the bigger men in the organization there is a growing uneasiness because things are not right—they feel our position weakening and our grip slipping. We are no longer sure when we plan increased facilities that they will be used. The buoyant spirit of confident expansion is lacking. And we know we have been defeated and licked in England. And we are being caught up [with] in the United States. With every additional car our competitors sell they get stronger and we get weaker.

No other high-ranking employee would have dared come to grips with Henry Ford in this manner. Eugene Farkas, for example, knew perfectly well that the Ford car needed a water-pump cooling system in place of the thermo-syphon system daily cursed by many Model T owners. But, he says frankly, "I thought it was much better to keep quiet on that subject," for after buying the Lincoln plant, Ford asked Farkas to design a thermo-syphon for the Lincoln motor! Farkas also knew that the Model T magneto had become hopelessly out of date. But one day in the dynamometer room he heard Ford harshly rebuking an engineer who had spoken on the subject: "I wouldn't put a high tension magneto on if somebody gave me the magneto free and gave me $500 to boot!" After this, relates Farkas, "I don't believe I made any suggestions because I didn't want to be knocked down."

Henry Ford in the summer of 1926 was sixty-three. Edsel, thirty-three that year, had been president of the company since 1919; Kanzler was thirty-four. They were young men of liberal views, progressive temper, and broad outlook. The company manifestly stood at a crossroads in its history. Could Henry have brought himself to retire, or to delegate increasing authority to these younger, better-educated, more flexible juniors, and devoted his energies to his many avocations, the future of the corporation and Henry Ford himself would have been far happier. Unfortunately, retirement was not in his nature.

Kanzler, in his memorandum, had written his own dismissal. Henry Ford made no known reply. But thereafter, when the executives met in the private dining room for lunch, he treated the young man with studied rudeness. For the most part, to Edsel's obvious pain, he ignored Kanzler; sometimes he cut him off abruptly in a speech, sometimes even ridiculed him. On July 26, 1926, precisely six months after he wrote the memorandum, Kanzler left the company.[2]

2.

We must do justice to Ford's point of view. Self-assurance, reluctance to face unpleasant facts, dislike of expert advice, and want of well-organized engineering and styling departments, were in great part responsible for his refusal to turn to a new model in time; but he had some defensible motives.

It was only natural that, taking a legitimate pride in his famous creation, a car which had changed the face of America and made him the greatest industrial pathfinder of his time, he should be reluctant to cast it on the scrapheap. He had put into it so much of his personality that it seemed almost an *alter ego*. As a believer in change, a preacher of incessant growth, effort, and adaptation, he had always recognized that ultimately even the Model T would be superseded. But he wished to bring out another model only when he could produce one as revolutionary in character; thus he would retain his position as a great innovator, not sink to the level of an imitator. Actually, he had begun thinking of a successor to the Model T in 1920, when he assigned some engineers to the development of the first of several X-engines (that is, engines whose eight or twelve cylinders would be arranged on an X pattern) with which he experimented. "It was definitely Mr. Ford's idea to have the X-type car replace the Model T," asserts Farkas.[3]

But for his stubborn immobility Ford had still another reason; his conviction that utility, and utility alone, was the foundation of sound automotive production. His cars were service-machines. He had no tolerance, any more than the engineers whom Thorstein Veblen praised in contrast to price manipulators, for mere frills; no patience with "conspicuous consumption." The idea that a car of 1923 should be thrown aside just because it did not look like a car of 1925 outraged him. In *My Life and Work* he emphatically condemned the new styling trends:

> It is considered good manufacturing practise, and not bad ethics, occasionally to change designs so that old models will become obsolete and new ones will have to be bought either because repair parts for the old cannot be had, or because the new model offers a new sales argument which can be used to persuade a customer to scrap what he has and buy something new. We have been told that this is good business, and that the object of business ought to be to get people to buy frequently, and that it is bad business to try to make anything that will last forever, because when once a man is sold he will not buy again.
>
> Our principle of business is precisely to the contrary. We cannot conceive how to serve the customer unless we make him something that, as far as we can provide, will last forever. . . . It does not please us to have a buyer's car wear out or become obsolete. We want the man who buys one of our products never to have to buy another. We never make an improvement that renders any previous model obsolete.

A great part of the rural population continued to think highly of the Model T. Of the farmers, stockmen, country doctors, and rural tradesmen who had been first to welcome the car, many had good reasons for clinging to it. The agrarian depression of the nineteen-twenties made every dollar count; road conditions in Western and Southern farming districts improved slowly; and the ordinary farmer cared little for advanced styling. A Ford dealer in rural Georgia wrote in 1927: "The greater part of our business comes from the rural districts where they are unfortunate in not having hard surface or paved roads. . . . There are thousands of people who are rather set and would be satisfied with nothing other than this Ford." The same view was expressed by a dealer of Iron Mountain, Michigan, who sent Ford a reminder that up to the spring of 1927 the Model T had accounted for about one-third of the total sales of the industry.

The Traffic is Getting a Little Impatient. (Des Moines *Register*, Sept. 30, 1927)

Rural areas would still take the greater part of the production, he declared: "I believe these buyers will continue to buy the Model T if you will make it." [4]

Thus while the Model T might be dying, it died hard. Even as city people spoke of the growing obsolescence of the Lizzie, tens of thousands who had difficult travel in prospect annually bought, used, and extolled the familiar car. When the English novelist Stella Benson, newly married, set out in the winter of 1924–1925 to cross the continent, a 4600-mile trip which bad roads made risky, her friends unanimously advised her: "Buy a Ford." She found Stephanie (most Model T's bore names) dependable and lovable. "Her voice is like that of the nightjar in midsummer; her profile is Grecian in its exquisite simplicity." Though her "knob-psychology" was at first difficult to master, she soon proved fool-proof. On goods roads she passed most cars, and on very bad ones all. She was in her full glory when she struck the mucilaginous ruts of a gumbo lane. "They are two feet deep or more, yet a hardy Ford can flounder along them at a spanking three miles an hour." Like all Model T's, Stephanie provided comedy as well as utility:

She had a hysterical trick of stopping dead with a horrifying coughing noise on the gangplanks of ferries at an angle of forty-five degrees. This she did in order to make her drivers appear fools in the eyes of ferrymen. We became familiar with the meaning silence of ferrymen as Stephanie settled down—a sheer derelict—upon their gangplanks. After an awkward silence the ferryman usually said, "Say, yu hevn't bin driving a Ford very long, I lay, hev yu?"

We blushed deeply and said, "I guess there must be something wrong with a sparkplug or what not."

The ferryman would then change his gum into the other cheek and get into the driver's seat of Stephanie, who at once, with a guttural roar of malicious amusement, slid faultlessly into her allotted place. [5]

The major part of the population, however, was changing its tastes. The restyled Model T of August, 1925, gave a temporary impetus to buying, but the impulse soon flagged. Some fresh spur was needed. One of Henry Ford's indirect answers to the Kanzler memorandum was therefore a fresh set of decisive price reductions, effective February 11, 1926, on all the closed models—for it was these which bore the brunt of Chevrolet competition. The Fordor sedan dropped $95 to a new price of $565; the Tudor sedan dropped $60 to a new price of $520; and the coupe came down $20 to a new price of $500. At the same time, prices were increased slightly on the less competitive open models. This was a confession that the company was feeling the pinch of market competition. But despite new features and lower prices, the decline of Ford sales soon reappeared. The flagging athlete was all the worse for his stimulants.

"It was the first time in the history of the company that price recessions, no matter how small, had failed to give a sharp impetus to demand," wrote one expert observer. During March, 1926, the Ford company manufactured only about 34 per cent of the industry's production; and Ford executives, remembering that not since 1918 had their share of the national volume in any year fallen below 40 per cent, found this figure highly disturbing.

Still Ford's faith in the efficacy of his formula appeared unshaken, and in June, 1926, he tried again. Cutting prices on the entire Model T line of cars, he brought all of them except the Fordor sedan below $500. The Ford runabout was now listed at $360, the touring car at $380, the coupe at $485, and the Tudor sedan at $495. At the same time he offered the electric self-starter, demountable rims, and balloon tires, previously optional, as standard equipment on the passenger models. Later in the year the sedans were given wire wheels without extra cost. Ford was striving hard, almost desperately, to move his dealers' stocks into the hands of buyers.[6]

But it was all in vain; the decline in sales continued. In 1926 General Motors sold almost half again as many units as in 1925, the Chevrolet accounting for most of the increase (its total mounted from 470,000 to 730,000, this despite a rise in price from $510 to $525). Ford's competitors restricted him to one third of the market, and threatened to reduce him in the coming year to a quarter or less; for the fall in sales of the Model T which began that spring became a precipitate drop by Thanksgiving and Christmas. Just why had the old formula lost its magic?

Henry Ford's answer was that it had not; that the failure lay not in the car or the formula, but in the defeatist attitude of those who handled it, particularly the dealers. In May, 1926, he and Gaston Plantiff made a tour of the New England agencies. They found that about three-quarters of the service work on the Model T was being done outside establishments authorized by the company, and Ford at once concluded that dealers who were losing money had only their own indolence to blame. The condition of many showrooms also disturbed him. When he unexpectedly visited Palmer, Massachusetts, the roadster on the floor was in deplorable shape. "How we can sell cars in that condition, God knows," exclaimed Plantiff later. In Worcester the dealer's display was feeble. "Mr. Ford was wild," reported Plantiff.[7]

Just after this tour Ford sat with nine men, Ryan, Martin, Sorensen, and six district supervisors, in earnest conference in the Dearborn Engineering Laboratory. The sessions continued for several days, Ford coming and going and making pithy pronouncements on general policy. The falling sales figures, he said, proved just one fact: the company had departed from its fundamental principles and lost its original verve. He demanded a return to the lost Sinai. From his lips the chiefs of the sales organization caught a shibboleth which became a steady refrain: "Most of your trouble at the present time is a question of your mental attitude."[8]

3.

But why the mental attitude?—for that was the real question. The Ford company had no such carefully-planned engineering department and no such research facilities as those which Alfred P. Sloan, Jr., had given General Motors. Of the great recent improvements in cars it had produced none. An electric vaporizer in the carburetor (1919) was a contribution from the Franklin. The use of hydraulic brakes and the fitting of four-wheel brakes on stock cars (1921) was credited to the Duesenberg, a leader also in fine body design. It was the Wills-Sainte Claire which first used molybdenum steel in construction (1921). Other companies led the Ford in introducing balloon tires, high-pressure chassis lubrication (Alemite), and lacquer finish for bodies. Packard brought in the hypoid gear drive in 1926, and that same year Stutz introduced the use of safety glass in body construction. Henry Ford regarded the Model T (to a great extent correctly) as a marvel of utility; yet by 1926 other cars not much more expensive were so much better equipped with improved devices that they were really more useful.

The Chevrolet in 1924 issued a handbill advertising its superiorities over "our nearest competitor." It boasted a water-pump cooling system; the Ford still had a thermo-syphon system, and its radiator still boiled under any engine-strain. The Chevrolet had an oil-gauge on the dash and an Alemite lubricating system; the Ford was still lubricated by a primitive "splash system." The Chevrolet's Remy ignition system operated accurately; the Ford still had the old device of four spark coils and a "timer" which constantly needed attention. The Chevrolet had its gasoline tank in the rear, which was both safer and more convenient; the Ford gasoline tank was still in front. The Chevrolet had four springs, the Model T two. The Chevrolet had a foot accelerator, the Ford a hand accelerator. The steering system on the Chevrolet was superior. Even those most attached to the Model T admitted that it needed constant care; that its sparkplugs had to be cleaned every two hundred miles, that the greasy transmission bands required endless adjustment, and that the "vibrator" on the coils had to be checked. Most people now grew irritable over such jobs. They did not enjoy the carbon-knocks uphill and the connecting-rod chatter downhill.[9]

A considerable industry had been built on devices for bettering the Model T. Sears, Roebuck, for example, sold a carburetor which helped the car start in cold weather, and gave it better mileage. Various devices kept four cylinders going when the Model T wished to run on three. As an ignition lock was not included on Fords, insurance rates were higher; and outsiders sold a lock for from $9 to $15. The cost of these additions brought Ford prices up nearer to the competitors' levels.

Most objectionable of all, to countless buyers who weighed the Ford against the Overland, Chevrolet, Essex, or Dodge, was the now-antiquated planetary transmission. Urban customers in particular wished a standard three-speed selective transmission. They did not want to keep a foot on a pedal for miles to hold the car in low gear. Even patient farmers were heard to remark scornfully that the planetary transmission was made of tin cans. And as roads improved, customers also asked for a larger car, faster, smoother, and better cushioned by springs. The Detroit branch manager sadly noted as 1926 ended that automobile-buyers everywhere used so nearly the same terms that it might be wondered whether they had not held a convention to discuss the situation. Price did not bother them. Raise charges if you like, they said, but "put on a speedometer, change your transmission, give us more speed, easier riding." People asked for a car which would take them to Flint and back without leaving them nervously exhausted. They denounced the intense vibration of the Ford; and when the manager pointed out that the Model T would run faster than the law allowed, they replied; "That is a joke!" [10]

A citizen of Canton, Ohio, who professed to be a champion of Ford cars, wrote Henry Ford that he would never buy another until a standard gear shift replaced the planetary transmission. A dealer in Peru, New York, was still more outspoken on the subject, declaring that a self-starter on the Model T counted for nothing in the absence of a throwout clutch. "I have a number of prospects that say they never will drive another Ford in the winter, one of the best mechanics in this section dropped dead last week from cranking a Ford Car with a starter on it, and I have a weak heart and when my car won't go I have to get it towed to start it." It would be possible to multiply indefinitely quotations of this sort from the mail addressed to Henry Ford or the Company. Even with its admonitions, much of it was friendly. A resident of Minneapolis, for example, who complained that the Model T with its 25 to 30 miles an hour was too slow for the new paved highways, and that it was excessively noisy, especially in low gear, added: "This is not a kick. . . . It is just that I have been a constant Ford booster, and hate to see evidence of waning popularity."

Most of those who desired a larger, faster, smoother-riding car of course demanded a six-cylinder engine. Some shared the view of the New York industrialist who frankly told Ford that the decline of the Model T was attributable to the desire to get into "another class." Others simply wanted more comfort; for example, a Chicago woman who confessed that she was of "the long, lean type," and that when she took a long drive in a Model T over a rough road "my bones will not talk agreeably to one another." Ford was even advised to acquire the Hudson-Essex line of six-cylinder cars and bring them out under his own name.

But quite as important as the growing volume of complaints upon engineering was the chorus of lamentations, ever louder and more plaintive, respecting design. With the roots of this dissatisfaction we have already dealt. A correspondent in Ithaca, N.Y., noting that the Model T appealed to the purse but not the eye, counselled Ford to commission some eminent architects (he suggested McKim, Mead & White, or Carrère & Hastings) to "clothe that machine with an exterior that shall be at once beautiful and simple in its form and lines." This would give it prized distinction. With equal shrewdness, a New Yorker pointed out that the Ford car had simply not kept up with the rising standard of living. Amid the general prosperity, he wrote, even the carpenter and plumber "wants a car which looks and handles a little more like his really rich neighbor's." [11]

These demands for better styling had a deeper significance than many people at first grasped. They pointed to a revolution not only in taste but in the conditions of automobile manufacturing; they marked the full inauguration of the annual style change, with all that it implied.

The exploitation of fashion, and the consequent rapid "dating" of older cars, was not deliberately adopted by manufacturers to speed the turnover of each year's new crop. But it was quickly accepted by them, and had that effect. Style touched the automobile as it touched women's gowns, and hats. As this condition made headway, the used-car market swelled in numbers and importance, and the pace of scrapping increased. "Obsolescence in style is an important factor in value to first owners at least, and induces early sale by first owners," declared a survey emanating in 1926 from the School of Business Administration of the University of Michigan. "It thus affects the elimination rate indirectly by so increasing the number of cars on the market that the value of all used cars is depressed. This depression . . . pushes the value of some of them at once, and of all of them more quickly, below the level of their value as junk."

The systematic alteration of styles from year to year can be attacked as socially wasteful and defended as socially useful, the discussion being pointless without exhaustive definitions of "waste" and "use." But for better or worse, the new system had come to stay. The Ford suffered heavily from it. Since no notable style changes had been made in the Model T from 1916 to 1925, owners had little incentive to trade in old automobiles for new. From its birth, the Model T had enjoyed an average road life substantially longer than that of other motor cars as a group. According to a study based on a careful sampling and analysis of registrations in 1923–1924, the Ford enjoyed an average life of eight years as against six and one-third years for all other makes.[12] Contributing to this longevity were the low cost of repairs and replacement parts for the Model T, and the large number of Ford service stations. The delight (not unmingled with exasperation) which many early drivers found in tinkering with their Fords was all the keener because it was good economy. What in a more complicated car seemed an irremediable breakdown was, in the Ford, simply a challenge to the amateur mechanic, and many a Model T toiled through its last years on a frugal stipend of baling-wire. The fact that its road to the automobile graveyard was so protracted retarded the rate at which the market could absorb new Fords.

Americans in the nineteen-twenties were consuming more goods than ever before; and the power of obsolescence in speeding the sale of consumer products, as Paul M. Mazur pointed out in his volume on *American Prosperity: Its Causes and Consequences* (1928), had become a vital ingredient in our precarious prosperity. Although this promotion of obsolescence violated every canon of Samuel Smiles frugality, although it outraged oldfashioned economists as much as Keynesian principles soon afterward outraged oldfashioned financiers, it now emerged as the dynamo of an expanding business world. The idea of obsolescence was carried home to Americans by advertisements which grew more and more strident in their announcement of "new," "revolutionary," and "epochal" changes in goods—washing-machines, vacuum cleaners, radios, refrigerators, furniture, lamps, stoves—that in half the instances had merely been restyled without essential alteration. Industry and business rapidly institutionalized the new factor. As Mazur wrote, "Wear alone made replacement too slow for the needs of American industry. . . . Obsolescence was made supreme."

And, as he added, the new formula specially applied to automobiles. What he wrote in Calvin Coolidge's last presidential year was to be true again in the 1950s.

Each year the new crop of automobile offerings casts into obsolescence the used and unused models of the previous year. The last year's model that is mechanically perfect and has never turned a wheel all of a sudden loses twenty to thirty per cent of its sales value. It has become undesirable because the consumer market is open only to this year's latest designs. . . . The greater visibility of the automobile brings into play the added impetus of rivalry with neighbors and friends. The neighbors' ready recognition of new as distinguished from old models adds greatly to the factor of obsolescence of the automobile.

Long before, the sculptor Horatio Greenough had preached the doctrine that functionalism can and must marry art; that a building, a bridge, a ship, a machine, should be designed primarily to fulfill its function, and in that design might well meet every aesthetic test. The clipper ships of Donald McKay, the bridges built by Eads and Roebling, the early skyscrapers of Root and Sullivan, with many an article of humbler usefulness, had proved him right. Streamlining had appeared in America in some railway cars in the eighteen-nineties, and was being slowly extended to a variety of products. The ungainly Model T, all functionalism, had not met Greenough's demands, and was now unable to breast the tides of fashion.

To Henry Ford, the consumer seemed mistaken—or misled. But to most motorists, the Model T exemplified an unwillingness to meet legitimate new tastes. To that extent, it went against the grain of the national consciousness. "We moved entirely too late," recalled a Ford executive years later. "The Model T lasted two years longer than it should have." [13]

4.

As complaints poured in, as sales dropped, and as evidence grew of the real superiority of rival cars in both engineering and design, the morale of Ford executives and Ford dealers naturally suffered. They felt that they were the victims of Henry Ford's inflexibility, for even as the end of the year in 1926 brought statistical proof of the disastrous situation, he stood firm.

"We have no intention of introducing a 'six'," he said that December. "We made 'sixes' twenty years ago. The Ford car is a tried and proved product that requires no tinkering. It has met all the conditions of transportation the world over. . . . Changes in style from time to time are merely evolution. . . . But we do not intend to make a 'six', an 'eight', or anything else outside of our regular products. It is true that we have experiments with such cars, as we have experiments with many things. They keep our engineers busy—prevent them from tinkering too much with the Ford car."

Because Ford dealers were suffering more heavily every season, they were now loudly voicing their discontent and apprehension. They had many grounds for resentment. As previously noted, city agents found it difficult to sell tractors; nearly all disliked peddling Ford fertilizer. Another irritant was the abolition, already noted, of closed territories in which each representative enjoyed the sole right to sell Ford cars. The effect of this sweeping change, by which any dealer could invade the territory nearest any other, had been softened by the general prosperity of the years following 1921. But when Model T sales began to fall, Ryan intensified the "crossroads policy" of multiplying dealerships, on the theory that more intensive sales effort would expand the volume of Ford business. This was in harmony with Henry Ford's view that nothing was wrong with the Model T that better salesmanship would not cure. The policy took no account, however, of the interests of the established dealer: his original investment, his bank loans, his expenditures for improvements, and his losses from Chevrolet competition. B. C. Forbes had much warrant for his statement in 1927: "Automobile men declare that no other manufacturer would dare act towards his dealers as Ford has acted." [14]

Within three years, 1923–1926, the company added 1300 dealers to its ranks without making a proportionate increase in production, raising the total from 8500 to 9800. Ryan's "crossroads policy" was specially resented by dealers who felt that the fruits of their long work for the Ford cars were being garnered by new agents who sometimes set up shop at their very doorsteps. For example, the Jennings Sales Company of Springfield, Illinois, had held a Ford franchise for many years; it had spent large sums in advertising; in 1921, at the company's request, it had built a three-story establishment at a cost of $200,000. Two years later the Ford Company gave a sales contract to a second dealer, who opened quarters only three blocks away. In the Colorado-Nebraska district, only six dealers had been added in the five years beginning 1919. But in 1924–1925, as Chevrolet sales began to gain, Ryan added thirty. Indeed, his general policy, as branch managers warned him that Model T sales would continue to fall, was to pepper the map with additional agencies.

At the same time, dealers who showed antagonism to company policies or who were accused of lacking enterprise were dropped. We can only guess at the number who by one means or another were eliminated; but unquestionably many who failed to overcome "sales resistance" or who criticized Ryan's course lost their contracts. Particularly hard hit were the dealers in urban areas where motorists demanded better-styled cars. In some instances the net profit of agents in cities was cut in half even though their total sales volume remained almost stationary—an indication that they were allowing huge discounts on used cars. Long-established dealers, like Clyde L. Herring of Des Moines, later governor of Iowa and Senator, gave up their agencies. "Our situation which you understand," Herring telegraphed Edsel Ford early in 1926, "will not permit continuing. Actual loss this year greater than last." [15]

That Ryan's policies should create bitter feeling against the company was only natural. A typical illustration is furnished by George B. Carter of Petersburg, Virginia. Anticipating a bright future, Carter had at great expense erected a building and purchased equipment. He was shocked when the principal roadman of the Ford branch in Washington, D.C., told him bluntly: "I am going to build a wall [of dealerships] around Petersburg." After several Ford agencies were established in the area, the disconsolate Carter wrote Ryan in January, 1926: "We are selling out to the other dealer here to try to avoid bankruptcy. God only knows what we are going to do with this big building we have built to house the business, as they are not able to rent or buy it." The local banks, said Carter, were no longer willing to lend money to Ford dealers, and one bank president had told him that "to put another dealer here was the rottenest thing he had ever heard of." Yet Carter had been signally loyal to the company. "It will probably interest you to know that at the time Mr. Ford was hard pressed for money we put in new Ford cars all the money we had. We then went to the bank and borrowed to the limit of our credit, storing the cars until such time as they could be sold." [16]

One important cause of discontent in both rural and urban districts was Ford's policy of reducing prices on delivered cars, trucks, tractors, and parts without prior notification to the dealer, and without compensating him for his consequent losses. The reduction in June, 1926, elicited from eight New Orleans dealers a telegram defining an attitude doubtless shared by thousands of others. As "old and loyal Ford dealers," they declared themselves distressed and disappointed. They could foresee little or no increase in volume to offset the loss in revenue, "and the grave injustice of making us stand the loss on stock in hand adds to our apprehension for the future." They had made no money during the past year, and they needed "a better and more complete line," with larger discounts, to meet the determined competition ahead. "We appeal to you for some assurance of early relief that will safeguard our investments, allay the fears of our financial connections, and restore our business to a profitable basis."

As Henry Ford took the view that the laziness and inertia of dealers constituted a main root of the company's difficulties, Ryan and his associates naturally resorted to bullying methods. One desperate California dealer wrote Mrs. Henry Ford that the slightest breach of policy provoked a vindictive retaliation. "The roadmen come into a dealer's place and cuss him out, give the dealer a lot of abuse and insults, and if the dealer goes to defend himself they threaten to cancel his contract and penalize him by not giving him cars for a certain length of time." He added that the trouble between the company and its dealers was notorious in the trade. An agent in Terre Haute who believed he spoke for a large majority of Ford dealers similarly situated wrote with equal bluntness to Edsel. It was not true, he declared, that dealers owed their losses to their own inactivity and incompetence; the heavy mortality roll of Ford agencies in 1925–1926 proved that even the best men could not survive indefinitely under existing conditions. The branch managers, he continued, knew the true state of affairs, but lacked the moral courage to make frank reports.[17]

It was undoubtedly true that in this company crisis the Ryan regime, striving to please Henry Ford, used the branch organization to suppress criticism. A California agent recalls: "Every dealer was in fear of that dictatorial setup. The fear of every dealer was that he might have said the wrong thing. . . . and that his contract might be cancelled. He did not know at any time where he stood. There was no basis of security." Suggestions that the Model T should be improved or supplanted stirred the branch managers to waspish accusations of disloyalty. Henry Ford probably never saw the crowding complaints that reached the home office in 1926. These communications from dealers came, as a rule, to the desk of either Ryan or Liebold—and they got no further.

In 1926, when the average gross volume of business done by Ford dealers fell to $72,720, some $8000 less than the previous year, it was asserted that about seven dealers out of ten were losing money. One former agent who, heading a protest movement, circularized dealers throughout the country, listed the familiar hardships: the repeated price-reductions without any protection for the dealer; the pressures of the Chevrolet and the second-hand market; the low discount rate; the failure of gross sales to keep pace with the cost of doing business. Only radical reforms, he believed—a 25 per cent commission on all cars and trucks, an increased sliding scale for larger volume, and reimbursement for price reductions—could save the dealers. One agent put his losses through Ford's price-reductions at $25,000 to $30,000. Another thought that few dealers were making a profit, and that three-quarters of them were discontented.[18]

The best Ford dealers, wrote the last-mentioned man, are going over to General Motors—and this statement contained much truth. Edsel Ford later estimated that the average turnover in dealerships was about ten per cent a year. In 1925–1926, however, it was much higher, and most of the cancellations resulted from request, or from forced sale. Many of those who could not meet the competition of the Chevrolet, Star, Whippet, or other low-priced cars, deserted to agencies selling them, and the exodus swelled with each passing month. Ford saw some of his most experienced dealers go over to his rivals. When a highly-valued agent in Buffalo announced that he was utterly discouraged and was taking on the Chevrolet line, Plantiff begged him to remain; but he was determined to rid himself of the dead weight of the Model T. The LaPorte-Heinekamp Motor Company in Baltimore cancelled its contract in the spring of 1927, and took the agency for Durant's Star. The firm, which was large and enterprising, explained that it could no longer withstand the public demand for a modern automobile of the gear-shift type. So the story went. We have no way of learning the precise number of such deserters, but the high turnover of the Ford dealers in 1926 indicates that it was large.[19] *

The onslaught against the Ford agencies extended even to their experienced salesmen, who were lured away by fat offers. In Texas, competitive dealers raided Ford offices and employed their best men, as a district supervisor reported to Edsel Ford, at salaries far in excess of what they had been getting. On the Pacific Coast the most effective salesmen developed by the Ford organization were seized upon by rival dealers, notably those in the Chevrolet camp. It would be a mistake to suppose that General Motors made its inroads primarily by winning over Ford agents, or by superior skill in sales; the important factors were its superior engines and styling. Nevertheless, by 1926

---

* In 21 months up to October, 1926, dealer changes reached 27 per cent in San Francisco and Portland, 34 per cent in Seattle, and 45 per cent in Salt Lake City. The vice-president in charge of sales for the Oakland Company (making Oaklands and Pontiacs for General Motors) sent form letters to Ford agents throughout the country inviting them to apply for "the Oakland-Pontiac Double-Profit Franchise" (W. R. Tracy, March 21, 1927, Acc. 285 Box 637).

Ford's field representatives were admitting that in not a few instances the drop in Model T distribution could be attributed to the shrewd marketing tactics and careful service of Chevrolet agencies.

Even Plantiff, who as Eastern District Manager had always sounded a booming note of confidence, became apprehensive when he learned late in 1926 that General Motors was devising even more intensive efforts. He told Ryan that Chevrolet had scheduled a production of a million cars in the coming year, "backed up with a ten million dollar advertising program." Moreover, he had ascertained that the sales program would be concentrated in sections where Ford cars had maintained their strength, and especially where one Ford and one Chevrolet dealer competed.[20]

It is not strange that morale steadily declined among the dealers. For Henry Ford to argue that the trouble was "psychological" indicated a curious inattention to the sources of the psychology. Efforts to whip men up to the mark by revivalistic methods—holding meetings of dealers and arranging inspirational talks—came to nothing. Nor was anything accomplished by measures of retrenchment which Ford, in characteristic fashion, applied during the summer of 1926 to the branch sales organizations. At the San Francisco branch, for example, the June slash removed 41 per cent of these employees; in Seattle 25 employees were discharged in a three-week period. Such cuts in personnel simply added to irritation and uneasiness. To permit of a reduction in branch clerical forces, the company ordered the wholesale elimination of record-keeping forms. This undoubtedly reflected Ford's aversion to "paper work." In Dallas 147 records forms were eliminated; in Atlanta, 237 forms.[21]

These were ineffectual, and perhaps injurious, stopgap measures. They did not strike at the root of the problem: the paralysis of engineering and the stagnation of design.

5.

But Ford, swearing that he would ne'er consent—finally consented. For one reason, his hopes for the X-engine completely collapsed; for another, not even his stubborn ear-stopping could shut out the rising clamor of derision and lamentation over the company's adherence to an obsolete model.

The X-engine project had been assigned, after the departure of an earlier engineer named Allan Horton in 1924, to Eugene J. Farkas. He and a little group detailed to him began work in the "fireplace room" of the old Dearborn tractor plant that year. At the same time that they tried to push forward the eight-cylinder X-engine, they were allowed to give some labor to a project for a six-cylinder engine, both on the in-line and V models. Henry Ford permitted this, apparently, as a slight concession to Edsel and Kanzler. "But he would only go so far," recalls Sheldrick, "and then something would happen to throw cold water on it, or wipe it out of the plans entirely." The six-cylinder engines died a-borning in the stage of blackboard sketches. It was the great dream of the X-eight, four cylinders facing downward, four upward on the X-figure, which occupied the experimenters.

A dream, or little better, the X-car remained. Farkas and his aides completed an X-eight engine in April, 1925. The motor had battery ignition, a single-unit starter and generator, and pistons of 3⅜ inch bore and 4 inch stroke. It had steel pistons, roller main bearings, a visible oil-level indicator, and a supercharger built into the flywheel. It was equipped with a three-speed planetary transmission. While it behaved with fair efficiency in brake tests, it was too heavy for the Model T chassis. The engineers bought an Oldsmobile, ripped out the motor, and installed the X-engine. "We drove that around quite a bit," Farkas recalls. But it failed to impress him. As the engineers had warned Ford, the lower sparkplugs picked up so much moisture and dirt from the road that frequent changes were imperative.[22]

Although operating tests convinced Ford that the engine was unsuited to the kind of light automobile that he desired, he ordered blueprints and layouts for other X-eight engines, and work proceeded into 1926. "There were so many of these X-eight engines under way at the same time," recalls Sheldrick, "that everyone was mystified." All the technicians viewed the project with skepticism, and some with sharp disapproval. Farkas reached the conclusion that successful adaptation of the engine would require years of research. Edsel Ford, like Kanzler, thought the X-eight too radical a departure which, even if efficient, would find public hostility almost insuperable. By the end of 1926 Ford, realizing that he had postponed too long the design of a new model, finally ordered experiments with the X-engine stopped. Six years of intermittent labor had come to nothing.

While Henry Ford thus dallied with the dream of a revolutionary engine, and the Chevrolet inexorably gained upon the Model T, he could not avoid hearing voices which echoed what Kanzler had written. At Edsel's conversations with him we can only guess, but Edsel was too sensitive to the company's interests not to speak up. Opinion on the effectiveness of Edsel's role in the great debate varies. Joseph Galamb says: "Edsel would talk about changing the model, but never in front of his father." Sheldrick differs, saying of Edsel: "He tried, in his mild way, to present the case to his father and argue in favor of the things the public wanted. His father would. . . . at least politely listen, but I don't think he ever went along with him at all." Sorensen goes further still: "Edsel had quite an argument with Henry Ford lasting a long time, but he finally forced his father to give up the Model T. That was Edsel's victory." In this matter Sorensen (who remained a mere me-too with Henry Ford) is a better witness than the other men. Edsel could use tactfully all the arguments Kanzler had marshalled. He could refer to such documents as a report which S. A. Stellwagen, a district sales supervisor, had sent him just after a meeting of two hundred dealers and salesmen in Denver on January 26, 1926; a report which declared that a new model was imperative, for "a winner must always lead." [23]

Other voices than Edsel's certainly found their way to Henry Ford. He may have heard from Ryan about Gaston Plantiff's alarmed letter of December 2, 1926, upon General Motor's plans for a million Chevrolets the coming year. For once shaken out of his chronic optimism, Plantiff sent a copy of this letter to Sorensen, with a news clipping which declared that Ford was losing ground in the industry. Sorensen, in reply, stated: "Every day this same sort of information comes in here by the bushel." Henry Ford must have seen some of it; he must have read a few of the hundreds of letters addressed to him berating the Model T and demanding a new car. He undoubtedly read articles in trade journals commenting on the heavy decline in his share of the market. If he came up suddenly on any little group of executives in the plant, he might have heard speeches that would make his ears tingle. Above all, he saw the monthly sales reports.[24]

At times he betrayed the fact that beneath his stubbornness burned an intense if spasmodic interest in public attitudes. When Frank Hadas would return from one of his periodic swings around the branch plants, Ford would ask: "Well, what did you see? What did the people say?" Hadas would reply: "The Chevrolet is making tremendous gains. Its dealers are disparaging the Ford, and especially the planetary transmission." He would tell of customers who grumbled over Model T peculiarities. "Is that what they are saying?" mused Ford. And although he would reiterate his determination to keep the Model T, he had obviously been given food for thought. A frank letter from his friend Edward A. Rumely, reflecting urban opinion, must have given him a certain shock. Rumely described a scene in June, 1926, on upper Broadway, as a crowd collected about a Model T which antedated the recent improvements. Three or four years earlier, people would have exclaimed over the sound workmanship; now, durable workmanship was taken for granted. The people wore pitying smiles, and "the only comments I heard were about its out-of-date appearance." [25]

Precisely when Ford changed his mind; just what inner turmoil accompanied the decision—this we do not know. But as 1927 dawned he prepared to cross his Rubicon.

Just before Christmas, declaring emphatically that he would offer no new model—"the Ford car will continue to be made in the same way"—he indicated his perplexed temper by some wistful words about public taste. "I sometimes wonder if we have not lost our buying sense and fallen under the spell of salesmanship," he told an interviewer. "The American of a generation ago was a shrewd buyer. He knew values in terms of utility and dollars. But nowadays the American people seem to listen and be sold; that is, they do not buy." And in mid-January he issued a public statement susceptible of varying interpretations. He admitted that in 1927 the company would produce fewer cars than in 1926. "The little let-down," he said, "will give us an opportunity for closer inspection and will be in every way desirable. We are not contemplating any extraordinary changes in models, although, of course, the whole industry is in a state of development and improvement." [26]

Rumor at once swept the nation. The entire history of the automobile industry holds nothing that parallels the public curiosity excited by reports that a new Ford car impended. By early spring it was commonly assumed that a fresh model with higher speed and a standard gearshift would appear soon; some said in July! But no authoritative announcement appeared. "Ford is keeping quiet and he will not even admit that he is building a new machine," said the automobile editor of the Baltimore *Sun* in May. "The public is burning with curiosity.

What will it look like? How fast will it travel? What equipment will it carry? . . . Will he still undersell his competitors? All of these are questions heard every day in all quarters of the United States."

Detroit, quite properly, had the first definite news. On May 18, 1927, the secretary of the police department appeared before the common council to request the immediate purchase of 111 Model T's for the police scout fleet. An "authoritative source," he declared, told him that the company would discontinue the Model T forthwith and begin production of a new gearshift car. This source appeared to be Martin B. Hanza, of the Ford agency handling the fleet sale, who told the common council: "Yes, we have information that the present model is to be discontinued. We are not seeking to sell these cars to the city to get rid of them. . . . The Ford Motor Company will continue to make parts for these cars for five years." Later that day W. J. Cameron, so often Ford's spokesman, said that *he* knew of no imminent change. But the cat was out of the bag; and on the evening of May 25, the Ford Motor Company announced that it would build a new car. This was front page news for every newspaper in the country.[27]

An elegiac statement was expected from Henry Ford, and he spoke with feeling. "The Model T was a pioneer," he said. Changing conditions demanded further refinement in automobile construction, but it would always hold a place in American history for its contributions to social welfare. Making the motor car available to all, it had been a great educator. "It had stamina and power. It was the car that ran before there were good roads to run on. It broke down the barriers of distance in rural sections, brought people of these sections closer together, and placed education within the reach of everyone." With the new car the company proposed to continue in the light-car field on the old basis of quantity production, high quality, low prices, and constant service. It expected to reach new heights. But—"We are all still proud of the Model T Ford car."

Even now the business is so brisk that we are up against the proposition of keeping the factory going on one model while we tool up for another. I am glad of this because it will not necessitate a total shutdown. Only a comparatively few men will be out at a time while their departments are being tooled up for the new product. At one time it looked as if 70,000 men might be laid off temporarily, but we have now scaled that down to less than 25,000 at a time. The lay-off will be brief, because we need the men, and we have no time to waste.

The changeover, however, was not to be as simple as this statement suggested.[28]

6.

On the morning of Thursday, May 26, 1927, the 15,000,000th Model T began its march off the assembly line. The ceremony was appropriately simple. No bands, no bunting, no speeches were provided. At 10 A.M. the engine was completed in the Rouge assembly plant. Each cipher of the serial number on the motor block was stamped by one of the eight oldest employees in proper order: John F. Wandersee, August Degener, Frank Kulick, Fred L. Rockelman, P. E. Martin, C. B. Hartner, Charles Sorensen, and Charles Meida.

The motor was then taken to the Highland Park plant, where Henry and Edsel Ford walked along the line as the chassis took shape. The finished vehicle, a touring car with "The Fifteen Millionth Ford" inscribed in silver lettering on its back and sides, approached the end of the conveyor line about three o'clock in the afternoon. Edsel took the wheel, and when Henry had climbed in beside him, started the motor. The car rolled off the line. With Martin and Sorensen in the rear seat, the automobile headed a motor procession of company officials and employees who made the fourteen-mile trip to the Dearborn Engineering Laboratory in a cold, drizzling rain. On the plaza in front of the building, under the gray skies, were Ford's first automobile and the first Model T. As a crowd of several hundred people applauded, Henry Ford grasped the tiller of his horseless carriage of 1896 and drove the old car around the plaza. Then the first Model T was started, its motor responding with vigorous gasps to a few turns of the crank. Once more Ford took the controls and went around the plaza. The ceremony was over.

That day found Ford, as observers noted, tired but happy. Eugene Farkas has left us a thumb-nail sketch of the man as the machinery for the Model T began to slow toward a stop. "He stretched himself. He usually made some exercises with his arm when he was tired. He said, 'Now, Gene, we've got to do it,' meaning that we've got to design a new car in a hurry." In announcing the discontinuance of the Model T,

Ford had said that work on the new model had been undertaken several years earlier. Though in a broad sense this was quite true, the fact remains that at the death of the Model T the Ford Motor Company had not fully shaped the plans for its successor.

It was inevitable that many should keenly regret the end of the familiar car. Indeed, the journalist Arthur Brisbane, adding a new Ford sedan and Ford truck to the several of each he already possessed, telegraphed Ford that he should keep one plant running indefinitely to make five hundred thousand Model T's a year; for they could easily be sold at increased prices by mail order. "I am much in earnest about this." One elderly lady of means in Montclair, New Jersey, indulged in a dramatic gesture. "When she heard that the old Model T was going out of use," an acquaintance told Henry Ford, "she purchased and stored away seven new Model T cars so that for the rest of her life she will not have to change." Countless owners on the morrow of Ford's announcement began to take better care of their cars than ever before, anxious to prolong their lives. The company continued to produce Model T parts for the next five years. In 1928, for example, it made 72,059 Model T motors. In July, 1927, Edsel wrote a San Francisco dealer: "It's most amazing the way the old models are selling in spite of the announcement of the new ones. We have been having 2200 to 2400 a day retail sales since the announcement."

All told, when the last Model T passed from wareroom to customer, the number manufactured came to 15,458,781.[29]

Meanwhile, all signs pointed to a continuing popular faith in the ability of the Ford Motor Company to make a popular-priced car that would bring it abreast of modern principles of engineering and design. It is a significant fact that Ford's competitors did not appropriate a large part of his market during the changeover period. In the first eight months of 1927, Ford registrations, measured against those for the same period the previous year, fell off by 490,472. The nationwide registration of cars during the first eight months of 1927, excluding Fords, was 1,649,839, as compared with 1,549,890 for the like period a year earlier. Thus the industry's gain was only about one fifth of Ford's loss. This fact indicates that two powerful forces were at work. First, many Ford owners were deferring the purchase of a car until the new model appeared; and second, many prospective buyers who would normally have been attracted to other makes were postponing a purchase until they learned what Ford would bring out.

Arthur Brisbane was one of those who waited for the new model, and as he did so, he made an interesting statement. "I think it most important that you should give the modern American plenty of color, and bright colors," he wrote Henry. "These are days of big wages and extravagance, the average American thinks more of the paint on the outside than of the engine under the hood, or the steel in the axles." [30] Ford, who had not yet set even an approximate date for the first new cars, was prepared to give the public plenty of color; but he would have angrily rejected Brisbane's assertion that the chassis was of secondary importance. To him, sound engineering and durable construction were still the primary values. The birth pangs of the new model were to prove as much. Whatever else the new model had or lacked, it would have integrity.

As the Model T vanished from the assembly line and joined the historic vehicles of the past, men could see that its most vital quality had been just that; integrity. Its pioneering usefulness had depended on its utility, its dependability, its versatility, and its tenacious endurance, all traits which reflected the honesty of its construction. Charles Merz called it "the first log cabin of the Motor Age," an apt image, for it sheltered almost precisely half of the automobile-owners of the United States in their swarming conquest of roads and lanes. It had the homely strength, economy, and all-round usefulness of the log cabin, and like it, fitted the demands of a hardheaded, hardworking, practical people venturing into a new domain. A farmer of the Pacific Northwest told a story eloquent of its basic characteristics. In 1915 he bought a second-hand roadster two years old. In the next thirteen years, using it as a farm truck (and also towing in "many cars of high and low price") he took the Model T to the repair shop only twice. The engine never required overhauling, and the car was never laid up. During these years, the owner, apart from the cost of demountable rims and a set of fenders, spent only $40 on upkeep. "I do not know how many hundreds of thousands of miles it has run," he wrote, "as the speedometer was worn out when I bought it and I never put another one on, but it has been in constant use." That car had integrity. Perhaps nothing in it was beautiful—but nothing in it was false.[31]

It would be easy to fill pages with impressive statistics about the Model T. No other model has ever been produced in such numbers, and it is safe to say that on this score alone its record will never be matched. Only one other model, the expensive Rolls-Royce Silver Ghost, built 1907–1927, had as long a life. During the existence of the car, the Ford Motor Company bought almost five billion dollars' worth of materials, paid well over a half-billion in taxes, and spent on wages and salaries nearly five and a half billions. The Model T, teaching the industry (indeed, numerous industries) the immense possibilities of mass production of goods, greatly stimulated the growth of the national economy. Before it was discontinued, automobile manufacturing was firmly established as the leading industry of the United States, and a pillar of world prosperity.[32] *

More striking than such statistics, however, are the innumerable evidences of the sturdy serviceability of the Model T to tens of millions of families, its extraordinary durability, and its impact upon social change. People told many stories of its spectacular feats in mountain-climbing and river-fording; but it was for its everyday reliability that it was really valued. With good reason, it early became known as the farmer's car. As his mechanical workhorse, it took his produce to market and returned laden with the articles he needed; as his all-weather carriage, it enlarged his family's horizons. Its motor power, transmitted by simple attachments while the rear wheels were propped on jacks, filled silos, operated portable sawmills, and ran feed-cutters, grinders, churns, and small power tools. It was equally the doctor's car, the engineer's car, the miller's car, the storekeeper's car, the school-teacher's car. It put its willing shoulder to a thousand tasks which costlier, better-looking automobiles declined. While its crotchety temperament and flagrant weaknesses gave rise to countless Ford jokes of Paul Bunyanesque exaggeration, all such jests were tinged with respect and flavored with affection.† So firmly fixed did the Model T become

---

* The changes made in the Model T may be found listed in Philip Van Doren Stern, *Tin Lizzie: The Story of the Fabulous Model T Ford*, and Floyd Clymer, *Henry's Wonderful Model T*, 1908–1927, both published in 1955.

† The Ford joke requires a separate treatise. It was probably an outgrowth of the broader class of automobile joke, a response of the folk-mind to an invention that invited satire. The various names of the Model T obviously emanated from the masses; the cattle hack, the Detroit Disaster, the Leaping Lena, the Bouncing Betty, the flivver, the bone crusher, the galloping snail, and the Spirit of St. Vitus. As Mark Sullivan says (*Our Times, The War Begins, 1909–1914*, IV, New York, 1932, 61–72), "this subject had best be left with some other and minor aspects of Ford history that seem to defy research."

in the folklore of use that in 1925 the Texas Court of Civil Appeals took judicial notice of its traits:

The use of the Ford is so nearly universal that its characteristic qualities have become matters of common knowledge. It is a light car, and is possessed of such agility as to excite the admiration, no less than the anger sometimes, of those who behold its antics. It can start, stop, back up or turn out, about, or over, almost in the twinkling of an eye. It neither runs on fixed rails nor does it require even a well-beaten path in which to move. It heeds not the ruts, halts not at ditches, and has been known in emergencies to negotiate fences even.[33]

It is proof of the durability of the Model T that in March, 1927, nearly nineteen years after the first one had been made, 11,325,521 of its kind were registered in the United States. As late as 1949 more than 200,000 were still registered, a figure exceeding the registration of all American cars in the year the Model T was born. In 1956 the car was still in daily use in a number of states, Sears, Roebuck still sold a few small parts, and the Ford Company still received many letters asking for its revival.[34]

The social impact of the Model T is not easily measured, and awaits the systematic assay of experts in the various social studies. That it helped to change the national psychology and national manners and mores as well as the national economy, cannot be questioned. No other single machine, in all probability, did so much to induce people of provincial mind to begin thinking in regional and national terms; none did so much to knit together different parts of the county, the state, and the country; none did more to create the sense of a freer and more spacious life. As a single item in the long roster of effects, a historian of the country store notes that the Model T gave people a new liberty of choice about what they would buy and where. Statisticians even reduced this liberty to figures: the farm buyer would travel on the average six to eight miles for hardware, fourteen for furniture, and twenty for women's fashions. Countless city wage-earners gained from the humble, honest flivver the same command over distance: their ideas changed as suburban living became feasible, and country escapes easy. Rural villages began to wither and county seats to expand. The pressure toward uniformity, in one sense, increased; but in another sense people found a far greater variety in life.

In the two decades of the Model T, a new nation had been born—and partly at its behest. "As the farmers bowled along the hard road in their tin Lizzies, elements of urban life were borne out along the main motor arteries to meet them; city newspapers, department store deliveries, string-along-the-road settlements made up of homes and businesses dependent on the road and the car." [35] America still hurries along this road, on a journey that would not be so far advanced had not the flivver, with all its absurdity and integrity, blazed the way.

XVII

THROES OF NEW BIRTH

"Sixty-four today and the biggest job of my life ahead," said Ford as July brought his birthday in 1927. When in the last week of May telegrams had been dispatched to every Ford dealer in the country announcing that the last Model T had left the assembly line, nothing had been said about the delivery date of the new model. Everyone knew that a larger, brighter phoenix would be born from the ashes of the old, but nobody could guess when. Even Ford could not guess, but he accepted the challenge of the new car as epochal. Like the ten thousand Ford dealers, like the millions of potential customers, he knew that his resourcefulness was on trial as never before.

The magnitude of the reorganization which had to be completed within the calendar year (a longer delay would be fatal) was something new in American industry. It was almost as if the Panama Canal had been closed by earthquake in a time of international tension, demanding the swift completion of a Nicaraguan waterway in its stead. After all, Ford production had represented almost half the automobile output of the world; the company normally employed over a hundred and twenty thousand men in and near Detroit; it had thirty-six assembly plants scattered over the country. Now its activities were largely paralyzed until a huge tripartite operation was successfully completed —the design of a new car; the retooling of the factory and assembly plants for mass-production of that car; and the reorganization of the sales force to market it. No wonder that the whole nation looked on with suspense. Rumors and reports about the new model constantly pushed into the headlines; and if the story of its parturition was not as thrilling as that of Lindbergh's flight, it vied in the news with the Hall-Mills murder case and the execution of Sacco and Vanzetti.

"Can Henry Ford come back?"—that was the great question. The sober *New York Times* remarked that no presidential campaign of the decade, no sports contest, aroused as much interest as "the fight for the heavyweight national automobile championship between Henry Ford and General Motors." Many were asking: "Can Ford create a new car that will do as much for America as the Model T?" [1]

When Ford had tinkered and hammered in the brick shed on Bagley Avenue, few besides Clara had known or cared. When he had assembled his first successful car on Mack Street, only a handful of associates had been concerned. Now, as people waited from spring till autumn frost, scores of millions caught up every rumor. The car was to have a revolutionary new engine; the car was to be called the Edison; the car was to be a hybrid of Lincoln and Ford named the Linford; the car was a secret disappointment and Ford in despair; the car was a dazzling success that would put Chevrolet with the dodo. Never in our industrial history, commented B. C. Forbes, had any product been awaited with half as much tension. One man who could not bear the suspense telegraphed: "Like millions, have been walking, waiting, wondering, wishing. Why don't you? Henry, oh please, Henry, why don't you?" [2]

2.

Henry Ford, betraying no sign of hurry or anxiety, attacked the basic problem of design with his principal objectives clearly outlined. He wanted a car built for speed, power, and comfort; a car suited to the improved roads and the quickened pace of life. "There are only so many hours in the day and there is much to be done," he told an interviewer. "Fifty and sixty miles an hour are desired today where thirty or forty would have satisfied in 1908." It would be completely new in design; new from front fender to tail-lights. Every one of the 5500 parts (for it proved to have that many) must be as nearly perfect as possible. Ford knew that his prestige was at stake; that his past achievement would avail nothing for the future; that many an automobile maker had sunk in ruin because of engineering defects that destroyed confidence in the dependability of his car. As always, he intended to lay special emphasis upon enduring qualities. He wrote two years later:

There is no business where chickens come home to roost more certainly than in the automobile business. The car has got to be good. And the only way it can be unquestionably good is through good workmanship. Even though the design be clumsy and antiquated, the car will be saved by the good workmanship put into it. But the latest and best design will be an unqualified failure if it lacks skill, accuracy, and honesty in the work put into its building.

Although in planning his car he naturally gave some thought to the market and to his lost leadership, he was ruled primarily by the instincts of the engineer and craftsman. Throughout his life, one generalization could be laid down concerning Ford: while as a mechanical genius, perhaps the greatest of his time, he was intensely practical, he had very little interest in competition. The integrity of the product was always the first consideration; consumer demand came second, and any thought of profits was incidental. One evidence of his preoccupation now with durability is the fact that from the outset he was determined to use expensive steel forgings in place of cheap stampings and malleable castings. Any other manufacturer would have paused to calculate costs, but Ford simply drove ahead to put more forged steel into the new model than could be found, probably, in any other car of the time. Because his instinct in mechanical matters was almost infallible, the automobile he built for himself did prove to be an excellent automobile for the general public.[3]

The first step was simple. As various engineers recall, dimensions were decided upon. Ford himself states: "Edsel and I decided on the wheelbase and size right away. . . . After that it was a matter of working things out on the drawing board until we got them right." On Edsel's insistence, the body was brought closer to the ground than in the Model T, and car-height was thus reduced. The overall length of the chassis was fixed at 113$\frac{7}{16}$ inches, and the wheelbase at 103.5 inches, a shade longer than the Chevrolet's. These basic matters settled, the grueling labor of design began.

Ford had certain advantages in dealing with the problem: unlimited funds, his own vast experience and insight, a group of able men still remaining on the staff in spite of all the discharges, and a factory spirit which recognized no impossibilities. "The money question did not bother us," he wrote later. At the close of 1926 the company possessed $246,209,040 in cash, and total assets stood just under $900,000,000. Had the figures been but a half or a third as great, he would still have shown his characteristic indifference to the dollar sign.[4]

As for his own talents, he threw them all into the undertaking. He presided over the labor of producing the prototype with unflagging vigilance and industry, exercising absolute authority. From diverse sources he drew the ideas and special skills needed, but he controlled their union into a functional whole. It was justly said of his work on the new model—indeed, on all models: "Mr. Ford remains tenacious, determined, unswerving. No part goes into a Ford car without Mr. Ford's critical—and often his creative—contribution to it."

Although discharges and resignations had left the Ford company without any single engineer of the stature of a Kettering or a Vincent, and although after the departure of C. Harold Wills no automotive designer of comparative talent had emerged in the Ford ranks, ample group ability was still available. It was group ability of the middling sort that Henry Ford prized; indeed, he would tolerate no other kind. The automotive expert who pointed out in 1927 that Ford "hasn't a single engineer in his whole organization who is regarded as outstandingly brilliant. . . . Ford himself is so dictatorial that the brainiest engineers in the country couldn't possibly get along smoothly with him," partly missed the point. The fact of the deficiency was true, but the reasons went well beyond personal friction. Nothing is strange or discreditable in the fact that Ford insisted on having engineers who, while capable of original solutions, were willing to subordinate their ideas to his own penetration and originality. He regarded their designs as raw material for change and adaptation. In an era of large industrial enterprise, group effort under one specially gifted leader is after all perhaps the best key for unlocking technological problems.

The group to whom Ford turned included Joseph Galamb, who had done much to help create the Model T, and who was in charge of experimental engineering; Eugene J. Farkas, formerly in charge of the X-engine project; Frank Johnson, chief engineer of the Lincoln division; and a newcomer named Laurence S. Sheldrick, almost unknown in the company. No formal administrative structure was created for the task—that was not Ford's way. These four men worked under him, and with constant advice from Sorensen, Martin, and above all Edsel, who was specially helpful in dealing with the body. But although at first they had coequal authority, it was inevitable that one man should rise to primary position; and it is revealing that the man Ford finally chose was Sheldrick. In such matters Henry liked to seek out a junior worker not hidebound by technological conventions, to test his abilities, and to give him an area of power roughly proportioned to the results he could achieve. Sheldrick achieved a great deal.

This new leader in the Ford factory, now in his late thirties, had learned drafting while a student in the Columbus, Ohio, high school. His father was an Englishman of uncommon abilities; he himself was studious and ambitious. He joined the Timken-Detroit Axle Company, rapidly rising to be chief tool designer; became a wartime officer in the Ordnance Corps, supervising the conversion of tractors to tanks; and after the armistice went into tractor design for firms in the Midwest and Canada. When Ford acquired the Lincoln, Sheldrick took a position in its engineering department, designing instrument panels, speedometers, ignition locks, and other parts. In time he was put to work on a supercharger and timing gears; and Ford, who often came into the building, began to take favorable notice of the young engineer. Sheldrick was becoming dissatisfied with his generally humdrum routine, and when another firm offered him $5000 a year—"a pretty nice improvement" over his Ford salary, he notes—he was tempted to leave; but Galamb, probably instigated by Ford, prevailed upon him to stay. To improve his position, he was then promoted to the Farkas squad working on the X-car project.

While a member of this squad, Sheldrick deepened the impression he made upon Ford, who learned to value him for his ability to shape ideas on the blackboard, his quickness, and his adaptability. On this X-car enterprise, recalls Sheldrick, individualism had free play. "There were so many independent designers who reported directly to Mr. Ford. . . . We really had no head, other than Mr. Ford." Under these circumstances, a promising technician could easily win Henry's favor. And while Sheldrick was energetic and original, he was not radical; on the contrary, observes a Ford research executive, "he was an orthodox engineer." This gave him precisely the balance that Ford desired. The new model, though it had to be a remarkable improvement over the Model T, was to be decidedly conventional from the standpoint of mechanical design.[5]

The group now working on it, like Ford himself, had complete confidence in their ability to make a better car than the Essex, Chevrolet, Overland, and other competitors. The bright lexicon of the Ford factory contained some queer words, but "fail" was not one of them. The tradition of success—success with the Models N and T, with mass production, with steady price decreases, with popular good will—was invaluable. The question, "Can Ford come back?" had no meaning inside the company; the answer was taken for granted.

3.

Ford's great disadvantages were his tardiness in doing any real preparatory work, his lack of scientific facilities or centralized engineering laboratories, and his predilection for rule-of-thumb procedure. His associates, who had been eager to start on the new car long before Ford gave the word, now, in mid-1927, realized the disastrous consequences of the delay he had imposed. The exact chronology of the work on the new prototype is hazy. It appears that Ford issued an oral order to proceed with design in August, 1926, still lustily denying that a new design was contemplated; that Sorensen that same month bade Farkas stop work on the X-car and "start right away" on the new model— "We've got to design a car for the market, a four-cylinder one;" that men began drawings for the body-layout, the simplest step, in December; and that the first blueprints were ready in January, 1927. In fact, one worker, Olsen, gives the date January 17 as the time when plans for body and chassis were first "gotten together on a sketch." [6]

But this sketch was tentative, a mere target to aim at, for to work out the fundamentals of any new car so that every part functioned not only well but triumphantly (as in a new Ford it must) was normally the work of a year or more. Now it must be compassed in months. The crew moved to the attack, working day and night. In March a chassis of some kind, with a bucket seat on top, was running well enough to be driven about; but a thousand jobs still had to be done. Meanwhile, Highland Park and the Rouge were for the most part inactive; competitors had cars to sell, but the Ford company had none. Ford himself, as we have said, was unhurried, but his associates labored in a nightmare of pace and pressure.

The laboratory facilities of the company, as noted earlier, were diffuse and disorganized. Ford wished them kept so. Fearing, as we have seen, that men would fall into ruts—perhaps sometimes also actuated by a Puckish sense of mischief—he liked to spur on competitive effort by assigning the same task to different men. J. L. McCloud, in charge of chemical and metallurgical research, recalls that during the nineteen-twenties two research laboratories in this field existed side by side, one under himself, one under William H. Smith. "I remember a couple of instances where Mr. Ford started me on some particular project, and Mr. Smith found out about it, and he started his boys working on the same thing."

Particularly revealing of Ford's loose research methods is a report made on them by the National Research Council in 1931. It shows (what every executive knew) that Henry Ford liked to perform research and testing in the most pragmatic way at the seat of the factory activity involved. Thus, although the Engineering Laboratory in Dearborn was supposedly the main center of company research, it was actually only one among many similar foci of study.

Unlike companies which possessed centralized laboratories and testing stations, declared the report, the Ford company had no one building which could be pointed out as the research department. "Considerable work of this kind is done in Ford laboratories, but the laboratories are scattered through the plant so that they may be closely connected with the type of work called for in actual production." A new type of axle was desired? Very well, experiments would be conducted just where axles were being made. Nor was research deputed to a picked and static group; instead, "suggestions and aid in the solution of problems may come from either chief executives or men in the shops." The more rivalry in experimentation the better; "competition is encouraged and even stressed not only among the factory departments, but also among concerns outside the company." [7]

While this policy encouraged practicality in experiment, it discouraged careful planning and deep-probing research. As was pointed out in an earlier chapter, the company had no advanced design engineering department at all. Said Harold Hicks of the conditions in 1927, "No money was being spent . . . to get highly trained young men out of the universities and technological schools. Expenditures for laboratory equipment and general research facilities were made according to Henry Ford's mood and whim. Only those in his good graces could spend any considerable sums of money, and his good graces were quite as likely to extend to the inexpert as to the specialist." Ford research, in short, was on the rule of thumb basis indicated by the habitual exhortation of the oldtime machine-builder, John Fritz: "Let's start her up and see why she don't go."

The rudimentary character of the equipment indeed harked back to an earlier day. Other companies—General Motors, Dodge, Packard—had excellent proving grounds for cars, running up to 1245 acres in extent; the Chrysler Corporation boasted of an engineering laboratory that would have done credit to Yale or Cornell. In contrast, as we have seen, the Ford Company had no proving ground at all. It used public highways in the Dearborn area, such as Van Born and Ecorse Roads, in trials of its experimental cars. The official tester, Ray Dahlinger, who was manager of Ford's farm properties and as such without any formal connection with the company, used methods which sorely exasperated the engineers. "There were only two kinds of reports he would bring back," one witness has recorded. " 'It is God damn good,' or 'The car's no damn good.' You could never get any details from him as to what was wrong or what needed improvement. It was either all wrong or all good, no intermediate whatever." While this verdict did not prevent some of the engineers from conducting their own tests, Henry Ford was much less likely to heed their findings than Dahlinger's rough summation. When the police gave warning that they would no longer tolerate use of public roads for testing cars, a Ford engineer suggested that the company might turn to the old airport at Dearborn; but Dahlinger rejected this idea out of hand, and the boss sustained him. Throughout the period covered by this book the "damn good" or "no damn good" fiats, a simple spectrum of black and white, took precedence over the delicate assessments of trained technologists.[8]

When one of the Ford engineers this year conducted spring vibration tests on the new model, he did not have any instruments for recording the results. Metals were placed under severe fatigue strains in the laboratory; if they came out intact, they were all right. Any more elaborate treatment, so far as Ford was concerned, was a waste of time and money. When Ford trucks were tested, they were simply loaded above their rated capacity, and driven over a rough terrain to see if brakes, steering gear, and engines survived the strain. This "seat of the pants" test, as engineers called it, sufficed—except for a dynamometer reading. Much as Henry Ford prized quality, he everywhere employed this principle of rough-and-ready experiment followed by rough-and-ready trials which eventuated in a rough-and-ready verdict. As Waldemar Kaempffert wrote:

He has two staffs, the one to design, the other to test. In the shop a defective part which can be saved is returned for correction. The inspector who discovers the defect does not even attempt to indicate how the correction should be made. He simply approves or rejects. Ford applies the same principle to the purely intellectual work of planning a new car. His designing hand knows not what his testing right hand does.[9]

It was in this atmosphere, without benefit of an outstanding engineer, of precision instruments, or of a tradition of continuous experiment, that the creation of the new model was undertaken. But Ford's orders gave the efforts of scattered workers cohesive force; his mechanical genius was worth more than laboratory refinements.

4.

Ford plunged into the new undertaking with an eagerness of spirit and clarity of vision that characterized him at his best. Then and later, his activity, enshrouded in thick clouds of rumor, became the theme of legend. It was said that he had donned overalls, taken up Spartan living quarters in the engineering laboratory, and, snatching frugal meals, toiled from dawn to midnight; that he deliberately fostered an atmosphere of crisis to whet public curiosity; and that he used the security precautions of the Czarist police to envelop the car in mystery. All this was sheer nonsense. But he did labor for weeks like a man possessed.

Separate duties were assigned to his chief associates. Farkas at first had charge of over-all design, and then moved on to special tasks like the axles and the four-wheel brakes; Sheldrick worked chiefly on the engine, but subsequently contributed to the improvement of the chassis; Galamb dealt with the design and engineering of the body and frame; Frank Johnson designed the clutch and transmission. In the beginning Ford, exhilarated by his sense of a great opportunity for creative action, bade Farkas choose at will his own quarters in the laboratory building. Farkas picked out a room. "That won't be big enough," ejaculated Ford, and took Farkas in tow for a tour of the large structure designed by Albert Kahn.

"That library is a nice place," commented Farkas as they halted at the threshold. "It has a nice fireplace." His old quarters in the Dearborn tractor building had possessed a fireplace which he liked. "Take it over," directed Ford. When Farkas showed reluctance to occupy the whole large library, Ford instructed Albert Kahn to erect a dividing wall with a built-in blackboard for full-scale drawings. "The wall cost a couple of thousand dollars," comments Farkas. "It was beautiful walnut." Mrs. Ford saw what was being done, and winced at the violation of the spatial integrity of the fine room. "That's awful to do that, Henry," she scolded. Nevertheless, the partition remained. A couch was fitted into one of the window-nooks. Here or in an easy chair Ford would rest as he watched the engineers at work, or studied the full-scale multi-colored drawings on the blackboard.[10]

The most vital segment of the car, the engine, was brought into proper shape by Sheldrick in an office and workshop on the west side of the laboratory. Only the general specifications were fixed at the outset, Ford, Sorensen, and Martin after long discussions agreeing with Sheldrick on a bore of 3⅞ inches and a stroke of 4¼. From that point the motor just grew like Topsy. "Mr. Ford was in the little room where I was working every day, sometimes as much as half a day at a time," recalls Sheldrick. Edsel lent a hand. Progress soon became rapid:

We were following the Model T engine only in the respect that it was to be a four-cylinder L-head engine of the same general type. There were to be a number of improvements. . . . It was to have a water pump; instead of being thermosyphon circulation it was to be forced circulation. It was to have battery distributor ignition; at that time, the ignition system of the Model T was recognized to be inadequate. . . .

Mr. Ford finally consented to some type of sliding gear transmission. One of his stipulations was that the collar shaft should become stationary when the transmission was shifted into high gear. In other words, he felt that the continually rotating countershaft, which was commonly accepted in all sliding gear transmissions, was inefficient. It ate up power, rotating the countershaft through the oil all the time it was in high gear.

Sheldrick also tells us just how Henry Ford controlled the work:

Mr. Ford had a great preference for seeing things full size, vertically, in front of him. Chalk on a blackboard was the most legible way of seeing them. He could see them at a distance; stand back and get an overall picture. It was a technique that Farkas developed to a fine point. We speak of a blackboard, but it really was a blackboard cloth stretched on a vertical drawing board. After we finished one of these we could roll it up and put it away.

We followed the practise of coloring these drawings too. We would fill in with colored pastel crayons certain parts in certain colors, so you could refer to the red piston, or pink cylinder block, and so on. . . . Mr. Ford could read blueprints, but I do think that in a very intricate drawing that showed a number of sections and views, one upon the other, it was a little difficult for him to follow. We kept as many complications out of these drawings as possible.

Mr. Ford would sit and direct us while we drew. . . . You might be drawing a main bearing, for example, and he would say: "Well, now, that's too big. Take a quarter of an inch off that," or, "That cylinder wall is too thick, reduce that a sixteenth of an inch," or, "Oh, that fly wheel looks too heavy."

He was constantly trying to keep down weight.

Although Ford's decisions were often made in an offhand, arbitrary manner which irritated the meticulous Sheldrick—"too much edict engineering," he says—they reflected his long, intensive experience and exacting craftsmanship, which were to make the new model unique in its class. No matter how intuitional his decrees, he was confident that Sorensen and Martin could translate them into economical production. Fortunately, in one area, that of the body, he left a free hand to Edsel, who had demonstrated with the custom-built Lincolns his discerning taste. And Edsel, as noted previously, worked in a different fashion.[11]

Where Henry Ford would say dogmatically, "Oh, that looks all right," or "Scrap it," Edsel showed a patient interest and a readiness to discuss details. Galamb submitted sketches and clay models, which the two debated at length. "He criticized the interior quite a lot, and the instrumental work," Galamb recalls. "When we made the first sample, Edsel criticized the trimming and the material. He was very particular about the cushions we used. He was very particular about the riding qualities of the car. He knew what he wanted and insisted that he get it." It was Edsel's idea, for example, to place a grille on the front end, a suggestion that Henry would never have tolerated in earlier days. It was Edsel's artistic eye which devised the various color schemes. His father had come to a belated realization of the young man's gifts, remarking with a real pride: "We've got a pretty good man in my son. He knows style—how a car ought to look. And he has mechanical horse sense, too."

By early spring, 1927, the body designs for the sedan were ready for shop work, and an experimental car was on the road. Ford, suffering from his automobile accident at the time, conferred with the engineers while confined to bed at Fair Lane. Numerous other experimental cars

—numbered in time by the score—were to follow. Though progress was being made, however, one element gave continuous trouble: the motor. Ford was insistent on a light engine, but equally insistent that it must furnish enough power to yield a road speed of between fifty and sixty miles an hour. To reduce motor vibration, economize gasoline, and ensure a long operating life, the engine was to be kept at a low level of revolutions-per-minute. In fact, Ford directed that the bore and stroke were to be only slightly greater than in the Model T, and that at least forty horsepower were to be delivered at but 2200 r.p.m. How could this exacting goal be met?

Despite Sheldrick's herculean labors, April found the motor still much too weak. To assist him, Harold Hicks, Ford's chief aircraft engineer, was temporarily assigned to the improvement of the new engine. Going to the engineering laboratory, he found Edsel, Sorensen, and Martin gathered about a motor which they disgustedly told him was furnishing only twenty-two horsepower. "If we should give you charge," demanded Sorensen, "how much could you get up?" Hicks, after a few rapid calculations, replied: "I can promise to get forty horsepower out of the engine if you will give me three weeks."

Hicks, working around the clock with Carl Schultz, found the seat of the difficulty in the intake and exhaust manifold. The first laborious alterations brought the horsepower up to thirty. Then, changing the water passages around the exhaust valves, Hicks raised it to forty. He deserves the principal credit for solving a knotty problem that threatened to delay the new model even longer—indeed, threatened to prevent it from reaching the market as a car whose combination of lightness and power won national applause. In his generous *Reminiscences,* however, Hicks declares that Henry Ford's insistence on this combination was fundamental, and takes care also to praise Edsel's contribution to the engine. Edsel, he writes, "knew that the right way to get power out of a job was to get the stuff in there and explode it." We might gather as much from Edsel's affection for high-powered European sports cars and experimental motorboats.

The engine had a quick take-off that later made the motor world marvel. As Hicks put it: "Up to thirty miles an hour the model could skin the pants off anything that was on the road." Its capacity for acceleration, too, was remarkable. It could leap from five to twenty-five miles an hour in just eight and a half seconds, a feat that six- and eight-cylinder cars had trouble in equalling. The engine gave the new car a speed of 65 miles an hour against 43 for the Model T.[12]

5.

Part by part, the new model was brought to the standards which Ford exacted. For him, the work was an adventure in the two fields of effort that furnished him the deepest satisfaction: the shaping of metal, rubber, and glass to the force of his inner vision as a sculptor shapes clay, and the distribution of his handiwork to waiting millions as a philanthropist might distribute largess. These fields were his true spiritual home as long as he had strength to labor. For his associates, however, the work was a long nightmare of nerve-racking absorption in design, experiment, rejection, and fresh experiment. Each man worked by the rule of trial and error.

"As parts of the new car were fashioned," wrote Waldemar Kaempffert, "they were turned over to the testing staff with hardly a word. The testers proceeded to crush, twist, bend, and pound. They sent back transmission gears out of which they had succeeded in tearing teeth, and rear axles which they had reduced to junk. No suggestion of a possible method of making a part stronger or shaping it more nicely to suit its purpose—nothing but the battered part and the baldest statement of what happened in the testing machine. The designers made their own deductions and began anew. Thus engines, transmissions, axles, steering gears were tossed back and forth."

As they labored, word drifted in that competitive companies were harvesting hay that Ford was temporarily unable to cut. Essex was making gains. Above all, Chevrolet was forging toward the front. In March it had reached and passed its goal of 4000 units a month; and though that was far short of the best Ford production rate on the Model T, it was ominous for the future. Nobody could miss the significance of the August announcement that during the first half of 1927 a total of 700,000 Chevrolet units had been produced, as many as in the entire previous year. Word came in, too, that many Ford dealers were in sad straits—particularly those in the large cities, with high overhead. By the thousands, in May they had bravely displayed window-posters flaunting the inscription: "Wait for the new Ford!" As the summer wore on they put up other signs: "Wait for the new Ford cars—Speed, Pick-up, Flexibility, Beauty, Comfort, Stamina—Coming Soon." Yet all too often the windows were dusty, the posters fly-specked, the general premises forlorn.[13]

The engine was almost the last Himalaya to be conquered. Ford was so delighted with what Hicks had accomplished that he ordered him to go out on the roads and race every car in sight. "Pretty soon they will get tired and then you go right on ahead of them all!" Hicks did just that. One day in late July, 1927, with a driver and a mechanic, he took out a car with the new engine, passed everything in sight, and finally headed home at fifty miles an hour. As he attempted to go around another car, it suddenly turned left directly in front of him. A tremendous crash ensued. The test car was carrying 750 pounds of lead in the rear section, which increased the force of the impact. Hicks was hurled through the windshield, and landed in a ditch, his arm mangled. As a consequence of the collision, Henry and Edsel Ford at once took an additional step to give the new model distinction: they equipped the windshield with safety glass.

But still another touch was needed. When the model seemed almost ready, Henry Ford stepped to the front with his jaw set. "Somebody must represent the public," he said. He slid his lanky form into a sedan, slammed the door, and stepped hard on the throttle. Always he drove at a reckless gait. He hurtled across a rough field, bumping over stones and fallen timber. Alighting on his return, he issued a curt demand: "Rides too hard. Put on hydraulic shock absorbers." This was a bold innovation in a popular-priced automobile. "Very expensive for a car of that class," records Sheldrick. "It was unheard of." No other feature of the model, however, did more to make the passenger comfortable.

On August 10, 1927, Edsel officially announced: "The new Ford automobile is an accomplished fact. The engineering problems affecting its design and equipment and affecting also its manufacture have all been solved." He revealed its speed. "The tests already made show it is faster, smoother, more rugged and more flexible than we had hoped for in the early stages of designing." [14]

6.

The Ford organization, its prototype car in hand, now stood face to face with a task of unprecedented magnitude and complexity—the retooling of the chief Ford factory for mass production. (This was the Rouge, as the assembly line was moved there in September, 1927.) Some advance planning, some anticipatory work, had already been done; but midsummer found the main labor hardly well commenced. "I don't think the management realized the problems involved in changing every component on a car and putting it into new production," observes one of the engineers.

Indeed, a change-over of such scope and urgency was then unknown in American industrial history. After Pearl Harbor a much more remarkable conversion to military production was accomplished by General Motors, Ford, Chrysler, Colt's, and other great manufacturers; but they had the help of the War Production Board, unlimited government money, and the accumulated experience of the past fifteen years. The retooling at the Rouge in 1927 was a feat unparalleled in peacetime. Meanwhile, a thorough overhaul was required in the thirty-four assembly plants of the United States and Canada, in twelve overseas factories, and in the shops of the major independent suppliers. Tens of thousands of hands previously laid off came back to assist. But in the succeeding months the skill of Clarence Avery, Hartner, Findlater and dozens of seasoned assistants, purged when the assembly line was moved to the Rouge, would have sped the task of increasing production, which was long to lag behind the demand for the new car.

Because almost all the 5580 parts of the model were entirely new, the mechanism of all Ford plants had to be rebuilt from the ground up. Factory layouts were changed; new construction work to fit these alterations was hurried forward; fresh power arrangements, with countless new electrical connections, were made; better conveyors were installed; machine tools of radical new design were made or ordered in thousands. It is "probably the biggest replacement of plant in the history of American industry," said the *New York Times;* "certainly never in the automobile industry" had it been approached. One and a half million square feet of factory space were added this year.[15]

Beginning in late May, thousands of toolmakers, die and pattern makers, millwrights, machine maintenance workers, and other skilled employees trickled back, to be employed on two and three shifts six days a week. By July, 17,000 of them were busy in the tool departments of the Rouge and Highland Park. Throughout the summer skilled mechanics were hired on the spot. In one department devoted solely to designing tools, more than 200 engineers and their assistants were kept busy, in relays, 24 hours daily. Some of the new machines were gigantic;

a set of power presses, costing a round million, towered 30 feet above the Rouge floor. The largest weighed 240 tons, more than twice the weight of the biggest presses used in making the Model T. New departments sprang into being, for many of the components, such as the sliding gear transmission and the water pump, had not been made by Ford during the old era. Once more, no attention was paid to expenditures. The machines for making the new steel-spoked wheel cost about $700,-000; the alteration of the machines for making two gears on the rear-axle assembly cost $500,000.*

The company policy of extreme specialization in machine tools created a heavy procurement problem. According to A. M. Wibel, during the changeover the Rouge ordered more specialized tools than any other factory in the world. As the new machines came in, old ones had to be torn from their foundation pits to be relocated. "We moved that machinery around so much," recalls Wibel, "that we had round corners on much of it." [16]

As often before, Ford posed engineering problems that experts were ready to pronounce insoluble. Of these, the electrical welding of essential components, such as the rear-end assembly, afterwards attracted perhaps the widest notice. The engineers designed self-indexing automatic welders for the purpose. With the cheap power from the turbogenerators at the Rouge, the company was able to cut costs and to usher in what F. L. Faurote called "a new day in motor fabrication, a new and surer way of assembly." Observers predicted that welding would displace the traditional bolting of major sub-assemblies; and they were correct, for the whole industry later adopted this innovation. Another engineering problem which challenged the ingenuity of the Ford engineers was the fabrication of the fuel tank placed under the cowl. Ford insisted that this two-section tank be made of plate steel covered with a rustproof alloy, and welded with watertight seams. Such plate was especially difficult to handle in welding. Even the indomitable Sorensen had grave doubts that the job could be done. But the engineers redesigned a standard welding machine, introduced the use of mercury to afford uniform heat at all points during the operation, and tri-

---

* The shutdown of May, 1927, found the company with some 45,000 machine tools valued at about $45,000,000. About 32,000 were production tools. In all, half of the tools were rebuilt; a quarter were kept without change, though often relocated; a quarter were scrapped. The company purchased 4500 new machine tools. The cost of the new machinery and overhaul came to $18,000,000. ("Preliminary Opinion on some Phases of Federal Tax Computations 1924–1926," Acc. 38, Box 61; N.Y. Times, April 19, 1928.)

umphantly overthrew every obstacle. Eventually the Rouge plant had ten machines producing more than 2500 perfect tanks daily.

From thousands of such episodes, knit into a throbbing whole by the busy brains and hands of tens of thousands of workers, emerged a memorable epic of industrial achievement. By mid-October, 1927, when the bulk of the machinery was in place at the Rouge, the Ford officials were hiring men at the rate of three or four thousand a week, and retooling had been completed except for the perfecting of a few small parts. Large-scale production had begun on pistons, cylinder-blocks, manifolds, and other components; outside suppliers were filling their initial orders. By this time about 150 hand-made experimental cars had been road-tested, though only a few had been given bodies. Ford felt sufficiently relaxed to make a journey East. At the Wayside Inn on October 14, he told reporters that the new model would appear soon. He added: "My work is all done. That's why I'm here. Edsel is taking care of the rest of it." [17]

7.

Shortly afterward Ford returned to Dearborn to welcome the first factory-produced Model A—for that was the name chosen. On the late afternoon of Thursday, October 20, he stamped by hand the serial number of the first Model A engine off the line. Next day this motor was incorporated in a Tudor sedan. Even yet, Ford withheld his final approval; he used this particular car for testing and inspection. On November 1, final changes were made in the tools of the main assembly line at the Rouge, and the new models began to roll away in very limited numbers—about twenty cars a day. No schedule was fixed as Ford and the engineers continued to iron out imperfections. So deliberate was the pace, so cautious Ford's attitude, that even in the first week of December the Rouge line was "creeping slowly as compared with normal production—but each day sees increasing speed." [18]

On December 1st readers of two thousand daily newspapers opened to full page advertisements of the new Ford car; next day another, and then another, until five in all had appeared. For these advertisements the company paid $1,300,000. But the unpaid publicity in a hundred forms dwarfed this effort. P. T. Barnum, contemplating it, would have died of envy.

Suspense and excitement among the general public had mounted by autumn to fever pitch. The tension was heightened by the fact that, as hundreds of thousands of automobile owners deferred purchasing a new car until the Model A appeared, a mild economic recession was attributed to that factor. Bankers, economists, and editors hoped that when the Ford plants fully reopened, business would regain its vigor. Most keenly interested of all were the Ford dealers, literally at the mercy of the starting whistle of the factory and worried about the market appeal of the car. In October, three Chicago dealers had become so desperate that they drove to Detroit, hoping that by some miracle they could see the automobile for themselves. As they rolled along Woodward Avenue toward Highland Park, an unknown car came toward them—and they were electrified to see Henry and Edsel Ford riding in it! Instantly they turned around and followed the car to the factory gates:

We stopped in back of it and sat tight. This was enough to get the Fords excited, so Edsel opened his window and waved us over to talk to him. When he found out we were dealers who had driven all the way from Chicago just for a glimpse of the new car, he asked us to come into the plant.

Henry Ford was extremely enthusiastic. He personally described the Model A from one end to the other. He took a tool off the work bench and showed us the proper adjustment of the brakes. Then we took a ride around the plant with Edsel.[19]

It was an event of national interest when in November a reporter on the Brighton (Michigan) *Argus* stumbled upon the new Ford parked outside a restaurant in his town while its passengers, two Ford officials, were dining. The reporter's photographs and news story were immediately published throughout the nation. "FIRST PHOTOS OF NEW FORD" ran the banner headline in red ink in a Detroit newspaper; "Perhaps this is the New Ford" was the more dubious appraisal of *Automotive Industries* when it reproduced the pictures. Indubitably, it *was* a Ford car, the new Tudor sedan. Meanwhile, some dealers were permitted to watch experimental models in road tests at Dearborn; and at long last, on November 30, press representatives were admitted to a demonstration there. They witnessed an impressive performance. "Through blinding eddies of snow and over rutty roads rim-deep in mud," wrote one, "the car was driven at sixty-two miles an hour, whirled about, brought to abrupt stops, and taken around curves at a breathtaking pace."[20]

Thus one of the memorable public events of 1927 thundered to a climax. This was a decade of naive mass-excitement over the arrival of celebrities—Charles Lindbergh, Gertrude Ederle, the Queen of Rumania; and when the Model A reached the principal cities of the nation it got an equally tumultous reception. On the first day a hundred thousand people crammed the showrooms in Detroit; mounted police had to be called out to control the Cleveland crowds; a mob almost burst the walls of Convention Hall in Kansas City. In New York people began gathering outside the main Ford showrooms on Broadway at three A.M.; by nine o'clock the street was so jammed that the police had to intervene; and that afternoon the manager hired Madison Square Garden. "Excitement could hardly have been greater," remarked the New York *World,* "had Pah-wah, the sacred white elephant of Burma, elected to sit for seven days on the flagpole of the Woolworth Building." The Stock Exchange registered the exultation of various interests in what the press described as a "Henry Ford market." The Ford Motor Company would make heavy purchases in many areas: four hundred thousand orders had come in before a single customer had seen the car! [21]

And what was the general verdict on the Model A? Dealers, automotive experts, competing manufacturers, and above all the general public, pronounced it a success—a car that exceeded expectations.

"There is nothing radical about the new car," Edsel admitted. "In fact, it is more conventional than old Model T." In detail, however, it embodied many innovations, all stamped with superior workmanship. The motor, combining strength with lightness and quietness, was unexcelled by any other product in the moderate-price class.* The pistons, made of aluminum alloy, weighed less than eighteen ounces apiece; other reciprocating parts were of alloy steel, light and strong. Although in adopting a selective sliding gear transmission Ford had bowed to current usage, his liberal employment of anti-friction bearings made this component better than that of rival manufacturers. All the gears were of heat-treated chromium steel. The ten-gallon gasoline tank, with gravity feed, was made an integral part of the cowl, and though some critics wagged their heads over its close proximity to the engine, actually it was entirely safe; insurance rates on the Model A were lower than on the Model T. Technicians saw at once that the generous use of steel

---

* At first, says V. Y. Tallberg, it was rough and showed excessive vibration; considerable effort was required to correct this fault.

forgings and the electric welding meant great durability. The battery ignition, with a coil and distributor of improved design that eliminated high tension cables to the sparkplugs, drew forth expressions of delight.[22]

As for the body, it satisfied all but the most fastidious of that day, for if it was not superior to those of the Chevrolet, Essex, and Whippet, it was their equal. Despite the short wheelbase, the car was comfortable and roomy. Esthetically, the only obvious defect was the lack of continuous line between the hood and the body, so that the latter "looked a little as if it had been put on as an afterthought." Of the seven body types, all were available in any of four colors—Niagara blue, gun-metal blue, Dawn gray (light or dark), and Arabian sand; except the Fordor, which was offered in Balsam green, Copra drab, Rose beige, and Andalusite blue! Edsel had designed the body so well that many likened the appearance of the Model A to a "baby Lincoln." With a minimum road clearance of nine and a half inches, the car now had the low contours of high-priced automobiles. Privately, Henry Ford said that he cared little for the improved styling, and even told a visitor to Dearborn that he still preferred the useful "tin lizzie" to its more graceful and comfortable successor. Publicly, however, he now acknowledged the importance of design: "Beauty of line and color has come to be considered, and I think rightly, a necessity in a motor car." [23]

No longer did a Ford car connote squeaks, chirps, and rattles, for the engineers, eliminating many joints, packing the interstices which remained with sound-deadening material, fitting the dashboard with a heavy insulator, and installing doors of heavier construction, had abolished most of them. No longer did the very name Ford make a passenger's spine ache, for the Houdaille hydraulic shock-absorbers, the stouter chassis, the rubber cushions at all points where the body was bolted to the chassis, and the improved transverse springs made the new model almost as smooth-running as a Pullman. In one of its features, the use of safety glass in the windshield, the Model A was in advance of all other low or medium priced cars, and of some in the high-cost range. This glass, developed by the Triplex Company, a British firm with a plant in Hoboken, was expensive.[24]

Altogether, it was a very superior car for 1927 and for its price. Ford was still intent on underselling his rivals, and when the schedule of charges was made public, people were astonished to find that prices had been held close to the Model T level and decidedly below those of the Chevrolet. The Tudor sedan sold at precisely the Model T figure, $495, and $100 below the Chevrolet charge. The Fordor sedan sold at $570, or but $30 more than its Model T counterpart, and $125 below the Chevrolet model. The coupe sold at $495, only $10 more than in Model T days, and $130 below the Chevrolet coupe. With a far better automobile than before, the Ford Motor Company was still serving the workingman, the farmer, the shopkeeper, the doctor—the plain American masses.[25]

8.

By any standards of measurement, this rebirth of the Ford automobile must be accounted one of the most striking achievements of twentieth century industrial history. Though Henry Ford's stubborn delay in recognizing the necessity of change had made the human and monetary costs greater than they need have been, they were lower than most observers had anticipated. The layoff of men in the spring of 1927 had been followed by a steady call-in of workers beginning in June, so that by Thanksgiving Week some 100,000 were busy at the Rouge and the now supplementary plant at Highland Park. Ford dealers had suffered, some becoming bankrupt, and many hanging on only by discharging sales and clerical staff and economizing to the bone; but banks were often ready to make loans on the mere strength of Ford promises of a new car, while the sale of Model T parts ($70,000,000 worth of them in the seven months that new car sales melted away!) provided a resource of real magnitude. What Edsel Ford called dealer-turnover was actually less in 1927 than in 1925 or 1926. Out of about ten thousand agents, the company in the last hard half of 1927 sustained a loss of only 1300 to 1500.*

* Of course dealers also had the remaining stocks of Model T to sell. They sold like hot cakes. "Though the Ford has been off the market nearly five months," commented the *New York Times* of October 23, 1927, "at the present time it is in third position, or better, in retail sales in the low-priced field in several cities. . . ." Edsel Ford's statement that turnover among dealers in 1927 had been less than the average of 10 per cent annually may be found in an interview in *Automotive Industries*, LVII, December 3, 1927, 845. Other evidence indicates that the turnover this year was about 15 per cent. Edsel put the total of dealers at 8500; Barron's *Financial Weekly*, quoted in the *New York Times*, August 30, 1927, estimated it at 10,000. Precise figures are now unprocurable. Keith Sward's statement that "hundreds upon hundreds" of dealers had been forced into bankruptcy is given (*The Legend of Henry Ford*, 205) without citation of any authority, and may safely be rejected. Of those who quit many took franchises for other makes. See John Billings, Jr., "10,000 Selling Agents Wait for the New Ford," Brooklyn *Daily Eagle*, October 15, 1927.

Least important of all to Henry Ford was the money cost of the changeover; for while it was staggering, it was well within the means of a company which had begun the year with a cash surplus of a quarter-billion. Ford, as we have said, had given the matter scanty thought, and when he did consider it, was satisfied with a glance at his bank balance. "All I know is that when we started actually to work out this change of models we had $350,000,000 in the bank," he said. "Now we have worked it out and we have $250,000,000 in the bank. That means we have spent $100,000,000 in the operation." Men who made a more patient and thorough calculation placed the total costs, including design, retooling, plant overhaul, and lost profits of $42,000,000 a month for a half-year, at roughly $250,000,000.

Acceptance even of that sum would not have troubled Henry Ford. In these matters his devotion to craftsmanship and to public service shone at their best. "We paid no attention to the cost or the time we took," he told a reporter. "When you are thinking about things like that you can't do a good job. This was a good job. We got things done the way we wanted them." At sixty-four he had confronted 'the biggest job of my life'; at sixty-four and a half the job was conquered.[26]

XVIII

MODEL A: A NEW ERA

WHILE from New York to San Diego crowds pushed and struggled to see the new Model A; while multitudes of Americans—50,000 in New York the first day—signed orders with cash deposits; while news came from Europe that special trains were being run to London for thousands anxious to view the car, that Berlin police were fighting back the throngs outside the exhibition rooms, and that 150,000 Spaniards attended the Madrid showing, Henry Ford and his lieutenants nevertheless had a grim comprehension that the impending year 1928 would be hard. Never in history had a vehicle aroused such excitement. It was estimated that in the United States more than 10,000,000 people inspected the model in the first thirty-six hours. But, with the Rouge works just painfully beginning their readjustment to production, with the branch assembly plants idle or barely stirring, how many cars could the company produce for the eager market? How patiently would the public wait? How successfully could General Motors and other competitors fight to hold the ground they had gained?

Some 400,000 orders went on the company books in less than a fortnight after the debut of Model A. But Henry Ford's optimism about filling them was soberly tempered. Although daily output stood at a hundred units, he said on December 2, 1927, that the company hoped to reach a thousand a day by the year-end. Then, he told reporters, "we will pick up much faster, for then it will simply mean an acceleration." But he was reluctant to set a date for the attainment of peak production; nobody knew better than Ford that the flexibility of his mass-production methods was to be tested on the factory floor.[1]

The army of Ford dealers in the first months of 1928 had a taste of the torments of Tantalus, chained where food and drink just eluded his lips. While public enthusiasm remained at a high pitch, deliveries hovered out of reach. "I feel positive that if we had had a thousand cars in the last three weeks we could have delivered every one of them," wrote a San Francisco dealer early in the year. "We have actual orders on our books, with a deposit of $25 or more, amounting to about five hundred, and have not made a single demonstration to a prospective customer." Far from lifting production to 1000 a day by New Year's, the company had brought it up only to 125–140. Not until February was each Ford dealer furnished with at least one sample car of most types in the Model A line. Inasmuch as Ford at first concentrated attention on the Tudor sedan and coupe, the Fordor sedan did not become available until May, and even in July was being made in such restricted numbers that several hundred agencies had not received a sample. Until late summer uncounted dealers tramped their Sahara wondering if the mirage of profits was ever to become a real oasis.[2]

2.

Why this costly delay? We can say in general terms that lack of early and adequate planning was responsible; it could have halved the time needed to reach full production. Designs could have been readied, layouts planned, new machines made and installed, much more rapidly. Some special threads in the story, however, demand notice.

No matter how astute the planning, the new tools and improved methods used to produce so advanced a car as the Model A would have cost much time. Not only did the car demand higher-speed tools than the Model T; every year the speed had to be increased. So far-reaching an innovation as the electric welding of parts (which one engineer, Bredo Berghoff, calls "the outstanding feature of the Model A tool-up") necessitated much readjustment of the assembly, and careful retraining of the men. Even for simple operations, it took time to break men in for new jobs; for complex processes, much more time. The two Fords and Sorensen, knowing that hurried work in these early months of 1928 would have meant defective workmanship, valued quality more than celerity. If the Model A did not stand up, the whole effort would be lost.

A certain number of factory delays, moreover, were practically inevitable. The slow delivery of machine tools was an impediment. Another difficulty lay in the new starter. Since Henry Ford objected to purchasing the Bendix starter-drive, he had ordered his aides to experiment with a new one. They spent much time and money on it with unsatisfactory results. "It jammed on the flywheel gear, and the motor would stick on the road. . . . It tore the teeth out of the ring gear of the flywheel. We had an awful lot of trouble with it"—so testifies Albert Smith. Finally the company went back to the Bendix. Manufacturing difficulties resulting from Henry Ford's insistence on bizarre details also caused delays. The valve guide bushings, the connecting rods and the large number of steel forgings required, presented even worse problems.[3]

Another set of delays clustered about the new single-system brakes of the Model A. Motor vehicle authorities in fifteen or sixteen States, the District of Columbia, Great Britain, France, and Germany raised sharp objections to a device by which foot and hand brakes acted on the same pressures; for if one failed, so did the other. Again, with the brake-rods used, an adjustment permitting the brakes to pull evenly was difficult. The governor of Washington telegraphed a protest; German officials withheld licenses; and the English plant wrote that British regulations specifying independent brakes were stringently enforced, and that if an accident befell any car which lacked legal equipment, the manufacturer might be held for serious damages.

Henry Ford for a time obstinately refused to yield ground. He was supported in this position by his chief experimental engineer, who prepared a memorandum arguing that the brake-arrangement was equal or superior in effectiveness to that of the Marmon, Pierce-Arrow, Rickenbacker, Stearns, and other higher-priced cars whose systems had been approved by every state. It was obvious that a new type of installation would delay manufacture of the car. As Sorensen wrote: "The addition of another brake, which would be absolutely unnecessary, would mean tremendous changes in the design of this automobile." But the objections were so weighty that Ford soon decreed the change.

"This will be taken care of at once," Sorensen finally cabled the Manchester plant in January, 1928. "Will meet all requirements." The company installed an emergency hand brake wholly independent of the four-wheel service brakes, announcing that all future Model A's would be equipped with it. This change, involving a rearrangement of machines and men, slowed down production for some weeks.[4]

"As frequently happens in the case of new models," explained *Automotive Daily News* in the summer of 1928, "actual use in the hands of the public brings to light the desirability of further improvements. It is these refinements of mechanical detail that up to the present have occupied Ford's time." Actually, the Model A placed the company in a far more fluid and mutable situation. Even after the faults which resulted from haste in designing the car had been cured, incessant changes had to be made to meet the demands of the new market. Apparently Ford had hoped that the bright, handsome vehicle would enjoy nearly as stable an acceptance as the Model T; if so, he was disappointed. The Model A was to live only four years. With not merely utility, but style, comfort, and freshness as the criteria, consumers wanted continuous alterations. By mid-1931, a half-year before the Model A died, two hundred major and 19,000 minor changes had been made in its construction. Where plant arrangements and machinery did not facilitate rapid shifts, the engineers had to restudy them.[5]

As a final delaying factor, the great upheaval of 1927–1928 in factory personnel was important. The car went into production just as Sorensen's purge of the "Model T" or Highland Park groups reached its climax. Avery, Hartner, Findlater, and scores of other capable men had left, their loss dealing a crippling blow. It is of course difficult to measure its effects, but we are safe in saying that they were disastrous. Looking back on the two battling factions, James O'Connor, then a foreman, has called the turmoil awful. "They were just like two companies. They weren't getting along at all." When no man could say whether the morrow would not bring his summary dismissal, morale and initiative sank. "We didn't make any preparations from one day to the other," recalls O'Connor. "I didn't make up any special tools." New men were often put in important supervisory posts without any knowledge of the techniques required. When they showed incompetence, their subordinates lost all respect for them. Many foremen became so unwilling to cooperate with such leaders that Mead L. Bricker administered stern lectures. "You've got to work with that man," he would growl, "or you're not going to be here."

Unable to express open disapproval, many foremen and workers resorted to slowdown tactics, obstructing the line. They were the more ready to do this because they suspected Sorensen of discharging some specially capable men, who seemed to be gaining Henry Ford's favor, out of mere jealousy. For example, Ford showed a high regard for one

Joe P., a first-rate mechanic in charge of body assembly. Sorensen heaped abuse and sarcasm on him. On one occasion he sneered: "Why don't you take a bath and get out of here?" Overhearing this, O'Connor remarked: "Gee, I don't know if I could take that, Joe." Joe imperturbably replied: "I get $3000 a month. If I stay here two more months that is $6000. I know I will go, all right, but what is the use of losing your head?" Three months later he was discharged. Since body assembly at this time was one of the most troublesome phases of Model A production, his removal was a blow to the whole factory.

Factionalism at the executive and supervisory levels was unquestionably in part responsible for the tardiness with which the Rouge got under way. Six months after the Model A made its debut, only 100,000 of them were on the road.[6]

3.

Hanging on grimly, many of the Ford dealers suffered heavy losses as they waited for cars. They took comfort from the resignation as sales manager of William A. Ryan, whom they had come to detest, and his replacement by the more considerate Fred L. Rockelman. But the *Automotive Daily News* correctly reported on April 23 that most of them were complaining and some were out of all patience. Late in 1928 a former large dealer in Cleveland, after some acrimonious exchanges with the company had resulted in the cancellation of his contract, asked for damages of $250,000. He had been promised deliveries, he said, and the promises had been broken.[7]

Deliveries of new cars were inevitably uneven, and this unevenness naturally bred two evils: charges of favoritism in the distribution, and the payment of bonuses by customers for preferential treatment. The air became thick with accusations that some agencies were being better treated than others. A group of New York representatives complained that Gaston Plantiff had given "pet dealers" more than half their requirements while others got only one-fifth. They telegraphed Henry Ford: "Won't you please instruct Rockelman come here personally investigate this great wrong as we are all now near bankruptcy?" Similar heartburnings were felt in Chicago, on the great plains, and along the Pacific Coast. Meanwhile, from prominent persons all over the map came pleas for a place at the head of the queue. Letters from politicians, financiers, industrialists, and film stars piled up on the desk of Edsel Ford. For, as Charles Merz writes: "To be the first owner of a new Ford in Hartford or Topeka became an honor as distinct as being elected member of an exclusive club." [8]

When Senator James Couzens placed a cash order, asking only that he be allotted the first car delivered in Washington, the Fords made him a gift of a Model A bearing the same motor number that he had owned twenty-five years earlier. "I am particularly impressed with your father's remarkable memory—that I drove motor No. 35 in 1903—and his desire to reincarnate that model," wrote Couzens to Edsel. He wished to pay, but Edsel insisted that "it is a very great pleasure to both Father and me to have it sent to you." A select list of others did get preference. Douglas Fairbanks and Mary Pickford were delighted to obtain an early coupe. "Mary uses new Ford in preference to all her other cars," telegraphed Fairbanks. "It surpasses our greatest expectations." The grant of priorities even to a few individuals, however, created such problems that in the spring of 1928 it was discontinued. To one petitioner Edsel, sending a polite refusal, wrote: "It would be hard to explain all the difficulties we are having to satisfy the clamoring public." The company nevertheless took pride in the fact that early purchasers of the Model A included Princess Ileana of Rumania, Carl Sandburg, and Franklin D. Roosevelt.[9]

Unavoidably, a system of resale at advanced prices sprang up all over the land. Men who obtained early deliveries parted with their new cars at a smart profit. Inevitably, also, some dealers who saw this done decided that *they* might as well get the profit. By selling through a third party they made a hundred or two hundred dollars per car extra. An outraged Hollywood technician telegraphed Henry Ford in the fall of 1928 that this practice was all too common. "The only parties getting legitimate delivery here have to have political drag. What can be done?"

On the whole, however, the sales department remained surprisingly healthy. The *Automotive Daily News* testified in midsummer that the loyalty and faith of the dealers were "amazing." Though a few had gone under, the mortality rate had been but slightly higher than in normal years, and the selling organization was "almost intact." Of course every weekly gain in output reduced the pressure. "Conditions are improving every day," wrote a California dealer in early fall. "In August we had thirty-one cars with a loss of only $152; and in September we delivered thirty-nine, so I feel confident we will be out of the red, and if the deliveries keep on increasing it won't be long until we are making a profit again." [10]

To assist the dealers, moreover, Henry and Edsel Ford chose the moment of the change-over to the Model A to inaugurate a striking new policy. Henry, as we have seen, had always disliked installment selling. Now, perceiving that if he were to market better-styled cars at higher prices he must follow his competitors in extending credit, he accepted it. Edsel Ford, long in favor of such a policy, was doubtless the moving spirit in the new departure. In the spring of 1928, when the company had more than 800,000 orders on hand and was constantly raising its production sights, the time seemed ripe. The actual work of organizing a Ford finance company began, indeed, as early as February, when a group of executives met to formulate plans and policies. Ernest C. Kanzler, who after leaving the company two years earlier had become executive vice-president of the Guardian Detroit Bank, played a leading role in this group. It was agreed that the new finance unit should have a close relationship with the parent motor corporation, but should not be a frank subsidiary, held in absolute ownership. It was also agreed that the capital should be furnished by two institutions, the Ford Motor Company and the Guardian Trust group of Detroit and New York. [11]

Thus it was that March, 1928, witnessed the birth of the Universal Credit Corporation, incorporated in Delaware with a capital of $11,500,-000, and with 15,000 shares of common stock so divided as to give the Ford Motor Company control with 7501; the Guardian Detroit Company taking 5000 shares, and Kanzler, as trustee, 2499. Edsel Ford announced to the dealers two months later that the corporation was ready to begin its business of financing Ford products on a time basis. It would furnish authorized agents for Ford and Lincoln cars generous assistance in accumulating stocks for delivery at the peak of the annual season. A dealer, in fact, had to advance only one tenth the list price of the car—the credit corporation supplied the rest of the money. At the same time, the corporation would assist retail customers. These might pay down as little as one-third of the cash delivery price, and would be given a year in which to complete the purchase. Fire and theft insurance were provided free.

Ford executives pointed out that the low finance charges amounted to a price-reduction on cars. "This cost of credit is just as vital as the cost of any of the material that goes into the building of the automobile. It is in every sense a commodity." [12]

4.

While the dealers, thus bolstered, held on, little by little the battle of production was won. By mid-year the output of finished cars rose to between 4000 and 4300 units a day, while the quickening rate of parts manufacture, which for certain items reached 6000 a day, lent additional encouragement. Ford spoke happily of his hope of attaining a mark of 10,000 cars a day by the opening of 1929. Practically all the domestic assembly plants were now making the new car; so were the large factories in Canada and England, and the smaller plants in Antwerp and Barcelona. Before the close of August, more than 275,000 cars had been delivered to purchasers, and the flow was rising.

As a new policy of installment credit helped sales, so a striking new policy in the use of outside parts manufacturers helped production. In old Model T days it had been Henry Ford's ambition to make most if not all of the parts of his car. The greater size, complexity, and finish of the Model A rendered this impossible. In August, 1928, Sorensen wrote Edsel Ford that, having gotten to the 4000-a-day rate, he could see a continued increase ahead. "This week we are working on stimulating the outside buying sources, so that we can make further jumps in production by getting as much help as we can from the outside and at the same time make the minimum amount of expenditure for tools, etc., in our own plants." This sound policy was energetically pursued.[13]

The company had once made all its wheels; the second half of 1928 found Kelsey-Hayes making one third of them. It had once made nearly all its own bodies; now Briggs was supplying 2500 daily, and the Murray Corporation had also begun to fill orders. Ford was buying shock-absorbers from the National Acme Company at the rate of 8000 a day, while he gave other orders to Houdaille and to Spicer. All of the storage batteries used in the new cars were purchased outside. The contracts for the starting and lighting systems were going in the main to Electric Auto-Lite of Toledo. Before many months the Muskegon Piston Ring Company had orders for about 90,000 rings daily. Indeed, it would not be long before 2200 firms would be supplying the Ford Motor Company, some of them devoting all their facilities to its needs.[14]

In the last month of 1928 the company was turning out about 6400 cars daily, and its total production for the year reached 788,572 units. Ford could feel that he had come back—back, in fact, from the verge of ruin. Even in September his output had been 22 per cent of the industry's total. He knew now that he had a superior car, that the public would wait for it, and that he was on the way to filling current demand. Before the year closed the company confidently announced that it expected to make two million units in 1929; and the nation, on the crest of its boom, believed that Ford really might.

It was time that the corner was turned. In the spring Ford had said: "Now, we've got to start saving money on these cars." In the year ending June 30, 1928, the company's cash had decreased by nearly $128,-000,000. For the calendar year 1928, it showed a net loss of almost $74,000,000, while the net reduction of its surplus was $48,512,000. To be sure, the surplus still stood at the fairly impressive sum of $582,630,-000! But actual cash on hand was $110,000,000 less than it had been in 1925; and the steady depletion of the surplus ran counter to one of Henry Ford's fundamental principles. Since its birth, the company had rigorously accumulated funds for expansion and contingencies. Nobody knew better than Ford that the industry was littered with the wreckage of companies, some of them once large and formidable, which had fallen because of inadequate liquid assets. Ford had lived through several panics and depressions; he was aware that inventions and veering taste might offer unexpected problems. Profits were imperative.[15]

To reduce costs and lift unit-income, the Ford executives took a number of steps in the summer and fall of 1928. It was fortunate for the company that Larry Sheldrick now became one of the most important of these executives. In the middle of the year Henry Ford delegated the control of engineering releases to him, and made him in all but name the chief experimental engineer. Responsible for important engineering decisions, Sheldrick made them with a celerity which speeded up all plant operations. At the same time, he gradually eliminated some of the over-costly parts and "fancy" production methods which had raised factory expenses. In this work he was manfully assisted by Joseph Galamb, P. E. Martin, Klann, and Sorensen.

Henry Ford, as we have seen earlier, had always shown himself hostile to the niceties of cost-accounting. "Heaven only knows, I don't," Sheldrick has said, "how the cost of a new Ford was determined at that time." Edsel, Kanzler, Crawford, and a few others had tried to do it scientifically. "But Mr. Ford never paid any attention. He just priced it to suit himself. I don't know what formula he used for that." In a pragmatic fashion, however, he was willing to economize. He was now prepared to drop some of the costlier features of the Model A if convinced that substitutes would be of equal or superior value.

It was Klann who heard Ford's remark about saving money, and he leaped at the opening it offered. "We can save ourselves $40 a car," he volunteered, "by putting malleable castings back in it." Of the original gestures of the Model A designed for durability, none was more expensive than the liberal use of steel forgings. For months after the car was introduced, nobody had dared to provoke Ford's wrath by even hinting that stampings would often be just as good. But Ford knew that Klann was right. He assented. "That knocked $30 off the car right away," recalls Klann. By the fall of 1928 the shift to malleable castings and stampings was under way. Galamb helped by demonstrating the strength of stampings. A trimly muscular little man, he sat down first on a forged piece, then on a stamped piece—and neither sagged. "That's all right," said Ford. "We'll save the money." [16]

Another measure adopted to dam back the creeping tide of financial loss was an increase in the prices charged for some Model A types. In November and December, 1928, the list prices f.o.b. Detroit were raised to $445-$495 for the pickup truck; $450-$460 for the roadster and phaeton; and $550 for the standard coupe. These increases were justified by a variety of facts. Ford had held his original price lists as closely as possible—and too closely—to the Model T schedule. His first Model A prices, in fact, were actually about $100 per unit below the Model T level when due allowance was made for increased weight. Factory cost sheets for March, 1928, prove that he was losing heavily on the two most popular body types:

	Factory Cost	Commercial Cost	Total Cost	List Price	Dealer's Price	Loss
Tudor	$655.38	$59.41	$714.79	$495	$396	$318.79
Phaeton	$592.43	$59.41	$651.84	$395	$316	$335.84

On each roadster the loss in March was $328.74, and on each coupe $246.81. Of course that was far from a typical month, for the limited production raised the unit costs. As output multiplied during the year, the overhead charges for each automobile fell sharply and the labor costs materially. Even the expense of materials dropped as Sheldrick and Klann introduced their substitutions. At first, too, much faulty work had to be rejected. It must be remembered that the Model A had about 5500 parts, and that practically all were of completely new design; it is not strange that early assembly work was often clumsy and many parts were spoiled. But even after all allowances are made, the cost figures remained a danger signal. The advances near the end of the year hardly absorbed the unit loss. Ford could not go beyond a certain point in raising prices, for he had to think of competitors and of his well-earned reputation for keeping good cars low. Loss could be turned into a profit only by careful economies, by improving plant efficiency, and by distributing fixed charges and production expenses over a tremendous number of units. Quantity was particularly important: the year 1929 must be one of expansion.[17]

5.

If expansion should not be steady and rapid, if production should not move well above 1,500,000 units, the Ford Motor Company in 1929 would lose ground to its rivals. The pace of competition was growing keener. Two evidences of this harsh fact must have troubled Henry Ford's pillow: the continued progress of the Chevrolet, and the rise of Walter P. Chrysler not only to third place, but to a formidable third.

The star of Chevrolet soared into the zenith in 1928, its factories working at peak capacity to fill the void created by Ford's slow change-over. By the middle of the year an average of 5300 Chevrolet units was coming each day from the assembly lines. More than a million units in all were built, or 24 per cent of the whole production of the industry as compared with Ford's 15.4 per cent. It was clear that the basic policy of General Motors as planned by the farsighted Alfred P. Sloan, and applied to Chevrolet by his brilliant lieutenants, Knudsen in manufacturing and Richard H. Grant in marketing, was thoroughly sound. The strategy was not to produce the cheapest automobile, but to hold the price at about $100 above the Ford, introduce engineering improvements every year, and to make changes in styling which emulated the lines and ornamentation of costlier cars. With a smoother engine than the Ford, a better body (by Fisher), and other original features, the Chevrolet gained a loyal following. The long wheelbase, 107 inches by 1928, gave it distinctive bigness in its price group.[18]

Everybody anticipated that the Model A would call forth a radically redesigned line of Chevrolets. Throughout 1928 the Chevrolet engineers were busy. They worked with the system, precision, and foresight of a picked body of experts, harmoniously controlled. At Thanksgiving the result of their labors was disclosed, and impartial observers at once pronounced it the most arresting car offered for the new season. Its six-cylinder engine especially delighted a host of Americans. For five years the march of automotive planners had been away from the four-cylinder car, and Sloan, Knudsen, and their associates had boldly decided to join it. This left the country with only the Ford, Whippet Four, Durant Four, and Plymouth as important four-cylinder models. The new Chevrolet engine developed forty-six horsepower, one-third more than its predecessor, had a rapid acceleration, and reached a speed of seventy miles an hour. The car also boasted a full-length frame, larger bearings, an oil gauge, oil filter, temperature indicator, an easier clutch, and other improvements. Its appearance was smarter.

All this General Motors made available at a moderate price. The six body types of Chevrolet were offered at $595 to $725, which meant a maximum increase of only $30 above prices of the previous year. Richard H. Grant could assert: "Here is a six selling in the price-range of the four." [19] It was in fact the lowest-price six-cylinder car in the world, costing about $100 less than its nearest competitors. The Model A had a rival which would not be easy to defeat.

This rival, moreover, at once reached the market in adeqaute quantities. Soon after Christmas, practically all of the ten thousand Chevrolet dealers had a new six on display, and deliveries had begun. Whereas Ford's factory changeover had been halting and costly, Chevrolet's was swift and economical. Setting a new record, it was a striking illustration of the possible flexibility of the new processes of mass production.* Only six weeks, in fact, elapsed between the building of the last four-cylinder and the first six-cylinder cars. Nothing had been left to chance or improvisation. Less than two months after the changeover began, dealers

---

* The careful advance planning of General Motors deserves remark. As early as 1925 the company began to investigate the possibility of a moderate-priced six-cylinder car. Soon afterward, Chevrolet engineers under James Crawford began designing and testing engines. More than a hundred were built, tested, and discarded before final approval was given one model in May, 1928. Meanwhile, Fisher engineers had designed new bodies, and other men improved various components. The changeover was then carried forward at a score of widely scattered plants. At Flint new machines were installed and thousands of workers instructed in the new methods. Knudsen also built a supplementary motor plant at Saginaw where, Sept. 1–Nov. 15, other thousands were familiarized with their tasks. Thanks to such preparations, even in December the production of motors averaged more than 2000 a day.

had been furnished with sample cars, regular production was moving smoothly, and output was steadily increasing. By February 1, 1929, less than three months after the beginning, all the Chevrolet plants were humming at full capacity. Thus only about 120 days intervened between discontinuance of the old models, and the attainment of high production on the new six.[20]

It is not strange that the whole industry, including Ford engineers, applauded Sloan's genius for organization and Knudsen's for leadership in what one trade journal called "a manufacturing miracle." To celebrate the feat, General Motors tendered Knudsen a banquet, where he was lustily cheered. Chevrolet output swiftly gained momentum. By the end of August, 1929, one million of the new sixes had come off the line. It seemed still uncertain in early summer whether the Model A or the "Chevvie," the product of Henry Ford's mechanical genius or that of General Motors team work, would bear off the blue ribbon for the year's sales. They were racing neck and neck. Had the price of the Chevrolet been lowered, Ford might have been doomed to defeat; as it was, the comparative cheapness of his excellent car still gave him an advantage. The Ford Motor Company had itself put a modestly improved line of types on display in January, 1929, including a town sedan, a cabriolet, a station wagon, and coupes. They had been well received, and demand seemed as insatiable as ever.

Meanwhile, no chapter in these years of the Coolidge-Hoover boom was more dramatic than that which chronicled the rise of Walter P. Chrysler and his company. Their swift emergence to power was the single exception to the rule that major rank in the automotive field could no longer be attained by a newcomer. All other would-be competitors with Ford and General Motors met frustration or disaster; William C. Durant, for example, failed to conquer a place for his enterprises during the period rather because he could not command the resources of the two giants than because he dallied with the stock market. But Chrysler succeeded where others collapsed. His bold personality made him, as one automotive historian has written, the last great individual constructive force in the industry.[21]

Big, tough, and brainy, Chrysler was a onetime master mechanic who never quite shed the rough ways of his early years in the railway shops. He was still a young man when he became plant manager of the American Locomotive Company, and only thirty-seven when in 1912 he joined General Motors. Four years later he became president and general manager of the Buick division (as well as G.M.'s vice-president in charge of operations) at a salary of $500,000 a year. He made so enviable a record as a cost-conscious executive with a creative grasp of factory techniques that by the end of the first World War he stood among the first dozen industrial leaders of America.[22]

Yet a greater career opened for him after 1920. Disgusted with Durant's erratic management of General Motors, he resigned. At forty-five, he was already a legendary figure; "a glittering personality with a rich railroadman's vocabulary, a short temper, and a showman's pride." At once a group of anxious bankers, an Eastern syndicate which had made loans of $50,000,000 to the Willys-Overland Company, bent their eyes upon him. The company seemed headed for ruin. Led by the suave James C. Brady, the syndicate by the offer of a net annual salary of $1,000,000 lured Chrysler in 1920 into the executive vice-presidency of Willys-Overland. By the exercise of his genius as a production engineer, he then quickly put the company on its feet. From this success he went on to salvage the Maxwell Motor Company. Chrysler sold the huge overstock of cars at a profit simply by doctoring the weak rear axles, he held off creditors, he reorganized production, he improved the automobile. By 1923 Maxwell was making $2,678,000, and in 1924 its profits went to well over $4,000,000.[23]

However, Chrysler wished to manufacture new and better automobiles under his own name. As president of Maxwell, he hired from the old engineering staff of Willys three engineers whom he had learned to admire: Fred M. Zeder, Carl Breer, and Owen R. Skelton. Bringing them to Detroit, he set them to work on a six-cylinder high-compression engine for which Zeder had already made certain designs.[24] In 1924 a new car, made by the Maxwell Corporation but called the Chrysler Six, was put on the market. When Chrysler in January of that year tried to exhibit it at the Grand Central show in New York, the officials there denied him space because the car had not yet been commercially sold. He resourcefully leased the lobby of the Hotel Commodore hard by, and displayed it with great effect. The attention it received not only encouraged him, but helped him obtain a $5,000,000 loan from bankers, so that the car was soon being shipped to dealers all over the country. It won unqualified praise. Selling at $1565, it was the first automobile in the medium-priced field to use a high-compression engine. Weighing only 2650 pounds, it was so styled and powered as to give the owner a sense that he was driving a far more expensive automobile. In its own class, it had unsurpassed speed and acceleration. Nearly 32,000 sold the first year.[25]

It was now possible for Walter Chrysler to stand alone. In 1925 he acquired the Maxwell business and properties, discontinued the line of that name, and formally organized the Chrysler Corporation. Beginning in thirty-second place in the industry, he rapidly scaled the ladder. In 1926, with four models and reduced prices, he reached fifth place. In 1927, selling nearly 200,000 units, he climbed to fourth. His profits, some $46,000,000 in three years, enabled him to carry through an ambitious program of plant construction and renovation, and to introduce the latest advances in industrial technology. By the spring of 1928, when the Model A was struggling to be fully born, he was manufacturing three sixes and a four, was planning a new six, the De Soto, and was firmly holding third place in the industry. His spectacular rise, the most astonishing since Henry Ford's, had been fairly earned by intellect, character, and enterprise; and though the Willys-Overland and Maxwell stages in his career indicated the extent to which finance capitalism had now moved into the business, he had shown a rugged independence. Still only fifty-three, he could look for new realms to conquer.[26] *

But to achieve the most important conquest—to capture part of the most profitable market—Chrysler must bring out a popular-priced car. And to do this he must have a plant sufficiently large, varied, and efficient to supply him with many of the parts which he was buying outside at excessive expanse. Lacking any foundry or forge-shop, he had to purchase great quantities of cast-iron parts and steel forgings. As he later reflected: "Without the better control of costs such as we could achieve with bigger plants, there was no hope of digging into that greatest of automobile markets, the one in which Henry Ford's only real rival was Chevrolet." Chrysler estimated that the facilities he needed, if built from the ground up, would cost $75,000,000. This placed him in a dilemma. If he erected new factories, the cost would over-

---

* Chrysler's industrial realism is illustrated by an incident related by Harold Hicks, who, discharged from the Ford company in 1932, soon found a position in the Chrysler research department. He experimented with streamlining, and by altering the body of a car, increased its speed from 83 to 98 miles per hour, with less fuel consumption. Chrysler had been about to abolish his research activities as an economy measure, but when told of what Hicks had done, he reflected for some seconds, then remarked: "Well, if that's what research will do, then we must always have research." (Hicks, *Reminiscences*.)

tax his capital reserves, and burden his new model with so many additional charges that it might not be low-priced at all; while the delay involved in construction would be a grave handicap. Yet if he merely expanded his existing plant, he might spend great sums without a really satisfactory result. What could he do?

He could merge with another corporation; and in 1928 the chance suddenly came. The Dodge Brothers Company, which in the middle twenties had been perhaps the strongest of the independents, by 1927 sank, as a result of weak management and poor styling, to so precarious a position that the bankers in control wished to get rid of their holdings. Clarence Dillon, of Dillon, Read & Company, undertook to manage the disposal. He knew that neither Ford nor General Motors would be interested in the purchase. But Walter Chrysler might, and Dillon approached him. Chrysler was receptive.[27]

For five days in May, 1928, Chrysler and Dillon were closeted in a suite at the Ritz-Carlton Hotel in New York, repeatedly twelve hours at a time. Finally an agreement was reached. As Chrysler insisted that it must be ratified by at least nine-tenths of the owners of each class of Dodge stock, for he wanted no trouble with minority stockholders, it was not until July 30 that the bargain was closed. No cash changed hands. But Chrysler paid $70,000,000 in stock, and assumed the interest payments on Dodge bonds aggregating $56,000,000. It was safe for him to do so, for experts agreed that the enlarged Chrysler interests had a potential earning capacity, under current conditions, of about $50,000,-000 a year.[28]

Even in a year which witnessed many large-scale industrial mergers, the absorption of the Dodge properties by Chrysler was outstanding: the largest such transaction, as the New York *World* said, in the history of the automobile industry. People everywhere noted that the Big Three who now dominated the business were producing in 1928 between 75 and 80 per cent of all the passenger automobiles made in the nation. That the Chrysler Corporation would become an aggressively efficient competitor in the low-priced domain everybody took for granted. No time was lost in effecting the merger of physical resources. In Detroit, Chrysler's chief production manager, the veteran K. T. Keller, had prepared gigantic canvas signs reading, "Chrysler Corporation, Dodge Division." A few minutes after the merger was sealed, Keller and his aides marched through the Dodge gates under the freshly painted streamers and took charge. They introduced extensive changes that soon saved Chrysler millions yearly.[29]

"The greatest thing I ever did was to buy the Dodge," said Chrysler years later. He got the plant facilities which had become indispensable to him, and which Keller quickly made doubly useful; and he at once supplemented them by building a new million-dollar engineering laboratory in Highland Park, where Zeder and his technicians began development work on the low-priced car. He also got about 4600 Dodge dealers, an accession which almost doubled his sales outlets. The *Automotive Daily News* congratulated him on thus "taking over a full-fledged and powerful merchandising army." Expanding the force, within a year he had close to 12,000 dealers, and stood on the same plane as the two leaders in the industry. He now had exactly the keys he needed to unlock the gates into the Elysium which a year earlier Ford and Chevrolet had occupied alone.[30]

In July, 1928, even before the final signatures were placed on the Dodge purchase, Chrysler introduced the Plymouth. The car descended from a model called the Chrysler 52, in turn a descendant of the old four-cylinder Maxwell. In its initial form, the Plymouth was not an automobile to create wild excitement in the breasts of the buying public. With a good 45-horsepower engine, hydraulic four-wheel brakes, and mediocre body design, it sold for from $670 for the roadster and coupe to $725 for the four-door design. It was not at first a close competitor of the Ford or Chevrolet, and when 1928 closed, only 76,000 had been distributed. But it was a threat for the future. Chrysler, as *Time* put it, had "gone into the low-priced field with the throttle wide open." He proved the fact by building a special Plymouth factory with a daily capacity of 1800 cars, and by raising production there in May of 1929 to 1000 automobiles daily.[31]

Like Sloan and Knudsen, Chrysler and Keller were not to be taken lightly.

6.

The nineteen-twenties were a decade in which great corporations, growing greater still, obeyed an apparent law of concentration fatal to many minor businesses. In the steel, oil, radio, railroad, banking, newspaper, and other industries, numerous weak competitors were crushed out of existence. The resolute survivors, in the favorable climate of the

Harding-Coolidge-Hoover administrations, usually adopted a policy of mutual tolerance. Midway between unrestricted competition, which no longer worked, and monopoly, which people and government attacked, sprang up a system labelled by the ugly word oligopoly. A few giants, not unreasonably hostile to each other, partitioned a given domain. Sometimes a mild price-competition survived, though even the state now tended to curtail it by laws against unfair trade practices. Sometimes the competition was confined to technological advances, to advertising, or to the dress of the article sold.

The automobile industry remained competitive, but the rivalry was more and more restricted to powerful organizations. Year by year the weaker companies dropped out or were merged. Manufacture of low-priced units in 1928 was practically confined to three leaders whose names were known to every child. Of these General Motors had total assets of $1,098,478,000; Ford of $742,056,000; and Chrysler-Dodge of $235,500,000. No other company was able to come within hailing distance of the Big Three. The Willys interests, including Willys-Overland, had assets valued at the respectable figure of $77,000,000; Durant Motors, Inc., was worth about $42,360,000. But neither really counted as a rival, and the Durant Company was destined for early extinction. This year the *Automotive Daily News* commented: "Many competent observers believe that the automobile manufacturing business is destined to simmer down to half a dozen big companies, run on the highest plane of efficiency and thus shutting off any competition." Between 1921 and 1930, the roster of exhibitors at the New York automobile show declined by nearly half.[32]

Chevrolet in 1928, as we have seen, outdistanced Ford, selling just over a million units as against not quite 800,000 for the Ford Motor Company. But in 1929 the tables were turned. When the year began, the Ford plants were racing into high gear. As the millionth Model A came off the line in February, Ford was producing about 7500 units a day, and by May he was making 8000. On June 26 his plants set a high record for a single day's work, building 9100 cars and trucks. The country still seemed riding the very crest of a wave of prosperity, and demand appeared almost insatiable. A month later, on July 24, the two millionth Model A rolled from the assembly, and in August production broke all monthly records but one. The industry as a whole this year was manufacturing 5,358,000 cars and trucks, or almost a quarter more than in any previous year. And to the very end of the year the Ford stride never slackened, although the rest of the industry began to falter as early as July. With the confusions and difficulties of 1927–1928 behind him, Ford was reasserting his power in factory and market.[33]

When New Year's eve came, the Ford executives could throw their hats in air. Their total output for the year 1929 was 1,851,092 units, the largest since 1925. Sales, as distinguished from factory production, came to 1,710,734 units. The company had outdistanced Chevrolet by about 400,000 units, a very satisfactory margin. It had taken 34 per cent of the business, leaving the Chevrolet far behind with only 20 per cent. The Plymouth toiled in the rear this year with sales of 85,700, a figure which did not deceive those who knew Chrysler's capabilities; the Whippet and the Durant car were nowhere. In all the prestige of achievement, it was a good year for the Ford Motor Company.

Financially, also, 1929 had been a highly encouraging year. By increased sales, lowered costs, and price advances, the company had repaired the gap that had been torn in its finances. With the market eagerly taking all the Model A's that could be made, Ford gradually, and without exciting comment, placed moderate increases on nearly all his popular types. The gross volume of his sales came to $748,000,000 as against $298,000,000 the previous year. It was the easier to make the increases because his finance company, the Universal Credit Corporation, was now busily offering credit throughout the country, and was rapidly raising the number of loans to customers close to the 400,000 mark. This, it should be noted, was accomplished with only the most trivial defaults. During the year the cash resources of the Ford Motor Company rose from $161,000,000 to 222,500,000, and the net current assets grew by $83,000,000![34]

What, however, would the next year be like? That was a question which hundreds of millions of anxious people on five continents were now asking. For on Thursday, October 24, 1929, the New York stock market had suddenly dropped, and had been checked only by a frantic pooling of bankers' funds to sustain it. The following Tuesday, October 29, it had plunged again so precipitously that prices fell forty points, and a host of speculators on margin were wiped out. Thereafter apprehension filled the air. All efforts to shore up the American economy to the old levels of activity proved futile. As optimism gave way to pessimism, merchants revoked their orders, builders cancelled their contracts, and plain citizens restricted all their activities. The farmers, who for several years had been in trouble, suffered more acutely than ever as mortgages were foreclosed; owners and employees of small shops, gasoline stations, amusements, and other marginal activities found their businesses in collapse; labor began to be laid off. Europe had ample economic problems of its own, and the sudden American depression made them worse.

It was certain that the contest between Ford and General Motors for leadership would go on. But it would go on under very different conditions, and as the depression advanced, observers began to wonder whether the main question for most automotive companies would not be one of simple survival.

XIX

PROJECTS AND PERSONALITIES

TEN miles from Detroit, driving west on Michigan Avenue, just beyond its junction with Southfield Road, the motorist of the nineteen-twenties came to a driveway turning northwest into mingled forest and farm land. It was the entrance to Fair Lane, the estate of Henry Ford, and the center of his personal life. Here the visitor who could pass the iron entrance gates and the guard stationed there might find Ford in a setting both remote and peaceful. Yet from Fair Lane radiated activities which engaged no small portion of the industrialist's energies, and helped define his multi-faceted personality.

The site of his own early rambles along the Rouge River, an area that preserved with little alteration the atmosphere of the eighteen-eighties which both he and his wife loved, a tract which for years had been their happy week-end haunt, Fair Lane was dear to both the Fords. It combined convenience with solitude and even wildness; for while only a few miles separated it from the throbbing Rouge, yet on any day, as a car sped to or from the highway, a rabbit, pheasant, fox, or deer might dash across in front of it. Fair Lane offered protection, too. During the last few years of their stay on Edison Avenue in Detroit, the Fords had literally battled with crowds of importunate visitors: seekers of gifts or of money for investment in fantastic schemes, cranks, admirers, and the merely curious. So at the Fair Lane entrance, a mile from where the gray stone house stood by the placid river, all who approached were halted. "I like privacy in my home," Ford explained frankly. "The people would make it a public park. It is to obtain the privacy that any man is entitled to in his own home, that I keep a guard at the gate. . . . Unless I did . . . my place would be overrun with strangers."[1]

What a visitor would see of the 2000-acre estate * was mostly forest, lawn, and garden. In general the wooded portions lay toward the river, to the left of the road as one entered. But beyond the house a smooth stretch of sward, originally prepared as a golf course for Edsel, extended half a mile northward to a small artificial lake, and the woods spread out on either side of it. The course had lain unused since Edsel's marriage, and the leg that fishhooked back from the lake into the woods was later developed into Clara's rose garden. Everywhere the greater part of the woods was second growth, but a number of patriarch trees—willows, oaks, elms—towered above the others, survivors from the older forest.

Clara had superintended the landscaping of the grounds, with the original intention to alter them little, and in making changes or additions to use flowers, shrubs, and trees native to the area. This plan was never abandoned, in that the natural look of the place was always preserved. But in her enthusiasm for gardening Clara Ford gradually introduced a number of alien but harmonious shrubs and plants. Particularly happy importations were the scilla, low, blue ground flowers which she finally established with snowdrops in dozens of areas along the woods and paths, where they spread carpets of white and cobalt in the crisp April days.

Aside from the flower beds edging the house, Clara developed a number of special areas, mostly near it—the English, Iris, Blue, Peony, and Trail gardens, and in 1925–1926 her crowning rose garden. This lay a full quarter of a mile northeast of the residence, in the woods. Clara had at first planted her roses near the house, in what later became the English Garden. Then she decided to attempt a more ambitious project, and arranged with Mrs. Harriet Foote of Marblehead, a well-known landscape gardener, to design and plant the new area. However, so great was Clara's interest in the enterprise that she made constant changes and modifications in the plans, and may fairly be regarded as a co-designer.

The completed garden covered an area of two and a half acres, stretching—from the summer house at the end nearest the residence to the pergola opposite—a distance of 610 feet, with a width from forest to

* This may be given as the size of the residence grounds. Actually, Ford had continually gone on acquiring farm lands adjacent to his holdings, and by 1918 possessed fully 5000 acres—a total which continued to increase. (Henry Ford, "Why Henry Ford Wants to Be Senator," *World's Work*, XXXVI, Sept., 1918, 525.)

forest of from 140 to 180 feet. The woodland setting gave it a natural beauty, which was enhanced by a large lily pond near the summer house and two rocky pools with a connecting stream at the pergola end; while the hundreds of thousand of blossoms, red, yellow, pink, salmon, white, damask, on bush or trellis against the turf of the garden floor, made a riot of color worthy of medieval legend. In 1926, 12,000 bushes all told were set out, with old and modern varieties both adequately represented.

While Clara Ford used to say that her pillow was a seed catalog, and while her notes and jottings show a wide range of interest in flowers and shrubs, the rose undoubtedly reigned unchallenged in her heart. A fragment, perhaps part of a paper for a garden club, brings to us some of the enthusiasm she knew in 1927:

I have had three lovely rose gardens in my life, one in Detroit, where I formerly lived, one much larger when I came out in the country to live 12 years ago, and last spring I planted still another with 10,000 roses, bush and climbers, with 600 varieties, many of the bronze yellow, Salmon, & apricot color that we have not seen until the last few years. I am a lover of roses, and hope to add to my collection from year to year, as new roses are introduced. I shall not make my garden any larger, but eliminate uninteresting ones for better ones. So large a garden is a great problem, with all the *pests* we have to contend with, but withall a great joy.[2]

Henry Ford, who enjoyed the outdoors in all its aspects, looked with a benign eye upon Clara's adventures with flowers, but reserved his greater enthusiasm for the wilder aspects of his estate, and for his farming activities. He loved to tramp along the Rouge River, to skate on frozen lake or stream, and to watch the birds and wild animals. "I like the outdoors. I like to walk across country and jump fences," he confessed. He had a reverence for unspoiled nature. "I never cut a tree down," he told Frank Stockbridge in 1918. He knew the exact day on which bobolinks arrived in Dearborn, knew what birds wintered there, and had 500 birdhouses on "the farm." "We call them our bird hotels," he said, "and one of them, the Hotel Pontchartrain,—a martin house —has seventy-six apartments. All winter long we have wire baskets of food hanging about on the trees, and then there is a big basin in which the water is kept from freezing by an electric heater."[3]

As to the farm, he set out apple and peach orchards, and gave close attention to grain and vegetable crops. Already in 1918 he had erected a 110,000 bushel concrete grain elevator, and in 1921 opened a flour mill

which operated for many years. Of course Ford was especially concerned
with the use of his tractor and its attachments for the cultivation of the
land, and for spraying and harvesting crops. He viewed this activity
as socially constructive; he stated more than once that eventually he
would cut up his thousands of acres into small farms, and "teach people
how to live on them." Although he "never cut a tree down," on one
occasion, doubtless for good reason, he himself felled an oak 41 inches
in diameter. It was estimated to be 250 years old, a contemporary of
Tecumseh's grandfather, and yielded four twelve-foot logs which produced 2540 board feet of lumber.[4]

Edsel had resided less than one year at Fair Lane before marriage
took him to his own Detroit home on Iroquois Avenue, then in 1919
to East Jefferson Avenue, and finally in 1926 to Gaukler Pointe. He
and his growing family often visited Clara and Henry. "We have built
a home in the country since I saw you," Clara wrote in October, 1919,
to an old friend, "and we love it very much, have a wonderful garden.
My son is married, and has a little son two years old and one three
months old. The eldest is named Henry II and the baby Edsel Junior
[the name, then in doubt, became Benson]. The eldest talks and runs
all over, calls Mr. Ford ga-daddie. We have them out with us a great
deal and could not love Edsel's wife more if we had picked her ourselves." Henry wrote notes to his grandchildren, played games with
them. In the end there were four—Henry II, Benson, and then after
a space of four years Josephine (July 7, 1923) and William Clay (March
14, 1925).[5]

The Edsel Fords' Gaukler Pointe home was built in 1926–1927, on
land deeded to them by Henry and Clara. According to Liebold, the
older Fords had intended to construct a residence there, but discovered
that they would be expected to assume community responsibilities, and
wanted complete freedom from such obligations. The situation of the
property—14½ miles from Detroit on the shores of Lake St. Clair—
was excellent, the entire 65 acres lying between the Lake Shore Drive
and the water. There were 3000 feet of shoreline, including a "peninsula"
which jutted out and curved back toward the shore to make a lagoon
admirably suited for mooring boats. A golf club and a country club
lay close by, while the Grosse Pointe Yacht Club was only a mile distant.

The estate as it finally developed included a lodge, a recreation pavilion (near which were a swimming pool and tennis courts), a power house, machine shop, greenhouse, garages, and the main building. All the structures were designed by Albert Kahn, who spent some time in Worcestershire studying the Cotswold type of architecture, selected as the general style. The two-storied main house included more than thirty rooms, an art gallery, and numerous baths and washrooms. It possessed an architectural distinction which the more expensive Fair Lane completely lacked.[6]

The two families had many friends in common, but also had their own particular groups. Edsel and his wife associated with what might be called the wealthy younger set in Detroit (the Books, Calkins, Jacksons, Potters, Macauleys), while Henry and Clara kept cordial ties with old friends and relatives of the Dearborn area, and with men and women the Fords had encountered as Henry had become better known. Undoubtedly the Edisons were closest to them. John Burroughs, until his death in 1921, and his associate Clara Barrus (who later continued the relationship), were both friends, and Ford in 1916 dedicated a grotto on the bank of the Rouge to the naturalist, Burroughs laying the cornerstone. A number of the stones facing the recess, and those leading to a bird bath below, came from the Burroughs homestead. A statuette of Burroughs was placed in the grotto in 1918. In connection with the larger memorial to Burroughs established chiefly through Ford's efforts, the latter met Hamlin Garland and his daughter. In England the Perrys were close friends until Perry left the company in 1919, and again after his return in 1929. On their first trip to England in 1912 the Fords had become acquainted with Lord and Lady Astor (born Nancy Langhorne of Virginia), and the two families remained in touch with each other by letter and visit for the next thirty-eight years. The Firestones in Akron, Arthur Brisbane the Hearst editor and columnist in New York, the Alvan Macauleys, Henry B. Joys, Dodges, and Livingstons in Detroit were among those with whom the Fords visited and corresponded. Clara found further social variety in her garden club and reading circle, while Henry maintained touch with old associates in the automotive field like Charles B. King, G. C. Flint, and James Bishop (who had helped him build his first car). Among Ford dealers Gaston and Ellen Plantiff in New York and Dutee and Rose Flint in Providence enjoyed a close personal relationship.

A number of those named were guests at Fair Lane; there too came

Charles Lindbergh, John D. Rockefeller, Jr., George Washington Carver, Chase S. Osborn (former governor of Michigan), and the then Prince of Wales, later Edward VIII. The house was well-staffed, but the atmosphere of Fair Lane was one of informality and simplicity. Ford himself was a sparing eater and seldom if ever served liquor. Clara, however, does not seem to have trimmed her menus to his taste; she loved rich desserts, and her papers contain many recipes for cakes, puddings, and candies. There is even one for a whiskey sour: two parts whiskey, one of lemon juice, and one of rock candy syrup—really a "whiskey sweet."

The Fords were pleasant hosts. Henry, incessantly active during the day, enjoyed the relaxation of talking with a variety of people; from fellow industrialists to writers, scientists, and young married couples. Alone, the two read aloud (that is, Clara to Henry: he himself read poorly and as he grew older disliked to use the glasses he needed), and talked about Ford's business affairs. "Anyone who knows the Fords," wrote Pipp in 1922, "knows that Mrs. Ford discusses nearly everything with Mr. Ford, reads to him a great deal, talks business matters and publicity with him, entertains reporters and correspondents at the home, when they are to write about him."

As their wealth and reputation increased both, Mrs. Ruddiman believes, were conscious of a certain isolation. "People wouldn't let them be people." They were justly wary of those seeking money or favors. Knowing this, a number of old friends and relatives forbore to approach them, lest their taking the initiative might be misconstrued. However, with friends like the Edisons, Ives, Flints, and Plantiffs, and with their closer relatives, Edsel and his family in particular, they could be fully at ease.[7]

Just as Ford liked to keep control in the Ford Motor Company indeterminate, so he liked to order his own movements with a kind of mystic intuition. Sometimes he arrived in strangely unorthodox fashion. John D. Rockefeller, Jr. told how, not long after World War I, he called on Ford at Dearborn and was ushered into his first-story office there. A minute later Ford strode up from outside, flung open a window, threw a leg across the sill, and leaped in!

Carl Sandburg visiting Ford as a journalist, saw him in comparable moments of antic action. But Sandburg found more than a Puck in

Ford. "One feels in talking with Ford that he is a man of power rather than of material riches." [8]

2.

An organizer even of his leisure, Ford from 1918 onward developed a kind of summer institution in the form of camping trips with a few chosen friends. He had always been a walker and nature lover, and from an early date went on brief outings. Clara records one in her diary for the spring of 1901. "Henry got home all safe," she writes. "Brought home fish and ducks. He had quite a time walking across the bay. But had a good time." The idea of the later camping trips seems to have germinated in a trip by the Fords and Edisons to the Florida Everglades, and to have taken firm root in California in 1915, when Ford, Edison, and Firestone, at the Panama-Pacific Exposition, went by private railroad car to Luther Burbank's home, and, at Firestone's suggestion, drove down southern California from Riverside to San Diego. Edison suggested that they repeat the outing the following year, and all agreed. Ford expected to go, but couldn't, and the first expedition, a success, was made without him, John Burroughs being persuaded to accompany Edison and Firestone. However, Ford joined the 1918 outing to the Great Smokies, and at once became the dominant spirit of this and later excursions.

The campers for that year were Edison, Firestone and his son, Harvey junior, Ford, Burroughs (who left a charming, 17-page typed account of the trip), Professor R. J. De Loach, an expert in plant pathology, and for a time Edward N. Hurley of the United States Shipping Board. They employed a group of six cars: two Packards for riding, two Model T's, and two Ford trucks; altogether they had seven drivers and helpers. Equipment, Burroughs observed, provided for what he called luxurious living (there were tents, chairs, stoves, a refrigerator, electric light, and tables). Their roads, however, were rugged, while, noted the eighty-year-old-Burroughs, they all craved direct contact with nature, and "cheerfully endure wet, cold, smoke, mosquitoes, black flies, and sleepless nights, just to touch naked reality once more."

Ford as a camper was a zealot. At a garage in Connellsville, Pennsylvania, to which they limped on the second day with a broken fan and a punctured radiator on one of their Packards, the mechanics shook their heads and suggested waiting for new parts from Pittsburgh. Ford snorted. "Give me a chance," he demanded, took off his coat, and in two hours had ingeniously repaired the damage. Their route led them to cold mountain camps at night, but Ford helped chop wood for the fires. He liked the people he met. When a little girl came to them with a pail of apples, he bought them all. He must have been delighted when Edison, bestowing five cents apiece on a group of youngsters, asked one of them if she knew his name, and drew the reply: "Yes, Mr. Graphophone." Burroughs himself attracted teachers, editors, clergymen, and nature lovers; but he was amused and somewhat dashed when a college president brought up a group of young women, saying, "Ladies of the college, this is Henry Ford," and failed to notice Burroughs, who had prepared a one-sentence speech in anticipation.

The friends built nightly campfires and talked of literature, mechanical progress, agriculture, and politics. Hurley and De Loach left; the others swung up into Tennessee and North Carolina, then back by way of Virginia and Maryland. Already the newspapers were beginning to follow their movements, although publicity had not become embarrassing.*

The 1918 trip is the only one for which a full account survives, and it was apparently a pattern for the others. As we have seen in Chapter IX, the party in 1919 included Kingsford, and followed a route through northern New York, Vermont, and New Hampshire. There was no camping trip in 1920, but a fall outing was held at Yama Farms, New York. Then, apparently, the wives demanded a share in the adventure; and in 1921 a journey through Maryland and Pennsylvania saw Mrs. Edison, Mrs. Ford, Mrs. Firestone, Mrs. Harvey Firestone, Jr., and Mrs. W. F. Anderson (wife of Bishop Anderson) with the party, as well as President Harding. Mrs. Harding had been invited but could not go. In 1923 the party visited Coolidge in Massachusetts, and in late April, 1924, on a journey across the upper peninsula of Michigan, Ford acted as engineer and Firestone as fireman for a train which carried the Fords, Edisons, Firestones, and Edsel Fords to various Ford properties—Iron Mountain, Sidnaw, and L'Anse among them. This was Pullman car camping; later in the year all assembled as Ford's guests at the Wayside Inn, in Massachusetts, and the men called upon Coolidge in Plymouth,

* For excerpts from Burrough's 17-page account of the 1918 trip, see Chapter I.

Vermont, who made Ford a gift of a four gallon maple sap bucket, fashioned about 1780 by one of his ancestors.[9] *

The summer of 1924 marked the end of the trips. The three surviving members of the original group (Burroughs had died in 1921) were older and busier, and apparently the work of organizing an expedition for the wives as well as for the men (there were at least five women to be considered) was a formidable undertaking. For the men, the rougher, more informal experience was what they wanted; the introduction of the women had undoubtedly conventionalized it. Again, novelty had worn off and publicity had come in. "The trips were good fun," said Ford in 1926, "except that they began to attract too much attention." [10]

In a more comfortable fashion he continued to seek the change and exploration of unfamiliar regions which they had provided. He made some use of his yacht the *Sialia,* which Mayo had bought for him in 1917, and from which he inspected his new upper peninsula properties in 1920. Repairs and alterations from 1921 to 1925, including a change from steam to diesel engines, cost more than a million dollars, and the salaries for a crew of 32 men totalled more than $5000 a month. The *Sialia* was fully and luxuriously equipped. Later Ford used the *Henry II* for lake voyages.[11]

When the Fords visited the Edisons at Fort Myers, Florida, in 1914, their hosts urged them to establish a winter home there. In December, 1916, Henry and Clara did so, buying a plot of land and a house for $20,000. In June, 1922, they acquired additional frontage for $13,500, giving them a total of four acres, next to the Edisons. The house, on which $22,000 was spent for improvements, was a two-storied building, with gables, and stood amid oaks, palms, mango, and grapefruit trees.

* The following anecdote may be partly or wholly the invention of an ingenious reporter. The friends were driving along one day when a noise developed in the front end of their car. They stopped at a small-town garage, and told a mechanic about it. He suggested that it might be a piston. "No," said one of the men in the car, "I'm Henry Ford, and it isn't due to motor trouble." The mechanic, a bit taken aback, then remarked that the difficulty might lie in an ill-fitting tire. "No," said a second voice, "I'm Harvey Firestone, and the tires are all right." Then, hazarded the mechanic, it might be faulty wiring. "No," pronounced a third voice, "I'm Thomas Edison, and the electric system is working fine." "Hmm," mused the now skeptical mechanic, "Ford, Firestone, Edison! And I suppose you'll tell me that that's Santa Claus riding with you!" (referring to Burroughs.) Another version places the occurrence in 1923 or 1924, and the mechanic has become a farmer. Edison, Ford, and Firestone have taken out the President for a ride, and the yarn ends: "And I suppose you'll tell me that that little shrimp in the back seat is Calvin Coolidge!" The basic anecdote is quoted by Bayard Johnson (see Note 9), but the two endings are supplied by Archives personnel, who do not know their sources.

It faced the estuary of the Caloosahatchee River, and lay toward the Gulf from the town of Fort Myers.

Ford had meanwhile become interested in the sea island region of Georgia, which Burroughs had described to him as rich in bird and wild animal life. While one account dates his interest in this area from 1921, the first deed for property there shows that on March 31, 1925, Ford bought 100 acres on the Ogeechee River, about twenty miles south of Savannah. This nucleus was to expand into a principality of one hundred square miles, stretching for thirty miles on both sides of the river, and including islands in the stream, marshes, plantations, standing timber, and villages. However, this property, with Richmond Hill as its center, was not intensively developed by Ford until 1935.[12]

A trip south could become a strenuous diversion for Ford, as we can see from a diary kept by Louis Ives for February and March of 1926. The Fords and Iveses, who were old Dearborn friends, boarded the Fair Lane, a special railroad car, and went by the D.T. & I. to Ironton, Ohio, where their hotel on wheels was switched to the Norfolk & Western. Ford showed a zest for physical activity. On February 18th, he and Ives ran around the train, and then trotted to the uptown district of Litchburg, where they stayed over night. They had a dance before retiring (Ford was almost 63 at the time, Ives almost 71!). The train took them to Charleston, South Carolina, where they took a boat for Savannah. They then made their way to the land on the Ogeechee which Ford had recently acquired. There he discovered an old steam engine, and had it shipped back to Dearborn.

On February 25, on a yacht large enough for dances, they embarked for St. Augustine, Florida, touched there, and continued to Miami, where the Firestones met them. In several days they sailed for Havana, then returned to Fort Myers to visit the Edisons. Ives "got the charlie horse in my right leg while running on my toes with Mr. Ford." [13]

In 1928 and 1930 Henry and Clara made summer voyages to England, where Ford professed to be on holiday, and gave scant attention to his British properties, although he showed an interest in Irish Free State tariffs, which were injuring his operations.[14] *

While the older Fords were establishing vacation homes in the south, Edsel and Eleanor had turned their eyes to Maine. Already in 1918 they

---

* The Fords on this trip went from England to the continent, where they visited Oberammergau and met Anton Lang, who took the role of Jesus in the passion play performed there.

had become delighted with Seal Harbor, a bay eight miles south of Bar Harbor on Mount Desert Island. "I am so crazy to have you come up here that I can hardly stand it," Eleanor wrote to Henry Ford in August of that year. "You would just love the forest walks revealing the mountain tops where you are unconscious of the existence of anything human." Edsel and she soon purchased property on the Harbor; by 1923 a contractor was working on the cellar of their future residence. Almost at the same time Edsel established a farm at Haven Hill, near Milford, in Pontiac County, Michigan, about sixty miles from his Gaukler Pointe property. Here he kept horses, and also operated the place as a general farm producing chickens, eggs, and milk.

The Seal Harbor house, later called Skylands, was "perched on a typical Maine ledge high above the village of Seal Harbor," to quote a news account, and half hidden in a tangle of spruce trees.[15]

Edsel owned a number of boats which he kept at Seal Harbor, among them the *Eleanor,* a M.D.I. sailboat, and the *Nordic,* a class R sloop. Thus Skylands gave the younger Fords an ideal situation for their growing family, with sea and forest beauty at hand, and sports on shore or water. Edsel took a keen interest in the races at the Harbor, and on one occasion bought five sailing craft at Quincy, Massachusetts, which were to be sold in Maine to any of his neighbors who wanted to participate in the contests.[16]

3.

By the nineteen-twenties Henry Ford believed that he knew how to live so as to improve and conserve his health. His were two prime recipes: first, the avoidance of "poisons" such as cigarettes, chewing tobacco, liquor, rich foods, and overeating in general; and second, the use of wholesome and particularly of nutritive foods. Just as he worked to better the farmer's lot through the tractor and village industries, so he labored incessantly to win a wide acceptance of his health program.

He was in a position to accomplish not a little. He could and did ban smoking and chewing on company premises, he warned employees against drinking, and he gave interviews in which he denounced drink. "Brains and booze will not mix," he declared, and again, "The brain of the man who drinks alcohol cannot be wholly quick and alert." Ford did not find it expedient to command all his employees to follow his doctrine. Ed Huff chewed with impunity; Fred Allison smoked; Cameron made periodic capitulations to whiskey; innumerable Ford employees smoked and drank away from the factory. Nevertheless, in general the reformer had his way, even enlisting habitual tobacco chewers like Bill Klann to reform himself and his associates. As early as 1911 Ford forbade the serving of liquor at conventions of branch heads and dealers. In the nineteen-twenties he even reached outside the company to the Dearborn Country Club, which he had established and supported, to ban smoking there. Liebold, whose responsibility it was to enforce the prohibition, felt that Ford had gone too far.[17]

Ford's interest in diet came later than his opposition to liquor. By the mid-nineteen-twenties he had become convinced that most people ate the wrong things, and too much of them. He even came to feel that eating should be made "a part of religion." Illness, drunkenness, and crime, he believed, were the indirect results of poor dietetic habits. "If people would learn to eat the things they should," he declared, "there would be no need for hospitals. Jails and prisons would have less to do." Now that the clergy had helped to abolish the use of liquor through prohibition, "let [them] teach people what to eat." He developed various theories about diet. He believed firmly that only one or several "harmonious" types of food should be eaten at each meal, that tea and coffee should be avoided, and that sound diet should comprise mostly vegetables and very little meat. (This was related to his prejudice against animal husbandry, an activity he thought unworthy of man. Speaking of cows, horses, and pigs, he pointed out on one occasion that the automobile would do away with the horse, while "we could make milk commercially and get by without eating meat, and so could cut out these wasteful animals.") [18]

In 1929 Ford began experiments at Dearborn to discover a farm crop that would have both food value and possibilities for industrial use. After an extended exploration, he chose the soybean, the value of which, particularly for nutritive purposes, was later to be confirmed scientifically. In this activity he was seeking once again to relate farming to manufacturing. Michigan farmers were soon urged to plant beans with the assurance that the Ford Motor Company would do everything possible to provide a market.

At Greenfield Village, a laboratory was established under Robert Boyer, a graduate of the Ford Trade School, who devised a process for extracting oil from the soybean. This was suitable for industrial use, and was soon employed in the manufacture of all Ford paint at the Rouge. An extraction plant was set up there, and others at Saline and Milan, Michigan. Soybean meal, the residue, was utilized at the Rouge foundry. Later Boyer experimented successfully with the production of a fiber. He and his associates were able to manufacture cloth for suits, and several plastics. Ford eventually brought about a yearly production of 3,000,000 bushels of beans by Michigan farms, taking a large part of the output himself.

To develop the nutritional possibilities of the bean, he employed his boyhood friend, Dr. Edsel Ruddiman, who, at his Dearborn laboratory, produced a wide variety of foods. Their range is suggested by the menu of a dinner served in August, 1934, at the Ford exhibit at the Chicago Century of Progress Fair. Every course was partially or wholly composed of the legume. The chief items were tomato juice with soybean sauce, celery stuffed with soybean cheese, puree of soybean, soybean croquettes with green soybeans, soybean bread and butter, apple pie with soybean sauce, soybean coffee, and soybean cookies and candy.

Ford also encouraged the great Negro technician George Washington Carver to utilize edible weeds in what Joe Galamb called "grass sandwiches." These were not popular: "It was just like eating hay." One boy, asked if he would like to make a trip with Ford and others, replied staunchly: "Not if I have to eat another of those sandwiches." (He didn't have to!) Again, the industrialist tried to get his research assistants to drink soybean milk. "He changed his ideas on diet all the time," Galamb asserted; "you could never tell what he was going to do next." William Lyon Phelps reported in 1929 to an audience at Town Hall, New York, that Ford trotted three miles on arising and did not eat until one in the afternoon. "Personally," remarked Phelps, "I would rather have a few millions less and breakfast." [19]

Ford believed that recreation was essential to health, and he had some strong preferences. He had courted Clara Bryant in gatherings at the Martindale House on Grand River Road, and at the Botsford Tavern. Both he and his wife loved the "old-fashioned dances," and Ford remembered nostalgically "these old inns with their fine ballrooms." The musicians and the dance calls, the ceremonious atmosphere, the ample space and the variety of the exercise—all appealed to him and Clara Ford. "The old American dancing was clean and healthful," Ford asserted in 1926. "In the square dances and the circle two-step one finds rhythm and grace of motion, and people are thrown together and have to know one another. The old dances were social. The modern dances are not. The same two people may dance together all evening, but the old dances gave one a dozen partners in an evening."

The Fords organized old-fashioned dances even before the first World War, but their interest seems to have taken a truly persistent form after the purchase by Ford of the Wayside Inn at Sudbury, Massachusetts, in 1923. In reviving square dances as a regular part of the Inn program, they brought to the hostelry Mr. and Mrs. Benjamin B. Lovett of Boston. The Fords found so close a harmony of interest between themselves and these teachers that they persuaded the Lovetts to come to Dearborn. There Ford set about finding a number of the old musicians of the region, and getting them to play and record their music. Finally he organized an "orchestra" which employed four instruments—the violin, cymbalum, dulcimer, and sousaphone. He made space in the Engineering Laboratories building for "classes" at which the Lovetts presided as instructors and master and mistress of ceremonies. Inviting employees, relatives, and friends, the Fords soon had large and lively groups dancing a number of the twenty-eight old dances (Ford later set the number at fourteen) which could be performed. Particularly favored were the waltz, polka, schottishe, Virginia reel, lancers, varsovienne, gavotte, ripple, and minuet.[20]

Here was Ford in a dashing new role in sharp contrast with the madding strife of the Rouge, and the newspapers gleefully publicized it. Radio, just out of the toddling stage, broadcast his dance music, and Ford took his hobby to Detroit. Asked in 1925 if in his opinion the old dances would now come back, he exclaimed in astonished indignation: "Come back? They're here!" He denied, however, that he was trying to oust modern dancing. "We are merely dancing in the way that gives us the most pleasure." Still, it was an obligation for a Ford employee to find the most pleasure in what his employer offered. McCloud recalled a night when Ford practically compelled him to break up a card party and bring his guests to the dance, while on another occasion when Sorensen wanted to leave early to keep an appointment his chief cheerfully protested, "Hell, Charlie, nothing is more important than this; you stay here," and released the Dane only when he "got very mad about it."

Ford was a lithe, easy dancer, and Clara Ford seemed to be as devoted to the dance project as he. Neither sat many dances out. He and

Clara brought out a guide, *Good Morning,* "by Mr. and Mrs. Ford," which became a textbook for thousands of Ford employees, guests, and pupils—for the schoolchildren at Greenfield Village, Sudbury, and elsewhere, all learned the dances, as did many classes in the Dearborn schools. The dancing assemblies were continued up to the second World War, and may be said to have been the most positive social activity of the Fords. If Howard Simpson was right in saying that "there never was an attitude of fun at these old-fashioned dances," that an indefinable stiffness prevailed, and that "a lot of people just came because Mr. Ford wanted them to come," still, Ford himself enjoyed the occasions, and felt also that he was accomplishing something socially desirable. To mix pleasure with accomplishment—that was of course close to the ideal.[21]

4.

In contrast to John D. Rockefeller and Andrew Carnegie, who practically put on philanthropy with long trousers, and never doubted the nobleness of giving, Henry Ford regarded charity with positive hostility. "Why should there be any necessity for alms-giving in a civilized community?" he demanded in 1923, and a few years later, when asked if he would endow a foundation, he stated implacably: "Endowment is an opiate of the imagination, a drug to initiative. One of the greatest curses of the country today is the practice of endowing this and endowing that. . . . No, inertia, smug satisfaction, always follow endowments."

Needless to say, this attitude did not indicate a lack of interest on Ford's part in his fellow man. He wanted almost desperately to aid broken individuals and promote the good of all individuals. He objected to giving because he regarded it as a dangerous crutch that, instead of helping a man to walk, might splinter, and wound or destroy him. The way to help men, Ford believed with a fervor that would have startled suave Ben Franklin, was to provide opportunity for them to help themselves. And he had done this abundantly, taking professed drunkards from the road or criminals issuing from prison gates, and devising work for the crippled, the consumptive, the aged, and the blind. He had lived out Whitman's text:

I seize the descending man and raise him with resistless will,
O despairer, here is my neck,
By God, you shall not go down! Hang your whole weight upon me.

But he wanted to rouse men, not coddle them. "Philanthropy . . . does not make for self-reliance. We must have self-reliance." And again, "It is easy to give; it is harder to make giving unnecessary." [22]

Accordingly, from 1908, when he may be said to have first had an excess of income over ample needs, on into the nineteen-twenties, Ford thought of himself as expressing his love of and service to mankind by providing more jobs, raising wages, distributing bonuses, and offering services to improve the lot of his employees. Nevertheless, during that period he also became a philanthropist in the narrower sense. He was pushed in that direction by a hospital.

The Detroit General Hospital was a civic project of Dr. William F. Metcalfe, considered the leading surgeon of the city. In the early nineteen-hundreds this eminent specialist had operated successfully on Clara Ford, and in 1909 Ford became a contributor to the hospital and the chairman of the finance committee for the undertaking, a role in which he was completely inactive. Some $700,000 was raised, and the essential buildings for the institution were started, but interest in the enterprise declined, and the Detroit press declared that it had been badly managed. Accordingly, when Ford was asked for a second contribution, "I refused because I thought that the managers should have known how much the building was going to cost before they started," and because he distrusted the management. But since he nominally shared responsibility because of his committee chairmanship, he offered to pay back all his fellow contributors and assume full control of the undertaking. His proposal was accepted, and Ford, who had contributed $10,000 in cash and about $100,000 in land, reimbursed from thirty to forty people at a cost of about $600,000. After a brief period in which all work had been suspended he then told Liebold, "Well, you had better go and finish it up."

However, between them they worked out a type of hospital differing from that which had originally been contemplated, and one which conformed to Ford's ideas of service to the public. The institution would be "closed;" that is, while any doctor could bring patients to the hospital, once within, they could be treated only by staff physicians and surgeons. The staff could not practice outside; their salaries were relatively high, but represented their entire income. All patients were examined upon entrance by several doctors, and sometimes by as many as eight, to insure correct diagnosis. All had standard rooms, each room with a bath. All, laborers or millionaires, were charged the same amount for the same service. Ford believed that most patients wanted to pay for the treatment they received, but did not want to pay excessively; he proposed to bill them for what the service cost, and was confident that once the institution was established, fees would be moderate.

To Liebold fell the chief responsibility for working out the details of building, management, and practice. He and several of the staff visited a number of highly regarded American hospitals; he also read widely and studied personally a number of problems, from the placement and relationship of the buildings (all eventually connected by tunnel) to the size and furniture of rooms and the character and use of equipment. Ford and Mrs. Ford participated in this study. The finished hospital incorporated many original and some revolutionary features.[23]

The hospital as it first opened on October 1, 1915, comprised only a few main buildings, but the twenty acre plot on which it was located (on West Grand Boulevard near Hamilton) offered ample room for expansion. However, in three years, on October 26, 1918—it was taken over by the Government, and not returned until September 20, 1919, and really began its life as the Henry Ford Hospital on November 10. By 1924 it comprised a group of nine buildings, chief of which were the main hospital, the educational building, the nurses's dormitory, the surgical pavilion, the power house, and the service building. While Ford employees were often sent to the hospital, it was not an adjunct of the Ford Motor Company, and was "open to any person of any color or religious belief." From the start, its standards were high, and it attracted a staff of able men, many from Johns Hopkins. After 1921, Edsel seems to have acted for the family with respect to the institution, supplanting Liebold as a general supervisor, and steadily improving the character of the hospital.*

This project alone established Ford as a philanthropist of no petty stature. Up to September 15, 1926, he spent $11,167,024 upon it, and his

---

* Liebold, who had done well in planning, building, and initial organization, by his autocratic and exacting methods had antagonized the staff and created an atmosphere of uneasiness and strain. He had also affronted the Detroit medical fraternity, who did not like a "closed" hospital in any case. Edsel, working through William L. Graham as superintendent, quickly won the loyal support of the staff, fostered research, and in general lifted the standing of the institution.

annual losses were then approximating $400,000 a year. Yet by this time he had an impressive list of other activities which he had supported in the public interest.

First, of course, had come world peace. He had worked for it more than half a year before he financed the peace ship, and his expenditures for the voyage and work in Europe afterward mounted to about $550,-000 for a cause to which his devotion would be life-long. However, after 1917 Ford apparently saw no reason for continuing monetary support, although as we have seen he staunchly supported the League of Nations in the *Dearborn Independent.*[24]

Another area that gradually engaged Ford's support was education. That he had an instinctive interest in it is shown by the fact that he served on the Dearborn Board of Education from 1911 onward. (That is, he lent his name; he did not attend meetings.) More important, by 1916 he had perceived the importance of training men as well as giving them jobs, for in that year he started the Ford Trade School. Technically, this was not a part of the Ford Motor Company but served it, and showed that Ford was alert to the creative part that the right kind of teaching could play in his own shops. And what was the right kind of teaching? It was, Ford made clear, the type which taught men useful skills and gave them knowledge they could apply to their daily working and living. In *Today and Tomorrow* he gives a disastrous example of education which was not practical. A Persian who came to the Ford Motor Company had been intensively educated, but chiefly by memorizing literary and religious texts. "He had been educated away from life. . . . He could do very little that a phonograph could not do—and it cost more to keep him than to keep a phonograph." However, while Ford wanted to relate teaching to practical living, he saw early that useful education spilled over purely industrial or vocational lines. In 1918, outlining his ideas for re-making rural life, he declared: "The key to the whole problem is education. We must teach men that they can live well and comfortably without spending every waking hour in drudgery, *and provide the means by which they can do this.*"

Ford seems to have pondered the meaning of education in these days. In 1919, when he talked with Upton Sinclair, we see his keen mind at work on the matter. Sinclair asked him what the purpose of education was, and Ford replied:

"I should say that the purpose of education is to make people do what they don't want to do."

"Do you really mean that?" demanded Sinclair.

"Yes, of course," Ford responded. "They'll do what they want to do without being educated." [25]

The replies expressed Ford's basic philosophy. Education led people to make an exceptional effort, to work—and that to his mind was good. Even at that time he was pondering the question of how he could best inform and instruct his fellow Americans. The publicity that attended his alleged remark in 1916 that "history is bunk" nettled him. He told Liebold on the way home from the Chicago *Tribune* trial in 1919: "You know, I'm going to prove that and give the people an idea of real history. I'm going to start a museum. We are going to show just what actually happened in years gone by." This was the germ of the center at Dearborn which now, as the Henry Ford Museum, includes Greenfield Village and the Greenfield Village schools. Ford soon began collecting materials. C. J. Smith says that on his camping trips (1918–1924) he would pick up farm implements, steam engines, and other articles and have them shipped to Dearborn. Ford had begun his restoration of the family homestead in 1919, and was collecting in 1920; office correspondence shows that this had become an organized activity by 1922, and that both Cameron and Frank Campsall were helping Ford, who went to Boston in the fall of that year to look at antiques. However, for some years he stored most of his acquisitions.[26]

In 1922 Ford took another step in philanthropy; he made his first contribution to the Berry schools. These comprised a group founded at Rome, Georgia, in 1902 by Miss Martha Berry, a woman of great charm and forcefulness who had given up a life in society to work for the mountain people of her state.* Her schools eventually took pupils from the primary grades through college. (Berry College was started in 1927.) The work appealed to the Fords because it combined schooling with pupil self-help, and emphasized instruction in the trades and agriculture. Their gifts were small at first, but by 1926 amounted to more than $126,000 a year, and grew in size after the college was started. A Ford Quadrangle with the Clara Ford Hall, the Mary Ford Hall,

---

* Miss Berry apparently began active work with the mountain children in 1900. See a pamphlet: "A Mountain Growing Since 1900," Fair Lane Papers, Box 44.

the Henry Ford Chapel, a gymnasium, recreation hall, and refectory eventually testified to their increasing interest. The only list we have of Ford's benefactions credits him with having given $2,759,281 to the Berry schools, and a list for Clara Ford shows her to have contributed $1,085,916. At least half of these sums seems to have been given by 1930, and there is a possibility that the total was larger than the record shows.

Henry Ford also showed interest for a time in the Lincoln Memorial University near Harrogate, Tennessee, an institution for mountain students which stressed self-help and vocational education. But his support was brief, and amounted only to $47,679. Apparently he was dissatisfied with the management and work of the college.[27]

Meanwhile his project for showing Americans what history really was had been taking form in his mind, and he had set aside a tract of land at Dearborn for buildings and exhibits. But while he was still planning this major enterprise he undertook two others which were really supplementary to it: the restoration of the Wayside Inn at Sudbury, Massachusetts, and the Botsford Tavern, on the Grand River Drive, sixteen miles from central Detroit.

The New England hostelry, built in 1686, was said to be the oldest in the United States, but was more notable as having been a tavern of high standing on an important post road, and one celebrated by Longfellow in his *Tales of a Wayside Inn*. It had thriven under different names (Howe's Tavern, The Red Horse Tavern, and the Wayside Inn after the publication of the *Tales*), had been closed for a time after the stage coaches ceased to operate, and had been reopened in 1897 by Edward R. Lemon. Ford bought it in September, 1923, from his widow, after the inn had again been closed.

While he paid only $65,000 for the inn itself and 90 acres of land, Ford at once began to buy both land and buildings to supplement the original purchase. In all, he acquired 2667 acres, much of which he used for a farm and some schools which he established as part of a community, with the inn as its center. Ford's idea was to restore an old American locality, and he devoted much thought, time, and money to remodeling and re-furnishing the inn, tracking down and buying many pieces of Howe furniture, and purchasing other period furniture and implements from places as far distant as Ohio and Pennsylvania. He also re-established on former sites a grist mill, a saw mill, and a blacksmith shop such as had operated in Colonial days, equipping them for use, but also set up in contrast modern shops and a modern dairy. Three notable houses of an early period were also purchased at other points in New England, carefully taken down, and reconstructed at Sudbury near the inn. Later, in 1928, he established a vocational school for boys in the vicinity.

Perhaps the most publicized of his activities at Sudbury was his purchase of a little red school house which had formerly stood near by in Sterling, Massachusetts, and which was alleged to be the one attended by Mary of "Mary Had a Little Lamb" fame. He remodeled this building as an actual school for Wayside Inn employees. Ford was not troubled when a spirited controversy broke out as to the authorship of the poem which celebrated Mary and the lamb, and as to whether or not Mary was imaginary and her pet "a paper lamb." *

Finally, to preserve the quiet atmosphere of his community, Ford made arrangements with the commonwealth of Massachusetts to relocate the highway, originally the main road from Boston to New York and now Route 20, an operation for which he eventually paid $280,-000.[28]

Altogether Ford reported $1,616,956.11 as "contributions" under the head of the Inn, and this sum seems to have approximated the cost of the land, buildings, remodeling, and equipment. From 1923 to 1945 he lost $2,848,177 on the hostelry as a business, although the greater part of this was on the farms and the schools.

The feelings which prompted him to make such expenditures and court such losses are voiced clearly in *Today and Tomorrow*. "I deeply admire the men who founded this country," he said, "and I think we ought to know more about them and how they lived and the force and courage they had. Of course, we can read about them, but . . . the only way to show how our forefathers lived and to bring to mind what kind of people they were is to reconstruct, as nearly as possible, the exact conditions under which they lived." And again, "We have both lost and gained in the movement of modern industry. Our gains are many times greater than our losses; we can keep all of the gains and repair some of the losses." These words show the broad view Ford

* Ford's experts claimed that Mary Elizabeth Sawyer, born March 27, 1806, in Sterling, Mass., was the original Mary, whose lamb followed her and behaved as the poem relates, and John Roulstone, Jr., an older fellow pupil, wrote the first three (and the best-known) stanzas of the poem, which was later expanded by Sarah J. Hale of Boston. Mrs. Hale's partisans asserted that she was the sole author, and that both Mary and the lamb were imaginary. (*N.Y. Times*, Jan. 18, Feb. 13, 1927.)

could take of the older life he had helped to destroy, and the new one he had helped to develop in its place. On the old Botsford Tavern near Detroit, he spent on acquisition and restoration $602,242.[29]

5.

The motivation for the Dearborn development, which for convenience can be called Greenfield Village, was similar to that for the inns.* However, in Dearborn Ford was attempting a far more complex and significant demonstration. It embraced the full range of American life, old and new, in so far as this could be presented in visible things: clothing, implements, machines, and even shops and houses.

Ford's conception of what he would attempt grew slowly. We have seen that in 1919 it was merely to show how Americans of another age lived and worked. By 1926 he distinguished various periods, saying: "We shall reproduce the life of the country in its every age." He had already acquired a collection which, says an informed observer, "had attained vast proportions," and had taken over the old Dearborn tractor factory for temporary storage. It was soon filled. In 1925 Ford bought from Edison the latter's tools and laboratory equipment at Fort Myers, but apparently only thought of devoting one room in the future museum to his friend.

But just as he had bought and moved buildings to the vicinity of the Wayside Inn about this time, he began now to plan a "village" in Dearborn to supplement his museum exhibits. Undoubtedly the Wayside Inn restorations started the idea, but he altered and expanded it: he would not select as exhibits colonial buildings only, but those of intermediate and even recent periods as well, particularly when he would associate them with important events and persons. Among the structures he included the house where he was born, although this was the last to be brought to the site. Soon he investigated the possibility of removing and reconditioning the entire group of buildings at Menlo Park, New Jersey, associated with Edison's electric light and other inventions. From the bricks of Clara Bryant's girlhood home he built a church—the Mary-Martha Chapel; he acquired Luther Burbank's

---

* According to W. A. Simonds, *Henry Ford and Greenfield Village* (1938), 115, the whole Dearborn development was termed the Edison Institute: "it comprises two units, the museum and the village." Today the official term for the whole is "The Henry Ford Museum." However, "Greenfield Village" is the accepted popular designation. Simonds, of course, used it with that meaning in the title of his book.

office; the Clinton Inn from Clinton, Michigan; a typical log cabin; a tintype studio; a general store; a noted machine shop; the Scotch Settlement schoolhouse where he himself began his education; a courthouse where Lincoln had practised law; and the railroad station from which Edison as a youth had been cashiered because of one of his chemical experiments. Each building contained appropriate furniture, implements, and—if a shop—machinery, and most were in operable condition—the machines and engines ran, the camera took pictures, the schoolhouse was filled with pupils.

Ford not only thus expanded the potentialities of his "museum," but also sharpened his purpose by emphasizing change from era to era. In 1931 he himself clearly indicated the full scope of his planning:

At Dearborn we have gathered specimens of nearly all the articles that have been used in this country since its settling, with the thought of assembling them so that anyone who cares to discover what the people of any past generation commonly used . . . will have only to go to the proper wing of the museum . . . and there see every household article, every kind of vehicle, every sort of tool. *One may review the common household articles from the handicraft stage, through the hand and machine stage, to the machine stage, and then through the progress of machine work.* (Italics ours.)

It was an ambitious plan, and when one recalls that it was being pursued at the very time Ford was supervising the last important construction at the Rouge, crusading for old-fashioned dances, working on his inns, getting started in aviation, launching a rubber plantation, and scrapping the Model T and creating a new car, one must wonder at his tireless interest and abounding energy.[30]

Naturally, he did not develop Greenfield Village unaided. Liebold, Campsall, Cameron, Edsel, and many others in Dearborn assisted, and he was aided constantly by Ford managers and dealers throughout the country and even abroad. Frank Vivian recounts enough adventures in California alone to suggest how Ford's collection increased with magical speed. Ford asked Vivian to procure for him in San Francisco one of the first arc lights to be used, and Vivian, with a promise of due credit, got it from the inventor free. The Californian then set out to acquire the Wohlbruck Collection, which contained a splendid array of old wagons, carriages, and automobiles, and had been successfully exhibited for pay. This assignment bristled with surprises. When

Vivian suggested to Wohlbruck that he donate his trove, the aging owner fell dead! "He was a very nervous sort of fellow." Vivian did not permit the casualty to daunt him; he comforted the widow, arranged for the funeral, and won her consent to ship the collection to Ford, along with at least one additional gift from her! Mrs. Wohlbruck was also nervous, and once, annoyed by one of Vivian's clerks, she withdrew the entire bequest. But with judicious admixtures of flattery and Scotch highballs, Vivian won it back, then hired a warehouse in San Jose to prepare the materials for shipment, and at length dispatched some 56 freight cars of exhibits to Dearborn!

He was quite as successful in getting a fine collection of arms, uniforms, papers, and other material related to the Confederate States of America—again free. "If you give it to the Edison Institute it will be there forever and your name will be on it!" he argued triumphantly. Similarly, he procured Luther Burbank's office and residence, with many of Burbank's books and implements. With this acquisition Ford was pleased but not satisfied: he wanted the remains of the little dog that had companioned the scientist for years. But the dog had been buried with Burbank, and his widow would not permit its exhumation. Vivian was frantic with frustration; he meditated on dickering with a pound to dig up a specimen of the right size. "After all, . . . it was just a dog, but it was causing me a lot of trouble."

Once the Village had been publicized, Ford received many individual gifts and collections from public-spirited Americans. His own cullings had been fabulous in quantity: "I don't know why he bought them," said Charles Voorhess of many duplicate specimens, "unless it was so he would have what there was, and there would be no more left." Ford discarded immense quantities of surplus antiques.[31]

The museum building, including its offices, was of course the heart of the development, and Liebold says that Edsel "had charge" (subject as always to Henry's veto) of planning for this important structure. He considered a number of designs, but a proposal that the structure be adapted from the Independence Hall in Philadelphia (which Liebold attributes to Robert O. Derrick) pleased both the Fords.* The Dearborn edifice was to cover eight acres, and hence would

---

* It is not certain that the suggestion was Derrick's. Fred Black and Frank Campsall were also active in considering possibilities for design, and one newspaper account makes Henry Ford himself the originator.

have a vast area under the roof beyond that of the original. But the task of reproduction was painstakingly carried out—local hand-made brick, Cold Springs gray granite, and blue-gray Georgia marble and soapstone (the stone for the base and trim) were used to achieve an appearance identical with that of the Philidelphia building.

The dedication of the Institute was so scheduled that it could be combined with a celebration of the fiftieth anniversary of the discovery of the electric light on October 21, 1929. Ford had invited hundreds of notable guests who would see the light again brought to birth, and get the first public glimpse of the museum and village. Edison, now eighty-two, arrived a few days in advance of the event, and was taken to the Menlo Park group in the village, now, with the aid of his former assistant Francis Jehl, completely restored.* As he entered the quadrangle, fenced in by a white picket fence, which contained his old laboratory, office, machine shop, and library (the Jordan boarding house where Edison workers stayed and Edison's Fort Myers laboratory were outside it), he noted the soil, carloads of which had been brought from Menlo Park.

"Hmm," he exclaimed, "the same damn old New Jersey clay!"

He wandered through the buildings, amazed at the preciseness with which they had been restored, down to desks, chemicals, and instruments. "Ford," he said finally, "it's ninety-nine and nine-tenths perfect."

His friend wanted to know what constituted the one tenth of one per cent of error.

"Oh, our floor was never as clean as this," chuckled Edison.

The day of dedication and celebration brought to Dearborn scientists and inventors like Madame Curie and Orville Wright, industrial leaders like Charles M. Schwab, Gerard Swope, and Owen D. Young (toastmaster at the dinner which closed the festivities), political leaders like Governor Fred W. Green of Michigan and Secretary of War James W. Good, labor leaders like President William Green of the A.F. of L., and other celebrities like Will Rogers, Will Hays, Jane Addams, Julius Rosenwald, and Albert Einstein. President Herbert C. Hoover arrived by special train to dedicate the Institute. It was the largest, most dis-

---

* Edison had helped lay the cornerstone of the Museum on September 27, 1928, driving a spade that had belonged to Luther Burbank into the unhardened concrete, walking across it to leave his footprints, and with a stick inscribing his signature beside them. The spade, footprints, and signature can be seen today in the completed building.

tinguished, most memorable gathering at which the Fords had ever acted as hosts. Liebold took the formidable arrangements in hand, with transportation, guards, lunch (at the Clinton Inn) and dinner (in the Museum Hall). Events went off smoothly on schedule, although the strain of the day eventually told on Edison, and at 8:45 that evening, when he was to enter the hall for the concluding radio broadcast, he broke down and for a time refused to go in. However, he recovered, and spoke briefly.[32]

The museum and the village, although not ready for exhibition, were sufficiently developed at this time to give a good idea of their fundamental character; the Institute, in the narrower sense of the school Ford was establishing, had yet to be launched. It was to take young men through high school and on to work at the collegiate level, but their entire course was to be related to doing as well as learning. Ford planned to feed into the institution promising graduates from the Greenfield Village, Wayside Inn, and other schools (which he planned to establish) exemplifying his ideas on education. The Institute students would have the museum and the village available as laboratory material. Indeed, one of their tasks would be to help complete the exacting work of setting up exhibits, particularly those of the museum. This activity went on for years; it was not until June 12, 1933, that the museum and village were opened to the public; and not a little of the museum material was still in the old Dearborn tractor factory, where it required appraisal, possibly reconstruction, and installation in the proper places with correct designations.

Ford's exhibits, museum and village, reflected the lack of historical knowledge and perspective which he and his chief assistants brought to their task. The final product contained outright mistakes, like the alleged Stephen Foster house, which seems never to have had any proved relationship to Foster (Ford didn't greatly care—he wanted a memorial that would call the attention of visitors to the great songwriter). More important, there was a lack of coherence. Some of Ford's most biting critics, like Keith Sward, have praised some details of his accomplishment, such as his exhibits showing automotive progress. There are other comparable groups of undoubted value. Unfortunately, the ground Ford covered was too vast, and the tremendously varied exhibits were not related to any clear central idea. (Ford's original conception of an educational center with the museum and village as a "library" *was* definite, but was never effectively worked out.) Sward's characterization of the whole is just:

> It is this striving for sheer mass and for "something of everything" that sets off the Ford collection from such an institution as the great Deutsches Museum of Munich. . . . It provides a cohesive and magnificent history of science and technology. By contrast, the Edison Museum is a hodge-podge, despite its core of excellent restorations. It has the appearance of an Old Curiosity Shop, magnified 10,000-fold.

Ford did not improve what he had started by his selection of men to administer the village and the museum. Ray Dahlinger had charge of the grounds, and James Humberstone, who had attended the Wayside Inn School, and had talent but scant experience, was given charge of the museum. Liebold thought Humberstone efficient, and he might have overcome his deficiencies, but clashed with Fred Smith, who succeeded him, and impressed Ford as quite too headstrong.

Ford's exhibits, museum, and village grew as the years passed. He acquired the McGuffey homestead, the shed in which he himself built his first car, the birthplace of Orville Wright, the Wrights' store in Dayton, Ohio, where they worked on their first airplane and its engine, and other structures.

Ford was greatly interested in Greenfield Village schools, of which eventually there were four: the Scotch Settlement (1929), the McGuffey (1934), the Miller (1943 *), and Ann Arbor House (1937). Many Ford employees sent their children to these schools, and Ford was a frequent visitor. For a time he dreamed great dreams about revolutionizing education, and early in 1930 announced that he would spend $100,000,000 in promoting the practical type of training that he advocated, and devote the remainder of his life to studying and promoting it. The news brought him enthusiastic messages, including one from the trial lawyer Clarence Darrow (then in Cannes, France), who announced: "If schools of this type could reach all the youth of America, in time it would result in the abolition of crime and poverty, both of which are a disgrace to civilization." [33]

Ford did establish a number of schools after 1930, some in Michigan

---

* The Ford farm lay part in one school district, part in another, and Ford's father, on the school board in both, sometimes sent his children to the Miller school, which lay in Springwells township, sometimes to the Scotch Settlement school in Dearborn. Henry Ford attended the Miller school for several years.

towns, chiefly those which were the sites of village industries, and some in Georgia. He continued to maintain the schools near the Wayside Inn. However, the depression deflected him from his formidable project, and with increasing age he had less creative drive for such understakings.[34]

Of all Ford's philanthropic activities, Greenfield Village was closest to his heart. It memorialized his best friend, Edison, and it expressed much of his own philosophy of life. He spent freely on it—$10,418,000, according to the Henry Ford Office records and his income tax returns, though the amount was undoubtedly considerably greater. Clara Ford contributed $278,380, and Edsel several times that sum.* With the Ford Hospital, the peace ship and the ensuing conferences, the Wayside Inn, and the Berry Schools, the Village was one of the projects on which Ford spent generously.

Altogether, from 1917 to 1947, Ford devoted $36,929,875 to philanthropies, which, for a man who did not believe in "alms-giving," was no negligible sum. Clara contributed $3,832,870.76 (1919 to 1950), making the grand total for both more than $40,000,000. Were the first Ford Hospital payments and the Peace disbursements of 1915–1917 included, the total would be higher by several millions.

On Edsel's contributions we have less information than on Henry's and Clara's. He was a more conventional giver than his father, in that he lent ready and liberal support to a wide variety of public causes, from automotive undertakings like the Lincoln Highway to musical groups like the Detroit Symphony Orchestra, from the Y.M.C.A. to the Detroit Aviation Society and the Byrd Antarctic expedition. Edsel was the chief instigator and supporter of this last enterprise, although John D. Rockefeller, Jr., gave almost as much financially. On one occasion Rockefeller telegraphed that if Edsel were raising a particular contribution to $100,000, he would match it. To a research laboratory in Maine, a memorial to a friend, Edsel gave $22,500 annually, and his files show pledges of $750,000 to the Y.M.C.A. (probably for a term of years), $125,000 to the University School, of which he was an alumnus, and $50,000 to Shenandoah National Park. In addition to supporting the Institute, he gave to the Henry Ford Hospital perhaps as much as $4,000,000, while the number of his small contributions is legion.[35]

---

* A biography of Edsel Ford (Acc. 23, Box 3, dated 1938) says: "With Mrs. Ford he has been one of the most generous donors of the Institute, enriching the collections for nearly every department of the Museum."

The question of contributions raises the question of income. How much did the Fords receive yearly? The amount was probably less than commonly supposed, for a large part of profits went back into the expanding business. Henry Ford's lowest annual income after taxes was $983,931 for the war year of 1918; his highest $13,832,590 for 1929. During the nineteen-twenties the average was $4,500,000. Edsel received about two thirds of what his father drew. Clara Ford had a smaller block of company stock and was paid as little as $145,494 (1926) and as much as $1,133,912 (1929), with an average of $350,000. Some relationship between income and philanthropies can be perceived in Henry's career: he received before taxes during the years 1917-1947 a total of $139,200,761, and during his lifetime contributed almost $37,000,-000 of this to public service. Of course, taxes took no small part of the total, $51,889,042, leaving $87,311,719 as net income. (However, contributions were of course not deducted from this, but from gross income, and they conditioned the tax levied for each year.) Of the $10,939,216 which Clara Ford received before taxes from 1919 to 1950 inclusive, she gave away while still living a total of $3,832,780.[36]

Henry Ford's ideas of service to his fellow man during the period from just before World War I on through the nineteen-twenties were infused with the same originality that marked his ideas on industry. They won attention, provoked discussion, and are still at work in some of his creations, notably Greenfield Village. His conception of education anticipated a trend toward relating instruction to work and living which is a major if not a dominant influence in most school curricula today, at both secondary and university levels.* The questions as to how far vocational instruction should be pushed in the colleges, and as to its unhappy influence on education in general, can be answered only in the light of long experience and evaluation. Of course the great legacy of Henry, Edsel, and Clara Ford to the future was the Ford Foundation, which lies beyond the time-span of this volume.

* Ford, of course, did not originate the idea of "learning by doing," which was implicit in early American cooperative ventures like that at New Harmony, Indiana, and had been developed as educational theory by John Dewey before Ford became active in the field. But the latter was a pioneer in the extensive and thorough character of his experiments in combined work and study.

XX

HOW THE WORKERS FARED

VISITORS to Highland Park and the Rouge in the middle nineteen-twenties saw an army of workers coming and going in a semi-continuous stream, for the movement of groups into and out of the plants had to be staggered. Lines of streetcars and busses disgorged their detachments; columns of automobiles rolled in and out of the company parking areas; squads of men, swelling sometimes to a battalion, came on foot. They represented almost every state and nation. Here were lanky mountaineers from Tennessee and West Virginia; moustached Hungarians and Croatians; farm boys from Indiana or Minnesota; Negroes from the deep South; Slavs bound for the blast furnaces or the cylinder-moulding floor; and Yankees, Britons, or Germans to operate the complicated machine tools. Now and then women would hurry by on their way to the magneto assembly or upholstering shop. The lame, the halt, and the deaf were there—even a few blind; the old and the young. Sometimes Manchester Avenue fronting the Highland Park factory, or Miller Road near the Rouge plant, filled with a restless body of men responding to a rumor of more jobs.

"What about industrial democracy?" the journalist William Stidger asked Henry Ford in 1923. Ford's answer was emphatic. "The average employee in the average industry is not ready for participation in the management. An industry, at this stage of our development, must be more or less of a friendly autocracy." When Stidger persisted, Ford said essentially what he had earlier said to Pipp: "I mean that one man must make the decisions; that one man must be responsible as the executive head." Although Sorensen, Martin, Hartner, Avery, and other executives made decisions on details, in the ultimate analysis the views of Ford did control the labor situation, and the lot of this army of workers was shaped by his hands.

By his hands—and by the general pressures of the time. The dozen years following World War I present a picture of retrogression in the American labor field. Union membership, after climbing to more than 5,000,000 in 1920, gradually fell, until in 1926 liberal estimates set it at less than 4,450,000. As the workers eligible for membership in unions then aggregated 20,000,000, only about 22 per cent, a proportion far lower than in England, were organized.

One blow after another, indeed, fell on the head of labor. The loss of the great steel and coal strikes of 1919; the depression of 1921; the hostile interventions of the Harding Administration in the railroad shopmen's strike; the Federal court decisions upholding anti-union ("yellow dog") contracts and the labor injunction; the aggressive campaigns of chambers of commerce, trade associations, and other organizations, abetted by some farmers, to maintain the open shop—all this rendered the era gloomy. The Clayton Act, which labor had hailed as a bill of rights, became a club to use against unions. Early in the nineteen-twenties representatives of some twenty manufacturers' associations laid plans in Chicago for a battle against the closed shop, adopting the name "American Plan." The chronic illness of coal mining, textile manufacturing, and other industries, and the displacement of labor on railroads and in factories by improved machinery, created a heavy volume of unemployment even in a generally prosperous decade.[1]

This was a period, moreover, in which labor was divided against itself. The inability of unions to penetrate such major industries as iron and steel, food packing, rubber, automobile manufacture, and chemicals was attributable in part to the frigidity of craft unions towards organizations of unskilled workers. The A.F. of L., under such conservatives at Samuel Gompers, Matthew Woll, and William Green, feared that new unions formed on a mass basis would be unstable, hard to control, and an element of weakness in labor battles. It fought the Industrial Workers of the World relentlessly. For all these reasons, paid union membership (excluding docile company unions) by 1929 sank to about 3,450,000, and labor leaders were decidedly unhappy.

The automobile industry, with its amorphous body of laborers and semi-skilled workers, and its rooted tradition of the open shop, remained throughout the period barren ground for union organizers. If San Francisco was the most highly unionized city of the nation, Detroit was the most refractory. All the chief automotive companies, led by

General Motors and Ford, stubbornly opposed any steps toward collective bargaining. This did not by any means imply that the position of automobile workers was specially depressed. In 1925 their average annual earnings, $1627, were higher than in any other great industry except iron and steel. They were well above the average earnings of book-and-job printers, $1561; of foundry and machine shop workers, $1422; of lumber-mill workers, $1274; and of men's clothing workers, $1009. Year by year automotive workers kept near the top of the list. But their position was not gained by aggressive unions, which did not and at this time could not exist.[2]

2.

The really basic issues respecting Ford labor policies in 1916–1930 have little to do with unions. The hour for organizing the mass-employment industries would not strike until Franklin D. Roosevelt became President. The important questions were of a different tenor. What were working conditions? What was discipline? What were wages? What, in general, was the spirit of the workers?

The term 'working conditions' embraces a variety of factors which determine whether a job, apart from its wages and hours, is satisfying. Tom Jones or Jacob Spitzka found himself spending a third of his year inside the much-vaunted Ford factory. He looked with critical eyes at his surroundings: floors, walls, windows, machine-arrangements. He surveyed his fellow workers, and still more sensitively scrutinized the foremen and superintendents. Factory rules bore sharply on his life. He soon found that a factory, like a ship, can be made pleasant or detestable by the mental attitudes of those who control it.

Physically, both Highland Park and the Rouge stood decidedly in advance of most American factories. Good light, ample ventilation, cleanliness, and efficient safety precautions were maintained. The many pictures in Arnold and Faurote's book on Highland Park show a plant well arranged, well managed, and well kept. Visitors came from all parts of the world to look and admire. Features that in 1915 were objectionable were soon altered. Thus the machinery at Highland Park was then driven by belts on overhead shafts, and because the machines were spaced closely, the forest of belting cut off much of the light; but beginning with World War I, Ford began running the machines by individual motorized drives. Again, the close spacing had meant that furnaces, welding machines, and other heating units stood near the activities they served, with the result that parts of the factory were excessively hot in summer; but Ford soon installed a system of blowers and exhaust fans which was recognized as a model for all industry. As for the Rouge, it was admirable from the outset. Considering that factories the world over had traditionally been sooty, smoky, dirty, littered places, the Ford plants possessed physical distinction.[3]

Pains had been taken at the Rouge in selecting interior colors. Upper walls, girders, and ceilings were painted an eggshell white to reflect the sunlight from the broad window spaces. A gray-blue was found best for the eyes below, and machines, housings, safety covers, and sheathings were painted that hue. The walls to high wainscot height were finished in a deep gray, the railings were black, the hydrants and alarm boxes red. One of Henry Ford's obsessions was cleanliness. He repeatedly said that as order and morale depended on it, he would tolerate no makeshift compromises. As we have seen, in 1929 the Rouge had more than 5,000 men engaged continuously in keeping the premises spick and span. Every month that year more than 11,000 gallons of egg-shell white and 5000 gallons of machine blue were used. Floors were kept scrubbed with hot water and cleaning soda. Rubbish cans were emptied every two hours. An intricate network of suction pipes with nozzles close to such machines as grinders kept the air free from dust. Many windows were washed once a week. The whole plant, as many observers testify, even to the power house and foundry, was spotlessly clean, and on bright days its interior was bathed in sunlight.

At both Highland Park and the Rouge systematic efforts were made to reduce the inevitable hazards of the factory. A multiplicity of warning devices alerted workers to danger, such as bells, signs, locks, shields, and red paint on cutting or crushing parts. The principal enemies were fatigue and monotony. Amid the steady clack-clack of machinery and the soothing whir of wheels, men performing repetitive motions tended to let their attention stray. However, among the major American industries, automotive manufacture usually ranked third or fourth safest in point of accident frequency, and second or third safest in accident severity. Men ran less risk in the Ford plants than on the farm or in old-fashioned blacksmith's shops. The Ford safety record was the best in the industry, and often the best in the country, as the National Safety Council recognized. Now and then, to be sure, some evidence of neglect appeared, as when in 1924 four men died in one month of blood-poisoning from dirty cutting oil. Workmen were at times needlessly burned or maimed. But it is impossible to eliminate all peril from any complicated mechanical employment.

The Ford Company often evinced a pioneering spirit in the areas of health and safety. Dr. J. E. Mead, head of the hospital and first-aid system, proposed in 1916 that a special officer supervise the detection and correction of unsanitary conditions. A Hygienic Department was created, and it pushed measures to protect health until it was absorbed by the Safety Department, an equally active, well-managed group. In 1918 a special mechanism was installed to remove iron dust from the air in the making of piston rings—"As far as is known," said the *Ford Man,* "the first of its kind in the country." Two years later a powerful suction system began removing smoke and dust from the foundry. Machine tools everywhere used the before-mentioned cutting compound, which reduced frictional heat, assisted the tool edge, and prevented rusting. Every cubic centimeter of oil contained millions of bacteria, which frequently gave operators a disease called oil dermatitis. Ford coolant was sterilized by a bacteriologist; and the company finally perfected a coal tar infusion which reduced infection to a fourth or fifth of what it had been.[4]

Careful attention was paid to drinking water and air. In 1929 the Rouge had no fewer than 2900 drinking fountains in its shops and yards, 200 of them in the foundry alone. Water temperature was controlled at between 55 and 60 degrees, and salt pellets were made available in summer. Rules at the Rouge called for admitting thirty cubic feet of fresh air a minute for every person working in an enclosed space, so that even in the furnace room the air was completely changed at short intervals. Telephones, goggles, respirators, and like sources of infection were sterilized every twenty-four hours, while the very coat racks were regularly disinfected.

Company regulations—"one of our strictest rules," said a foreman—required that the slightest scratch or pinprick or even a trifling indisposition be reported immediately to a first-aid station. In cases of serious injury or infection, the employe went to the hospital in the general assembly building. Here, amid thousands of machines, was a structure which shut out all noise, its long hallways, painted a snowy white, having "something colonial" in their aspect. With at least two doctor-surgeons in constant attendance, it offered two operating rooms, an x-ray room, eye and dental rooms, and other special facilities. Men might be kept here several days, but serious cases were removed to the Henry Ford Hospital in Detroit.[5]

Workers could bring lunch from home, or buy part or all of it from lunch wagons in the plant. Several firms of outside suppliers operated competing wagons. The company supplied inspectors and laboratory men to supervise the food. Sometimes complaints of bad quality were made. But Edwin P. Norwood, who lunched more than fifty times from the wagons in 1929, speaks well of the fare. A boxed lunch containing three sandwiches (one jelly, two cheese or meat), a piece of fruit, and some cake, cost fifteen cents, a pint of milk seven cents, and a pint of tea or coffee five. Tests of weight and quality were incessant. The medical officers of the plant tried to see that the worker got 800–900 calories from his boxed lunch, and boasted that their pure food regulations were more exacting than those of the state of Michigan. The wagons of course sold large quantities of ice cream, candy, peanuts, and other packaged goods. Commissary plants, though not on Ford property, were adjacent to it, and in 1929 the fleets of lunch wagons numbered 220.

In 1924 the company, to promote health and efficiency in the plant, created what it called the medical transfer division to see that employment was more closely adapted to special physical requirements. Tubercular men were placed, at least in theory, in areas where the air was specially clean; those with defective vision were given jobs free from hazard; workers with throat ailments received warm, dry employment, and so on. Many of the transfers were temporary; a worker in the cement plant who showed tokens of pulmonary weakness would be sent outdoors for six months, and when cured brought back. This transfer department had its own investigators, who made a point of looking for ill-placed men: during a period of five years, they shifted 50,000 men. Following the tradition which Henry Ford had early established, the factory took many workers without regard to their manifest physical handicaps—took even epileptics and mental cases—and of course it had to exercise special care in placing them.

This effort to help handicapped people presents one of the best facets of the company's employment record. Klann, the exceedingly able superintendent who began as a machine hand, relates that the personnel office once sent him seventeen blind men. He set them to work on a

gasket-making routine involving the separation of tin, copper, and asbestos parts, which they could perform by touch. "They did a marvelous
job." On another occasion he received a war veteran who frankly said
that now and then he lost nervous control of himself. Taking care to
keep him away from machinery, they set him to weighing pistons. One
day he threw a piston at another worker, explaining later that it was
"just an impulse." They then transferred him to the task of attaching
fenders to a paint conveyor which carried them into a 500-gallon tank
of enamel ten feet deep. Presently he dove into this tank. When his associates fished him out, he told them: "I dreamed I was crossing a river in
Germany!" The company persisted, however, in keeping this veteran,
who like thousands of other handicapped men, and like large numbers of
paroled convicts, finally made an excellent workman.[6]

3.

Working rules in the Ford plants differed little in essentials from
those in other large automotive factories, though in a few respects they
were more severe. As in all mass production industries of the time, they
were the rules of an army, not of a cooperative community. One regulation, never completely enforced, required complete silence. The men
were forbidden to whistle, sing, or talk. Since most tasks demanded
complete concentration, the men were supposedly too busy to chat;
while safety was also a factor, for talking men might forget due precautions. A much harsher rule forbade sitting down at any time. "When
we were not working," recalls W. Allen Nelson, who served many
years at Highland Park and the Rouge, "we *stood* at our benches. There
wasn't a place to sit down, and if you sat, or even if you leaned against
a machine, you were liable to be fired. . . . You didn't sit down *at all*."
It was a leg-weary body of men who tramped out of the factory. General Motors laid the same interdict on talking and sitting, but it was
less strictly enforced.

As in other American factories, time margins were strictly watched.
Because the assembly lines and feeder lines kept moving inexorably,
tardiness was intolerable: if a few key men were late, half the factory
was late. When the starting bell rang, men had to be standing at their
machines, the time-clock punched, their clothes changed, and their tools
taken from the crib. The lunch period of fifteen minutes included whatever time was taken for washing hands and getting food from the lunch

wagon. The company hired "spotters" to report workers who seemed to be stealing time, and of course over-zealous spotters sometimes wronged innocent men. A man who had spent seventeen years on the production line was dismissed one day because a few seconds before the quitting bell rang he took a piece of waste and wiped the grease from his arms. Another worker who drove cars off the end of the assembly line often began work five or ten minutes early, but—

One day, just about thirty seconds before lunch period, he delivered a car to the inspection, and knowing he did not have time to deliver another before the bell rang he stepped over to the lunch wagon and bought a bottle of coffee. As he was paying for this the bell rang.

That evening when he went to punch his clock-card it had been removed from the rack. The time clerk referred him to the superintendent, who at once ordered the clerk to make out a quit-slip for this employe because he had bought a bottle of coffee before the lunch bell rang. Once more the "spotter" had got in his deadly work as an aid to natural attrition.

No one was big enough or little enough to feel sure he was exempt from these spotters. So the haunting fear that their every movement was being watched was present in the minds of all.[7]

In the days of John R. Lee so abrupt a dismissal would have been impossible, and appeal against any injustice easy; the main difficulty here was in the despotic enforcement. One rule required men to wear their badges at all times. Martin repeatedly sent men home for a week or two for failure to keep on their badges—another abuse of power.

The arrangement of shifts was a complicated matter. The starting and quitting schedules had to be so patterned as to avoid congestion at the plant gates and on the transportation lines. Since the simultaneous arrival or departure of one third of the working force of 60,000 or (in 1929) 96,000 men would have disrupted the plant, shifts had to be put on an elaborate time-pattern. The Rouge by 1929 had 126 departments, which were fitted into a varied program. Arrival of the No. 1 shift was staggered between nine in the evening and half an hour after midnight; the No. 2 shift between five and nine in the morning; and the No. 3. shift between 1:30 and 5 p.m. Thus bodies of men were coming and going half of the time. The largest single mass of men to report at once, about 8000 in 1929, came at 7:30 a.m. That number was clearly too large, and the company was trying to reduce it. Of the total force that year, it was estimated that about 50,000 used street-cars and busses, and about the same number rode in privately-owned cars, while a considerable number walked. Adequate parking space was provided, with a separate area for cars carrying the crippled.[8]

Company practise in the rotation of shifts during the nineteen-twenties was open to grave criticism. All factories operating on a three-shift basis have to find some mode of distributing the experienced men among all three shifts. They may simply require most employees to take their turn with each shift. Alternatively, they may make the less desirable shifts more attractive by a wage premium. They may even shorten the late night ("graveyard") shift or exempt it from the more difficult tasks. The Ford Company made no concessions whatever during this period, but required workers to rotate shifts without regard to seniority, or to any other factor save illness. Inasmuch as shifts were changed every two weeks, a hand hardly got adjusted to one schedule of work and sleep before he was thrust into another.

"It was a miserable business," wrote one man who changed shifts fortnightly for seventeen years. "How anyone could adjust to two-week changes I don't understand. I had stomach trouble for the first few days every time I changed. The chief problem was loss of sleep; for the first week after a change, I didn't get over four hours' sleep in twenty-four." [9] After Henry Ford passed from the scene, the plant adopted a system of monthly shift-changes, and required men to adhere even to this only if their departments voted for rotation. High seniority men were given their choice of shifts, and the necessary distribution of skilled workers was achieved by special inducements.

Smoking was of course strictly forbidden in the plant. At one time during the nineteen-twenties Ford even attempted to stop chewing. "Bill," he said one day to Klann, "Do you chew tobacco?" "No," responded Klann, "I chew gum." (Actually he chewed both.) Ford inquired about a number of other executives, learning that Hartner, Findlater, and Scofield all chewed. Klann reminded him that Thomas A. Edison did so, and that on a visit to the Rouge Mrs. Edison had rebuked him for having tobacco juice on his chin. "Yes," said Ford defensively, "but he doesn't believe in smoking cigarettes." After further talk, Ford informed Klann, "I have a job for you."

"What's that?" said Klann.

"You go and stop the chewing in the whole plant right now," ordered Ford.

Klann could hardly believe his ears, but he set to work. When he ordered Hartner to quit, he was told to go to hell. When he spoke to Findlater, the sturdy Scot replied: "That's just one of Ford's cranky ideas; skip it." Nevertheless, Klann made a valiant effort. Whenever he found an employee disobeying his orders, he would send the man out to chew on the street for an hour without pay. "I sent hundreds of fellows out," he later recalled. But at the end of five months he reported to Ford that the crusade was a failure. "A lot of the men see me coming," he said, "and they swallow the stuff and make themselves sick, and I've got to take them to the doctor." Ford finally compromised on a requirement that every chewer pay a cent apiece for a portable paper cuspidor.[10]

One evidence that the Ford discipline after 1920 was that of an army, and not a cooperative community, was furnished by the failure to invite and pay for suggestions from the workers for technological or operational improvements. We have seen that in the period before American entrance into the World War, the Suggestion Committee had collected many fruitful ideas. For a time in 1920–1921 the *Ford News* continued to gather proposals, but gave the program decreasing publicity until it seems to have died completely during 1922. After that year the ideas of rank-and-file employees, though still an important source of progress in the factory, received little recognition from the company, and little reward. In keeping with the more severe labor policies in the nineteen-twenties, the suggestions of men at the benches and machines were treated with an approach to indifference.

Yet the workers did continue to make proposals. A sweeper, for example, devised a better method of grinding drills. W. A. Nelson, with the company over a long period, believed that such suggestions still counted for half of the technological improvement. "I know this is so, because it has been my experience for many years. Many times these ideas were picked up by alert supervisors and put into practice." He thought that this appropriation of ideas took place on all levels of supervision, and that it aroused resentment against the management. Judging by the experience of other corporations at the time, and of the Ford company later (for it instituted a modern suggestion plan in August, 1947, and by July, 1954, had paid $2,377,000 for almost 47,000 suggestions adopted out of more than 210,000 submitted, with large profit to itself) the loss to the company through failure to maintain its excellent pre-war scheme was very heavy.[11] Such a scheme, unfortunately, did not consort with the disciplinary ideas of the men who ran the great plant. The spirit of the factory after 1920 was not stimulating, but repressive.

4.

In design and arrangement the factories were superior; in their literal meaning, most rules were fair enough. But what of the spirit of the plant? It was a spirit created by half a dozen men who ran it under Henry Ford: by Charles Sorensen, P. E. Martin, W. C. Klann, Charles Hartner, and others. Dean Marquis, resentful over the destruction of the labor reforms instituted by John R. Lee, Clarence Avery, and himself in the days when Highland Park was called "the House of Good Feeling," lashed out at these bosses. They had soured Henry Ford's early idealism and perverted his humane approach, Dr. Marquis believed. Unquestionably, as we have seen, the spirit of the establishment changed sharply for the worse in 1920–1921. When a full working force was rehired after the shutdown caused by the depression, the men found the pace of production accelerated, enforcement of the rules tightened, and the whole atmosphere harsher.

John R. Lee and Avery had believed not in driving but leading the worker, and the Sociological Department under Marquis had been built on this faith. After the departure of Lee and Marquis, rough treatment of the hands was temporarily encouraged. While the huge growth of the labor force and the fierce competition among automotive firms would inevitably have meant a sterner discipline, for a time severity was pushed to extremes. Formerly a working foreman or straw boss had dealt with thirty men, keeping them up to their jobs, substituting whenever one went to the toilet, and meeting any emergency. Now an assembly line foreman dealt with fifteen men; scrutiny of individual effort was twice as close as before, and production schedules were constantly raised. The output of cars went in 1922 to 8000 a day; then to 9000 and even more. A period of hard driving set in which lasted about three years before more moderate practises prevailed.

"They say Sorensen was the worst driver there was," recalls Klann, "but I don't think he was much of a driver. All he wanted a man to do was to get out a day's work. Hartner was a great driver in the same way. Hartner and I were the worst in the shop so far as driving was concerned. Hoffman was no soft mark either. He was a good driver."

This is a frank admission that there was competition in hard driving. And Klann was equally candid in saying: "Ford was one of the worst shops for driving the men." On that point all observers in the early nineteen-twenties are agreed. "The influence of Mr. Martin at this stage had begun to wane," declares one observant worker, "and that of Sorensen and Bennett was rapidly expanding. An evil influence in Ford affairs had set in; from that time on we were subjected to whip-cracking, a very poor substitute." The morale of Ford employees in 1921–1924 inevitably declined. Actually Bennett's influence on discipline did not become marked until 1927, when he became head of the personnel department at the Rouge.[12]

One means of extorting more work from the employees was to threaten a layoff, for even after the depression of 1920–1921 ended, workers were aware that new jobs would be hard to find. Just before the shutdown in the winter of 1920–1921, the *Auto Workers' News* reported that although the Ford works were employing 4000 fewer hands than before, and using them only five days a week instead of six, production had remained constant. "This has been accomplished," the paper observed, "by having men run five or six machines where they used to run three." The speed-up at this time and just after the shutdown, a period when the company heads felt that ruin was impending, was probably the most intense in Ford history. Many employees would doubtless have liked to write Henry Ford in the terms used by one worker. "While on production," his letter complained, "conditions are so rushed it's awful. Human power and endurance cannot stand the speed, grind, awful strain, and continued hurry-up call of the bosses. And old faithful employees will shake their heads and say they will have to look elsewhere as soon as possible." The frenzied pace continued even when prosperity appeared on the horizon. "Increased labor efficiency," reported *Automotive Industries* in the spring of 1921, "has made it possible to operate the plant at approximately eighty per cent of capacity with sixty per cent of the normal labor quota." [13]

Under the prodding of Sorensen, Martin, and Klann, the foremen of each shift tried lustily to outdo the production records of the shifts immediately preceding and following theirs. They drove their men for all they were worth. It was this hurry and tension which led labor leaders to term Sorensen a Simon Legree, and caused a Detroit labor journal to cartoon the "Ford autocracy" as a Prussian martinet with a whip lashing a muscular workingman to madness. Foremen were constantly yelling, as Knudsen said he once did, "Hurry up! Hurry up!" This English phrase haunted many an Italian or Slav immigrant in his sleep.

Yet by 1924 the speed-up was being mitigated. Whether it was actually excessive after that date is a moot question; whether it was worse in the Ford factories than in General Motors or other plants is still more questionable. Edwin P. Norwood maintains, on the basis of long and careful observation, that the assembly lines in 1928–1929 were moderate pace-makers, regulated to the natural gait of the men who worked on them. In the last analysis, he argued, the men set the pace. "To ask them to perform beyond their capabilities would be to defeat the very end that is being sought." Excessive speed would result in a deterioration of nerves or muscles fatal to sound workmanship, would frequently mean the scrapping of valuable materials, or even the tearing down and reassembling of a complicated product. It would also mean a costly labor turnover as disgruntled employees quit work. A natural tempo was less fatiguing than one either too fast or too slow.[14]

The operator could protect himself, moreover, against being swamped by an excessively rapid flow of work. If materials came too fast, or if an unexpected hitch occurred, a worker was expected to halt the line by throwing a switch, or reaching upward and jerking a cord. A light then glowed in the central control booth. If it lasted only a few seconds the difficulty was minor; if it shone longer, it meant a breakdown of machinery or other serious impediment, and help was dispatched. But all stoppages, long or short, were tabulated; and when a cluster of stoppages indicated that some conveyor was running too swiftly, its gait was reduced. Obviously, an average speed had to be fixed—too fast for some men, too slow for others; and obviously, men of placid temperament endured the inexorable demands of the carriers better than the nervous types. Experience also counted. When work began on the Model A, F. L. Faurote wrote:

At this writing, early in December (1927), about 550 Model A Fords of the several different styles have been made. Others are coming off the assembly line slowly. I stood and watched the men for a time. The job is new to all of them and they make haste slowly. There are stops for fitting, stops for parts and minor adjustments. In fact, the assembly line now is just crawling.[15]

In studying the pace of work in the Ford factories the glib generalizations of outsiders who used statistics with a bias, or who made a hasty tour of the plant looking for something to criticize, are worthless. Some writers have treated statistics of increased productivity as if they were an index of managerial pressures alone. Actually a great part of the steady rise in Ford output was attributable to superior tool steels and improved machinery; another great part to more scientific methods and economical management; another to the winnowing out of poorer workers in the discharges and reemployment of 1920–1921, and still another, at times, to a rise in the morale of workers, such as followed wage increases. The impartial-minded employee previously quoted, Nelson, regards Keith Sward's account of the speed-up of 1921–1922 as inaccurate because Sward made no proper allowance for the contribution to production by the Ford Company's efficient new machines, some of them installed as part of the war effort. "The men were pushed harder, but at the same time they were working with machines better able to turn out the higher production." [16]

The same contention that pace and production offered a complex problem, not to be dismissed with a hasty verdict, comes from Murray Godwin, writing after he had been a wage-earner in the Highland Park plant for two years, and an observer of Ford industrial processes for three. Like Klann and others, he emphatically contradicts Louis Adamic's assertion that when assembly conveyors carried 180 motor blocks an hour in 1925 as against 120 in 1919, the difference was supplied in human energy. Not at all, he writes; the difference was largely supplied by mechanical aids. In this period many common tools were changed first to the "speed" and then to the "power" type. A certain operation might first be accomplished by a socket-wrench with a T-form handle. This would be replaced by a speed-wrench having a knob for one hand and a crank for another; it could be turned at enhanced speed, with less energy. Presently it too would be replaced by an electric-driven wrench unit, suspended from above and counterweighted for ease of manipulation—a common power-tool in the Ford plants. The operator now had only to apply the socket to the bolt head and touch the grips, spinning the shaft. Speed increased again, but the job became far easier. [17]

Such changes, writes Mr. Godwin, were multiform and incessant.

Improvements in precision eliminated the filing or grinding of parts on the line (by 1919 files were no longer used), and the laborious discarding of defective pieces. Ford's acquisition of the Johansson gauge rights in 1923 made interchangeability of parts much more certain. Another improvement was the assignment of certain sub-assemblies on the main line to positions further back in the production pattern, so that units which once needed adjustment now came ready-assembled to the central conveyor. A new jig might halve the time for making a specific alignment. Multiple-gauging devices might merge three or four inspections into one, saving both time and energy. Improved mechanization and the subdivision of labor also played their parts in a painless increase of speed. Once Godwin came upon a die-casting job which was being put on a conveyor, a department boss timing its speed. Forty feet away the same job was being taken off the conveyor by three experimental automatic machines. "This," he writes, "is not untypical of the way improvements tread on one another's heels at Ford's."

Louis Adamic had pictured Ford workers on the chassis assembly as working like fiends, sweat pouring down their cheeks, their jaws set, their eyes on fire; some of them lying all day on their backs on little carts under the machines. Mr. Godwin pronounces this a grotesque distortion. The Ford company did its best to bring a host of visitors into the plant, and hour by hour guided them alongside the lines of workers, whose aplomb it thought a good advertisement. It also took countless photographs of the Rouge chassis line in operation, doing this on the jump without posing or prettification; the employees looked busy but unharassed. Even the men on the little carts, who did not work on their backs nor get underneath anything but the fenders, did not appear unhappy. The truth, in Mr. Godwin's view, was stated by Stanley B. Matthewson, a student of labor economics who, while surveying the output of unorganized workers, went to observe conditions in the Ford factory:

> I had heard indeed that that particular assembly process was "the fastest line in America." I begged for a job on that line and got it. To my surprise, I found . . . the job required only a constant application of physical energy, not at all beyond my capacity or the capacity of others about me. In fact, we were a jolly, normal group of workers whose talk, as we rode home in a packed bus after eight hours in the "madhouse," was never of fatigue or oppression. We kidded each other a lot, and sometimes we wished we could put in six days a week instead of five.[18]

Like a French machinist, H. Dubreuil, who came to America to study scientific management as a workman and labored in a number of shops, recording his impressions in *Robots or Men,* Godwin thought that at the Rouge (and elsewhere) noise was a major factor in the fatigue of workers. The shrieking of drills, the pounding of presses, the roar of furnaces, made a clamor which wore on the nerves with ceaseless attrition. He thought that the Ford establishment had its full share of danger, discomfort, and indignities. But on a balanced estimate he regarded the Rouge as a much better factory than many others. Its rigorous discipline might seem callous. "But my attitude is that the hardest places to work are shops which are easygoing and slovenly; for there one is continually running afoul of the carelessness and egotism of gone-to-seed employees, tripping over debris, getting hurt by faulty equipment, and straining one's muscles in attempting to function as a truck or a chain-fall."

It would be easy to pile up quotations on the exhausting hurry, the tyranny of the foremen, the unpleasantness of an atmosphere redolent of motor fumes and heat-treating gases, and the dangerous character of some tools. It would be equally easy to accumulate statements like those of a member of the Yale Industrial Research Group who, after spending six months in the summers of 1925–1926 working in thirteen departments of the Ford works, concluded that "if one is not unusually nervous or slow, he has no difficulty in working on the conveyor line;" that the charge of monotony was invalid, for men had "abundant opportunities" to change their jobs; that the relation between foremen and workmen was too intimate (foremen rising from the rank and file) to permit of much tyranny; and that many men "got tired, not because they have too much, but because they have too little to do." * No simple statement on pace, fatigue, discipline, and morale is possible, because the Ford operations were too multitudinous, the changes too incessant, and the psychological factors too numerous to permit of easy conclusions. What to a dozen workers seemed a matter-of-fact segment of industrialism might seem to one slow or nervous worker sheer purgatory; and for that matter, an employee who in one mood regarded his job as an enviable way of making a good living might in another mood loathe it as a frustration of all his finer potentialities.†

---

* V. Y. Tallberg, who was at the Rouge during this period, disagrees. He states that the men *were* worked hard, and that there *was* tyranny.

† See p. 524.

A few generalizations are permissible: that in the Lee-Marquis-Avery era, 1913–1920, Highland Park presented in everything but its lack of union organization an almost Utopian example of enlightened, kindly, progressive labor relations; that the speed-up of 1920–1923, with the scrapping of old procedures, converted the Ford works into a hard-bitten, roughly managed establishment of familiar type, partly redeemed by vestiges of its early character and by its dynamic engineering policies; and that from 1923 to 1930 the Ford factories stabilized their discipline on a plane satisfactory enough but for the erratic harshness shown by Sorensen and others—the way of the bucko-mate on a hard-driven ship. We may add that about 1927–1928 the emergence of Harry Bennett to a position of real power over personnel introduced an element of arbitrary brutality previously unknown. His dismissals, however, affected foremen, draftsmen, engineers, and other skilled workers much more than the rank and file. As we have seen, when in 1927 the final assembly line was closed down at Highland Park and a great body of employees was shifted to the Rouge, Sorensen with the help of Bennett instigated a shake-up which inspired general apprehension.

Klann, as one of the men used in this high-handed, hit-or-miss decimation of the force, stated: "I discharged close to two thousand men in the shop." As soon as the hands learned of Bennett's authority over personnel many saw that a storm loomed ahead: "A lot of the boys saw it coming and they quit their jobs." Klann tells how the relentless policy was applied to even the best Highland Park foremen. For example:

We started building the cars the first of November, 1927. I took Pederson and Ed Gartha out to the Rouge plant with me to run the line.

Sorensen said, "Who are these guys?"

I said, "Sorensen, you know Pederson. You brought him in the shop yourself twelve years ago. . . . He is a Scandinavian the same as you are. You know who he is. He has had charge of the line for the last twelve years. You know who Gartha is."

He said, "Fire them."

† The question of monotony in work is also intricate and controversial. That able social worker and journalist William L. Chenery in 1924 questioned Ford superintendents about the boredom of repetition. They told him that a majority of the workers preferred routine. Said one: "Lots of fellows get to thinking that the machine belongs to them. They want to work at a particular machine; they don't even care to change to another of precisely the same sort. Others hate to learn new things. They prefer the comfort of keeping at what they already know." A great deal of evidence leans in this direction. But it does not invalidate the criticism that such routines were destructive of mind and spirit, and one superintendent said as much. (*N.Y. Times*, Aug. 10, 1924, Sect. VIII.)

So I did. I fired both of them. He didn't tell me why to fire them. He just said, "Fire them."

He said, "You go and see Bennett and see who he wants to take charge of this job." [19]

Comprehension slowly spread through the Rouge after 1928 that the oldtime Ford who had taken pride in the five-dollar day and the Sociological Department was dead. In his place reigned a Ford who flatly declared, "A great business is really too big to be human." This new Ford asserted that he encouraged brusqueness, friction, and competition. "I pity the poor fellow who is so soft and flabby that he must always have 'an atmosphere of good feeling' around him before he can do his work," he wrote in 1930. Sorensen and Bennett certainly illustrated Ford's further statement: "We make no attempt to coddle the people who work with us." [20] Partly because this pair had differing spheres of authority, for the time they did not clash, though they soon began to regard each other with covert jealousy. Ford seemed to stand aloof from factory routines, and many employees believed that he was ignorant of the harsher acts. But astute observers suspected that he not only saw them but inspired some of them.

Despite growing uncertainties, working conditions (for those surviving the 1927–1928 purge) remained good until the end of the nineteen-thirties. Many men preferred the Rouge to any other plant; many, as the reminiscences of workers show, cherished a sense of personal or institutional loyalty that could not be matched at General Motors or Chrysler. Partly because of what Veblen terms the instinct for workmanship, they took pride in the latest engineering advances and the renown of Models T and A. At times they even made a zestful game of breaking old records. This Stakhanovite spirit, encouraged for patriotic reasons in the First World War, continued to crop out later. Nelson tells us that the foremen set goals and the men, anxious to push production above 10,000 cars a day, voluntarily responded:

Men actually worked until they dropped in front of their machines trying to contribute to it. They just went to it until they were exhausted. This was on both the Model A and the Model T. . . . There was actually a feeling of exultation when a certain goal was reached on time, and this was prevalent among large numbers of the men. . . . Men would go over to the superintendent's office and look at the chart showing the production of the day before, and you would see them at quitting time looking at it. Every time ten more motors were added, they would come back and some of them would say: "Come on, boys, tomorrow we will do better." [21]

The statement suggests how much might have been accomplished had the Ford Motor Company clung to the Lee-Marquis-Avery program of leading the men instead of falling back on the Sorensen-Klann-Bennett tactics of driving them.

5.

The fact remains that to the end of the nineteen-twenties many workers felt themselves fortunate to have a job in the Ford plants. One perplexity of the superintendents was indeed to stop the traffic in jobs. Mike Stubas would say to Tony Giovanetti: "Give me ten dollars, and I'll get you a place in the shop." And Mike would then speak to Alec Sparks or Henkel of the personnel department: "This is my cousin. The next vacancy, I wish you would give him a trial." For years every effort was made to root out this abuse. If the superintendents learned that any man had collected money on the pretext of finding another a job, he was discharged on the spot. Klann relates that one grateful Jewish youth, on being hired, brought in a pair of meerschaum pipes as gifts to his immediate superiors; Klann dismissed him as a lesson, but immediately rehired him. After Bennett took charge of personnel in 1927–1928, rumor had it that jobs were sold on a wide scale. The significant fact is that men were anxious, not altogether from economic pressure, to get within the Ford gates.

One of the principal reasons for this, of course, was Ford's reputation for paying exceptionally high wages and benefits. That reputation, at one time well earned, was maintained by a good deal of ill-informed talk and writing. An article in the *New York Times* in 1924, for example, credited Ford with paying about $1.58 a day more than the average rate for similar work in Michigan. Occasional incidents tended to confirm the popular notions on the subject. When Ford took over the factory of the Allegheny Plate Glass Company in Glassmere, Pennsylvania, for example, all wage rates there were raised 80 per cent. This went to prove that the automobile industry offered much higher levels of pay than most others; it did not prove that Ford's position in his own industry was unusually generous. As a matter of fact, Ford wages from one point of view *were* exceptionally high; from another point of view, they went in the mid-twenties below the industrial average. The difference was made by Ford's adoption of the five-day week in 1926. After that event, his daily *rates* of pay continued high, but weekly *earnings* were low.[22]

Of course some workers preferred the short week, which left two free days for gardening, recreation, or odd jobs, to the larger weekly earnings; many did not. But the dry statistics of the Federal and State governments leave no doubt that Ford's announcement of the five-day week in 1926 meant lower weekly pay. Labor leaders were quick to state this fact, and they were right. The average hourly earnings in all Ford plants and branches in the United States moved from 87 cents an hour in 1921 to 80 cents in 1925, 89 cents in 1928, and 96 in 1931. Ford hiring-in rates in 1928–1929 were definitely at the top of the automotive industry at 62.5 cents an hour. However, a survey of the automotive industry made in 1928 by the Federal Bureau of Labor Statistics proves that weekly earnings in the Ford establishments in 1925 were $4.21 below the industry's average, and in 1928 were $1.37 below. At Highland Park the showing would have been somewhat better than that here indicated, and at the Rouge somewhat worse.[23]

The five-day week movement in industry was still something of a novelty in 1926, and Henry Ford's espousal of it stimulated its progress. Soon after he announced it, the American Federation of Labor, holding its annual convention in Detroit, favored its gradual extension by means of union contracts. Labor in general was still required to toil for excessive work-periods. As recently as 1909 the Federal Manufacturing Census had shown that large numbers of wage-earners worked seventy-two hours each week in iron and steel, paper-making, flour-milling, sugar-refining, and petroleum refining. Henry Ford had long insisted that the working day should not run over eight hours; he now descanted with equal vigor on the economic advantages of the five-day week. But ideally the shorter week should not have meant reduced earnings. Ford himself had emphatically maintained that "we can find methods of manufacturing which will make high wages the cheapest of wages," and that "if you cut wages, you just cut the number of your own consumers." He might have argued that the extra day was well worth the $1.37 difference in pay found in 1928; but he could have kept an undisputed claim to leadership in wages if he had given the extra day with no cut in earnings at all.[24]

Indeed, in the final instalment of his autobiography, *Moving Forward,* Henry Ford admitted this. "Events have fully demonstrated," he wrote, "that the five-day week is as productive as the six-day week. . . . Of course, the full case for the five-day week cannot be proved unless it carries with it a six-day pay. The purpose of the five-day week is not to compel people to live on five sixths of their present income, but to enable them to earn their present income, or more, in five sixths of the time." He added that it was the responsibility of management to enable them to do this. One critic of Ford for permitting a drop in real wages was the business analyst B. C. Forbes. In 1927 he quoted a responsible Ford employee as saying that not one Ford employee in twenty had been financially benefited by the five-day week, while numerous men had been injured. A still sharper critic was Reinhold Niebuhr, then a pastor in Detroit, who wrote in the last days of 1926: [25]

> Mr. Ford declares that a third of his men receive increases. Most of these increases are either $2 or $4 a week. Which means that even the best of his men are still short from $2 to $4 in their weekly pay envelope. That is, they receive either $32 or $34 instead of $36. At the present moment the five-day week has been reduced to four and one-half days throughout the plant, and many workers have even less work than that.

The Ford company, to be sure, did increase the pay of large numbers of men from time to time. Just how many were thus benefited, just when and how, are questions difficult to answer. A single report survives on wage increases granted at the Rouge during a twelve month period in 1926–1927. They totalled a little more than 45,000 of which 22,000 were first increases, 17,000 second, and 6000 third, with a few above that level. Most of the grants were less than 10 cents an hour. Indeed, we have evidence that the usual rate of increase was 40 cents a day, that increases continued for competent workers until they reached $7.20, and that above that figure men found it difficult to go. Wage increases depended on the nature of the job, the skill of the worker, and the willingness of the foremen to make favorable recommendations. An exceptionally quick, intelligent, or ingenious worker, soon became known as such to officers above his own foreman, so that it was difficult for a prejudiced boss to hold a good man back. [26]

Because of these slow but fairly steady increments, the criticism of Ford's five-day week based on a drop in real wages gradually lost part of its force. The average weekly wage at the Rouge rose from 1925 to 1927 by $4.68, workers being paid an average of 93.6 cents an hour in the latter year. But these statistics are not wholly trustworthy, for the large-scale layoff in 1927 incident to the introduction of the new model, during which the more skilled workers were retained, had the effect of raising average hourly payments. It was not until Ford dramatically announced his seven-dollar-a-day minimum and made it effective on December 1, 1929, that he confuted his assailants and regained much of his old prestige in the wage field. This step created a sensation almost rivaling the five-dollar day announcement fifteen years earlier. Its advertising value to him and the company was tremendous.

Whatever the precise motivation of Ford's seven-dollar day announcement—and a desire to gain favorable publicity, a readiness to dramatize himself in the role of a lone adventurer rejecting all the accepted canons of sound business behavior, and striding forth as the paladin of the common man, may well have helped shape his decision —it came at a moment of great psychological effectiveness. In October the stock-market crash had shaken the country. President Hoover in November convoked a conference of business leaders: Secretary Mellon, Walter Teagle, Julius Rosenwald, Owen D. Young, Myron C. Taylor, Eugene G. Grace, Pierre du Pont, Henry Ford, and others. This gathering provided a sounding-board of great power. When Ford at the close of the conference released his announcement, it astonished and apparently dismayed the other magnates, who had expected that no important statement of policy would be enunciated by any member except through President Hoover. Besides, was this a time, with prices and profits breaking sharply, to come forth with a sweeping wage increase? The conference had stood emphatically for holding the economic line: its official statement had declared that employers should not initiate wage reductions, and labor should not ask increases.

But it can be said for Henry Ford that he had been contemplating a wage increase for several months. Late in July his prediction that the minimum wage in his factories was certain to be raised "at no very distant time" had seized the front page of Detroit newspapers and been published far and wide. The company was then prosperous, with large profits and roseate prospects. The economic troubles of the autumn had clouded these prospects; but like most other people, Henry Ford thought that the storm would soon blow past and the skies brighten.

We can give him credit for a sincere desire to raise wages and to hearten the country by a bold gesture. His announcement had been at least partly prepared before he went to the conference, and would apparently have been issued at about this date in any event.[27]

In releasing his news immediately after the conference Ford declared that the purchasing capacity of the nation must be stimulated by lower prices and better pay. "Wages must not come down, they must not even stay on their present level; they must go up." In the usual style of his homilies he declared that this was no startling, miraculous plan of recovery; "it is all as plain and familiar as a copybook maxim." President Hoover would show the country "that there is nothing to fear and that if every one will attend to his own work, the future is secure." In a time of general alarm and gloom this statement was psychologically sound, and Ford could claim the unusual distinction of supporting his theories with concrete action. His first announcements gave no details as to the precise amount of the wage changes; he merely said that the increases would be general, and would be by percentages based on the class of employment. The three representatives of labor at the conference, Secretary Davis, William Green, and John L. Lewis, expressed natural gratification.

When the details had been worked out, Edsel Ford stated that the minimum wage would be advanced from six to seven dollars, and that general increases, effective December 1, would be given all wage-earners and salaried employees. The estimated cost would be $19,500,-000 a year. "Lately," he said, "we passed on the benefits of some of our economies to our customers in the form of reduced prices on our cars; and now we share up with our workingmen." Thereafter new employees were hired at six dollars for a probationary period of sixty days, when their wages went to the seven-dollar minimum. General readjustments were made all along the line. Former employees receiving less than six dollars (mostly minors) went to that figure immediately; all those with rates between six and seven dollars were advanced to the higher wage; and skilled workers and salaried folk getting more than seven dollars received five per cent increases. As a result of these changes, among other factors, average wage rates in all American plants and branches of the company rose during 1930 about fifty cents a day over the average for the previous year.

The seven-dollar day was maintained for two years lacking about two months; two years of deepening economic depression. Full credit is due Ford for this attempt to shore up the disintegrating economy of the nation. That he meant well there can be no doubt, and editorial comment indicates that his seven-dollar day had some real effect in encouraging frightened people, and in blunting the edge of wage-slashes. The actual results of the nominal wage-increase within the Ford empire, however, have offered a subject for acrimonious debate. Two elements exerted a downward pressure on real wages even while they seemingly rose; the fact that as the depression reduced the size of the working force, Ford (like other employees) tended to keep the skilled men who would have gotten high wages anyhow, and discharge the ill-trained; and the fact that the Ford company diverted an increasing proportion of its work to suppliers who paid wages much below the Ford level.

The first element is obvious, and was beyond the company's control. If the nation had made a prompt and vigorous recovery from the economic blows of 1929–1930, Ford might have hired a full force in 1931, and given the benefits of the seven-dollar day to a normal quota of unskilled workers. But the downward spiral went unchecked. All over the world factories were closing and unemployment was rising. In the United States empty passenger trains ran through cities where hardly a wisp of factory smoke stained the skies. It was inevitable that hard-pressed plants, forced to discharge their workers, should keep their best men. Throughout the nearly two years of the seven-dollar day, the three-day week prevailed in most Ford departments. In that period of soup lines and lengthening relief rolls, men employed even three fifths of the time felt lucky. It would have been insane for the company to retain the most inefficient part of its force, and the good men discharged would have suffered as much as the poor hands.

The question of diversion of work to low-wage suppliers is even more complex. To what extent did it take place? To what degree was it a deliberate evasion of the seven-dollar day?

That Ford's use of suppliers during this period increased, perhaps considerably, is unquestionable. Two interpretations may be put on this enhanced use: that it was Ford's way of escaping the consequences of his publicity-courting gesture as labor's benefactor, or that it represented Ford's effort to assist hard-pressed manufacturers struggling on the verge of bankruptcy. It may even have been a combination of the two! The sinister interpretation is pressed by Keith Sward, with no little manipulation of evidence. The favorable interpretation is given us by Ford himself. He did not need, in 1930, to tell Americans that plants all over the country were grasping eagerly at straws to keep from drowning, and that managers, stockholders, and employees regarded any contract as a heaven-sent boon. His statement in *Moving Forward* could therefore be read as the boast of a generous spread-the-work policy: "In 1929 we were giving work to 2200 concerns; this year we constantly use 3500 concerns out of a total of 5800 who [can potentially] supply us." [28] *

Officers of the Ford Company were aware that they could be attacked because their suppliers' wage rates were so much lower than their own. Theodore F. MacManus published an advertisement in the *New York Times* of February 24, 1930, pointing out in acrid language how much use the high-paying Mr. Ford made of low-paying firms. This prompted Sorensen to write the major suppliers listed by MacManus asking them for their wage rates. Among the eight companies whose answers are on file, hourly rates ranged from 45 to 85 cents, with average piece-work earnings ranging from 61 cents an hour upward. The typical work week was 50 hours. Two large suppliers, the Briggs and Murray Body companies, who three years later were revealed to be paying abominably low wages, sent no recorded replies. Company officers used the answers to give a writer for the Detroit *News* material for an article which put the best face on the matter possible. After saying that he had scrutinized "typical" reports on supplier wages, the writer declares that from "letters taken at random" he found that the average wage rate paid was 69.67 cents an hour. Inasmuch as Ford workers averaged about $1 an hour, he concluded that the hand employed full-time by outside concerns making Ford parts received $35.25 a week, while the Ford hand got $40.

Savage price-cutting and wage-cutting were then the order of the day. Numerous instances are on record in the East and South of factories hiring women at $3 to $6 a week. According to the Detroit *Labor*

---

* As an instance of Mr. Sward's all too frequent manipulation of data we may note the following. The Dow-Jones service issued a report early in 1931 stating that Ford had 3500 regular suppliers, and a complete supplier-list of 5500. Ford himself, as noted above, spoke of increasing his use of suppliers from 2200 concerns to 3500 concerns. On the basis of this information, Mr. Sward writes: "The number of suppliers to whom Ford sublet his work rose steadily from 2200 concerns in 1929 to 3500 the following year, then to 5500 outside establishments in 1931." (*The Legend of Henry Ford*, 220). This last clause is a clear misinterpretation of the sources quoted, and is fairly typical of the methodology repeatedly employed by Mr. Sward to support his hostility to Ford.

News, the Murray Body Company in the spring of 1930 was paying some 500 women employed on a Ford contract as little, on a piece-work basis, as $3 a day. Formerly men in this factory department had earned $7 to $8 a day; they had been discharged in favor of women, who at first were able to make $4.50, but who since a recent drop in the piece-rate were glad to earn $3 in nine hours. No doubt this allegation was true. In many shops and stores women were receiving less. The times were out of joint, and economic injustice would run rampant until drastic measures by the government protected the helpless.

And actually a better defense of Ford's increased use of suppliers is available than company officers made at the time. This increased use had three roots which stood quite apart from wage advantages. (1) The Model A was so much more complex than the Model T that it required a much ampler range of manufacturing facilities. The standard Fordor model in 1928 weighed 420 pounds more than the same model of its predecessor, had more than 5500 parts, and included among these parts many added items which had *never* been made by the Ford Motor Company, among them the oil pump, windshield wipers, the distributor, water pump, air cleaner, oil filters, and various gauges. Had Ford tried to manufacture these parts he would have had to expand his facilities enormously in a time of economic strain. He naturally turned to specialized suppliers. (2) In this period of frequent company bankruptcies, labor turmoil, and general uncertainty, it was important to guarantee a steady flow of parts. This could be done, in some degree, by allocating orders to a greater number of suppliers. (3) To save freight, obtain prompter delivery, and win local good-will, the branch assembly plants were expanding a local purchase program; and this obviously added to the number of suppliers, but not to the total purchased.

As a matter of fact, although the use of suppliers rose, the amount of labor expended on cars inside the Ford plant did not fall, but increased. In 1930, Ford assembled 1,267,034 units, paying for 238,908,506 hours of work; in 1935 the company assembled 1,116,693 units and paid for 213,681,353 hours of work. In other words, while production in this period declined 11.9 per cent, work hours declined only 10.6 per cent. Many company officers, indeed, thought Henry Ford was altogether too reluctant to go to outside sources. He hated to admit that the Rouge could not manufacture an item more efficiently than an alien concern.[29]

Once more we must say that easy generalizations are dangerous. Many complex factors affect any estimate of wage rates or working periods. But we are safe in asserting that as respects both, Ford throughout the nineteen-twenties occupied much the same plane as General Motors. The Rouge and Highland Park possessed one signal advantage in payment by the hour, not by piece-rate. Testimony from men who worked for both companies is decisive on this point. Piece-rate pay, which Henry Ford always condemned, created tension, hurry, and uneasiness, and put men at the mercy of any mishap.

6.

The principal grievance of workers throughout the automotive industry did not pertain to wages, hours, or the pace of the assembly line. It dealt with uncertainty of tenure and the almost total lack of seniority privileges. Ford workers, after the end of the enlightened Lee-Marquis-Avery era, were subject to discharge at any time and for any reason. They had no tenure and no appeal. An economic slump, failure in sales, or stoppage of work for retooling resulted in layoffs; and in choosing men to be kept while others went, no preference whatever was given to old employees. "We would just keep those we thought were the best men," says one former boss. A mechanic who had been with the company since Piquette days was discharged as quickly as one who had joined only three months ago. On the assembly line, in fact, the bosses had a natural liking for young, vigorous, quick men not past thirty-five. Experienced hands past that age, if they did not possess some indispensable skill, were thus often the first to be dismissed and the last to be re-engaged.

This was an injustice which rankled. On the railroads senior employees, protected by strong brotherhoods, had various much-prized advantages over juniors; in the mass-production industries they were penalized. Another grievance was the frequent failure of the management to give workers any advance notice whatever of a layoff.

It was clear that only a strong union could protect seniority rights, insist on pensions, and gain other privileges which, taken in combination, would offer faithful workers a boon far beyond high wages or short hours—security. But as we have noted, the automotive industry was poor ground for unions. Not only did General Motors, Ford, and practically all other companies take an attitude of belligerent resistance; most of the workers were indifferent. The immigrant from Poland,

Italy, or Jugoslavia, the Negro from Georgia, the restless mountaineer from Tennessee, were slow to comprehend the advantages of united action. They were suspicious of walking delegates; their ingrained individualism made them chilly toward union meetings; they were quick to resent union fees. Education would be needed before they gained the discipline and tenacity to wage successful labor offensives.

Henry Ford's own attitude was uncompromising, while his bosses, led by Sorensen, were fiercely antipathetic. They would hire union men, but would countenance no unions. Ford's philosophy, however mistaken, was sincere and was based on some real thought. Inevitably prejudice entered into it; the prejudice of a self-made man who thinks that others could succeed if they just had equal grit, industry and brains; the prejudice of the rural mind which distrusts all urban organizations; the prejudice of an inveterate individualist suspicious of any restrictions. But he had thought beyond his prejudices. One reason why he detested unions was that he saw lurking in them the threat of class warfare. He always argued that the United States was fortunate in having no fixed classes—it simply had "men who will work and men who will not"—and that incitation to class was almost treason. He gropingly expressed this idea when he talked with John Reed in 1916.

"Do you believe in labor unions?" Reed asked.

"No, I don't," answered Ford. "Labor unions mean war, and I don't believe in war. Perhaps labor unions are necessary when people haven't got any other defense against special privilege. But I believe that when we get all the facts before the people, special privilege will die out."

Ford always indulged the notion that his lot was identical with that of the workingmen. He so spoke of himself in *My Life and Work*— "We who have been and still are a part of the laboring class." A farmer's son, a whilom mechanic, a man who still worked with his hands, a hater of parasites, a leader who built larger plants to make more goods and jobs, what was he if not a workingman? "I stand for the best interests of my enployees," he said in effect in more than one interview. "I do all I can for them. Nobody should try to draw a line between us. That would be the surest way of hurting us both." * In badly managed,

---

* Ford wrote Charles Edison October 6, 1933: "I have never bargained with my men, I have always bargained for them. It would be strange to see my men and me trying to get the better of each other. I think we have made better bargains for them than any stranger could, or than they could make for themselves." (Acc. 1, Box 117.) Edsel had no such illusions. Henry Ford also opposed unions because he felt that they "would be dominated by racketeers." (Voorhess, *Reminiscences.*)

exploitative industries (particularly those under the thumb of Wall Street!) unions might be necessary, but never at Highland Park and the Rouge. Down to 1930, at least, Ford did not think of himself as a paternalistic employer, but as a fellow-participator with his workers in the great game of industry.

This was absurd, but it was sincere. Even while becoming one of the richest men in history, Ford was sincere in inveighing against riches and privilege; *his* wealth was different, for it was productive wealth. He was probably sincere in questioning the motives of union leaders—"Some of them are very rich." He showed a childlike sincerity in arguing, as an individualist, that men should keep out of armies, unions, employers' associations, and even rigid political parties. "People are never so likely to be wrong as when they are organized," he proclaimed in the *Ford News*. "And they never have so little freedom. . . . People can be manipulated only when they are organized. . . . The safety of the people today . . . consists in this fact, that the people are unorganized and therefore cannot be trapped." [30]

Once enrolled in a powerful union, Ford held, workers were likely to be led willy-nilly into strikes, boycotts, and other rash movements. Sometimes the manipulator would be a labor leader. Sometimes he would be a tool of large financial interests in the background. Late in 1919 Ford stated on his *Dearborn Independent* page that many strikes had a concealed design. He gave as an example the strike engineered in some parts-supply factory not to raise wages, but to bring down in ruin the huge industry to which the parts were essential. Ford's utterance came just after the Wadsworth strike, which affected his supply of closed bodies. In 1923 his views were even more emphatic. "Labor unions are part of the exploitation scheme," he told the *Christian Science Monitor*. "The men probably don't know it, and maybe even their leaders don't know that they are really but tools in the hands of the master exploiters of production." A little later he spoke of the Ku Klux Klan, the Masons, the Knights of Columbus, and various patriotic societies as organizations open to Wall Street (that is, wicked financial) influences. "That goes for labor unions, too," he added, "they also are organized and used by Wall Street." This was a reckless echo of Populist days. He really believed that unions were a limitation on freedom. Edsel, in various statements in the nineteen-twenties, took a much more liberal view. [31]

Had a powerful union movement developed in the automotive industry before 1930, the Ford Company, like General Motors, would
have come into conflict with it, but none did. When World War I
closed, an Auto Workers' Union existed, but it had only 40,000 members
in the spring of 1919, and was suspended from the A.F. of L. that year.
Its heads believed that if they could win one important strike in a well-
organized factory, they would soon be able to sign up most employees.
But they never won that strategic strike, and the union shortly collapsed. Ford factories never blacklisted union men, but continued to
employ them, even employing a former head of the Detroit Federation
of Labor; they could afford this indifference.

One of the most painful features of the employers' movement against
unionism in the nineteen-twenties was the widespread use of espionage.
This had been given a pronounced impetus by the war, when Central
or East European elements were suspected of disloyal activities. Many
companies began using paid informers. Attorney-General A. Mitchell
Palmer encouraged and even required a close wartime watch on German sympathizers, creating a broad network of agents for the protection of factories pursuing war war, whose activities were assisted by a
privately-organized secret service called the American Protective
League.

During the war the detective force in the Ford plants, part of the
Eighth Industrial Division under government supervision, recruited
scores of operatives, each expected to report any suspicious word or act.
While nearly all the reports bore upon pro-German activities, a few concerned sabotage, and a sizable number dealt with "radical" leanings.
Even refusal to buy Liberty Bonds was a ground for suspicion. Soon
after the armistice the attorney-general severed his connection with all
private detective agencies, declaring that he feared harmful results from
their work. But in many industries the espionage organizations persisted. In the Ford plants the force of operatives was reduced, but the
managers had become imbued with the idea that large-scale espionage
would be highly useful, and determined to keep and improve the tool.

A highly illuminating sheaf of espionage records written just after
the war by a well-trained agent, B. J. Liccardi, who worked under the
superintendent's office in the Highland Park plant, survives in the Ford
Archives. He moved from department to department as his superiors
suspected some baleful outcropping of inefficient management, theft,

radicalism, or union propaganda. Liccardi, who after gaining experience in various metal industries had helped break strikes in Chicago and New York, and had been an investigator for Liebold during the Chicago *Tribune* trial, kept busy day and night. After eight hours of heavy work in the shops, where he was expected to set an example, he often attended evening meetings of I.W.W. locals, of Local 82 of the International Association of Machinists, or of some branch of the Socialist Party. This type of activity continued right through the decade. Klann says frankly, "We always had spies or agents to get information" —on Communism, union activities, and general employee attitudes toward the management.

This espionage system, in the Ford factories as elsewhere, generated an atmosphere of apprehension and distrust, and was met by labor groups with counter-espionage. E. G. Pipp declared that a number of the spies were men of vicious character. The editor believed that Ford would be shocked to know how these gentry used money, drink and complaisant women to compromise and discredit certain victims. He would like to tell Ford this face to face, not in a public article; but, he added, "you have permitted those responsible for the conditions to build a wall about you that makes it impossible to get the information to you in any other way." [32]

7.

Among labor leaders the nineteen-twenties naturally witnessed a slow erosion of faith in Ford and his labor policies. The greater their distance from Detroit, the more likely they were to retain much of the admiration which had sprung from the five-dollar day and the early labor reforms; the more weight they gave to the five-day week and seven-dollar day as substantial moves toward betterment of the worker. But little by little even peripheral groups became disillusioned. In 1925 Professor S. M. Levin of the City College of Detroit undertook to discover how representative labor men of the country regarded Ford. He found a surprising amount of ignorance, some approval, and a growing skepticism. William Green declared that the Ford minimum, then $6, was "not an extraordinary wage," that the labor turnover was distressingly large, and that the spying practised on union men was "very objectionable." James O'Connell, president of the A.F. of L. Metal Trades Department, admitted that he knew little, but of the general impression that Ford paid exceptionally high wages, he was convinced that the public was deceived both as to real working conditions and real wage levels.

The astonishing fact is that union leaders were as slow and hesitant as they were in expressing a loss of confidence. Or is it, after all, so astonishing?

For one reason, even without the lingering memory of the five-dollar day and the bright era in which the Ford plant had been a little welfare state, and even without consideration of the special regard which Ford still paid to the Negro, the physically handicapped, and the hope-bereft graduates of the penitentiaries, he compared favorably with many prominent employers. In the steel mills the twelve-hour day survived the great strike. In the coal fields throughout the nineteen-twenties low wages, unemployment, and company stores kept hundreds of thousands in chronic poverty. Textile factories sweated their labor; big mercantile establishments paid girls barely enough to live on. Many concerns blacklisted union men. Automobile manufacture ranked as a high-wage industry, and the Ford Company was still arguably a leader in the wage-hour field. For another reason, union leaders knew that however mistaken Henry Ford's philosophy of labor relations was, he had one, and he held it honestly. He was a queer mixture of good and bad, and they felt a natural regard for the constructive aspects of his mind and personality. It is perhaps not so strange, after all, that an A.F. of L. organizer, addressing the Michigan Federation of Labor in 1926, prefaced his criticism of Ford policies with the words, "Here in our State we have fine employers like Mr. Ford and others," and concluded by saying: "It is not for the purpose of minimizing the greatness and humanity of Mr. Ford that I mention these things." [38]

Some of the happiest pages in this variegated record chronicle the company's generous treatment of Negro workers. One day in 1914 Henry Ford had led an oldtime Negro friend, William Perry, with whom he had often manned a crosscut saw during his farming years, into the Highland Park plant, explained some of the machinery, and bade the superintendent to "see to it that he's comfortable." Perry was the first Negro employee. Within a half dozen years after the Armistice, more than five thousand colored people were working for Ford. By 1926, the roster had lengthened to ten thousand or more, a tenth of the whole force. Indeed, during the open-shop era, the Ford Company employed well over half the Negroes in the motor industry. Henry Ford and Sorensen developed special confidence in two colored pastors of Detroit, the Rev. R. L. Bradby of the Second Baptist Church and the Rev. Everard W. Daniel of St. Matthew's Episcopal Church, who helped them find capable men, break up the use of knives, and compose differences between the races. One of the Episcopalian parishioners, D. J. Marshall, became the leading Negro-relations agent for the company from 1923 until his death some twenty years later; and he did good work until he fell too far under the influence of Harry Bennett.

Henry Ford had a firm conviction that the races should labor as partners, "the colored man at one end of the log and the white man at the other." Still more important, he held that merit, not color, should govern promotion; and Edsel and he made Sorensen and Martin support their position. The result was that at a time when practically all large industries paid grudging attention to skilled and semi-skilled Negroes, and almost none would give a foremanship or white-collar position to a colored person, Ford practised real equality. Negroes got the same wages and chances; Negro foremen gave orders to whites and blacks alike, and two or three Negroes had the authority to challenge plant superintendents on questions of discrimination, and to get white foremen discharged for unjust acts. The Rouge was the only plant in the industry where Negroes shared in all the manufacturing operations.[34]

But the great underlying grievance of labor became more prominent year after year. The depression was certain to accentuate it. Until labor organizations were created strong enough to face the automobile companies as equals, until wages, hours, seniority rights, and other conditions essential to security became a subject of negotiation instead of dictation, the American ideal would remain unfulfilled. A sweeping reform was overdue.

XXI

FORD OVERSEAS:

THE YEARS OF STORM

As Henry Ford and his associates looked about the globe in 1927–1928 they saw that a more systematic organization of their foreign business had become imperative. American motor production had grown beyond all expectation. Out of 4,163,000 automotive vehicles manufactured in the world in 1927, the United States supplied more than 3,400,000; out of 5,200,000 units in 1928, a total of 4,360,000. The export trade took 7.1 per cent of all American automotive production in 1926, 11.3 per cent in 1927, and 11.6 per cent in 1928. Naturally, automobile manufacturers, including Henry Ford, were in general strong believers in lower tariffs and freer global trade. Down to the change-over from the Model T to Model A, the Ford company was consistently the largest exporter. But it had depended too long on the waning popularity of the "tin Lizzie," had done too little to plan its foreign business, and felt the shadow of an increasing threat.[1]

That threat, in part, came from General Motors and the Chevrolet; in part from the growing vigor of British, French, Italian, and other foreign makers of small cars. The apprehension which Ford officers felt concerning the General Motors rivalry was reflected in their pains to gather careful statistics on it. As the Model A was introduced the figures became ominous. In Spain during 1929 new Ford cars accounted for 18.3 per cent of all registrations, Chevrolet 19.5 per cent; in Sweden new Ford cars comprised 20.7 per cent of registrations, Chevrolet 20.9 per cent; in Iraq the figures were 35.2 and 37.4; in the Philippines 24.1 and 25.9.[2] Throughout most of Latin America the Fords still led by a comfortable margin, but their position was precarious. Meanwhile, the Austin and Morris in England, the Citroën in France, and the Fiat in Italy, excellent cheap cars all, were formidable antagonists.

In conferences dominated by Henry Ford, Edsel, and Sorensen, the

541

company decided that distribution should be systematized from three main centers, Michigan, Ontario, and England. Besides intensively cultivating the home market, the Rouge would send parts for assembly mainly to Japan and Latin America. Ford Motor of Canada, the largest automotive factory under the British flag, would principally distribute (chiefly through affiliated companies) to most of the Empire-Commonwealth. As for England, a large and efficient factory to be erected there would generally serve and produce vehicles for all parts of the continent, Turkey and the Middle East, and Africa north of Rhodesia.

The consistent aim of the Ford organization had been to combine two types of savings; one from the technological advantages of mass production, one from lower transportation costs. The proposal now was for three great mass-production factories in Dearborn, Ontario, and England to turn out cars at the lowest possible figure, and distribute them, or parts for assembly, as economically as possible. It was a simple idea, but in practice a complex task.

The first step was to choose the ablest head possible to conduct the reorganization of the business in Europe. Early in 1928 Henry Ford revisited England. While in London he sent word to Sir Percival Perry, living in the Channel Islands, to come see him; and Perry, then at the height of his powers—a man radiating vitality and charm—had several long talks with Henry, and accompanied him to his ship at Southampton. During the visit Ford had inspected the site bought at Dagenham, just below London on the Thames, two years earlier, and had shown enthusiasm for it. He also responded cordially to Perry's ideas for lifting the European reorganization to a high plane; these harmonized with his own and Sorensen's. It was agreed that Perry would at once reenter Ford employ as head of European operations. April found him hard at work in the Regent Street offices, planning the revolutionary new program.[3]

When Ford returned to Dearborn, Sorensen asked him: "Well, what did you accomplish?" "I've hired Perry again." "That is the best news you could have brought me," exclaimed Sorensen.[4]

The first step was to form the Ford Motor Company Ltd. for the purpose of unifying all the Western European interests. By agreements dated December 7, 1928, it acquired the old Ford Motor Company of England, with the Manchester plant; Henry Ford & Son, of Cork; and a controlling interest in Ford companies in France, Belgium, Germany,

Italy, Holland, Spain, Denmark, Sweden, and Finland. The new English company was given certain rights to manufacture and assemble Ford products to be supplied principally for the British Isles, the continent (except Russia), the Middle East, Northern Africa, and Afghanistan, together with all required patents. It was also to undertake the manufacture of Fordson tractors for world distribution.

Under the new plan, the factory to be erected at Dagenham would not only make cars for the British market tariff-free (for the product would be entirely British), but engines, other parts, and whole cars and tractors for the associated companies. Continental imports from Ford in Detroit came to about $7,000,000 in 1930; most of this business would be transferred to England. The advantages of mass production could be seized once a level of 100,000 units a year was reached; and the Ford executives hoped that Dagenham would produce 120,000 units as soon as it began running full force. The Model A car and Model AA truck would be the standard European units, but some thought was entertained of a smaller automobile as well for Britain, where "baby cars" were increasingly popular.[5]

Edsel Ford, striking a spade into the boggy soil at Dagenham on May 16, 1929, formally commenced construction of the new works, which were expected to surpass in size and equipment those of General Motors at Luton. The 500-acre area, a low, water-soaked tract overgrown with coarse grass, looked highly unpromising. These were the Essex marshes which Dickens had vividly described in *Great Expectations*. But during the next year more than 11,000 concrete piles were driven into the bog. Rarely if ever had a site been so tightly packed with piles, many of them sunk to an eighty-foot depth. Under those parts of the factory which had to bear specially heavy weights, the columns were hammered down so closely that the foundations represented almost solid steel-reinforced concrete. Four large buildings were soon erected— one for the foundry and machine shop, one for manufacturing, one for assembly, and one for offices. Ore and coal yards rose in gray and black hillocks. A blast furnace with a five hundred ton daily capacity reared its stacks; alongside stood forty-five coke ovens to provide fuel. Close at hand were a powerhouse of unique design, and a connecting refuse-preparation house—for Henry Ford, who wished to do London a good turn and to illustrate anew his ideas on salvaging waste materials, had agreed to burn as much as a thousand tons daily of the city's garbage.[6]

Perry never liked the site. He always maintained not only that South-ampton was far better, but that Dagenham was about the worst possi-ble choice! The cost of the piling was tremendous. Because of this cost, space was economized, and the operations had to be too closely con-stricted. The rail and road facilities, moreover, seemed to him distinctly inferior to those of Southampton. Henry Ford, however, was pleased by the frontage of nearly half a mile overlooking the wide and busy Thames. A concrete jetty more than 1800 feet long and 51 feet wide, coming right up to the main buildings, gave ample shipping facilities; one section of it accommodated barges full of London refuse, which was unloaded by conveyors, another section vessels of 20 feet draught taking cars out, and still another ships up to 28 feet draught bringing in coal, iron ore, and limestone. The main London-Tilbury railway and an arterial road were close at hand. Perry's architects, Charles Heath-cote & Sons, cooperated with the Detroit executives and H. B. Hanson, who had final authority in planning, in erecting one of the most efficient and attractive industrial works yet seen in Great Britain. In general plan, it followed the Rouge, but because of space limitations was "compressed." [7]

Just as Henry Ford had placed the tractor factory in Cork partly be-cause he wished to lessen the flow of Irish emigration, so in choosing Dagenham he was partly actuated by a wish to help the people of Eng-land solve some of their problems. "I regard Great Britain as still being the center of world trade," he said in 1928, adding: "I am sure Great Britain can manufacture better for the Continent, for India, and for other places on that side than any other country." He took pride in re-claiming a waste area and burning refuse (which Hanson indicates had some advantages for the plant); while on a much more important plane, he wished to do something to cure the chronic unemployment of East London. He hoped that a body of floating labor there, drawn to Dagenham, might find new and better homes in neighboring Essex towns.

The English company had a nominal capital of £7,000,000, of which £2,800,000 were sold by public offering in December, 1928, and the other £4,200,000 assigned to the Michigan company, in exchange for the old Manchester properties, patent rights, and other assets. The flota-tion of the minority block of stock had some novel features. In offering the shares for public subscription at £1 each, Perry made no forecast of future earnings. He merely summarized the earnings of the previous four years by the British and continental companies involved—earnings which averaged more than 13 per cent of the new capital of £7,000,000. Perry had first proposed that the English branch of Lee, Higginson & Company be allowed to place the stock on the market at a premium, which would be used to give Ford, Ltd. a reserve; but Henry and Edsel Ford objected to any markup of shares, and to the commission which the brokers would charge. Everyone underestimated the demand. In the event, an eager public awaited the offering, while American investors were eager to buy shares. They had never been able to purchase stock in the Ford Motor Company in the United States, but here at last was an opportunity to participate in a Ford enterprise.

To the dismay of Perry, Henry Ford, and Sorensen, American buyers, bidding up the shares to a high premium, soon obtained most of them.* Edsel Ford learned in January, 1929, that almost two million shares were in American hands, while at the beginning of February the Guaranty Trust Company placed the figure at 2,400,000. But even if only half a million shares were left in Great Britain, and were well distributed about the country, Perry believed that the business would be greatly helped. Ford shareholders would naturally tend to buy Ford cars. Early in 1929 the stock was quoted at better than £4½; then it fell early in 1930 to £3, at which price it gave a yield of nearly 3.5 per cent. This, of course, was at the height of the American bull market. The first report of the English company, covering the period from incorporation to the end of 1930, showed profits of slightly more than a million pounds, and made possible a dividend (after ample allowance for depreciation) of ten per cent on the value of the stock. These profits included £104,500

---

* Henry Ford, who saw clearly that he could never maintain American companies in foreign lands, and had no desire to do so, at first wished to divide the stock of the new British company 50-50; it was Perry who, in conversations with Henry, insisted that Detroit should keep 60 per cent.

Perry's idea was that Lee, Higginson's London branch be allowed to take £2,500,000 of the £2,800,000 of stock, and distribute it among British investors; Henry and Edsel Ford insisted that the Ford Motor Company, Ltd., offer it directly to the public at par. "We do not wish international distribution," cabled Edsel in November, 1928. "Prefer shares held by English small investor." This was a commendable position. But a brokerage house might have done better in protecting the small investor, while speculators got much of the eventual rise in price. Hanson, *Reminiscences*, tells how he demanded and received 200 shares of the Dutch company, which he got at "about 40," and soon sold at 100. This operation, with a profit of approximately $12,000, gives some idea of the possible gains realized on British shares.

from the net income earned by affiliated companies before their re-organization, received in dividends and premiums on the sale of their shares.[8]

It was obvious that if the English company had offered its shares at a higher price than £1, it could easily have sold them, for purchasers lucky enough to get stock at that figure quickly trebled or quadrupled their money. On this score Henry and Edsel Ford had no regrets, but they did regret the fact that so much of the offering was seized by Americans acting through English agents. They had underestimated the demand; Perry in particular, uneasy about the flotation and working hard to make sure of a market, was astonished by the response. When early in 1931 the company increased its capital to £9,000,000 by creating 2,000,000 additional shares of £1 par value, it not only sold them at £3, the current rate, but took precautions to keep American bankers and brokers from getting large blocks.*

The British motor industry at this time was highly competitive, and because of horsepower and gasoline taxes was increasingly dominated by the small inexpensive automobile of from seven to sixteen hp.† Approximately three fourths of the total private cars made in the kingdom were the product of five firms—Morris, Austin, Singer, Humber, and Rover; the remainder being made by about thirty companies. Buyers who had only £250 or less to spend enjoyed a wide range of choice in 1930: the Austin four-cylinder and the Morris Minor at £130–£140; the M.G. Midget at £185–£240; the four-cylinder Ford (still made at Manchester) at £170 up; the four-cylinder Morris Cowley at £180–£195; the Singer Junior at £140; the six-cylinder Chevrolet at £190–£240; and others. British production in the four years 1927–1930 had ranged between 212,000 and 237,000 units, while exports had run from 30,000 to 42,000 annually.

"It is obvious," said the London *Economist* on April 11, 1931, "that the incursion of the Ford Motor Company on a large scale into the British market will intensify the precarious struggle for existence of the

---

* However, in addition to the 1,200,000 shares purchased by the American company at this premium, only 339,451 of the 800,000 minority shares were purchased at the £2 premium. The remaining shares were sold in 1933 and 1934 at premiums well under one pound.

† In 1928 the home sales of British cars of 16 hp. or less were 82 per cent of the whole; in 1929 they were 88 per cent. P. W. S. Andrews and Elizabeth Brunner, *The Life of Lord Nuffield: A Study in Enterprise and Benevolence* (Oxford, 1955), 187. Gasoline duties were imposed in 1928. It should be remembered that British motor horsepower differs from American, and has more strength per unit.

thirty firms now responsible for only about 40,000 cars." Not only would the new Dagenham plant compete in the home market; it would also be formidable in the British export trade. Already the Ford Company furnished from Manchester more than half of the British automobile exports; Dagenham might do better, while the continental Ford companies, obtaining supplies from Britain instead of Detroit, would probably meet even more of the European demand.[9]

Yet the Ford "incursion" was no more a foreign invasion than the almost simultaneous purchase of the Vauxhall works by General Motors. The Ford company had been entrenched at Manchester for a quarter century; the Ford car was made by British workers almost entirely of British materials, and at Dagenham would be wholly British-made. Moreover, as the *Economist* noted, both the British home market and British export activities needed expansion. If the new Dagenham plant "leads to a more intensive export sales campaign and more efficient manufacturing methods on the part of the British motor industry," Ford's new effort "will have a great national value."

The British company, as time proved, had to contend against unexpected adversities. The officers had hoped to begin certain manufacturing operations there in 1930, but were unable to do so because the expenses involved in providing temporary accommodations—roads, jetties, drainage, and the like—were thought to be unwarranted. At the end of that year about two million pounds of capital were locked up in the still uncompleted plant. It did not open until March 19, 1931, and its output did not count until later still. Then, too, the British scheme of taxation bore more heavily on the new Model A than it had on the lighter Model T, and so discouraged Englishmen from buying it. Perry complained bitterly of the whole revenue system as applied to vehicles; horsedrawn carriages were undertaxed, while the levy on engine power, calculated according to diameter of cylinder, encouraged the production of cars uneconomically small. He pleaded for a moderate tax, permitting the use of larger automobile bodies.

Worst of all, while Dagenham was still half-finished, the Wall Street crash ushered in the Great Depression. This at first struck the world's motor industry by a moderate reduction in its rate of expansion rather than by a staggering setback, but total new registrations fell in 1931 and again in 1932. For these and lesser reasons the Ford Motor Company, Ltd., after doing well down to June 30, 1931, showed in the ensuing fiscal year a loss of £80,978. Although business deficits were at that time the rule rather than the exception all over the world, this bad balance-sheet was a source of great humiliation to Perry. Henry Ford took the position that while the economic hurly-burly raged the continental companies should pay no dividends, but use all their surplus funds to assist Dagenham and the German plant, which were making high capital outlays. This policy was more easily formulated than put into practice; for one reason, continental shareholders were clamorous for some return, and for another, European governments restricted the movement of funds.[10]

In a defensive mood, Perry repeatedly stated to Henry and Edsel Ford that prior to the 1931 capital increase the American company had never remitted any cash to Britain or the continent. The businesses there had been developed almost entirely by profits of the several companies, and by receipts from the sale of stock. The American company had steadily furnished credit in the form of goods, but it had just as steadily been paid for these goods. During the three fiscal years ending June 30, 1931, Europe in fact remitted to Detroit almost $5,000,000 in dividends and fees. The financial embarrassments of 1931–1932 he attributed in no small degree to Sorensen's serious under-calculation of the costs of the Dagenham plant, and to Henry Ford's insistence on the great power plant (power could have been bought from the outside), which had to be built on tremendous piles.*

Given time, Perry believed that the British company could overcome its difficulties and pay handsome profits; meanwhile, he concluded, the American company must furnish a loan. He wrote Sorensen on February 16, 1933, that the once hopeful outlook of Dagenham had been clouded by forces beyond his control:

The frequent changes of model, the building of the German plant, the growth of tariffs, quotas, and other international commercial restrictions, have altogether upset what you and I thought to be the prospects of Dagenham. . . . When the German factory was decided upon I pointed out that Dagenham could not afford to lose the output which we had figured we

---

* On costs, see Perry's statement in the annual report for 1929 (London *Times*, March 8, 1930): "Contracts have been placed already to the value of £1,400,000. Contracts are now being negotiated to the value of over £1,000,000, and payments to date in respect of work done amount to approximately £390,000." As for profits, he wrote Sorensen August 30, 1932, that in the three years ending June 30, 1931, the reorganized European companies had earned profits of approximately $25,000,000. (Acc. 6, Box 310.)

should get from the German demand. . . . Similarly, in respect of finance, I have repeatedly and continuously pointed out that we were getting out of our depths with financial commitments, but have always been reassured, *even by Mr. Henry Ford himself, that I was to "forget money."*

Perry asked for concurrence in accepting an order from Sir William Letts, the British head of Willys-Overland-Crossley Ltd., for a supply of engines and axles, even though the contract would assist a competitor. He got neither the concurrence nor the loan. Instead, Sorensen visited England, looked into the situation, and by reductions and rearrangements in manufacturing, general stores, and car financing, made £500,000 available. But the economic affairs of the world at this moment were falling into a yet more lamentable state. To see just how grave the relapse was, we must turn to the continental companies.[11]

2.

One basic object of the European reorganization had been to nullify, so far as practicable, the general hostility to foreign-owned companies. Long before the Great Depression, "Buy British," "Buy German," "Buy French," and "Buy Italian" signs had sprung up everywhere. A majority of the voting stock of the new continental companies was vested in the Ford Motor Company, Ltd., itself an affiliate of the American company. But each concern was to have prominent citizens of its own nation for directors and officers; each was to provide for some public stockholding participation; and each was to press toward a car made entirely from home materials by home labor. After the organization of the new English corporation in 1928, the European reorganizations occupied many months. Under the oversight of Dearborn, Perry astutely managed all details. He helped see to the building of new and enlarged factories at Rotterdam, Antwerp, and Stockholm. Meanwhile, he laid plans for continuous supervision through what he called a mechanical audit department.

"Our various plants in Europe," he wrote Sorensen on October 11, 1929, "are badly laid out, inadequately equipped, and improperly managed. Heroic measures such as changing the Superintendents would not correct the existing evils, which can only be eliminated by constant attention and audit, going over the operations, checking up minute costs, teaching all the new tricks that are constantly being learnt for ensuring efficiency, and so on." [12] As he later declared, he replaced haphazard price-making by systematic procedures based on exact costs and adjusted to competition.

The general rule was that 60 per cent of the stock should be held by the American-controlled British company, and 40 per cent by outside shareholders; the important exceptions being Italy, where "Fordita" remained wholly owned by Ford, Ltd., and Scandinavia, where the Danish company owned 60 per cent of the Swedish company, which in turn held 60 per cent of the Finnish concern. Henry Ford had demurred to this arrangement when Perry first proposed it to him. Why not give each company independent status? He had exercised no such control over the Canadian corporation, and it had grown like a green bay tree. To this Perry rejoined that the Ontario factory was just across the river from Detroit and run by men in close rapport with the Rouge managers; the European companies were 3000 miles away, and needed the guiding hand which he and the Detroit executives could furnish.

The French corporation, Ford Société Anonyme Française, initially the most important on the continent, had a capital of 130,000,000 francs, of which 52,000,000 were subscribed by the public; they bought the 100-franc shares so eagerly that at the beginning of 1930 the company heads believed nearly 100,000 French citizens were stockholders. The Danish company, second in importance (it appointed the dealers for Norway, Latvia, and Lithuania, and supplied associated companies in Sweden and Finland), had a capital of 30,000,000 kroner, the company itself holding one third. The Belgian company, at first third largest, began with a capital of 100,000,000 francs, of which 30,000,000 were subscribed by some 17,200 new stockholders.[13]

In Germany, which Perry hoped would become the largest of the continental units, the new company made no public stock offering; instead, selected Germans were allowed to invest, 15 per cent of the stock going to men associated with the "dye trust," I. G. Farbenindustrie, and 25 per cent to selected Ford dealers. Of course stock of Farbenindustrie was itself widely held. This step was taken partly to forestall the export of the stock to America during the Wall Street "Ford boom" which accompanied the British reorganization, and partly to gain the support of the powerful interests identified with Farbenindustrie—for the uneasy political situation in the Reich made such support crucial. The whole capital was 15,000,000 reichsmarks, a sum which would be increased as the company grew. General Motors invested $32,000,000 in the Opel Company in the spring of 1929, and the Ford planners hoped to rival Opel.[14] The Spanish company had a capital of 15,000,000 pesetas, 12,000 of its 30,000 shares being held in Spain. The Dutch company, which proved exceptionally prosperous, had a capital of 5,000,000 florins; the Swedish firm, 5,000,000 kroner; and the Finnish, 20,000,000 Finmarks.

A cardinal element in Perry's European policy was the selection of public men and leading financiers or industrialists for his boards of directors. In Great Britain he obtained the services of Lord Illingworth, prominent textile manufacturer and onetime Postmaster-General; John T. Davies, once private secretary to Lloyd George and government director of the Suez Canal; and Roland D. Kitson, later Lord Airedale, a director of the Bank of England. In Holland one director was R. J. H. Patijn, former ambassador to the United States, and another August Philips, a large manufacturer of electric light bulbs.

The Belgians included Baron Moncheur, a leading statesman, and Comte Adrien van der Burch. Among the French directors was the Marquis de Solages; among the Spanish another cabinet minister, Conde de Guell, Marquis de Comillas. In Denmark, Count Carl Moltke, former Minister of Foreign Affairs, was a director. The German directors were Dr. Carl Bosch, the leading figure in I. G. Farbenindustrie; A. Schurig, an important agriculturist; and Dr. Heinrich F. Albert, who had been in the German service in America in the early years of the First World War, and had later become Minister of National Economy.*

Like the British company, in the two years before the Great Depression fully set in, the reorganized continental companies were decidedly profitable. Denmark led with net earnings in 1929 of $1,566,000, and in 1930 of $1,626,000; France and Belgium were on her heels with annual earnings of between $1,200,000 and $1,380,000 each.

Altogether, the net earnings of the British and continental companies in 1929 exceeded $10,280,000, and in 1930, $10,930,000. Ford of England returned profits more than twice those of any of its continental associates. This was natural because of the greater capital investment at Dagenham, Manchester, and Cork, and because of the important export

* Perry was chairman of all the continental companies but the Swedish, while Edsel Ford and Sorensen also had seats on the boards.

and re-export part the British company played in European distribution. Indeed, Perry expected Ford of England soon to earn nearly as
much as all the continental companies combined. It was well for the
British company that in these early years, while it had nearly $10,000,-
000 locked up in the Dagenham plant, which would not get into full
operation until 1932, the associated companies needed little financial
help from it. During the process of reorganization and expansion they
obtained merchandise credits and some cash loans without interest, but
this was all.[15]

What should be done with the profits made on the continent? All
the companies paid dividends in 1929 and 1930 of at least 10 per cent;
in Belgium and Spain in the latter year the rate reached 15 per cent,
and in Holland 20. If dividends were sent to Britain, however, they
were subject to a tax of 22.5 per cent. Once more Perry complained bitterly about British policy. It was outrageous, he declared, that after a
Ford unit had paid the Swedish or Italian government 20 per cent on
its earnings, and the German government 41 per cent—for Reich taxation reached that level—it should incur this high additional levy on payments sent to British shareholders.

Europe, happily for Perry, then had one country which played somewhat the special role taken by Delaware in the United States—Luxembourg. To avoid a double taxation, in 1930 he formed a holding company, Ford Investments Corporation, under Luxembourg laws; its
function being to hold the dividends of the associated companies until
Ford, Ltd., called for them or else liquidated this special company. As
part of this plan to avoid paying British taxes, the sum of $3,680,000 was
added as a book item to the capital reserves of Ford, Ltd. Since this
addition to reserves roughly equalled the total of dividends received
from the associated companies on their 1929 activities, it was inferred
that future profits from the same sources would be shown from time
to time as accretions to the capital reserve of the British company; and
British law laid no tax on capital gains.*

Meanwhile, facilities of the continental companies were, as we have
said, greatly expanded. Perry, making a hasty tour of the various plants,
was shocked by their inadequacy, some being little better than "shan-
ties." Henry Ford had given him full authority to make changes, and in

---

* The first holding company, which lasted only four months, was in Lichtenstein. At this time
Perry also created the "Office of Sir Percival Perry to coordinate the European operations."

cooperation with Sorensen he instituted sweeping reforms. He held frequent conversations by transatlantic telephone, beginning in 1929, with the Detroit executives, including Edsel; usually choosing a Sunday for its greater leisure. Finding that some authorizations were summarily withdrawn, and some decisions countermanded—the old Ford rule was "Verbal orders don't go"—he attached a recording apparatus to his telephone. After that he was better able to hold the Detroit officials to all their statements.[16]

In the fall of 1930 Henry Ford revisited Europe,* planning to lay the cornerstones of new Ford factories in Germany and Holland. Some months previously Perry and Sorensen had inspected various sites in the Rhine valley, concluding that the choice lay between Cologne and Dusseldorf. Sorensen, returning to Detroit, wrote that the hour had struck for some real effort to obtain more business in Germany, for "the way the other makers, including Americans, have beat us there is shameful." After talking with Henry and Edsel, he decided that Cologne was after all the better place, and instructed Perry by telephone to acquire land there, using the threat of alternative sites to obtain the best possible tax concessions. This Perry did.

From Konrad Adenauer, mayor of Cologne and later Chancellor of the republic of Western Germany, he obtained a guarantee of specially low tax rates. "As compensation," wrote Adenauer, "you will agree to obtain your workmen and office employees, so far as possible, from the Cologne area." At the same time Perry took a five-year lease on premises in Berlin, at the corner of Unter den Linden and Wilhelmstrasse, for office and exhibition space. "The company will possess the best showrooms in Germany situated in what is almost an ideal location," he wrote.

Ford laid the cornerstone in Cologne, on the banks of the Rhine, amid general salvos of applause. Mayor Adenauer entertained him at lunch in City Hall, with numerous industrial leaders of the Reich. The German press lauded him as "the American automobile king." Numerous special articles discussed the technological innovations he was

---

* This year, visiting England, Ford conceived the plan which grew into the Henry Ford Institute of Agricultural Engineering. The object was to show how agriculture could be improved and made more profitable; to stop migration from land to city; and to increase the farm laborer's return. The Fordson Estate was created by the purchase of about 10,000 acres at Boreham, Essex, and here the Institute was supported by Ford until his death. See Lord Perry, *Ten Years' Romance: An Agricultural Experiment* (London, 1934).

expected to bring to Germany, and the employment he would furnish in the Rhineland—2000 men as soon as the factory opened. "To Europe," Harold Callender wrote the *New York Times,* "Ford is a genius, a rather bewildering genius. He is also a symbol of a second industrial revolution that had developed in America, as André Siegfried puts it, a type of civilization essentially different from Europe's; and he is regarded as now offering to Europe a taste, at least, of this specifically American industrial and social system." About two-score engineers were sent over from Dearborn, some of them remaining in Cologne several years, and much of Dearborn machinery was put into the plant.[17]

In Holland, unfortunately, Ford was unable to carry out his planned ceremony. The previous spring Perry had chosen a factory site in Rotterdam; but as it was not on the waterfront, Sorensen had cabled him to get one where boats could dock directly alongside. "Please go into this matter," he urged, "trying to lay out plans similar to Copenhagen and Yokohama all our new plants should be along these lines." But the Rotterdam authorities did not wish factories on their waterfront, and as they were adamant, Ford refused to visit the city. A little later Amsterdam stepped in with an offer of thirty-eight acres, well-situated, for only $320,000, and promised to spend more than that sum in harbor facilities, railway sidings, and other improvements. During 1931 the factory was therefore built in Amsterdam. In Belgium, meanwhile, the old Hoboken plant was given up and a better factory begun on land leased from the city of Antwerp.[18]

This expansion was maintained as vigorously as the iron times permitted. Larger storage and office facilities were erected in Stockholm, where the Swedish company acted as distributing agent only. Assembly operations in Barcelona were improved. Spain stood fifth among European countries in 1931 in the number of cars, and offered a profitable market. In Istanbul by that year Ford had an assembly plant, planned in Dearborn by its American manager, capable of turning out 37,000 cars annually, and so supplying not only most of Asia Minor, but any Russian trade that could be developed through Odessa. Unfortunately, no Russian or Near Eastern market ever justified the plant.

Over all the associated continental companies, Perry (advised always by Detroit) exercised supervision which pleased some and irked others, although not he, but some of his arrogant agents, caused ill feeling. Not only was he chairman of the board for the French, German, Spanish, Danish, Belgian, and other companies; his Luxembourg holding company acted both as policy-coödinator and banker for the whole group. The "Office of Sir Percival Perry" maintained a close scrutiny of details from Lisbon to Vienna. Sorensen had written Perry on January 29, 1930: "I think Mr. Ford, like myself, is very anxious not to interfer with your organization, and not to make any decisions that would be burdensome to you."

It was fortunate that Perry was a man of cultivated mind, broad cosmopolitan outlook, and marked tact. He travelled from country to country, corresponded widely, and held an annual dinner for all available directors. Everyone knew the basis for the preëminent position of the British company: Dagenham was the one mass-production plant outside North America, expected as such to fill much of the European demand for Ford products, while Perry was by all odds the ablest Old World executive. But national interests and rivalries being what they were, his position inevitably created friction and jealousy. In a world full of poverty, unemployment, and trade warfare, ill-feeling found quick root.[19]

3.

Instead of brightening, after 1930 the political and economic skies steadily darkened. In nation after nation, tariff increases, import quotas, restrictions on the transfer of money, and political pressures grew heavier. Not only in countries ruled by the dictators—Mussolini, Hitler, Pilsudski, Stalin—but in lands with democratic regimes, any dependence on reasonable and stable business conditions became impossible.

The situation in France was typical. When Congress was giving final shape to the Smoot-Hawley Tariff, which President Hoover signed in 1930 despite the protest of a thousand American economists, France was one of the nations which took retaliatory action. Her government enacted a law (April 18, 1930) which sharply raised rates on foreign automobiles, bodies, and parts. Fortunately for Ford S.A.F., its increasing use of French materials largely parried this blow, the company manager announcing that the rise in the tariff amounted to only about four per cent for each Ford car. Some competitors, notably Chevrolet, Chrysler, and Essex, were much harder hit. French manufacturers however, organized a spirited crusade against foreign car manufacturers.

Louis Renault, assembling the motorcar editors of the Paris newspapers, rallied them to the fight. "If Ford and General Motors dominate the French market," declaimed Renault, "one and a half million Frenchmen will have died in vain in the last war. We shall have escaped German suzerainty only to fall under the sway of America. Idleness will confront several million workers. Our rusting factories can no longer supply war materials." [20]

Additional duties followed. Citroën and Renault instigated the Manufacturers' Association to demand them, and governments proved compliant. Late in 1933 Perry termed them "enormous." The two French manufacturers had struck directly at the Ford interests by getting rates on certain stampings imported by the company increased five times! A high official of the Ministry of Commerce had declared with savage emphasis that his department expected yet to stop Ford business entirely. Profits were vanishing. Perry wrote Sorensen: "I spent last weekend in Germany. The problem is much the same in both countries, viz.: Can a manufacturing plant be made to pay when output is confined within the limited areas which national tariffs are building up? Just at the present time international business is awful, and no one can tell from one day to the other what is likely to happen." [21]

The managing director of the French company, a big, handsome man named M. Dollfus, a former banker, so strong of will that he often clashed with Perry and Sorensen, was determined not to give up without a battle. He advocated a combination with the Mathis company, which had a factory at Strasbourg, the result to be a new corporation known as Matford. Using the facilities at Asnieres and Strasbourg, it would produce a light car with Mathis four-cylinder engines and various Ford elements, so completely French that it would compete on even terms with Renault and Citroën. For several reasons, one being his dislike of the Mathis engine, Henry Ford objected to the project. "I cannot get anywhere with him," reported Sorensen to Dollfus. "He will not take any interest in a four-cylinder engine." Perry also was at first opposed to the combination. But finally Sorensen and Perry made a special trip to Strasbourg, where they found a neat little factory, well run, with a skillful, industrious body of Alsatian and German workmen. Much impressed by it, they decided that the merger would be advantageous, and Dollfus was given permission to negotiate it—only to encounter new difficulties and delays.[22]

Meanwhile, the French government, as the depression deepened, was under greater pressure than ever to reserve the home market to home producers. At the close of 1933 it fixed quotas on long lists of imports; and Dollfus was stunned to find the automobile quota only one fourth of the 1932 importations! He believed that this was a special blow, instigated by Renault and other manufacturers, against Ford of France. At once he sent the French premier a long argumentative letter. His company was building new plant facilities to render it independent of other nations, he declared—including a pressed-steel unit, gearbox unit, and metal wheel unit, none of which existed in France. They would be finished in the fall of 1934, making Ford S.A.F. quite self-contained, and augmenting the defense-potential of the republic; meanwhile, Ford should be supported, not attacked. Two interviews with the premier followed, and protracted talks with other ministers. By frenzied effort, the manager got the quota raised to the 1932 level.

This concession, however, was temporary and precarious. French car manufacturers maintained their stubborn pressure, receiving covert support from American importers like General Motors who hoped to profit from any blow to Ford S.A.F. All over the world nations were withdrawing economically behind their own frontiers. Firms controlled from abroad risked the most serious troubles, and even extinction. It was true that Ford S.A.F. employed thousands of Frenchmen and paid high French taxes. "But I have not ceased to warn you," wrote the company's French attorney, "against 'instructions,' far too imperative, which you constantly receive from organizations holding the majority of your shares. . . . I must again emphasize the fact that your highest interests dictate the effective transfer of a majority of your shares to French holders." [23]

Such was economic nationalism in France.

4.

In Italy the fever of the time raged no less violently. Mussolini's government, with the powerful Fiat interests at its elbow, would not cede an inch of ground to a foreign company. "Fordita," with principal offices now in Genoa, had conducted a modestly profitable business with the Trieste assembly plant, but was unable to make satisfactory progress. When Perry attempted to put vigorous new policies into force, the Duce blocked him on every path.

First, Perry bought late in 1929 a tract in the industrial zone of

Livorno, intending to erect an efficient new assembly plant which would be partially financed by selling two-fifths of the stock of Fordita to Italian citizens. A representative of the government at once called to say that it would not permit such a plant. In vain did Perry try to obtain a refund for the land. When the manager of Fordita, an able and forceful Englishman named Thornhill Cooper, gained an interview with Mussolini, the Duce advised him to make some arrangement with Fiat.

It soon became plain that an alliance with some Italian manufacturer was a necessity. A decree at the end of 1929 increased Italian duties on car parts by about thirty per cent ad valorem, and next year the tariff on Ford imports was raised 211.7 per cent! This was prohibitive. The Ford executives therefore visited the Fiat offices in Turin. Here they received an astonishing proposal: Fiat would consent to an alliance if Fordita, using Fiat facilities in Turin, would make five per cent of all Ford vehicles produced in the world. Such an arrangement was of course quite incompatible with the existing structure of Ford manufacture and distribution.

Thereupon Fordita (the cable code name), encouraged by the prefect of Milan, went to that city for negotiations with a weaker Italian company, Isotta Fraschini. The government, said the prefect, would approve of a fusion to be called Isotta-Ford. Heads of the two companies reached an agreement by which a new joint corporation would be organized, the Ford interests would contribute a large capital in return for forty-nine per cent of the stock, and the expanded Milan factory would manufacture Ford cars and trucks for the Italian market. But the rejoicings of Isotta and Milan were more than outweighed by the anger of Fiat and Turin! The government, under pressure from this quarter, quickly forbade the consummation of the arrangement.

Protests were quite useless. Italy was filled with resentment over the Smoot-Hawley Tariff, while Mussolini was determined to keep the Italian market for purely Italian companies. Thornhill Cooper wrote the Minister of Corporations that Fordita had been established since 1922, that some 7000 cars and trucks and 12,000 farm tractors of Ford make were being used in the peninsula, that the company had made large investments at Trieste, Naples, Livorno, Genoa, and Bologna, and that some 150 dealerships in the kingdom represented an investment by Italians of more than 200 million lire—but all this was in vain.

It was questionable in the early nineteen-thirties whether Fordita could ever keep its organization alive. On November 18, 1930, Mussolini decisively told Senator Scialoja, the Ford legal representative, that he did not approve of any Ford establishment in Italy except in conjunction with Fiat—and the Fiat terms were impossible. Only a few cars, imported principally from the Spanish and British plants, could be sold over the steep tariff wall. "I confirm my understanding," wrote the despairing Perry to Sorensen on February 1, 1934, "that you approve of a gradual evacuation of Italy." [24]

Until Hitler came into power, Ford of Germany, despite the exorbitant 41 per cent tax on profits, promised to do well. Out of not quite 80,000 cars distributed in 1930, Opel, the General Motors subsidiary, sold 24,000, Ford 11,150, and Daimler-Benz 7500. The spring of 1931 found the new Cologne assembly plant in operation, using a large amount of rather badly made German parts, while 500 Ford service stations were active. True manufacturing at Cologne had not yet started, but was expected to begin soon. The manager, Edmund C. Heine, was an American trained by Sorensen. At that time the great adverse factor was the economic depression. Industrial production in the Reich was steadily declining, and nobody knew when financial stability could be restored. Nevertheless, Ford sales increased markedly in 1930 and the first months of 1931, and in March of each year a ten per cent dividend was paid. Perry sent hopeful reports to Detroit.

After the financial collapse of 1931, however, and still more after the Nazi revolution, the efforts of Ford of Germany to conduct a business justifying its great outlay at Cologne became a prolonged torture. It was harassed in every possible way. When the Reich enacted a law forbidding officials to hold more than a limited number of directorships, the German company almost lost the valuable services of Dr. Carl Bosch. German motor interests, abetted by the Nazis, raised a clamorous agitation against Ford Aktien Gesellschaft as not making a German product. The Nazi Party issued certificates of German origin, without which it became almost impossible to do business; and to procure one the board of the Ford A.G., meeting in June, 1933, passed at Perry's insistence a resolution stopping all imports except V-8 motors. The Nazis, wrote Perry to Edsel Ford, "interfere with everything, and although their interference is not exactly officially Government, yet it is political and influential." [25]

Ford of Germany had expected to pay for its huge investment in land, factory, and equipment at Cologne in the ordinary fashion; but the collapse of German internal and external credit in 1931, with the ensuing Hoover moratorium agreement of July that year, made the usual money-raising measures impossible. The result was that the German company by the spring of 1933 owed Ford, Ltd., of England, about three million reichsmarks for construction at Cologne, and three million more for goods supplied from Dagenham, these sums being frozen. Moreover, until Perry told Heine that he would get no more credits from Detroit or Dagenham, they continued to import British and American materials, paying for them in notes. "They are losing at the rate of 400,000 marks a month," lamented Perry, "and really losing the money of the British and American Ford companies." Total net losses of the German company in 1932 exceeded six million marks; additional losses in 1933 made necessary a drastic capital reorganization.[26]

As financial troubles thus thickened, it became evident that Ford of Germany faced a momentous choice. It could align itself with the Nazi regime, take orders supinely, and possibly gain temporary profits, or it could struggle along isolated from politics, hoping for an economic reconstruction of Germany guided by such conservative industrialists as Dr. Bosch. Perry was emphatically for the latter course. His disgust, and his detestation for Hitlerism, taxed his ample vocabulary.

"Really the Germans have behaved disgracefully," he exploded in 1933, "because they have borrowed every cent they could lay their hands on, and made their laws in such manner that foreigners were bound to go into their country with heavy investments in order to get any German trade, and having done this they turn round and virtually confiscate all investments." He abominated Hitler's anti-Semitism, his sabre-rattling, and his demagogic speeches. When Dr. Albert was forced to resign his position as head of the North German Lloyd, and Dr. Bosch, the leader of I.G. Farbenindustrie, was on the verge of a nervous collapse—both men had been ceaselessly bullied by the Nazi chieftains—he condoled with these two directors. He hoped that, like Albert, Dr. Bosch would resign from Farben rather than accept Nazi dictation.[27] *

Other officers of Ford of Germany, however, took a different view. E. C. Heine, for all his American citizenship, became an ardent admirer

* Dr. Albert, says Tallberg, then at the Cologne plant, was not really anti-Nazi, although when with Perry he pretended to be.

of Hitler. He carried this attitude so far that Bosch and Albert became deeply worried by his activities. They feared he was plotting a Nazi seizure of the plant. The FBI, some years later (1937–1938), suspected Heine of trying to obtain secret designs of American aircraft for the Nazi government. Subordinates in the Cologne establishment disliked him; one American engineer later asserted that he would crawl to any-one superior in rank, but kick any inferior—"conditions were very, very bad when Heine was there." His strong Nazi connections, however, made his recall a difficult matter, and during critical months he stayed on.[28]

Meanwhile, Prince Louis Ferdinand of Prussia, a handsome grand-son of the Kaiser, holder of a doctorate from the University of Berlin and friend of Franklin D. Roosevelt, who in 1933–1934 was in Henry Ford's employ as "free lance roadman" in various countries, including Germany, also looked favorably on the Nazi regime. He had an inter-view with Hitler, who spoke of his admiration for Ford and his desire to motorize Germany. Actually, the prince learned, Hitler cherished some ill-feeling for Ford, who on one of his visits to Germany had not taken pains to meet the future Fuehrer in Munich. But Louis Ferdinand nevertheless conveyed certain of Hitler's wishes to the Ford executives. He wrote Liebold:

Yet all this ought not to keep us from going ahead. I already wrote to you, that in my opinion Mr. Ford has only two ways to choose with his German plant: to close down, or to go ahead in a real Ford way, which means a big way. This of course Mr. Ford only himself can decide.

I repeat, that the way things are now in Cologne we will be put out of business within a year. It is absolutely beneath the dignity of the Ford Motor Company to be satisfied with five per cent of the German business, whereas Opel-General Motors sells almost fifty per cent of all cars made in Germany. It will be necessary to change the name of the car into a German name, and also change the location of the plant, and build a real production plant, where we can produce everything, and not have to rely on other firms.[29]

This proposal turned out to be precisely what Hitler wished. In 1934 he undertook a program for making the use of automobiles universal in Germany. According to its plan, within five years approximately three million cars were to be distributed, sturdy enough for high speed on the new autobahns, but sufficiently low-priced to appeal to the masses. Replacements would be needed at the rate of 600,000 cars a year. Generous government aids would be given to manufacturers and road-builders. In the summer of 1934 approaches were made to both Ford and General Motors. Leading citizens of Hamburg, with the approval of the Fuehrer, held conferences with Dr. Albert, Heine, and Prince Louis Ferdinand, suggesting that a great new factory be erected in that city to use Ford capital and skills in making the *Volkswagen*. Finally Mayor Krogmann of Hamburg took steps to obtain definite promises, through a deputy, from Hitler, and the deputy reported in effect:

That the Fuehrer stated positively that he would support Ford as well as any other foreign enterprise, which would invest its capital in Germany, and thereby give the German workman wages and bread. He further stated that the Government wishes, for reasons of national defense, that the Cologne factory should not be extended, because of the leading automobile factories of Germany that are now in the so-called danger zone. It is therefore the wish of the Government that new buildings and extensions of automobile factories be transferred into Central Germany, under which he also indicates Hamburg.[30]

Prince Louis Ferdinand, urging Henry Ford through Sorensen to have faith in the future of Germany, and through Liebold to ignore Perry, who was "trying to mess things up," was anxious to see the Volkswagen go through. What a pity it would be, he wrote, "if Mr. Ford, who is the father and creator of the motorcar age, would abandon Germany and leave the task to his Jew competitors the General Motors people, who have invested a tremendous sum of money and are now producing on a large scale." He was hostile not only to Perry but to Dr. Albert, who, he assured the Dearborn executives, belonged to an outworn regime. In short, both the managing director Heine and the free lance salesman Prince Louis Ferdinand believed in hitching Ford of Germany to the rising Hitler star.

In this clash upon policies, Heine and Ferdinand lost. Henry Ford, Edsel, and Sorensen had no intention of throwing a fortune into a Hamburg factory, to make not Fords but some new Volkswagen model, and to lie at the mercy of the unscrupulous Nazi regime. They preferred continuing with the Cologne plant. Down to the beginning of 1934 this never carried true manufacturing operations, but continued to assemble parts, made to an increasing extent within the Reich, for two cars: the Model A Ford, and the V-8, and the small "Eiffel." While Perry throughout 1933 wished to get rid of Heine, who was constantly running from Cologne to Berlin on political errands, he hesitated for fear the Nazis would put some bungling tool in his stead. "I believe you understand," Perry wrote Sorensen late in the year, "that the Nazi Government are putting their nominees everywhere. Under the flimsiest of excuses they discharge public and private officials for the sole purpose of supplanting them by their own supporters." They already had an agent in uniform parading the Ford works.[31] *

For the time being Heine was retained, but under strict orders to cease meddling with politics. Then came his summary recall to Dearborn. On his arrival there Sorensen told him flatly: "You are not returning to Germany." When Heine asked the reason, the Dane replied tartly: "None of your business. You're just not going back." Until the Second World War opened, the German company had to be left in an unsatisfactory state; then, of course, it went under strict Nazi control.[32]

5.

In some continental countries, business after 1930 became absolutely impossible. Czechoslovakia raised her tariffs to a prohibitive level. In Hungary the currency restrictions became an unbreachable wall. "Whilst nominally it is possible to import goods freely," reported Perry, "the National Bank carefully supervises all trading activities, and a special permit has to be obtained for all imports; the issue of these permits is so bureaucratically handled that the result is an open embargo." For a time Ford, Ltd., thought of establishing an assembly plant at Gydnia in Poland, and hired Prince Nicholas Mirsky of Warsaw as adviser. But Mirsky was not useful, Government officials refused to take any firm action on Ford proposals; and the general position of Poland was so hazardous that London dropped the idea, leaving what little business it could get to the Danish company.[33]

But despite the grip of the depression and the growth of economic nationalism, the continental companies as a whole in the early nineteen thirties held their own. The devaluation of the American dollar, following Roosevelt's inauguration, made payment on materials imported from the United States less onerous. Trade in some countries, after reaching a nadir in 1932, revived the following year. Thus the Dutch corporation, completing its Amsterdam factory, increased its turnover

* Actually, many employees at this time wore Nazi uniforms when working.

of products, and made a small but hopeful profit in 1933 (about 630,000 florins). The Spanish company did the same (nearly 2,000,000 pesetas); so did the Greek, Rumanian, and Egyptian corporations (with consolidated net profits of £31,000). The Swedish company just about broke even, while the Belgian and Danish companies made, as always, substantial profits. Perry was able to tell his stockholders that wherever a vestige of fair competition remained, the Ford interests could still do well.

Because of the depression, reducing both income and expenditures, by 1933 the capital of the four companies in Holland, Denmark, Belgium, and Spain was manifestly too large. For at least the time being, little further expansion was contemplated. The dizzy changes in exchange rates, speculation in currencies, and uncertainties as to tax policies, made the holding of surplus liquid resources hazardous. For these reasons the four companies decided on a return of two fifths of the paid-up capital to investors. The total amount thus repaid came to nearly £1,100,000 in English money, of which about £660,000 went to the holding company in Luxembourg.

The brightest ray of light in 1933 was the record of Ford, Ltd., of England. It was plain to everybody soon after the reorganization that the Model A was unsuited to the British market—too expensive, too costly in taxes and gasoline, too large for narrow roads. American Ford executives had talked for years of a small English car; and Perry, himself at first somewhat reluctant, finally converted his English associates to the idea. Two companies in particular, Morris Motors and Austin, threatened to run away with the market.

Perry's general requirements went in 1931 to Dearborn, where technical experts led by Larry Sheldrick set to work on what was called Model Y. At various stages of this engineering effort Dagenham executives, including Sir A. R. Smith and Sir Patrick Hennessy, visited the Rouge to lend their assistance. Their general specifications were simple: the car must have a small-bore engine of about eight English horsepower, a ninety-inch wheelbase, a narrow tread, and a limited weight. The design had to be finished quickly, and it was. Work was begun in October, 1931, and the prototype car released February 1, 1932. "It was a characteristic Ford in all respects," Sheldrick recalled later, with torque-tube drive, transverse springs, and certain valve and push-rod features on which Henry Ford insisted. At about the same time Dearborn also designed a special taxicab for England, able to turn within narrow compass. Dagenham was tooled for the new Model Y in the spring and summer of 1932, and production in quantity began that fall.[34]

The "Baby Ford" not only met a keen British demand, but proved marketable on a considerable scale in parts of the continent. The old twenty-four horsepower two-door saloon had cost £180; the new eight horsepower two-door saloon cost but £120, and a fourteen horsepower four-door saloon £199. The V-8 Coupe, a regular American Ford, cost £258. In addition, Dagenham offered three types of vans, and three sizes of trucks. It was evident that whereas Model A had failed to penetrate the British market, the "Baby Ford" would give Morris and Austin very stiff competition. Domestic sales for 1933 ran above £6,187,000, and foreign sales—despite the shrinkage from quotas, tariffs, exchange restrictions, and so on—above £6,653,000. The trading loss of nearly £291,000 in 1932 was transformed into a profit of £1,386,719. President Roosevelt's measures had assisted in the bright showing by the company, for thanks mainly to dollar depreciation, a profit of £462,239 had been made on exchange. Perry was able to wipe out all the old debit balances, and, inasmuch as the directors decided to pay no dividend, to replace them by a credit balance of some £388,000. He was to be congratulated on the energy with which he and his associates had pulled the company around.[35]

What was more, Ford, Ltd., now had its own special line of cars, made for its own public; it had the largest and best-equipped automobile factory in the British Isles; and it could count on an expanding market in countries where the gasoline price was so high that a light vehicle was wanted. The English car was soon assembled in Australia, New Zealand, and South Africa, and being imported complete by Ford Motor of Canada; and the time would come, though nobody then foresaw it, when, much altered and improved, it would sell in sizable numbers in the United States. It should be added that since 1928 all Ford tractors were being made in the Cork plant, their production in the United States having ceased; and this fact gave the British company another important asset. The French and German companies, however, were restive under British control.

6.

The millionth Ford to be built in Canada left the line March 24, 1931, just three weeks before the twenty millionth Ford car left the Rouge plant. Like most industrial concerns throughout the world, the company suffered heavily from the depression. In 1933 the net operating loss was $1,175,000, partly offset by returns of $555,000 from affiliated companies. Nevertheless, even in that gloomy year it sold 26,400 units, and felt able to pay a dividend of one dollar a share from its surplus of nearly $30,000,000. Its plants were then conservatively valued at almost $28,000,000, and it could well be accounted one of the strongest manufacturing enterprises in the Dominion. In essential respects it was autonomous. Neither Henry nor Edsel Ford, who had a high personal regard for W. R. Campbell (its head), would have thought of issuing an order to him on plant operation. In engineering, design, and production methods, however, the company constantly profited from its close connection with the Rouge plant just across the river. It of course took over the Model A at once. Of all the foreign affiliates of the American corporation, it inspired the greatest confidence. However turbulent the political scene in Europe and Latin America, Canada was quite as stable as the United States, with vast possibilities of growth in population and wealth.[36]

In the Far East, as the "Mukden incident" of 1931 and the ensuing Japanese occupation of South Manchuria showed, the outlook was as murky as in Europe. Ford interests in that area had never been pushed far beyond the exploratory stage. The assembly branch operated in Japan during the 1920s, first in Yokohama and then in Kobe, had done something to replace rickshaws on the Japanese streets with Model T's, but its total output was small.

Then in 1928–1929 a somewhat larger assembly plant was built at Koyasu, near Yokohama, at a cost of 2,700,000 yen. It was opened early in 1929 with the usual ceremonies: a speech by the mayor of Yokohama, a reception to 1500 selected guests, and a luncheon at the new Hotel Grand in Yokohama. A band played and flags fluttered in the breeze as men in Prince Alberts stood in talkative groups about the handsome structure of steel, concrete, and glass. Inside, a bunting-draped Model A moved along the assembly line till it rolled away from the end. Henry and Edsel sent congratulations. But trade restrictions and international friction limited the Yokohama plant mainly to the depressed Japanese market.

The story in China was even less cheerful. Henry Ford in 1930 decided it might be both profitable to the company, and helpful to the Chinese people, if he erected a factory in that troubled republic. He dispatched two agents across the Pacific with orders to find a good factory site on deep water in the vicinity of Shanghai. "How big?" demanded the agents in an interview before leaving. "Well, as big as we need," was Ford's informative reply. After some months of hard work in the Shanghai area, the transmission of many maps and reports to Dearborn, and inch-by-inch inspection of several sites that seemed specially promising, the two agents discovered that they faced an insuperable obstacle.

Returning to the Rouge, they reported it to Henry Ford: "This is the deal. If we buy a site in China, the site has to be in the name of a Chinaman because a foreigner can't own land in China."

Ford disposed of the matter in one word: "No." [37]

The company was not going to spend millions in China and then let a Chinese hold title to its investment. The Ford agents in Shanghai, Messrs. Dodge & Seymour, Ltd., were doing a fairly good business, and they could continue to run it on an importing basis. This decision the Ford Company never had reason to regret.

All in all, the Ford interests had made an heroic effort to create and maintain a flourishing group of companies abroad. The European reorganization planned by Sir Percival Perry and supported by Edsel Ford and Sorensen deserved a greater success than it achieved. For reasons beyond company control, the story was largely one of frustration; depression, trade warfare, and political tensions all but wrecked the undertakings. One main object was the conversion of American operations abroad into true foreign businesses, making European cars out of European materials. As Perry told the first general meeting of the British company, the effort was marked by largeness of view:

Business had been already created which was immensely profitable and in every commercial sense highly satisfactory. This was handed over to us for a consideration which as you will see from the balance sheet before you, we have been more than able to discharge out of the first year's profits. By the magnanimity and altruism. . . . of Mr. Henry Ford and his son, Mr. Edsel Ford, we were guaranteed the provision of capital sufficient to . . . . erect and equip manufacturing resources in this country adequate to carry on and extend the profitable business which already had been created and developed. At the same time, British investors were offered an opportunity to participate in this enterprise upon the same terms and with remuneration exactly equal to that of its founder. . . . I personally consider this to be a gesture of international importance which has not yet been paralleled in the industrial history of the world.

Even had the era been less turbulent, however, the reorganization would have been exposed to misunderstanding. Frenchmen and Germans, looking at a Model A, did not see the home materials in it; they saw the name Ford, which meant a foreign car. Britons did not think of their own share in the ownership of the Dagenham company; they thought of the larger American Detroit ownership. Some Ford executives, too, were dissatisfied. They inevitably, if mistakenly, thought of a Ford factory in France as a completely Ford-owned factory. When it paid dividends, why should not *all* dividends go to Detroit? They did not stop to consider that, as Perry correctly insisted, until 1931 the new factories abroad had been built out of profits and stock sales in each country, with little cash from Detroit. Nor did they stop to consider that Frenchmen had paid for stock under guarantee of forty per cent of the dividends from the French factory, as Britons had paid for stock under a guarantee of forty per cent of the dividends of the British and associated companies.[38] Exposed to these misunderstandings, the reorganization would in any circumstances have been precarious. But it should be saluted as a gallant effort at internationalism in business affairs in an era of intransigent nationalism.*

---

* And also to raise living standards, for Henry Ford regarded industrialization as leading to that end. It is difficult to obtain exact information on Ford wage-rates in Europe, for differences in living costs and incessant currency fluctuations complicate the picture. "Attempts have been made," Perry declared in 1929, "to apply the well-known principles of Mr. Henry Ford concerning wages and labour among Ford employees in Europe, and . . . . it is accurate to state, in a general sense, that the same principles which Mr. Ford practises on so large a scale and with such beneficial social results amongst the workers in America have been applied to European employees." Ford himself announced that year that he would establish the same scale of real wages for all employees regardless of the country in which they lived. This inspired Edward A. Filene to offer the League of Nations $25,000 to defray the costs of compiling data on which to base real-wage rates, and to offer the Ford companies his coöperation. Warmly praising Ford's lead, he asserted that it should be imitated by every American concern with foreign branches. The British wage-scale, directly controlled by Perry, was maintained at a fair equivalent of the American wage for some time, and above the prevalent rate in other British motor factories. (See Perry to Liebold, June 21, 1929; Perry to Filene, same date; Filene to Perry, June 8, 1929; Filene to Ford, June 3, 1929, all in Acc. 285, Box 976. See also the N.Y. Times, May 29, 30, 1929.) As for Germany, an article in the N.Y. Times of March 9, 1930, stated that the Ford factory had established new wage standards for that country, a skilled workman earning about 70 cents an

No one can deny that Henry Ford and the Ford Company had treated the European organizations in a large-minded way. They had made every possible concession to national feeling. They had contributed their ideas, designs, technological innovations, and patent rights at a low valuation. The two Fords, Sorensen, and others labored with Perry and the lesser European executives in the friendliest cooperation. As the hard years of the nineteen-thirties passed, a sense of the defects of the European system—if so loose an arrangement can be called a system—steadily grew. The pyramided corporate structure was awkward and inefficient. The possibilities for conflict between the British company on the one side and the continental establishments on the other were numerous. The arrangement made profits excessively vulnerable to double or triple taxation. In time the hastily improvised organization would have to be supplanted by one of more logical and practical character; but while it lasted it was a symbol of the American company's generosity of outlook.

---

hour as compared with 35 cents paid in other German plants, and white collar workers receiving pay half again as high as that given elsewhere. "There is contentment all around." But the Great Depression and the rise of the dictators played havoc with Ford's plans.

XXII

IMPACT OF DEPRESSION

THE Ford Motor Company had changed from Model T to Model A in the nick of time. In 1929 the United States suddenly swung from riches to rags. At the beginning of the year the economic skies seemed almost cloudless; the nation's appetite for automobiles, radio sets, electric washers, refrigerators, and other evidences of higher living standards appeared insatiable. The stock market was rising to its speculative peak. Then with the fall came a series of recessions, culminating on "Black Tuesday," October 29, in the frenzied sale of nearly sixteen and a half million shares. The crash initiated a depression which spread ruin throughout the land, at first slowly, then with gathering speed. Within twelve months six million men were walking the streets unemployed. Five thousand banks failed, multitudinous factories shut down, foreign trade sank to a trickle, and as soup-lines lengthened, a great part of the population experienced genuine misery.

Inevitably, the automobile industry was one of the chief sufferers. The high-pressure sales campaigns of recent years had so glutted the used-car market that the *New York Times* in November, 1929, estimated the second-hand automobiles in dealers' lots at anywhere from a half-million to a million. According to the chief statistician of the Chrysler Corporation, "the American people had over a trillion miles of transportation in their garages when the depression began."

Because of the solid merits of the Model A, the Ford Company weathered the first phase of the depression better than its competitors. The demand for the new car kept output for the whole industry in 1929 almost level, indeed, with that of the previous year; the drop was only 81,000 units. Ford's percentage of the total output rose as competitors felt the force of the rising storm. In the first five months of 1929, the boom months, the company made 30.5 per cent of all cars built; in June

570

it made 40 per cent; and in October its share increased to 44 per cent.[1]

During this phase, most people still hoped, along with the Hoover administration, that the depression would prove transitory. Practically nobody in the country realized what an ordeal lay ahead. Professional venders of optimism were beating all their tom-toms; they predicted prosperity even on this side of the corner. Henry Ford had special reason for indulging his natural cheerfulness.

Particularly could he be cheerful in counting his profits. The Ford Company, according to figures later gathered by the government, had lost $30,447,000 in 1927, and $70,641,000 in 1928, years of the changeover. In 1929, however, it made profits (after taxes) of $91,522,000, a figure all the more impressive when the substantial profit reductions of other companies were considered. General Motors, titan in the field, slipped from $296,256,000 profits (after taxes) in 1928 to $265,825,000 the ensuing year; while profits of the nine major independent companies dropped by about $35,000,000. Many of the smaller independents were in the direst peril.[2]

Then during 1930 the automotive industry sank steadily further, like most other businesses, into the morass of depression. As the market became stagnant, both manufacturers and dealers felt the keenest anxiety. General Motors sales dropped from roughly one and a half billion dollars in 1929 to just barely a billion dollars; Ford sales from $1145 millions to $874 millions. General Motors profits went down to $116,740,000, a reduction of roughly $149,000,000 in the twelvemonth. Ford profits sank to roughly $40,000,000, a drop of $51,000,000.[3]

All indications pointed to what was the fact: that the worst was yet to come. Our available evidence suggests that between one quarter and one third of the nation's automobile dealers went out of business this year. "There are many towns," declared the manager of the Michigan Automotive Trade Association, after a first-hand survey, "where retailers of well-known makes have been obliged to give up the ghost." The sales manager of an unnamed motor company brutally remarked that dealers were dropping off like flies sprayed with insecticide. Although General Motors protected its agents rather better than any other company, they suffered bitter losses. Nor was it the "weak" dealers alone who went under. Numerous companies had deliberately overstocked their agents, holding to their heads the gun of a possible franchise revocation; and often it was the bigger automobile merchant, with a large investment in organization, buildings, and vehicles, who slid into the abyss.[4]

A lengthening roster of small independent manufacturers went out of business forever. Hudson, Nash, and Studebaker managed to hold on, though Hudson had the first of four deficit years in 1930, and both Studebaker and Nash the first of four in 1932. But among the firms which disappeared in 1930–1931 were the makers of the Stearns, Moon, Kissel, Gardner, Locomobile, Elcar, and Jordan automobiles, while the Marmon Company soon followed them. These failures emphasized the growing concentration of the industry in a few strong hands. The fact that all the firms named were situated in cities other than Detroit also hastened the well-established trend toward concentration in Michigan. The depression was a powerful winnowing agency. The spirit of Darwin rode the economic storm. Early in the crash of values the *Automotive Daily News,* in an editorial headed "Jungle Law," had predicted that the survival of the fittest would be illustrated anew—and it was.[5]

Henry Ford's numerous statements for the press make it evident that throughout 1930 he retained his belief that the depression was simply a healthy punishment for various economic follies—among them the neglect of the impoverished farmers, and the abuse of instalment buying—and that good times would soon return. After all, his $40,000,000 profit for the year was fairly good in itself, and very good indeed compared with the tiny $771,000 profit of Chrysler. Undoubtedly all the Ford executives perceived by the close of 1930 that competition among makers of inexpensive cars was becoming grimmer and fiercer. As the market contracted, the chief manufacturers naturally made efforts to gain a larger share of it. Ford in 1930 had outsold the entire line of General Motors by about 300,000 units, and had outsold Chevrolet by a wide margin.[6]

But would the company be able to hold its position? As General Motors and Chrysler improved the Chevrolet and Plymouth, would the Model A maintain its high standing?

The answer was quickly given. In 1931 the Ford Company felt the full blow of the depression, now more prostrating than ever. The industry as a whole was operating at about a third of capacity. Only General Motors and Nash continued to make returns reasonably satisfactory as measured by the yardstick of the middle 'twenties, both earning more than 20 per cent on investment; only Chrysler improved its position over the preceding year. Ford went into red ink. The Model A was beginning to experience the same disfavor which had overtaken the Model T before it. Total Ford sales for 1931 (619,757 cars) slipped down to $460,000,000, not much more than half of those the preceding year, while the net loss reached $37,181,000.[7] Could Ford executives have looked ahead, they, like other businessmen, would have been aghast. The world was entering upon a convulsion which was to mean want for hundreds of millions, revolution in Latin-America, the rise of Hitler, chaos in China, creeping economic paralysis in the United States, and the advent of Franklin D. Roosevelt with a sweeping program of changes.

2.

Ford executives were later to look back with a sense of unreality upon the policies adopted during the first two depression years, 1930–1931. The company had to deal with prices, models, wages, dealers, and labor problems. Compared with General Motors, Ford leadership had seldom been prescient. The decisions now made were bigger with fate than men knew, for the nation's economic and social structure was being drastically reshaped. Labor in particular was about to open a new era, which its historians would date from the hardships, discontents, and rebellions of the depression years.

First, a series of emergency measures was undertaken in the winter of 1929–1930, when men still hoped for an early lifting of the clouds. They included expansion of plant, reduction of car prices, raising of wages, improvement of the design of Model A, augmentation of the sales force, and reduction of the commissions paid dealers. On the postulate of an early return of prosperity, it was a fairly rational program. The postulate proved unsound. The history of 1930–1931 is therefore a record first of the application and then the sharp modification of these measures.

Henry Ford stood in the van of the public-spirited industrialists who believed that the first acts required by the crash were plant-expansion and price-cutting. Busy before it occurred building Greenfield Village, planning what is now the handsome Dearborn Inn, hard by, pushing his agricultural and educational ventures, and watching the reorganization of the European businesses, he interrupted none of these activities. The erection at Dagenham of the largest automobile plant in Europe

(1930–1931) contributed to the battle against depression in Britain. The formal dedication of the yet incomplete Greenfield Village took place just as the Wall Street bubble was about to be finally pricked. Work on it continued.

Early in 1930, seizing advantage of reductions in building materials, Ford announced a program of branch factory construction to cost about $25,000,000. Of the new plants, that at Edgewater, N.J., replacing the old Kearny plant sold to Western Electric, was the most important. Looking from a thirty-three-acre site at the foot of the Palisades toward the apartment houses of upper Manhattan, it was opened to visitors early in December as one of the largest industrial establishments in the East. At capacity, 6000 men working on shift could make about 800 cars a day, though only 4500 men were initially employed. Other new branch plants were built in Buffalo, in Seattle, and at Richmond and Long Beach, California. Then as the depression deepened, construction, though never stopped, had gradually to be reduced. The industry was already overbuilt.[8] *

Meanwhile, the most obvious blow at the under-consumption which had done so much to produce the crash was price-cutting, and Ford and some rivals were quick to turn to it. Beyond doubt Henry Ford vividly recalled his experiences in 1920. Many people in the industry hoped that lower charges, better models, and vigorous advertising might persuade even frightened consumers to scrap their old cars and buy new ones. Car-buying was actually falling much more rapidly and heavily than personal income. Farmers and wage-earners especially were stubbornly refusing to purchase.†

Following his general precedent nearly nine years earlier, Ford led the way in November, 1929, by lowering prices on the Model A coupe $35 and the tudor sedan $5. He and his engineers were then working on a redesigned version of the Model A which he expected to advertise

---

* The Ford Company made additions to the Rouge power-house in 1930–1931; it built its two-mile water tunnel from the Detroit River to the Rouge during the next two years. See *Ford News* 1930–1935, *passim;* Roscoe A. Smith, *Reminiscences.*

† In 1930 personal income fell about 10 per cent from the level of the previous year, but expenditures for new cars dropped more than one third. In 1931 personal income dropped another 15 per cent, but automobile purchases went down about 30 per cent. Next year the story was even worse. Over the three-year period, personal income declined 42 per cent, automobile production 75 per cent, and expenditures for automobiles 75.4 per cent. These figures, furnished by the Department of Commerce, are calculated on a sounder basis than those in E. D. Kennedy's *Automobile Industry.* In 1929 farmers had bought 650,000 new passenger cars, and in 1932 they bought only 55,000! (See John W. Scoville, *Behavior of the Automobile Industry in Depression,* published by the Chrysler Corporation, no date, probably 1936).

extensively. This car, appearing on the last day of the year, was mechanically almost identical with its predecessor, but embodied distinct improvements in styling: the interior was roomier, the entire front of the automobile raised, stainless steel was used generously in the headlights, radiator shell, hub-caps, and cowl finish-strip. The public was indeed temporarily pleased, as a flood of orders showed. Moreover, the company supported the revised model by a vigorous advertising campaign, on which Ford spent $8,700,000 during 1930. In the first few days of the year, Ford dealers took almost $60,000,000 in orders, a gleam of sunshine in the spreading gloom of the period.

As he lowered prices, Ford also raised wages to a minimum of $7 a day. President Hoover and others, trying to stop the panicky wage-reductions which came on the heels of the Wall Street collapse, found his action (which Edsel assuredly influenced) very encouraging. Price reductions and wage increases were an old Ford formula. Henry had always denounced wage deflation as a means of achieving price deflation.

"I was never able to reduce the price of automobiles until I could first increase wages," he said. And he added a bit of characteristic economic theory: "I would rather put ten men to work at $7 a day than twenty men at $3.50, because the $7 men would have a surplus to spend which would put other men to work, while the $3.50 men would be barely living. The higher the wage the greater the purchasing power and the wider the variety of work that is set in motion." [9]

Other firms followed Ford's price lead, but not his action on wages. The Chevrolet coupe was lowered $30 in price; the Plymouth coupe $65. Competition was growing sharper.

And while in 1921 the price reductions in the automobile and other industries had unquestionably helped shorten the depression, 1930 was by no means another 1921. To begin with, the range of possible price-cutting was much more limited because car prices were now far lower than in the earlier years; the average standing at $830 as against a previous $1200.[10] The industry had grown accustomed to higher volume sales and lower profit margins. In the second place, price-cutting operated in such a changed social climate that nobody could predict that it would stimulate sales. Not infrequently, indeed, it might have just the opposite effect, leading possible customers to believe that still greater reductions lay just ahead, and that it would be wise to wait. Because automobile prices had been dropping for a decade, the depression merely accelerated the general trend. Average wholesale charges declined almost precisely one-third from 1927 to 1933, and retail prices (because of generous trade-in allowances for old cars) probably fell yet more steeply. But no company found the results satisfactory, and Ford executives thought them highly discouraging.[11]

The battle between the two giants, General Motors and Ford, would have been bitter enough had they stood alone; but Walter Chrysler's improved Plymouth car soon heightened the competition. As we have seen, Chrysler introduced the Plymouth in the summer of 1928, built a factory which by the following May was producing a thousand cars daily, and in 1929 sold 87,500 of the model. At a new engineering building in Highland Park, Fred M. Zeder and his technicians meanwhile toiled to make the Plymouth better. They used the best appliances and most expert knowledge of the day.

"No one," said Zeder, "will question the infinite superiority of present day scientific methods over the hit-and-miss, trial-and-error methods of the past." [12] The Chrysler plants were remodelled for cheaper production and lower prices, so that they were able slowly to pull out of the market stagnation which was destroying the weaker independents. When in March, 1930, Chrysler announced sweeping price reductions, it was evident that he might become formidable. The four chief low-priced cars stood that spring in fairly close proximity:

	Plymouth	Ford	Chevrolet	Willys-Overland Whippet
Coupe	$590	$500	$565	$525
Four-door sedan	625	625	625	585

The gap between the Ford and its pursuers was narrowing, and both Chevrolet and Plymouth clearly intended to set a hot pace. When a new and larger Chevrolet for 1931 was announced, the reductions ranged from $20 to $60 according to type. Moreover, the Chevrolet by that time had won a reputation for automotive engineering distinctly more advanced than that of the Model A. Its engineers were about to bring in free wheeling (introduced by the Studebaker in 1930) and synchromesh transmission, with more powerful engines and higher speed. But the most striking development in the low-priced market in 1931 was the entrance of a new Plymouth, with eight body-styles ranging in price from $535 to $645. It was an automobile to arrest wide attention. A genuinely "new" car, the product of two and a half millions spent on research and retooling, it made free wheeling for the first time standard in the low-priced field.* Its wheel base of 110 inches was 6.5 inches longer than the Ford's; it had a double drop frame and constant mesh transmission; and above all, it boasted of "floating power," a two-point rubber engine-mounting that reduced motor vibration and enhanced the value of the remarkably efficient four-cylinder engine. In price, the Plymouth was rather the competitor of the Chevrolet than the Ford, but its mechanical innovations attracted many who were willing to pay an extra hundred dollars for the new features.[13]

At once, in 1931, competition among popular-priced cars became a race among three strong entrants. It was clear that Ford would soon have to bring out a new model, and that it would have to embody advances over both the new Chevrolet and new Plymouth.

When the first of the improved Plymouths came down the assembly line in June, 1931, Walter Chrysler was waiting impatiently at the end. He climbed into the driver's seat of the third car, and set out for the Ford office in Dearborn. Leaving his car at the curb, he spent an hour or two with Henry and Edsel Ford touring the Engineering Laboratory. Then, guiding his hosts to a window, he quietly remarked: "I have something I want to show you." After inspecting the car, the Fords were delighted as Chrysler took them on a demonstration ride. Then the triumphant engineer presented the car to the Fords, and went home in a taxicab. A month later the Plymouth was leading both Chevrolet and Ford in the Wayne County area, and was a favorite with New York buyers. Although the total sale for the year, 94,000 cars, was small compared with that of the Ford, it is unquestionably true that it ate into Ford's lead—that Chrysler's gain was Ford's loss. And when Ford sales kept going down, the distribution of Plymouths continued to climb.[14]

The industry speculated over Henry Ford's future course, now that price cuts alone had availed him so little. Selling a total of 619,757 units, the Ford Company in 1931 took only 26 per cent of the industry's market. Some observers predicted that Ford would bring out an eight-cylinder automobile. The trend to the eight, with its enhanced

* Free-wheeling proved a will-of-the-wisp. For a time it was regarded as an improvement; but it was eventually abandoned, and a number of states have prohibited its use by statute. By taking the car out of gear, free-wheeling saved gasoline at the expense of safety.

speed and flexibility, had gathered impetus in the late nineteen-twenties and became marked in 1930. Paul Hoffman of the Studebaker Company declared that as these models became available at reasonable prices, "motorists in ever-increasing numbers are entering the eight-cylinder market." [15] Would Ford enter this field?

Buick abandoned the six for the straight-eight in 1931, while others prepared to follow the example. To be sure, the eight would cost more; but the Ford Motor Company had already evinced a willingness to develop "de-luxe" models, made with special smartness. Lincoln was influencing it. Two extracts from company letters to agencies at this time are revealing. "We have provided these two deluxe body types," ran one, "to meet a constantly growing demand, particularly from women buyers, for smart rich body interiors." Women were getting their innings! These two types, the letter added, "should favorably impress all owners of medium and high-priced cars." The other letter urged dealers to reach new purchasers with the new Victoria coupe. Without injuring business in other types, "it should appeal to buyers of medium and high-priced closed models because of its special features." [16]

Faced with a critical decision, Henry Ford never lacked nerve. In August, 1931, he shut down production of the four-cylinder Model A "indefinitely." He was pondering a bold step. Gossip slipped around Detroit that he was wavering between a new six and a new eight, each with strikingly novel features.

3.

When we turn to Ford policies toward dealers and workers in these initial depression years 1930–1931, the human element in our story becomes more pronounced. Many tens of thousands of men, numbering with their families hundreds of thousands, looked for bread to the commissions and the wages which the company offered. Hasty or callous new plans might mean direct suffering. The depression was a terrible tragedy to fully a quarter of the American population, and wise industrial leadership was needed to soften its rigors. Ford was so great an employer that he had a peculiar responsibility. From the beginning of 1930 he was under heavy fire from critics who declared his $7 wage largely illusory, in that he discharged many of his own highly paid men while letting contracts for parts to sub-manufacturers who paid their hands wretchedly. It is unquestionably true that all manufacturers, in nearly all industries, were hammering down prices of materials or parts from suppliers who in turn hammered down wages; that was part of the descending spiral of the depression.* Ford was also severely criticized for the shutdown in the last weeks of 1931 while he worked on the new model that he hoped would retrieve his disappearing sales. Men declared that it aggravated the already severe economic breakdown in Detroit.[17]

For years the Ford policy toward dealers and workers had been grim-tempered; would it so continue? We may look first at the dealers.

The eve of the depression had witnessed indications that the company was altering the policy of rowelling dealers that had taken shape while Ryan rode with whip and spur in the sales department. But this was only an evanescent adjustment to temporary circumstances. The limited stocks of Model A in 1928 and the keen demand for it throughout most of 1929 had made it unnecessary to overload dealers, and then hammer them to sell. A happier development of the period was a scientific planning of distribution. For the first time in its history, the Ford company had begun in 1929 to gear its production schedules to long-range sales possibilities carefully projected from field reports and analyses of market conditions. Had the depression not come, the results of this policy might have been highly beneficial.[18]

When late in 1929 Ford reduced car prices, raised wages, and announced his expansion program, he also adopted a bipartite sales policy. As one element, he cut the discount or commission given to dealers. From 20 per cent they were brought down to 17.5 per cent. Simultaneously, and even more unfortunately, he increased the number of agencies.

We must remember that at that moment people expected the depression to be brief. Ford was influenced in part by the recent profitable sales of the Model A, which led him to suspect that dealers had been making too much money, and making it too easily. (Some large Detroit dealers had.) He was influenced also by the expectation that his improved design of the Model A, about to appear, would open to dealers a new lode of gold.

The new policy, however, proved an error. As the depression closed in fast, Ford found that the smarter design and the advertising cam-

---

* This particular charge, which was also made against other automotive manufacturers, has already been shown to be baseless.

paign gave sales only a brief fillip. When the gross volume dropped in 1930 by about $200,000,000 as compared with the previous year, dealers were gripped by the worst crisis in their experience—one transcending even the lean days of the Model A changeover. Of course the agents for practically all other companies were suffering; indeed, nearly all business men were keeping but a jump ahead of the wolf. Tales of desperate poverty and bankruptcy were growing too common for special notice. But Ford dealers did feel that the multiplication of agencies and the reduced commission, imposed just when many were recouping the losses of the changeover period, were specially unfair. They felt that *they* were being asked to foot the cost of most of the price-reduction, for the new rate trimmed the dealer's return on Ford cars by an average of $15 for each unit sold. For the popular types of Ford, noted one trade journal, this meant that the dealer shouldered most of the burden.

"On the Tudor sedan," explained the journal, "there is a reduction in price of $25. On the basis of the reduced discount, the dealer would assume $17.50 of this reduction, whereas the Ford Company would assume only $7.50. On the roadster the reduction is $15, of which the dealer would assume $13 and the Ford Company $2." [19]

Receiving this lessened return, the Ford dealer had to carry on his business with the smallest margin of cash profit in the whole industry. His handicap was especially severe because, as competition grew keener in the depression years, the dealers lost much of their oldtime profits from accessories and became dependent as never before on new cars and trucks. "Few people realize the bitterness," commented the *Automotive Daily News* in April 30, 1930. And the pill was made harder to swallow when the brusque, domineering Sorensen was entrusted with the execution of the program. Believing that many dealers had become rich and lazy, he went to work with a will.[20] Rockelman, in charge of sales, disapproved of the program, but had to stand by helplessly.

A Ford branch manager, Henry C. Doss, has given us an account of Sorensen's ironfisted approach. Having seen some of the worst effects of the Ryan "cross-roads" program, Doss was against both the reduced discounts and the increase in dealerships. He was called in to give his opinion.

"Get Doss a raincoat," Sorensen sneered. "I'm going to tell him something and he's going to weep all over the place."

Sorensen explained that the 8300 dealers affiliated with the Ford

Company must be increased to 10,000, and that every dealer would be expected to give extra effort to his work. He looked at Doss defiantly.

"I think that will be a great mistake and it will be disastrous," replied the branch manager. "You will be years living it down. You'll lose a lot of your dealers to Chevrolet and others." [21]

But Sorensen was adamant. Fresh dealers were given contracts in droves. Experienced agents who opposed the new policies and spoke their minds frankly were replaced as rapidly as possible. Stressing the importance of weeding out "undesirables," the company reminded branch managers of their wide powers in cancelling franchises. The "cross-roads" program was now at its worst. Many newcomers went into business in corner stores with the most rudimentary service facilities. "No objection," states *Motor,* "was raised to dealers getting locations as close as possible to established operators with large investment." Doss recalls that new agencies were even planted within three blocks of ones long established. "It was a hell of a program," he states. "I couldn't agree with it and wouldn't sell it." He resigned—but in vain.

"Lukewarm, indifferent, and halfhearted sales representation is not wanted," thundered the home office to the branch managers. "It will not be tolerated, and your dealers must understand this if they expect to continue selling the Model A." [22]

As indignation spread among the Ford dealers, their outcry reverberated across the country. Even agents for other cars, who still enjoyed discounts ranging from 20 to 24 per cent, and who perhaps felt themselves threatened, joined their voices in the protest. One Detroit newspaperman termed the clash of interest "the biggest factory-dealer battle in the automobile industry since its start thirty years ago." A convention of Illinois bankers attacked the Ford policy on the double ground that failing dealers were a financial problem, and that the multiplication of agencies had stimulated excessive allowances for old cars and fomented an unhealthy condition in the industry. So incensed were the bankers that they refused to give credit to any of the newly-established "cross-roads" agencies. Meanwhile, the defections from the Ford ranks which Doss had predicted grew into a steady stream. Chevrolet in particular recruited many able Ford dealers, who added strength to the already well-schooled and well-protected General Motors corps.

Even amid the nation's varied troubles that winter of 1929–1930, the rebellion of the Ford dealers attracted the sympathetic gaze of industrial analysts. Farmers were gathering with pitchforks to stop foreclosure sales; hard-pressed or greedy factory owners were beginning to grind the faces of labor—some small New England establishments would soon pay women workers $2 a week. But still the dealers, rallying for their rights like the patriots at Concord, claimed some special notice. *Business Week* offered a measured appraisal of the outbreak:

Specifically, many Ford dealers object to: (1) roadmen who tour the country and report all violations of factory rules and enforce strict discipline upon the dealer organization; (2) reduced discounts by which the possible margin for net profit has been reduced to approximate invisibility; (3) treating contracts as "scraps of paper" as was done with the demand upon dealers to sign riders to their franchises accepting 17.5 per cent discount at the peril of their business lives; (4) ironbound, factory-set quotas which frequently have little relation to sales possibilities in the dealer's territory but are ever before them; (5) inclusion of Lincoln cars and Ford trucks in quotas for localities where sales of either may be practically impossible; (6) failure of factory to consider dealer's needs in distributing models and colors; (7) having to buy all garage equipment from a recognized Ford source regardless of relative need or price of equipment; (8) factory exercising authority over amount of money to be spent for show rooms, garages, and similar investments in the business.[23]

Ford and Sorensen, seeing that if they persisted the network of dealers would be torn to shreds, had to retreat. In making concessions, they threw up a dust-cloud by trying to put responsibility for the unfortunate program on Rockelman. He had not only disapproved of the cut in the discount, but had courageously pleaded against it. As a convenient scapegoat, he was summarily dismissed in March, 1930—almost immediately joining the Chrysler corporation, and soon becoming head of the Plymouth division. His place should have been given to the experienced J. R. Davis, who had been assistant to Ryan and later to Rockelman; but Sorensen and Ford created a clumsy duumvirate, giving Claude Nelles equal authority with Davis.

Under a new decree effective late in April, 1930, a sliding scale of discounts was adopted. It ranged from 17.5 per cent for dealers who sold less than fifty cars and trucks up to 20 per cent for dealers selling 151 to 500, and 21 per cent for those who sold more than 500. The new rates were based upon replies to a questionnaire circulated among dealers. Relatively few, of course, would qualify for the highest rate, for it was estimated that only one dealer in seven handled more than 500 new units a year. But a great many Ford agencies did sell 200 or more units, and the average gain was expected to be about $800 annually. It was obvious that the new sliding scale distinctly favored city dealers with a large market, and did little for agents in small centers. The latter group, and especially country dealers, remained vocally discontented. The profits of Ford dealers in general were unquestionably lower than those of their rivals in the Chevrolet camp; according to some estimates, they averaged one third lower. In justice to the company, however, it should be noted that Ford cars were priced at lower levels than Chevrolets, and that Ford was trimming costs sharply all along the line. In June, 1930, the company announced its second depression price-cut, reaching all but two types in its line, and ranging from $5 to $25 a car.[24]

"Dealers naturally are gratified over their victory," wrote a newspaper observer, "but they are not wildly enthusiastic because they have no illusions as to what it presages." They had two fears: that the company would force cars upon the well-established dealers by high-pressure methods, and that it would multiply small new dealers with contracts calling for low quotas, and hence earning lower commissions. Both fears proved to have some justification. As competition grew hotter, all companies did a certain amount of forcing. All applied various kinds of pressure; and the Ford Company was not behind its rivals. In practically all companies, too, the turnover of dealers was high. Ford records show that at the beginning of 1930 the company had 8275 dealers, that during the year it lost nearly one sixth of them, and that it nevertheless acquired enough new agents to begin 1931 with 9450 dealers. Probably most of the newcomers did have small quotas and clung to solvency only by frantic efforts and frenzied economies. A declining market, a rising roster of dealers—this meant trouble.[25]

Nevertheless, the company had honestly turned its back on the unhappy policy which Ford and Sorensen had so hastily inaugurated, and now proceeded along a more enlightened pathway. A new sales manager, a still more liberal discount, and a more judicious attention to public demands in engineering and design, all gave heart to dealers.*

* Of the 8275 dealers who began the year 1930, no fewer than 829, or more than 10 per cent, voluntarily dropped their sales contracts, while 395 had contracts cancelled by the branch offices. The 9451 dealers with whom the company began the year 1931 represented a net increase of 1176 over the figure a year earlier. If we add the number of replacements, the new Ford dealers authorized during 1930 number 2400. This was the "cross-roads" or hyper- (cont'd on p. 584)

4.

Tiring of the inefficient duumvirate, Ford and Sorensen appointed a new sales manager for the year 1931, William C. Cowling. A tall, hulking man with a huge beaked nose, he was a transportation expert who had been with the company for twenty years, had operated the D.T. & I., and had done valuable work helping the Ford organization expand its nation-wide network of branch assembly plants. Earlier he had headed the traffic department. He possessed brains, courage, and a liberal outlook.

The Cowling regime began auspiciously by raising the dealers' discount (February 6, 1931) to a flat 22 per cent. No more of the iniquitous sliding scale! The small-quota dealers cheered its passing, for they had been penalized just in proportion to their lack of strength. "This action," said Edsel Ford, "should reassure our dealers that we want all dealers both large and small to receive adequate returns from their business when conducted with sound merchandising practice." Hopefully, Edsel urged an increased volume of sales.

Telegrams of congratulation and appreciation poured in from all parts of the country, a proof that the morale of representatives had risen immediately. One dealer called the announcement the best news from Detroit in five years. Another, in Charleston, South Carolina, telegraphed that it had come just in time. "We have felt that as we made no money last year, and in fact have lost about $4000, in spite of having sold 500 new cars and 700 used cars, that the situation facing us for 1931 was without hope." Many assured the company that the new discount would help them meet the Chevrolet allowance for old automobiles. Some added a plea for still further concessions.

They were made. A kindlier tone pervaded company correspondence with dealers; and in the fall (October 21, 1931) further discounts, ranging between $20 and $150, were authorized on seven of the higher-priced types in the Ford line.[26]

Perhaps these were partly measures of desperation, for in the whole year, as we have seen, the industry (including Ford) worked at about one-third its capacity, and Ford production dropped nearly one half.

(cont'd from p. 583) competitive policy at its zenith. ("Classification of the Reasons for Cancellation," December 12, 1930, Acc. 38, Box 63.) The F.T.C. *Report on Motor Vehicle Industry*, 842, which distinguishes between dealers (retailers only) and distributors (both wholesalers and retailers) gives the average profit of dealers in 1935, for the industry as a whole, as only $3096.

At this dark moment, nothing seemed to succeed. A new group of low-priced cars, the DeVaux (Durant of California), the Rockne (Studebaker), and the Willys (replacing the Whippet) all proved unprofitable; and so did a group of new midget cars, notably the Littlemac and the Austin. General Motors was about to drop its Oakland (1932) and Hudson its Essex (1933) as impossible to sell. The Ford Company, like others, resorted to special expedients. A night-selling scheme was introduced under which dealers kept showrooms open evenings, and salesmen called on possible customers after dinner. Ford caravans travelled from town to town selling cars and trucks for instant delivery. The phrase "sales resistance" had gained currency, and Cowling's associates vigorously scolded any branch manager incautious enough to use it. "QUICK ACTION is what we want," the company admonished these managers late in 1931. All the new devices and scolding, however, availed nothing against the depression. Sales continued to fall toward the nadir of 1932.

Yet the wishes of dealers were now being given consideration, and it was partly in consequence that this period of intensified strain saw some positive achievements. One was the before-mentioned introduction of deluxe models. This, in effect, was diversification applied to a single product, and in its broadening of the price range, was Ford's partial answer to the General Motors policy of "a car for every purse."

Another achievement which encouraged many agents was the development of truck bodies useful for a wide variety of purposes. A special assistant sales manager was appointed to push them. They were fitted to the new model AA truck chassis with four-speed transmission, dual rear wheels, and a wheelbase of either 134 or 157 inches, which met a keen demand. "This new truck has so extended the usefulness of the Ford," noted a trade journal in 1930, "that, within the first half of this year, it has found its way into many fields in which it had not previously been a factor." An almost endless list of commercial types appeared: buses, furniture vans, garbage trucks, coal trucks, refrigerator trucks, heavy-duty hoist trucks, and even hearses. This was partly a response to the growing use of trucks and vans in American life. As highways improved and cities expanded, dealers could point out to customers fresh ways of using these vehicles and of invading the railroads' domain.

This diversification of Ford production, along with the broadened activity of General Motors, meant that the largest manufacturers were moving into markets previously the safe preserve of small independents. Little companies had made profits by specialization. As *Fortune* observed years later: "The independents have existed—and sometimes flourished—over the years by producing for segments of the market that have not attracted the mass manufacturers." By making products more advanced in style, or embodying features too radically new for large-scale manufacture, the little firms had kept a measure of prosperity. Now their happy exemption was being ended by the depression. But as the Ford line became more variegated, the dealers found in it new resources.[27]

5.

Having seen what happened to other general Ford policies in 1930–1931, we must turn to the workers; and there we need a larger view, extending into 1932–1933.

It was of course labor which suffered most during the depression. By the time that President Hoover urged Congress to establish the Reconstruction Finance Corporation (December, 1931) unemployment was appalling, and the hardships of the poor were more acute than in any previous crisis. Detroit was naturally one of the principal centers of misery. In 1932, the worst depression year for the automobile industry, production was only one-fifth of the 1929 capacity, and every company of note lost money. Falling output and rising unemployment naturally meant onerous tasks of relief. Many hardworking people, as social workers testify, were in despair; many were rebellious.*

At the very beginning of the depression James Couzens, speaking to the Michigan Manufacturers' Association in a Detroit hotel, warned members that the problems of seasonal unemployment, low aggregate wages, and fair treatment of unions still awaited wise attention. "If you do not solve them soon," he prophesied, "government will step in and solve them for you. That will be just too bad!" Few who heard these words in December, 1929, then had any idea that the evil genie just let out of the bottle would soon tower into a frightful monster. Three

---

* As to losses, even General Motors in 1932 showed a seven million deficit on motor vehicles, although it made ten millions on accessories and parts. (F.T.C., *Report on Motor Vehicle Industry*, 491–493.) General Motors, which had employed 233,286 people in 1929, at a yearly average of $1670, in 1932 employed only 116,152, at a yearly average of but $1233. F.T.C., *Report*, 547.

years later they knew. Michigan was now a state of nearly five million people. The number of gainful workers out of employment ranged in 1932 from just over half a million in January to nearly three-quarters of a million in October. During a considerable part of the next year unemployment stood at well over the three-quarter-million mark. Social agencies and state authorities were quite unable to cope with the general want. While the story was sad enough everywhere in America, Michigan was one of three states (the other two Ohio and Illinois) which by the spring of 1932 particularly needed more national help.

In Detroit as in other great cities, lawyers, engineers, architects, toolmakers, journalists, and schoolteachers stood in the breadlines. "Brother, can you spare a dime?" was a phrase of poignant meaning. Some men who had occupied highly respected stations lived at the city dump in shacks made of stray boards and pieces of sheet metal. It was by no means true that the automobile workers were worse off than others. The Upper Peninsula had a much larger proportion of unemployment than the Detroit area; employed automobile workers earned much more than those working in agriculture, mining, building construction, and the lumber and furniture industries. Nevertheless, the automobile factories had their ample store of harrowing tales. Theodore A. Mallon, of Ford's testing department, recalls seeing one man withdraw at noon with his lunch-box into an obscure corner. Inquiry showed that he was lunching on boiled potato-peelings in order to send food to his wife and children, who had gone to a low-rent area! The medical department in the Ford factory, like those in others, found many workers catching infections simply because they were too undernourished to resist germs.[28]

Special conditions in the automobile industry complicated the relief problem. Seasonal unemployment had always been a difficulty; when models were changed, when demand shifted, when for any reason trade slackened, men were thrown out of work. Technological unemployment, growing throughout the nineteen-twenties, had a sharper tooth in 1930–1935, for hard-pressed companies instituted all the economies possible. Moreover, superintendents in most factories during the depression years showed a disposition to speed up the working forces. We do not know just what happened in the Chevrolet, Hudson, and Studebaker plants, but we can guess. All foremen knew what Knudsen had meant when he said, "I learned to shout 'Hurry up!' in fifteen languages," and if factory workers had not learned before, they learned now.

Along with the great majority of American employers, Ford soon had not only to reduce his working force drastically but to cut wages. Year by year the payrolls fell. In 1929, when the Model A was moving fast and the minimum wage was raised to $7 a day, the company paid out $181.5 millions to Rouge wage-earners; the next year, $145 millions; and in 1931, when the minimum wage receded to $6, only $76.7 millions. Thence the total sank until for 1933 it stood at the tragic figure of $32.5 millions.* The company's minimum pay in 1932, the worst depression year for the whole industry, ran $6 for skilled men, $5 for semi-skilled, and $4 for laborers. In November of that year Ford compared favorably with other automobile plants:

2,500 men were at $6 a day	9,600 men were at $4
12,000 men were at $5	400 men were under $4

"Attempts were made," recalls Theodore A. Mallon, "to equalize the work during the depression period, but only after the force was cut way down." Instead of hiring one man a week, the company might employ one man for two days and another for three. With heads of families desperately seeking places, jealousy and suspicion ran rife. Accusations of favoritism were numerous. "I remember very well," relates one worker, Ernest Grimshaw, "certain individuals who were friends of the foreman worked every week; other fellows wouldn't get any work at all." [29]

The atmosphere of some great industrial centres was so full of fear and anger by the winter of 1932–1933 that observers regarded the election of Roosevelt as a safety-valve, forestalling a revolutionary outburst. Detroit later recalled this period as the darkest in her history. The economic storm had loosed all the winds of radical discontent. A Congressional committee which held hearings on the Red peril in the summer of 1930 heard witnesses (including General Motors and Ford officials) estimate the city's Communists at from 1500 to 5000. Jacob Polansky, an officer of the Metal Trades Association, believed that his district, which included all Michigan and part of Ohio, had 10,000.

---

* Ford's average number of payroll employees in 1929 had been 101,069, at an average wage of $36.97 for a forty-hour week. In 1932 the average number was 56,277, at an average wage of $31.53. (F.T.C., *Report*, 668.)

Sorensen, testifying that the Ford Company had experienced no difficulties with the Russians sent to study Ford methods, added: "But don't think we're not always on the watch." [30] No doubt by 1932–1933 Communism was still stronger. Other radical isms spread like fire in tinder.

Gangster activities, largely a product of prohibition and the lucrative rum-running from Canada, were at their height during these years. The city had a swarm of bootlegging kings, vice overlords, hi-jackers, blackmailers, and miscellaneous extortionists; it was popularly supposed to have Italian racketeers affiliated with the Mafia or Camorra; it certainly had murder-men, and kidnappers who terrified such magnates as Henry Ford. ("I can replace factories but not grandchildren," he was reported once to have said.) Lawlessness flourished. Nearly every issue of the Detroit newspapers chronicled some horrifying crime of violence. Inasmuch as any great factory was pretty nearly a cross-section of the male population, no establishment so large as the Rouge could be without its criminal element. Racial antagonisms sometimes flared high in this city of so many ill-digested national groups. Gentiles who hated Jews, Poles who hated Germans, and above all, whites from the Southern hill-regions who hated Negroes, were numerous. The Klu-Klux Klan by the late nineteen twenties had many fanatical adherents, and not a few inside the Ford plants.[31]

Ford workers could hardly complain of discharges and wage-cuts, the universal products of depression; but they did complain, and with rising bitterness, of other ills. The arbitrary, irrational harshness of a good many foremen and other bosses; the failure to give warning of shutdowns; the total lack of regard for seniority in discharges and re-hiring; the antagonism to union men; and the growing ascendency of Harry Bennett and his janissaries of the service department, generated a deep rumbling spirit of revolt. These abuses more than offset certain good features of the Ford factory: the temporary effort to keep wages high, the movement to spread the work, the special regard for handicapped men and Negroes, and the provision of widely-used gardens where employees might grow some of their own food.* Nearly all of

---

* Employee gardens were of long standing in Ford history, for the company had long set land aside in periods of strain. In 1921 gardens had been encouraged. Various Ford employees testify that work in them was never compulsory (though Keith Sward mistakenly declares it was), that the privilege of raising vegetables was much appreciated, and that the additional food really helped in the Great Depression. See T. A. Mallon, Albert Smith, and Willis (cont'd on p. 590)

the complaints, when analyzed, could be related to one fundamental grievance, the lack of union protection. That grievance had not been keenly felt in the old prosperous days when Detroit's long tradition of open-shop rules, and the chilliness of craft union toward unskilled automotive workers, had been taken for granted. But now the depression was generating demands which would lead straight to the C.I.O. and the sit-down strikes.

The contempt for seniority was specially resented. The laying-off and rehiring of men was an unhappy process at best. In most factories, not merely the Ford plant, veterans would see junior workers, the proteges of somebody with influence, taken back in their stead. No doubt in the Ford plant the ousting of senior employees was occasionally just incidental to the hurry and confusion of plant management. No doubt an apparent act of favoritism occasionally had some justification. A physician would telephone, "Here in my office is a man whose wife needs an immediate operation—he has no money or work;" or a Negro minister would write, "The Smith family in my congregation is totally destitute, and the son must find a job." The company tried to heed such calls. But two forms of real favoritism were bitterly resented. Whenever a dealer reported, "I have a customer ready to buy, but he wants a place for his nephew," this tacit trading of a job for a car-sale was likely to go through. Still more galling was the tendency to re-hire men of docile temper as against men ready to defend the workers' rights.[32]

In these depression years arbitrary procedures were bad enough; but arrogance gave them a brutal edge. Sorensen's rough example was copied by underlings. Foremen knew what was demanded of them. So long as the Rouge had a strong middle echelon of highly trained supervisory workers—some of them engineers of standing, and most of them decent fellows—the lower ranks enjoyed a certain protection. But now this echelon was broken down. Word would come from the head office, as sales fell and losses grew, that overhead was too high. Discharges came in recurrent waves; and the best men, being the highest paid, were likely to suffer most. The Motor Department in the boom years had a half-dozen salaried men doing managerial work, and most other departments at least four; cuts left the Motor Department just one, and

---

(cont'd from p. 589) F. Ward in their reminiscences. "It was a tremendous expense that the Ford Motor Company went to to plow that ground up and to put guards over it to keep people from taking somebody else's tomatoes," recalls Ward.

some others none. The foremen left were likely to be drivers after Sorensen's own heart.

A great many industrial establishments—steel mills, coal mines, packing plants, clothing factories—were seats of arrogance and brutality in those years; the bosses were under orders to save money, raise production, and take advantage of the plethoric labor market. But one special element marked off the arbitrary regime at the Rouge from that elsewhere: the rising power of Harry Bennett. By 1930 the close-knit, athletic figure of the former pugilist, with his blue shirt, bow tie, and dapper suit, was familiar to all Ford men. He was one of the four most powerful figures under Henry and Edsel Ford at the Rouge: Liebold's and P. E. Martin's stars were sinking, Sorensen's was stationary, Bennett's was rising. Legend was soon to weave about his name an intricate web, much of which—as he was not the kind of man to write letters or leave papers—rests on newspaper stories and the reports of his intimates.

The legends dealt with his various homes, and especially three; his costly house on Grosse Ile, with rooms decorated in Chinese style, intricate hallways, and a secret stairway descending to the enclosed dock of his steel motor-boat; another costly stronghold not far from Ann Arbor; and a cottage on Lake St. Clair. They dealt with his prowess as a boxer—he could still knock down hard-muscled plug-uglies, and did. They dealt with his fondness for painful practical jokes, such as tripping men into the Detroit River. They dealt with the elaborate espionage system his Service Department offered in the Rouge; with his very dangerous friends and minions; and with the enemies who hated him and repeatedly tried to kill him. They dealt with the revolver he carried and the target-practise range in his office.

Most of all, legend dealt with his influence over Henry Ford, the chilly co-existence between him and Sorensen, and the unquestioned (and helpless) detestation in which Edsel Ford and decent executives held him. The whole fountain of his power lay in his relation with Henry Ford. The owner (according to report) brooked no criticism of him. Assigning task after task to him, Ford was pleased by the unswerving, hard-hitting execution of orders. After some peculiarly disagreeable job had been done in a specially disagreeable way, Ford would remark appreciatively: "Harry gets things done in a hurry." Harry, though often embroiled in quarrels, meanwhile boasted of his power. "When anybody says he will take the question to higher author-ity," he enjoined on one lieutenant, "tell him we'll always take it one stage higher than he does!" Sorensen in *Forty Years with Ford* tells of seeing Mrs. Ford in tears over "this man Bennett who has so much control over my husband and is ruining my son's health."

Though the reasons why his ascendency grew are complex, three seem of salient importance. First and most important, his open rela-tions with the Detroit underworld gave him a supposed capacity for protecting Henry Ford and his family from criminal molestation. Ben-nett not only associated with but befriended men of gang affiliations. Chester La Mare, a handsome, flashily dressed Sicilian, with a com-manding personality and sonorous voice, who supplied fruit and vege-tables to the Ford commissary, was much in evidence. Joe Tocco, a leader in one of the river gangs, once showed a Ford employee how he carried his .45 automatic revolver stuffed into the waistband of his trousers. Another Italian-American with a long police record some-times lounged in a Rouge office. All three were eventually assassi-nated.[33]

Bennett had other channels for dealing with the underworld. It was natural for Ford, when frightened about his grandchildren, to consult with him; even Clara Ford, after her husband's automobile accident, was said to have appealed to him. The gangster menace was real—one man, Walter Simek, was convicted of threatening to kidnap Edsel's children, and was deported to Czechoslovakia. A circumstantial story yet circulates in Detroit of a gangster plot (instigated from New York) to kill Henry Ford, and of the lethal fashion in which it was brought to an end in a Detroit hotel room.[34] But Bennett exploited the peril for a great deal more than it was worth.

The spread of radicalism and discontent inevitably also gave Ben-nett's Service Department a larger role in plant affairs. Whether the danger of disturbances or sabotage increased or not, many industrial-ists thought it did and took precautions. Ford was one. The service men, writes one Ford veteran, were constantly searching for labor "agi-tators;" they treated the hands "like dogs." Another relates that it came to be a question, by 1933, whether Bennett or Hitler had first thought of the gestapo idea. Henry Ford responded to urgent demands of labor and its champions by heavier reliance on the service force. And, as a third factor, the psychological element cannot be ignored. Ford had long tried to remold his son in his own image; he had failed. In Bennett he saw a number of the traits and attitudes he had vainly tried to implant in Edsel, and with the blindness of a stubborn, limited man of seventy, he gave the cocky, ruthless, little police-chief a scope he had denied his highly civilized son.

The atmosphere which enveloped workers at the Rouge as Bennett took firmer grip on the reins is well indicated by a story told by W. C. Klann. In the fall of 1928 this able official, with his long record of invaluable service, was discharged, receiving a final check for $10,000. When asked a little later to return, he declined, for (he said) he did not wish to get the treatment given Frank Kulick. What had happened to Kulick? He also had been discharged arbitrarily. He had appealed to Henry Ford, who told him to go and see Sorensen, who would put him back to work. Sorensen thereupon sent Kulick to perform a special task for Bennett in getting a defective car ready for use. Inspecting it, Kulick found that a camshaft had been inaccurately ground. With Klann's assistance he made a perfect cam, and after much trouble, for Bennett's service men interposed all kind of obstacles, he delivered it. Klann continues:

Frank Kulick put the camshaft in the car, and he started the motor. It was very quiet. He called up Harry Bennett and told him about it. Bennett said, "We'll take it for a ride."

Bennett told Frank it was still noisy. He told Frank to lie on the running board and listen through the hood. He drove out of the gate on Miller Road and turned the corner so fast he threw Kulick off the running board. Bennett drove back into the plant through another gate and left Kulick outside. Frank started to go back into the plant, but the service men would not let him in.[35]

The one certain and adequate protection for labor in the Ford factory, as in American factories in general, was a strong union. When Roosevelt took the oath of office on March 4, 1933, a law guaranteeing workers the right to form unions and bargain collectively was not far distant; and nowhere was its application to be more dramatic than in the automotive industry.

6.

Whatever his blunders and shortcomings, Henry Ford was still a mighty power in his industrial world. As the depression grew, the pace of competition with the Chevrolet and Plymouth forced him to a new engineering achievement—the V-8 car. The prick of necessity was sharp indeed when 1932 opened. Chevrolet the previous year had sold $386,644,000 worth of cars; Chrysler sales had reached $172,330,000. While net Ford-Lincoln sales of $460,000,000 still looked substantial, obviously the Model A was declining sharply and Plymouth was climbing. For a time Ford wavered between a new six-cylinder and a new eight-cylinder model.

He made the bolder choice. On February 11, 1932, James Sweinhart gave the Detroit *News* an authorized announcement which press associations carried throughout the country. Ford was building a new model, with a new eight-cylinder V-shaped motor; he would continue building four-cylinder cars, an improved Model A known as Model B; both the V-8 and the Model B would have roomier bodies, a longer wheelbase, a lower-hung chassis, and a heavier frame than in any earlier Ford car—so the announcement ran.

"We developed a corking good four, and were all ready to let it go," Ford told Sweinhart, "but we found it is not the new effort which the public is expecting. That's why we're bringing out the eight now." Hoping the new car would assist in national recovery, he added an appeal to suppliers of raw materials. "If American manufacturers do their utmost to start the wheels of industry and the material men begin to raise prices, the whole effort may be throttled. In times like these everyone has to take some risk."

Behind the introduction of the V-8 lay one of the interesting Ford stories. When the Chevrolet late in 1929 had gone from a four-cylinder to a six-cylinder model, Ford had halted at the desk of an engineering assistant, Fred Thoms, to say, "We're going from a four to an eight because the Chevrolet is going to a six. Now, you try to get all the eight-cylinder engines that you can." Actually, Ford had experimented much earlier with both eight- and twelve-cylinder engines, and had not yet made up his mind. But Thoms and his aides now picked up nine eights in various places, cleaned them, and placed them in a row. These engines, made in two or three segments, were costly. Ford knew that cheapness was vital, and began work with his helpers on a one-piece cylinder block. "Everybody said it couldn't be done," recalls Thoms, "but Ford said it could." [36]

Under Ford's supervision, Carl Schultz and other engineers working in the Edison laboratory had laid out the first V-8 engine in May,

1930. The second was ready in November. Then in rapid succession came twenty-five or thirty more, the engineers trying everything to reduce costs. Thomas A. Edison rode around in one of them. Thought was given to bringing out a new eight-cylinder model at once, but the time was not ripe, and Ford still played with the idea of a six, even ordering six hundred experimental pistons. According to assistants, his worry had become intense by the fall of 1931. "He seemed to be getting madder and madder. Of course we didn't know what he was thinking —but we knew he felt we weren't yet on the right track." Then on December 7, 1931, after a long conference with Edsel, he had suddenly reached his decision.

"From that moment Henry Ford personally became the dynamo of the works," wrote Sweinhart. "He was here, there, everywhere, ordering, directing, changing. A task immeasurable by words confronted him. The whole works had to be changed. Building of the eight would require certain finished parts which Ford did not make; these had to be designed, contracted for, put into production elsewhere. A vast amount of machinery had to be taken out; new machinery, not yet in existence, had to be designed, built elsewhere, brought in, and installed." In reality, the plant reorganization was by no means so extensive or costly as that in 1927. Only certain sections had to be shut down while new machinery was installed. Production of the V-8 could be introduced gradually.

When the V-8 went on display March 31, 1932, in fourteen body types, the country was preoccupied with unemployment, commercial failures, hunger in the great cities, a revolt of farmers against foreclosures, and preparations for the Presidential contest. Yet the car received a warm welcome. The governor of Michigan attended a celebration in Dearborn. Across the nation nearly six million people visited Ford showrooms. At prices ranging from $460 to $650, the V-8 was much the handsomest of all the company's creations. Streamlining began at the very front of the V-type radiator shell, and was carried back in the gracefully curved lines of top, sides, and rear. New riding comfort was provided by low seats, deep cushions, increased use of rubber mountings to absorb noise and vibration, and the basic Ford principle of transverse springs. Gear-shifting was synchronized; tires were larger; wheel nuts were concealed behind hub-caps; safety glass was standard in all windshields. In the 65 hp. engine, two banks of four cylinders each were cast in a single piece with the crankcase, and the cylinders were set at an angle of ninety degrees. An automatic spark, a double drop frame designed to lower the body, and bright rustless steel for exposed parts, with two-light depressible beam headlights, added to the attractions of the car.[37]

Reporters in these weeks found Ford smiling, alert, and optimistic. "I've got back my old determination," he declared with a jaunty wave of his hand. Almost seventy, he was breasting the depression as cheerfully as any man half his years. Like the Model T nearly a quarter-century earlier, he declared, the V-8 embraced in a car of low prices numerous features theretofore found only in expensive automobiles; like its homely predecessor, it gave the public innovations of lasting value. It was an achievement which shone doubly bright against the gloom of the times.

The automobile industry, like other industries and the nation as a whole, stood in 1932 on the threshold of an entirely new era. The Ford Company, so long one of the greatest money-makers in the United States, was passing through rough waters; but unlike many smaller automotive companies, it was destined to emerge safely. In the years from its foundation to 1927, it had registered profits exceeding nine hundred millions. The three worst years of the depression, 1931–1933, were to see it pile up losses of more than $125,000,000. Despite the V-8, Ford-Lincoln sales fell in 1932 to $254,680,000, and in 1933 rose only to $297,147,000. This was in the deepest trough of one of America's worst decades. But financial recovery, of a modest sort, did lie just ahead. In 1934 and the two succeeding years the company would return a modest profit.

Concentration was now the ruling principle of the industry. The general effect of the Great Depression was to place most production in the hands of the Big Three: General Motors, Chrysler, and Ford. Could the Ford Motor Company regain that third of the national market which it had held so triumphantly in 1929, and once more lead the field in the sale of low-priced cars throughout the world? Henry Ford had his answer to these questions: "I've got back my old determination." But even he must have realized that he faced a heightened competition with a deteriorating organization.

XXIII

FORD: SYMBOL, LEGEND, REALITY

AMID the early bewilderments of the depression, Henry Ford (with Samuel Crowther collaborating) published his book *Moving Forward,* which seemed a challenge to the gloomy business situation. He dealt with technology, management, wages, production, and the distribution of goods. The tone was hopeful, the advice constructive. With them he combined comments on the curing of economic maladies, and glimpses into a chromatic future. Certain of his insights and predictions were remarkable. "We are not beyond the creeping stage in business," he wrote. "When business begins to walk then we shall begin to learn something more about wages and probably destroy the lines that separate wages and salaries." Above all, he called for boldness. Men should assist in the constant birth of new ideas and new eras. We have hardly begun to perceive the wonders open to us, he preached; to rub the scales from our eyes, we must accept and follow revolutionary concepts.

As proof of the plasticity of our society, Ford pointed to motor transport: "That has developed many millions of mobile horsepower, and this in turn has caused a start toward rebuilding the country." Let the reconstruction go on! He was for a courageous program of public development such as the New Deal presently launched: more railroads, more waterways, more dams for flood control and power, more highways for cars and trucks. The moment, with the advance of engineering and growth of population, was right. "Their cost is not important. We have the money. And from a national standpoint they should not be looked at in terms of dollars spent but rather in terms of dollars circulated." Let the people resolve on more work, more production, more use of new scientific and technical ideas, and more buying, and the depression would vanish. Let them also cast aside old bogies, such as exaggerated fears of technological unemployment.

It was characteristic of Henry Ford, his restless energy, incessant theorizing, and flair for publicity, that amid a multitude of other pursuits he helped Crowther write a book ready for the turn from prosperity to hard times. It was also characteristic that he should unabashedly rephrase nearly all his old ideas.

Most of them were good ideas, worth repetition. Men strive for goods and should have them abundantly at low cost, for "the day of actual overproduction is the day of emancipation from enslaving materialistic anxiety." High wages and ample leisure are vital to the economic machine. As for pay, he had proved that "there is no conflict between low costs and high wages;" as for leisure, "our buying class is our working class, and our working class must become our 'leisure class' if our immense production is to be balanced by consumption." Money is only a tool, a means to an end, never to be valued in itself. "Today none of our real leaders is working for money. All of them have more money than they can use, and they continue to earn money in large amounts as part of the machinery of monetary supply for the whole of society. All so-called private fortunes are nothing less than public reserves." The fundamental test of any activity is service to society, and people should always be discontented with the quality and quantity of the service they give. Contentment means decay; "everyone is capable of doing at least twice as much as he or she is now doing."

Automotive manufacture was the greatest single industry in America, and Henry Ford much the greatest figure in the automotive world. He was also the liveliest, most changeable, most picturesque figure. The Ford Company, in public esteem, had more and more boiled down to Henry Ford. The book threw some light on the company, as in its chapters on Model A and the Johansson gauges; some light even on Henry Ford. Most of all, however, it contributed to the image of Ford the symbol.[1]

2.

A second industrial revolution had been wrought by the complex system of mass production and its appurtenances, offering the richest cornucopia of goods the world had yet known. This revolution required a personal symbol. Men instinctively find some figure who sums up a movement or trend, as Bismarck summed up autocracy and Cecil John Rhodes imperialism. Just as Rockefeller was the symbol of industrial consolidation, and Krupp of munitions making, Ford became the symbol of the mass-production era. Before long Aldous Huxley was to satirize this tendency in *Brave New World* by presenting the intellectual acolytes of the new age, worshippers of uniformity and machines, as singing hymns not to Our Lord but Our Ford.

For a man to become the symbol of a movement it is not enough that he be one of the principal figures in it; he must also make a reverberant success, preferably on a world scale. This was true of Bismarck and Rhodes, Krupp and Rockefeller. It was true also of Ford, whose factory gave birth to mass production, whose Model T was as instantly recognized on every street in five continents as Charlie Chaplin on the screen, and who became possibly the richest person on the globe. His success impressed titans of finance and politics while somehow appealing to the masses as a contribution to their welfare.

The man who symbolizes a great change must meet another requirement: he must take a positive stand on the issues bound up in it. He must believe with fervent intensity in the new forces released. No storm of attack could move Rockefeller from his faith in industrial concentration: "The age of individualism has gone, never to return." Bismarck's devotion to autocracy was as unshakable as Gibraltar: "It is not by parliamentary speeches that these great problems will be settled, but by blood and iron." Henry Ford's faith in mass production, lower prices, and higher wages as moulders of a better age was as ironclad as Rhodes's belief in the beneficence of the British Empire.

It is also important that the symbolic figure have, if possible, picturesque gifts and traits, that he be the kind of human being about whom anecdotes and legends cluster. Few men of his time had the salience of Henry Ford, who aroused curiosity by his unpredictable, many-faceted, and contradictory nature, and who constantly made news by his acts and utterances. He was as unmistakably American as Orville Wright, Mark Hanna, or Walt Whitman; and he possessed one Lincolnesque quality, an identification with common men even when he was most uncommon. His figure and physiognomy contributed to the hold he took on the general imagination. Though but of average height, five feet nine, he was so spare, lithe, and erect that he looked tall; though rather nondescript of feature, only eyes and mouth being at all remarkable, he appeared arrestingly vital and individual. Nobody who once saw him ever forgot him. John Reed was struck by his vitality: "A slight, boyish figure, with thin, long, sure hands, incessantly moving; clean-shaven—the fine skin of his thin face browned golden by the sun; the mouth and nose of a simple-minded saint; brilliant, candid, green eyes, and a lofty forehead rising to shining gray hair like the gray hair of youth; the lower part of his face extraordinarily serene and naive, the upper part immensely alive and keen. He spoke swiftly, easily, without raising his voice, without hesitating, and his vocabulary consisted chiefly of words of one syllable." John Gunther years later was impressed by the same vitality. "He is swift as a shadow. . . . He is lean, with a stomach long and flat like an ironing board; his hair is carefully kept and lustrous; the years have written long, deep parentheses at each end of his quick, sensitive mouth. He is able neither to sit nor stand for long. When he stands, his hands flutter across his chest or by his sides." [2]

A cartoonist who so drew Ford as to show that sense of spare tireless vitality, could have made him seem the archetype of the swift new industrial age.

3.

It is not enough, as we have suggested, that a man symbolize a movement; he should also symbolize an epochal controversy. It was Ford's fate that the controversies surrounding him affected the whole planet and reached into a diversity of social areas. The domination of the machine over the individual, foreshadowed by Samuel Butler in *Erewhon;* the growth of uniformity in dress, furniture, and social habits caustically arraigned by Sinclair Lewis in *Main Street;* the role of the personal autocrat in industry and politics at a time when both were full of new Caesars; the lot of workers as they became richer in goods but poorer in initiative and independence; the struggle between capitalists eager to speed up their factories and labor unions using the slowdown to exact better terms—discussion of any of these subjects involved Henry Ford. His name appeared in a hundred contexts as men debated the issues of the day. The personal disputes in which he figured, such as the Dodge brothers and Chicago *Tribune* suits, were of transient importance compared with these great basic controversies of the economists, sociologists, and journalists.

Ford as an international and national symbol emerged by successive steps. The first was the worldwide adoption of the Model T, as homely as a burro, as useful as shoes, an article of prime utility carrying the Ford name everywhere. The second was the Selden Patent suit, from which Ford stepped forth a triumphant Perseus holding aloft the Medusa's head. The Peace Ship, advertising his idealism and naivete, and the contrast between the practical industrialist and impractical meddler in public affairs, helped enlarge the symbol. The announcement of the five-dollar, six-dollar, and ultimately seven-dollar days, and the five-day week, all had their impact. The five-dollar day in particuar, resounding along every civilized coast and losing none of its force in countries where five francs or marks seemed good daily pay, was long remembered. The London *Economist* declared in 1954: "It may well rank as the most dramatic event in the history of wages." The publication of *My Life and Work* in 1925 and *Today and Tomorrow* in 1926, loosing waves of comment around the world, gave Ford more than ever the aspect of a versatile ideologist, a preacher with a gospel delivered to the bass drum obligato of pounding machinery.

Once well started, the controversies never stopped. They projected Ford's figure against a motion-picture screen of fighting groups. In the combat over mass production, its benefits and liabilities, labor leaders and skilled workers tended to take up their cudgels against almost everything that Ford represented; but farmers, unskilled workers, salaried people, and others who wanted standardized goods at low cost tended to range themselves beside him. The populations of industrially retarded countries, such as Russia and Argentina, were in general enthusiastic over the forces symbolized by Ford, while the nations with well-developed industries and a high level of mechanic skill, like Britain and Germany, were prone to hostility. Lovers of handicraft arts of course aligned themselves against believers in quantity production for utility alone, the ghosts of Ruskin and William Morris fighting against the shades of the men who had filled the world with standardized goods from Birmingham, Lyons, Munich, and Pittsburgh. People honestly impressed by bigness, including Americans proud of the Rouge plant as the nation's No. 1 industrial giant, and others whom bigness depressed, entered the controversy. Of course the unending battle between capitalism and socialism was part of the general meleé.

Ford, quite conscious by the early twenties of his position as philosopher of a new era, and exhilarated by the noise of conflict, rose to the demands on him. "I think he felt comfortable in this challenge," states

Fred L. Black, close to him in the *Dearborn Independent* days. "I think that he enjoyed it by that time thoroughly." His enjoyment was all the greater for his inability to understand some of its ramifications.

Naturally farmers, white-collar men of low income, restless American youth, Negroes, and others had a special regard for Ford the symbol. To millions of rural families he meant an end to social isolation, cheaper transport of crops, and more amusements. They correctly felt that he was one of themselves. "Henry Ford," declares W. J. Cameron, who knew him intimately, "was a product of an agrarian society with their basic thoughts. He never got out of it. The city was all on the edge of his life; the farm and the tool shed were always in the center of it. He always had the agrarian point of view." (Of course he was also the agrarian rebel, the child of farm life dedicated to its partial destruction and its transformation by water-power, tractor, and an alliance with industry through the conversion of farm crops to oils, paints, and plastics.) A thousand evidences of his rural quality, from interviews on bird-watching and crop-prices to his long absorption in tractors and soy beans, reached the farm population. "Land is the Basic Fact," proclaimed a typical editorial of "Mr. Ford's Page" in the *Dearborn Independent*. Small-town people and suburbanites also found wider horizons in Ford's new era.

At the same time Ford, to many labor leaders and skilled mechanics, was becoming a symbol of other and sinister tendencies. The five-dollar day, a brilliant beacon of hope, lost much of its lustre when, as we have seen, other employers made comparable advances. For the high wages a price had to be paid—a price, many thought, which made the toiler a mere robot. The vice-president of the Brotherhood of Electrical Engineers declared in 1922: "The Ford operatives may enjoy high pay, but they are not really alive—they are half dead."

Admittedly, Ford's minute subdivision of labor (declared critics) was an irresistible tendency of the time; admittedly, it held great economic advantages; and admittedly, many employers, including Ford, were making experiments to save the worker from its injurious effects. Still, Ford became the chief representative of what many called a new age of joyless tedium in industry. "The Ford plant," as one magazine writer put it, was "the symbol of everything that most automobile workers cry out against in this industry. There is, for instance, no personal animus against Walter P. Chrysler or William S. Knudsen; the

enemy there is the impersonal corporation or the mass-production machine system itself. This cannot be said for the Ford Company, because
there exists a definite dislike of Ford himself." [3]

Ford, regarding this criticism as unjust, argued that the skills and
happiness of oldtime craftsmen were exaggerated; their products often
very crude, their lives hard and narrow. He argued that as mass-production evolved it required unprecedented numbers of highly skilled
workers. "A few years ago," he wrote in *Moving Forward,* "we had no
production job which could not be learned by any man of average intelligence within a month, and perhaps one-half of our jobs could be
learned in a week. Today the proportion of jobs which can be learned
in a week or less is rather small and to learn any of the more important
production tasks requires a training of from two weeks to a month—
provided the man has some native mechanical ability. The more delicate jobs of inspecting and balancing require from six to eight weeks
to learn and a slow-witted man can never learn them." Mass-production forced a steady growth of the machine-tool industry, which also
required a multitude of master-craftsmen. Ford asserted that the corps
of one hundred thousand men the company normally employed in the
Detroit district could muster a greater variety of expert skills than any
oldtime nation of two million people. But all this did not convince his
opponents.[4]

4.

Overseas, the nations from China to Peru which desperately wanted
industries of their own of course regarded Ford and his methods as
offering the key to a storehouse rich with goods. We have seen that in
Russia after the First World War, Ford became the great exponent of
the idea of plenty-for-all. Soviet workers who dreamed of a forty-four
hour week were told that Ford had introduced a forty-hour week. The
Russian peasant with his mattock heard of the Fordson tractor as a
deliverance from drudgery and crop failure.

Maurice Hindus, writing in 1927, described Russian villages where
the people, eager for a new agricultural era, ascribed a magical quality
to the name of Ford. At a village wedding the bridal cart was drawn
by a Fordson, to which speakers at the wedding banquet pointed as
evidence of Soviet progress. Hindus was bombarded with questions
about the man:

It is really extraordinary how popular Ford has become in Russia. Incredible as it may seem, more people have heard of him than of Stalin. . . . Next to Lenin, Trotsky, and Kalinin, Ford is possibly the most widely known personage in Russia.

Whence has come this amazing popularity, in Bolshevik Russia of all places, of the richest capitalist in the world? Ford has not sought it. For all I know, he may not even be aware of its extent or intensity. Only in part can it be attributed to the widespread and diversified use of the Fordson tractor. Nor is it a mere accident or manoeuvre artifically stimulated by some invisible power. Ford just happens to be the symbol of something which the Russian craves with all the flaming fervor that is in his soul.[5]

Trotsky praised the Ford production methods; *Pravda* chronicled the progress of "Fordization" in Russian factories; *My Life and Work,* translated in revised form, sold in huge quantities in the Union, being used as a text in universities and technical schools. Foremen, clerks, and factory managers studied manuals based on Arnold and Faurote's analysis of Highland Park operations, while some agricultural communes adopted the name of Fordson.

This popularity of a capitalist in a Communist country was not really incongruous, for Soviet leaders thought of Ford not as a capitalist but as a revolutionary. As Lenin had broken new political paths, Ford was the chief economic innovator of the age, the leader who had scrapped established methods and hewed out direct roads to well-being. His work touched some of the deepest yearnings of the Muscovite soul.[6]

In Western Europe the attitude toward "Fordism" was more hesitant and equivocal. On one side stood admiring businessmen, wage-earners dazzled by the five or seven-dollar day, and champions of modernity; on the other was the tradition of individual craftsmanship rooted in the medieval guilds, and the belief that a worship of efficiency destroyed the poetry of life. Many workers had divided minds. Harkening to Ford's slogan, "High wages to create large markets," and thinking enviously of American blessings as depicted in Hollywood films, they nevertheless retained a stubborn attachment to their ancestral ways of life and work. Thus when in 1928 the British Labor Party was calling for a weekly minimum wage of £4, the Ford minimum of about £8 seemed alluring; but British toilers knew that their trade union organization was far in advance of America's, and that Ford was hostile to unions in Manchester and later at Dagenham. When the Ford factory was established in Cologne, German mechanics, who had always liked complex operations demanding varied skills, would not readily accept assembly-line routines. Danish workers presented an iron opposition to what they termed the speed-up, while Frenchmen simply ignored it.[7]

Another widely-felt attitude was expressed by the Irish author who wrote: "Cork was built by the Danes and destroyed by Henry Ford." He added: "God forgive Henry Ford, and he only a generation or two removed from the Rebel City." This was the position of liberals and intellectuals who made Ford the symbol of an all-potent industrialism trampling down individuality, beauty, and serenity, and erecting machine-altars to Mammon and Moloch. Many things in modern life which sensitive men detested, from the signboards defacing country roads to tasteless motion pictures, from giant skyscrapers to jerrybuilt suburbs, were by an unfair metastasis connected with Ford's angular figure. Countless artists, poets, novelists, and musicians felt a repulsion at his name. Britons looking at a Wolseley factory denounced Ford; Frenchmen seeing a Citroën car throw a veil of dust over the landscape anathematized him. Seumas O'Brien, recalling how Cork had sold its race-course to the Ford Company, saw that mad act as ending a golden age. "Take your blasted old factory out of Cork," he demanded of Ford; "give us back our race-track touts, our drunken aristocracy, our philosophic longshoremen, our venders of pigs' feet, and our jaunting-car jarveys, the great entertainers, as much a part of Cork as Aristophanes was of Greece." [8]

However divided the attitudes of Europe, the power of Ford's name as a symbol was indisputable. Lord Northcliffe extolled him as the exemplar of American energy and resourcefulness; in Paris Charles M. Schwab electrified Baron Rothschild's dinner table by describing his achievements. For months his *Mein Leben und Werk* was one of the best-selling books in Germany, outdistancing fiction. From Sweden to Turkey the term "Fordismus" epitomized the new mass-production engineering and low-price economy of abundance. Just as Waddill Catchings and William Trufant Foster, in books popular in England and America, assumed that advanced nations were emerging (particularly America) on a brighter economic plane in which Ford's methods and ideas furnished much of the sunshine, so William Zimmerman in Germany became an apostle of "Ford's Evangelium," and the econ-

omist Yves Guyot in France wrote enthusiastically of him. Italy offered
an interested student of his ideas, now admiring, now critical, in the
eminent historian Guglielmo Ferrero. In Britain Alfred Kinross, M.P.,
hailed *My Life and Work* in the *English Review,* as Lord Leverhulme
did in the *Spectator,* as epochal, every page full of light. "It embodies a
far truer Socialism than the Socialism of our Labour members." Ford,
in Kinross's opinion, had neither a capitalist nor Socialist ideology. "He
has stated a new theory of business and in practice he has proved that
Socialist and ordinary capitalist are alike in that each is at the mercy of
a false idea of economics."

The retort of collectivist thinkers to such writers was of course pungent, but it was qualified by admiration for Ford's managerial miracles,
his more benevolent policies, and his hostility to Wall Street. H. J.
Massingham, replying to Leverhulme, called capitalism bad. Ford, in-
sofar as he was a despot and a foe of trade unions, represented some of
its worst aspects. But his hatred of finance capitalism, his liberal wage
practises, his hostility to patent controls, and his desire to produce goods
in vast quantities made him in the main a happy biological sport of the
capitalist system. "He is not a monopolizer; he is a vitalizer."

So thought others. Although the London *New Statesman* wished to
see the Socialist commonwealth supplant the capitalist state, it thought
Fordism well worth adopting—under strict limitations. As the old industrial revolution had been worth while despite its attendant miseries,
the new industrial revolution would be worth while too—"but let us
learn from the past to control the future." In America Upton Sinclair,
as his little book *The Flivver King* shows, shared this position. He was
against Ford as a symbol of capitalist enterprise, but all for Ford as a
symbol of revolutionary change in industry.[9]

It will be seen that the symbolic Ford was a complicated concept,
meaning many things to different men. Nowhere was this more true
than in his own country. By 1930 some thoughtful men condemned him
fiercely, but many others took the position of John A. Ryan, director
of the National Catholic Welfare Council, who wrote: "I realize more
strongly than ever that he has made the greatest contribution toward a
solution of more than one of our industrial problems that has yet been
made by any captain of industry." And somehow, amid the chorus of
attack and praise, Ford maintained all through the nineteen-twenties
a hold on the amused, puzzled, respectful, skeptical liking of the masses

unmatched by any other business leader. He was an economic giant, a political child, a philanthropist, a tyrant, a messiah, a devil—but as a symbol he was tremendous.

5.

The Ford legend was born simultaneously with the symbol, but was a much less spontaneous creation. It grew with his fame, and at times was inextricably tangled with it. Both came into existence late in his life, for he was past fifty when the five-dollar day startled the globe. His name until then connoted a product, not a man; as Mark Sullivan wrote, Ford long meant just a cheap car as Fairbanks meant scales and Colgate soap. He was not in *Who's Who in America* in 1914. But as Ford's fame expanded and brightened, so did the Ford legend. It was no time at all until a commentator, parodying the Ford Motor Company slogan, exclaimed: "Watch the Ford myths go by!" [10]

In the creation of the legend Ford himself played an active part. He discovered himself at the same time the world did, and signalized the fact by pontifical pronouncements and essays in self-portraiture that sometimes wove Oriental embroideries about the real man. "I think," says E. G. Liebold out of long daily association, "that Mr. Ford felt a news story on the front page was of more value than a paid advertising campaign. He went on the theory of keeping the name Ford before the public, not particularly as an advertising factor so much as a means of upholding his popularity." Modest in shrinking from public appearances, he enjoyed the publicity of the printed page. He meant to imprint his personality on his time, as he proved in making the *Dearborn Independent* a personal organ, and to drive home his social and political ideas. He soon comprehended that to become a personal force he must dramatize himself, and that dramatization meant boldness.

"He wasn't cautious in ideas as in mechanics," observes W. J. Cameron; "he ranged."

Among the masses the Ford legend was largely bound up with the popularity of his greatest product, the Model T, and it had all the democratic quality of that universal car. Indeed, one homely exponent of American democracy disappeared when the Model T's ceased to be ubiquitous. With them went the Ford joke, which had much in common with jokes about other cheap universal items—mail-order catalogues, nickel cigars, hot dogs, five-and-ten cent stores—and yet a

quality all its own. "Henry can make 'em faster'n you can wreck 'em"
—that type of joke tended to make men brothers in a warm appreciation of Henry. A distinct element of affection went into the "lizzie
labels" specially used by college youth: "Danger, 100,000 jolts"; "Come
on, baby, here's your rattle"; "If you must bump me, use your head";
"Galloping snail"; "If we had milk and sugar, it would be a milk
shake"; and "Don't laugh, girls, think how you look without paint."
The magazine *Judge* once paid $5 for the best lizzie labels. Then, with
the emergence of Model A, came the final Ford joke, "Henry's made
a lady out of lizzie," and after it the final label, placed on loyally preserved antiques, "Henry's first go-cart." [11]

Though neither Ford nor the company had any public relations
department, both had men, as previously noted, who dealt unofficially
with publicity. Charles A. Brownell briefly, and W. J. Cameron for
many years acted as Ford's spokesmen, and E. G. Liebold frequently
contributed something. In general, however, Ford spoke for himself,
often all too volubly.

He was shrewd in parrying troublesome reporters, and at news conferences would sometimes score off them, raising a general laugh. "They
got in there to grill him," recalls W. C. Cowling, "and *he* did the
grilling." At times his retorts would be worth a news story in themselves. When the Model A was brought out in New York, for example,
he stood with Edsel and Thomas A. Edison among a group of press-
men. One lad kept asking impertinently, "Mr. Ford, how much are
you worth?" Ford ignored him. But at the third or fourth inquiry he
turned in anger, snapping out: "I don't know and I don't give a
damn!" The youth grinned happily. He had his story. In general,
however, Ford was communicative, making associates wonder that so
shy a man could have so large a sense of publicity values.

"He would talk freely on almost anything," recalls Fred L. Black,
who adds that some of the talk bore little relation to "reason and judgment." It was one of Cameron's and Liebold's duties to weed out of
interviews any snap judgments that would have unpleasant repercus-
sions. Since Ford's offhand statements were often curt and orphic, they
could advise reporters not to repeat some sententious indiscretion: "I
don't know what he meant myself." When Ford sat down for a long
discussion with favored writers, such as Charles W. Wood of *Collier's
Weekly,* Garet Garrett, Samuel Crowther, B. C. Forbes, or (later) Anne

O'Hare McCormick, he took greater care, for he knew that magazine articles had a more lasting impact than a newspaper column.[12]

On a first reading, his almost innumerable interviews seem a chaotic jumble of observations, three-fourths of them platitudinous. No wonder that Mrs. McCormick called him a hard man to interview. "His associates say that he has a twenty-four track mind, and that the signals do not cross; but certainly he jumps from track to track." Sometimes he jumped the track altogether, as when he impulsively said late in the nineteen-twenties that he meant to retire and devote the rest of his life wholly to education.

Close examination of his interviews, however, reveals a hammer forging a well-conceived pattern. When he sat down at the Rouge to discuss happiness, health, antique furniture, railroads, dancing, or the national debt, talk seemed to flow as artlessly as from a loquacious villager—but part of it was artful. Inevitably, a good many strokes on the self-portrait he was so carefully painting revealed traits he would have liked to conceal. The result was complex. It was the portrait of an ingenious, determined, self-willed mechanic with a rural education, a set of firm agrarian prejudices, a belief in old-fashioned simplicities joined with incessant change, a faith in hard work combined with broad leisure and in thrift combined with steady spending for self-betterment, a set of superstitions that would have astonished an Elizabethan crone, a group of suspicions that would have awed a Russian conspirator, a passionate love of invention, and an H. G. Wells confidence in the future. The portrait was of a vulgar puritan, a millionaire ascetic, a belligerent pacifist, and a prophet of the morrow with feet fixed in the past.

Behind his talk often ran a good deal of concentrated thought, and sometimes a deep vein of originality. When he offered opinions on the harmfulness of granulated sugar (its crystals cut blood vessel walls), the mendacity of written history, and the ruinous effect of installment selling on the economy, he spoke with insouciant ignorance. This was not true, however, when he made an observation about the machinery he loved so well: "You can't tell much about a machine until it is old. Then you can see what it has done and how well it did it. It is like an old man." It was not true when he expressed his neo-Franklinesque beliefs upon thrift: "Let us earn our money. . . . But then let us spend it intelligently. Money is made to be spent for improving ourselves and our life." Nor was it true when he expounded his deeply pondered dynamism. His statement that "the only thing permanent in life is change" sounds banal. A greater subtlety, however, lurked in his applications of the idea. When effort, innovation, and struggle died, the man or institution died. "I don't believe in quitting work," he said in 1926. "Happiness is on the road, not in reaching the peak. I am on the road, and I am happy." [13]

Sometimes he was crisply epigrammatic. Discussing credit in the heyday of the Coolidge boom, he remarked: "Debt has become a national industry." Discussing the bull market, he said sententiously: "The only stock I take any stock in is the stock in the stock room. I am sure of this, however: the high-water mark in stocks means that someone will soon reach the low-water mark in pocket." He could be cynical. "The world always has been, is, and will be run by mediocre men." In general, however, he dispensed a serious, homely philosophy of life. A book of aphorisms entitled *Henry Ford Self-Depicted* might be compiled from his interviews:

No one will ever get anywhere in this world unless he becomes a teacher, one who can show others how to do things. Edison and I, in working out our plans, had to teach others to make every piece of machinery we needed.

In Mexico villages fight one another. If we could give every man in those villages an automobile, let him travel from his home town to the other town, and permit him to find out that his neighbors at heart were his friends, rather than his enemies, Mexico would be pacified for all time.

The unfortunate man whose mind is continually bent to the problem of his next meal or the next night's shelter is a materialist perforce. Now, emancipate this man by economic security and the appurtenances of social decency and comfort, and instead of making him more of a materialist you liberate him.

Of course the steady desertion of the farm cannot continue forever. Too many people have believed that Santa Claus lives in the city. They were raising a million dollars to advertise Detroit and bring more people here. I told them the money would be better spent to educate people how to get away from the city.

What we call waste is only surplus, and surplus is only the starting point of new uses.[14]

No unimportant contribution to the Ford legend was made by the company broadcasting station, WWI, which began operations in 1921. It was characteristic of Ford that he chose an amateur, not an expert, to run it. Seeing Fred L. Black in the Highland Park office building one day in the fall of 1919, he accosted the young man: "Say, Fred, what do you know about wireless?" When Black admitted that he knew nothing, Ford promptly told him to learn; and soon WWI was going on the air every Wednesday night with two hours of music and talks.[15] His "page" in the *Dearborn Independent,* which gave birth in 1926 to a book in his name called *Ford Ideals,* also extended the legend.[16]

A small library rapidly grew up about Ford. Beginning in 1916, when a young Western writer, Rose Wilder Lane, sought Detroit for articles on Ford which, first published in a San Francisco newspaper, were reissued as *Henry Ford's Own Story* (1917), the demand for books grew. All were journalistic, nearly all were favorable. Sarah Bushnell's *The Truth About Henry Ford* (1922) has been mentioned. James Martin Miller the same year issued *The Amazing Story of Henry Ford.* The Socialist Allan L. Benson, once candidate for President, enrolled himself among Ford's admirers, and in 1923 gave the world a ragged account of achievements at Highland Park and of Ford's ideas entitled *The New Henry Ford.* Ford finally cut Benson's visits short. Several other authors made themselves something of a nuisance. One was Ralph Waldo Trine, an inspirational writer whose *The Power That Wins,* "an intimate talk with Henry Ford on the inner things of life," came out in 1929. More obnoxious still, from Ford's point of view, was Elbert Hubbard. Invited to Dearborn, he came, wrote an article, and sent Ford a bill for $800.[17]

Somewhat better was William L. Stidger's *Henry Ford—The Man and His Motives* (1923), which contained a fulsome but useful record of talks. Stidger, a Methodist clergyman in Detroit, contributed to truth and myth alike. Much more realistic and refreshing was Charles Merz's *And Then Came Ford* (1929), by one of the ablest journalists of his time, then associate editor of the New York *World.* It may be called the first really detached and objective book about Ford, which strove with success to disentangle fact from legend. And meanwhile, of course, a special place had been taken by Dean Samuel Marquis with his humane, incisive, and revealing *Henry Ford: An Interpretation* (1923).

Dr. Marquis, scornful of journalistic eulogies, essayed a portrait, not a biography, and used the X-ray, not the calcium light. He had known Ford intimately, was an observant man of complete integrity, and possessed marked literary skill. His two hundred pages, while quite fair, offered more material for revising the symbol and exploding the myth than all the other books combined. Explaining that Ford was the most elusive man he had ever known, he tried to analyze both virtues and faults—with the caveat that he had "lights so high and shadows so deep that I cannot get the whole of him in proper focus at one time." A paragraph condensed from the index indicates this characterization:

Ford, Henry, his love of sensations; cleverness; love for the limelight; his altruism; a dreamer; not a gambler; generosity to employees; love of home life; his gospel of work; temperamental and erratic; lacks traits of true greatness; lack of sustained interest; enthusiasm in new enterprises in social justice; his courage and tenacity; dislike for quarrels but a good fighter; complexes; a supernormal perception in certain lines; his courage of his convictions; an affable and democratic man; difficult of access; the isolation of his mind; contributions to social activities of the church; employment for old men and cripples; does not believe in old-age pensions; thinks and acts quickly; normal state that of mental agitation; no wholly satisfactory portrait of; mental and moral qualities of high order; no one really knows; endless conflict in.

No one really knows! An apt subtitle of Dr. Marquis's book would have been, "A Study in Contradictions." One central thesis was that Ford's early idealism had been blunted by certain hardfisted, hardjawed plant executives whom Marquis, borrowing a term from Lloyd George, called scavengers. Another (borne out by other men) was that his remarkable intellectual qualities had never been organized, and his moral traits (including "some of the highest and noblest I have ever known") had never been blended into a unified character. He also noted that Ford's moods seemed to follow changes in physical health:

Today he stands erect, lithe, agile, full of life, happy as a child, and filled with the child spirit of play. Out of his eyes there looks the soul of a genius, a dreamer, an idealist—a soul that is affable, gentle, kindly, and generous to a fault. But tomorrow he may be the opposite. He will have the appearance of a man shrunken by long illness. The shoulders droop, and there is a forward slant to the body when he walks, as when a man is moving forward on his toes. His face is deeply lined. . . . The affable, gentle manner has disappeared. There is a light in the eye that reveals a fire burning within altogether unlike that which burned there yesterday. He has the appearance of a man utterly wearied and exhausted, and yet driven on by a relentless and tireless spirit.

Dr. Marquis's book pained Ford, and the Ford organization made efforts to buy up and suppress the volume, so that it became scarce. It deserved a better fate. One of its best chapters paid warm tribute to the ability, courage, justice, and generosity of Edsel Ford.[18]

No book about Ford, however, had a tithe of the influence of the three volumes which Samuel Crowther wrote with the aid of Ford, Cameron, and Liebold. Selling all over the globe, they vastly expanded the Ford legend. Crowther, a graduate of the University of Pennsylvania, a versatile journalist and something of an economist, was forty-two when *My Life and Work* was published. Its resounding success made *Today and Tomorrow* and *Moving Forward* inevitable. Those who knew Crowther thought highly of his intelligence, honesty, and literary craftsmanship. He also wrote about Ford in numerous magazines. Some of his letters suggest that he could expand an ounce of Ford into a pound of Crowther-Ford—though of course the ounce was vital. When *System* asked him for an article on how Ford overcame the summer slump in 1923, for example, he wrote Liebold: "I could do the interview in about two minutes with Mr. Ford."

It was Crowther who gave Ford's ideas on Muscle Shoals their best form in articles for *Collier's* and other vehicles. He felt a warranted elation over the eager reception of *My Life and Work,* the heavy sales, and the careful reviews. "In England I think every manufacturer has read it," he wrote when he came back from Europe in 1923. Crowther also penned for Ford the radio talk to England which he made in a test transmission on November 26, 1923. Company executives recognized the basic ideas of the Ford-Crowther writings as essentially Henry's, demurring only that Crowther made them seem too fixed; actually Ford was always revising them, always pushing ahead. But of course the literary dress was almost entirely Crowther's.[19]

6.

Ford's associates had to live not with the symbol or legend, but the reality. Their Ford was a protean, wayward, unpredictable company head who for a time improved in knowledge, experience, and grasp with the passing decades, but who steadily became harder, more inflexible, and more capricious. His temper changed for the worse not merely because of the influence of certain associates, and the hard buffets he took, but because of the corrosive effects of autocracy. "Power corrupts"

—Lord Acton's law holds in industry no less than politics. Yet he remained a man of charm, philanthropic instincts, and many inspiring traits; a very complicated human being. We can here illustrate only a few of his main qualities.*

He had an insight which associates recognized as wholly superior to their own. His success was founded on a clear perception of five related facts: that the American people needed cars in millions; that a single durable inexpensive model could meet that demand; that when new technological elements were woven together to create mass production, they could furnish the millions of cheap vehicles; that price reduction meant market expansion; and that high wages meant high buying power. This was as obvious, when demonstrated, as Columbus's art of standing an egg on end. Until then it was so far from clear that Ford had to battle his principal partner and the current manufacturing trend to prove it. A special kind of genius lies in seeing what everybody admits to be obvious—after the exceptional mind thinks of it; and Ford had that genius. It changed the world.

Next to this insight, Ford's most striking gift was unquestionably his peculiar engineering talent. He combined something of Da Vinci's creative quality in mechanics with James Watt's superb practicality. Ford had the faculty of divining almost any mechanism at a glance; he *read* engines. Indeed, W. J. Cameron said that the great engine collections he made in his museum were his historical library. "They were living things to him, those machines. He could almost diagnose the arrangement by touching it. There was a peculiar sympathy between him and a machine." Curious stories of his mechanical genius gained circulation. Rouge men told John Gunther that if six carburetors were laid on a table, identical in aspect but five good, one faulty, Ford could

---

* It would be possible to fill a volume as large as this one with anecdotal material on Ford's personal habits, quirks, and adventures. It would relate how he quoted McGuffey, played the fiddle as badly as Thomas Jefferson, ran for his life when a buck deer treed him at Fair Lane during the rutting season, skated at seventy on the laboratory pond, went for long walks with farmer cronies, tinkered with watches in the shop over his garage, yawned when a literary visitor came to his house to read a manuscript letter by Robert Burns but awoke to delighted life when he understood this visitor to express an interest in old furniture, got President Harding to let him out of the basement door of the White House to avoid reporters, spoke harshly of Grosse Pointe society people as parasites rather than builders, deputed disagreeable measures of discipline to others but then watched their execution with visible enjoyment, helped mix the batter for johnny-cakes in the old oven at the Wayside Inn, and so on. Such material explains how a sense of his charm, originality, and wayward genius permeated the great establishment on the Rouge along with a sense of his prejudices, blunders, cruelties, and constant autocracy. Some of the more significant materials are included in this volume; but anecdotal trivia may be found abundantly in other books, and are not within the scope of this history of the Ford Motor Company.

tell the bad one at a glance; that walking past a brick wall, he could instantly estimate within two per cent the number of bricks it contained. Old associates agreed that, pondering over a piece of machinery, he took special delight in simplifying it—in reducing the parts. The axle shaft and differential gear, for example, had always been two pieces; Ford made them in one, and that became standard practice.[20]

This passion for machinery helps explain his remarkable power of hard, concentrated work. The relaxed air which he wore in public, with his well-advertised recreations in square dancing, collecting Americana, and making trips with Edison and others, concealed from some observers the fact that from boyhood till age he led a singularly intense and laborious life. Knudsen concluded that his greatest single asset was his power of mental absorption. Sorensen, who knew him when he had "nothing but his wonderful energy," has recorded that in his early years he often toiled long after midnight to expand his technical knowledge. At Highland Park and the Rouge his responsibilities were always enormous, but his flair for engineering made much of the work pleasure —particularly his mechanical experimentation.[21]

Study of his daily activities gives us the impression of a quick brain through which moved a steady succession of technological ideas. A helical type of spring band to use in planetary transmission for holding the drum; a new element in the carburetor; a bolder mode of casting the engine block—always he had some ingenious novelty in mind. That side of his mind never rested. "He was up at Harbor Beach one time," writes Liebold, "where he had a summer cottage, and he was coming home with Edsel. Suddenly he said: 'I've got the idea. We're going to put a worm drive on the tractor.'" This, he hoped, would solve the vexatious problem of power transmission to the rear axle.

During his prime he experienced his greatest happiness in a pioneering quest for new technical ideas. Anything was worth trying. We have seen that at one time he was interested in making an improved electric automobile; at another was fascinated by the idea of plastic bodies for cars, an outgrowth of his work with soy beans. (Unfortunately, plastics could not then be machined to the close adjustments required, or endure sharp changes in temperature.) He tried a five-cylinder car. While experimenting with his X-car, he tested a number of bold innovations —a four-wheel drive, a radical new steering gear, the placing of the engine on the rear axle, and so on. Meanwhile, he found recreation in simpler mechanical activities. Once on a trip to northern Michigan his party saw an old traction engine sawing logs, and Ford insisted on stopping. They soon noticed that the operator shut the engine down occasionally to get up steam. "I'm going over there," exclaimed Ford, "and ask him if I can't set that valve." The engineer gladly consented. So Ford fetched some tools, took off the plate, and adjusted the valve. "He was just tickled to death," says C. J. Smith.

His almost infallible grasp of detail and mechanical vision made him swift of action. "You didn't have to tell him much or show him," says Smith. "He'd see things right away, quick." Because details illustrated mechanical principles, each part was alive to him. "He'd show as much interest in taking off one nut as in the whole job." On a trip he might crack jokes, but in the factory or experimental room the mature Ford was all concentrated attention. His memory for facts was uncanny. Once he turned his attention to a slide-valve engine on which another maker held patents. Reflecting that he might wish sometime to build such an engine, he decided to protect his rights by recovering an old slide-valve that, as a humble mechanic, he had put in a Westinghouse steam-engine. He recalled that the engine had been No. 345, and had been shipped to McLean County, Pennsylvania. A searcher found the battered old engine, found a bill of sale which proved that it was No. 345, and found the slide-valve. Brought to Dearborn, it was triumphantly put in the condition in which Ford had known it.

His technological genius was one aspect of a remarkably intuitive mind; he hit on truths rather by divination than ratiocination. Many associates noted what Dean Marquis called a "supernormal perceptive faculty." Marquis termed him a dreamer, with a different view from other men of what was possible or impossible. "I suppose the reason is that men who dream walk by faith, and faith laughs at mountains." He frankly told Carl Sandburg, Fred L. Black, and many others that he worked largely by hunches. Even his understanding of his associates was partly intuitive. He had "a faculty to sense the thought of others," remarked his lifelong friend, George M. Holley. "When I first went to the Ford Motor Company," states W. J. Cameron, "nobody dared to lie to Mr. Ford. He would have *smelled* a lie." Naturally, his intuitions worked badly at times. His reliance on subconscious processes helps explain why he was so unsystematic and erratic. It also helps explain the increasing isolation of his mind after 1920, for in proportion as he believed his instincts infallible, he thought discussion and criticism—the clash of ideas—unnecessary. This isolation "is about as perfect as he can make it," wrote Marquis in 1923. Sorensen believes that from middle age on he had only two really close friends, Sorensen himself, and the head of the British company, Sir Percival (later Lord) Perry. (This view ignores Edison, certainly a close friend, but makes an important point.) [22]

His complex, inconsistent nature lent itself to a Jekyll-and-Hyde interpretation which greatly oversimplified the facts, for he was not two men but a dozen. Yet the tendency to explain him, like such other contradictory personages as Edwin M. Stanton and Woodrow Wilson, by a simple theory of dual personality, is understandable.

Highly modest in most ways, he had an insatiable desire for headlines. Along with an appealing inarticulateness, which kept him from making public speeches (the longest ever recorded was twenty-eight words), he was voluble to trusted writers. He was kindly in most personal relationships; Liebold never heard of his personally discharging a man, Marquis testified that "he hates to say no," and Cameron assures us that he was by instinct always a gentleman. Yet we have seen how he countenanced desk-smashing. He had such simple tastes that when his fortune first grew he lamented that "Mrs. Ford no longer does the cooking," but his mansion was costly, and he had a private railroad car. He was contemptuous of organization, derided cost-accounting and shocked Perry by making a bonfire of forms, yet he integrated a variety of complex undertakings—coal-mining, logging, the making of steel, glass, cloth, leather, cement—with a high talent for organization.

What keys can we find to the puzzle presented by this Dearborn wizard? Perhaps it is a mistake to look for any. Pattern-making is inappropriate to so unpatterned a man. Yet two partial clues may be suggested.

Ford the countryman, the son of farming people, the child of Springwell Township lately wrested from the forest, was projected to leadership of the industrial and urban age. The result was internal conflict. This resulted not only because Ford deplored and revolutionized important aspects of farm life, but because along with some of its virtues he clung to certain of its limitations.

He remained a countryman in his regard for work as a virtue in itself. His cure for most current ills was more work, more striving.

"Anybody looking for a job had Mr. Ford's heart right off," says one lieutenant. True to the frontiersman's instinct, he preferred trial and error to precise planning, and was ready to whittle at anything: tractors, a tri-motored airplane, a weekly journal, a railroad, a model farm in England. He had the farmer's hatred for monopoly and special privilege. He had gained his own leadership without favor and without warring on competitors. His earnest counsel to George Holley to take out no patent on his carburetor, his opening of Ford machines and Ford methods to public view and general use, his battle against Selden, all harmonized with frontier attitudes. When his radio engineers at WWI worked out the first good directional airplane control and gained a patent, he shared it with all. In the spirit of frontier democracy, he believed that an amateur could quickly be made an expert, and proved it—as by turning a sweeper into an efficient metallurgist.

Meanwhile, his early environment laid penalties on the industrialist. Like other untutored men, he had a suspicion of the uncomprehended, a susceptibility to bad counsel, and a tenacious hold on prejudices. His antagonism to Wall Street may have owed something to Populist influences, and to his anxieties in 1920–1922; but surely three fourths of it was distrust of what he did not understand. His hostility to the "international Jew" was also mainly founded on ignorance. Part of it was ideological, but it was the ideology of misinformation, not malice. It is significant that his suspiciousness, which was hardly visible in his first years of success but whch grew marked when he came under fire, was a suspiciousness of men and institutions that would naturally seem alien to most rural people of his youth. Even in religion, his unorthodox wanderings—he leaned to a belief in reincarnation—recalled the loose spawning of sects on the frontier.[23] A few men in the plant who catered to his likes and dislikes gradually gained special influence over him. Sorensen earned his influence by efficient service and in the main used it well; but the same could not be said of Harry Bennett.

Conflict between Ford the countryman and Ford the industrialist offers one clue to his nature; the other is quite different. The dreamer, the man of intuitive mind, is usually an artist; and many vagaries, many contradictions, many triumphs and failures, become comprehensible in Ford if we view him as a man of imaginative and artistic temperament. His detachment, his wry humor, his constant self-dramatization, his ability to see affairs in large terms, and above all his creative zest, all bespeak an artistic bent. He was like Emerson, one author he enjoyed reading, in his combination of the homely and starry. Sandburg, hearing him remark, "Man can do whatever he can imagine," thought the touch of the ridiculous in him just right—"as though all creative, inventive geniuses must expect misunderstanding and in order to live must have a little element of the clown." [24]

Highland Park was perhaps the most artistic factory, in architecture, shining cleanliness, and harmonic arrangement, built in America in its day. Ford, out of a deep instinct, refused to make its power house the usual dark, greasy shed in the rear. Instead, he made it the costliest and handsomest power house in the country, put it on the avenue alongside the office building, installed great plate glass windows to show the machinery, tiled the floors, and kept it as scrubbed and shining as an art museum. His Model T, his tractor, airplane, and truck, might seem ugly to some; to him they had a functional artistry. The Rouge plant possessed a majestic beauty which the painter Charles Sheeler caught. And the aesthetic element was plain in the old dances, old folk songs, old historic buildings, and old machines Ford loved so well.

Above all, he had the artist's desire to remake some part of the world after his own pattern. His gospel on wages and prices; his plan for decentralizing industry to combine it with rural life; his enthusiastic forays into "better" agriculture, recreation, and education; his warm promotion of the Sociological Department for half a dozen years; his combined school and museum at Dearborn; his books—what were they but the artist's effort to impose his vision on life? We may wish he had shown more constancy of purpose, and had kept out of areas where he blundered badly. But he could hardly help himself. He was convinced that society was serving itself badly, and he could assist it. Had Walt Whitman lived on into Ford's time, he might have enjoyed Ford's excursions with Burroughs. The three men could be called unaesthetic, but all were artists in the energy of their vision and the bigness of their style.

Ford's saddest creative failure lay in his relationship with his son, to whom he gave intense devotion and total incomprehension. Edsel was a man of the finest qualities, upright, idealistic, public-spirited, and highly intelligent. The father's mistaken belief that he lacked toughness and drive led to sadism and tragedy. "He tried to remake Edsel in his own image," says Sorensen—and whether this is true or not, he certainly acted with a tragic lack of insight or sympathy.[25]

Ford should have tried to mould the future by means of a partnership. Edsel had virtues all his own which would splendidly have supplemented the father's gifts. He was more just and considerate than Henry, so that many of the factory executives felt a warm affection for him. He had a finer spirit—"the spirit that guides private wealth in channels that make for social and industrial betterment," wrote Marquis. Some of his father's acts, such as the anti-Jewish campaign, grieved him. Henry Ford's efforts to remake the son included not only nominal grants of authority followed by abrupt withdrawals of it, but also harsh treatment of men like the able Clarence W. Avery, who, coming close to Edsel, aroused Ford's jealousy. "I do think," declares Laurence Sheldrick, "the old man set Sorensen against Edsel a great many times deliberately. Edsel was aware of this, and I think it broke his heart." [26] Sorensen declares that he set Bennett against his son, and that Sorensen was caught between the two.

Henry Ford's greatest single error was that he did not let his son take over responsibilities as fast as he was able to assume them, and become a real partner in building the company. Had he done so, its outlook in 1933 would have been much brighter. But Ford, like other temperamental creators, worked alone.

7.

Like other autocrats, moreover, Ford could not bear to surrender power. Since 1919 he had been one of the last great despots of the industrial world, his dictatorial sway backed by complete ownership and large financial reserves. The decisions of the Ford Motor Company were as much his personal fiat as Abdul Hamid's had been the decisions of oldtime Turkey. He ran one of the two or three greatest manufacturing enterprises in modern history as absolutely as if it had been a medieval principality. When Mussolini rose to power, writers instinctively compared the two: each a dictator, each professing humanitarian objectives, each selfishly ambitious, each responsible for so much that was good and so much bad that a balance sheet was difficult. When Ford said, "There's too much tradition in all human activity, too much respect for mere precedent; if it stands in the way of real progress it must be broken down," he was talking like Mussolini. When he fixed wages and hours, ordered a two million dollar coke plant built and then torn down, decided to keep $300,000,000 cash on hand, and had high officers dismissed at his nod, he was behaving on the Rouge much as Mussolini did on the Tiber.[27]

Happily, the Ford Motor Company was far greater than its chief author. That complex and powerful corporation represented a pooling of the energies and brains of countless men. Into it had gone the devotion of superior spirits—Avery, the farsighted exponent of mass production; Harold Wills, the gifted designer; Norval A. Hawkins, the brilliant sales manager; James Couzens, the ironwilled, public-spirited business organizer; Ernest Kanzler, of versatile talents; the two Lelands, maker of the Lincoln car; and many more. Memorable contributions to its growth had come from Percival Perry, strongest of its overseas servants; from John R. Lee, expert in labor relations; from Sorensen and Martin, production heads; from Klann, Liebold, and others. Into it had gone the sweat and strain of countless laborers, Negroes, Poles, Germans, Italians, and Southern mountaineer stock; the best efforts of thousands of foremen and straw bosses. "We'll build this as well as we know how, and if we don't use it somebody will," Ford had said. "Anything that is good enough will be used."

NOTES

APPENDICES

BIBLIOGRAPHICAL NOTE

NOTES

All reminiscences cited in the following notes, unless otherwise designated, are in the Oral History files of the Ford Archives, Dearborn, Michigan; and all references to Fair Lane Papers (Accession 1 in Ford Archives), and to numbered accessions and boxes (e.g. Acc. 260, Box 4) are to materials in these archives.

CHAPTER I
Scene and Actors, 1915 (*Pages 1–25*)

1. Frank Morton Todd, *The Story of the Exposition* (New York, 1921), IV, 247; *Ford Times,* VII, July, 1915, 1; Frank Vivian, *Reminiscences.* As described by Horace L. Arnold and Fay L. Faurote, *Ford Methods and the Ford Shops* (New York, 1915), the moving assembly was practically a complete process in April, 1914, but the assembled chassis was run out of the factory and the body, coming down a chute on John R St., then added. The completely integrated assembly in which the body was installed on the assembly line apparently was perfected late in 1914.

2. Ira E. Bennett, *History of the Panama Canal* (Washington, 1915), 181–182. W. Leon Pepperman, *Who Built the Panama Canal?* (New York, 1915), 355, states that the American ss. *Pleiades,* Aug. 16, was the first vessel to carry a cargo through the canal, proceeding from the Pacific to the Atlantic.

3. N.Y. *Herald,* Jan. 24, 26, 1915.

4. *The Growth of American Economy* (New York, 1946), ed. Harold E. Williamson, Chap. 22 (Samuel Rezneck), 501–504; Oscar T. Barck, Jr. and Nelson M. Blake, *Since 1900* (New York, 1952), 10.

5. Arnold Bennett, *Your United States* (New York, 1912) and André Siegfried, *America Comes of Age* (New York, 1927). The quotation is from Siegfried, 347–348.

6. *Recent Economic Changes in the United States* (New York, 1929) I, 50; Leland R. Robinson, *An Introduction to Modern Economics* (Phila., 1951), 467.

7. *Recent Economic Changes in the United States,* I, 59; Hugh Dolnar (Horace L. Arnold), "Bicycle Tools," *American Machinist,* XVIII, Oct. 3, 1895, 781; "The Automobile and Machine Tools," *American Machinist,* LIX, Jan. 23, 1916, 261; *The Growth of American Economy,* Chap. 22 (Samuel Rezneck), 513. Rezneck notes that mass production demanded control of parts and coordination of activities, and adds: "In supplying that control and coordination the automobile industry became particularly important in the evolution of mass production; its history in fact epitomizes the triumph of mass production in the United States."

8. *Automobile Topics,* XXXV, Jan. 16, 1915, 827; Alfred L. Reeves, "It's a Billion Dollar Industry," *Automobile Topics,* XLIV, Jan. 6, 1917, 954. Reeves gives the total number of dealers as 30,000; *Automotive Industries,* LVII, Feb. 18, 1918, puts Ford dealers at 6910 and others at 21,850, a total of 28,760. The total for 1915 would naturally be somewhat less than either of these later estimates.

9. Darwin S. Hatch, "Production the Genie of 1916," *Motor Age,* XXVIII, Dec. 20, 1915, 7; *Automobile Topics,* XXXVI, Jan. 2, 1915, 573–575. XXXVII, May 8, 1915, 1062a, and XLII, July 8, 1916, 867 and July 22, 1916, 1064; LI, Sept. 21, 1918, 649; "Engineers in Session," *Automobile Topics,* XXXVI, Jan. 9, 1915, 744.

10. *Ford Times,* VIII, Oct., 1914, 13; April, 1915, 310–311; June, 1915, 387, and IX, Nov., 1915, 150; Branch Audit Reports, Acc. 260, Box 4.

11. Henry Ford in Collaboration with Samuel Crowther, *My Life and Work* (Garden City, N.Y., 1923), 51, hereafter cited as *My Life and Work;* Directors' Minutes, Ford Motor Co., Ford Archives, July 14, Aug. 24, and Sept. 7, 1906, hereafter cited as Directors' Minutes, or, for meetings of stockholders, Stockholders' Minutes. The stockholders were Henry Ford (585 shares), James Couzens (110, including one share held for his sister), Gray Estate (104), David Gray (1), John F. Dodge (50), Horace E. Dodge (50), J. W. Anderson (50), and H. H. Rackham (50). For dividends see Allan Nevins, with the Collaboration of Frank Ernest Hill, *Ford: the Times, the Man, the Company* (New York, 1954), Appendix VIII, 649, hereafter cited as *Ford: the Times, the Man, the Company.* As to plant expenditures, these had been chiefly for land, construction, and equipment at Highland Park. Appendices II, V, and VI in the same volume give dividends, price, and production figures.

12. *Ibid.,* chaps. XI–XXI: these trace the roles of Ford, Couzens, and the Dodges in earlier company affairs.

13. "Whose Brains?", *Pipp's Weekly,* IV, Jan. 19, 1924, 3–4.

14. Max F. Wollering, *Reminiscences.* For other references to the Ford-Wills relationship, see notes, Chap. VI, present volume.

15. William N. Mayo, R. T. Walker, Joseph Galamb, Eugene J. Farkas, John Wandersee, Fred L. Black, H. L. Maher, and J. L. McCloud, in their reminiscences. William N. Mayo is the son of William B. Mayo.

16. Samuel S. Marquis, *Henry Ford: An Interpretation* (Boston, 1923), 136, 147, 148, hereafter cited as Marquis, *Henry Ford.* For Marquis's work with Lee, see S. S. Marquis Papers, Ford Archives.

17. Biography of Edsel Ford (mimeographed), Acc. 23, Box 3; undated clipping from E. C. Clinkscales, Columbia, Mo., Ford dealer, Fair Lane Papers, Box 27; *Ford Times,* IX, Oct., 1915, 117–123 (Edsel's transcontinental trip).

18. J. M. Waggoner, Alex Lumsden, Frank Hadas, Frank C. Riecks, and McCloud, in their reminiscences; *Ford: the Times, the Man, the Company,* 267, 366.

19. *Ibid.,* 460–461; Norman Beasley, *Knudsen* (New York, 1947), 1–32, 52–80.

20. William C. Klann, Hadas, A. M. Wibel, Theodore F. Gehle, Maher, and others in their reminiscences; for further details on Hawkins and Brownell, see *Ford: the Times, the Man, the Company.*

21. *My Life and Work,* 43; Liebold, *Reminiscences; Ford Times,* VIII, June, 1915, 387.

22. C. J. Smith, Logan Miller, and Farkas in their reminiscences.

23. Fair Lane Papers, Box 97; Cork *Examiner,* March 19, 1917 (clipping in Acc. 44, Box 14); *Ford Times,* IX, Feb., 1916, 295. Burroughs wrote a 17-page typescript account of the 1918 vacation trip, from which the description in the text is taken. For an account of the camping trips, see Chap. XIX.

24. Liebold, *Reminiscences; Ford Times,* IX, Dec., 1915, 213; N.Y. *Herald,* Jan. 23, 1915.

25. Correspondence, Fair Lane Papers, Boxes 97, 127, 134, 135, 141.

26. Fair Lane Fact Sheet, Ford Archives; Acc. 23, Box 31 (Fair Lane in Ireland); Mary Louise Gregory Brand, *Reminiscences.* Fair Lane in Ireland, to judge from references in letters, seems to have been a street in the city of Cork, but was also referred to as a neighborhood.

27. *My Life and Work,* 25, 26, 199; Margaret Ford Ruddiman, Written Memoir, Ford Archives, V, 3 (on Ford's work with steam engines); Galamb, Farkas, Richard Kroll, and Liebold, in their reminiscences.

28. Detroit *Journal,* June 17, 19, 1915.

29. For details concerning the Dodge Company and its plants, see Chapter IV.

30. *Tribune* Suit Record, 6637–6638 (for full citation, see Chap. V). Dr. Johannes H. M. A. Tiling deposed on Nov. 13, 1918, that on May 7, 1915, Ford came with John Burroughs to his office, and that when Tiling told them that the *Lusitania* had been lost, Ford made the remark quoted. In the same record, 589–590, Ford is quoted as to the burning of his plant.

31. Detroit *Free Press,* Aug. 22, 1915; Liebold, *Reminiscences* (on Delavigne).

32. *Pipp's Weekly,* as cited in Note 13, above; Theodore F. McManus and Norman Beasley, *Men, Money, and Motors* (New York, 1929), 169—hereafter cited as *Men, Money, and Motors.* The two accounts agree in the main; the text uses details from both.

33. *Pipp's Weekly, op. cit.;* William A. Simonds, *Henry Ford: His Life, His Work, His Genius* (Indianapolis, 1943), 148–149—hereafter cited as Simonds, *Henry Ford;* Directors' Minutes, Oct. 13, 1915.

34. Dodge Suit Record, I, 419 (Horace Dodge's letter) and 509–510. For form of citation to Dodge Suit, see Chap. IV, Note 6.

CHAPTER II

Peace Crusade *(Pages 26-54)*

1. Louis P. Lochner, *Henry Ford: America's Don Quixote* (New York, 1925), 13—hereafter cited as Lochner, *Henry Ford;* John Bainbridge and Russell Maloney, "The Innocent Voyage" (in series: "Where Are They Now?"), *New Yorker,* March 9, 1940, 23 ff; Pamphlet published by International Committee for World Peace Award to Rosika Schwimmer, Fair Lane Papers, Box 53; Marie Louise Degen, *The History of the Women's Peace Party,* in Johns Hopkins Studies in Historical and Political Science (Baltimore, 1939), 28 ff. Lochner's career prior to his association with Ford is outlined in the booklet: "Henry Ford's Peace Expedition: Who's Who," Dec., 1915. This was distributed on the *Oscar II* after its sailing on Dec. 4, 1915.

2. Bainbridge and Maloney, *op. cit.;* Degen, *op. cit.,* 85; Lochner, *Henry Ford,* 8–12. Schwimmer proposed the resolution which committed the Congress to its continuous mediation policy; it was seconded by Julia Grace Wales. Schwimmer claimed to have been the first to propose mediation by neutrals, and Degen, 46, concedes that she was, but adds that the "details of the plan" were developed by Miss Wales, who published a widely circulated pamphlet about it, and was generally credited with being the originator.

3. Lochner, *Henry Ford,* Chaps. V, VI (Dearborn events and first days in New York), and VII (conference with Wilson); N.Y. *World,* Nov. 23, 1915; Jane Addams, *Peace and Bread in Time of War* (New York, 1922), 34. "I was alarmed," writes Miss Addams of the peace ship proposal, but states that Ford argued the more publicity the better.

4. Oswald Garrison Villard, *Fighting Years* (New York, 1939), 302–305; Lochner, *Henry Ford,* 26–28; N.Y. *Evening Post,* Nov. 24, 1915; N.Y. *World, Tribune, N.Y. Times,* Nov. 25. The *Times* alone states that Miss Addams and Miss Tarbell were present.

5. N.Y. *Tribune,* Nov. 25, 1915; N.Y. *Evening Post,* Nov. 26; N.Y. *Times, World,* Nov. 27; N.Y. *Herald,* Nov. 28. The *Herald* quotes the Hartford *Courant* and the Balt. *Sun.*

6. *The Romance of the Automobile Industry* (New York, 1916), James Doolittle, ed., 73.

7. Margaret Ford Ruddiman, *Reminiscences;* Ann Hood, *The Boy Henry Ford,* unpublished MS., Ford Archives; McGuffey's *New Fourth Eclectic Reader,* 113–114, 115–117; *Fifth Reader,* 229; *Sixth Reader,* 336; all reprints of Wilson, Hinkle & Co. edition, 1857; Harvey C. Minnich, *William Holmes McGuffey and His Readers* (Chicago, 1936), 171 (McGuffey's patriotism).

8. Merle Curti, *Peace or War: the American Struggle, 1636–1936* (New York, 1936), 23–27; 44; A. C. F. Beales, *The History of Peace* (New York, 1931), 231–242.

9. *Ibid.,* 244, 249 ff.; Julius Moritzen, *The Peace Movement in America* (New York, 1912), vi, 3–9. Jane Addams, *Newer Ideals for Peace* (New York, 1906), phrased the conviction that the forces of a new morality would "in the end, quite as a natural process, do away with war." One of the authors, at Stanford University when David Starr Jordan and E. H. Krehbiel were offering a course in "International Conciliation," participated in discussions as to the probable extinction of armed conflict.

10. Lochner, *Henry Ford,* 29–35. There may have been 50 workers on the business staff prior to sailing; on shipboard the number may be placed at 23. See list in a collection of papers, clippings, and photographs assembled by Mary Alden Hopkins, and in Special Collections Department, Columbia University Library, and hereafter cited as Hopkins Papers. A text of the tele-

gram of invitation commonly used may be found in Lochner, 31. The Hopkins Papers contain a briefer form signed by Katherine Leckie.

11. Lochner, *Henry Ford*, 41–44; Degen, *History of the Women's Peace Party*, 134; *N.Y. Times*, Nov. 27, 1915. The *Times* reports that Ford first stated "that he had never made a speech and that this was the first time he had ever faced a public audience." He went on, "I simply want to ask you to remember the slogan, 'Out of the trenches before Christmas, never to go back,' and I thank you for your attention." Miss Degen gives the same words.

12. *N.Y. Tribune*, Nov. 29, Dec. 2, 3, 1915; Lochner, *Henry Ford*, 32; *Detroit Saturday Night*, IX, Dec. 4, 1915; Joseph Rappaport, *Hands Across the Sea; Jewish Immigrants and World War I* (typescript Ph.D. thesis), 162–163. As to students, Ford told Lochner: "I want fellows with sand, who'll even quit their college to go on the peace voyage." From 18 to 25 students sailed on the *Oscar II*; enough followed on the *Frederick VIII* to bring the total on a January list to 36. (Hopkins Papers.) Rappaport shows that the radical Jews were anti-war in principle, but also approved Ford's project because it promised a negotiated peace which presumably would leave Germany strong. They were pro-German because they regarded Germany as enlightened in attitude toward the Jews, while Russia, the sponsor of pogroms, typified barbarism.

13. Fair Lane Papers, Box 53; Pamphlet: "Henry Ford's Peace Expedition: Who's Who," Dec. 1915, Hopkins Papers; *ibid.*, passenger list; *N.Y. Tribune*, Dec. 1, 2, 1915; Acc. 62, Box 40 (Bryan's letters); Lochner, *Henry Ford*, 38. Bryan in writing to Ford, offered to speak on peace in Detroit without fee, paying his own expenses. Miss Addams discusses her illness, which was both serious and protracted, in *Peace and Bread in Time of War*. Ford returned from Detroit on the night of the 30th, arriving in New York on December 1.

14. *Reminiscences*, Roger Marquis and Barbara Marquis Carritte (Marquis's son and daughter); *N.Y. Herald*, Dec. 5, 1915. Burroughs, who on this occasion may not have voiced his disapproval of the peace ship, later quoted Ford with approval on the 1918 vacation trip about the necessity for winning the war, adding: "His unfortunate Peace Ship expedition did more credit to his big heart than to his judgment." (Fair Lane Papers, Box 97.)

15. *N.Y. Evening Post*, Dec. 4, 1915; Lochner, *Henry Ford*, 48; *N.Y. Herald*, Dec. 5, 1915; Phila. *Public Ledger*, Dec. 7, 1915.

16. *N.Y. World*, Dec. 5, 1915 (description of crowd); Lochner, *Henry Ford*, 49–50.

17. Hopkins Papers; Irving Caesar, "How I Stopped World War I," unpublished magazine article, Ford Archives. Caesar, a personable and able youth engaged by Lochner and Schwimmer as a clerical assistant, also covered the cruise in his *Reminiscences*. He later became a song writer of reputation. Unfortunately, lack of space forbids extensive use of his lively and often spicy accounts of the cruise.

18. William C. Bullitt, Phila. *Public Ledger*, Jan. 9, 1916; MS.: "The Ship of Fools," Hopkins Papers; Lochner, *Henry Ford*, 70, 75.

19. The best account of the resolutions dispute is Bullitt's, Phila. *Public Ledger*, Jan 6, 1916 (dispatch of Dec. 10, 1915). See also his Jan. 8 article (dispatch of Dec. 9). Theodore Pockman, *N.Y. Tribune*, Jan. 9, 1915, also deals with the dispute, as do Bainbridge and Maloney, *op. cit.*, Mary Alden Hopkins, Hopkins Papers; Lochner, *Henry Ford*, 70–75, and Florence L. Lattimore, "Jitney Diplomacy," *Survey*, XXXV, Feb. 12, 1916, 587.

20. Bullitt, Phila. *Public Ledger*, Jan 8, Jan. 31, 1916; Mary Alden Hopkins, Hopkins Papers; Lochner, *Henry Ford*, 68, 77.

21. Bullitt, Phila. *Public Ledger*, Dec. 23, 1915, Jan. 9, 1916; Hopkins, MS. article, "The Ford Peace Expedition in Scandinavia," Hopkins Papers; letter, Plantiff to Henry Ford, Jan. 11, 1916, Acc. 66, Box 1; Lochner, *Henry Ford*, 80, 84.

22. Lochner, *Henry Ford*, 85–92; *Reminiscences*, Roger Marquis and Barbara Marquis Carritte.

23. *N.Y. Tribune*, Dec. 24, 1915; Fair Lane Papers, Box 53 (Plantiff's statement); Bullitt, Phila. *Pub. Ledger*, Dec. 25, 1915, Jan. 10, 1916; Lochner, *Henry Ford*, 91; *N.Y. Times*, *N.Y. Tribune*, Jan. 3, 1916.

24. Bullitt, Phila. *Public Ledger*, Jan. 24, 1916; Lochner, *Henry Ford*, 93–96; 97–99; Hopkins, untitled MS. article, Hopkins Papers; letter of Anti-Oorlag Raad to Henry Ford, Feb. 5, 1916, Fair Lane Papers, Box 53.

25. Plantiff in The Hague to Henry Ford, Jan. 11, 1916, Acc. 66, Box 1; Aked to Ford, Fair Lane Papers, Box 53. For Dutch attitude, see Note 24.

26. Acc. 66, Box 1; B. W. Huebsch, *Reminiscences*, Special Collections, Columbia University Library; Lochner, *Henry Ford*, Appendix III.

27. Bullitt, Phila. *Public Ledger*, Feb. 1, 1916; Lochner, *Henry Ford*, 113–116, 131–137; Plantiff in The Hague to Henry Ford, Jan. 11, 1916, Acc. 66, Box 1; N.Y. *Tribune*, Jan. 30, 31, 1916; Florence L. Lattimore, as cited in Note 19.

28. Lochner, *Henry Ford*, 65–69; letters, Aked in Stockholm to Ford, Feb. 5, 13, 1916, Acc. 53, Box 1; Irving Caesar, *Reminiscences* (Caesar was Schwimmer's "agent"); Liebold, *Reminiscences*.

29. Lochner, *Henry Ford*, 137–153, 154 ff., 237–240.

30. N.Y. *Evening Post*, Feb. 22, April 28, 1916; Lochner, *Henry Ford*, 179–185, 207–224; cable, Liebold to Ada Clark, The Hague, Feb. 7, 1917, Acc. 62, Box 19; Liebold, *Reminiscences*.

31. For example, Lochner's persistent pleas for a fair settlement with Emily Greene Balch. Miss Balch asked pay for a substitute she had employed to take her place while she acted as delegate. Correspondence in Acc. 62, Box 26, shows that Lochner did all in his power on her behalf, but Miss Balch recently stated to Mrs. John A. Randall, Jr., her biographer, that she never received the money.

32. Mark Sullivan, *Our Times: Over Here: 1914–1918*, V (New York, 1933) 182–183; Elmer Davis, *Reminiscences*, Columbia University Library; Walter Millis, *Road to War, America, 1914–1917* (Boston, 1935), 243; Curti, *op. cit.*, 245; Lochner, *Henry Ford*, 159–160; William L. Stidger, *Henry Ford: the Man and His Motives* (New York, 1923), 25, hereafter cited as Stidger, *Henry Ford*. In *My Life and Work*, 245, Ford gives a statement similar to what Stidger quotes, but longer. Millis, while blaming the press, expresses the opinion, 245, that "its [the peace ship's] actual effect was to cloud the whole neutral peace movement with an imbecile buffoonery."

33. Liebold, *Reminiscences*; "Whose Brains?" *Pipp's Weekly*, IV, Jan. 19, 1924, 4.

CHAPTER III
Producing for War (*Pages 55–85*)

1. Fair Lane Papers, Box 53 (Balch telegram); Acc. 23, Box 4 (Cragin); Lochner, *Henry Ford*, 214, 220; N.Y. *Herald*, Feb. 6, 1917.

2. Lochner, *Henry Ford*, 225; N.Y. *Herald*, April 18, 1917. Ford's statement appears in a dispatch from Detroit about producing tractors for England.

3. *My Life and Work*, 245, 246; N.Y. *Herald*, April 3, 1917; N.Y. *Tribune*, April 3, 7 (Kirchwey and Bryan). Miss Balch and Jordan, as members of a peace delegation, left New York for Washington April 2. Failing to procure an interview with Wilson, Jordan said: "Well, if it's war we're all in for it."

4. McManus and Beasley, *Men, Money, and Motors* (Detroit reporter); N.Y. *Herald*, April 30, 1917 (Nova Scotia statement); *Scientific American*, CXVI, Feb. 24, 1917, 196 (submarine); N.Y. *Tribune*, Nov. 13, 1915 (quoting Admiral Grant); *Detroit Saturday Night*, CXVI, Feb. 24, 1917, 13.

5. Acc. 62, Box 95 (Cork site); Acc. 6, Box 260 (Perry's cable to Edsel); Acc. 62, Box 519 (other cables); C. J. Smith, Liebold, *Reminiscences* (on trip to England).

6. W. F. Bradley, "Ford Tractor Makes French Debut," *Motor Age*, XXXI, May 17, 1917, 29–31 (lists chief models); "46 Makers to Show Farm Tractors," *Automobile Topics*, Aug. 18, 1917, 143 (Fremont, Neb., exhibition); L. W. Ellis, "Progress in Small Farm Tractors," *Scientific American*, CXII, April 3, 1915, 306–308; Victor W. Page, "Modern Agricultural Designs," *ibid.*, CXV, July 29, 1916, 100–101 (growth of tractor); Acc. 62, Box 56 (Yerkes correspondence); *Ford Times*, IX, Nov., 1915, 187; Henry Ford Office Files, Acc. 2, Box 31; *Automobile Topics*, XLIII, Aug. 12, 19, 1916; *Motor Age*, XXXII, Aug. 23, 1917, 12.

7. *Automobile Topics*, XLVII, Aug. 18, 1917, 143; J. Edward Schipper, "Ford Tractor Ready to Help the Farmer," *Motor Age*, XXXII, Aug. 23, 1917, 26–28; Articles of Association, and Minute Book, Henry Ford & Co., Ford Archives. Schipper's illustrated article contains the best contemporary description of the Ford tractor.

8. Perry to Edsel Ford, May 8, 1917, Acc. 44, Box 14 (Perry's resignation); W. F. Bradley, cited in Note 6 above; *Westminster Gazette*, May 22, 1917; Liebold, *Reminiscences;* P. Hanson, Director General Munitions Contracts, to Henry Ford, Acc. 62, Box 51; Robert H. Larson, "Dearborn in the First World War," *Michigan Historical Magazine*, XXVII, No. 2, Spring, 1943, 302–316; Kroll and Charles Voorhess, *Reminiscences* (tractor plant). Bradley reports that a group of British manufacturers offered to produce 10,000 tractors. However, the British press was on the whole favorable to Ford. As to production, Larson says that in sixty days after the signing of the contract, tractors "were being shipped," and Schipper, Note 7 above, says that in August the Fordson was "ready for production," but both doubtless echo optimistic press notices of the day. See Note 10 for production figures.

9. Northcliffe to Ford, Oct. 19, 1917, Acc. 6, Box 34; *Detroit Saturday Night, XI,* Nov. 24, 1917 (reprint Northcliffe's article).

10. Fordson Salesfax, Acc. 179, Box 3; *Motor Age*, XXXIII, Feb. 14, 1918, 12; XXIV, July 4, 1918, 17; H. C. B. Underdown to Ford Motor Co., Feb. 21, 1919, Acc. 6, Box 260; "An 85-Tractors-a-Day Plant," *Motor Age*, XXXIII, April 11, 1918, 26–27. Underdown was director of the Agricultural Machinery Department, Ministry of Munitions of War.

11. Interview of authors with Lord Perry, Nassau, March 28, 1952; Acc. 62, Box 8 (Government inquiry about ambulances); *Ford Times,* VIII, June, 1915, 413 ("The Fords Behind the Firing Line"); N.Y. *Herald,* June 25, 1916; Brochure issued in England by Perry defending Ford, 1917, Acc. 44, Box 14.

12. *Ford Man*, III, June 17, 1917, 1; Liebold, Galamb, *Reminiscences*.

13. Fact Sheet on Ford Motor Co. War Work, Dec. 17, 1917, Acc. 572, Box 26; Fair Lane Papers, Box 125 (cables about airplanes); Joe Toye, "Ford Says We Can Lick Germans by Airplanes Built for 25 Cents a Lb.," Boston *Herald*, Oct. 7, 1917.

14. Isaac F. Marcosson, *Colonel Deeds, Industrial Builder* (New York, 1947), 237–247; Interview authors with Harold H. Emmons, Detroit, June 8, 1955; Hughes Report (See P. 14, n.).

15. Marcosson, Emmons, *op. cit.;* "Summary of War Activities of the Ford Motor Company," Sept. 27, 1918, summary of Dec. 17, 1917, and Report: "When the Ford Motor Company Espoused the Liberty Motor," Nov. 13, 1918, all Acc. 572, Box 26. The Sept., 1918 Summary states that the Signal Corps discussed the building of Liberties with the company in July, 1917; the Dec. 17, 1917 report notes "Airplane Cylinder Job," with a first request on Aug. 7, 1917, and 5 cylinders shipped Sept. 27, 1917; The Report of Nov. 13, 1918 states categorically that the cylinders were first made, and that a contract for engines followed.

16. Report of Nov. 13, 1918, *op. cit.;* Hughes Report, *op. cit.;* Emmons interview, *op. cit.*

17. "Summary of War Activities," Sept. 27, 1918, and Report, Nov. 13, 1918, *op. cit.;* Col. G. W. Mixter and Lt. H. H. Emmons, *United States Army Aircraft Production* (Washington, 1919), 22 (bearings); Liebold to John D. Ryan, Bureau of Aircraft Production, July 27, 1918, Acc. 62, Box 18 (bearings); Memorandum, Carl Emde to Edsel Ford, Acc. 6, Box 36 (Liberty production); Klann, Farkas, Galamb, and Kroll, reminiscences (detail of Liberty production); Summary of Ford Motor Co. War Activities, Oct. 31, 1921, Acc. 572, Box 26 (cost of Liberty contract); correspondence, J. Gilmore Fletcher of Aircraft Procurement Division and John R. Lee, Ford Motor Co., Oct. 17, 1918, Acc. 572, Box 26 (additional order for 7000 Liberty engines).

18. See Chap. IV, Notes 6 and 19.

19. Liebold, *Reminiscences;* N.Y. *Tribune,* Nov. 17, 1917 (Ford on Shipping Board); "Great Submarine-Chaser Factory Produces 'Eagles' by Indoor Shipbuilding System," *Engineering News-Record*, LXXXI, Oct. 17, 1918, 698–702 (on design); Secretary of Navy to Henry Ford, Dec. 24, 1917, Acc. 572, Box 26 (progress in patrol boat design).

20. Liebold, *Reminiscences;* Correspondence, Henry Ford Office Files, Acc. 62, Box 106; Production Records, Acc. 38, Box 42 (contract).

21. *Engineering News-Record,* as cited above in Note 19; Beasley, *Knudsen,* 86; *Ford Man,* II, May 17, 1918, 1.

22. Telegrams, Acc. 62, Box 106; Beasley, *Knudsen,* 85–87; Charles Lundberg, "Manufacturing Eagles at Ford Shipyard," *Iron Age,* CII, Sept. 19, 1918, 679–684; *Ford Man,* II, July 17, 1918, 1.

23. Letter, Charles C. West, Superintending Constructor for Navy at Ford Motor Co. to company, Sept. 9, 1918, Acc. 6, Box 34; Memorandum, Whitford Drake, Superintending Constructor at Ford Motor Co. to Bureau of Steam Engineering and Bureau of Construction and Repair, May 29, 1918, in Production Records, Acc. 38, Box 42; Frank Riecks, *Reminiscences; Ford Man,* III, Oct. 3, 1919 and Liebold, *Reminiscences* (Eagles on Lakes St. Clair and Erie).

24. Tribune Suit Record, 5419 (Edsel Ford, July 11, 1919); Folder, "Eagle Boats and Rouge Shipyard," photographs and records, Ford Archives; Josephus Daniels to Ford Motor Co., May 18, 1918, Acc. 62, Box 6; *Detroit Saturday Night,* XIII, Jan. 11, 1919, 3; Charles C. West, letter of Dec. 30, 1918, Acc. 6, Box 34; Ford Motor Co. to Navy Construction Board, July 21, 1920, Acc. 33, Box 94; Table of Eagle Boat Completions, Acc. 572, Box 26; *Ford Man,* III, Feb. 17, 1919, 4; May 3, 1. Edsel Ford estimated the maximum number of employees on Eagle boats at 8000; work records for September 30, 1918, the final figure available, shows 7930 men at work. Employees were transported to and from work by fleets of buses. As to Eagle boats completed, the sources above indicate that seven boats had been completed by mid-November, and —the company's statement to the Board—two delivered by Armistice Day. The Table says that seven had been "accepted" by Nov 24, 1918.

25. *Detroit Saturday Night,* XIII, Jan. 11, 1919, reprinting material from issues of *Daily Iron Trade and Metal Market Report* of Dec. 26, 27, 1918; excerpts from hearings, Acc. 23, Box 4; Tribune Suit Record, 5525–5526 (Edsel Ford, July 14, 1919); Ford Motor Co. to Navy Construction Board, as cited in Note 24.

26. *Ford Man,* III, Dec. 3, 1919, 1; West to Ford Motor Co., Dec. 30, 1918, Acc. 6, Box 34; Letter of Commander, Eagle 1 (copy), Acc. 6, Box 258; *ibid.,* letter T. Roosevelt (Theodore Roosevelt, Jr.) for U.S. Navy to Ford Motor Co., April 3, 1924; Tribune Suit Record, 5419 (Edsel Ford, July 11, 1919, on costs); Summary of War Activities, 1921, *op. cit.* (also on costs). Roosevelt states that Eagles 1, 2, and 3 went "on a cruise to northern Russia" in April, 1919, and that "the ships underwent some severe weather and on the whole withstood it well, although they were very uncomfortable at sea." Edsel set costs at about $50,000,000; the Summary sets figure cited in text.

27. *Ford Man,* III, June 17, 1919, 1; Summaries of war activities, Sept. 27, 1918 and Oct. 31, 1921, *op. cit.;* Tribune Suit Record. 4515–5416 (Edsel Ford, July 11, 1919); Philip E. Haglund, *Reminiscences* (armor plate); Auditing Records, Acc. 33, Box 94 (contracts for war materials). The *Ford Man* lists "1,000.000 worth of work on special devices for the British Navy" as among Ford war accomplishments.

28. N.Y. *Herald,* March 25, 1918; Bricker, Galamb, Farkas, reminiscences; Tribune Suit Record, 5416, 5467–5468 (Edsel Ford, July 11, 1919); correspondence and memoranda, Acc. 33, Box 93.

29. Daily Car Reports, Acc. 6, Box 34; Acc. 62, Box 8; Tribune Suit Record, 5595–5597 (Edsel Ford, July 14, 1919).

30. G. S. Anderson, assistant secretary Henry Ford to John E. Cox of Kalamazoo, Mich., Sept. 10, 1918, Acc. 62, Box 61; *N.Y. Times* Sept. 8, 1918; Tribune Suit Record, 6628–6629; 6632–6633 (Henry Ford, July 23, 1919); R. J. Pearse to Edsel Ford, Oct. 7, 1917, and Edsel to Pearse, Oct. 20, 1917, Acc. 6, Box 34; "Facts About Edsel Ford," *Pipp's Weekly,* I, May 15, 1920, 6–8.

31. Liebold, *Reminiscences;* Tribune Suit Record, 5436–5450 (Edsel Ford, July 11, 1919); Hughes Report, *op. cit.,* 909; Simonds, *Henry Ford,* 174–178; Farkas, Klann, in their reminiscences. Edsel's testimony gives the Ford version effectively, as do Liebold and Klann. Klann remarks: "Carl Emde was a German, Charlie Hartner was a German, and I was a German, and there were a dozen boys on this job and they claimed that these German boys were holding the job back." Klann describes the work done on Liberty engines, and praises Emde as having

worked "so blamed hard" on both the Liberty and the Eagle boat jobs (the mockup at Highland Park).

32. See references in Note 27 above to Ford war production.

33. *Ibid.*, letter of March 19, 1919, Acc. 62, Box 107.

34. Acc. 6, Box 260; Clyde L. Herring, Des Moines, to Edsel, Feb. 22, 1919, Acc. 6, Box 32.

35. N.Y. *Herald*, March 22, April 30, 1917; N.Y. *Tribune*, Sept. 22, Nov. 18, 1918; Tribune Suit Record, 7143 (Frank Klingensmith, July 28, 1918) and 5392–5393 (Alfred Lucking, July 11, 1919).

36. *Pipp's Weekly*, IV, July 7, 1923, 2, also II, March 25, 1922, 7–8.

37. *Ibid.*, III, May 6, 1922, 1–3; Sarah T. Bushnell, *The Truth About Henry Ford* (Chicago, 1922), 96; telegrams, Ford to Glass, Glass to Ford, June 23 and June 27, 1919, and correspondence, Mellon–Liebold, Acc. 572, Box 26; *N.Y. Times*, April 20, 1922 (general account).

38. Auditing Records, Acc. 33, Box 94.

39. Ford Motor Company to Navy Construction Board, July 21, 1920, Acc. 33, Box 94.

40. H. L. Leister to E. G. Liebold, Feb. 17, 1923, Acc. 572, Box 26. Leister explains the effect of the Dent Act, and notes the activities of the "Revenue Department" officials. Liebold, in letters to Lawrence Godkin and James Couzens, early 1923, same accession and box, comments at some length on war profits.

CHAPTER IV

Drive for Power (*Pages 86–113*)

1. Wedding invitation, Fair Lane Papers, Box 27. The invitations were sent by Mrs. William Clay, sister of Joseph Lowthian Hudson, founder of the Hudson Department Store. William Clay, who had died in 1908, had for some time been manager of the store. Hudson had died in 1912. With Roy Chapin and Howard Coffin, he had founded the Hudson Motor Car Co. in 1909, owned 8 per cent of the stock, and for a time was its president. (Chris Sinsabaugh, *Who, Me?* (Detroit, 1940), 326, 328.) After his death his sister continued to reside in his former home. For details of the wedding, see Detroit *Evening News*, Oct. 31. 1916 and Detroit *Free Press*, Nov. 2, 1916.

2. For Edsel's rise in the company, see mimeographed Biography, Acc. 23, Box 3. Liebold, Harold Hicks, Galamb, and others (reminiscences), speak of his interest in quality automobiles. Lochner, *Henry Ford*, 15, relates that on his visit to Ford in November, 1915, Edsel after lunch played a drum solo to music from a phonograph record. His later interest in music and art is shown in Accs. 6, Box 76 and 23, Box 3. A letter from Edna Hemer, Fair Lane Papers, Box 32, indicates Eleanor Clay's interest in amateur theatricals.

3. Detroit *Evening News*, Oct. 31, 1916, describes the two attending dancing classes together, and contains a sentimental description of Eleanor Clay.

4. Edsel to Henry and Clara Ford, April 8, 1916, Edsel to Thomas C. Whitehead, postmarked Sept. 27, 1916, in Fair Lane Papers, Box 27; *Ford Times*, IX, Oct., 1915, 117–123 (transcontinental trip, 1915).

5. *Detroit Saturday Night*, X, Nov. 4, 1916; Detroit *Free Press*, Nov. 2, and Detroit *News*, Nov. 4, 1916. The latter states that at the wedding Ford had been "chatting freely" with John Dodge.

6. John F. Dodge and Horace E. Dodge v. Ford Motor Company, Henry Ford, *et al.*, 204 Michigan Records and Briefs, Jan. term, 1919, hereafter cited as Dodge Suit Record. Because the printed record is not continuously paginated, additional references will be given as follows: (1) Dodge Suit Record, I, for testimony taken in 1916, and accompanying documents; (2) Dodge Suit Record, II, for testimony taken in 1917, and the opinion and orders of the circuit court; and (3) The title of the brief and the court with which it was filed—e.g., "Dodge Suit Record, Brief and Argument for Defendants, Circuit Court."

7. Dodge Suit Record, I, 351–352; *Dearborn Independent*, Oct. 8, 1915; *My Life and Work*, 162.

8. Dodge Suit Record, I, 260–261 (Ford's version of interview); II, 589 (Wills's version); II, 509–510 (John Dodge on tractor), and II, 490 (Dodge on rumors of tractor activity, and interview with Ford).

9. *Ibid.*, 490–492.

10. Detroit *Free Press*, Aug. 17, 1913 (announcement of Dodge car); *Iron Age*, XCI, Jan. 2, 9, 1913, 1–10, 144–146 (size and value Dodge plant). The site covered 25 acres, and four buildings, including a brass foundry, are noted. Construction had begun in Feb., 1911. John F. Dodge under questioning by Lucking (Dodge Suit Record, II, 512) admitted: "It is true that the Dodge Brothers have extended their factory greatly in the last three or four years." Pipp's statement in *Pipp's Weekly*, IV, Jan. 19, 1924, 5, if accurate, would make the Dodge properties worth considerably more in 1916; they were sold in May, 1924, for $146,000,000 (*Automotive Industries*, LII, May 7, 1925, 832). As to profits earned by the Dodges on Ford contracts, Ford estimated these at $10,000,000 (Detroit *News*, Nov. 4, 1916.) For details of their original $10,000 contribution, see *Ford: the Times, the Man, the Company*, 238.

11. Dodge Suit Record, II, 491, 492, 505.

12. Stockholders' Minutes, June 4, Dec. 9, 1915. The state limitation on capitalization, increased from $25,000,000 to $50,000,000, is noted by Justice Ostrander in 204 Michigan 459, 259 and 461. Company profits for 1915–1916 are cited in Dodge Suit Record, I, 4–6.

13. *Automobile Topics*, XLV, Feb. 24, 1917, 253–254 (Highland Park plant). For cars and price ranges, see newspapers and technical magazines, 1915–1917, e.g. *Scientific American*, CXIV, Jan. 1, 1916, 32, 34. Leonard P. Ayres, "The Automobile Industry and Its Future," (quoted in Additional Tax Case, Transcript of Hearings, 701) gives figures for Ford cars made in 1915. Willys's statement will be found in *Automobile Topics*, XLV, July 17, 1915, 815; Chevrolet's production and plans, *ibid.*, XLI, Feb. 19, 1916, 115 and April 22, 1916, 970. Wills's statement about Ford competitors appears in Dodge Suit Record, II, 648.

14. Some low-priced cars were cycle cars, or cheaply made models that soon dropped out of competition. Of Ford's chief rivals, the Chevrolet was priced at $550, the Overland at $595, and the Dort at $650. Ayres, cited in Note 15, gives statistics showing the percentage of Ford cars to the total. For Ford on competitors, see Dodge Suit Record, I, (Henry Ford, Nov. 14, 1916), 198, 201.

15. Directors' Minutes, Feb. 2, and Stockholders' Minutes, Feb. 3, 1916; *Automobile Topics*, XLII, Aug. 5, 1916, 1273; Detroit *Journal*, Aug. 1, 1916.

16. Detroit *News*, Aug. 31, 1916; the Dodges to Henry Ford, Sept. 23, 1916; Ford to Dodges, Nov. 2, 3, 1916, all in Dodge Suit Record, I, 9–11, 12–13, 13–14, 331–332; Directors' Minutes, Oct. 31, Nov. 2, 8, 1916, May 17, Aug. 14, 1917, and April 9, 1918.

17. W. J. Cameron, *Reminiscences;* Dodge Suit Record, I, 434–436 (Edwin G. Pipp, Nov. 21, 1916). Pipp was describing a casual encounter between Ford and Couzens while Ford, Pipp, and others were working on an article for the *News* (Nov. 4). For Rackham's testimony see *ibid.*, II, 616. Earlier (p. 608) Rackham further clarified his attitude: "I have quite an interest in profits, the same interest as any of the stockholders have. I believe in the distribution of profits strongly."

18. *National Cyclopaedia of American Biography*, XXV, 95, on Lucking; Detroit *Free Press*, May 15, 1919; "Elliott G. Stevenson, the Goat-Getter," *Detroit Saturday Night*, XIII, June 28, 1919, 2 ff.; "Ford at Bay," *Forum*, LXII, Aug. 1919, 130.

19. Dodge Suit Record, I, Bill of Complaint, 1–20.

20. Detroit *News*, Nov. 4, 1916. Pipp testified that this article was prepared mainly by him, after a conference with Ford, Lucking, and others.

21. Dodge Suit Record, I, 95–109 (injunctions), 122–123, 143, 165, 168–169, 215 (Henry Ford, Nov. 14, 1916). There was considerable truth in Stevenson's charges as to Ford's use of his power. Years later, David Gray testified that he had been "a mere figurehead" and that his actions as a director were "purely perfunctory." (Memo. of Interview of Messrs. David Gray and Luman Goodenough with S. T. Miller, Oct. 27, 1926, Acc. 96, Box 11.) Gray seems to have been the most resentful of the stockholders, but Couzens sometimes showed an independent attitude. However, Ford as the majority stockholder did much as he pleased. For his behavior as a

witness, see Dodge Suit Record, I, 259–260, 180, 188 (Nov. 14, 15, 1916). As to payment of dividends Ford, under questioning, said (120–121, Nov. 14, 1916) that he had made up his mind to pay only "regular dividends" (i.e., 5 per cent per month on the $2,000,000 capitalization) "for the present," had fixed in his mind no future time when he would pay special dividends, and that such payments were "indefinite for the future." This testimony gave Stevenson a strong basis for asserting that Ford would not pay unless compelled to, and impaired the force of Lucking's argument that special dividends had already been paid and would continue to be.)

22. *Ibid.*, II, 582–660 (C. Harold Wills, c. May, 1917).

23. *Ibid.*, Opinion of Circuit Court, 109–138; Detroit *News*, Oct. 31, 1917.

24. Dodge Suit Record, Brief for Defendants and Appellants, Supreme Court, 52–53, 57, 149, 168, 171; *ibid.*, Plaintiffs' Reply Brief, 16–17, 32–38.

25. Dodge v. Ford, 204 Michigan 459, *passim*.

26. Liebold to Plantiff, Feb. 19, 1919, Acc. 62, Box 107. Plantiff had written on Feb. 10: "Are you pleased with the Dodge decision; are you going to appeal it on the dividend question?"

27. Directors' Minutes, Dec. 31, 1918. Ford's letter, dated Dec. 30, 1918, is folded into the minutes.

28. Los Angeles *Examiner*, March 5, 1919; Liebold to Plantiff, March 19, 1919, Acc. 62, Box 107; *Automobile Topics*, LIII, March 15, 1919, 655.

29. Detroit *Journal* and Philadelphia *Press*, March 11, 1919; Los Angeles *Sunday Times*, March 16, 1919 (Liebold); *Motor Age*, XXXV, April 3, 1919, 15. Liebold's interview carries a March 14, Detroit date line.

30. Walker, *Reminiscences;* Dana Mayo, memorandum, Ford Archives; William N. Mayo, *Reminiscences;* Tribune Suit Record, 6627 (Henry Ford, July 23, 1919); News Release, Mt. Clemens News Bureau, July 11, 1919, Acc. 53, Box 9; Detroit *Times*, Feb. 15, 1927. Dana Mayo was the older brother of William N. Mayo. He was working at the Ford Motor Company in 1919, and would have a fuller knowledge of what was then occurring than his brother, who was not.

31. Ford Minority Stockholders' Tax Suit, 159, in Acc. 84, Box 1; affidavit of Stuart W. Webb, probably June 26, 1925, Acc. 96 (see also Ford Minority Stockholders' Tax Suit, 25–25); F. W. Holmes to Edsel Ford, Oct. 17, 1919, Acc. 6, Box 34; Walker, *Reminiscences*.

32. Opening statement of Joseph E. Davies, with exhibits, Ford Minority Stockholders' Tax Suit, 68–78.

33. Copy of Couzens option (June 14, 1919, photostat), Acc. 33, Box 41; Dana Mayo, Memorandum, *op. cit.* (on Ford's jig), Acc. 33, Box 41 (Berger option and other purchases, with dates).

34. "Memo of Financial Transactions re Purchase of Stock," letter of Ford Motor Co. of Delaware to Ford Motor Co. of Michigan, Sept. 2, 1919 (photostat), Acc. 352, Box 1.

35. Gray interview, as cited in Note 21; Additional Tax Case, Transcript of Hearings, 1336 (John W. Anderson, Jan. 21, 1927); Couzens Option, *op. cit.;* Secretary's Office File, Ford Motor Co., unnumbered box; Directors' Minutes, July 10, 1919.

36. F. W. Holmes in Boston to F. L. Klingensmith, Detroit, Aug. 11, 1919, Secretary's Office File, Ford Motor Co., Box 4. A full list of the banks invited to participate, with the share proposed, their offers and allotments, is attached.

37. "Certificate of Incorporation of Eastern Holding Company," Acc. 96, Box 9; letter of F. L. Klingensmith to Chase Securities Corporation *et al.* (photostat), Secretary's Office File, unnumbered box; *Automobile Topics*, LVIII, June 5, 1920, 293.

38. Letter, W. L. Graham to Mrs. Clara J. Ford, May 28, 1920, Acc. 62–1, Box 6.

CHAPTER V

Forays in Politics (*Pages 114–142*)

1. Simonds, *Henry Ford*, 159; J. P. Tumulty, *Woodrow Wilson as I Knew Him* (Garden City, N.Y., 1925), 185.

2. *N.Y. Times*, March–May, 1916; Ray Stannard Baker, *Life and Letters of Woodrow Wilson*, VI (Garden City, N.Y., 1939), 253; *Independent*, LXXVI, May 15, 1916, 241, 242.

3. *N.Y. Times*, May–July, 1916; for Jenkin Lloyd Jones' attitude see files of his weekly journal, *Unity;* for Hudson Maxim's, his *Leading Opinions Both For and Against National Defense* (New York, 1916).

4. N.Y. *Herald*, March 28, 1915; N.Y. *Evening Post*, March 11, 1916.

5. N.Y. *World*, Sept. 15, 1916; Baker, *op. cit.*, 288.

6. Josephus Daniels, *The Wilson Era: Peace, 1913–1917* (Chapel Hill, N.C., 1944), 463 ff.; Liebold, *Reminiscences.*

7. N.Y. *World*, Oct. 7, 1916.

8. Baker, *op. cit.*, VIII, 209.

9. Letter of Bernard M. Baruch, June 9, 1918, Acc. 62, Box 60; *N.Y. Times*, June 17, 1918; Grand Rapids *Herald*, June 22, 1918; *Detroit Saturday Night*, XII, June 22, 1918, 13.

10. For a full sketch of Newberry, see *Detroit Saturday Night*, XII, Oct. 26, 1918.

11. Gaston Plantiff to E. G. Liebold, Sept. 16, 1918, Acc. 62, Box 26; *Detroit Saturday Night*, XII, June 20, 1918, 9.

12. Omer *Progress* and Ishpeming *Iron Ore*, as quoted in *Detroit Saturday Night*, XII, July 13, 1918, 2; *ibid.*, July 6, 1918, 5 (Newberry advertisement); *N.Y. Tribune*, Sept. 8, 1918.

13. Spenser Ervin, *Henry Ford vs. Truman H. Newberry* (New York, 1935), 21, n.

14. Records, Acc. 62, Box 61; Firestone to Henry Ford, Oct. 26, 1918, *ibid.; Congressional Record*, LVI, Pt. 10, 10,386b; Ervin, *op. cit.*, 28 ff.

15. *Congressional Record*, LX, Pt. 3, 2, 445; *N.Y. Times*, Nov. 8, 1918; *Congressional Record*, LVII, Pt. 2, 1061d, 1760c.

16. *Ibid.*, LIX, Pt. 2, 65, 66; Ervin, *op. cit.*, 41, 42.

17. Liebold, *Reminiscences;* Robinson to Liebold, Jan. 14, 1920. Acc. 62–1, Box 20.

18. Newberry vs. United States, 256 U.S., 232; *Congressional Record*, LX, Pt. 3, 2445.

19. *Pipp's Weekly*, I, Feb. 5, 1921, 1; II, Sept. 17, 1921, 1–15; Black, Cameron, in their *Reminiscences.*

20. The reminiscences of Black, Liebold, and Cameron give a rather full idea of how Ford's comments were gathered and processed.

21. Black to Liebold, Aug. 21, 1919, Acc. 62, Box 81; *ibid.*, E. B. Sinclair to Liebold, Jan. 29, 1919; speech of E. G. Pipp, April 5, 1921, as reported in the Detroit press; Pipp in *Pipp's Weekly*, II, March 25, 1922.

22. Records, Acc. 62, Box 81 (especially report on N.Y.C. sales and on special representatives' operations in the fall of 1919); *Dearborn Independent*, April 19, 1919, 4 (on Wilson and the masses); *ibid.*, 10 (on League of Nations defeat).

23. Liebold, *Reminiscences;* Tribune Suit Record, 1 ff.

24. *Ibid.*, 2156 ff.; Det. *Free Press*, May 12, 1919; Det. *Times*, Aug. 15, 1919.

25. Det. *Free Press*, Det. *News*, Chicago *Tribune*, and N.Y. *World*, May 12–16, 1919.

26. "Henry Ford at Bay," *Forum*, LXII, Aug. 1919, 136.

27. State of Michigan. On the Circuit Court for the County of Macomb, Henry Ford v. The Tribune Company et al. Transcript of Court Record, May 13, 1919–August 14, 1919, *passim.* Hereafter cited as Tribune Suit Record.

28. Detroit *News*, May 25, 1919.

29. Tribune Suit Record, 3472, 3473.

30. *Ibid.*, 793–845 (May 20, 21, 1919); Grand Rapids *Press*, Chicago *Tribune*, May 19, 1919.

31. Tribune Suit Record, 3467 ff.

32. "Henry Ford at Bay," *op. cit., passim; Pipp's Weekly*, II, Oct. 15, 1921, 1; Tribune Suit Record and press reports covering July 14–26, 1919.

33. Tribune Suit Record, 5729, 5733, 5670 ff., 5872 ff. (July 15, 1919).

34. *Pipp's Weekly*, II, Oct. 22, 1921, 5.

35. Tribune Suit Record, 5747 ff., 5868, 5869 (Ford on history); Cameron, Liebold, *Reminiscences;* Bushnell, *The Truth About Henry Ford*, 141, 143. *Ford Methods and the Ford Shops* (see Chap. I, note 1) was written by Horace L. Arnold and F. L. Faurote.

36. Tribune Suit Record, 8681–8688, 8703, 8715 ff.

37. Chicago *Tribune*, Aug. 21, 1919 (citing *Neb. State Journal*, Sioux City *Journal*, and *N.Y. Times*); Portland *Oregonian*, Aug. 15, 1919; *Nation*, CIX, July 26, 1919, 102.

38. Henry Ford Office, Correspondence, Acc. 62, Box 5; McCormick to Ford, July 30, 1941, Acc. 572.

CHAPTER VI
Postwar Crisis (*Pages 143–170*)

1. "Whose Brains?", *Pipp's Weekly*, IV, Jan. 19, 1924, 2; Typescript of talk by Pipp at Temple Israel, Akron, Ohio, April 5, 1921, Acc. 6, Box 456; Klann, *Reminiscences*.

2. N.Y. *Tribune*, Dec. 1, 1918 (Hughes); *Commercial and Financial Chronicle*, Nov. 23, 1918; *Automobile Topics*, LII, Nov. 9, 1918, 20, 58; *ibid.*, Nov. 16, 1918, 116 (for shipments); N.Y. *Tribune*, Dec. 1, 1918, Part II, 7 (Macauley).

3. Irving Bernstein, *The Automobile Industry: Post-War Developments, 1918–1921* (U.S. Bureau of Labor, Division of Historical Studies of Wartime Problems, No. 52), 2, 6, 7, 9, 10–16, 20, 21, 35, 37, hereafter cited as Bernstein, *Automobile Industry;* Robert A. Gordon, *Business Fluctuations* (New York, 1952), *passim; Automobile Topics*, LII, Nov. 9, 1918, 16, 23, 30. The industry early took a firm position on the disposal of vehicles in Government possession, which by mid-1919 numbered 180,000 for the War Department alone. The vehicles abroad were disposed of there, 30,000 in the United States were taken over by the Bureau of Public Roads, the Post Office, and the Public Health Service, and the remainder had so deteriorated by the time they were sold to the public that they did not affect the industry.

4. Pioch, E. A. Walters, N. H. F. Olsen, *Reminiscences; Motor Age*, XXXIV, Dec. 12, 1918, 11 (Ford production); Bernstein, *op. cit.*, 24 (for industry as a whole). Bernstein cites Federal Reserve Board figures.

5. The resignations of the three men are noted in the Detroit *News*, Mar. 15, 1919 (Wills); Detroit *Free Press*, Mar. 21, 1919 (Lee); and *Motor Age*, XXXV, May 1, 1919, 13 (Hawkins).

6. *Pipp's Weekly*, III, July 22, 1922, 5 (quoting Ford); Detroit *News*, Mar. 15, 1919 (Wills on leaving); *Automobile Topics*, LIII, Mar. 22, 1919, 783–784 (Wills's talents, conflict with Ford); Wollering, *Reminiscences;* Charles E. Sorensen, conversation with the authors, June 29, 1954; Memorandum of Release and Agreement (photostat), Secretary's Office File, Box 13 (final payment to Wills). In testifying in the Dodge suit, Ford stated that his agreement with Wills was oral, undated, and that he sometimes paid him ten per cent of his own dividends, or more, or less. However, there *was* an agreement in writing.

7. R. T. Walker, *Reminiscences* (Hawkins's methods, Wills's attitude); Plantiff to Liebold, Sept. 29, 1916, Henry Ford Office Files, Acc. 62, Box 54; *Ford: the Times, the Man, the Company*, 361–362 (Ford and Hawkins); Liebold, *Reminiscences;* Directors' Minutes, Dec. 31, 1918.

8. Tribune Suit Record, 6711–6712 (John R. Lee, July 23, 1919); *Motor Age*, XXXV, May 1, 1919, 13 (Ford production).

9. *Automobile Topics*, LIII, Jan. 25 (Hubbs), Feb. 1, 1384 (Clifton and Kaye), and Mar. 22, 1919, 781, 784; May 3, 1578, *ibid.*, LXV, Sept. 13, 635; E. D. Kennedy, *The Automobile Industry* (New York, 1941), 105, 107; "Production Takes an Optimistic Slant," *Motor Age*, XXV, April 10, 1919, 16; "Plans for G.M. Expansion in 1919," *Motor Age*, XXXV, April 10, 1919, 17, and "Makers Estimate Car Output for 1920," *ibid.*, Sept. 11, 1919, 10.

10. Bernstein, *op. cit.*, 24, 31; *Automobile Topics*, XLII, Aug. 5, 1916 (1915 prices) and "Ford Seeks Return to Pre-War Levels," LIX, Sept. 25, 1920, 653 (higher prices); and *ibid.*, LII, issues of Nov. 16, 23, 30, Dec. 7, 1918 and Jan 11, 1919; *Automobile Topics*, XLII, July 8, 1916, 867; *ibid.*, XLV, Feb. 24, 1917, 241.

11. *Motor Age*, XXXV, May 1, 1919, 13 (Ford production and orders); Bernstein, *op. cit.*, 32, 33, 35; Detroit *Labor News*, May 23 and June 6, 1919 (Studebaker strike).

12. Mark Sullivan, *Our Times: The Twenties*, VI (New York, 1935), 156–160; Detroit *Labor News*, April 25, May 2, 1919; *Auto Workers' News*, May 22; "Labor Troubles Curtail Car Pro-

duction," *Motor Age*, XXXVI, July 3, 1919, 10; "Labor Disturbances Cut August Output," *ibid.*, Sept. 11, 1919, 28; S. H. Slichter, "The Period 1919–1936 in the United States: Its Significance for Business-Cycle Theory," *Review of Economic Statistics*, Feb., 1937, 6; Klann, *Reminiscences* (Wadsworth strike). The Ford body plant by November, 1919, was turning out 800 bodies a day, and "within a few weeks" promised to supply all the company's requirements, which actually it never did. See Chapter VIII for details, and Chapter IX for Ford's sources of raw materials.

13. Bernstein, *op. cit.*, 39; Kennedy, *op. cit.*, 105; "Production Takes an Optimistic Slant," *Motor Age*, XXXV, April 10, 1919, 16; *Ford: the Times, the Man, the Company*, 644.

14. Bernstein, *op. cit.*, 26–27, 35; "Makers Estimate Car Output for 1920," *Motor Age*, XXXVI, Sept. 11, 1919, 10; Kennedy, *op. cit.*, 115, 117; *N.Y. Times*, Jan. 7, April 25, 1920.

15. Bernstein, *op. cit.*, 42, 55–56; "Established Names Serve Trade Well," *Automobile Topics*, LVIII, July 3, 1920, 831; "Trade Reacts to Stagnant Business," *ibid.*, Aug. 7, 1920, 1468; "Conditions Dictate That Prices Stay Up," *ibid.*, July 3, 1920, 830. In this last article Edward S. Jordan of the Jordan Motor Co. reported on the hostile attitude of bankers but stated that while they may have "practically forbidden" the purchase of cars, and justifiably, yet by doing so they had intensified the desire of people to purchase them. As to the index for cars, it never ran far ahead of that for other commodities, although it has frequently been stated to have been completely out of line with them. Automobile prices held at 124.9 for September, but dropped to 111.5 with October.

16. "Prices Still Move But Upward Only," *Automobile Topics*, LVIII, June 12, 1920, 417, 424, also August and Sept. issues of same publication; General Sales Letter, Aug. 12, 1920, Acc. 78. The suggestion in this letter about converting the bankers was not Henry Ford's; Klingensmith wrote the copy. However, Ford undoubtedly approved the effort to increase sales.

17. Bernstein, *op. cit.*, 46, 47; Kennedy, *op. cit.*, 124. The highest figure for stocks had been 231 in Nov. 1919, and in April, 1920, it stood at 222 (as against 1918 level of 100).

18. *My Life and Work*, 170; Kennedy, *op. cit.*, 125–126 (on expenditures at the Rouge, which check with our knowledge of what was being done). For expenditures on the Upper Peninsula, for the D. T & I., and for coal mines, glass works, silica deposits, etc., see Chap. IX. Ford's remarks about high prices and costs apparently refer to the period April–July, 1920.

19. *My Life and Work*, 171; Black, *Reminiscences; N.Y. Times*, Sept. 22, 1920. In *My Life and Work*, Ford said: "We had to do something to bring our product within the purchasing power of the public," which expresses his sense of the importance of volume production and sales to the Ford Motor Company.

20. *Automobile Topics*, LIX, Sept. 25, 1920, 649, 652; Oct. 9, 1920, 897, and Oct. 30, 1281; *N.Y. Times*, Sept. 26, 28, 29, Oct. 3, 1920; Bernstein, *op. cit.*, 61; *My Life and Work*, 171.

21. *Automotive Industries*, XLIII, Oct. 14, 1920, 791, Oct. 28, 888, and Nov. 25, 1094; Kennedy, *op. cit.*, 120; Plantiff to Liebold, Oct. 10, 1920, Acc. 62–2, Box 29; Sorensen in Dearborn to Edward Grace in Cork, Nov. 11, 1920, Acc. 38, Box 43 (closing of tractor plant), and Letter 929 (Ryan) and Special Letter, Dec. 7, 1920, Acc. 78. In Detroit, according to Kennedy, Mayor James Couzens suggested a share-the-work program to give all automotive workers some employment, but the manufacturers rejected the idea, asserting that they had only been laying off "inefficient workers."

22. *My Life and Work*, 171; Kennedy, *op. cit.*, 124–125; *Men, Money and Motors*, 229–231; Alfred P. Sloan, Jr., in collab. with Boyden Sparkes, *Adventures of a White-Collar Man* (New York, 1941), 123–126, hereafter cited as Sloan, *Adventures of a White-Collar Man*.

23. General Letter 877, Sept. 25, 1920, Acc. 78; *Automotive Industries*, XLIII, Oct. 21, 1920, 837; memorandum, Fred Diehl to Edsel, Klingensmith, Sorensen, Nov. 2, 1920, Acc. 6, Box 34 (on consolidations); *My Life and Work*, 170, 173; *Automobile Topics*, LIX, Oct. 23, 1930, 1156, and Oct. 30, 1280; General Sales Letters of Dec. 7, and Mar. 11, 1921, Acc. 78; Kennedy, *op. cit.*, 126. The sales for October and November are given in the General Sales Letter of Dec. 7, 1920, those for Dec. on Mar. 11, 1921. Kennedy sets the Dec. production at 78,000.

24. General Sales Letters of Oct. 21, Dec. 2, Dec. 7, and others, 1920 (on economies) and Letters 928, 929, and 938, Dec. 1 and Dec. 10, 1921. Edsel wrote a short statement on Dec. 1, 1928, Ryan a much longer and definitive one, which was amplified by his letter of the 10th.

25. *N.Y. Times,* Nov. 23 (Nash), Jan. 4, 5, 6, (other firms) Dec. 25, 1920 (Ford); and Feb. 11, 1921 (data on unemployed).

26. *Ibid.,* Dec. 29, 30, and 31, 1920; *My Life and Work,* 172.

27. Klann, *Reminiscences;* L. E. Briggs, *Reminiscences;* James Sweinhart, "Henry Ford Tells How He Paid His Way Out," Detroit *News,* July 22, 1921 (figures on office force cuts); Memo to all Departments from C. E. Ridgeway, Telegraph Operator, Feb. 8, 1921, Acc. 62-2, Box 9; Charles Martindale, *Reminiscences.* While Sweinhart's article is a glowing account from the Ford point of view, his figures on the reduction of the office force may be accepted, as they would have been furnished or checked by Liebold.

28. Sweinhart, *op. cit.* (quoting Ford); Theodore A. Mallon, William N. Mayo, R. T. Walker, Klann and others, in their reminiscences. Ford in *My Life and Work,* 173–174, gives the same general picture as in his interview with Sweinhart. Mallon's estimate of $7,000,000 does not seem exorbitant when the sweeping character of salvage activities is considered, and the high cost of many of the machine tools.

29. *My Life and Work,* 169–170. Ford cites the amount used as $70,000,000. His figures were doubtless checked by Ford officials, but as we have seen the amount actually utilized was $60,000,000. Durant's resignation from General Motors late in November, and subsequent transactions with the bankers in connection with it, undoubtedly prepared the public and the financiers to believe that Ford would need help. The first suggestion of a loan seems to have seen print in *Automobile Topics,* Jan. 15, but the rumors were circulating before this. See Note 30.

30. Acc. 6, Box 35; *N.Y. Times,* Jan. 11, 21, 1921; Brisbane to Liebold, Acc. 62-2, Box 2. Rumely sent copies of his letters to both Edsel and Liebold, indicating the possibility that he had discussed his ideas with them.

31. Emory W. Clark, First and Old National Bank, Detroit, to Edsel Ford, Jan. 6, 1921, Acc. 6, Box 31F. On Nov. 30, 1920 Edsel had sent Clark a balance sheet. For Liebold's activities, see Acc. 62-2, Boxes 1, 6, and 12. There can be no question of Liebold's merely listening to proposals; there was an extended exchange of information and ideas, clearly looking toward action.

32. Karl Bickel of the United Press is responsible for this explanation of the situation. His syndicated story was published in numerous papers on Feb. 1, 1921; the Newark *Evening News* carried the full Bickel article, often shortened in other papers.

33. Plantiff to Liebold, Acc. 62-2, Box 9; *N.Y. Times,* Jan. 4, 7, 15 and Feb. 25 (Macauley), 1921; Sweinhart, *op. cit.* (Ford); Liebold, *Reminiscences;* Ford to Briscoe, Feb. 3, 1921, Acc. 62-2, Box 9.

34. Hicks, Liebold, in their reminiscences; Sweinhart, *op. cit.; My Life and Work,* 173–176. Sweinhart's account of the actual interview is the fullest, and is followed in the text. Ford's account is detailed as to the way in which the situation was met; he notes the interview, and his asking Edsel to assume the post of treasurer.

35. Liebold, *Reminiscences; N.Y. Times,* Jan. 28, Feb. 1, 1921; *N.Y. Tribune,* Feb. 9, 1921.

36. General Sales Letter, Feb. 5, 1921; McManus and Beasley, *op. cit.,* 228. Beasley, *Knudsen,* 105–106, credits Knudsen with suggesting the shipments to dealers.

37. Branch Auditing Reports, Acc. 260, Box 5; James H. Collins, "Management Problems in the Automotive Industry," *Bulletin of the Taylor Society,* X, Aug., 1925, 192–195 (on dealers in general); Letter, Ernest C. Kanzler to the authors, June 11, 1956; Willis J. Hakes, *Reminiscences.*

38. *N.Y. Times,* Feb. 23 and April 13, 1921.

39. General Sales Letter, Mar. 11, 1921, Acc. 78; *My Life and Work,* 175 (on sources of funds Ford raised); Acc. 33, Box 41 (balance sheet for Dec. 31, 1920). The balance sheet, supplied by the company in 1926 in connection with the Additional Tax Case, shows Real Estate, $94,036,997.81; other tangible goods, $103,243,786.20; cash, $12,974,041.14; good will, $20,517,985.82; credits, $40,717,343.94; miscellaneous (bonds, etc.), $19,568,596.05, a total of $291,058,750.96 for assets. Liabilities are given as capital stock, $17,264,500.00, liability on unsecured indebtedness, $129,483,042.93, and surplus, $144,311,208.03. Another

balance sheet cited by Lawrence H. Seltzer, *A Financial History of the American Automobile Industry* (Boston and New York, 1928), 115, differs considerably from this. It is cited from the Annual Report of the Michigan Secretary of State. The surplus is $124,265,141. Sales figures as cited above are of course mainly from the Sales Department. Figures given in the *N.Y. Times* for April 13, 1921 tally with these, are doubtless from the same source, and furnish the March figure. Branch Auditing Reports (Acc. 260, Box 5) do not agree, giving December 67,664, January, 37,263, and February, 33,308 for both cars and tractors. Ford cited still different figures to *Automotive Industries*, XLIV, Feb. 24, 1921, 481, giving sales for January as 57,000 (to Sweinhart, *op. cit.*, he gave 50,000).

40. Kennedy, *op. cit.*, 120–137. Willys's troubles are described in detail. He lost the Willys Corporation, a holding company, in November 1921, and the Willys-Overland never again attained its former position, both the Chevrolet and the Chrysler giving it stiffer competition than it had previously known.

41. Martindale, *Reminiscences* (for estimate of savings in office salaries); Bernstein, *op. cit.*, 54, for labor's role in bearing the burden of the depression. Material in the Ford Archives on the cases of individual workers is too scattered to be of real value.

42. Resignations can be checked from current newspapers or periodicals, e.g. *N.Y. Times*, Jan. 3, 1921 (Brownell); Detroit *News*, Jan. 3, 1921 (Klingensmith); *N.Y. Times* Jan. 7 (Turrell); *Automobile Topics*, LX, Jan. 29, 1921, 1224 and *N.Y. Times*, Feb. 1, (Anderson and Marquis); *ibid.*, Feb. 18 (Hartman). Beasley, *Knudsen*, 107, fixes Knudsen's resignation as "early in March," and *Automotive Industries*, XLIV, March 17, 1921, refers to it as "recent." Actually, the records of the Ford Personnel Office show that Knudsen left February 28. For further comment, see Liebold, Hicks, in their reminiscences; Lord Perry in interview with authors, Mar. 28, 1952 (Edsel and Klingensmith).

43. Beasley, *Knudsen*, 107–109; Anderson to Edsel Ford, Feb. 22, 1921, Acc. 6, Box 30, and Liebold to Klingensmith, draft of letter (undated), Acc. 62-2, Box 9.

CHAPTER VII

The Lincoln Story (*Pages 171–199*)

1. Undated memorandum by Edsel Ford, Acc. 6, Box 276; article by James Sweinhart, Detroit *News*, Jan. 11, 1922; interview by authors with Harold H. Emmons, Detroit, June 8, 1955. Edsel's memorandum was evidently prepared in 1927 when the Lelands brought suit against Ford. While not signed by him, it is from internal evidence ("we," "my father," "my mother" etc.) clearly his.

2. Interviews by the authors with Wilfred C. Leland, Feb. 13, March 20, 1955; comments by Mr. Leland on Edsel's memorandum, May 25, 1955; Chronology prepared in 1924 by Mr. Leland, and statement by him, March 8, 1923, "To the Stockholders of the Lincoln Motor Company," both given to the authors.

3. *Ford: the Times, the Man, the Company*, 211–212; Sinsabaugh, *Who, Me?*, 198–199; Arthur Pound, *The Turning Wheel* (Garden City, N.Y., 1934), 101–110. See also Note 6.

4. *Ibid.*; Wilfred C. Leland to the authors, April 30, 1955 (on leaving General Motors and founding Lincoln, 1917); Emmons, cited in Note 1 (on the same). Considerable planning and some activity preceded the chartering of the Lincoln company. J. M. Eaton, "Vestibule School of the Lincoln Motor Co.," *Industrial Management*, LIV, Dec., 1918, 452–453, who states he was then "welfare manager" of Lincoln, says that the company was founded in June, and "came into being" in July.

5. Pound, *op. cit.*, 109, 125; *Lincoln Motive*, II, Nov. 7, 1921, 1; interviews with Wilfred Leland, cited in Note 2.

6. Sinsabaugh, *op. cit.*, 163 (Leland's role in S.A.E.); "Personal Liberty to Violate Law" (pamphlet reprinted from *Manufacturers Record*, Feb. 18, 1926, a reply by Leland to Henry B. Joy, who called him a "fanatic" on prohibition); J. Bell Moran, *The Moran Family* (Detroit,

1949), 88 (smoking at Cadillac). The introduction to Leland's pamphlet by Judge Pliny W. Marsh of Detroit tells of Leland's civic work: Marsh calls him "Detroit's best citizen," and in the pamphlet Leland tells something of his early life.

7. Hughes Report (see Chap. III). Wilfred Leland told the authors, March 20, 1955, that he and his father could have raised all the funds they needed, but that the Government insisted on advancing the major part of the money.

8. Hughes Report, 906, 907; "Aviation Engine History" (see Chapter III, p. 68, n.)

9. Lincoln Motor Co. Minute Book, Acc. 331, Box 1; Wilfred C. Leland to the authors, April 30, 1955; Frank Johnson, *Reminiscences.* Leland states that during the war no work was done looking to activities after the war. However, with peace the Lelands determined to design a car, and began work on it, borrowing $2,000,000 for that purpose. Johnson states that he worked on the projected Lincoln while Liberties were still being produced, doubtless in the period Nov. 11–Jan. 31, 1918–1919.

10. Report of H. M. Leland (as president), March 10, 1921, Lincoln Minute Book, *op. cit.; Lincoln Motive,* II, Sept. 26, 1921, 1, 3 (a house organ); Emmons, *op. cit.* (bodies); Ralph C. Getsinger, *Reminiscences* (bodies and general conditions); Lincoln Minute Book, July–Nov. (attitude of Dr. Murphy and supporters) and J. Bell Moran, letter to authors, March 19, 1956 (same).

11. Lincoln Minute Book, minutes for Oct. 10, 20, Nov. 2, 8, 1921; "The Lincoln Motor Company Record," memorandum to authors by Wilfred Leland, June 6, 1955. The account in the text is necessarily simplified. Wilfred Leland came to believe that Dr. Murphy, after becoming a director, wished to precipitate a receivership and buy the company at a low price. He asserted also that Murphy instigated the Government claims against the Lincoln Motor Co. There is evidence that Murphy and his associates, on the other hand, regarded the Lelands as poor business men, who employed relatives and friends unfitted for their tasks. The moot case is that of Angus Woodbridge, H. M. Leland's son-in-law, who had charge of body design, was held responsible for the first unpopular bodies, and was said to have been a "lady's milliner." Walter Wagner, who purchased machinery and checked tools for Lincoln, states in his *Reminiscences* that Woodbridge was incompetent, and that Archer, the chief inspector, a choir singer in the Lelands' church, had a fine speaking voice, but "didn't know a gauge from a washboard." It seems useless to explore this controversy, evidence on which is both prejudiced and fragmentary. However, one point that Wilfred Leland makes is that when he, Platt, and his father went to New York on Nov. 5, they had been told by Kissell-Kinnicutt that a $10,000,000 loan had been made available, and they should "pick it up." But in New York, says Leland, the three learned by telephone from Detroit of the Government claim of Nov. 4, and felt that they must inform the bankers, who suggested that the claim be cleared up before the loan was made. In 1955 Wilfred Leland stated that on returning to Detroit he had told the directors at the Nov. 8 meeting of the possible loan, but that they would not wait for the claim to be settled. The minutes do not report such a statement by him or Platt, and Leland's 1923 account of events leading up to the receivership makes no mention of the possible loan. Of course, the conflict between the Lelands and the Murphys does not bear directly upon the disagreement between the Lelands and the Fords.

12. Affidavit of Henry M. Leland, Detroit, Jan. 7, 1931, Acc. 62-2, Box 48. This contains his explanation of why he wished to repay the stockholders, and also states that the Lincoln Company, if bought in late 1921 or early 1922, could have operated at a profit of $10,000,000 a year. In view of Getsinger's explanation of the sales situation, it appears that a considerable period would have been required before custom-made bodies in sufficient quantity could have been supplied to make profitable operation possible. Edsel Ford, as will be seen, challenged the figure of $10,000,000 as unrealistic.

13. Wilfred C. Leland, interview with the authors, Feb. 13, 1955; memorandum by Edsel Ford, cited in Note 1; statement of Wilfred Leland of March 8, 1923, for Lincoln stockholders, given by him to authors.

14. *Ibid.;* Affidavit of H. M. Leland, cited in Note 12; Wilfred Leland, interview of Feb. 13, 1955.

15. "Comments on Amended Bill of Complaint" (1929), by Edsel Ford, Acc. 6, Box 276. Like the memorandum cited in Note 1, this is unsigned and undated, but clearly Edsel's.

16. He not only denied such a pledge in his two memoranda, but also in a release, Acc. 285, Box 36, in the Detroit *Free Press* of Nov. 19, 1927, and by implication in many letters to former Lincoln stockholders.

17. "The Passing of the Lelands," *Pipp's Weekly*, II, Jan. 21, 1922, 1–2.

18. "What Judge Tuttle Said," *Pipp's Weekly*, III, Feb. 3, 1923, 4 ff. Pipp, in comment on p. 2 of this issue, states that at the meeting at Leland's house a promise was made "to reimburse all the original stockholders." A reading of Tuttle's account shows this not to have been the fact. Tuttle stated that Emmons discussed the stockholders, saying that Ford would like to see "a little something" done for worthy stockholders "like schoolteachers," but not for speculators. Wilfred Leland in a letter to Henry Ford, March 19, 1924 (original in Acc. 6, Box 276, reprint in *Detroit Saturday Night*, April 5, 1924) stated that he himself had said nothing about stockholders at this meeting because Emmons asked him not to, pointing out that the judge would be interested in the creditors only. Emmons, however, told the authors that he had *not* made this request of Wilfred Leland (interview of June 8, 1955), and had himself discussed the stockholders (as Tuttle relates), telling all that he then knew of Ford's intentions.

19. *N.Y. Times*, March 10, 1923 (Stone's $5,000,000 estimate), and Jan. 13, 1922 (Detroit Trust appraisal); W. C. Leland to Henry Ford, March 19, 1924, *op. cit.* (Leland appraisal). The Lelands valued the Lincoln property at $16,131,159.

20. Minute Book, Lincoln Motor Co. (Ford-owned), Acc. 331, Box 1; Racine, Wis., *Call*, Jan. 12, 1922 (Ford on Leland); Detroit *News*, Feb. 4, 5, 1922; *Automobile Topics*, LXIV, Feb. 11, 1922, 1213–1214.

21. Wilfred Leland to Henry Ford, May 23, 1922, Acc. 6, Box 276 (production); Leland to Ford, March 19, 1924, as cited above (new prices); *Automotive Industries*, XLIV, Feb. 9, 1922 (prices); Edsel Ford, "Comments on Amended Bill of Complaint," *op. cit.;* Acc. 133, Box 1 (profits on Lincoln, 1925).

22. W. C. Leland to Ford, March 19, 1924, *op. cit.;* Klann, Liebold, Getsinger, *Reminiscences; Automotive Industries*, XLVI, Feb. 9, 1922, 303 (W. C. Leland on changes in Lincoln plant). "The probabilities are," said the article, "that Ford engineers will work with the Lelands in an advisory way in determining changes."

23. Letters, W. C. Leland to Ford, May 23, 26, 27, Acc. 6, Box 276; deposition of John H. Bourne, Detroit *News*, Dec. 26, 1929; E. A. Walters, *Reminiscences.*

24. Liebold, *Reminiscences;* E. C. Kanzler, interview with authors, June 11, 1956.

25. W. C. Leland to Ford, March 19, 1924; Liebold, *Reminiscences;* Chronology, 1924, given to authors by W. C. Leland.

26. Leland to Ford, March 19, 1924; Bourne, as cited in Note 23; Chronology, *op. cit.*

27. Letters, W. C. Leland to Ford, May 23, 26, 27, 1922; Leland letter of March 19, 1924, Liebold, Getsinger, *Reminiscences.*

28. A. J. Lepine of Edsel Ford's office to Harold D. Colter, Sarnia, Ont., Acc. 6, Box 37; Edsel to Mrs. H. M. Kuehner of Phila., Jan. 25, 1922, *ibid.;* Acc. 62, Box 2, 62-2, Box 44, and 285, Box 81 (Liebold's letters).

29. Bourne deposition, *op. cit.,* Emmons interview, *op. cit.;* Charles W. Zaring, Bloomington, Ind. to Henry Ford, April 17, 1922, Acc. 285, Box 81 (quoting Leland letter); Detroit *Times,* Dec. 29, 1929 (Lelands on Bourne letters).

30. Bourne deposition; W. C. Leland letter of March 19, 1924; Detroit *Free Press,* Nov. 19, 1927 (Edsel Ford on H. M. Leland payment); Acc. 285, Box 636 (listing Leland payment as "additional compensation"). Edsel stated that the $363,000 represented the value of H. M. Leland's B shares.

31. Statement, A. F. Hosmer of Ford Auditing Dept. to B. J. Craig, Acc. 285, Box 636; *N.Y. Times,* March 10, 1923 (payment of creditors). Hosmer's statement shows the payments to the Lelands and Nash, also $312,052.56 on March 15, 1923 to Joseph Boyer, and payments on that date of $359,968.37 and $359,968.38 to W. H. Murphy and John Trix, respectively. Ford also paid $460,857.49 to banks on Lincoln company notes, and $1,481,899.45 to merchandise

creditors, a total of $11,655,699.21 excluding the payment of $363,000 to H. M. Leland, but including the $8,000,000 paid at the Receiver's sale.

32. Liebold, *Reminiscences;* Edsel Ford to Robert Crawford of the Atlas Foundry Co., Detroit, Dec. 4, 1923, Acc. 6, Box 44; Walter Wagner, *Reminiscences;* Michigan Supreme Court, 245 Michigan Record and Briefs, 606 (Judge Fellows on Ford's right to discharge Lelands: he gives citations).

33. Production Records, Walter T. Jacobowski, Ford Archives; General Sales Letter 1259, June 15, 1922 (discontinuance of Lincoln as separate company); *Ford News,* II, July 1, 1922, 1 (Lincoln parts made at Rouge); III, June 15, 1923, 1 (plant addition in use); III, Sept. 15, 1922, 1, 5 (addition, and assemblies); *Automotive Industries,* XLVII, Sept. 14, 1922, 537 (new building); Memorandum of E. R. Nyland to Ford officials, Nov. 23, 1922, Acc. 6, Box 265 (changes by Edsel); General Sales Letters 1259, 1293 (Sept. 23, 1922), and 1480 (Feb. 16, 1924), all in Acc. 78 (dealers).

34. *American Machinist,* LIX, Dec. 20, 27, 1923, and Jan. 3, 1924, pp. 897–901, 943–947, and 5–8 respectively; Correspondence, Lincoln Motor Co., and general sales letters, Acc. 6, Box 265 (body types); *Ford News,* III, April 8, 1924, 3 (precision); III, June 1, 1923, 1, and V, June 15, 1925, 7 (police use); III, Aug. 15, 1923, 3 (English comment); IV, Sept. 1, 1924, 7 and VI, Oct. 1, 1926, 1 (prizes); "Lincoln Motor Co.," Acc. 6, Box 255 (Milan show). As to special fees for bodies, see Edsel Ford to Gaston Plantiff, in above correspondence, April 23, 1924: "The fee of $9,000 per job is only payable provided the bodies are finally adopted . . . as production models."

35. Note 31 above (creditors); Gilbert Butler of Bossert Corporation of Utica, N.Y., to Ford Motor Co., March 10, 1923, Acc. 62, Box 2 (on payment); *Automotive Industries,* XLVIII, March 15, 1923, 643; "Ford Pays," *Pipp's Weekly,* III, March 10, 1923, 1; Stidger, *Henry Ford,* 75–76 (pro-Ford comment on payments).

36. W. C. Leland letter, March 19, 1924, *op. cit.; Pipp's Weekly,* III, March 3, 1923, 6–7; *N.Y. Times,* Oct. 17, 1927 (Leland to stockholders).

37. *N.Y. Times,* Nov. 16, 1927 (the suit and Gallagher's comment); Liebold, *Reminiscences;* 245 Michigan Supreme Court, 604 (summary of the Ford position); *ibid.,* 602, 607 (Fellows' comments); 252 Michigan Supreme Court, 547 (amended bill).

38. *Ibid.,* 551 (rejection of amended bill); Keith Sward, *Legend of Henry Ford* (New York, 1948), 174 (Leland's letter to stockholders, and death).

39. *Automotive Industries,* XLVI, Feb. 9, 1922, 303. The quotation is from a statement issued by the Lelands.

CHAPTER VIII

The Rouge: Concept and Growth (*Pages 200–216*)

1. Mary Louise Gregory Brand, *Reminiscences.*

2. "River Rouge" (pamphlet), Wm. Graham Printing Co., Detroit, 1891, Ford Archives; L. J. Thompson Papers, Acc. 384, Box 1; "Ford Buys Thousand-Acre Site for Blast Furnaces and Plant," *Automobile Topics,* XXXVIII, June 19, 1915, 433. In Springwells, the Thompson Papers show, between May 22, 1915 and Oct. 10, 1918, Fred E. Gregory purchased 1439 acres at a total cost of $2,207,393.27; and in Ecorse township during the same year, 1030.13 acres at a cost of $1,001,440. It may be assumed that of this total Gregory had acquired at least 2000 acres by July, 1915. *Automobile Topics* notes the purchase of 1000 acres. The Springwells purchases were all north and east of the Rouge. Mrs. Brand says that William Gregory, her father's brother, J. Hudson, Fred Brand, and Dave McGinnity assisted Fred Gregory. The latter died May 20, 1918, and William Gregory took over his work.

3. Norman Beasley, "Henry Ford Says," *Motor,* XLI, Jan. 1924, 292; Wibel, Liebold, and Walker in their reminiscences. See also D. J. Hutchins, *Reminiscences,* for an account of shortages.

4. Detroit *Journal,* June 15, 19, 1915.

5. Editorial, Detroit *Journal*, Oct. 19, 1925 (on Livingston, at his death); Livingston to Henry Ford, July 14, 1915, Fair Lane Papers, Box 141. Other correspondence with Ford in this box reveals Livingston's alertness and his friendly relationship with the Ford family. He took them sailing, and on July 30, 1915, sent Ford a birthday present of fifty-two American Beauty roses.

6. Liebold, William F. Verner, *Reminiscences*.

7. Fay L. Faurote, "Henry Ford Still on the Job with Renewed Vigor," *Factory and Industrial Management*, LXXIV, Oct., 1927, 197; *Today and Tomorrow*, 3, 6, 41–42. Ford's comments on raw materials and parts as quoted in the text are from the last citation. Faurote quotes him, as interviewed at the Rouge itself, on change and growth, and on the necessity of using facilities creatively: "You must get the most out of the power, out of the materials, out of time." Ford's effort to create flow in manufacture is illustrated in many phases of the Rouge, which the reader will perceive as the chapter progresses.

8. John H. Van Deventer, "Mechanical Handling of Coal and Coke" (in the series, Principles and Practice at River Rouge), *Industrial Management*, LXIV, Oct., 1922, 196; Verner, *Reminiscences*. Verner thinks that Couzens favored a Detroit River site.

9. "Eagle Boats and Rouge Shipyard, 1918" (photographs and reports on construction and employees), Ford Archives; "Progress Being Made on Ford Plant," *Iron Age*, CII, Dec. 19, 1918, 1520.

10. F. L. Prentiss, "Making Ore Pile Part of Automobile Plant," *Iron Age*, CV, May 6, 1920, 1295, gives an excellent map of the Rouge in its early stage.

11. Detroit *Journal*, Mar. 4, 1918 (description of work at site, although at an earlier period); Verner, Riecks, and G. R. Thompson, in their reminiscences. Other reminiscences in the Archives, such as those of R. T. Walker, Frank Hadas, and E. G. Liebold, supply some details as to Mayo and early planning.

12. John H. Van Deventer, "Links in a Complete Industrial Chain" (first article in his series), *Industrial Management*, LXIV, Sept., 1922, 134; Fay L. Faurote, "Planning Through Obstacles and Not Around Them," *Factory and Industrial Management*, LXXV, Feb., 1928, 302–306; Verner, H. B. Hanson, *Reminiscences*. While both Van Deventer and Faurote described planning after the preliminary stage, it is apparent from Verner and Hanson that there had been little if any change in method. Hanson, who arrived in 1921, felt that Ford and Sorensen discussed plans in advance.

13. Moritz Kahn, "Plan the Plant for the Job," *Factory and Industrial Management*, LXXV, Feb., 1928, 316–318; F. L. Prentiss as cited in Note 10 above, 1302.

14. A. M. Wibel, R. T. Walker, W. F. Verner in their respective reminiscences. Wibel quotes Ford's remark about "feeling it out" in connection with the plannning of steel operations, but it expressed his general attitude.

15. Riecks, *Reminiscences*.

16. Verner notes Sorensen's appearances at the Rouge prior to the transfer of the tractor plant, also his participation in conferences.

17. *Ford Man*, III, Dec. 17, 1919, 1; *ibid.*, IV, Dec. 31, 3, 4; Jan. 17, 1920, 4.

18. Van Deventer, as cited in Note 12, 133–134.

19. *Ford Man*, III, Nov. 17, 1919, 4 (body production); Dec. 17, 1 (coke ovens); *ibid.*, IV, June 3, 1920, 2 (Furnace A); July 3, 1 (saw mill); Detroit *News*, May 18, 1920.

20. Walker, *Reminiscences* (on work at the Rouge); *Automotive Industries*, XLVI, Feb. 16, 1922, 442; *Ford News*, II, Feb. 15, 1922, 1. The latter reference gives a fairly full account of tractor operations, with the date of first production, and its progress during the first year.

21. Riecks, H. B. Hanson, *Reminiscences*.

22. *Ibid.* (Sorensen); Van Deventer, "Plant Facilities of the World's Biggest Foundry" (fifth article in his series), *Industrial Management*, LXV, Jan., 1923, 1; *Ford News*, I, Nov. 1, 1921, 1, 8; *ibid.*, III, Feb. 1, 1923, 1.

23. Van Deventer, "The Power Plant" (seventh article), *Industrial Management*, LXV, March, 1923, 149–160; Dearborn *Press*, July 30, 1938, Sec. I, 7 (for later developments).

24. Detroit *News*, Aug. 4, 1917; Directors' Minutes, Aug. 14, 1917; *Ford Man*, IV, May 3,

1920, 1; Advertisement by War Department, "Improvement of River Rouge, Mich.," in envelope, "C. W. Zauger, River Rouge," Acc. 285, Box 19.

25. The resolution for an investigation was introduced by Senator Lawrence Sherman (Republican) of Illinois (Senate Resolution 279, 66th Cong., 2nd Session, Jan. 13, 1920), and was noted in the N.Y. *Tribune* of Jan. 14. It was alleged to have been a political move to embarrass Ford, who had pushed the Newberry investigations, and it later died in committee. Ford's difficulties in acquiring or getting condemned the properties along the Rouge necessary for improvement are covered by correspondence in Acc. 62, Box 14. He was compelled to post a $2,000,000 bond with the Federal Court in Detroit in connection with these operations, and even after having settled with most of the owners involved, failed to get even a partial return of his money (N.Y. *Times*, April 18, 1922). However, the *Times* of Jan. 5, 1926, reports his victory in the Supreme Court in a suit against the Dodge Brothers, J. Calvert Sons, and others, "arising out of the condemnation of land in improvement of the Rouge River at Detroit," and this apparently settled the matter.

As to Markham's work, Livingston praised it in a letter of Dec. 27, 1923, to Ford: "Colonel Markham is a man of great executive ability." The engineer's term had expired, but Livingston hoped he would remain on the job (Fair Lane Papers, Box 141).

26. *Ford News*, III, Feb. 15, 1923, 3 (transshipment of cargoes); Aug. 1, 1923, 1 (first steamships). For the contractors' obligation to dump under Army direction, see advertisement cited in Note 24 above. One of the low areas built up with fill lay to the west of the slip, and later became the site for the Ford steel plant. As to coal, it was later (1926) dispatched by rail to Toledo, then transshipped direct by boat to the Rouge.

27. *Ibid.*; also IV, July 15, 1925, 1; "Chart of Rouge Plant Traffic Operation, Jan. 1, 1917 to June 30, 1923 incl.," Acc. 38, Box 55.

CHAPTER IX
Projects in Expansion (*Pages 217–248*)

1. Jennie Folley, *Reminiscences*. Of the 1919 trip, on which he was a driver and helper, C. J. Smith, *Reminiscences*, notes Kingsford's presence. Kingsford had married a first cousin of Henry Ford, Mary Flaherty, daughter of Nancy Ford Flaherty (Fair Lane Papers, Box 28).

2. A. G. Wolfe, *Reminiscences;* Upton Sinclair, "Henry Ford Tells Just How Happy His Great Fortune Has Made Him," *Reconstruction*, I, May, 1919, 129–132. Wolfe's father in 1910–1912 was operating Ford's farms in the Dearborn area; Ford knew the Wolfe children, and took them for long drives on which Wolfe concluded in retrospect, he was locating sites for future factories. The Sinclair article, extremely interesting, is mostly in dialogue, apparently taken down, perhaps in shorthand, by Mrs. Sinclair.

3. Fair Lane Papers, Box 97 (camping trips); Liebold to Kingsford, Nov. 7, 1919, and Kingsford to Ford, Feb. 12, 1920, both in Acc. 284, Box 16; *ibid.*, other correspondence between Liebold and Kingsford; Liebold, *Reminiscences; Detroit Saturday Night*, XIV, July 31, 1920 (on property); Stockholders' Minutes, Michigan Iron, Land, & Lumber Co., Nov. 17, 1920, Acc. 339, Box 1 (ratification of purchase).

4. Liebold, Folley, *Reminiscences; Ford News*, IV, Sept. 15, 1923, 1; *N.Y. Times*, Jan. 7, 1921; *Automotive Industries*, XLIII, Sept. 23, 1920, 642; Walker, *Reminiscences* (construction, Iron Mountain); *Ford News*, II, Jan. 15, 1922, 4; III, Jan. 15, 1923, 3; Albert Olsen, *Reminiscences* (all on Iron Mountain sawmill and lumber camps); Marquette (Mich.) *Daily Mining Journal*, July 19, 24, 1920 (sawmill).

5. "Imperial Mine Makes Big Ore Shipment," *Ford News*, II, Aug. 1, 1922, 1; "Ford Iron Mine at Michigamme Shows Progress," VI, Jan. 15, 1925, 5; D. L. Newkirk to Kingsford, Sept. 18, 1931, Acc. 38, Box 66 (on Imperial iron); *N.Y. Times*, Sept. 9, 1923 (Pequaming purchase); *Ford News*, IX, June 1, 1929, 123 (Blueberry mine); *Literary Digest*, LXXIV, Aug. 26, 1922, 56 (Ford as producer); Russell Gnau to Albert E. Dunford, Feb. 18, 1924, Acc. 28, Box 107; unsigned report from Iron Mountain to B. J. Craig, Ford Controller, May 12, 1925, Acc. 38, Box 53 (activi-

ties, and valuation of plant). Gnau wrote at length to Dunford in Berkeley, Cal., who was preparing a B.S. degree thesis on Ford use of raw materials.

6. Evans Clark, "Ford Works a Miracle in Mining Coal," *N.Y. Times*, Sec. 10, April 15, 1928; *Ford News*, II, May 1, 1922, 1, 8 (Ford coal needs); Sept. 1, 1922, 1 (Ford's statement); Detroit *Times*, Sept. 19, 21, 1922 (I.C.C. orders); *Ford News*, III, April 1, 1923, 1, 4 (mines and capacity); *N.Y. Times*, Feb. 10, 1923 (Fordson Coal Company); *Ford News*, 1922-1928 (offers of coal and coke to Ford employees). As to the three new mine groups, the *Ford News* estimated that the Dexcar property at Twin Branch, W. Va., contained an 18,000,000 ton reserve, had a 2000 ton daily potential, and a working force of 500. To the Pond Creek mines, in E. Kentucky near Williamson, W. Va., a 28,000 acre tract, it allotted a 300,000 ton reserve, a 7000 ton daily output, and a work force of 1000, and to the Peabody properties (120,000 acres with 500,000 bd. ft. of timber) a 200,000,000 ton coal reserve. Clark's estimates are somewhat less for all three properties.

7. Liebold, *Reminiscences* (on plants); Liebold to John Barton Payne, Payne to Liebold, Acc. 62, Box 79 (prices of govt. ships). A number of vessels were then being finished for the Govt. under war contracts, and Ford considered buying some. However, other expenditures, the unfinished condition of the Rouge River, then depression difficulties, apparently caused postponement.

8. H. E. Hoagland, "Ford's Revolutionary Railroading," *N.Y. Times*, Sec. 7, Aug. 14, 1921 (general account of road); statement on D.T. & I., Acc. 285, Box 13 (1920 deficit); Liebold, *Reminiscences* (Osborn and Ford). The 1920 deficit is cited elsewhere as smaller (*N.Y. Times*, Feb. 21, 1924, $1,481,158, and Samuel Crowther, "Ford's Story of His Railway," *World's Work*, XLVIII, June, 1924, 161-166, $1,769,460), but the Archives figure is apparently taken from the railroad's records. Hoagland was Professor of Transportation at Ohio State University.

9. Hoagland, *op. cit.*, and Liebold, *Reminiscences* (terms of acquisition); *ibid.*, and *N.Y. Times*, Sept. 11, 1920, Nov. 13, 1921, and Feb. 4, 1923 (Tannenbaum and Strauss); Acc. 285, Box 472 (Tannenbaum and Strauss at stockholders' meeting); *N.Y. Times*, March 11, 1922 (Ford's attempted lease). Ford, according to the *Times* of March 11, sought to lease the D.T. & I. "to a company owned exclusively by the Ford family" (the Detroit and Ironton). Profits could then be taken by this company, and not by the D.T. & I. The I.C.C. ruled against him, minority stockholders receiving notification on March 10, 1922.

10. Hoagland, *op. cit.;* Liebold, *Reminiscences;* "Henry Ford's Railroad Experiment," *Railroad Magazine*, XXIV, July, 1938, 11. The first quotation is from Hoagland, the second from the *Railroad Magazine*.

11. Hoagland, *op. cit.*, *N.Y. Times*, June 7, 1929 (comments on purchase); Liebold, *Reminiscences* (early period of Ford control); D.T. & I. Minutes, Treasurer's Office, Ford Motor Co; W. L. Graham, Treasurer's Office, Ford Motor Co., to Liebold, Dec. 24, 1920, Acc. 62-1, Box 6 (1920 expenditures); *N.Y. Times*, Jan. 19, 1921 (further disbursements); Hoagland and "Henry Ford's Railroad Experiment" (changes in equipment, wages, work attitudes).

12. Memorandum of report submitted to Directors, July 21, 1921, Acc. 62-2, Box 24; *N.Y. Times*, June 15, 1922 (proposed lower rate); *ibid.*, Oct. 16, 1921 (Ford and railroad strike); financial statements, Acc. 285, Boxes 221, 447; *N.Y. Times*, Feb. 21, 28, March 21, 1924 (comments railroad executives, financiers); *ibid.*, Aug. 14, 1921 (editorial); correspondence, Liebold and railroad men, Acc. 285, Boxes 144, 210, and 267; "Henry Ford's Railroad Experiment," *op. cit.*, and *Ford News*, III, July 1, 1923, 1, 8, and V, July 15, 1925, 1, 8 (cutoffs and electrification); Liebold *Reminiscences* (on sale). At least several groups visited Dearborn and examined the railroad while Senator Robert M. La Follette (Acc. 62, Box 115) and William G. Mc Adoo (Acc. 62, Box 2) both sought facts about the railroad which they could use in public statements.

13. *Ford News*, IV, March 15, 1924, 1, 4; May 1, 1, 8; June 1, 1; Aug. 1, Aug. 15, 1; and V, Feb. 15, 1925, 1, 8; Liebold, *Reminiscences (Lake Ormoc)*; Norman J. Ahrens, Memorandum, Ford Archives; financial statements, Acc. 38, Boxes 62, 63 (ships in operation, profits and losses); Departmental Communication, Acc. 285, Box 496.

14. Frank Parker Stockbridge, "Henry Ford, Amateur," *World's Work*, XXXVI, Sept., 1918, 515; Folder, "Travel," Fair Lane Papers, Box 97 (purchases of Lenawee Co. sites); Liebold, *Reminiscences* (early purchases, announcement of general program); Dearborn *Press*, Aug. 23,

1918 (Hamilton and Rouge sites); Troy (N.Y.) *Record,* Aug. 29, 1918 (Green Island); "Mr. Ford's Own Page," *Dearborn Independent,* April 19, 1919, 3; *My Life and Work,* 204 (farming and machines); Henry Ford, "Why Henry Ford Wants to Be Senator," *World's Work,* XXXVI, Sept., 1918, 525–526.

15. *Today and Tomorrow,* 141–147; Voorhess, Liebold, William Mielke, in their reminiscences.

16. *Today and Tomorrow,* 141–143, 145, 149; Voorhess, *Reminiscences* (farm boys like factories); Liebold, *Reminiscences.*

17. *Ibid.* (start of glass experimentation); Riecks, Klann, *Reminiscences* (Avery, Hanson); *Ford News,* II, Nov. 15, 1921, 1 (first manufacture); *ibid.,* III, May 1, 1923, 1, 5 (Glassmere); VII, Sept. 1, 1927, 3 (Twin Cities plant and total production); D. J. Hutchins, *Reminiscences.*

18. Alfred Lief, *The Firestone Story* (New York, 1951), 144–153; E. G. Holt, *Marketing of Crude Rubber* (Trade Promotion Series, Dept. of Commerce, No. 55, Washington, 1927), 1, 3; P. W. Barker, *Rubber: History, Production, and Manufacture* (same series, No. 209, 1940), 23–25; Firestone to Ford, Acc. 62, Box 2. Many British economists and business men opposed the Stevenson scheme. In practice, it did not exert an even control, for prices shot up and down, mounting to $1.23 in June, 1925. The plan collapsed in 1928, as Dutch production became larger.

19. John F. Melby, *Rubber River: . . . the Rise and Collapse of the Amazon Boom* (Chicago, 1942), 452 ff.; Wickham (cited in text); Barker, *op. cit.,* 4, and Holt, *op. cit.,* 1, 3.

20. Lief, *op. cit.,* 166, 180. Edison estimated the cost of his rubber at $2.00 per pound. Records of payments to him by Ford appear in Acc. 285, Box 956.

21. Correspondence, Cuthbert Christy and Liebold, Oct. 13–Nov. 8, 1924, Acc. 285, Box 214; De Lima correspondence, Acc. 284, Box 139 and Acc. 38, Box 61; Barker, *op. cit.,* 24 (rubber prices). Christy, an English author and naturalist, claimed knowledge of rubber culture in both Africa and the Far East, and sought a position with Ford. He later served on a League of Nations commission reporting on forced labor in Liberia.

22. Barker, *op. cit.;* John C. Treadwell *et al.,* "Possibilities for Para Rubber Production in Northern Tropical America" (pamphlet, Washington, 1926), 1–8; McCloud, O. Z. Ide, Carl La Rue, in their reminiscences; "History of the Companhia Ford Industrial do Brazil," and letter, Schurz to Ford, Aug. 21, 1925; text of contract, Acc. 38, Box 61. The History, a typescript, is of only moderate value. Ide discovered that Jorge Dumont Villares, a Brazilian highly useful to him as a translator, advisor, and intermediary, owned a tract of land which Ford would require, and would probably share his profit on it with the governor. Ide did not grudge Villares a profit, but ignored an Englishman, who claimed a payment for having introduced Villares to Governor Bentes. Ide originally asked for 6,000,000 acres, but was satisfied with 2,500,000!

23. Detroit *News,* Nov. 4, 1928 (description of site); "A Dependable Supply of Distinctive Brazilian Hardwoods from the Ford Plantation in the Amazon Jungle," (pamphlet, probably 1934), Acc. 38, Box 17 (varieties of trees); *N. Y. Times,* Oct. 12, 1927 (approval of contract); "History," *op. cit.;* Ide, Kristian Orberg, Liebold, *Reminiscences; Ford News,* VIII, March 15, 1928, 49–50; Aug. 1, 159, Aug. 15, 169–170 (on converting ships and their departure *ibid.,* Nov. 1, 1928, 240; Detroit *News,* Nov. 4, 1928 (work on site); Sorensen letters, Acc. 38, Box 64. "VP" (doubtless Victor Perini) wrote to Sorensen on June 9, 1930, after Oxholm's departure, noting the captain's confusion. Sorensen had sent H. Braunstein of the Rio de Janeiro office, J. S. Kennedy of the Para office, and W. E. Carnegie of the Ford Motor Co.'s Accounting Department to report on the situation and assist Oxholm.

24. Cablegram, Kennedy to Sorensen, Aug. 28, 1929, in "History" (progress of work); *N.Y. Times,* Nov. 25, 1928, Sec. 5 (climate and diseases); June 6, 1929 (loss of case for transportation of seedlings); "History," (seedlings and general conditions).

25. Carnegie's report to Sorensen, Acc. 38, Box 64; correspondence, A. Johnston and Sorensen, 1931, Acc. 38, Box 68; "Forty Years, 1903–1943," a history of the Ford Company, Ford Archives; Desmond Holdridge, "A Native Returns to the Amazon," *Living Age,* CCCLX, April, 1941, 153–158; Charles Morrow Wilson, "Mr. Ford in the Jungle," *Harper's Magazine,* CLXXXIII, July, 1941, 181–187.

26. "Ford Experiments May Give U.S. New Source of Rubber," release by McCann-Erickson, Dec. 19, 1941, Acc. 23, Box 17; Holdridge, *op. cit.,* 158. The release calls the Brazilian project

"the $20,000,000 Ford Project," but Holdridge estimates the cost at $8,000,000. The latter figure is clearly inadequate, and the McCann-Erickson estimates, approved by the company, should be approximately correct.

27. William B. Stout, *So Away I Went* (Indianapolis, 1951), 160-163; Henry Ladd Smith, *Airways* (New York, 1942), 467-82, 122; Lloyd Morris and Kendall Smith, *Ceiling Unlimited* (New York, 1953), 227-233, 242-250.

28. William B. Stout, *Reminiscences* (a memoir later than his book, tape-recorded); Liebold, *Reminiscences* (early Ford interest in aviation); *Automotive Industries*, XLIII, July 22, 1920, 189 (Mayo's 1920 European trip); data and correspondence, Stout and Edsel Ford, Acc. 6, Box 562, Acc. 285, Boxes 148, 277; Stout to Edsel, with attached memorandum from Mayo, March 21, 1923, Acc. 6, Box 562 (Mayo's suggestion as to help); Stout, *So Away I Went*, 176-182 (performance of *Maiden Detroit*); Detroit *Free Press*, April 27, 1924 (Henderson on Stout plane); Glen Hoppin, *Reminiscences* (selection of landing field); *Ford News*, IV, Sept. 1, 1924, 1 and V, Nov. 15, 1924, 1 (airport).

29. Hoppin, *Reminiscences*; Stout, *Reminiscences* and *So Away I Went*, 183-189; Detroit *Times*, Feb. 13, 1925; *Michigan Manufacturing and Financial Record*, Feb. 14, 1925; Brisbane to Edsel, Feb. 13, 1925, and Edsel to Brisbane, Feb. 19, Acc. 6, Box 354.

30. Stanley Knauss, *Reminiscences*; N.Y. *Times*, April 14, 1925; *Ford News*, V, April 15, 1925, 1; Life of Edsel Ford for *Encyclopedia of American Biography*, Fair Lane Papers, Box 27 (first Dearborn-Chicago flight); Detroit *Times*. N. Y. *Tribune*, April 14, 1925; *Ford News*, V, June 1, 1925, 1, 4, and July 1, 1925, 1, 4; correspondence, Mayo and Edsel, Acc. 6, Box 562; Minutes of Stout Metal Airplane Co., July 4, 31, 1925, Ford Archives.

31. Smith, *Airways*, 94-95; Mayo to Edsel, July 22, 1925, Acc. 6, Box 562 (Henderson-Stout-Mayo conference); Hicks, *Reminiscences*; *Ford News*, V, Oct. 1, 1925, 1, 8; VI, Nov. 1, 1925, 1, 8; Jan. 15, 1926, 1, 7 (Florida plane). Hicks had worked with E. J. Hall on the Liberty engine.

32. Hicks, *Reminiscences*; Stout, *So Away I Went*, 209, and *Reminiscences*; *Ford News*, V, March 1, 1926, 8. No account of the fire was published in the *Ford News*; the March 1 issue contains the first reference to it.

33. *Ford News*, V, March 1, 1926, 8; VI, July 1, 1926, 1, 2; Leslie S. Gillette, "Ford's Progress in the Air," *Automotive Industries*, LV, Dec. 16, 1926, 1004; Hicks, *Reminiscences*.

34. *Ford News*, VI, Oct. 1, 1926, 5 (first sale to National Air Transport); *ibid.*, March 1, 1926, 1, and VII, March 15, 1927, 1.

35. *Ford News*, VII, April 1, 1927, 1, and IX, Jan. 2, 1929, 3 (Buffalo line); Hicks, *Reminiscences*, and *Ford News*, VIII, Dec. 1, 1926, 253-254 (improved tri-motors); Aviation Records, Acc. 479.

36. Hicks, *Reminiscences*; Stout, *So Away I Went*, 241, 242; Aviation Records, Acc. 479; *Ford News*, X, Sept. 15, 1930, 206, and Oct. 15, 1930, 230; IX, Aug. 1, 1929, 170 (production for June, 1929, and list of customers).

37. Designs at the Ford Archives, preserved from this period, show great advances over the types produced by the company at this time, and anticipate many features of later successful airliners. Ford, however, would not approve them.

38. Aviation Records, Acc. 479.

CHAPTER X

The Greater Company (*Pages 249-278*)

1. Sinsabaugh, *Who, Me?*, 115.

2. Galamb, McCloud, Farkas, in their reminiscences; interview with C. Harold Wills, Jr., March 12, 1953.

3. Walker, Klann, Wibel, in their reminiscences. Many former Ford employees described experiments carried on in the Ford plants.

4. *Ford News*, III, April 1, 1923, 1, 8 (laboratory building); IV, April 1, 1924, 1, 4 (character of Johansson blocks); Liebold, *Reminiscences*. Liebold discusses the character and ac-

curacy of the blocks, which he says were precise to forty-one millionths of an inch, and their use by the U.S. Bureau of Standards and comparable foreign agencies.

5. Voorhess, Donaldson, Charles Thomas, William Gassett, Liebold in their reminiscences.

6. *Ford News*, III, April 1, 1923, 1, 8; Howard Simpson, *Reminiscences*.

7. "Ford Motor Company Engineering Chart," Nov. 1, 1919, Ford Archives; McCloud, Liebold, *Reminiscences*.

8. Fay L. Faurote "Splitting an Inch a Million Ways," *Factory and Industrial Management*, LXXVI, Sept., 1928, 510–513 (on gauges); *ibid.*, "Research Is Back of All Ford Manufacturing," LXXVI, July, 1928, 74–77 (on laboratory work, particularly testing); Simpson, Olsen, E. Zoerlen, and Sheldrick in their reminiscences. Faurote lists many measuring devices, such as micrometer calipers, "measuring machines both domestic and foreign, comparators, interferometers, microscopes, reference, plug, and ring gauges," etc. Many Ford engineers note Ford's fetishes and taboos —e.g., McCloud, Hicks, Farkas.

9. McCloud, *Reminiscences;* Sloan, *Adventures of a White-Collar Man*, 142–144.

10. World Production Report, 1903–1952, Acc. 62, Box 49; *Ford News*, II, Jan. 15, 1922, 1; III, Feb. 1, 1923, 1; IV, Jan. 15, 1924, 1; V, Jan. 15, 1925, 1.

11. World Production Report, *op. cit.;* "Ford Truck Ready Soon," *Motor Age*, XXI, April 19, 1917, 15; *Ford News*, II, Jan. 15, 1922, 1, and III, Feb. 1, 1923, 1 (truck production); *ibid.*, V, June 1, 1925, 3 (African endurance contest) and V, July 15, 1925, 8 and Oct. 15, 1925, 1 (truck bodies and truck sales). Klann, *Reminiscences,* states that the truck used the Model T motor, and describes truck bodies.

12. *Ford News*, II, Aug. 1, 1922, 4, 6; III, May 1, 1923, 6; IV, March 1, 1924, 1; V, Feb. 1, 1925, 1 (all for uses of Fordson); VI, Feb. 15, 1926, 1, and VII, Feb. 15, 1927, 1 (Russian orders); IV, Feb. 1, 1924, 7 and V, Oct. 15, 1925, 1 (English and American contests); IX, Feb. 1, 1929, 27, and Simpson and Liebold, *Reminiscences* (shift to Ireland).

13. *Ford Times*, VIII, Oct., 1914, 13, and IX, March, 1916, 345, N.Y. *Herald*, July 25, 1915 (Ford branches in pre-war period); "Memorandum Pertaining to Establishment of Branches," Acc. 96, Box 9; Hadas, *Reminiscences*.

14. *N.Y. Times*, Dec. 22, 23, 1922 (Chicago plant); B. R. Brown, *Reminiscences* (construction work); Klann, *Reminiscences* (general program, and Edsel's and Kanzler's role); *N.Y. Times*, Jan. 2, 1924 and *Ford News*, IV, March 15, 1924, 1 ff. (scope of program).

15. Max Wiesmyer, Hadas, *Reminiscences* (general planning, technical and architectural details); *Ford News*, III, May 15, 1923, 6–7, June 1, 1923, 1, Sept. 1, 1923, 1 ff., and IV, June 1, 1923, 1; *ibid.*, June 1, 1925, 1, 4 (Twin Cities Plant).

16. *N.Y. Times*, Jan. 2, 1924; *Ford News*, IV, July 15, 1924, 1; Wiesmyer, Hadas, *Reminiscences*.

17. Unnumbered General Letters, "Instructions to Branch Roadmen," Jan. 11, 1923, "Reductions in Branch Road Forces," April 11, 1922, and General Letter 1405, July 20, 1923, Acc. 78. For data on numbers of dealers and roadmen, and for supervisors' recommendations, see Acc. 6, Boxes 445, 446, and 447.

18. Branch Auditing Reports, Acc. 260, Box 5 (1921 figure); *Automotive Industries*, LVII, Dec. 10, 1927, 853–857 (for 1925).

19. General Letter 1358, March 22, 1923 (contacts between branch managers); General Letter 1107, Aug. 15, 1921 (dealers); both in Acc. 78.

20. General Letter 1529, July 15, 1924 (Edsel's comment); John H. Eagal, *Reminiscences*.

21. Unnumbered Letter, April 11, 1922, *op. cit.* For work of special roadmen, see Acc. 78, *passim;* for zone roadmen, see Unnumbered General Letter, "Instructions to Branch Roadmen," Jan. 11, 1923, Acc. 78.

22. Report on St. Louis Branch, A. W. L. Gilpin to Edsel Ford, Oct. 1, 1923, and R. S. Abbott to Edsel, Jan. 22, 1924, Acc. 6, Box 445 (dealer activities); report on H. B. Seitzer & Co., St. Peter, Minn., March 28, 1922, no accession number, Ford Archives (on farmers); unnumbered General Letter, "Dealers' Cars," Feb. 15, 1922, Acc. 78 (dealers); Report on St. Louis branch, A. W. L. Gilpin to Edsel, Oct. 1, 1923, Acc. 6, Box 445 (photographs); La Porte Heinekamp Motor Co. vs. Ford Motor Co., 24 Fed. Rep. (2nd) 861 (1928), 862–863

(dealers' contracts, etc.); Federal Trade Commission, *Report on Motor Vehicle Industry* (Washington, 1939), 106 ff. (general company-dealer practices), hereafter cited as FTC, *Report on Motor Vehicle Industry*.

23. R. S. Abbott to Edsel Ford, Jan. 22, 1924, Acc. 6, Box 445 (attitude of supervisors); Charles C. Hildebrand to Henry Ford, March 16, 1922, Acc. 285, Box 68 (shipment without notification); General Letter 1242, April 21, 1922, Acc. 78 (commissions); Eagal, *Reminiscences* (general conditions).

24. *Ford News*, IV, June 15, 1924, 1 (5,000,000th car); unnumbered General Letters, "Handling Second-Hand Cars," July 11, 1922, and "To All Minneapolis Branch Dealers," Dec. 27, 1923; General Letter 1589, April 14, 1925 (on handling trade-ins); General Letter 1248, May 4, 1922; Report on Chicago Branch, Gilpin to Edsel Ford, Feb. 19, 1925, Acc. 6, Box 445; General Letter 1572, Mar. 2, 1925 (company's warning). All general letters above are in Acc. 78.

25. Report on New Orleans Branch, May 7, 8, 9, 1924, R. S. Abbott to Edsel Ford; Report on Milwaukee Branch, A. W. L. Gilpin to Edsel, Jan. 27, 1925, both Acc. 6, Box 445.

26. The resentment of dealers with respect to fertilizer, the *Dearborn Independent,* and tractors, is reported in supervisors' letters, indicated in general letters, and discussed in various reminiscences.

27. Birmingham (Ala.) *News,* Jan. 7, 1924 (Brownell). Citations in preceding chapters on the Rouge, price cuts, etc. indicate the extent of "free publicity" about the Ford company.

28. *Automotive Industries,* XLIX, Aug. 16, 1923, 344 (on home office inactivity and advertising by dealers); E. G. Liebold to F. E. Lawrence, June 25, 1920, Acc. 284, Box 13; General Letter 1200, Nov. 19, 1921 (on more dealer advertising); General Letter 830, July 21, 1920 and unnumbered General Letter, "Newspaper Advertising Copy," Feb. 8, 1922 (materials supplied dealers); *N.Y. Times,* Aug. 17, 1923 and *Automotive Industries,* first citation in this note (restoration of advertising department); General Letters 1421, Sept. 5, 1425, Sept. 7, and unnumbered letter "Advertising Assessment to be Absorbed by Dealers," Oct. 22, 1923, and *Automotive Industries* article (on company-dealer advertising cooperation).

29. Unnumbered General Letters, "Dealers' Imprints in Advertising," Oct. 18, 1923, and "Newspaper Advertising," Jan. 7, 1924; supervisor's report on Charlotte Branch to Edsel Ford, Jan. 28, 1924, Acc. 6, Box 445; General Letter 1556, Dec. 11, 1924 (on advertising by competitors); Edsel Ford to Wetmore Hodges, April 30, 1924, Acc. 6, Box 56, and unnumbered General Letters, "Institutional Advertising," June 17, 1924, and "Institutional Advertising Discontinued," Sept. 30, 1924; *Wall Street Journal,* March 31, 1925.

30. James Dalton and Harry Tipper, "Percentage of Ford Gain Slips Behind Other Leaders," *Automotive Industries,* XLVIII, March 22, 1923, 651; Norman G. Shidle, "Has Ford Lost His Big 'Sales Punch' in the Low-Priced Field?" *ibid.,* Oct. 29, 1925, 727-729; Ford Motor Co. v. Parker Rust Proof Co., *op. cit.,* Leister's testimony, 2721-2725 (comment on changes in car); *Ford News,* V, Dec. 1, 1924, 1 (Dec., 1924 price cuts); James Dalton, "What Will Ford Do Next?" *Motor* (N.Y.), May, 1926, 106 (cuts from 1921 to Dec., 1924). Dalton lists cuts made on June 7, 1921, Sept. 2, 1921, Jan. 16, 1922, Oct. 17, 1922, Oct. 2, 1923, and Dec. 2, 1924.

31. Leister, as cited in 30 above, 2326 (Ford and price cuts); *Ford News,* IV, June 15, 1924, 1 (10,000,000th Ford); *Automobile Topics,* LXXIV, May 24, 1924, 122 (estimate of 7,000,000 Ford cars); Leister, *op. cit.,* 2377 (spare parts).

32. "Ford Industries, 1925," typescript dated Nov., 1924 (dealers and outlets); *Ford Owner and Dealer,* 1921-1924, Acc. 170; General Letters 1135, Sept. 14, and 1121, Aug. 30, 1921, unnumbered General Letter, "Parts Sales," June 23, 1923 (company attitudes); *Automotive Industries,* XLVI, Jan. 5, 1922, 37 (discounts); unnumbered General Letter, Jan. 25, 1922 (sales by dealers, 1920, 1921); article, *Automobile Topics,* cited in 26 above (profits).

33. Harry Tipper, "Automobile Finance Companies Needed to Help Dealers," *Automotive Industries,* XLVII, July 27, 1922, 182; E. A. Rumely to Liebold, Nov. 19, 1926, Acc. 285, Box 545; Liebold to Midwest Reserve Trust Co., Aug. 24, 1921, Acc. 285, Box 36; General Letter 1363, March 30, 1923, *N.Y. Times,* April 8, 1923, and *Automotive Industries,* XLVIII, April 12, 1923, 841 ff. (all on the plan); *Ford News,* III, May 15, 1923, 5, and Oct. 1, 1923, 1 (plan at

home and abroad); *N.Y. Times,* Oct. 6, 1929 (Ford on origin of plan); General Letter 1363, March 30, 1923 (Ryan).

34. *Ford News,* IV, Oct. 1, 1924, 1 (completions), V, March 15, 1925, 1 (later status); C. C. Housenick, *Reminiscences.*

35. Herman L. Moekle, *Reminiscences;* correspondence, Edsel and Crowther, with typescript of article, Acc. 6, Box 108, carrying Edsel's comments. In early 1929 Crowther submitted the article, for the *Youth's Companion,* to Edsel. His first sentence ran: "Edsel Ford at thirty-six is the richest man in the world." Edsel wrote in the margin: "Not true." Crowther substituted: "is one of the richest men in the world."

36. Black, Walker, *Reminiscences.*

37. U. Sinclair, "Henry Ford Tells," *Reconstruction,* I, May, 1919, 131; *Pipp's Weekly,* IV, July 28, 1923, 3; Galamb, *Reminiscences* (Ford and administration).

38. Galamb, Klann, *Reminiscences.* Foregoing sections on branch assemblies and marketing indicate the character of Edsel's and Kanzler's work. Some of Kanzler' letters to Edsel, Acc. 6, Box 270, reveal his fine cultural background and his gift for expression.

39. Memoranda, Conferences of June 22, 1920, and J. J. Harrington, Memorandum of Subjects Discussed with and Decided by Edsel Ford, July 19, 1921, both in Acc. 6, Box 34; *Pipp's Weekly,* I, May 15, 1920, 6; Hicks, Black, Walker, in their reminiscences; Ernest C. Kanzler, interview with authors, June 11, and letter to them June 24, 1956.

40. Liebold, *Reminiscences;* correspondence, Crowther and Liebold, Acc. 285, Boxes 164, 217 (on Crowther's relationship to Liebold and Ford); Black, *Reminiscences.*

41. *Ibid.,* (Liebold and the press, Liebold's ambitions); *Pipp's Weekly,* I, April 9, 1921 (detectives); Marquis, *Henry Ford,* 73–74; Walker to Ford, May 25, 1922, Acc. 285, Box 80; English to Edsel Ford, Jan. 2, 1920, Acc. 6, Box 31.

42. For Sorensen's rise, see Chaps. I, III, VIII, XI. Moekle, *Reminiscences,* notes Sorensen's entrance into branch and sales matters after Kanzler's departure.

43. *Pipp's Weekly,* I, May 15, 1920, 7; Black, Hicks, *Reminiscences* (blackbirds, conferences, and the "silent cure"); McCloud, Klann, *Reminiscences* (discharges). Ford's policy of playing one man against another is noted by Hadas ("Mr. Ford might have thought, 'Let's you and him have a fight and see how we come out' "), Haglund, and others. Haglund was a potential rival to Lumsden, his chief. Later he himself was "crowded" by an assistant named Wolfe.

44. Black, Hadas, *Reminiscences.*

45. Gehle, Miller, *Reminiscences.* Hadas gives the Sorensen-Edsel episode, and Simpson also notes how Sorensen would beat Edsel down in conference.

46. Hicks, Black, Gehle, in their reminiscences.

CHAPTER XI

The Rouge: Industrial Colossus (*Pages 279–299*)

1. The summary of Rouge activities is based on Van Deventer's articles (September, 1922 to September, 1923) and reports on progress in the *Ford News,* 1923–1924. Mr. Erwin Dasher, Assistant Superintendent of the Dearborn Assembly Building (formerly B Building) stated on July 21, 1955, in an interview, that in the middle 1920's transportation was chiefly by street car, bus, and jitney. The latter charged 10¢ per person to or from River Rouge (the village), 15¢ for Ecorse, and 20¢ for Wyandotte. Relatively few workers used their cars—Dasher had one, but kept it for Sundays.

2. Sorensen's position in 1919, as head of the Fordson plant, was an important one, but until after July he was of course not in the Ford Motor Co. When last employed there he had been Martin's assistant, while in the early 1920's Kanzler, who had been *his* assistant in the tractor plant, was Martin's superior and became a company vice-president. Kanzler states that Martin gave Sorensen orders for a time, but that Sorensen increasingly evaded them (interview with authors, June 11, 1956). Norman J. Ahrens, *Reminiscences,* speaks of Sorensen as "the man who made the deepest impression on me" of all Ford executives—"the most brilliant man I have

ever known with the ability to render the right decisions on the instant." Kanzler, referring to his complete loyalty to Ford, called him "a great soldier who carried out orders." For the European trip correspondence, see Acc. 38, Box 45.

3. Haglund, *Reminiscences*. Hanson confirms Haglund's account in all essential details.

4. Folder, "European Trip, 1921," Acc. 38, Box 45; Galamb, *Reminiscences*.

5. J. A. Spender, *Through English Eyes* (New York, 1928), 23; Van Deventer, "Links in a Complete Industrial Chain," *Industrial Management*, LXIV, Sept. 1922, 137.

6. Van Deventer, "Mechanical Handling of Coal and Coke" and "By-Products from Coke Oven Gases," (second and third articles in his series), *Industrial Management*, LXIV, Oct., Nov., 1922, 195–201, 280–287.

7. *Ibid.*, "How the Blast Furnace Unit Fits Into the Ford Industrial Chain," (fourth article) Dec., 1922, 321–328; Haglund, Hanson, Joe Lawry, in their reminiscences. Hanson gives a full and interesting account of the process, which was rather complicated.

8. Van Deventer, as cited in Note 7.

9. *Ibid.*, "Plant Facilities of the World's Biggest Foundry," "Operations in the World's Biggest Foundry," "Machine Operations on Ford Cylinders and Fordson Pistons," (articles five, six and ten in his series), LXV, Jan., Feb., June, 1923, 1–11; 67–76; 359–368; Verner, *Reminiscences*.

10. Lawry, *Reminiscences* (on moving the foundry machine shop from Highland Park); *Ford News*, II, Aug. 1, 1922, 1; *ibid.*, III, June 15, 1923, 1; IV, Feb. 1, 1924, 1 (on foundry production); Spender, *op. cit.*, 25–26.

11. Matthew W. Potts, "Mechanical Handling at the River Rouge," *Industrial Management*, LXVIII, Aug., 1924, 85; Fay L. Faurote, "Planning Production Through Obstacles and not Around Them," *Factory and Industrial Management*, LXXV, Feb., 1928, 305.

12. Riecks, *Reminiscences*.

13. Faurote, as cited in Note 11, 302, 304–305; *ibid.*, "Single-Purpose Manufacturing," *Factory and Industrial Management*, LXXV, April, 1928, 769–772, and "What Is Going On Behind the Scenes at the Ford Plants," LXXIV, Nov., 1927, 257.

14. Van Deventer, as cited in Note 5, also *ibid.*, "Machine Tool Arrangement and Parts Transportation" (article nine), *Industrial Management*, LXV, May, 1923, 259; Faurote, "Make Time and Space Earn Their Keep," *Factory and Industrial Management*, LXXV, March, 1928, 545; *The Ford Industries: Facts About the Ford Motor Company and its Subsidiaries* (Detroit, 1924), 44–45; Hanson, *Reminiscences*.

15. *Ford News*, V, Feb. 1, 1925, 5 (motor assembly); Feb. 15, 1925, 1 (turbo-generator); June 15, 1925, 1 (pressed steel); Aug. 1, 1925, 4 (Spring and Upset); Oct. 15, 1925, 5 (concrete); and *ibid.*, VI, Feb. 1, 1926, 1 (Spring and Upset); Hanson, *Reminiscences*. Hanson gives an admirable account of the entire steel development at the Rouge, for which he had overall planning responsibility.

16. James Sweinhart, "Ford Building Steel Factory," Detroit *News*, Dec. 26, 1924; Harold F. Baker, "Steel Mills in Detroit Base Sales on Time Savings," *Automotive Industries*, LXIII, Sept. 13, 1930, 362 f.

17. Wibel, Haglund, Hanson, *Reminiscences*.

18. Production Records, Acc. 38, Box 108; *Automotive Industries*, XLIX, July 2, 1923, 89; Haglund, Lumsden, *Reminiscences*.

19. Lumsden, Hanson, *Reminiscences*.

20. *Ford News*, VI, March 15, 1926, 1; Lumsden, *Reminiscences*. Haglund gives a briefer account which tallies with Lumsden's. Hanson, *Reminiscences*, says that the real trouble lay in a failure to follow specifications for ladle steel, which caused warpage in both of these units.

21. Haglund, Hanson, *Reminiscences*.

22. *Ibid.*; *N.Y. Times*, Feb. 11, 1929 (Ford steel production); *Ford News*, VI, Feb. 15, 1926, 3, 4. While the Purchasing Department asserted it could buy steel cheaper than the Ford plant could make it, Hanson states that they had no dependable figures to back this assertion, that the savings in transportation were enormous, and that in times of scarcity the company could produce at a half or a third of inflated market prices.

23. Fay L. Faurote, "How Ford Plans His Layout of Grounds, Buildings and Plant," *Factory and Industrial Management*, LXXV, June, 1928, 1196 (area and buildings); L. J. Thompson Papers, Acc. 384, Box 1 (sale of land); Dearborn *Press*, July 30, 1938 (plant cleaning); *Ford News*, V, Nov. 1, 1925, 1 (employees). As to land, Ford sold 399.2 acres in 1917 for $709,856, its exact cost, 293.9 acres in 1921 for $442,709.59, and 429.689 acres in 1924 for $669,734.43 (both again for the purchase price).

24. *Ford News*, VII, Oct. 1, 1927, 1, 8; *ibid.*, IX, July 15, 1929, 158, 167.

25. McCloud, Anthony Harff, Haglund, Klann, Hanson, Logan Miller in their reminiscences; *N.Y. Times*, Nov. 18, 19, and Dec. 12, 1927.

26. Haglund, Logan Miller, *Reminiscences*.

27. Haglund, *Reminiscences*.

28. *Ibid.*; Miller, *Reminiscences*.

29. Van Deventer, "Machine Tool Arrangement and Parts Transportation" (ninth article), *Industrial Management*, XLV, May, 1923, 259; Faurote, "Make Time and Space Earn Their Keep," 545, and "Planning Production Through Obstacles, Not Around Them," 305, both cited above. For the effects of Ford's arbitrary price reductions on factory pace, see Chapters VI, X, and XVI. Hanson, *Reminiscences*, notes that the intensive mechanization kept men closely to their work.

CHAPTER XII

From Muscle Shoals to Anti-Semitism (*Pages 300–323*)

1. Mark Sullivan, *Our Times: The Twenties*, VI (New York, 1935), 522–523; Erwin, *Henry Ford vs. Truman H. Newberry*, 99, 100, 101.

2. Collier to Ford, July 7, 1923, Acc. 62-2, Box 88; Commons to Ford, June 8, 1918, Acc. 62, Box 60; *Wall Street Journal*, Oct. 3, 1922; *Detroit Saturday Night*, XVI, Aug. 3, 1922; *Pipp's Weekly*, II, Feb. 25, 1922, 5 (Vandenberg statement).

3. Black, Liebold, *Reminiscences; Pipp's Weekly*, II, Feb. 18, 1922, 9, 10; Hammond to A. Hussey, June 25, 1923, Acc. 572. A. R. Pinci in the *Forum*, LXXVIII, Aug., 1927, 181–189, asserts that Woodrow Wilson wished Ford to run in 1924.

4. *Ibid.*; William L. Stidger, *Henry Ford*, 80–87; Black, *Reminiscences*.

5. Liebold, *Reminiscences;* Collier to Ford, July 5, 1922, Acc. 62-2, Box 88; Record to Lucking, June 5, 1922, *ibid.*; Charles Merz, *And Then Came Ford* (Garden City, N.Y., 1929), 217–237 (Chap. 11); *N.Y. Times, N.Y. World*, Aug. 10, 1923; *N.Y. Times*, Dec. 20, 21, 1923.

6. *N.Y. Times*, Jan. 9, 1924 (Cameron interview); C. J. Smith, *Reminiscences*.

7. Sixty-seventh Congress, 2nd Session, House Doc. 67.

8. Gray Silver to Ford, June 2, 1921, Acc. 62-2, Box 1; J. W. Worthington to Liebold, July 21, 1921, Acc. 285, Box 81; Sixty-seventh Congress, 2nd Session, House Doc. 167, 14–18 (text of Ford offer).

9. Acc. 285, Boxes 248, 256 (support of Ford offer); Gifford Pinchot to W. G. McMurchy of St. Paul *News*, Acc. 285, Box 81; *N.Y. Times*, May 10, 1922 (Norris's statement).

10. Sixty-seventh Congress, 2nd Session, House Doc. 167, 18–24; House Report 1084.

11. Worthington to Liebold, Aug. 13, 1921, Acc. 285, Box 81; *N.Y. Times*, Jan. 12, 1922.

12. Interview, Detroit *News*, March 17, 1922; *N.Y. Times*, March 18, Sept. 7, 1923; *Collier's Weekly*, July 26, 1924.

13. Liebold, *Reminiscences; N.Y. Times*, Oct. 16, 1924 (Ford withdraws offer); *Collier's Weekly*, Oct. 18, 1924.

14. Statement, Controller's Office, Ford Motor Co., on "Earnings and Losses of Foreign and Domestic Companies, 1920–1927."

15. Liebold, Reminiscences (in general, and on Tannenbaum and Strauss); Detroit *Journal*, Oct. 26, 1914, *Boston Traveller, Herald*, Nov. 21, 1914, and correspondence, Fair Lane Papers, Box 134, on Edison. E. T. Berger's stock option is covered in Chap. IV.

16. *Pipp's Weekly*, I, March 5, 1921, 1; J. L. McCloud, *Reminiscences;* C. à Court Repington,

The First World War, 1914–1918 (London, 1920), 384. Repington here talks with Maurice Rothschild on the subject. Romain Rolland's classical novel *Jean Christophe* contains a sharp arraignment of Jewish writers for their alleged vulgarization of the theater and the novel. Anatole France vigorously expressed anti-Semitic opinions. In pre-Hitler days such utterances were taken less seriously than later. On the European continent anti-Semitism had political connotations; never in England or America.

17. J. J. O'Neil to Liebold, Nov. 26, 1919, Acc. 62, Box 81.

18. Address of E. G. Pipp, Temple Israel, Akron, O., April 5, 1921, Acc. 6, Box 256.

19. Street Sales Reports, Dearborn Publishing Co., Acc. 62-2, Box 23; Merz, *And Then Came Ford*, 183, 184; *N.Y. Times*, April 24, 1927 (Bernstein suit). As stated in a note in the text, the suit was settled out of court.

20. *Pipp's Weekly*, I, June 11, 1921, 1; *N.Y. Times*, Jan. 6, 1921 (Franklin's statement).

21. London dispatch, *N.Y. Times*, July 10, 1927; Circulation Reports, Dearborn Publishing Co., Acc. 62-2, Box 52.

22. *Dearborn Independent*, Dec., 1921, March, 1922; *Pipp's Weekly*, II, Jan. 28, 1922; *N.Y. Times*, Jan. 6, 1922. "Mr. Ford's Page" in the *Independent* still lustily attacked the "international financiers" and the "international power," of which, Ford asserted, bankers and foreign ministers were merely pawns. See his article in the *Independent* of Oct. 28, 1922.

23. The attacks on Sapiro were signed Robert Morgan, and were supported by editorials. For typical attacks see issues of Dec. 13, 1924 and April 11, 1925, the second alleging a plan for "world cotton domination."

24. The *Dearborn Independent* professed to welcome this suit. "The main thing is to get this Sapiro system of cooperation presented to the farmers of the United States more fully and fairly. . . . In a court of law that system can be turned, even to its inmost corners, to the bright light of competent and impartial scrutiny." (*Dearborn Independent*, Jan. 31, 1925.)

25. The trial was fully covered by the *N.Y. Times* and *World*, and the Detroit *Times* and *News*, March 15–April 22, 1927. Sapiro at first alleged 141 distinct libels, but later reduced the number by 54. Senator Reed cross-examined him mercilessly on the stand, asserting that he had collected exorbitant fees (which does not seem to have been the fact), and that his motives in organizing farm cooperatives were bad. William C. Richards in *The Last Billionaire: Henry Ford* (New York, 1948), quotes Bennett. Both Sward, *The Legend of Henry Ford*, 155, and Harry Bennett, *We Never Called Him Henry* (New York, 1951), 48–56, cast doubt on the reality of Ford's accident. Liebold, as indicated in the footnote on p. 31, states emphatically that there was one, and this is borne out not only by the Ford Hospital doctors but also by other Ford employees in a position to know.

26. The woman juror was Mrs. C. Hoffman; Judge Raymond publicly cleared her, and blamed the "depraved journalism" of the Detroit *Times* for the mistrial. The *N.Y. Times*, in an editorial, "Still a chance for Mr. Ford," April 24, 1927, suggested the course which he shortly took.

27. *Dearborn Independent*, July 31, 1927 (text of apology); *N.Y. Times*, *World*, and *Tribune*, July 8, 9, with editorial comment. Louis Marshall commented in the *N.Y. Times*, July 14, 1927. and N. D. Perlman described the Davis-Perlman-Marshall-Palma conferences in the *Times* of July 11.

28. This was the period of an organized revolt of grocers and butchers against Ford's food stores for employees. (*N.Y. Times*, March 28, 1927). Ford's letter to Bernstein is noted in the *N.Y. Times*, July 25, 1927.

CHAPTER XIII

A Bright Dawn Pales (*Pages 324–354*)

1. Edwin P. Norwood, *Ford Men and Methods* (Garden City, N.Y., 1931), 41–116; *Ford: the Times, the Man, the Company*, 512–567.

2. For a thorough analysis of the labor situation as America entered the first World War, see

W. Jett Lauck and Edgar Sydenstricker, *Conditions of Labor in American Industries* (New York, 1917).

3. Samuel M. Levin, "Ford Profit-Sharing, 1914–1920," *Personnel Journal*, VI, Aug., 1927, 77 ff.; Frederick C. Mills, "Price Movements and Related Industrial Changes," in *Recent Economic Changes in the United States*, II, 603–655; Frederick L. Paxson, *America at War, 1917–18* (Boston, 1939), 150, 151.

4. Hadas, *Reminiscences; Ford Man*, II, Oct. 3, and III, Dec. 31, 1918, Jan. 17, 1919; IV, Dec. 31, 1919. *The Auto Workers' News*, issued by Local 127 of the United Automobile, Aircraft, and Vehicle Workers of America, for two years beginning May 15, 1919, covers the 1919–1920 agitation for higher wages. Top management was then discussing labor policies, considering plans which would have eased the pressures of high prices and rents. In the spring of 1920 a strike in the Ford foundry gave workers there an increase of 40 cents an hour (*Auto Workers' News*, April 22, 1920). The *Ford Man* of Dec. 31 contained a full company statement of the bonus plan, pointing out that "the recent purchase of the holdings of minority stockholders and the great financial obligations incurred thereby" made it difficult to offer more generous benefits. See also "The 1920 Ford Plan: Bonus and Stock Sharing," *Dearborn Independent*, Jan. 10, 1920.

5. *N.Y. Times*, Nov. 25, 1920; S. M. Levin, *op. cit.*

6. See records of the Ford Motor Company, Industrial Relations Planning and Analysis Department, Ford Archives. The average hourly earnings in all American Ford plants and branches in 1920 were $.8545; in 1921, $.8665. They then declined to $.8036 in 1925, rose to a maximum of $.96 in 1931, and fell with the depression.

7. One employer, James Inglis of the American Blower Company, wrote Henry Ford in Oct., 1920 regretting that he did not accompany his price reductions with a statement that wages must also be reduced, "and that profiteers in the laboring class would have to be dealt with." (Acc. 62-1, Box 9.)

8. *Ford Man*, IV, April 3, 1920; General Letters 771 and 778, May 18 and June 22, 1920, Acc. 78; W. M. Cunningham, "*J.8*": *A Chronicle of the Neglected Truth About Henry Ford D.E. and the Ford Motor Company* (Detroit, about 1931), 50–52; General Letters 1181, 1251, Oct. 26, 1921, May 10, 1922, Acc. 62-2, Box 24.

9. General Letter 1283, Aug. 31, 1922, Acc. 62-2, Box 24; *Ford News*, Aug.–Sept., 1922, *passim;* J. E. Bossardet, *Reminiscences;* data from Planning and Analysis Section, Labor Relations Department, Ford Archives.

10. *Idem.; Ford News*, III, March 15, 1923, 1; Sward, *op. cit.*, 78, 79; Detroit *Times*, Jan. 24, 1921.

11. Talk to Investigators, April 15, 1914, S. S. Marquis Papers, Ford Archives, hereafter cited as Marquis Papers; George Heliker, interviews with Buren Webster and E. D. Brown, Nov. 2, 1952; Report, Acc. 62, Box 59; Instructions, Marquis Papers.

12. *Ibid.*, for general details; Memorandum, Sept. 10, 1917, Marquis Papers (changed character of inquiry under Marquis).

13. Testimony before Judge Alschuler, Nov. 23, 1920, Acc. 63, Box 1.

14. Marquis, *Henry Ford*, Chap. 6.

15. *Idem.;* John R. Lee, "So-called Profit-sharing in the Ford Plant," *Annals of the American Academy of Political and Social Science*, LXV, May, 1926, 297–310.

16. George Heliker, interview with W. A. Nelson, Aug. 1, 1954.

17. Boyd Fisher, Detroit Chamber of Commerce, draft of article, Acc. 62, Box 58.

18. "Criticisms of the Ford Plan" (no date), Marquis Papers.

19. "Comments by Church Officials," "Comments by Judges and Police Officials," etc., Marquis Papers.

20. "Human Interest Story, Number Thirty-Four," June 18, 1915, signed A. C. Tait, Marquis Papers.

21. S. M. Levin, *op. cit.*

22. *Ford Man*, I, Dec. 17, 1917, and later issues; S. M. Levin, *op. cit.*, 84, 85 (English School).

23. F. E. Searle, *Reminiscences; Ford News*, V, June 1, 1926, 2; Detroit *Free Press*, March 10, 1952.

24. Searle, *Reminiscences;* Superintendent's Reports, Ford Archives.

25. Fred Nicholson, "An Evaluation of the Training Program of the Henry Ford Trade School," M.A. thesis, Wayne University (typescript); Jerome Davis, "Henry Ford, Educator," *Atlantic Monthly,* CXXXIV, June, 1937, 804–806.

26. "Ford Schools," Mimeographed Report, June, 1928, Acc. 6, Box 157; Davis, *op. cit.;* Searle, *Reminiscences.*

27. Superintendent's Report, Feb. 5, 1934, Acc. 6, Box 162; Searle, *Reminiscences.*

28. Minutes of Operating Committee, March 23, 1916, Acc. 85, Box 5; Minutes of Executive Committee, Feb. 28, 1917, Acc. 85, Box 75; Memorandum on Policy, Feb. 28, 1918, Acc. 75, Box 88.

29. Complaints, Fair Lane Papers, Box 126 (letters to Clara Ford); S. S. Marquis to Edsel Ford, June 28, 1920, Marquis Papers.

30. *Ford Man,* III, Dec. 3, 17, 1919; IV, Jan. 17, Feb. 3, 17, March 3, and later dates, 1920; *Ford News,* IV, Sept. 1, 1924, 1, 5; A. S. V. Brenton, "Henry Ford's Stores," *Hays System News,* June, 1940, 24; W. A. S. Douglas, "The Row About Henry Ford's Grocery," *Literary Digest,* XCIII, April 16, 1927, 12–13; *N.Y. Times,* April 5, 1927.

31. Minutes of Operating Committee, March 7, 1916, Acc. 85, Box 5; *N.Y. Herald,* March 10, 1919; Liebold to Robert Gair Company, Brooklyn, Dec. 21, 1920, Acc. 62-2, Box 4; Liebold, *Reminiscences.* The investment was not less than $1,750,000, on which annual profits of $30,000 give 1.7 per cent interest. (Acc. 62-2, Box 4.)

32. *N.Y. Times,* Jan. 26, 1921; Mrs. Barbara Carritte (Marquis's daughter), *Reminiscences.*

33. Marquis, *Henry Ford, passim,* contains enlightening evidence on this change.

34. *Recent Economic Changes,* II, 433–464; *Statistical Abstract of the United States, 1940* (Washington, Government Printing Office, 1941), 349–351.

35. Ford's announcement is in the Detroit *Times, News,* March 25, 1922; his statement is in the *N.Y. Times,* March 25; comments by Gompers and Woll appear in *N.Y. Times,* March 26, 1922.

36. See Detroit *Labor News,* July 27, 1923, for Ford's interview in the *Monitor,* and editorial comment.

37. W. L. Chenery, "Ford Backs His Ideas After Ten Years' Test," *N.Y. Times,* Aug. 10, 1924; Dean Marquis, *Henry Ford: An Interpretation,* 127.

38. Klann, *Reminiscences;* Marquis, *op. cit.,* 103, 155.

CHAPTER XIV

Ford Overseas: The Expansive Years (*Pages 355–378*)

1. *Ford: the Times, the Man, the Company,* 358–362, 408, 510.

2. *Automobile,* XVII, Aug. 29, 1907, 308 (Couzens); *Ford Times,* IX, November, 1916 (Boyle). The *Times* contains many examples of Model T efficiency in the war.

3. *New International Year Book,* 1920; *Ford News,* II and III: Nov. 1, 1921, 1, 6; Oct. 15, 1923, 3, 7 (general foreign news); Nov. 15, 1921 (China); April 15, 1922 (Canada); Jan. 15, 1923 (Russia); Feb. 15, 1923 (Uruguay); VII, Jan. 1, 1927, 2 (Ford pinion in Palestine).

4. *New International Year Book,* 1922–1925; *N.Y. Times,* Dec. 17, 1922 (Chinese students); *Ford News,* VII, Feb. 15, 1927, 1 (Russian orders); July 1, 1927, 7 (Dutch army classes); July 15, 1927, 6 (Spanish tour). Files of the *Ford News* contain many such items.

5. On this conference, see unsigned 19-page memorandum, Nov. 8, 1923, Acc. 572.

6. Knudsen Report and related materials, Acc. 6, Boxes 260 ff.; Russell I. Roberge, *Reminiscences.*

7. Roberge, who had important responsibilities in foreign operations, outlines the standard modes of development in his reminiscences.

8. Klann, Roberge, Briggs, Gehle, Wiesmyer, in their reminiscences; Correspondence, Acc. 6, Boxes 260 ff., 551. Wiesmyer states that layouts were made in Detroit for the Belgian and

later the Dutch plants. As to design, Sir Stanford Cooper, vice-chairman of the Ford Motor Co., Ltd., in August, 1952 cited to Allan Nevins numerous instances of the harm done Ford sales abroad by adherence to outdated styling.

9. Pound, *The Turning Wheel*, 245–251.

10. On policy differences, see Knudsen Report, Note 6 above.

11. Perry, Aug. 18, 1914, to Norval Hawkins on Empire marketing, Acc. 572; Lord Perry in Nassau, interview with the authors, March 28, 1952. In the recorded conversations of March, and in July–August conferences with Nevins alone, Lord Perry emphasized the cancellation of plans for the Southampton factory (which he said Ford had definitely promised to build), as the reason for his resignation.

12. Klingensmith to Perry, March 22, 1918, and Perry to Klingensmith, April 10, 1918, Acc. 6, Boxes 260, 551; Minutes, special meeting Ford Motor Co., Ltd., May 13, 1919, Acc. 6, Box 551 (acceptance of Perry's resignation and election of W. C. Anderson as his successor); Henry Ford to Perry, Oct. 9, 1919, Fair Lane Papers, Box 145. Copies of Klingensmith's letter went to Ford executives.

13. Particularly for his services as Deputy Controller, Mechanical Warfare Department, and Director of Traction, Ministry of Munitions, Perry was made K.B.E. Couzens had been unwilling when war began to permit the British company to do anything officially for the families of men in service, but after he left, Perry with the approval of Edsel Ford and other Ford officers created a fund consisting of one-half the average earnings of the servicemen. Later a trust was established which took over the fund on April 15, 1918; the trustees included the well-known manufacturer and sociologist, H. S. Rowntree, as well as some Ford officers. Perry also made the most of Ford's wartime service in supplying tractors to Britain, and of the home for Belgian refugees which Henry and Clara Ford maintained at Oughtrington Hall. His activities in placing Ford in a better light are covered in the London *Times* and in his March, 1952 interview with the authors. See also his correspondence with Edsel Ford, Acc. 6, Box 551.

14. Perry, interview with authors, *op. cit.*; Sorensen, interview with authors, June 29, 1954. Numerous letters in the Ford Archives testify to the cordial relationship between Sorensen and Perry, and Sorensen spoke of it at some length, and warmly.

15. *Automobile Topics*, LV, Sept. 20, 1919, 773; *Automotive Industries*, XLI, July 24, 1919, 195; Oct. 23, 1919, 836; Nov. 13, 1919, 992.

16. Gehle, *Reminiscences;* correspondence, Acc. 6, Box 551 (Anderson). Recalled from London Dec. 31, 1920, Anderson was succeeded a month later by Charles L. Gould, who in turn resigned April 15, 1924, and was succeeded by H. S. Jenkins. Gehle corroborates Perry's belief that Gould was a failure. For one reason, his training was in sales: he knew nothing of manufacturing. Jenkins, who had served in Rio de Janeiro, did better.

17. See the *Motor Trader*, May 9, 1923; and other materials from that journal in Acc. 38, Box 108.

18. Figures supplied by the Ford Motor Co., Ltd., from its files in Dagenham.

19. Gehle, Klann, *Reminiscences;* Perry to Clara Ford, Dec. 31, 1918, Fair Lane Papers, Box 145; E. L. Clarke, Manchester, Dec. 24, 1926, to Sorensen, Acc. 38, Box 54. Gehle was sent to England early in 1923 with authority to make necessary changes, and remained two years. He and Klann, who accompanied him, discharged Gould and others. Gehle discovered that British cars covered 10 miles more to the gallon than the Ford, and were more pleasing to British customers. He brought back a sheaf of figures, statements, and recommendations for the improvement of the British Ford, and Edsel and Kanzler supported him in urging them. As to wages and workers, Clarke in 1926 reported to Sorensen: "We have raised our line foremen and charge hands 2d. per hour effective December 1. This showed the foremen in a practical fashion what the five-day week meant and they got after their jobs with a great deal more energy. . . . We are firmly establishing the thought in the minds of the charge hands and men that by increasing their output and giving a better return they will enable us to pay them that extra rate which we are planning."

20. Perry, interview with authors, *op. cit.*; N.Y. *World*, Nov. 23, 1916; Cork *Examiner*, March 19, 1917; Sorensen to Daniel T. McConnell, Irish National Bureau, Acc. 38, Box 43.

21. Edward Grace to Sorensen, Dec. 4, 1920, Acc. 38, Box 43; Grace to W. C. Anderson, Nov. 2, 1920, Acc. 38, Box 46.

22. Stewart to Sorensen; Grace to Sorensen, Oct. 22, 1920, both in Acc. 38, Box 43.

23. N.Y. Times, Feb. 27, March 2, 7, 8, 11, April 12, 1922.

24. Edsel Ford took a keen interest in British operations, and played a direct part in improving them (1923–1924), as his letters and cablegrams show (Acc. 6, Box 260.)

25. Citroën to Ford Company (cable), June 30, 1919; Sorensen to Citroën, July 1, 1919, Acc. 572.

26. W. E. Davis and E. Grace, Report on French Survey, June 22, 1921, Acc. 572; ibid., J. J. Harrington, cablegram to Edsel Ford, Paris, Dec. 11, 1926; Schedule of European Registrations in 1929, sent to Sorensen Nov. 17, 1931, Treasurer's Office, Ford Motor Company.

27. Ford News, II, Oct. 15, 1922, 1; V, Jan. 1, 1925, 1, 4.

28. Sorensen to Liebold, Jan. 1, 1922, Acc. 38, Box 43; N.Y. Times, Oct. 26, 1930 (Section III).

29. Ford News, VI, April 15, 1926 (general on German plant); N.Y. Times, Aug. 22, 1926, Section II (on shop council).

30. Schedule of Nov. 17, 1931, op. cit.; N.Y. Times, March 4, 1928. This article reviews German tariff history after the import embargo on cars was removed in October, 1925.

31. Perry to Sorensen, Feb. 1, 1934, Acc. 38, Box 23 (Fordita and the Italian government); Ford News, V, Dec. 1, 1925, 5 (Trieste plant); letter, Ford employee, Trieste (name illegible) to J. J. Miller, Detroit, Dec. 30, 1926, Acc. 572.

32. The Ford Times, Canadian edition, which began monthly publication at Walkerville, Ont., in Aug., 1913, is the fullest general source of information about the Canadian company. The Ford News (American) contains numerous brief articles about Canada. For the Australian company see Ford News, IV, Feb. 15, 1924, 3, 8, and V, July 15, 1925, 1, 5.

33. Orberg, Reminiscences; Briggs, Reminiscences; Ford News, V, Nov. 15, 1924, 1, Jan. 1, 1925, 5 (on Latin American plants and methods of shipment to them); Automotive Industries, XLIX, Nov. 8, 1923, 971 (Latin-American trade); Report, 1930, on "Results Obtained in South America and Orient," Acc. 38, Box 4.

34. Ford News, IV, Nov. 1, 1924, 1; Nov. 15, 1; Dec. 1, 1; VI, June 1, 1926, 1.

35. Statement of assets made by Russell I. Roberge, Sales Department, Ford Archives.

36. Roberge, Moekle, Klann, in their reminiscences; J. J. Harrington, Brussels, to Ryan in Detroit, Dec. 7, 1926, Acc. 572.

37. Ford News, IV, Nov. 1, 1923, 1 (Japan); Ford Times, VIII, Oct., 1914, 1, 7, 41; Dec., 1914, 138. Of Japan, Roberge wrote Edsel from Tokyo Sept. 7, 1924: "Practically all passenger cars are chauffeur driven, and the law requires an assistant Chauffeur or footman on the front seat of all hired cars except taxicabs."(Acc. 6, Box 267.) For more on Japan, see Roberge, Reminiscences.

CHAPTER XV

Winds of Challenge (*Pages 379–408*)

1. Preston W. Slosson, *The Great Crusade and After* (New York, 1931), *passim;* Robert S. and Helen M. Lynd, *Middletown: A Study in Contemporary American Culture* (New York, 1929), especially Chap. XVIII, "Inventions Re-Making Leisure."

2. "Tenting on the New Camp Ground," N.Y. Times, Aug. 13, 1922; R. L. Duffus, *The Independent*, CXVI, Feb. 13, 1926, 183, 184.

3. N.Y. Times, Feb. 3, 10, Aug. 13, 1922.

4. Jean Labatut and Wheaton J. Lane, Eds., *Highways in Our National Life: A Symposium* (Princeton, 1950), 95, 96; N.Y. Times, March 23, 1926; *Recent Economic Changes*, I, 246.

5. *American Yearbook*, 1926, 581–585; Department of Agriculture Bulletin No. 1279; *Recent Economic Changes*, I, 246; L. E. Van Norman, "Motors and Highways End Isolation," N.Y. Times, May 29, 1927; Slosson, *op. cit.*, 231–234.

6. Ralph C. Epstein, *The Automobile Industry: Its Economic and Commercial Development* (Chicago and New York, 1928), 9; *Recent Economic Changes*, I, 273; *U.S. Statistical Abstract*, 1940, 417.

7. Liebold, Hakes, *Reminiscences*.

8. Murray Fahnestock, "Reviewing Ten Years of Ford Development," *Ford Owner and Dealer*, XXI, April, 1924; N.Y. *World*, Aug. 27, 1916.

9. Leslie Henry, "The Ubiquitous Model T," *Antique Automobile*, XVI, June, 1952; F. A. Ames, Inc., Owensboro, Ky., in *Ford Owner*, XIII, April, 1920.

10. Frederick Lewis Allen, *Only Yesterday* (New York, 1931), 6–7; Fahnestock, *op. cit.*

11. Earnest Elmo Calkins, "Beauty the New Business Tool," *Atlantic Monthly*, CXL, Aug., 1927, 146.

12. Additional Tax Case, Hearings, Norval A. Hawkins, 1689; Klann, *Reminiscences;* J. C. Young, "Ford to Fight It Out with His Old Car," N.Y. *Times*, Dec. 26, 1926; Galamb, *Reminiscences;* Ford Motor Co., General Letter 712, March 29, 1920.

13. Murray Fahnestock, *ut. sup.;* Hadas, Galamb, in their reminiscences.

14. Kroll, *Reminiscences;* Fahnestock, *ut. sup.*

15. L. V. Spencer, "Metamorphosis of the Motor Car," *Motor Age*, XXIX, March 9, 1916, 5–11; *Automobile Topics*, XL, Jan. 22, 1916, 1081–1082; *ibid.*, XLIV, Dec. 23, 1916, 698; N. G. Shidle, "Economy and Efficiency Increased by New Final Assembly System," *Automotive Industries*, XLV, July 14, 1921, 69–72; series of articles by P. S. Hanna on Hudson plant in *Wall Street Journal*, Oct. 8, 21, Nov. 10, 22, 1926.

16. Henry M. Jewett, president of Paige-Detroit, N.Y. *Times*, June 14, 1925; N.Y. *Times*, Aug. 1, 1926.

17. Sloan, *Adventures of a White Collar Man*, 113–118; *Automotive Industries*, XLVI, March 30, 1922, 732.

18. Additional Tax Case, Hearings, 1690; James Dalton, "What Will Ford Do Next?", *Motor*, May, 1926, 114.

19. N.Y. *Times*, Jan. 8, 1923; Kennedy, *The Automobile Industry*, 164–165; files of *Automobile Topics*, 1922–1925.

20. H. A. Tarantous, "Better Motor Cars This Year," N.Y. *Times*, Jan. 7, 1923, and "Motor Cars of 1924 Better in Every Way," N.Y. *Times*, Jan. 6, 1924; E. R. Plimpton, "Four-Wheel Motor Car Brakes," N.Y. *Times*, Aug. 12, 1923.

21. Tarantous, N.Y. *Times*, Jan. 6, 1924.

22. Booth Tarkington, *The World Does Move* (Garden City, N.Y., 1928), 149, 150, 264; Slosson, *op. cit.*, 130 (episode of Lincoln car); F. J. Keppel in *Recent Social Trends in the United States*, one-vol. edition (New York, 1933), 876–980, and especially 958, 966; Ford Motor Co. v. Parker Rust Proof Co., III, 2345 (H. L. Leister).

23. *Automobile Topics*, LIII, Feb. 8, 1919, 54, 55; J. M. Worthing, "Woman's Place is Now in the Driver's Seat," N.Y. *Times*, Jan. 6, 1929, Sec. XI; *Motor Age*, XXI, May 10, 1917, 85, 86; Kennedy, *The Automobile Industry*, 164–165.

24. James Dalton, "Cautious Production Is Need," *Motor*, XLIV, Sept., 1925, 33; N.Y. *Times*, Aug. 16, 1925, Jan. 7, 1926.

25. Lawrence H. Seltzer, *Financial History of the American Automobile Industry* (Boston and New York, 1928), 121–122; Epstein, *op. cit.*, 281–284; J. C. Young, "Ford to Fight It out with His Old Car.," N.Y. *Times*, Dec. 26, 1926.

26. Pound, *The Turning Wheel*, 192–229; Sloan, *Adventures of a White-Collar Man*, 125, 139–140; FTC, *Report on the Motor Vehicle Industry*, 427; Beasley, *Knudsen*, 117; *Ward's Automobile Yearbook*, 1952, 85.

27. N.Y. *Times*, May 9, 1922; Sloan, *op. cit.*, 103–111, 140–141; C. McD. Puckette, "General Motors: A Romance of Business," N.Y. *Times*, Aug. 14, 1927; Pound, *op. cit.*, 193–199; R. L. Duffus, "The Rise of a Billion Dollar Corporation," N.Y. *Times*, Nov. 18, 1928; Seltzer, *op. cit.*, 211.

28. *Automobile Topics*, LXIII, May 211921, 19–20 (Hawkins); W. S. Knudsen, "For Economical Transportation," *Industrial Management*, LXXIV, Aug., 1927, 65–68; "General Motors II: Chevrolet," *Fortune*, XIX, Jan., 1939, 37 ff.

29. *N.Y. Times*, Dec. 3, 1926; "Chevrolet," *Motor*, Oct., 1942, 114, 162.

30. Galamb, Kroll, in their reminiscences.

31. *N.Y. Times*, Jan. 6, 1924; Ford Motor Co. General Letter 1425, Sept 7, 1923, Acc. 78.

32. *Automotive Industries*, XLIX, Aug. 23, 1923, 399; General Letter 1425, Sept. 6, 1923; Hadas, *Reminiscences.*

33. *Ford News*, V, Sept. 1, 1925, 1, 3, 4.

34. *Automotive Industries*, LIII, Aug. 27, 1925, 326; *Ford News*, IV, Nov. 15, 1925, 1.

CHAPTER XVI

The End of Model T *(Pages 409-436)*

1. Sheldrick, Gehle, *Reminiscences.*

2. Unsigned memorandum by Ernest C. Kanzler, Jan. 26, 1926, Fair Lane Papers, Box 116; Farkas, Sheldrick, *Reminiscences; N.Y. Times*, July 27, 1926 (Kanzler's resignation).

3. Sheldrick, Farkas, *Reminiscences.*

4. *My Life and Work*, 148, 149; E. G. Kingsford to Henry Ford, May 12, 1927, Acc. 285, Box 756.

5. Stella Benson, *The Little World* (New York, 1925), 117 ff.

6. *Ford News*, V, Sept. 1, 1925, 1 ff.; James Dalton, "What Will Ford Do Next?", *Motor*, May, 1926. 101; *Automotive Industries*, LIV, June 24, 1926, 1113.

7. "Chevrolet," *Motor*, Oct., 1942, 114, 162; Plantiff to W. A. Francis, May 14, 1926, Acc. 66, Box 1. Some of Plantiff's pungent reports to Edsel are found in Acc. 6, Box 447. He was then (1925) acting as a district supervisor.

8. S. A. Stellwagen, report on San Francisco branch, June 17-19, 1926, Acc. 6, Box 447.

9. *Automotive Industries*, LXII, April 12, 1930, 592-593; Chevrolet handbill in letter, Edsel to Henry Ford, March 20, 1924, Fair Lane Papers, Box 27.

10. J. M. Leonard, *The Tragedy of Henry Ford* (New York, 1932), 224 ff.; E. A. Rumely to Edsel Ford, Sept. 11, 1926, Acc. 6, Box 82; Report of Charles L. Lathus, Sales Department, Dec. 6, 1926, Acc. 23, Box 4.

11. S. G. Stewart to Henry Ford, May 13, 1927; E. R. Preston to Ford Motor Co., Feb. 10, 1927; Noble Widows to Henry Ford, Aug. 1, 1926, all in Acc. 285, Box 756.

12. C. E. Griffin, *The Life History of Automobiles*, Michigan Business Studies, I, No. 1 (Ann Arbor, 1926).

13. Paul M. Mazur, *American Prosperity: Its Causes and Consequences* (New York, 1928), 92-97; Wibel, *Reminiscences.*

14. J. C. Young, "Ford to Fight It Out with His Old Car," *N.Y. Times*, Dec. 23, 1926; B. C. Forbes, "Ford Loses Motor Leadership: Amazing Facts," *Forbes's Magazine*, April 15, 1927, 32.

15. *Automotive Industries*, LVII, Dec. 10, 1927, 855; *Motor*, LIV, Nov., 1930, 31; Report, S. A. Stellwagen to Edsel Ford, Jan. 28, 1926, Acc. 6, Box 447; Herring to Edsel Ford, Jan. 7, 1928, Acc. 6, Box 78.

16. Carter to W. A. Ryan, Jan. 14, 1926, Acc. 285, Box 457.

17. Manafee Motor Co. *et. al.* to Henry Ford, June 22, 1926, Acc. 285, Box 528; H. C. Apgar to Mrs. Henry Ford, Nov.. 25, 1926, Acc. 285, Box 497; George C. Nichols to Edsel Ford, March 13, 1926, Acc. 6, Box 81.

18. Eagal, *Reminiscences: Automotive Industries*, LVI, Feb. 19, 1927, 225; S. J. Vinson, circular letter, Feb. 10, 1927, Acc. 38, Box 444; William P. Young, *A Ford Dealer's Twenty Year Ride* (Hempstead, N.Y., 1932), 67.

19. *Automotive Industries*, LVII, Dec. 3, 1927, 845; Baltimore *News*, April 28, 1927; Stellwagen to W. A. Ryan, with report, Nov. 1, 1926, Acc. 285, Box 648; Plantiff to Edsel Ford, Oct. 14, 1926, Acc. 66, Box 1.

20. A. J. Langford (Dallas, Tex.) to Edsel Ford, May 29, 1926, Acc. 6, Box 446; Plantiff to W. A. Ryan, Dec. 2, 1926, Acc. 38, Box 138.

21. Stellwagen to Ryan, Nov. 1, 1926, Acc. 285, Box 648; A. J. Langford to Edsel Ford, May 29, June 7–9, 1926, Acc. 6, Box 446.

22. Sheldrick, Farkas, in their reminiscences.

23. Galamb, Sheldrick, in their reminiscences; Stellwagen to Edsel Ford, with report, Jan. 28, 1926, Acc. 6, Box 447.

24. This exchange is in Acc. 38, Box 138. Sorensen pooh-poohed the matter—nobody was "worried one bit."

25. Hadas, *Reminiscences;* Rumely to Henry Ford, June 16, 1926, Acc. 6, Box 82.

26. James C. Young, interview with Ford, *N.Y. Times,* Dec. 26, 1926; *ibid.,* Jan. 19, 1927.

27. See notices, Clipbooks 43, 44, Ford Archives; Avery McBee in Baltimore *Sun,* May 22, 1927; Detroit *News, Free Press,* May 19, 1927; *N.Y. Times,* N.Y. *World,* May 26–30, 1927.

28. *N.Y. Times,* N.Y. *Tribune,* May 26, 1927.

29. Detroit *News, Times,* May 26, *Free Press,* May 27, 1927; Farkas, *Reminiscences;* Brisbane to Henry Ford, June 17, 1927, Acc. 6, Box 86; E. A. Rumely to Ford, Dec. 2, 1927, Acc. 285, Box 696; Edsel Ford to W. L. Hughson, July 5, 1927, Acc. 6, Box 89; Folder: "Statistics—Mr. Cameron, Misc. Worksheets, June 15, 1935," Martindale Papers, Ford Archives. Another figure given is 15,457,868.

30. *N.Y. Times,* Oct. 30, 1927; Brisbane to Ford, Sept. 13, 1927, Acc. 23, Box 1.

31. Tim Wilson, Kapowsin, Wash., to Henry Ford, July 27, 1928, Acc. 285, Box 904.

32. Leslie R. Henry, *Antique Automobile,* XVI, June, 1952, 3.

33. San Antonio & Arkansas Pass Railway Company vs. Singletary, as quoted in *N.Y. Times,* May 31, 1925.

34. *Automotive Industries,* LVII, July 30, 1927, 147; Henry, as cited in Note 33.

35. Gerald Carson, *The Old Country Store* (New York, 1954), 288.

CHAPTER XVII
Throes of New Birth (*Pages 437–458*)

1. *N.Y. Times,* July 31, 1927 (Ford's comment) and Sept. 29, 1927 (Ford and General Motors); Frederick Lewis Allen, *Only Yesterday,* 162, 163 (popular interest).

2. *N.Y. American,* Sept. 11, 1927; J. W. Swain to Henry Ford, Nov. 25, 1927, Acc. 285, Box 708.

3. *N.Y. Times,* Nov. 29, 1927 (speed): Ray Priest, "Ford, Sixty-Six, Spends Birthday on Job," Detroit *Times,* July 30, 1929 (Ford quoted); Sheldrick, *Reminiscences.*

4. *Ibid.;* Charles Vining, "Bunk' Says Henry," *Toronto Star Weekly,* Jan. 4, 1928; *Moving Forward,* 165; FTC, *Report on the Motor Vehicle Industry,* 657.

5. "Mr. Ford Doesn't Care," *Fortune,* VIII, Dec., 1933, 65; B. C. Forbes, "Ford Loses Motor Leadership," *Forbes,* April 16, 1927, 32; Galamb, Hicks, Sheldrick, McCloud, reminiscences.

6. Farkas, N.F.H. Olsen, Sheldrick, reminiscences.

7. McCloud, *Reminiscences,* E. Y. Watson, "Ford Research Conducted on Competitive Basis," Detroit *News,* Oct. 31, 1931.

8. Hicks, *Reminiscences;* John Billings, Jr., Brooklyn *Daily Eagle,* Oct. 16, 1927; "There Are No Automobiles," *Fortune,* II, Oct., 1930, 73.

9. N. F. H. Olsen, Sheldrick, Dale Roeder. *Reminiscences;* Waldemar Kaempffert, "The Dramatic Story Behind Ford's New Car," *N.Y. Times,* Dec. 18, 1927.

10. *N.Y. Times,* Nov. 29, 1927; Vining, "Bunk! Says Henry," *op. cit.;* Farkas, *Reminiscences.*

11. Sheldrick, *Reminiscences.*

12. Kaempfert, as cited in Note 9; Galamb, N. F. H. Olsen, Sheldrick, Hicks, reminiscences; *Automotive Industries,* LVII, Dec. 10, 1927, 856.

13. Kaempfert, *op. cit.; N.Y. Times,* Aug. 14, Oct. 29, 1927; Doss, *Reminiscences;* J. C. Wetmore, N.Y. *Sun,* Sept. 21, 1927.

14. Kaempfert, *op. cit.;* Hicks, *Reminiscences; N.Y. Times,* Aug. 11, 1927.

15. Roeder, A. M. Wibel, *Reminiscences; N.Y. Times,* July 25, 1927.

16. *Cram's Automotive Reports,* July 9, 1927, 6; Wibel, Pioch, *Reminiscences; Ford News,* VII, Sept. 1, 1927, 1; Kaempffert, *op. cit.*

17. *Ibid.* (quoting Sorensen); F. L. Faurote, "Planning and Mass Production Coordinated," *Factory and Industrial Management,* LXXV, May, 1928, 986; *Ford News,* VI, July 15, 1926, 2 ff.; Aug. 1, 1926, 1 ff.; and VII, March 1, 1927, 1 (all on welding); *Cram's Automotive Reports,* Oct. 8, 1927, 6–7; *N.Y. Times,* Oct. 15, 1927 (Ford's statement).

18. *Cram's Automotive Reports*—"Confidential Ford Report" (special release), Oct. 22, 1927, also Nov. 26, 1927, 6, 7; *N.Y. Times,* Oct. 23, 25, Nov. 2, 1927; *Ford News,* VIII, Dec. 1, 1927, 1.

19. *N.Y. Times,* Dec. 4, 1927 (effect of car on general conditions), and Dec. 21, 1927 (advertising); *The Ford Dealer Story* (Dearborn, Mich., 1953), 80–81.

20. *The Westward* (weekly newspaper), Nov. 16, 1927; *Automotive Industries,* LVII, Nov. 12, 1927, 735; *N.Y. Times,* Dec. 1, 1927.

21. Merz, *And Then Came Ford,* 300–301. For accounts of the various unveilings, see also the press in key cities for early December.

22. *N.Y. Times,* Dec. 2, 1927 (Edsel); Galamb, *Reminiscences; N.Y. Times,* March 23, 1928.

23. E. D. Kennedy, *The Automotive Industry,* 200; *The Rebel Prince: Memoirs of Prince Louis Ferdinand of Prussia* (Chicago, 1922), 159.

24. Liebold, *Reminiscences; N.Y. Times,* Dec. 2, 1927.

25. *N.Y. Times,* Nov. 28, Dec. 1, 1927; *Ford News,* VIII, Dec. 15, 1927, 1.

26. Detroit *News,* Dec. 8, 1927; Klann, *Reminiscences;* Charles Vining, *Toronto Star Weekly,* Jan. 4, 1928.

CHAPTER XVIII
Model A: A New Era *(Pages 459–478)*

1. *N.Y. Times,* Dec. 4, 1927. Said the Pittsburgh *Press,* Dec. 4, 1927: "There are only two kinds of people in Pittsburgh today: those who have, and those who have not seen the Ford." In Detroit, the first day brought 115,000 persons to Convention Hall to see the car. (Detroit *Free Press,* Dec. 4, 1927.)

2. William L. Hughson to Edsel Ford, Jan. 5, 1928, Acc. 6, Box 101; Ford Motor Co., General Letter on Model A Deliveries, Feb. 22, 1928, Acc. 235, Box 15; Edsel Ford to John A. Gerhauser, July 30, 1928, Acc. 6, Box 276.

3. Bredo Berghoff, Klann, and Albert Smith, in their reminiscences.

4. *N.Y. Times,* Jan. 10, Feb. 13, 1928; telegram, Gov. Roland H. Hartley to Henry Ford, Dec. 7, 1927, Acc. 38, Box 56; H. S. Jenkins to Sorensen, Dec. 16, 1927, Acc. 38, Box 51; *ibid.,* Jenkins to Production Dept., Dec. 23, 1927; Sorensen to L. E. Titus, Acc. 38, Box 56; Sorensen to H. S. Jenkins, Jan. 3, 1928, Acc. 38, Box 51; *N.Y. Times,* Feb. 19, 1928; *Ford News,* VIII, Aug. 1, 1928, 158 ff.

5. Sorensen to Thomas Farmer, May 21, 1928, Acc. 38, Box 113; "Monthly Production of Cars and Trucks," March 5, 1929, Acc. 38, Box 59; Russell Gnau to Herman Maise, April 24, 1928, and Sorensen to Thomas Farmer, May 21, 1928, Acc. 38, Box 113; *Automotive Daily News,* July 27, 1928; Phil S. Hanna, "Ford Plans No Radical Change," *Wall Street Journal,* June 8, 1931. By April, 1928, the company's unfilled orders had swelled to 800,000, and by May to 1,000,000.

6. James O'Connor, *Reminiscences; N.Y. Evening Post,* May 12, 1928 (Model A's in use after six months).

7. E. W. Alexander to Edsel Ford, Nov. 12, 1927, Acc. 6, Box 85; Rockleman's undated letter, May, 1928, Acc. 235, Box 15; *Automotive Daily News,* Dec. 10, 1928.

8. New York dealers to Henry Ford, June 26, 1928, Acc. 285, Box 735; correspondence, 1927–28 in folder "Ford Model A," Acc. 6, Box 276; Merz, *And Then Came Ford,* 303.

9. Couzens to Edsel Ford, Dec. 7, 1927, and Edsel Ford to Couzens, Dec. 15, 1927, Acc. 6,

Box 87; *ibid.,* Douglas Fairbanks to Edsel Ford, Jan. 3, 1928; correspondence, Edsel Ford, 1928, in Acc. 285, Box 734; "A Few Famous Owners of Model A Cars," *Ford News,* VIII, Dec. 15, 1928, 276.

10. David Ragin to Henry Ford, Oct. 2, 1928, Acc. 285, Box 870; *Automotive Daily News,* July 27, 1928; Hughson to E. G. Liebold, Oct. 1, 1928, Acc. 285, Box 821.

11. Confidential Report, Universal Credit Corp., from inception to Dec. 31, 1928, Minute Book, Acc. 33, Box 97; Epstein, *The Automobile Industry,* 115–122 (general use of finance companies). Under Norval Hawkins, a Ford policy of depositing funds in banks serving Ford branch areas had been inaugurated, with the understanding that the banks would extend credit to Ford dealers, who would assist customers. This policy had been continued under Ryan.

12. Minute Book, Universal Credit Corp., Consolidated Balance Sheet, Dec. 31, 1929, Acc. 6, Box 116; press release, April 18, 1928, in Minute Book; *N.Y. Times,* May 4, Sept. 19, 1928; folder, "Re: Authorized Ford Finance Plans," Acc. 33, Box 95; *Ford News,* IX, March 15, 1929, 71.

13. *N.Y. Times,* July 8, Aug. 18, 29, 1928; *Ford News,* VIII, July 2, 1928, 133 ff.; "Monthly Production of Cars and Trucks," March 5, 1929, Acc. 38, Box 59; Sorensen to Edsel Ford, Aug. 10, 1928, Acc. 6, Box 276.

14. Ray Priest, "Million New Fords Out," Detroit *Times,* Feb. 4, 1929; *Automotive Daily News,* Dec. 19, 1928, Jan. 24, 1929.

15. *Ford News,* VII, Dec. 1, 1928, 253; General Letter, "December Exhibits," Nov. 15, 1928, Acc. 235, Box 15; Ford advertisement, *N.Y. Times,* Dec. 20, 1928; Klann, *Reminiscences;* "Statement of Net Cash Expenditures," etc., Acc. 38, Box 57; FTC, *Report on Motor Vehicle Industry,* 645.

16. Sheldrick, Klann, Olsen, Galamb, in their reminiscences; *N.Y. Times,* Nov. 4, 1928. The *Times* stated that the cast iron content of the car had been increased from 20 to 35 pounds in the previous fortnight.

17. General Letters, "Price Changes," Nov. 8, 20, 1928, Acc. 235, Box 15; Charles Morgana, *Automotive Daily News,* Dec. 8, 1927 (price and weight); "Comparison of Cost and Sales of Automobiles and Trucks Produced . . . March, 1928 and Nov., 1926," statement by W. E. Carnegie, Acc. 38, Box 57.

18. *Automotive Daily News,* Jan. 3, 10, 1928. The latter issue gives details of the 1928 Chevrolet.

19. *Automotive Daily News,* Nov. 16, 1928.

20. "General Motors, II: Chevrolet," *Fortune,* XIX, Jan., 1939, 40; "Chevrolet Production Change Over to 6-Cylinder Car Held Industrial Feat," *Automotive Daily News,* Feb. 8, 1929.

21. Editorial, *Automotive Daily News,* Jan. 18, 1929; Kennedy, *The Automobile Industry,* 313; *Men, Money, and Motors,* 249–259.

22. "Chrysler," *Fortune,* XII, Aug., 1935, 31.

23. Walter P. Chrysler, in collab. with Boyden Sparkes, *Life of an American Workman* (New York, 1950), *passim,* hereafter cited as Chrysler, *Life of an American Workman;* "The Chrysler Operation," *Fortune,* XXXVIII, Oct., 1948, 151 ff.; Kennedy, *op. cit.,* 135; T. F. McManus, *The Sword-Arm of Business* (New York, 1927), 154; FTC, *Report on Motor Vehicle Industry,* 549 ff.; J. C. Gourlie, "Dodge-Chrysler Merger United Two Great Properties," *Automotive Industries,* LVIII, June 9, 1928, 864; Chrysler, *op. cit.,* 175 ff.

24. *Ibid.,* 179–181.

25. Walter Boynton, "Sparks from the Show," *Automotive Daily News,* Jan. 11, 1929; "The Chrysler Operation," *Fortune,* loc. cit., 151.

26. In addition to the sources just cited, see *Automotive Industries,* LII, June 25, 1925, 1163; *Automotive Daily News,* Dec. 5, 1929.

27. Chrysler, *op. cit.,* 191–192; Kennedy, *op. cit.,* 170 ff.; William Z. Ripley, *Main Street and Wall Street* (Boston, 1927), 86 ff.

28. Detroit *News,* July 31, 1928; *N.Y. World,* July 31, 1928.

29. Editorials, *Automotive Daily News,* June 4, Aug. 6, 1928; *N.Y. Times,* Jan. 6, 1929.

30. *Automotive Daily News,* June 4, Aug. 6, 1928.

31. *Ibid.,* July 5, 1928.

32. Norman G. Shidle, "Mergers Past and Present," *Automotive Industries*, LVIII, June 9, 1928, 865–866; editorial, *Automotive Daily News*, June 4, 1928.

33. *Ibid.*, May 11, June 30, Aug. 4, Sept. 5, 1929. The highest daily record for the Model T had been 9109, on Oct. 31, 1925. (*Ford Motor Co. Facts and Figures*, 1953.) The *N.Y. Times* of July 6, Aug. 4, and Sept. 5, 1929, has interesting material on daily and monthly records.

34. Confidential Report, Universal Credit Corporation, Acc. 33, Box 95; "Ford Motor Company, Current Assets, Current Liabilities, and Net Current Assets," in folder, "Financial Statements . . . 1918–1933," Acc. 134, Box 45; FTC, *Report on the Motor Vehicle Industry*, 648.

CHAPTER XIX
Projects and Personalities (*Pages 479–507*)

1. *Detroit Saturday Night*, X, June 24, 1916, 13.

2. "Fair Lane: the House and Gardens," (pamphlet), Bull., No. 3, Ford Motor Co. Archives, 1955; Fair Lane Papers, Box 93 (fragment about rose gardens); *ibid.*, Box 38 (correspondence about and description of rose garden).

3. *My Life and Work*, 236; Frank Parker Stockbridge, "Henry Ford, Amateur," *World's Work*, XXXVI, Sept., 1918, 515.

4. *Ibid.; Ford News*, V, April 1, 1925, 3 (flour mill); *Ford Man*, IV, June 3, 1920, 1 (oak tree).

5. Letter, Clara B. Ford to Mrs. Meade, postmarked Oct. 24, 1919, on exhibit, Ford Archives; Mimeographed Biography, Edsel Ford, Acc. 23, Box 3.

6. Acc. 6, Box 261 (property deeded to Edsel); "The Edsel B. Ford Lake Shore Estate at Grosse Pointe Shores, Michigan," (Folder) Ford Archives; Liebold, *Reminiscences.*

7. "Fair Lane," cited in Note 2 above; Correspondence, Fair Lane Papers; *ibid.*, Box 94 (notes and recipes); *Pipp's Weekly*, III, May 6, 1922, 2; Margaret Ford Ruddiman, *Reminiscences.*

8. Carl Sandburg, "Carl Sandburg Chats With Henry Ford," Chicago *Daily News*, Dec. 25, 1928; interview by Allan Nevins with J. D. Rockefeller, Jr., Jan. 12, 1952.

9. Correspondence and exhibits on camping trips, Fair Lane Papers, Box 97; Bayard Johnson (Dartmouth College), "The Four Vagabonds," Research Papers, Acc. 423; Alfred Lief, *Harvey Firestone: Free Man of Enterprise* (New York, 1951), 164–167, 171–177; 181 ff., 214; Harvey Firestone, in collab. with Samuel Crowther, *Men and Rubber* (New York, 1926), 190–194.

10. *My Life and Work*, 240. Firestone, in *Men and Rubber*, 194, says, "We became a kind of travelling circus."

11. Fair Lane Papers, Box 98 (on *Sialia*); Norman J. Ahrens, *Reminiscences* (*Henry Ford II* and vacations).

12. Correspondence, photographs, and reports, Fair Lane Papers, Box 41 (on both Georgia and Florida properties); Acc. 384, Box 1 (financial details, Georgia properties).

13. Folder, "Travel," Fair Lane Papers, Box 97.

14. See files of *N.Y. Times*, April, 1928 and October, 1930.

15. Eleanor Clay Ford to Henry Ford, August 16 (?), 1918, Fair Lane Papers, Box 32; Acc. 6, Box 269 (early Seal Harbor); Acc. 6, Box 378 (Haven Hill); Portland (Maine) *Telegram*, July 7, 1929 (description of Seal Harbor house).

16. Acc. 6, Boxes 269, 272.

17. *Moving Forward*, 281; Hicks, Voorhess, McCloud, Klann, and Liebold in their respective reminiscences.

18. *N.Y. Times*, May 10, 1929 and March 5, 1930; Johnson, as cited in Note 9 above.

19. William A. Simonds, *Henry Ford and Greenfield Village* (New York, 1938), 224–235 (on soy bean experiments); McCloud, *Reminiscences* (on Boyer and Dr. Ruddiman); Galamb, Sheldrick, Wibel, Hicks, C. J. Smith, in their reminiscences; *N.Y. Times*, Feb. 17, 1929 (Phelps); Simonds, *Henry Ford*, 30, 38–39, 201.

20. George Brown, *Reminiscences* (dances in 1909–1911); Simonds, *Henry Ford*, 30, 38–39, 201; Simonds, *Henry Ford and Greenfield Village*, 74–75; *Today and Tomorrow*, 222–224; McCloud, *Reminiscences; Ford News*, VIII, Jan. 15, 1928, 3 (Ford orchestra and 28 dances).

21. *N.Y. Times*, Dec. 14, 1925; *Ford News*, VII, Jan. 15, 1927, 1 (radio broadcasts); Mr. and Mrs. Henry Ford, *"Good Morning"* (Dearborn, 1926), 7–17; McCloud, Simpson, in their reminiscences.

22. *My Life and Work*, 206, 210; H. V. Wilkins, "Ford Working on New Car," Detroit *Times*, Feb. 15, 1927.

23. *My Life and Work*, 214–219; Liebold, *Reminiscences;* W. L. Graham, "The Henry Ford Hospital, Detroit: Its Organization, Policies, Plant," *Hospital Management*, (Chicago), Nov., 1924 (series of articles), Acc. 6, Box 264.

24. *Ibid.; Ford Times*, IX, Dec., 1915, 213–221; Detroit *News*, Oct. 27, 1918; Detroit *Journal*, July 31, 1919; Liebold, *Reminiscences;* Correspondence, Acc. 6, Box 264 (showing Edsel's role); *ibid.*, report of Sept. 15, 1926 to Edsel and Henry Ford (finances); Simonds, *Henry Ford*, 157.

25. *Today and Tomorrow*, 177, 180; *The Sun* (N.Y.), Nov. 26, 1929 (Dearborn Board of Education); Henry Ford, "Why Henry Ford Wants to Be Senator," *World's Work*, XXXVI, Sept., 1918, 523; Frederick Searle, *Reminiscences;* Upton Sinclair, "Henry Ford Tells Just How Happy His Great Fortune Has Made Him," *Reconstruction*, I, May, 1919, 130. The *Ford News* throughout the 1920's carried many news articles on the trade school.

26. Liebold, C. J. Smith, in their reminiscences; Detroit *News*, Oct. 1, 1920 (first collecting in Akron, O.); Correspondence, Nov.–Dec., 1922, Campsall–Cameron, Campsall–Boston Antique Shop, Campsall–Henry Ford, Acc. 285, Box 83.

27. Pamphlets and Correspondence, Berry School, Fair Lane Papers, Box 44; data on Henry and Clara Ford's contributions, Ford Archives; Fair Lane Papers, Box 43. The figures given on contributions, 1919–1950, are drawn from the Henry Ford Office Files, and can only be approximate, as they are based on income tax reports and recorded expenditures, and neither of the Fords left any complete record of their gifts or other disbursements. However, the totals may be taken as approximately correct, but somewhat below what was given. A sheet in Box 44, cited above, shows that contributions to the Berry Schools began in 1922 with $139, and by February 11, 1928 totalled $1,118,602. Since extensive construction for which the Fords were paying was then in process, and since both 1929 and 1930 were good years as to Ford income, it is possible that including 1930 about $2,000,000 were spent on the Berry Schools.

28. Samuel Chamberlain, *Longfellow's Wayside Inn* (Boston, 1938), *passim;* Israel Sack, *Reminiscences* (furnishings); *Ford News*, VII, March 1, 1928, 45; *Today and Tomorrow*, 225–228; Acc. 384, Box 1 (financial); *N.Y. Times*, July 20, 1923, Dec. 6, 1925 (furnishings from Ohio and Penna.); *ibid.*, Jan. 18, Feb. 13, 1927 (Mary and her lamb); Dec. 12, 1928 (highway alteration); May 24, July 14, Sept. 22, 1928 (colonial homes).

29. Acc. 384, Box 1; *Today and Tomorrow*, 222, 225, 227.

30. *Ibid.*, 225; Simonds, *Henry Ford and Greenfield Village*, 117, 179–211; *N.Y. Times*, Feb. 20, 1925 (purchase of Edison equipment); *ibid.*, April 24, 1928 (toll house), July 16, 17 (Menlo Park group), and Oct. 15 (Burbank's office); Liebold, *Reminiscences;* Henry Ford in Collab. with Samuel Crowther, *Moving Forward* (New York, 1931), 125, hereafter cited as *Moving Forward*.

31. Frank Vivian, *Reminiscences; N.Y. Times*, Feb. 12, 1929, and March 4, Aug. 17, 1930; Voorhess, *Reminiscences*. The *Times* articles cover various gifts to Ford.

32. Liebold, *Reminiscences; Ford News*, IX, June 15, 1929, 135, 137, and Nov. 1, 1929, 242–245; *N.Y. Times*, Sept. 28, 1928 (laying cornerstone); Simonds, *Henry Ford and Greenfield Village*, 134–135 (Edison and Menlo Park group).

33. Simonds, as in Note 32, 115, 147, 215 ff.; Sward, *The Legend of Henry Ford*, 263–265 (exhibits); Voorhess, Liebold, *Reminiscences* (museum personnel); Acc. 292, Box 6 (schools); Acc. 23, Box 2 (Darrow); *N.Y. Times*, Feb. 14, 1930 (Ford's announcement).

34. Liebold, Maher, *Reminiscences*. The Edison Museum never developed as Ford had

planned it, perhaps because he was more interested and confident with respect to primary and secondary education than in more advanced training.

35. Data on Henry and Clara Ford's contributions (see Note 27). For Edsel's contributions, see correspondence and memoranda in boxes of Acc. 6. No reliable estimate exists for his total gifts.

36. Data on Henry and Clara Ford's contributions, *op. cit.*

CHAPTER XX
How the Workers Fared (*Pages 508–540*)

1. Stidger, *Henry Ford*, 188 ff.; Selig Perlman and Philip Taft, *History of Labor in the United States* (New York, 1935); Norman Ware, *Labor in Modern Industrial Society* (Boston, 1935); Leo Wolman, *Ebb and Flow in Trade Unionism* (New York, 1936) and *Industry-wide Bargaining* (New York, 1938).

2. Robert Dunn, *Labor and Automobiles* (New York, 1929); A. J. Muste, *The Automobile Industry and Organized Labor* (Baltimore, 1936).

3. Arnold and Faurote, *Ford Methods and the Ford Shops*, 330 ff.; Norwood, *Ford Men and Methods*, Chaps. IV, V, 49–82.

4. Reports of the Safety and Hygienic Department for 1918 *et seq.*, Acc. 62, Box 28; Norwood, *op. cit.*

5. Klann, Wibel, *Reminiscences* (various aspects of safety); *Ford News*, IV, March 1, 1925, 3 (analysis of safety hazards, and table of accidents for Ford plants at home and abroad).

6. Klann, *Reminiscences;* Chen-Nan Li, "A Summer in the Ford Works," *Personnel Journal*, VII, June, 1928, 18 ff.

7. Cunningham, "*J 8*": *A Chronicle of the Neglected Truth About Henry Ford, etc.*, 23 ff. W. A. Nelson, interviews with George B. Heliker, August, 1953.

8. Norwood, *op. cit.*, 46–47.

9. W. A. Nelson, as cited in note 7 above.

10. Klann, *Reminiscences*.

11. W. A. Nelson, as cited above. Records of the Treasurer's Office, Ford Motor Company.

12. Klann, *Reminiscences;* Orry Barrule (Leslie MacDonald), "Life with Uncle Henry," unpublished MS., Ford Archives.

13. *Auto Workers' News*, Dec. 9, 1920; W. J. Renwick to Henry Ford, Nov. 10, 1920, Fair Lane Papers, Box 126; *Automotive Industries*, XLIV, April 21, 1921, 876.

14. Norwood, *op. cit.*, 9–10.

15. *Factory and Industrial Management*, LXXV, Jan., 1928, 62 ff.

16. W. A. Nelson, as cited above.

17. Klann, *Reminiscences;* Louis Adamic, *Dynamite: the Story of Class Violence in America* (New York, 1931), 401–402; Murray Godwin, "Apology for Ford," *New Freeman*, III, 105 ff.

18. *Ibid.*

19. Klann, *Reminiscences*. Similar stories are told by other employees in their reminiscences.

20. Henry Ford in collaboration with Samuel Crowther, *Moving Forward* (Garden City, N.Y. 1931), 48 ff., 118–119; 141–152; *My Life and Work*, 263–264.

21. W. A. Nelson, as cited above.

22. Klann, *Reminiscences; N.Y. Times*, Feb. 17, 1923, Aug. 10, 1924.

23. Industrial Relations, Planning, and Analysis Dept., Ford Motor Co. (figures); "Entrance Wage Rates for Common Labor," *Monthly Labor Review* (Dept. of Labor), XXVIII, May, 1929, 179–181; *ibid.*, "Wages and Hours in the Motor Vehicle Industry," 181–187.

24. *Today and Tomorrow*, 153–154, 158.

25. *Moving Forward*, 81–82; Reinhold Niebuhr, "How Philanthropic Is Henry Ford?" *Christian Century*, Dec. 9, 1926.

26. Report of April 19, 1927, Acc. 185, Box 2; Chen-Nan Li, *op. cit.*

27. *N.Y. Times*, Nov. 22, 1929; Detroit *Times*, Nov. 23, 1929.

28. *N.Y. Times*, Dec. 4, 1929; correspondence, Acc. 38, Box 14, and Acc. 285, Box 971; Reports, F.M.C. Industrial Relations, Planning, and Analysis Dept., Ford Archives; *Moving Forward*, 74.

29. Correspondence, Acc. 38, Box 64; Detroit *News*, March 25, 1931; Statistics, Treasurer's Office, Ford Motor Company; Albert Conn, *Reminiscences*.

30. John Reed, "Industry's Miracle Man," *Metropolitan Magazine*, Oct., 1916; *My Life and Work*, 262–263; *Ford News*, II, Sept. 15, 1922, 2.

31. *Dearborn Independent*, Nov. 22, 1919, 3; *Detroit Labor News*, July 27, 1923 (quoting Ford from *Christian Science Monitor*); *N.Y. Times*, Oct. 31, 1925 (Wall Street influences).

32. Papers, A. H. Buhl to Henry Ford, Ford Archives, particularly letter of March 2, 1918 (American Protective League, founded about April 1, 1917); Reports, B. J. Liccardi, Ford Archives; "Ford's Secret Service," *Pipp's Weekly*, II, June 11, 1921, 1–4.

33. William Green to S. M. Levin, May 5, 1925 and James O'Connell to Levin, Jan. 18, 1926; *Detroit Labor News*, Feb. 5, 1926 (Michigan Federation of Labor convention, and remarks of William Collins).

34. Willis Ward, *Reminiscences;* "The Negro in Detroit," Prepared for the Mayor's Interracial Committee by. . . . the Detroit Bureau of Governmental Research; Herbert R. Northrup, *Organized Labor and the Negro* (New York, 1944); David L. Lewis, "History of Negro Employment in Detroit Area Plants of Ford Motor Company 1914–1941," a University of Michigan typescript essay (1954), 56, and *passim*.

CHAPTER XXI
Ford Overseas: the Years of Storm (*Pages 541–569*)

1. FTC, *Report on Motor Vehicle Industry*, 34–36; London *Economist*, May 10, 1930.

2. Tables in Sorensen File, Acc. 6, Box 310.

3. *N.Y. Times*, Dec. 3, 1927, May 6, 1928 (Sec. III). Ford created a stir by refusing to visit Ireland in protest against Free State tariff on motor cars and parts.

4. Conversation, C. E. Sorensen with authors, June 29, 1954.

5. Perry to Sorensen, March 1, 1929, Acc. 6, Box 310; London *Economist*, Nov. 29, 1930, April 11, 1931.

6. In the summer of 1952 Allan Nevins visited Dagenham, talked with the principal executives, and examined company records. He also talked at length with Lord Perry in London. Klann, *Reminiscences*, deals with choice of Dagenham site and early operations.

7. Ford Motor Co., Ltd., First Annual Report, March 8, 1930, contains a history of building operations. Perry reported: "We own approximately 491 acres of freehold land, and our factories will, in the first instance, occupy approximately 71 acres with 41 retained for immediate development." Hanson, *Reminiscences*, recounts his part in the operation, in which he was assisted by Boyd, an English engineer supplied by Perry.

8. "It is most annoying," Perry wrote Sorensen of the American gobbling of shares earmarked for Britons (Acc. 38, Box 115). The London *Economist* followed the operation; see, e.g., the issue of March 8, 1930. See also Report of the General Meeting of the Ford Motor Company, Ltd., March 18, 1931, published as a pamphlet. Hanson discusses the burning of garbage. After being dried in a preliminary operation, it could be used as fuel.

9. The London *Economist*, March 31, 1934, gives production figures 1929–1933 by major companies. See also E. C. Lester, "With £250 the Limit," *Autocar*, March 7, 1930; and for prospects of the Ford Motor Co., Ltd., London *Economist*, March 31, 1931.

10. Report Second General Meeting F.M.C., Ltd., March 18, 1931; Perry to Edsel Ford, Dec. 2, 1931, Acc. 38, Box 115.

11. Perry to Sorensen, Feb. 16, 1933, Acc. 6, Box 310; Sorensen, conversation with the authors, *op. cit.*

12. Acc. 38, Box 111.

13. Annual Reports, Ford Société Anonyme Française, 1929, 1930, 1931; Lord Perry, conversations with Nevins, June, July, 1952.

14. Kennedy, *The Automobile Industry*, 220-221.

15. Annual Reports of F.M.C., Ltd., 1930, 1931, 1932; "Ford Progress in Europe," *Barron's Weekly*, May 18, 1931; "World Production Report Through 1952" (Ford Motor Co.), Acc. 6, Box 49.

16. Lord Perry, interview with authors, March 28, 1952.

17. Gehle, *Reminiscences*, gives a vivid picture of the backwardness of the German motor industry and of Ford contributions to its improvement. Ford standards and tolerances were much more accurate than the German. "The blueprints for the parts would come from the States, pass through German engineering under Tallberg, and be issued in German." Annual reports, F.M.C., Ltd., deal with German taxation. See also Sorensen to Perry, Sept. 27, 1930; Perry to Sorensen, Oct. 25, 1929; and Adenauer to E. C. Heine, Oct. 18, 1929. These letters are in a select file in the Ford Archives. For Callender quotation see *N.Y. Times*, Oct. 19, 1930.

18. Sorensen to Perry, May 10, 1930, Select File; Annual Report Nederlandsche Ford Automobiel Fabrik, 1932.

19. Annual Reports, F.M.C., Ltd., 1931, 1932; London *Economist*, April 14, 1934 (Ford record); Patijn, The Hague, Jan. 8, 1932 to Perry and Perry to Edsel, April 27, 1932, on European operations, 1930-1932, Acc. 6, Box 310; V. Y. Tallberg to authors, Jan., 1957 (on Perry's subordinates).

20. *Automobile Topics*, XCVI, Jan. 4, 1930, 745 (Renault).

21. Perry to Sorensen, Dec. 19, 1933, Acc. 38, Box 14.

22. Sorensen to Dolfuss, Sept. 7, 1934 (Select File); conversation of authors with Sorensen, *op. cit*. Moekle, *Reminiscences*, states that machinery and techniques in the Mathis plant were far below the Detroit standard, but Sorensen and Perry used a European measuring rod.

23. Dolfuss to Sorensen, Jan. 23, 1934, and G. F. Bergery to Dolfuss, Jan. 10, 1934, Select File.

24. A summary by Perry for Count Volpi of the Italian Ministry of Ford work in Italy, Nov., 1930, is in the Ford Archives.

25. Perry to Edsel Ford, June 15, 1933, Select File.

26. Perry to Sorensen, July 7, 1933, Select File; Annual Reports to F.M.C., Ltd., 1932, 1933; Gehle, Klann, *Reminiscences*.

27. Perry to Sorensen, June 6, 1933, March 13, 1934, Acc. 38, Boxes 13, 21.

28. Klann, V. Y. Tallberg, *Reminiscences;* Conversation of authors with Sorensen, *op. cit.*

29. Prince Louis Ferdinand, Stettin, April 26, 1934, to Liebold, Select File.

30. Dr. Albert's summary, Acc. 38, Box 23.

31. Perry to Sorensen, Dec. 19, 1933, Select File.

32. Conversation of authors with Sorensen, *op. cit.*

33. Perry to Sorensen, Dec. 19, 1930; memorandum to Sorensen, Dec. 7, 1931, both in Select File.

34. Sheldrick, *Reminiscences;* Nevins, conversations with Dagenham executives, 1952; Annual Reports F.M.C., Ltd., 1932, 1933.

35. The entire trading profit was made on sales in the United Kingdom. "The Ford 'baby' car," said the London *Economist*, April 14, 1934, "has secured a profitable share of the market on this side of the Atlantic, into which its elder brothers failed to penetrate." See F.M.C., Ltd., Annual Report, 1934.

36. George Dickert, *Reminiscences*.

37. Frank Bennett, *Reminiscences*, who went to Japan in 1921 for the company, gives a full account of experiences in that country. When he began operations in Kobe just after the earthquake of 1923, he worked so rapidly that he forgot to get a permit for the plant, and was under arrest two weeks. Frank C. Riecks and W. C. Cowling, *Reminiscences*, cover the Chinese experience. Cowling remarks of Henry Ford: "I think he wanted to contribute something to the industrialization of China through the Shanghai plant."

38. The Detroit executives charged European companies for certain services performed for

them. "Europe showed a loss in 1928," Perry wrote Sorensen Aug. 30, 1932 (Acc. 6, Box 310), "but has paid to Detroit almost five million dollars in dividends and service fees during the last three years." Dagenham alone in 1932 paid $210,000 for Detroit aid in designing the "baby" Ford and furnishing 14 model cars. (Directors' Minutes, Dec. 14, 1932, Dagenham Archives.)

CHAPTER XXII
Impact of Depression (*Pages 570–596*)

1. R. A. Gordon, "Cyclical Experience in the Interwar Period," in *Conference on Business Cycles* (National Bureau of Economic Research, New York, 1951), 189 ff.; Joseph A. Schumpeter, *Business Cycles* (New York, 1939) II, 753–794; Thomas Wilson, *Fluctuations in Income and Employment* (3rd ed., London, 1948), 118 ff.; John K. Galbraith, *The Great Crash* (Cambridge, Mass., 1955), *passim;* John W. Scoville, *Behavior of the Automobile Industry in Depression* (address, Dec. 30, 1935, publication date not given, probably 1936—published Chrysler Corporation); *N.Y. Times,* Nov. 4, 1929; FTC, *Report on Motor Vehicle Industry,* 35, 36, 649 (world, American, and Ford production). The impression that the automobile boom in the nineteen-twenties was a chief factor in producing the depression has no basis. See Simon Kuznets, *National Product Since 1869* (National Bureau of Economic Research, New York, 1946).

2. FTC, *Report on Motor Vehicle Industry,* 489 ff.; 601 ff.; 662 ff.; *Automotive Daily News,* Aug. 4, 18, Sept. 5, 1929. The two millionth Model A was turned out on July 24, 1929 (*Ford News,* IX, Aug. 15, 1929, 182.)

3. FTC, *Report, op. cit.,* 535–537, 645–649.

4. *Automotive Daily News,* Oct. 28, 1930; *ibid.,* Chris Sinsabaugh, "Sparks from Detroit," Dec. 18, 1931; "G.M. III: How to Sell Automobiles," *Fortune,* XIX, Feb., 1939, 105.

5. *Automotive Daily News,* Nov. 21, 1929; FTC, *Report,* 649, 676, 718.

6. *Ibid.,* 430, 649, 651.

7. *Ibid.,* 649; Kennedy, *The Automobile Industry,* Chaps. X, XI.

8. Numerous articles in the Detroit *Times,* 1929–1930, cover expansion plans; see also Henry Ford's interview-article in *N.Y. Times* magazine, May 24, 1931.

9. *Ibid.*

10. Scoville, as cited in Note 1.

11. Kennedy, *op. cit.,* 229; Schoville, *op. cit.*

12. McManus, *The Sword-Arm of Business,* 154; "Chrysler," *Fortune,* XII, Aug., 1935, 31.

13. *Automotive Daily News,* Nov. 8, 1930, July 3, Dec. 4, 1931.

14. *Ibid.,* July 16, 1931; "Ford, Chevrolet, Plymouth," *Fortune,* IV, Oct., 1931, 939; "Mr. Ford Doesn't Care," *Fortune,* VIII, Dec., 1933, 66.

15. Norman G. Shidle, "Competition Sharpens Ford Dilemma," *Automotive Industries,* LIV, June 20, 1931, 939; "Notes Eight-Cylinder Trend," *N.Y. Times,* Jan. 5, 1930 (Hoffman).

16. Ford Motor Co., General Sales Letters, Jan. 16, 1929, March 5, 1930; Oct. 23, 1930. Acc. 78.

17. For these criticisms, see Upton Sinclair, *The Flivver King* (Pasadena, Cal., 1937), 76 and Sward, *Legend of Henry Ford,* Chap. XVII.

18. Gaston Plantiff to Sorensen, Feb. 8, 1929, W. A. Francis to George H. Sprague, April 30, 1929, Acc. 38, Box 115; General Sales Letter, "1929 Estimates," Oct. 19, 1928, Acc. 235, Box 15.

19. *Automotive Industries,* LXIV, June 20, 1931, 940; FTC, *Report,* 859 ff.; George Crimmins, *Reminiscences; Automotive Daily News,* Nov. 9, 1929.

20. *Ibid.,* April 30, 1930; "The Rebirth of Ford," *Fortune,* XXV, May, 1947, 207.

21. Henry C. Doss, George Crimmins, *Reminiscences.*

22. Ford Motor Co., General Sales Letters, Feb. 7, Oct. 10, 1930, Jan. 20, 1931, Acc. 78; Doss, *Reminiscences:* "Bankers Condemn Ford Policy," *Motor,* LIV, Nov., 1930, 144.

23. Ray Priest, "Ford Discount War Ended," Detroit *Times*, April 28, 1930; "Bankers Condemn Ford Policy," *op. cit.*, 31, 144.

24. *Business Week*, April 2, 1930, 9.

25. Priest, as cited in Note 23; *N.Y. Times*, June 2, 1930; James Dalton, "Ford Dealers Win Discount Victory," *Motor*, June, 1930, 82.

26. William C. Cowling, *Reminiscences;* General Sales Letter, "Dealers' Discount," Feb. 11, 1931, and "Model A Wholesale Prices," Oct. 20, 1931, both in Acc. 78; Acc. 66, Box 1 (letters of appreciation from dealers).

27. General Letter, "Q-A Selling Plan," Nov. 20, 1931, Acc. 78; Letter of May 14, 1931, Acc. 38, Box 68 (on night selling); William B. Harris, "Last Stand of Auto Independents?" *Fortune*, L, Dec., 1954, 114 ff. (on independents).

28. Mallon, *Reminiscences;* George F. Granger and Lawrence R. Klein, *Emergency Relief in Michigan, 1933–39* (Lansing, 1939); William Haber and Paul L. Staunchfield, *Unemployment Relief and Economic Security* (Lansing, 1936); see also the brochures in *Michigan Census of Population and Unemployment*, First Series (Lansing, 1935–1936). The quotation from James Couzens is in Arthur Pound, *Detroit, Dynamic City* (New York, 1940), 316.

29. Mallon, Ernest Grimshaw, *Reminiscences;* figures furnished by J. E. Bossardet, Payroll Department, Ford Motor Company.

30. Detroit *Times*, July 26 and *News*, July 27, 1930 (hearings). Rep. Hamilton Fish, Jr., presided.

31. Richards, *The Last Billionaire*, 173 (quoting Ford); Klann, Willis F. Ward, *Reminiscences*. Retroactive light was thrown on Detroit gangsterism by the Kefauver Committee hearings of 1953–1954.

32. Hicks, Grimshaw, *Reminiscences*. Hicks states that in July, 1932, Sorensen abruptly cut his salary from $750 to $500 a month. However, such cuts were common in business and industry in general, along with discharges. Grimshaw gives abundant detail on favoritism in re-employing men at the Rouge.

33. Albert Smith, Grimshaw, *Reminiscences;* Orry Barrule (Leslie MacDonald), "Life with Uncle Henry," *passim;* Richards, *The Last Billionaire*, Chap. XV; Klann, Wibel, Gehle, in their reminiscences. The authors have received much confidential material on Bennett, some of it not now usable. Of his own slender volume, *We Never Called Him Henry*, the best comment that can be made is that it is worthy of its author.

34. For the criminal career of Vaslov Simek, see Elmer L. Irey, *The Tax Dodgers* (New York, 1948), 83. For other material the sources are confidential.

35. Orry Barrule, *op. cit.;* Mallon, Klann, *Reminiscences*.

36. Thoms, *Reminiscences;* Sweinhart as cited in text. The *News* article is reprinted in the *Ford News*, XII, March, 1932, 3, 17, and the following month XII, 3–5, the *News* carried an article "A New Car: the Ford V-8," with photographs and further details.

37. Thoms, Emil Zoerlin, in their reminiscences cover the development of the V-8. See also Ralph Graves, *The Triumph of an Idea: the Story of Henry Ford* (Garden City, N.Y., 1935), Chap. VII. Further articles in the *Ford News*, 1932–1933, add interesting details.

CHAPTER XXIII
Ford: Symbol, Legend, and Reality (*Pages 597–621*)

1. *Moving Forward*, 56, 57, 113, 119, 123–127, 203 ff.

2. John Reed, "Industry's Miracle Man," *Metropolitan Magazine*, XLIV, Oct., 1916; John Gunther, *Inside USA* (New York, 1947), 399.

3. Fred L. Black, W. J. Cameron, *Reminiscences;* Sinclair Lewis, *Main Street* (New York, 1920), 51; *N.Y. Times*, April 7, 1922; J. H. O'Brien, "Henry Ford's Commander in Chief, Harry Bennett," *The Forum*, XCIX, Feb., 1938, 67–72.

4. *Moving Forward*, Chap. IX: "The New Craftsmanship."

5. Maurice Hindus, "Ford Conquers Russia," *The Outlook*, CXLVI, June 29, 1927, 280–283.

6. For Ford's reputation in Russia, see Moscow dispatch, *N.Y. Times*, Feb. 17, 1928.

7. London *Economist*, April 11, 1928. For details concerning German and Danish workers, see Chap. XXI.

8. Seumas O'Brien, "Henry Ford and Romantic Cork," *The Commonweal*, XIX Jan. 19, 1934, 322–324.

9. Waddill Catchings and W. T. Foster, *The Road to Plenty* (Boston, 1927); William Zimmerman, "Ford's Evangelium von den Teknischsocialen Dienstleistung," *Schmollers Jahrbuch*, XL, 491–523; Yves Guyot, *Journal des Economistes*, Oct., 1924 and Oct., 1926; Lord Leverhume, London *Spectator*, CXXXI, Oct. 27, 1923, 585–587; Albert Kinross, *English Review*, XXXVII, Nov., 1923, 649 ff.; H. J. Massingham, London *Spectator*, CXXXI, Nov. 3, 1923, 629–630; Sinclair, *The Flivver King*, 27 ff.

10. Mark Sullivan, *Our Times; The War Begins*, IV (New York, 1932), 49–50; Gerald Stanley Lee, "Is Ford an Inspired Millionaire?", *Harper's Weekly*, LVIII, March 14, 1914, 9–11.

11. Liebold, Cameron, Howard Simpson in their reminiscences. Two good books on the Model T contain some of the popular jokes associated with it: Philip Van Doren Stern, *Tin Lizzie: the Story of the Fabulous Model T Ford* (New York, 1955), and Floyd Clymer, *Henry's Wonderful Model T, 1908–1927* (New York, 1955).

12. Garet Garrett, "Henry Ford's Experiment in Good-Will," *Everybody's Magazine*, XXX, April, 1914, 465; Julian Street, "Detroit the Dynamic," *Collier's Weekly*, July 4, 1914, 10; *N.Y. Times*, Aug. 1, 1914.

13. For representative interviews, see *N.Y. Times*, May 11, June 20, 1926, Feb. 5, 1927.

14. These quotations are compiled from the newspaper clipping scrapbooks, Ford Archives. For cynical comment on Ford's publicity methods, see "The Real Henry Ford," *Pipp's Weekly*, III, June 24, 1922, 2–12.

15. Black, *Reminiscences*. The Ford station was one of the first to pay its talent well. The Sunday Evening Hour, with Cameron as chief speaker, was not instituted until 1934.

16. The full title: *Ford Ideals: Being a Selection from Mr. Ford's Page in The Dearborn Independent* (Dearborn, 1926).

17. Of Benson, Liebold says in his *Reminiscences* that Ford had little confidence in him, and "he got to be rather a pest." Liebold also tells of Elbert Hubbard's bill. Ida M. Tarbell in *New Ideals in Business* (New York, 1916) included flattering references to Ford and his company.

18. Marquis, *Henry Ford*, 170, 196–198.

19. A considerable number of interesting letters by Crowther are in Acc. 285, Box 217, and show energy, zeal, and discretion, and also that Crowther saw Ford little, and depended on Liebold, Cameron, and "Mr. Ford's Page" in the *Dearborn Independent*, in which numerous passages can be traced in the three Ford-Crowther books, particularly *My Life and Work*. Considering the indirect character of the "collaboration" one marvels at the vigor and coherence of these three volumes. Crowther on Sept. 12, 1924, complained to Liebold that Ford advertising was bad. "The Ford industries are built on ideas . . . None of the ideas which made Mr. Ford what he is get into the advertisements." It was to Crowther that John A. Ryan wrote the appreciative letter on Ford's great contribution to industrial problems previously quoted—see Crowther to Liebold, April 1, 1924.

20. Cameron, Howard Simpson, *Reminiscences; Gunther, op. cit.*

21. For Knudsen and Sorensen comments on the earlier years of Ford activity, see *Ford: the Times, the Man, the Company*.

22. Liebold, Cameron, Voorhess, McCloud, Simpson, C. J. Smith, Hicks, George M. Holley in their reminiscences. The immense store of oral history materials in the Ford Archives would supply a fresh and interesting volume devoted to the personality of Ford. Such a character study does not lie within the purpose of this history of the Ford Motor Company.

23. William C. Richards in *The Last Billionaire*, Chap. XXIV, credits the writings of Orlando J. Smith, a Confederate veteran who became a Mississippi planter and editor, with the conversion of Ford to a faith in metempsychosis or the transmigration of souls. Marquis, *Henry Ford*, 80–92, deals with Ford's relations with the Episcopal Church, in which he was baptized

and confirmed, stating: "He is not an orthodox believer according to the standards of any church that I happen to know."

24. "Carl Sandburg Chats with Henry Ford." Chicago *Daily News,* Dec. 25, 1928. Ford had read Sandburg's *Lincoln: the Prairie Years* (or Clara had read parts of it to him), and recalled with amusement the account of Jefferson Davis, as Secretary of War under Buchanan, experimenting with camels for carrying supplies in the Southwest.

25. Conversation, Sorensen with authors, *op. cit.*

26. Sheldrick, *Reminiscences.*

27. Waldemar Kaempffert, "The Mussolini of Highland Park," *N.Y. Times,* Jan. 6, 1928.

APPENDIX I

THE RUSSIAN ADVENTURES

It would be difficult to conceive of two economic philosophies more sharply opposed than those of Henry Ford and Lenin or Stalin. Yet these quintessential figures of Capitalism and Communism did achieve certain working relations, so that the Ford Motor Company had several striking adventures on Russian soil. Henry Ford, as a contribution to world peace and prosperity, was ready to help promote the industrial advancement of the Soviet Union. And the Russian leaders, seeing in the Ford methods of mass production the epitome of all their country most needed, were eager for his machines, procedures, and engineers.

The initial relationship was purely commercial: Russia bought and Ford sold. We have noted that beginning in 1920, when crop failure and famine were ravaging Russia and Herbert Hoover's Relief Administration was coming to the rescue, the Soviet Government placed orders for Fordson tractors which in the next half-dozen years aggregated about 25,000 machines. A single shipment from the Rouge carried 1930 tractors, each with its replacement parts and crate weighing nearly two tons. As Lenin wished to scatter them widely over the country, consignments were sent to various ports—Leningrad, Odessa, and Vladivostok. The Russians opened schools for the operation and care of the machines, where their own experts gave erratic training. "Eighty-five percent of the trucks and tractors in Russia," boasted the company in 1927, "are Ford built." [1]

These tractors and the considerable imports of Model T cars heightened the impact of the ideas in "Fordismus" or "Fordizatsia": ideas of high industrial efficiency, mass-production, and large-scale distribution of cheap goods. While Henry Ford was alternately denounced as a slave-driver and lauded as a mighty innovator, these ideas were thirstily accepted as promising the regeneration of Russia. An Englishwoman touring the country in 1926 reported that she saw Ford's name emblazoned on banners in workers' processions, as emblematic of a new era; long articles appeared on Ford methods; and the Communists eagerly devoured translations of Ford's *My Life and Work* and *Today and Tomorrow*. [2]

673

Then early in 1926 the Russian Government invited Henry Ford to send a delegation to find out just what was being done to service the 20,000-odd tractors working the Soviet soil, and to commence training the staffs of service organizations along Ford lines. The government hoped to interest Ford in the erection of a tractor factory in the Union, and in enlarged export activities. Ford accepted and sent five men, including William G. Collins of the Italian Ford Company and the engineer Bredo H. Berghoff. This was a year of crisis in Russia; of political tensions, after Lenin's death, destined to end in Stalin's dictatorship and the exile of Trotsky, and economic distress caused by peasant resistance to state grain collection. The five experts alighted from the train in Moscow April 18 to find Amtorg representatives waiting on the platform to greet them. They spent more than four months in the country, travelling about seven thousand miles in all; they toured the Volga and Don valleys and the Crimea, stopped for service work in Kharkov, Rostov, Taganrov, and Odessa, proceeded to the Trans-Caucasus, and from Batum went to Tiflis to erect a Ford exhibit at an agricultural fair. Wherever they could they gave lessons to Soviet technicians. As one illustration of the work they did, they later noted that at Rostov-on-Don their instruction in the proper way of pouring new bearings and manipulating the burnishing machine had reduced the cost of this work from twenty rubles to six ($10 to $3).[3]

The delegation found Ford products everywhere. Of 5700 tractors owned by the Ukrainian Government, 5520 were Fordsons; of 700 automotive units which the Baku authorities used in petroleum production, 420 were Ford cars or tractors. While International Harvester tractors were also to be seen, and were preferred in some districts as having slightly more power, in general, writes Berghoff, "they liked the Fordson better than any other make that they had tried." In Moscow the Putilow Works were making a rather poor copy of the Fordson at an admitted production cost of some $2200, although it was being marketed by the government at the same price as the genuine Fordson, about $900 including plow. The party saw no tractors of Russian design in operation, but heard that Soviet engineers were building (not manufacturing) experimental machines. Servicing was wretched. The Russians seemed entirely mad on the subject of charts, diagrams, and colored tables of figures, but these meant nothing:[4]

During our preliminary talks with officials of the servicing organizations in Moscow, whose offices were chuck full of such charts, we were commencing to wonder why we had been sent over, as it appeared beyond all doubt from the charts shown to us that the Russians themselves had the situation well in hand. For instance, this chart showed the great number of repair shops which were to be found in the Ukraine, the North Caucasus, and the Volga regions. Still another chart indicated the number of instructors that were attached to each such repair shop, the number of times each tractor was being visited each month, the excellent spare parts service established. . . .

Our surprise can be imagined when we arrived in the Ukraine, the richest tractor district in Russia, and were unable to find a single Fordson repair shop worthy of the name. No special repair equipment existed anywhere, although fourteen full sets of Fordson [repair] equipment have lately been received for the Ukraine alone. . . .

Spare parts when imported were good; when Russians made them, poor. They were roughly cast, the pistons, for example, varying considerably in thickness. The Ford party discovered to their horror that when some tractor users ran out of gasoline, they poured crude oil into the tanks—which ruined the engines. "I would say," declares Berghoff, "that most of the time about forty percent of the tractors were inoperable." When the Ford party pointed out that discs would be better for certain soils than ordinary plows, the Russians had never heard of them, and were reluctant to try them.

The farther the delegation travelled, the more they were impressed by the general crudity, discomfort, and backwardness evident in Russia. Some allowance, of course, must be made for the novelty of the scene, and still more for the terrible ravages of war. But in the trans-Caucasus the Americans gazed in wonder at twelve oxen drawing a single home-made wooden plow, at men threshing with flails, and at women baking bread in clay holes dug in banks. After looking at the primitive methods of logging and sawing timber, the group concluded that light portable sawing units with Fordson power would greatly reduce the cost of lumber in all parts of Russia. No tractors, so far as they could see, were being put to industrial uses. The housing shortage resulted in horrible overcrowding in town and country alike; the visitors commented on rooms completely filled with beds, and on the popularity of workers' and businessmen's clubs simply as places of refuge for people without real homes. They decided that the largest industry in the country must be the one making signs, "Elevator out of order." Everywhere grandiose plans for the future contrasted with scenes of neglect. At Taganrov, for example, they saw a large factory which the British had built during the war and filled with good machinery, now rusting.

Yet the Russians were obviously anxious to learn, and happy when they found how to use good tools. In parts of the Volga region farmers were driving Fordsons with electric headlamps twenty-four hours a day, and sometimes plowing more than a thousand hours a season. The Tiflis fair, with exhibits of American, British, German, Swedish, and other machinery, drew great crowds. It appears that the Fordson did better there than its competitors. A plowing contest was held in a field of stiff clay never before broken, the shares to go at least seven inches deep. Most tractors were quite unable to meet that requirement. When the Fordson tended to stand on its rear wheels, the party insisted that its fattest member must ride on the front axle. In fact, they tied him there. "He sure got more exercise that day than he ever got in years," Berghoff remarks. Later the Russians arranged a contest in hauling cannon over mountain roads; but the delegation, protesting that Henry Ford would never consent to this, drew a supply wagon instead. No results of the contests were ever published. Night after night throngs filled the tent where the Ford men showed motion pictures; day after day they punched and patted the machinery.

Studying Russia as a field for a possible Ford factory, the party was not impressed. They found Russian industry lacking in managerial talent. For example, the distribution of spare tractor parts had not been organized; one service warehouse would be full of two or three types, while another warehouse several hours away would totally lack them. Visiting thirteen large industrial establishments, the party found only one, the Red Giant rubber factory in Moscow, where four thousand workers made galoshes and other articles, in a high state of efficiency. It was orderly and clean. Other plants, however, were dirty, slack, and ill-equipped. "Factory buildings as a rule were good, and labor very inefficient." Of course a Ford factory would have to use Russian labor and foremen. The want of plant-managers with sufficient brains, drive, and authority to get work done was glaring. This seemed primarily the result of a system of management by political-minded committees.

For several reasons, the delegation decided, a Ford factory in Russia was really unthinkable. In the first place, no owner could feel any confidence that the government would not take over the plant itself, without compensation, any time it liked to do so. The Soviet leaders admitted openly that they could not make the tractors they needed for ten years or so; and thus "a Ford plant would come in handy." Various means of expropriation could be found. In the second place, any American factory would have to be protected against "political commissars sitting next to the man who knew the business." No concessionaire could be named in Russia who was not experiencing great difficulty in operating his business. And in still other ways the Soviet Government was not to be trusted. Though nominally it respected foreign patents, actually it stole them freely. Just as the Fordson tractor, after many delays and blunders, was being reproduced in Russia under the name of the Krasny Putilowitz tractor, the Fiat truck was being reproduced at another place, and the Bosch magneto was being manufactured at a third. At the Putilowitz plant, the jigs, fixtures and methods reflected practices at the Highland Park works so faithfully that it was evident the

Russians had studied the encyclopaedic work of Arnold and Faurote on that factory with minute care, and done their best to reproduce its achievements.[5]

Berghoff on his return in 1926 talked with Sorensen. "When I told him about the political bosses in the factories, he said, 'Well, that settles that. We're not going to try to run a business under those conditions.'"

I

Finding that Henry Ford and his advisers took a chilly attitude toward the construction of a plant in Russia, the Soviet authorities tried a different tack. In the late summer of 1928, four Russian officials, including representatives of the Amtorg Trading Corporation and of the Moscow Automobile Trust, visited Detroit with a more promising proposal. They suggested that the Trust should build a factory to make Ford units, at first using parts shipped from Detroit, but gradually shifting to Russian components. The Ford Company should consent to reproduction of its models, furnish blueprints, install machinery, and provide technical and mechanical assistance. The Soviet officials contemplated a plant making up to 25,000 cars a year when working one shift, or 50,000 when working two. Henry Ford and his advisers at once said that such a factory was too small to interest them.[6]

After complicated negotiations, the Ford Motor Company on May 31, 1929, signed a contract with the Supreme Economic Council of the USSR, acting through Valery I. Meshlauk and the Amtorg Trading Corporation. This agreement fitted into Stalin's first five-year plan, which had been initiated the previous year with the object of raising Russia's industrial production 136 percent. The Ford Company engaged to furnish detailed plant layouts and working projects for the erection and equipment of a factory able to produce 100,000 units a year—partly Ford Model A cars, partly AA trucks, and partly heavier trucks. (The Russian names were Gaz-A, Gaz-AA, and AMO-3.) In return, the Russian Government contracted to buy through Amtorg a total of 72,000 Ford units (cars, trucks, and equivalent parts, in any proportion it liked) on a four-year schedule: 6000 units the first year, 18,000 the second, and 24,000 in each of the two final years. It would use Ford-made parts exclusively for repairs.[7]

Henry Ford manifestly took a generous position. His company agreed to give Russia the full rights to make, sell, and use Ford units throughout the USSR, to make and use Ford machinery and other equipment, and to use all Ford inventions or technical advances patented or unpatented. Ford would furnish detailed drawings of all the departments of a complete factory, specifications and schedules of machinery, and operation sheets. The company would supply two or more detailed sets of drawings of all tools, jigs, fixtures, and other special equipment at the Rouge plant. Ford would permit access to the American plants by Russian engineers and other employees, to learn by actual floor work the methods in use. Finally, the company would send to Russia its own skilled engineers and foremen to help plan the new works, install the equipment, and train the working force. The actual cost of furnishing drawings, plans, staff, and services would be paid by the USSR.[8]

Thus Russia would get a supply of cars and trucks, well-equipped factories, and careful Ford tuition; the Ford Company might or might not get a fair profit—the price of units and parts was to be cost at the Rouge plus fifteen per cent. The Soviet Government actually planned two distinct plants. The more important, a complete factory called the Molotov Works, was to rise at Nizhni-Novgorod (after 1932 called Gorky); the smaller, merely an assembly plant termed the KIM Works, was to be in Moscow.

At this time Russia was almost wholly dependent on importations in the automobile field. Stalin himself said in 1933 that prior to the first five-year plan "we had no automobile industry." Two small factories in Moscow, the AMO and Il'ich, and the small Yaroslav plant, offered only rudimentary and utterly inadequate production. The government program as late as 1927 had included the building of no passenger cars whatever, and only two thousand light pickup trucks, a figure probably never reached. The Ford delegation in 1926 had found that while the Putilowitz managers claimed they were making two tractors a day, the true rate was only about twenty a month! The Russians built a new tractor factory at Stalingrad in 1928, and the next year reequipped the tractor plants at Leningrad and Kharkov; but just what these steps meant outsiders could only guess.[9]

It was certain that Russian automotive engineers badly needed Ford instruction. A Ford expert who visited Russia in the fall of 1929 at Soviet request, Peter MacGregor, inspected the Putilowitz tractor factory thoroughly, and submitted a blunt report to the authorities. He found the shop layout, placing of machinery, and general planning poor but passable. A tractor which he disassembled was rough in workmanship, but quite usable. But he discovered much to criticize:

If my boss owned or had charge of this works tomorrow, he would immediately call it to attention, by shutting off power and not allowing a single wheel to turn until everybody in the plant, including the staff, cleaned out everything from their office or department that is not used in the manufacture of the product of the factory. He would abolish all piece work and get everybody into good spirits by giving them just a little more salary or wages than they ever made by piece work. . . . All factory department foremen would get their men, skilled and unskilled, to pull out every piece of steel, wood, pipes, paper, empty barrels, etc., to the center of the floor. The yard boss would be instructed to get his tractor and haul out tons of junk that has been accumulating for years. You have enough cast iron and steel lying around in shops and yards to build at least ten years' production of tractors, and I mean only the metal that is lying around in the way.

MacGregor was distressed by the listlessness of the workers:

What is the matter with the factory heads and foremen? I have only met one in the place that seems to have any initiative, and he cannot go ahead because the general system of getting work done is so bad that no speed can be put into it. For instance, to get a job going the machine or fixture is drawn up; then it takes from one to four weeks to get a blueprint made from the tracing. The blueprinting machine should be in the drawing office. In our American and Irish plants you can get a blueprint made and dried in less than five minutes. . . .

In the machine shop nearly every place you look you see from two to six men sitting around in groups smoking during working hours with no apparent work near them, and no one making any effort to give them any.

By taking the debris off the floor, moving the machines closer and in better line, installing gravity conveyors, putting a stop to idling and smoking, giving women light work instead of heavy shovelling ("the surprise to me is that the law and doctors allow it"), raising wages, and checking insubordination, MacGregor believed he could increase production one-third while making the workers happier. But he did credit the factory with one achievement. "The Russians are making a radiator core that has our design beat every way," he wrote Sorensen.[10]

II

Henry Ford took satisfaction in the Russian contract as a means of promoting world concord. "Russia is beginning to build," he told *The Nation's Business,* adding that the Soviet Government had done wisely in coming to America for industrial guidance. He thought it the duty of an advanced nation to help laggards in the field. "I have long been convinced that we shall never be able to build a balanced economic order in the world until every people has become as self-supporting as possible."

The time was coming, he continued, when Russia, China, India, and Latin-America would no longer accept nearly all their manufactures from other lands. Only stupid greed "can think of the world as continuously dependent on us, or of our people as the perpetual factory hands of the nations. No, the nations will do as Russia is doing." They would get the benefit of a half-century of experience. Industrialization, he repeated, meant prosperity, and prosperity made for world peace.

"The adoption of high wages, low prices, and mass production in all countries is only a matter of time. Instead of reducing our foreign markets, it will serve to define them." [11]

Agreements supplementing the original contract enlarged the exchange of personnel. The summer of 1929 found four Ford experts hunched over drawing tables in Moscow and Nizhni showing Soviet engineers details of their plans. Russian technicians, a few of them English-speaking, meanwhile began to arrive in Detroit, and shortly became a large group. The company gave them complete on-the-job instruction, and as it shipped blueprints and machinery to Nizhni it returned some of them as newly-made experts. It was a gala event, hailed by *Pravda* in a front-page story, when the first units were completed on February 1, 1930. For the next two years this assembly work continued in Nizhni and Moscow.[12] *

Excitement filled the area as the walls of the Molotov Works began to rise some eight miles from the old city of Nizhni, between the Volga and Oka Rivers. Construction of the factory and the new workers' city for 25,000 people was in the hands of the Austin Company of Cleveland, O., advised by Ford engineers. "Here," wrote the press correspondent H. R. Knickerbocker in 1930, "where five months ago there were at most a few families of peasants, are today ten thousand men at work, erecting a plant that by the end of 1932 is intended to turn out 140,000 cars a year." (He had listened to Soviet planners!) The builders ran into shortages of materials and labor, the latter a surprising fact in a country where ever since the revolution the cities had been crowded with jobless men. Nevertheless, progress was made. As in 1931 the works approached completion, with the opening fixed for the coming New Year's Day, a body of almost 150 Russians arrived at the Rouge for final training. Furnished with interpreters, and housed partly in one of the Rouge buildings, they got on amicably with the Americans. They included not only many assembly and machine shop specialists, but metallurgists and two women chemists.[13]

Meanwhile, Ford men went to Russia in party after party. Once forty mechanics left in a body on the *Leviathan*. To help in getting the Nizhni production line under way, a final group of seventeen—tool designers, electric welders, experts in heat treatment and pressed steel work, operators of Erie hammers—finally went over under the captaincy of Frank Bennett. Though the arrangement was that they should remain but a half-year, two were still there in the early winter of 1933. Before leaving, Bennett had a farewell conference with Edsel Ford and Sorensen. He always remembered the quiet courtesy with which Edsel remarked: "Mr. Bennett, when the first car comes off the assembly lines, would you send us a cable? It means very much to this company."

* Sorensen, in *My Forty Years with Ford*, 195 ff., tells of a visit to Russia which seems to have been preliminary to the arrangement for the Molotov factory. His observations on Russian industry at that time much resemble MacGregor's.

When Bennett reached Nizhni Novgorod, he found that the almost-completed factory had not yet begun turning out cars and trucks. It could not start because while the Russians had established conveyor-lines like those of Detroit, the subsidiary feeder-lines were partly incomplete. "It was maybe a week or ten days before we got started rolling," recalls Bennett. As most workmen were new to the complex machine tools, Bennett's most onerous task was teaching them. But great was the jubilation when the factory made a satisfactory start! The townspeople, wild with elation, entered in droves to watch operations, and grave professional men begged to help on the assembly line just to see how it produced its wonders. "Look at what we have done," people would exclaim with pride. "Think of what we are going to do in the future!" A banquet was held with wine and speeches; and to show their appreciation, the banqueters tossed Bennett in a blanket—as they did a bemedalled general.[14]

At first the Russian operatives needed constant watching. They could not be trusted with fine precision work, and made some strange mistakes. For example, they put the drums of highly inflammable paint right beside the ovens which baked the paint sprayed on the cars. Once when the ovens got overheated and the paint on the trucks, reaching flash point, burst into flames, they had difficulty in rolling the drums away in time. But Frank Bennett took an immense liking to the Russian people.

After finishing at Nizhni he went to Moscow, where he found architects and builders directed by Albert Kahn, Inc., of Detroit, rapidly completing the assembly plant. It was equipped with the best machinery; "almost everything there was made by the Ford Motor Company." When the Moscow plant was running as smoothly as that in Nizhni, he asked a high official about transportation home. The man was gracious. "But, by the way, comrade," he remarked, "you haven't had a vacation. You are entitled to a month at our expense."

Bennett replied that he would take it in America. "No, no," expostulated the official, "we wish to send you to a sanatorium on the Black Sea."

The protesting Bennett was hustled off the night before Christmas to the Crimea. He was given baths, massage, well-planned meals, and some mountain-climbing. At the end of the first month he was forced, against his will, to stay for another. Finally it was over.

"I came back to Moscow," he recalls, "and it dawned on me why they had sent me down there. They didn't want to let me go until they were sure the factory would run without my presence."[15]

Altogether, under this Muscovite project, about two hundred Russians came to the Rouge for training, while a somewhat smaller number of Americans went to the Soviet Union, a few of whom remained five or six years. After the Yankees came back a veil of secrecy shut down on Nizhni operations. Ford officers, getting one of the Putilowitz-Fordson tractors sent over, found that it fell short of their specifications, and believed that the Models A and AA from Nizhni were equally below standard. Russia completed its contract for 72,000 units and continued buying for a time under the terms of the 1929 agreement; but on November 22, 1934, in accordance with Soviet policy of discontinuing direct foreign aid, Amtorg terminated the arrangement.[16] Just what the production at Nizhni was no American ever learned. Soviet statistics, even when obtainable, were notoriously inaccurate. A writer who took pains to ascertain the truth, Freda Utley, wrote in *Foreign Affairs* early in 1941 that in 1932 the total Russian passenger-car production had been 23,879, and tractor production 50,640; while in 1937 the output of cars was about 200,000, and that of tractors was unknown. The Soviet authorities, reluctant to acknowledge how much they had leaned upon foreign technical aid in the first five-year plan, naturally minimized the Ford contribution. But the *Technical Encyclopaedia* did admit in 1937 that "the Soviet automobile industry was oriented in the advanced technological experience of the United States." [17]

III

Henry Ford's substantial creation of two automotive factories in Russia must be appraised in the context of world history. When the contract was made, Western distrust of the Soviet Union was abating. A contract between the General Electric and Amtorg in the fall of 1928 had broken the so-called credit blockade restricting Russo-American business relations. The United States recognized the Soviet Government in 1933. Many Westerners regarded Stalin's first five-year plan as in general sound and promising. They hoped that it would multiply the production of goods, raise the standard of living, wipe out illiteracy, and improve the nation's culture. And although it had a heavy debit side in its terrorism, its frightful hardships to labor, and its calculated liquidation of millions of peasants and kulaks, its achievements actually proved to be important. They contributed to Russian power—and Hitler's seizure of the reins in Germany and the ensuing armaments race made power important.

Ford and his company, like some other American corporations, assisted in giving Russia a mechanized industry at a critical hour in world affairs. When America and the USSR became active although mutually suspicious partners in the Second World War, the Ford executives could feel confident that their undertaking had been justified. It did not matter much to Henry Ford that they lost money. Under the Amtorg contract, sales 1929–35 came to $18,116,000; the cost of materials to Ford $15,928,000; the commercial expenses to $2,766,000; and the final loss to $578,000.[18] To give his ideas a practical illustration on the world stage, Henry Ford would gladly have sacrificed twice that sum.

NOTES

Appendix I: The Russian Adventures

1. The first Russian orders had come in during the fall of 1918, while civil war raged, but volume trade began in 1921. *Ford News*, August 15, 1924; January 15, 1925; for quotation, February 17, 1927.

2. The *Bol'shaia Entsiklopedia* (Moscow, first edition, 1936, volume 58) contains a long article on "Fordism." See also *N.Y. Times*, November 13, 1926, September 14. 1927.

3. Report of Delegation, Acc. 531, Box 1; Bredo H. Berghoff, *Reminiscences*.

4. Report of Delegation, *ut. sup.*, p. 2; Ford *News*, December 1, 1927.

5. At Odessa the delegation found the November Revolution Works turning out plows copied from Oliver and John Deere models. Report.

6. E. W. Moke to Gaston Plantiff on the negotiations, September 21, 1928; Acc. 66, Box 1.

7. The contract is in Ford Archives, Acc. 531, Box 1.

8. Ford executives queried some New York bankers about the financial trustworthiness of the Soviet Government and received favorable answers; Acc. 66, Box 1. The Russians agreed not to export Ford units, and to put the Ford name on them.

9. For Stalin's statement see his *Problems of Leninism*, Russian edition, Moscow, 1933, II, 373; see also *Maliia Entsiklopedia* (Moscow, 1928, I, 88), article Automobile Industry.

10. MacGregor's interesting report, dated September 16, 1929, is in Acc. 38, Box 61. His letter to Sorensen, Cork, October 3, 1929, is in Acc. 38, Box 1.

11. *The Nation's Business*, June, 1930, pp. 20–23.

12. *Pravda*, also *Izvestia*, February 2, 1930; *Technicheskaia Entsiklopedia*, second edition, volume 6, 1937, pp. 285, 286.

13. H. R. Knickerbocker, *The Soviet Five-Year Plan and Its Effect on World Trade*, London, 1931, 30–34; Frank Bennett, *Reminiscences*.

14. Frank Bennett, *Reminiscences*.

15. *Idem.*

16. Liebold, *Reminiscences*, describes the defective tractor; the letter of termination is in Acc. 6.

17. Freda Utley, "The Enigma of Soviet Production," *Foreign Affairs*, XIX, 385–401; *Technicheskaia Entsiklopedia*, as cited in note 12, p. 285.

18. Figures furnished authors by the Treasurer's Office, Ford Motor Company, December 9, 1954. Russian orders to the Rouge for parts, though continued for some years, proved small. As the Russian flow of cars and trucks was slender, spare parts were simply not needed in large quantities.

APPENDIX II

FORD MOTOR COMPANY SALES, 1918–1934

(From World Production Report, 1903–1952, Acc. 62, box 49, For Archives)

1. Total Sales, United States, all vehicles

1918	532,509	1927	518,401
1919	998,029	1928	758,299
1920	530,780	1929	1,870,257
1921	1,006,948	1930	1,451,574
1922	1,373,331	1931	731,601
1923	2,120,898	1932	395,956
1924	2,012,111	1933	429,638
1925	2,024,254	1934	757,931
1926	1,651,424		

2. Total Sales, trucks and tractors, United States

Trucks		*Tractors*	
1918	62,444	1917	254
1919	120,597	1918	34,167
1920	43,934	1919	56,987
1921	67,796	1920	67,329
1922	127,322	1921	35,338
1923	193,234	1922	66,752
1924	172,221	1923	101,898
1925	268,411	1924	83,010
1926	186,082	1925	104,168
1927	61,100	1926	86,101
1928	110,342	1927	93,972
1929	355,453	1928	8,001 *
1930	272,897		
1931	186,394		

* After 1928, tractor production was shifted to Cork, Ireland

685

3. Total Sales, World

1918	572,154	1927	555,796
1919	1,047,858	1928	833,514
1920	582,647	1929	1,967,741
1921	1,050,741	1930	1,517,023
1922	1,425,830	1931	771,444
1923	2,201,188	1932	451,591
1924	2,083,481	1933	515,488
1925	2,103,541	1934	872,849
1926	1,752,075		

APPENDIX III

FORD MOTOR COMPANY EMPLOYMENT
TOTALS, UNITED STATES
ANNUAL AVERAGE, *1915* THROUGH *1933*

(From the Ford Company Industrial Relations Analysis Department)

	U.S. Area			Rouge Area	Highland Park
	Hourly	*Salaried*	*Total*	*Hourly*	*Hourly*
1915	18,028	864	18,892	—	18,028
1916	31,298	1,398	32,696	—	31,298
1917	35,246	1,165	36,411	—	35,246
1918	32,531	1,168	33,699	—	32,531
1919	46,861	1,393	48,264	8,822 *	43,080
1920	61,708	1,860	63,568	8,073	49,337
1921	49,424	934	50,358	6,592	31,745
1922	80,189	1,171	81,360	20,491	44,194
1923	126,719	1,469	128,188	35,912	63,168
1924	138,275	1,732	140,007	40,378	61,759
1925	153,666	1,886	155,552	56,908	50,565
1926	139,758	1,971	141,729	56,773	41,326
1927	100,532	1,497	102,029	49,195	31,051
1928	141,590	2,843	144,433	74,055	33,125
1929	170,502	3,624	174,126	98,337	13,444
1930	148,138	4,224	152,362	88,519	3,661
1931	104,171	4,401	108,572	61,010	1,840
1932	86,710	3,996	90,706	56,264	780
1933	46,282	2,675	48,957	28,915	524

* Rouge Area employment data reflects only 5 months in 1919, August through December.

NOTE ON BIBLIOGRAPHICAL
AND OTHER SOURCE MATERIALS

To SAVE SPACE for the text, we have omitted a formal bibliography for this volume. Few general readers will require it; specialists will find all books, pamphlets, reports, legal transcripts, and magazine and newspaper articles used by the authors in the notes—either those numbered and listed by chapter toward the end of the volume, or asterisked notes placed beneath the text on various pages. The importance of respective items is indicated in the text or the notes. An extended bibliography appeared in *Ford: the Times, the Man, the Company,* by Allan Nevins with the collaboration of Frank Ernest Hill (New York, 1954), and this includes a large number of items which apply to the present volume.

No group of materials has been so important for this study as the accessions, oral history reminiscences, and special exhibits available at the Ford Archives in Dearborn. The accessions comprise tens of thousands of letters, cables, telegrams, memoranda, financial records, photographs, and general statistics. The reminiscences, now numbering more than three hundred, contain the testimony of former or present Ford officials and workers, and of other persons who have had knowledge of the events covered in this volume. Since these records deal with important persons, conditions, and happenings, usually with full comment, they often supply explanations of policies and events which letters, figures, and even news reports do not give. Thus they fill in gaps which might have necessitated conjecture. In addition, various activities are covered by several reminiscences, permitting a check of one account against another or others. Many tape-recorded memoirs reflect independent points of view, since a considerable number of the authors have left the Ford Motor Company years ago, and are financially independent, or working for other organizations, sometimes automotive rivals.

In addition to the sources listed above, the authors were able to interview or correspond with various individuals, among them Harold H. Emmons, Wilfred C. Leland, Ernest C. Kanzler, Charles E. Sorensen, J. Bell Moran, and William A. Ryan. The wealth and variety of available material has permitted an intensive examination of Ford Motor Company activities, few of which are undocumented.

A.N.
F.E.H.

INDEX

689

COMPANIES AND MEN

Business Enterprise in America

An Arno Press Collection

Allen, Hugh. **The House of Goodyear:** A Story of Rubber and of Modern Business. 1943

Bennett, Howard F. **Precision Power:** The First Half Century of Bodine Electric Company. 1959

Broehl, Wayne G., Jr. **Precision Valley:** The Machine Tool Companies of Springfield, Vermont. 1959

Broehl, Wayne G., Jr. **Trucks, Trouble and Triumph:** The Norwalk Truck Line Company. 1954

Bruchey, Eleanor S. **The Business Elite in Baltimore, 1880-1914.** 1976

Burgess, George H. and Miles C. Kennedy. **Centennial History of the Pennsylvania Railroad Company, 1846-1946.** 1949

Cleland, David Ira. **The Origin and Development of a Philosophy of Long-Range Planning in American Business.** 1976

Darr, Richard K. **A History of the Nashua and Lowell Rail-Road Corporation, 1835-1880.** 1976

Engelbourg, Saul. **International Business Machines:** A Business History. 1976

Gibb, George Sweet. **The Whitesmiths of Taunton:** A History of Reed & Barton, 1824-1943. 1943

Gibb, George Sweet and Evelyn H. Knowlton. **History of Standard Oil Company (New Jersey): The Resurgent Years, 1911-1927.** 1956

Giddens, Paul H. **Standard Oil Company (Indiana): Oil Pioneer of the Middle West.** 1955

Gloster, Jesse Edward. **North Carolina Mutual Life Insurance Company.** 1976

Gras, N[orman] S. B. **The Massachusetts First National Bank of Boston, 1784-1934.** 1937

Hidy, Ralph W. and Muriel E. Hidy. **History of Standard Oil Company (New Jersey): Pioneering in Big Business, 1882-1911.** 1955

Holbert, Hayward Janes. **A History of Professional Management in American Industry.** 1976

Hungerford, Edward. **Men and Iron:** The History of New York Central. 1938

James, Marquis. **Biography of a Business, 1792-1942:** Insurance Company of North America. 1942

James, Marquis. **The Metropolitan Life:** A Study in Business Growth. 1947

Kaufman, Charles N. **The History of the Keller Manufacturing Company.** 1976

Kuniansky, Harry Richard. **A Business History of Atlantic Steel Company, 1901-1968.** 1976

Larson, Henrietta M. and Kenneth Wiggins Porter. **History of Humble Oil & Refining Company:** A Study in Industrial Growth. 1959

Loth, David. **Swope of G.E.:** The Story of Gerard Swope and General Electric in American Business. 1958

Marcosson, Isaac F. **Anaconda.** 1957

Morison, Samuel Eliot. **The Ropemakers of Plymouth:** A History of the Plymouth Cordage Company, 1824-1949. 1950

Myers, Kenneth Holston. **Marketing Policy Determination by a Major Firm in a Capital Goods Industry:** A Case Study of Bucyrus-Erie Company, 1880-1954. 1976

Nevins, Allan. **History of the Bank of New York and Trust Company, 1784-1934.** 1934

Nevins, Allan and Frank Ernest Hill. **FORD:** Volume I, The Times, the Man, the Company; Volume II, Expansion and Challenge, 1915-1933; Volume III, Decline and Rebirth, 1933-1962. Three vols. 1954/1957/1963

Payne, Peter Lester and Lance Edwin Davis. **The Savings Bank of Baltimore, 1818-1866:** A Historical and Analytical Study. 1956

Plavchan, Ronald J. **A History of Anheuser-Busch, 1852-1933.** 1976

Puth, Robert C[hristian]. **Supreme Life:** The History of a Negro Life Insurance Company. 1976

Sanderlin, Walter S. **The Great National Project:** A History of the Chesapeake and Ohio Canal. 1946

Schwarzman, Richard C. **The Pinal Dome Oil Company:** An Adventure in Business, 1901-1917. 1976

Thomas, Norman F. **Minneapolis-Moline:** A History of Its Formation and Operations. 1976

Twyman, Robert W. **History of Marshall Field & Co., 1852-1906.** 1954

Wainwright, Nicholas B. **History of the Philadelphia National Bank:** A Century and a Half of Philadelphia Banking, 1803-1953. 1953

White, Gerald T. **Formative Years in the Far West:** A History of Standard Oil Company of California and Predecessors Through 1919. 1962

Williamson, Harold F. and Orange A. Smalley. **Northwestern Mutual Life:** A Century of Trusteeship. 1957

ECONOMIC PLANNING IN FRANCE

JOHN HACKETT

B.Sc.(Econ.) Honours, London School of
Economics. Docteur d'Etat ès-Sciences Econ-
omiques, Université de Paris. Maître de
Conférences à l'Institut d'Etudes Politiques,
Paris. Principal Administrator at the
Organization for Economic Co-operation
and Development.

ANNE-MARIE HACKETT

Ancienne Elève de l'Ecole Nationale
d'Administration, Paris. Maître de Conférences à l'Institut d'Etudes Politiques, Paris.
Conseiller Référendaire à la Cour des
Comptes.

ECONOMIC PLANNING
IN FRANCE

JOHN HACKETT

AND

ANNE-MARIE HACKETT

with a Foreword by
PIERRE MASSÉ
Commissaire Général du Plan

HARVARD UNIVERSITY PRESS
CAMBRIDGE, MASSACHUSETTS
1963

TO OUR PARENTS
IN FRANCE AND ENGLAND